AMERICAN PHILOSOPHIC ADDRESSES, 1700–1900

Number 17 of the
Columbia Studies in American Culture

AMERICAN PHILOSOPHIC ADDRESSES

1700 - 1900

Edited by JOSEPH L. BLAU

1754 1893
COLUMBIA
UNIVERSITY
PRESS

IN LITTERIS LIBERTAS

COLUMBIA UNIVERSITY PRESS

NEW YORK

Columbia Studies
in American Culture

EDITED AT COLUMBIA UNIVERSITY

A series bringing together scholarly treatments
of those aspects of American culture
that are usually neglected in political histories and in
histories of American literature and education
THE ARTS AND SCIENCES
PHILOSOPHY AND RELIGION
FOLKWAYS
INDUSTRY AND AGRICULTURE
in short, whatever has contributed significantly
to the patterns of American life and to its heritage

BOARD OF EDITORS

HARRY J. CARMAN
Professor of History

MERLE E. CURTI
Professor of History, University of Wisconsin

JOHN A. KROUT
Professor of History

DUMAS MALONE
Professor of History

HERBERT W. SCHNEIDER
Professor of Philosophy

B
851
.B5

First printing 1946
Second printing 1947

7/5/67

FOR

Judith Leona

PREFACE

THE chief purpose of the editor of this collection of addresses is to provide materials for students of the history of American thought. Herbert W. Schneider's *History of American Philosophy* is another, closely connected aspect of the same enterprise. Experience in teaching this subject has shown that it is essential to provide both a historical account of the career of ideas in America and examples of the elaboration of these ideas in works of literary value. The *History of American Philosophy* is designed to meet the first of these needs; *American Philosophic Addresses, 1700–1900,* to meet the second.

After considering the various types of material which might be used for the second purpose, the editor decided to use these addresses, because: (1) each is an outstanding example of a literary form much cultivated in America; (2) each is a carefully prepared and clearly expressed formulation of a characteristic philosophic position; (3) together they give impressive evidence of the degree to which American thinking for particular occasions in the major areas which the addresses span was universalized by general considerations and led to philosophical formulation. A further consideration was that each address could be presented in full as a finished composition and an adequate development of a theme.

In the introductions to the addresses an attempt has been made to place each speech in its historical context, to define its relation to the total thought of its author, and to indicate its salient points. Additional data on the first topic can be found in the *History of American Philosophy.*

In general the texts of the addresses have been reproduced as they were found, with their many inconsistencies of typography and spelling unchanged. Obvious typographical errors have been corrected, and in a few cases forms of spelling and punctuation which would hamper the modern reader have been altered to conform to present-day usage. Except where indicated, all footnotes to the texts are those of the authors. In a few cases, a complimentary closing bearing no relation to the theme of the address has been eliminated; with these exceptions, the texts are complete.

The New York Historical Society has kindly consented to the publication of Cadwallader Colden's "Introduction to the Study of Phylosophy" from its manuscript collections. The editor has taken more liberties in editing this manuscript than he has taken with the previously printed texts. While attempting to retain the flavor of the original, he has revised the spelling and punctuation throughout. In this case the version here printed makes no claim to literal fidelity.

The editor is grateful for the facilities of the Columbia University Library and the co-operation of its staff. Herbert W. Schneider gave freely of both assistance and advice at all stages in the preparation of this book; Eleanor W. Blau helped immeasurably, not only by such tangible aids as the preparation of the manuscript and correction of proof, but also in many intangible ways. The editor's debt to them can only be acknowledged, never repaid.

J. L. B.

Far Rockaway, New York
June, 1946

CONTENTS

INTRODUCTION

PHILOSOPHICAL AND CULTURAL THEMES IN THE AMERICAN ADDRESS

THE trends of thought which are exemplified in the addresses reprinted in this collection surely show that the young American nation had a vigorous intellectual life. Emerson's comment that no literature of moment had been produced in America from about 1800 to his own day reflects a narrowness of vision on his part rather than a just analysis of the intellectual life of the country. His comment was not isolated, however; it was repeated by many men on both sides of the Atlantic. It carried the more weight because the American nation was passing through a period closely analogous to human adolescence; its physical growth was phenomenal; in the presence of the older and more settled nations of the earth, the United States was either aggressively boastful or extremely self-conscious. Alternately cocksure and uncertain of itself, the young American people engaged in a great deal of self-criticism.

The perennial question in the early stages of this discussion was, "Is there an American cultural life," and this question was usually expressed in terms of a "national literature." Charles Jared Ingersoll said that there was no national literature and could not be one, but that "the influence of America on the mind" was practical. He declared boastfully that America led the world in scientific and mechanical pursuits, and he minimized its literary culture. The first half of his position was generally agreed to, but it was by no means universally conceded that there could be no literary culture in America. His emphasis on practicality led in its day to a controversy over the proper function of education, which is represented here by one extreme statement, that of Willis Hall, a lawyer and one-time Attorney General of New York State. Hall, under utilitarian influence, defended the position that the liberal arts or humanities have not benefited civilization and that American education, if it is to have any value, must minimize the study of the humanities and concentrate on utilitarian, practical studies. In his argument Hall shows the result of wide and critical reading in the humanities. John Neal's *American Writers*, a series of articles in English periodicals, is a good illustration of an alternative view of literature in America. So, too, Edward Everett in "The Circumstances Favorable to the Progress of Literature in America" pointed to elements of geography and of politics, which, he declared, should make for the development of an original and vital cultural life in the United States.

The discussion took a more significant turn, however, when the possibility of a national literature was admitted, and attention was given to the question "What kind of literature is appropriate to a democracy?" or "What are the peculiar obligations of an educated group, or a group of literati, in a free society?" Various answers to this type of question came from various sources. As a rough generalization, critics who were politically Democratic, like George Bancroft, the historian (whose *History of the United States,* said J. F. Jameson, was a vote for Jackson), declared that the ultimate source of strength and of ideas for the literary men of America had to be in the common people; whereas Whig critics pointed to the dangers of rooting a culture in the uncultured mass. Orestes A. Brownson, a radical Democrat, went even farther than Bancroft, declaring that a popularly based culture would come about only by revolutionary force of arms. Gulian C. Verplanck called attention to "The Advantages and Dangers of the American Scholar," and the dangers he saw were shallowness and insincerity. On the frontier men like Alexander Kinmont insisted that American culture and American freedom issued from the same historic sources and that both were rooted in the people. It remained for Ralph Waldo Emerson to place the discussion on its highest, as well as its most democratic ground, by his representation of "The American Scholar" as the delegated intellect of the community, as "Man thinking." The scholar and man of letters was to be rooted in the past and in the everyday practical life of his own time, but was to be the intellectual representative of his kind, even as the Senator was their political representative, to think the thoughts of his people, not under compulsion from them, but under the influence of a deep and abiding kinship. Emerson gave this theme a characteristically individualistic treatment, but a more radical transcendentalist, Henry James the Elder, transmuted an idealism like that of Emerson into a belief that anti-individualistic social democracy was to become the keynote of American cultural life. Henry James declared this doctrine at an apt time: during the Civil War, which separates sharply the maturity of American culture from its adolescence.

With Emerson's "American Scholar" and James's "Social Significance of our Institutions" must rank Wendell Phillips' discourse on "The Scholar in a Republic." Phillips declared that the duty of the scholar was to make of himself a leader of the people in the democratic agitations of the day. He excoriated scholars for living in ivory towers and for failing to take the popular side of the most vital problems of their age. Inheriting the themes of both Bancroft and Emerson, Phillips thought it the duty of the scholar in a republic to hold his learning in trust for the people, to use it for their benefit only. He asked, not subservience to the people, but informed and wise leadership of the people. In the views of Emerson and Phillips there is contained a sound and worthy answer to the question of what type of culture is desirable in a democracy.

Because they are necessary for the formation of an enlightened public opinion for the maintenance of democracy, the arts of communication are *par excellence* the democratic arts. The written and spoken word is one of the many luxuries which are mass-produced in a democracy. The central freedom is not freedom of thought; it is the freedom to express one's thought. What one merely thinks and does not communicate to others cannot possibly affect the established order. Only when the attempt is made to convince and persuade others does thinking become dangerous. This is the heart of Ralph Barton Perry's distinction between "ideas" and "ideals." Ideals appear when ideas, "by evoking a community of emotion and will, play a social and not merely an individual role in human affairs." [1]

Today the propagation of ideas has become a major industry in America. Books, magazines, newspapers, the radio, the pulpit, and the lecture platform descend into the arena and compete for the public eye and the public ear. Freedom of expression has become a commonplace of our culture. In an earlier age the avenues of expression were less numerous. Books were fewer, magazines but a handful, the radio not even a fantastic dream. The pulpit and the lecture platform were the chief roads to public attention, and the art of public speaking was the vehicle for the expression of ideas. During the period which began with the stirrings which gave birth to the American revolution and ended with the beginning of modern journalism, the spoken rather

[1] Ralph Barton Perry, *Puritanism and Democracy*, New York, 1944, p. 19.

than the written word formed the American mind. During that period of about a century and a half, oratorical ability played a central role in American life. "Mostly U.S.A. is the speech of the people." [2]

The opportunities for the exercise of this art were many. Public holidays of national or local importance, which are now only an excuse for a long drive into the country, were formerly the occasions for celebrations at which at least one, and often more than one, orator spoke at length. The public dinner and the public after-dinner speaker were both usual; but the speaker was likely to deliver a lengthy oration rather than a string of empty platitudes or second-hand witticisms. Even college clubs held meetings at which orators were heard. The lyceum and the chautauqua circuits were developed, and their lecturers usually spoke to full houses. Pulpit oratory was prized; an exceptionally well-delivered sermon provided table-talk for a week. Political oratory was the determining factor in elections, not merely a concession to the public.

Charles Jared Ingersoll, in 1821, pointed with pride to the skill of American speakers and to the ability of American listeners. In these respects he contrasted America and England. More surprising to us today is the respect for their audiences which is implicit in the selection of themes of some of these older orators and in the development which they gave to these themes. They seem to have believed that nothing was over the heads of their audiences. Illustrations are too numerous to catalogue; one example should, however, fix the point. On May 19, 1725, there occurred in Maine a minor episode in the history of the struggle between the Europeans and the American Indians for possession of the territory. A young officer named Lovewell and his men were ambushed and destroyed by hostile Indians after heroic resistance. At Fryeburg, Maine, on May 19, 1825, the centenary of Lovewell's Fight was celebrated, and a local celebrity named Charles Stewart Daveis was the orator of the day. After recounting at length the details of the fight and the heroism of its participants, he continued by delivering what made in print a thirty-page essay of very high quality on the nature of popular government. This occurred in what was at that time a backwoods community, part of the frontier.

[2] John Dos Passos, *U.S.A.*, Modern Library Edition, p. vii.

I do not mean to suggest that all the addresses, orations, lectures, speeches, and sermons delivered between 1730 and 1890 were of so high an intellectual caliber. It is not even true that most of them were. There were speeches of incredible inanity, dreariness, and bombast, which fully merit oblivion. They were bad enough to justify the comment of Richard Hildreth in the first sentence of the preface to his *History of the United States:* "Of centennial sermons and Fourth-of-July orations, whether professedly such or in the guise of history, there are more than enough." Interspersed among the mediocre and the bad, however, there were enough good addresses to leaven the mass and to justify this collection.

Some of the addresses collected here were delivered before academic audiences, some before church members, some before heterogeneous popular audiences. All have one distinguishing characteristic: all are speculative in nature. Although the reasoning in most is an attempt to present a universal solution for a particular question, it is philosophical reasoning. Each address represents the attempt of a speaker to put his position on record before a mixed audience, to persuade or convince its members to share his point of view, and thus to influence the course of events. Each of these addresses is, then, a popularized statement of a philosophic outlook as well as a call to a particular action or belief.

In both of these ways these addresses reveal their democratic character. They are attempts to form public opinion on the issues out of which they arose. They are also attempts to inform and enlighten, to educate, the public, whose opinion is the true court of final appeal in a democracy. In their time these speeches were a part of the education of their auditors, and, in the sense in which Wendell Phillips uses the term, the speakers were "agitators."

The central problem of democracy is to keep open the channels of communication. All citizens of a democratic country must be able to find out what leaders of thought and leaders in practical life are thinking about the problems confronting the nation; each citizen must be able freely and publicly to express and to defend his own opinion. This open statement of diverse views leads to the formation of a public opinion which represents the majority view of an informed electorate. It is the cardinal tenet of the democratic faith that this public opinion is sounder than the opinion of the wisest individual, for it includes his opinion, but transcends his prejudice and his self-interest. This is the background of such a paean to enlightened public opinion as that spoken by William Crafts before the Harvard chapter of Phi Beta Kappa in 1817:

Publick opinion! How shall I describe that invisible guardian of honour—that eagle eyed spy on human actions—that inexorable judge of men and manners—that arbiter, whom tears cannot appease, nor ingenuity soften—and from whose terrible decisions there is no appeal? . . . I see it, watching with parental eye over the chastity of virtue, relaxing the grasp of avarice, and melting the heart of cruelty. I see it impelling youth to fight for their country, and soothing them in death. I see it standing in the stead of religion, and enforcing it by penalties, more expeditious than its own. I see it fortify the weakness of law, and preserve the moral sanity of states. In these delightful offices, publick opinion is an angel on earth, and we love and cherish, while we obey it. Such is publick opinion, when it is enlightened. Laws cannot counteract, nor legislatures repeal, nor magistrates suspend it. . . . A nation cannot be virtuous, unless it be enlightened, for it will be subject to its passions,—nor independent, for freedom is never allowed to those, who do not know how to govern themselves—their rights are always in danger, their liberties forever on the wing—nor great, for ignorance generates selfishness.[3]

Perhaps the most interesting intellectual characteristic of the United States and its citizens has been the rapidity with which scientific discoveries have been utilized in practical inventions and have vastly altered the economic life of the country. Although scientists themselves may have been concerned only with the theoretical outcomes of their research, popularizers have never been lacking to simplify their work for public education. Nowhere has the interest of the average person in science been greater; nowhere has he been more willing to take a chance on a new tool or a new technique. Although this readiness has led to excesses, especially on the part of advertisers, it has been most valuable, especially in its by-product of a high standard of living.

Just as the practical results of scientific development have played an important part in American economic and social life, its theoretical re-

---

[3] William Crafts, *An Oration on the Influence of Moral Causes on National Character*, Cambridge, Mass., 1817, pp. 5–6.

sults have played a major, if always controversial, part in intellectual life. Scientific discoveries may be kept for a time from transgressing the bounds of the established world-view. The stimulation which these discoveries give to the speculative mind leads ultimately to the formulation of new views, which inevitably conflict with the old. Thus, while Cotton Mather was able to accept the Newtonian world-view as support for the traditional Christian theology, it was clear not very long afterwards that Newtonianism was complemented by Deism rather than by Christianity. The significance of the sciences in American intellectual life can be measured by the extent to which they have come to terms with religious belief.

Thus, the mechanistic physics of Cadwallader Colden, America's most distinguished early Newtonian, exemplified in this collection by his "Introduction to the Study of Phylosophy," was in itself not particularly dangerous to the religious tradition. When, a little later, Benjamin Rush applied the same type of mechanistic thinking to biology and spoke of "The Influence of Physical Causes upon the Moral Faculty," he was leading straight into infidelity. His doctrine undermined such theological standbys as the doctrine of original sin and led to a completely untraditional view of moral responsibility. The orthodox reply to this position was well stated by President Wayland, of Brown, who attempted to reconstruct the logic of science in such a way as to make the Christianity of the scientist the criterion of his science.

John Neal and Job Durfee, stimulated by the science of their time, stand here as representatives of those thinkers who followed Rush's lead. They believed that, through science and its results, man and his institutions would develop and prosper. Durfee thought this progress was inevitable; he believed that it would come regardless of the form of government or the social or economic status of the people. Science itself became creative, and, to that extent, divine. To counteract this point of view, men such as Andrew Preston Peabody of Harvard, editor of the *North American Review,* recognized the possibility of conflict between religion and science in areas such as morals, but declared that religion rather than science must be the ultimate authority.

All of this thinking preceded the Darwinian revolution. The full effects of Darwin on philosophical and religious thought in America did not come until about 1870. From that time, a fight has been waged from which religion is only now recovering. The Darwinian hypothesis brought to a focus the tendencies toward a mechanistic or a biological ethics which had been gathering strength since the time of Rush. Within the arena of this conflict many minor engagements were fought, one of which is exhibited here in the Phi Beta Kappa addresses of Oliver Wendell Holmes in 1870 and Noah Porter in 1871. Holmes accepted Rush's belief in the influence of physical causes upon ethical and social behavior, and, in general, advocated the continuance of mechanistic thinking in science; in addition, he carried the fight into the opposing camp by his insistence that religion itself applied an all-too mechanistic calculus to the moral life. Porter's reply described ethics as "the science of man," and asserted its supremacy over physical science, "the sciences of nature." Meantime, even such a conservative as James Woodrow lost his position at the Presbyterian Theological Seminary at Columbia, South Carolina, because he accepted the evolutionary theory and insisted that it heightened the glory of God and strengthened the design-argument. Newton and Darwin and American thinkers who followed out the implication of their science shook American intellectual life to its foundations.

From time to time, as we have seen, the attempt to solve the immediate problems of cultural life led to the formulation of the solutions in terms of a philosophy of culture; similarly, the attempt to come to terms with newer scientific developments led to the construction of speculative scientific philosophies. In much the same way, from time to time, when there was some pressing issue to be discussed, the occupants of American pulpits transcended the expression of purely pastoral or merely doctrinal thoughts in their sermons and discussed the current religious issue on the broad base of a philosophic theology. These sermons were not summaries or popularizations of theological treatises. They were original and trail-breaking developments in theological thinking, and, as such, their influence was felt far beyond the limits of theology. A selection of these sermons, each sensational in its age, is presented in the third section of this anthology.

Oliver Wendell Holmes's "Deacon's Masterpiece; or, The Wonderful One Hoss Shay" that "ran a hundred years to a day" and then collapsed all at once symbolized the course of the New England theology. The sermon "God Glorified in Man's Dependence," by Jonathan Edwards, illustrates how, in his theology, two of the points of earlier Calvinist theology, that man's chief end is to glorify God and that man is totally dependent upon God, were joined to provide a pietist basis for the later New England theologians. Edwards maintained that the sense of total dependence is man's chief way of glorifying God. By so doing, he at one and the same time psychologized the belief in total dependence into the sense of total dependence and reinstated the catechetical doctrine of man's chief end. The last fruit of the New England theology is to be seen in the sermon of Edwards A. Park, "The Theology of the Intellect and That of the Feelings." In this sermon Park turns back to an Edwardean pietism with his theology of the feelings as a corrective to the overextension of the sphere of the intellect in theological thinking.

The conflict over the separation of church and state has passed through several crises in American history. One such crisis is represented here by Ezra Stiles Ely who, in 1827, moved towards the idea of a Calvinist-dominated state. Ely cleverly based his attack on religious freedom on the constitutional guarantee of freedom of religion. His plan led liberal thinkers everywhere in the country to rush to the defense of secularism.

Of the Unitarian development in American theology several stages are exemplified. The earliest of these is William Bentley's "Sermon in Stone Chapel," where the position taken is that of natural religion, in which belief in God and in a future life are accepted, but greatest emphasis is placed upon moral development. In the next stage, represented by William Ellery Channing's "Likeness to God," a transcendentalist belief in the immanence of God in man leads to the belief that through his likeness to God man's moral development takes place. In the third stage, that of Emerson's "Divinity School Address" of 1838, the belief in a God immanent in man produces an extreme religious individualism which denies eternal value to the Scriptures and places emphasis on the religious inspiration of each man. Even farther than Emerson went Theodore Parker, the most critical of the transcendentalists, who accepted the idea of progress not only as applied to ceremonies and to the Scriptures but even as applied to man's beliefs about the nature of God. While Emerson and Parker were moving in these new directions, a conservative development of Unitarian thought was also taking place, and within this movement James Walker asserted that religion should be a matter of meeting an emotional need rather than setting up an intellectual science, but denied the radical individualism of the transcendentalists by insisting that this religious need was to be satisfied through an ecclesiastical organization. The final stage in the development of Unitarian thought was taken by Francis Ellingwood Abbot, who took the short step outside the boundaries of Christianity, and formulated a humanistic "free religion" as the logical outcome of the rejection of the divinity of Jesus.

A third, more conservative trend in American philosophical theology is represented by the so-called "New Theology," which is here given in an early form in Horace Bushnell's "Christian Nurture" and in a later, more systematic form in Theodore T. Munger's "Man the Final Form in Creation." This school of thought places much emphasis on religious training rather than on catastrophic conversion, on the social rather than the individual aspects of religious belief and practice, on the sense of community with men rather than communion with God. In Munger's sermon it produced an excellent expression of the coming to terms with evolutionary science which was the most frequent intellectual activity of the end of the nineteenth century. Evolutionary thought was the more readily acceptable because this school of theology was historically grounded.

Even thus hastily passed in review, the addresses in this collection are seen to stem from various sources, to be rooted in various soils. As the problems of American life arose, solutions were sought in terms of American philosophy and culture. In the diversity of the solutions lies one of the most vital forces in the development of the United States. Confronted by a real problem and offered alternative solutions, the people of America were stimulated to thought. When, as in these addresses the solutions were expounded in a philosophical way, the people were stimulated to reflective thought. Thus, diversity has served the ends of democracy as unity never could.

Federalist and Republican, Democrat and Whig, Newtonian, Darwinian, Edwardean, Unitarian, Transcendentalist, Swedenborgian—all have spoken their thoughts. They have placed their solutions of immediate problems in the context of their total philosophical positions and by speaking freely of ideas have contributed to the development of an American public opinion. They have expressed themselves, some with charm, some awkwardly, but fully in the public eye. They have not retired into solitary musing, but have presented their ideas in the open competition of the market place. They found listeners and disciples, and though they dealt in ideas, they reached the masses. This is the true dignity and function of the address in American life, to bring "Man thinking" forth as "Man discoursing" to men listening and themselves learning to think.

— I —

PHILOSOPHY OF AMERICAN CULTURE

CHARLES JARED INGERSOLL

1782, born October 3, at Philadelphia, Pa.

1796–99, student at Princeton; was not graduated

1801, *Edwy and Elgiva*; a tragedy

1802, admitted to bar

1808, *View of the Rights and Wrongs, Power and Policy, of the United States of America*

1810, *Inchiquin; the Jesuit's Letters*

1812–14, elected by Republicans to Congress; chairman of the House Judiciary Committee

1815–29, U.S. District Attorney

1823, *The Influence of America on the Mind*

1831, *Julian; a Tragedy*

1830–31, elected to Pennsylvania State Assembly

1840–49, elected to Congress; later years, chairman of Committee on Foreign Affairs

1845–52, *History of the War of 1812*; four volumes

1861, *Recollections*; two volumes

1862, died May 14

AMERICAN independence was not achieved at one stroke. The Declaration of 1776 and the bitter battles of the Revolution served well to fix a political independence which, in its origins, antedated both. Another war, that of 1812, was necessary before the United States could begin to feel themselves economically independent of Britain. Finally the country began to move in the direction of cultural independence—a movement as yet incomplete, and one which many people consider impossible of completion.

Hints of the struggle for cultural independence came very early in the existence of the United States as a nation. On the Fourth of July, 1788, for example, Simeon Baldwin, in his oration at New Haven, declared:

The United States are particularly happy in a general diffusion of knowledge and in the prospect of a greater improvement. Science cannot flourish in a land that is blasted with a tyrant's breath.—She is the companion of freedom, the child of independence. Dependency of government insensibly carries with it a fatal dependency of mind.—Men are too apt to think, that superior power is necessarily connected with superior wisdom, and for modes of acting and modes of thinking, with reverence look up to those, on whom they are dependent. Even in these States, we have found it a more difficult task to root out those unnatural prepossessions, which tend to idolize the persons and productions of foreigners, to the prejudice of humble merit among ourselves, than to break the chains of political oppression.

Noah Webster's attempt to force cultural independence on the United States by the deliberate creation of an American English seems naïve; the mere change in the spelling of certain classes of words is unlikely to produce a revolution in thought. Yet, when Joel Barlow wrote his *Columbiad*, he accepted Webster's reformed spelling as part of a conscious intention of supplying the new country with an epic illustration of its principles. Barlow's Preface and Postscript to the *Columbiad* should both be read as an essay in cultural nationalism. Again, in his address on being installed as president of the University of Vermont in 1815, Samuel Austin appears as a defender of American culture.

If, in America, book-making is less a business than in Europe, and intellectual effort has less excitement from the expectation of reward; yet the proper and purest motives are as strong here, as in any other part of the world. We are less exposed to be swayed by authority, and are less liable to be interrupted by revolution and war. That the mind is as vigorous and piercing, and as adequate to the highest attainments here, as any where, we have evidence enough in the names of Edwards, Rhittenhouse, Franklin, Washington, Parson, Rush and many living characters, whose names it might be somewhat indecorous to mention.

The true declaration of cultural independence, however, did not come until 1823, when Charles Jared Ingersoll, then United States District Attorney for Pennsylvania, delivered before the American Philosophical Society "A Discourse concerning the Influence of America on the Mind," which is reprinted here. In his earlier work, *A View of the Rights and Wrongs, Power and Policy of the United States of America* (Philadelphia, 1808), which was chiefly concerned with economic questions, Ingersoll introduced a brief comment on the dependent state of American literature, which he deplored as "a matter of regret to every friend of American literature." His later discourse has as its purpose "to sketch the philosophic condition of this country and explain the influence of America on the mind." The success of American culture, he asserts, is founded on public-supported education. The studies are practical and progressive; there are no vested interests in any particular form of training. Therefore, "American education is better adapted to enlarge and strengthen the mind, and prepare it for practical usefulness." The universality of American education is "the hand-maid of universal suffrage," "every husbandman understands the philosophy of politics better than many princes in Europe." The common language shared by England and the United States is a handicap in the establishment of an independent literature; however, "independent of this foreign oppression, the American mind has been called more to political, scientific, and mechanical, than to literary exertion." Also important in the development of an educated citizenry are the press (free from government control) and the cheapness and the number of books published. Here Ingersoll discusses the need for a better copyright law to stimulate American authorship.

Political, scientific, and mechanical development is the burden of Ingersoll's remarks. He discusses the number of inventions for which patents have been granted as an indication of the degree to which the useful arts and sciences flourish in the United States; the advances of medical science especially in the control of disease as a sign of scientific growth. As the American contribution to political life and theory, he describes the system of representation, which he calls "the great distinction between ancient and modern government." Representation in America is "real"; "thousands of springs, gushing from every quarter, eddy onward the cataract of representative democracy, from primary self-constituted assemblies, to the State Legislatures, and the national Congress." The effect of this multiplication of organizations in the members is "to sharpen their wits, temper their passions, and cultivate their elocution," and to familiarize many of the inhabitants of the country with the methods and practices of the deliberative and legislative assembly. An incidental result is the high quality of American oratory.

The talent of effective oratory is much more common in America, where laws are made, controversies are settled, and proselytes are gained, by it, every day. . . . Crowds of listeners are continually collected in all parts of this country to hear eloquent speeches and sermons. . . . Thought, speech, and action, must be perfectly free to call forth the utmost powers of this mighty art.

A further result is the multiplicity of laws which has led to a more careful study of jurisprudence and ultimately will lead to a simplification of the law. Ingersoll maintains, too, that there has developed in America an "American church . . . as justly entitled to that distinctive appellation as the church of Rome, the church of England, the Gallican church, the Greek church, or any others, to theirs respectively." The American church is preeminently Christian, for "whoever reads the text book of Christianity must be convinced that it is the religion of self-government." The cardinal principles of the American church are "segregation from political connection and toleration." Tolerance in America does not mean that a dominant majority permits the mere existence of a minority religion, but "the absolute independence and equality of all religious denominations." Segregation means "that no human authority can in any case whatever control or interfere with the rights of conscience." Under these conditions of freedom, all churches flourish; infidelity and indifferentism are rare.

Ingersoll's discussions of all these points are rather statistical and quantitative than qualitative. He seems to be concerned to point out that there is a large and flourishing American culture, which is to be attributed to the "influence of America on the mind." He concludes with a very brief and hardly successful attempt to "explain the political and physical causes of the results, to which attention has been invited." In substance, his explanation is contained in his closing sentence: "Let our intellectual motto be, that naught is done while aught remains to be done: and our study to prove to the world, that the best patronage of religion, science, literature, and the arts, of whatever the mind can achieve, is SELF-GOVERNMENT."

THE INFLUENCE OF AMERICA ON THE MIND

APPOINTED to deliver the annual discourse of the *American Philosophical Society*, I propose to sketch the philosophical condition of this country, and explain the influence of America on the mind. The task is not an easy one, owing to the extreme dispersion of the materials. Elsewhere intellectual improvements are collected in the accessible repositories of a metropolis, absorbing most of the intelligence of a whole nation, and flourishing with artificial culture long applied. In the United States we have no such emporium; the arts and sciences are but of recent and spontaneous growth, scattered over extensive regions and a sparse population.

We will begin with the base of the American pile, whose aggrandisement, like the pyramids of Africa, confounds the speculations of Europe. While the summit and sides elsewhere are more wrought and finished, America excels in the foundation, in which we are at least the seniors, of all other nations. Public funds for the education of the whole community are endowments exclusively American, which have been in operation here for several ages, while the most improved governments of Europe are but essaying such a groundwork, which indeed some of them dread, and others dare not risk. It is nearly two hundred years since school funds were established by that aboriginal and immortal hive of intelligence, piety, and self-government, the Plymouth colony. These inestimable appropriations are now incorporated with all our fundamental institutions. By the Constitution of the United States it is the duty of government to promote the progress of science and the useful arts. Not one of the eleven new States has been admitted into the Union without provision in its constitution for schools, academies, colleges, and universities. In most of the original States large sums in money are appropriated to education, and they claim a share in the great landed investments which are mortgaged to it in the new States. Reckoning all those contributions federal and local, it may be asserted that nearly as much as the whole national expenditure of the United States is set apart by laws to enlighten the people. The public patronage of learning in this country, adverting to what the value of these donations will be before the close of the present century, equals at least the ostentatious bounties conferred on it in Europe. In one State alone, with but 275,000 inhabitants, more than forty thousand pupils are instructed at the public schools. I believe we may compute the number of such pupils throughout the United States at more than half a million. In the city of Philadelphia, without counting the private or the charity schools, there are about five thousand pupils in the Commonwealth's seminaries, taught reading, writing, and arithmetic, at an expense to the public of little more than three dollars a year each one. Nearly the whole minor population of the United States are receiving school education. Besides the multitudes at school, there are considerably more than three thousand under graduates always matriculated at the various colleges and universities, authorised to grant academical degrees; not less than twelve hundred at the medical schools; several hundred at the theological seminaries; and at least a thousand students of law. Nearly all of these are under the tuition of professors, without sinecure support, depending for their livelihood on capacity and success in the science of instruction. In no part of these extensive realms of knowledge is there any monastic prepossession against the modern improvements. Not long since chemistry, political economy, and the other great improvements of the age were excluded from the English universities as innovations unfit to be classed with rhetoric, logic, and scholastic ethics. Oxford and Cambridge, in the fine metaphor of

Dugald Stewart, are immovably moored to the same station by the strength of their cables, thereby enabling the historian of the human mind to measure the rapidity of the current by which the rest of the world are borne along. The schools are equally stationary. Notwithstanding their barbarous discipline, and the barbarous privileges of the colleges, they have always produced good Latinists and Hellenists. But American education is better adapted to enlarge and strengthen the mind, and prepare it for practical usefulness. In that excellent institution, the Military Academy, the dead languages are not taught, and that kind of scholarship is postponed to sciences certainly more appropriate to a military education. This is not the occasion to inquire whether those standard exercises of the faculties and roots of language may ever be supplanted without injury. But as it is certain that the many great men who have received education at the English seminaries is not a conclusive proof of their excellence, though often cited for the purpose, so it is also true, that eminent individuals have appeared in literature and science, without the help of that kind of scholarship. The founder of the American Philosophical Society was not a scholar in this sense; yet his vigorous and fruitful mind, teeming with sagacity, and cultivated by observation, germinated many of the great discoveries, which, since matured by others, have become the monuments of the age: And whether science, politics, or polite literature, was the subject of which *Franklin* treated, he always wrote in a fine, pure style, with the power and the charm of genius.

Successive improvements in the modern languages, continually perfecting themselves under the prevalence of liberal ideas, have brought them to a degree of moral certainty and common attainment, which must render the dead languages less important hereafter. Their study will be confined probably to a few; and may, perhaps, in the lapse of time, perish under the mass of knowledge destined to occupy entirely the limited powers of the human understanding. While, therefore, we are discussing whether the learning of the ancient languages ought to be maintained, innovating time is settling the question in spite of unavailing efforts and regrets for the immortal authors of European literature. Thus we may understand why the Latin and Greek languages are less cultivated in America than in Europe. Unfettered by inveterate prepossessions, the mind, on this continent, follows in its march the new spirit that is abroad, leading the intelligence of all the world to other pursuits.

Since the career of this country began, education on the continent of Europe has severely suffered by political fluctuations, and continues to be thwarted by political superintendence. Whatever science and literature accomplish there must be in spite of a perplexing and pernicious education. Wanting the stability and tranquillity and security of free institutions, their existence is in perpetual fluctuation and jeopardy. The schools are regulated by one dynasty to-day, by another on opposite principles to-morrow, as the instruments of each in its turn, employed as much in unlearning what had been taught, as in learning what is to be inculcated, continually molested and convulsed by state intrusion. The arts and sciences which war requires and requites, may be encouraged and advanced: and fortunately for mankind, their extensive circle embraces many in which peace also delights or may enjoy. The northern universities have best preserved both their liberality and their usefulness. But in southern Europe, learning appears to be disastrously eclipsed where it has never ceased to receive Pagan and Christian sacrifice for more than two thousand successive years.—Liberty, says Sismondi, had bestowed on Italy four centuries of grandeur and glory; during which, she did not need conquests to make her greatness known. The Italians were the first to study the theory of government, and to set the example of liberal institutions. They restored to the world, philosophy, eloquence, poetry, history, architecture, sculpture, painting, and music. No science, art, or knowledge could be mentioned, the elements of which they did not teach to people who have since surpassed them. This universality of intelligence had developed their mind, their taste, and their manners, and lasted as long as Italian liberty. How melancholy is the modern reverse of this attractive picture! When even freedom of thought can hardly breathe, and freedom of speech or writing has no existence, revolution is the only remedy for disorder; sedition infects the schools, rebellion the academies, and treason the universities. In America, where universal education is the hand-maid of universal suffrage, execution has never been done on a traitor; general intelligence disarms politics of their chimerical terrors; our only revolution was but a temperate transition, without mobs, massacres, or more than a single instance of signal perfidy; every husbandman understands the philosophy of politics better than many princes in Europe. Poetry, music, sculpture, and painting may yet linger in their Italian haunts. But philosophy, the sciences, and the useful arts, must establish their empire in the modern republic of letters, where the mind is free from power or fear, on this side of that great water barrier which the creator seems to have designed for the protection of their asylum. The monarchs of the old world may learn from those sovereign citizens, the ex-presidents of these United States, the worth of an educated nation: who, having made large contributions to literature and the sciences, live in voluntary retirement from supreme authority, at ages beyond the ordinary period of European existence, enjoying the noble recreations of books and benevolence, without guards for their protection, or pomp for their disguise, accessible, admired, protected, and immortalised. The Egyptians pronounced posthumous judgment on their kings: we try our presidents while living in canonised resignation, and award to those deserving it, an exquisite foretaste of immortality.

In adult life we may trace the effects of the causes just indicated in education. The English language makes English reading American: and a generous, especially a parental nationality, instead of disparaging a supposed deficiency in the creation of literature, should remember and rejoice, that the idiom and ideas of England are also those of this country, and of this continent, destined to be enjoyed and improved by millions of educated and thinking people, spreading from the bay of Fundy to the mouth of the Columbia. Such is the influence of general education and self-government, that already over a surface of almost two thousand miles square, there are scarcely any material provincialisms or peculiarities of dialect, much less than in any nation in Europe, I believe I might say than in any hundred miles square in Europe; and, what is perhaps even more remarkable, the German, Dutch, and French veins which exist in different sections, are rapidly yielding to the English ascendancy, by voluntary fusion, without any coercive or violent applications. Adverting to the great results from the mysterious diversity of the various languages of mankind, the anticipation is delightful in the effects of the American unity of tongue, combined with universal education throughout this vast continent,—the home of liberty at least, if not the seat of one great empire.

But speaking and writing the language of an ancient and refined people, whose literature preoccupies nearly every department, is, in many respects, an unexampled disadvantage in the comparative estimate. America cannot contribute in any comparative proportion to the great British stock of literature, which almost supersedes the necessity of American subscriptions. Independent of this foreign oppression, the American mind has been called more to political, scientific, and mechanical, than to literary exertion. And our institutions, moreover, partaking of the nature of our government, have a levelling tendency. The average of intellect, and of intellectual power in the United States, surpasses that of any part of Europe. But the range is not, in general, so great, either above or below the horizontal line. In the literature of imagination, our standard is considerably below that of England, France, Germany and perhaps Italy. The concession, however, may be qualified by a claim to a respectable production of poetry; and the recollection that American scenes and incidents have been wrought by American authors into successful romances, some of which have been re-published and translated, and are in vogue in Europe; and that even popular dramatic performances have been composed out of these incidents. The stage, however, is indicative of many things in America, being engrossed by the English drama and English actors. But as a proof of American fondness, if not taste, for theatrical entertainment, I may mention here that an English comedian has lately received for performances before the audiences of four or five towns, whose united population falls short of four hundred thousand people, a much larger income than any of the actors of that country receive in which this sort of intellectual recreation is most esteemed. There would be no inducement for strolling across the Atlantic, if the largest capital in Europe afforded similar encouragement, taking emolument as the test, and London with 1,200,000 inhabitants as the standard. As another remarkable proof of the state of the stage in the United States, I may add that an eminent American actor appears in the same season, (and it is practicable within the same month) before audiences at Boston and New-Orleans, compassing two thousand miles from one to the other, by internal conveyance. Such is the philosophical, as well as natural, approximation of place, and the unity of speech throughout that distance.

In the literature of fact, of education, of politics, and of perhaps even science, European pre-eminence is by no means so decided. The American schools, the church, the state, the bar, the medical profession, are, all but the last, largely, and all of them adequately, supplied by their own literature. Respectable histories are extant by American authors of the States of Kentucky, Georgia, North Carolina, South Carolina, Virginia, Maryland, Pennsylvania, New York, New Jersey, Vermont, Maine, Massachusetts, Connecticut, and New Hampshire; besides some general histories of New England, and several geographical and topographical works on Ohio, Indiana, Illinois, and Missouri, containing histories of their settlements. Our national histories, inferior in subordinate attractions to the romantic historical fictions of Europe, are composed of much more permanent and available materials. In biography, without equal means, have we not done as much since we began as our English masters? In the literature as well as the learning of the sciences, botany, mineralogy, metallurgy, entymology, ornithology, astronomy, and navigation, there is no reason to be ashamed of our proficiency. In mathematics and chemistry, our comparative deficiency is perhaps the most remarkable. In grammatical researches, particularly in the interesting elements of the Indian languages, American erudition has preceded that of Europe, where some of the most learned and celebrated of the German and French philologists have caught from American publications, the spirit of similar inquiry. In natural and political geography our magnificent interior has produced great accomplishments, scientific and literary. The maps of America have been thought worthy of imitation in Europe. Mr. Tanner's Atlas, lately published, is the fruit of a large investment of money and time, and reflects credit on every branch of art employed in its execution. The surveys of the coast now making by government, will be among the most extensive, accurate, and important memorials extant. Several scientific expeditions have likewise been sent by the government at different times into the western regions, whose vast rivers, steppes and deltas have been explored by learned men, whose publications enrich many departments of science, and are incorporated with applause into the useful literature of the age. One of the most copious and authentic statistical works in print, is an American production, which owes its publication to the patronage of Congress. The public libraries, particularly those of Cambridge University,[1] of the New York Historical Society, of the American Philosophical Society, of the city of Philadelphia, of Congress, and others which might be enumerated, abound with proof and promise of the flourishing condition and rapid advances of literature and science throughout America. A single newspaper of this city, contains advertisements, by a single bookseller, of more than one hundred and fifty recent publications by American authors from the American press, comprehending romance, travels, moral philosophy, mineralogy, political and natural geography, poetry, biography, history, various scientific inquiries, and discoveries, botany, philology, oratory, chemistry applied to the arts, statistics, agricultural and horticultural treatises, strategy, mechanics, and many other subjects. From this ample and creditable catalogue I may select for especial notice the Journal of the Academy of Natural Sciences as a work of uncommon merit; and the profound and elaborate report on Weights and Measures, as a laudable specimen of official function.

The first and the present Secretaries of the Department of State, who have both made reports on this important branch of scientific politics, rank among the foremost scholars of the age by their eminence in various literary and scientific attainments. The American state papers, generally, have received the homage of the most illustrious statesmen of England, for excellence in the principles and eloquence of that philosophy which is the most extensively applied to the affairs of men: and their publications afford large contributions to its literature. Whether any policy be preferable to another, is generally a merely speculative topic. But I may with propriety assert that the United States have been the most steadfast supporters of maritime liberality, of international neutrality, and of the modern system of commercial equality. They were the first to outlaw the slave trade, and the first to declare it practical. Great Britain is imitating their example in commercial, colonial, navigation, penal, and even financial, regulations. France, Spain, Italy, Portugal, parts of Germany, and South America, have in part adopted their political principles. And in all the branches of political knowledge, the American mind has been distinguished.

The publication of books is so much cheaper in this country than in Great Britain, that nearly all we use are American editions. According

---

[1] This is, of course, *Harvard* University, at *Cambridge*, Mass. Ed.

to reports from the Custom-houses, made under a resolution of the Senate in 1822, it appears that the importation of books bears an extremely small proportion to the American editions. The imported books are the mere seed. It is estimated that between two and three millions of dollars worth of books are annually published in the United States. It is to be regretted, that literary property here is held by an imperfect tenure, there being no other protection for it than the provisions of an inefficient act of Congress, the impotent offspring of an obsolete English statute. The inducement to take copyrights is therefore inadequate, and a large proportion of the most valuable American books are published without any legal title. Yet there were one hundred and thirty five copyrights purchased from January 1822 to April 1823. There have been eight editions, comprising 7500 copies of Stewart's Philosophy published here since its appearance in Europe thirty years ago. Five hundred thousand dollars was the capital invested in one edition of Rees' Cyclopœdia. Of a lighter kind of reading, nearly 200,000 copies of the Waverley novels, comprising 500,000 volumes, have issued from the American press in the last nine years. Four thousand copies of a late American novel were disposed of immediately on its publication. Five hundred dollars were paid by an enterprising bookseller for a single copy of one of these novels, without any copyright, merely by prompt republication to gratify the eagerness to read it. Among the curiosities of American literature, I must mention the itinerant book trade. There are, I understand, more than two hundred wagons which travel through the country, loaded with books for sale. Many biographical accounts of distinguished Americans are thus distributed. Fifty thousand copies of Mr. Weem's Life of Washington have been published, and mostly circulated in this way throughout the interior. I might add to these instances, but it is unnecessary, and would be irksome. Education, the sciences, the learned professions, the church, politics, together with ephemeral and fanciful publications, maintain the press in respectable activity.

The modern manuals of literature and science, magazines, journals and reviews, abound in the United States, although they have to cope with a larger field of newspapers than elsewhere. The North American Review, of which about four thousand copies are circulated, is not surpassed in knowledge or learning, is not equalled in liberal and judicious criticism, by its great British models, the Edinburgh and Quarterly Reviews, of which about four thousand copies are also published in the United States. Written in a pure, old English style, and, for the most part, a fine American spirit, the North American Review, superintends with ability the literature and science of America.

Not less than a thousand newspapers, some of them with several thousand subscribers, are circulated in this country; the daily fare of nearly every meal in almost every family; so cheap and common, that, like air and water, its uses are undervalued. But a free press is the great distinction of this age and country, and as indispensable as those elements to the welfare of all free countries. Abundant and emulous accounts of remarkable occurrences concentrate and diffuse information, stimulate inquiry, dispel prejudices, and multiply enjoyments. Copious advertisements quicken commerce; rapid and pervading publicity is a cheap police. Above all the press is the palladium of liberty. An American would forego the charms of France or Italy for the luxury of a large newspaper; which makes every post an epoch, and provides the barrenest corners of existence with an universal succedaneum. Duly to appreciate the pleasures of it, like health or liberty, we must undergo their temporary privation. Nor is our experience of the licentiousness of the press too dear a price to pay for its freedom. It is a memorable fact in the history of American newspapers, that while some of the most powerful have been consumed in the combustion of their own calumnies, on the other hand, the most permanent and flourishing are those least addicted to defamation. It is also a fact, that the most licentious newspapers which have appeared in America, were edited by Europeans. The American standard is equally removed from the coarse licentiousness which characterises much of the English press, and the constraints of that of the rest of Europe—and this standard has been established, while state prosecutions have been falling into dislike. Our newspapers are regulated by a public tact much truer and stronger than such ordeals. The same ethereal influence in a free temperature, is equally effective to preserve the good from obloquy, and to consign the unworthy to degradation. Where the press is perfectly free, truth is an overmatch for detraction. Many of our public men have constantly enjoyed the public favour, in spite of intense abuse; and have survived its oblivion, to receive a foretaste of posthumous veneration.

Under the light of these results, the press has learned the value of temperance, and while all the avenues of private redress are open to those who choose to seek it, state prosecutions have nearly disappeared. Irreligious, obscene, and seditious publications, are infinitely more common from the English than from the American press: scurrilous and libellous newspapers exist to be sure, but they are the lowest and most obscure of the vocation; whereas in England, some of the most elevated and best patronised, are the most scandalous and personal. In the darker ages, dungeons, scaffolds, torture, and mutilation, were the dreadful, but vain restraints put on the understanding. Can it be supposed, that in this enlightened æra, punishment, however mitigated, will do more than inflame it? And what is the English law of public prosecution for libels, but a milder remnant of those principles? By which, infidelity, blasphemy, sedition, treason, and individual calumny, are provoked, disseminated and infuriated. Experience has taught us, that the freedom of the press is the best protection against its abuse, and that its transient licentiousness is part of the very nature of the blessing itself. The splendid skies, forests and foliage of America, with which Europe has nothing of the kind to compare, are inseparable from those vicissitudes and extremities of weather and seasons, which, while menacing desolation, purify and sublimate existence. This American deduction of the much apprehended postulate of the press, is obviously and rapidly gaining converts in England, whence perhaps it may ultimately spread over Europe, and abolish the pernicious alternatives there prevalent. Without it, the press must cause convulsions, and retard the progress of the mind. The English newspaper press, much less free by law than the American, is in practice much more licentious. A late number of the Quarterly Review, (which is no mean authority on such a point) admits, in so many words, that the occupation of the English daily press is, to 'do every thing that honor and honesty shrink from': to which character the absence of decency should be superadded. The Attorney General protects government from libels; but the Chancellor has brought about a most preposterous state of things between the right of literary property, and the want of right in obscene, blasphemous, or otherwise illegal subjects of that property. English party vituperation is much coarser and more personal than ours. But, without going into politics, it may suffice to notice the difference in other things. There are vented in the London newspapers, regular and perennial streams of defilement—polluting police reports, details of inhuman amusements, pugilistic and others, indelicate particulars of various private occurrences, the infamous amours of the royal and noble, are catered for every day's repast, and demanded with an eagerness which bespeaks a vitiated appetite. It seems to be thought that publicity, like execution, deters from crimes, when assuredly, they both stimulate their perpetration. There is another office of the English press, extremely derogatory to the press itself, and injurious to society. I mean the journalising private and domestic concerns, and the most trivial transactions of social intercourse, for the gratification of a vanity, peculiar to the aristocracy of that kingdom. The effects of this proclamation of the common affairs of private life, can hardly fail to be injurious to the female character in particular, whose modesty and retirement are thus perpetually broken in upon. The American newspaper press is conducted in better taste, and with more dignity.

From literature the transition is natural to the arts, which minister to usefulness, comfort and prosperity, individual and national. Under their authority to provide for the encouragement of the arts and sciences, the United States, in thirty years, have issued about four thousand four hundred patent rights for new and useful inventions, discoveries, and improvements. By the prevailing construction of the acts of Congress, American patentees must be American inventors or improvers, and are excluded from all things before known or used in any other part or period of the world. The English law allows English patentees to monopolise the inventions, discoveries, and improvements of all the rest of the world when naturalised in Great Britain. Notwithstanding this remarkable disadvantage, I believe the American list of discoveries is quite equal to the English. The specimens and models open to public inspection in the national repository at Washington, are equal, I understand, to any similar collections in England or France, and superior to those of any other country. It will hardly be expected that I should undertake to mention even the most remarkable articles of this immense museum, containing every element of practical science, of mechanism, of refinement, and of skill. I may be allowed, however, to say that the cotton gin has been of more profit to the United States, than ten times all they ever received by internal taxation; that our grain mill machinery, applied to the great staples of subsistence, is very superior to that of Europe; that there are in the patent office models of more than twenty different power looms, of American invention, operated on, and weaving solely by extraneous power, steam, water, wind, animals, and otherwise; and that the English machines for spinning have been so improved here, that low-priced cottons can be manufactured cheap enough to undersell the English in England, after defraying the charges of transportation. Where American ingenuity has been put to trial it has never failed. In all the useful arts, and in the philosophy of comfort,—that word, which cannot be translated into any other language, and which, though of English origin, was reserved for maturity in America, we have no superiors. If labour saving machinery has added the power of a hundred millions of hands to the resources of Great Britain, what must be the effect of it on the population and means of the United States? Steam navigation, destined to have greater influence than any triumph of mind over matter, equal to gunpowder, to printing, and to the compass, worthy to rank in momentum with religious reformation, and civil liberty, belongs to America. A member of this Society, in his eloquent appeal to the judgment of Great Britain, has argued this claim ably on abstract reasoning. But, without disputing the conceptions and experiments of England, France, and Scotland, of Worcester, Hulls, Juffrou, or Miller, or entering at all into the question of prior imagination, it has always appeared to me that there is a plain principle on which to rest the rights of this country. Steam navigation was reserved for the genius of those rivers, on a single one of which there is already more than a hundred steam boats, containing upwards of fourteen thousand tons, and in whose single sea port, fifty steam boats may be counted at one time. This was the meridian to reduce to practical results, whatever conceptions may have existed elsewhere on this subject. Necessity, the mother of this invention, was an American mother; born, perhaps, on the shores of the Potomac, the Delaware, or the Hudson, yet belonging to the Missouri, the Arkansas, the Mississippi, and the Pacific ocean. By a very useful book called the Western Navigator, (published in this city,) it appears that the entire length of the Mississippi river is 2500 miles, of the Missouri 3000, of the Arkansas 2000, of the Red 1500; and from the recent works of Major Long and Mr. Schoolcraft, it is ascertained that a large number of great tributaries unite their waters with these prodigious floods, washing altogether, according to the summary of the author of the Western Navigator, in the valley of the Ohio, 200,000 square miles, in the valley of the Mississippi proper, 180,000, in that of the Missouri, 500,000, and in that of the lower Mississippi, 330,000, giving a total of 1,210,000 miles as the area of what is termed the Mississippi basin. Most if not all of these vast streams are innavigable but by steam boats, owing to the course of their currents and other circumstances. These then are the latitudes of steam boats, which have been abandoned in some parts of Europe, as too large for their rivers, and too expensive for their travelling.—In less than ten years from this time, steam boats may pass from the great lakes of the north-west by canals to the Atlantic, thence to the isthmus of Darien, and across that to China and New Holland. They now ply like ferry boats from New York to Pensacola, New Orleans and Havanna, with the punctuality and security, and more than the accommodation, of the best land carriage of Europe. Wherever this wonderful invention appears, overcoming the winds and waves by steam, measuring trackless ocean distances by the quadrant, and protected from lightning by the rod, it displays in every one of these accomplishments the genius of America.

In the ordinary art of navigation, the construction, equipment, and manipulation of vessels, commercial and belligerent, America is also conspicuous. The merchant vessels of the United States, manned with fewer hands, perform their voyages, generally, in one third less time than those of the only other maritime people to be compared with them. And without referring to the achievements of the American navy as credentials of courage or renown, I may with propriety remark, that an intelligent and scientific fabrication and application of arms, ammunition, ships, and all the materials of maritime warfare, are unquestionably demonstrated by their success in it.

The mechanics, artisans, and laborers of this country are remarkable for a disposition to learn. Asserted European superiority has been of great advantage to America in preventing habitual repugnance to improvement, so common to all mankind, especially the least informed classes. Superior aptitude, versatility and quickness in the handicrafts, are the consequences of this disposition of our people. A mechanic in

Europe is apt to consider it almost irreverent, and altogether vain to suppose that any thing can be done better than as he was taught to do it by his father or master. A house or ship, is built in much less time here than there. From a line of battle ship, or a steam engine, to a ten penny nail, in every thing, the mechanical genius displays itself by superior productions. The success of a highly gifted American mechanical genius now in England, seems to be owing in part to his adapting his improvements, by a happy ingenuity, to the preservation of machinery, for which several English mechanics have been enriched and ennobled, but which would have been superseded as useless had it not been thus rescued.

If a ship, a plough and a house be taken as symbols of the primary social arts of navigation, agriculture and habitation, we need not fear comparisons with other people in any one of them. In the intellectual use of the elements, the combinations and improvements of the earth and its products, of water, of air, and of fire, no greater progress has been made in Europe within this century than in the United States. The houses, ships, carriages, tools, utensils, manufactures, implements of husbandry, conveniences, comforts, the whole circle of social refinement, are always equal, mostly superior here to those of the most improved nations. I do not speak of mere natural advantages, of being better fed, more universally housed and more comfortably clothed, than any other people; but excepting the ostentatious, and extravagant, if not degenerate and mischievous, luxuries of a few in the capitals of Europe merely; looking to the general average of civilisation, where does it bespeak more mind or display greater advancement? Internal improvements, roads, bridges, canals, water-works, and all the meliorations of intercourse, have been as extensively and as expensively made within the last ten years in the United States, as in probably any other country; notwithstanding the sparseness of a population, of which scarcely half a million is concentrated in cities, and a slender capital. Five thousand post offices distribute intelligence throughout the United States with amazing celerity and precision over eighty thousand miles of post roads. The mail travels twenty-one thousand miles every day, compassing eight millions of miles in a year. There are twelve thousand miles of turnpike roads. Our facilities and habits of intercourse are unequalled in Europe; almost annihilating the obstacles of space.

Within two years from this time, when all the great canals now in progress shall be completed, an internal navigation of ten thousand miles will belt this country from the great western valley to the waters of the Hudson and the Chesapeake. The New York canal and the Philadelphia water-works are not surpassed, if equalled, by any similar improvements in Europe within the period of their construction.

The polite arts, painting, engraving, music, sculpture, architecture, the arts of recreation, amusement, and pageantry, flourish most in the seats of dense population. Few of them thrive without the forcing of great capitals, the reservoirs of the refinements of ancient, sometimes declining, empire. Architecture is an art of state, whose master works are reserved for seats of government. The public edifices of Edinburgh or Liverpool, for instance, or those erected at any other provincial town within the last twenty years, bear no comparison to the costly and magnificent capitol, built, burnt, and rebuilt, within that period at Washington. Indeed, I believe that there are no public buildings which have been constructed at London during this century in so expensive and splendid a style. The Halls of the Senate, and of the Representatives at Washington, are in the relation of contrast with the Houses of Commons and the Lords in London, as to magnitude, magnificence and accommodation. And, if I am not mistaken, the only historical paintings of national events, which have ever been paid for by legislative appropriation, are those executed by an American artist for the walls of the capitol.

To these imperfect views of education, literature, science, and the arts, I will add sketches of the American mind, as developed in legislation, jurisprudence, the medical profession and the church; which, in this country, may be considered as the other cardinal points of intellectual exercise.

Representation is the great distinction between ancient and modern government. Representation and confederation distinguish the politics of America, where representation is real and legislation perennial. Thousands of springs, gushing from every quarter, eddy onward the cataract of representative democracy, from primary self-constituted assemblies, to the State Legislatures, and the national Congress. Three thousand chosen members represent these United States, in five and twenty Legislatures. There are, moreover, innumerable voluntary associations under legislative regulations in their proceedings. I am within bounds in asserting, that several hundred thousand persons assemble in this country every year, in various spontaneous convocations, to discuss and determine measures according to parliamentary routine. From bible societies to the lowest handicraft there is no impediment, but every facility, by law, to their organisation: And we find not only harmless but beneficial, those various self-created associations, which in other countries give so much trouble and alarm. It is not my purpose to consider the political influences of these assemblies, nor even their political character. But their philosophical effect on the individuals composing them, is to sharpen their wits, temper their passions, and cultivate their elocution: While this almost universal practice of political or voluntary legislation, could hardly fail to familiarise a great number of persons with its proprieties. The mode of transacting business is nearly the same in them all, from the humblest debating club to Congress in the capitol. Legislation in the United States is better ordered, more deliberative, decorous, and dignified, much less tumultuous or arbitrary and more eloquent than in Europe. Continual changes of the political representatives, afford not less than ten thousand individuals spread throughout the United States, practically familiar with the forms and principles of legislation, who, through the vivid medium of a free press, constitute, as it were, an auditory greatly superior to that of any other nation. A large proportion of this great number of practical legislators, is qualified by the habits of discussion incident to such employment, and perfect freedom, to deliver their sentiments in public speaking; which, being in greater request, of greater efficacy, and at greater liberty in America than in Europe, is naturally more prevalent and powerful here than there. It is a striking view of the ideas of legislation in Europe, that within the last thirty years France and Spain have waged destructive wars for legislatures, consisting of single assemblies; a constitution, which in America, would not be thought worth so much bloodshed.

The much abused French revolution, has given to that country a Legislature of two houses, and a press of considerable freedom. But the peers are lost in the secrecy of their sessions: and the deputies can hardly be called a deliberative assembly. Few speak, inasmuch as most of the orations are read from a pulpit: and still fewer listen, amidst the tumults that agitate the whole body. To crown these frustrations of eloquent debate, when it becomes intense and critical, as it must be, to do its offices, the proceedings are sometimes closed by an armed force, marched in to seize and expel an obnoxious orator. This is certainly not the philosophy of legislation.

In Great Britain, an excessive number is crowded into an inconvenient apartment, where but few attempt to speak, and few can be brought to listen: and where both speakers and hearers are disturbed by tumultuous shouts and unseemly noises, not, according to our ideas, consonant with either eloquent or deliberative legislation. In theory, the House of Commons contains nearly 700 members: in practice the most important laws are debated and enacted by sixty or fifty. Owing to the want of personal accommodation, when the house is crowded, its divisions to be counted are attended with great confusion. Most of the bills are drafted, not by members, but by clerks hired for that purpose: to which is owing much of the inordinate tautology and technicality of modern acts of Parliament. In theory and principle there is no audience, and in fact, bystanders are not permitted but occasionally, under inconvenient restrictions. Reports and publications of the debates are unauthorised, and of course imperfect, notwithstanding, the exploits of stenography. Although Parliament is omnipotent, yet a member may not publish abroad what he says in his place, without incurring ignominious punishment as a libeller: which punishment was actually inflicted not long ago on a peer, proceeded against by information, for that offence. In France, the press is, in this respect, freer than in England. The publication of speeches in the Legislature is considered an inviolable right, which, among all the revocations of the present government, has never been molested or called in question. By a perversion of the hours, unknown, I believe, in any other country or age, most of the business of Parliament is done in the dead of night, to which, probably, many of the irregularities now mentioned are ascribable. The great popular principles which have preserved the British Parliament, while every other similar attempt in Europe has failed, or nearly so, and its brilliant political performances, have recommended it to admiration, notwithstanding these disadvantages; and indeed sanctioned them as part of the system. But unprejudiced judgment must allow, that all these are imperfections which have no place in Congress. Hence it is, that there are not now, and probably never were at any one time, more than two or three members of Parliament actuated by the great impulses of oratory: and that the talent of extemporaneous and useful eloquence always has been much more common in Congress. Burke's inimitable orations, which all ages will read with delight, were delivered to an empty house. A member, now a peer, himself one of the most eloquent men of England, whose political and personal ties bound him particularly to remain during the delivery of one of these master-pieces, after nearly everybody else had withdrawn, actually crawled out of the house to escape unnoticed from an intolerable scene. Johnson, the editor of Chatham's famous speeches, in a number of the Rambler, treats the graces of eloquence with elaborate ridicule and contempt; and Hume, in his Essay on Eloquence, and Blair, in his Lectures on Rhetoric, acknowledge that they are not characteristics of British oratory. The printed speeches of England are among the finest specimens of the art of composition; but it is notorious that in parliament and at the bar the most celebrated speeches avail nothing with those to whom they are addressed; and eloquence, in the pulpit of the established church is, I believe, a thing unheard of. The talent of effective oratory is much more common in America, where laws are made, controversies are settled, and proselytes are gained, by it, every day. An eloquent professor or lecturer, in England, is very rare, if there be any such. While it is well known that the medical school of Philadelphia owes its success, in part, to the mere eloquence of its lecturers. Crowds of listeners are continually collected in all parts of this country to hear eloquent speeches and sermons. The legislature, the court house, and the church, are thronged with auditors of both sexes, attracted by that talent which was the intense study and great power of the ancient orators. Thought, speech, and action, must be perfectly free to call forth the utmost powers of this mighty art. It requires difficulties; but it needs hopes. Its temples in free countries are innumerable. When its rites are administered the most divine of human unctions searches the marrow of the understanding; the orator is inspired, the auditor is absorbed, by the occasion.

Annual sessions of five and twenty legislatures multiply laws, which produce a numerous bar, in all ages the teeming offspring of freedom. Their number in the United States has been lately computed at six thousand; which is probably an under estimate. American lawyers and judges adhere with professional tenacity to the laws of the mother country. The absolute authority of recent English adjudications is disclaimed: but they are received with a respect too much bordering on submission. British commercial law, in many respects inferior to that of the continent of Europe, is becoming the law of America. The prize law of Great Britain was made that of the U. States by judicial legislation during flagrant war between the two countries. The homage lately paid by the English prime minister to the neutral doctrines proclaimed by the American government, in the beginning of the French revolution, which declares them worthy the imitation of all neutral nations, may teach us that the American state papers contain much better principles of international jurisprudence than the passionate and time-serving, however brilliant, sophisms of the British admiralty courts. On the other hand, English jurisprudence, while silently availing itself of that of all Europe, and adopting without owning it, has seldom if ever made use of an American law book, recommended by the same language, system, and subject matter. American translations of foreign jurists, on subjects in which the literature of English law is extremely deficient, appear to be less known in England than translations of the laws of China. This veneration on our part, and estrangement on theirs, are infirmities characteristic of both. Our professional bigotry has been counteracted by penal laws in some of the States against the quotation of recent British precedents, as it was once a capital offence in Spain to cite the civil law, and as the English common law has always repelled that excellent code from its tribunals. I cannot think, with the learned editor of the Law Register, that late English law books are a dead expense to the American bar; or that, in his strong phrase, scarcely an important case is furnished by a bale of their reports. But I deplore the colonial acquiescence in which they are adopted, too often without probation or fitness. The use and respect of American jurisprudence in Great Britain will begin only when we cease to prefer their adjudications to our own. By the same means we shall be relieved from disadvantageous restrictions on our use of British wisdom; and our system will acquire that level to which it is entitled by the education, learning, and purity of those by whose administration it is formed.

In their national capacity, the United States have no common law, but all the original States are governed by that of England, with adaptations. In one of the new States, in which the French, Spanish, and English laws, happen to be all naturalised, an attempt at codification from all these stocks is making, under legislative sanction. In others, possibly all of the new States, which have been carved out of the old, a great question is in agitation whether the English common law is their inheritance. Being a scheme of traditional precepts and judicial precedents, that law requires continual adjudications, with their reasons at large, to explain, replenish, and enforce it. Of these reports, as they are termed, no less than sixty four, consisting of more than two hundred volumes, and a million of pages have already been uttered in the United States; most of them in the present century; and in a ratio of great increase. The camel's load of cases, which is said to have been necessary to gain a point of law in the decline of the Roman empire, is therefore already insufficient for that purpose in the American. Add to which, an American lawyer's library is incomplete without a thousand volumes of European legists, comprehending the most celebrated French, Dutch, Italian, and German treatises on natural, national, and maritime law, together with all the English chancery and common law. I have heard of an American lawyer of eminence whose whole property is said to consist in a large and expensive law library.

Notwithstanding this mass of literature, the law has been much simplified in transplantation from Europe to America: and its professional as well as political tendency is still to further simplicity. The brutal, ferocious, and inhuman laws of the feudists, as they were termed by the civilians, (I use their own phrase,) the arbitrary rescripts of the civil law, and the harsh doctrines of the common law, have all been melted down by the genial mildness of American institutions. Most of the feudal distinctions between real and personal property, complicated tenures and primogeniture, the salique exclusion of females, the unnatural rejection of the half-blood, and ante-nuptial offspring, forfeitures for crimes, the penalties of alienage, and other vices of European jurisprudence, which nothing but their existence can defend, and reason must condemn, are either abolished, or in a course of abrogation here. Cognisance of marriage, divorce, and posthumous administration, taken from ecclesiastical, has been conferred on the civil tribunals.

Voluminous conveyancing and intricate special pleading, among the costliest mysteries of professional learning in Great Britain, have given place to the plain and cheap substitutes of the old common law. With a like view to abridge and economise litigation, coercive arbitration, or equivalents for it, have been tried by legislative provision; jury trial, the great safeguard of personal security, is nearly universal, and ought to be quite so, for its invaluable political influences. It not only does justice between the litigant parties, but elevates the understanding and enlightens the rectitude of all the community. Sanguinary and corporal punishments are yielding to the interesting experiment of penitential confinement. Judicial official tenure is mostly independent of legislative interposition, and completely of executive influence. The jurisdiction of the courts, is far more extensive and elevated than that of the mother country. They exercise, among other high political functions, the original and remarkable power of invalidating statutes, by declaring them unconstitutional: an ascendancy over politics never before or elsewhere asserted by jurisprudence, which authorises the weakest branch of a popular government to annul the measures of the strongest. If popular indignation sometimes assails this authority, it has seldom if ever been able to crush those who have honestly exercised it; and even if it should, though an individual victim might be immolated, his very martyrdom would corroborate the system for which he suffered. Justice is openly, fairly, and purely administered, freed from the absurd costumes and ceremonies which disfigure it in England. Judicial appointment is less influenced by politics; and judicial proceedings more independent of political considerations.

The education for the bar is less technical, their practice is more intellectual, the vocation is relatively at least more independent in the United States, than in Great Britain. Here, as there, it is a much frequented avenue to political honours. All the chief justices of the United States have filled eminent political stations, both abroad and at home. Of the five Presidents of the United States, four were lawyers; of the several candidates at present for that office, most, if not all, are lawyers. But without any public promotion, American society has no superior to the man who is advanced in any of the liberal professions. Hence there are more accomplished individuals in professional life here, than where this is not the case. Under other governments, patronage will advance the unworthy, and power will oppress the meritorious. Even in France, where there are, and always have been lawyers of great and just celebrity, we sometimes see that for exerting the noblest, and, in free countries, the most common duties of their profession, for resisting the powerful and defending the weak, they are liable to irresponsible arrest, imprisonment, and degradation, without the succour and sanctuary of a free press, and dauntless public sympathy. In Great Britain, it is true, there is no such apprehension to deter them: and equally true, that professional, as well as political dignities, are free to all candidates. But the ascendancy of rank, the contracted divisions of intellectual labour, the technicality of practice, combine with other causes to render even the English individuals, not perhaps inferior lawyers, but subordinate men.

British jurisprudence itself, too, that sturdy and inveterate common law, to which Great Britain owes many of the great popular conservative principles of her constitution—even these have been impaired by long and terrible wars, during which, shut up within their impregnable island, the offspring of Alfred and of Edward, infusing their passions, their politics, and their prejudices into their laws, have wrenched them to their occasions. The distinguishing attributes and merits of the common law are, that it is popular and mutable; takes its doctrines from the people, and suits them to their views. While the American judiciary enforces this system of jurisprudence, may it never let wars, or popular passions, or foreign influences, impair its principles.

There are about ten thousand physicians in the United States, and medical colleges for their education in Massachusetts, Rhode-Island, Connecticut, New York, Pennsylvania, Virginia and Ohio. There are also two medical universities in the state of New York, one in Pennsylvania, one in Maryland, one in Massachusetts, and one in Kentucky; containing altogether about twelve hundred students. Under the impulses of a new climate and its peculiar distempers, the medical profession has been pursued and its sciences developed with great zeal and success in this country; whose necessities have called forth a bolder and more energetic treatment of diseases, more discriminating and philosophical, as well as decisive and efficient; a more scientific assignment of their causes, and ascertainments of their nature. Many medical errors and prejudices, now abandoned in Europe, were first refuted here.

What is justly termed a national character, has been given to the medical science of America, and American medical literature is circulated and read in Europe, where several American medical discoveries and improvements have been claimed as European. Anatomy, the most stationary of the medical sciences, is ardently cultivated, and has been advanced by discoveries in the American schools. Valuable contributions have been made to physiology, and more rational views inculcated of animal economy. An American discovery in chemistry has distinguished its author throughout Europe: Where the achievements of this master spirit of sciences, while, to be sure they leave ours behind, yet encourage it to an application full of promise. It is a merit of the American schools, at least, to have accurately defined the bounds of chemistry and physiology. Our diversified soils and climates, afford inexhaustible healing and balsamic plants, many of which have been adopted into the materia medica, and displayed in publications creditable to the literature and some of the fine arts, as well as the science of this country. And the bowels of this continent are rich with sanative minerals, some of which, likewise, have been extracted and made known both to science and by literature. Mr. Cleaveland's treatise on mineralogy is, I believe, used as a text book in Great Britain.

American physicians are probably unrivalled in the knowledge and use of what are termed the heroic remedies. They have introduced new and rational doctrines respecting the operation of remedies; combatting the notion of their reception into the circulation, and referring it to the principle of sympathy. They deny the asserted identity of remedies; believing, that they have succeeded in proving an essential difference in their operation, not only in degree, but in effect. The American improvements in Surgery are too numerous, and though not the less important, too minute and technical, to be generalised in a summary. Its apparatus, mechanism, and operations, have been improved by a theory and practice equal in science, skill and success, to any in the world. But its greatest melioration is philosophical. The founder of most of the improvements in surgery alluded to, deeming its most skilful operations, but imperfections in the preserving art, reserves them for its last resort, never to be performed till all means of natural cure prove abortive. On this exalted principle the great Hunter taught and practised; uniting humanity and philosophy to science and art;

a benefactor, whose original and admirable suggestions it is the merit of American physicians and surgeons to have introduced into their practice in this country, before their imputed innovations were reconciled to pre-conceived opinions in his own.

Midwifery, both practical and theoretical, has also received essential improvements in the American school, some of which have been declared by high authority to mark an æra in the obstetric practice. In the theory and practice of medicine, the improvements are too many and important for my recital. The gastric pathology, the prevailing treatment and theory of hydrokephalus, and of dropsies in general, the boasted European practice in marasmus, the cure of the croup, of gout by evacuations, the arrest of malignant erisipelas, and of mortification, and of inflammation of the veins; in short, a long list of remedial systems, which might be enumerated, though claimed in Europe, belong to America. The vaunted suggestion of Europe, that fever originates in sympathetic irritation, and that venesection and other evacuations are requisite in the primary stages of it, have long been the established doctrines of America, where they were first demonstrated. American medical science and skill have outstripped those of the rest of the world, Europe included, in the character and treatment of epidemics and pestilences. In this great field, Europe has done little, while the progress of America has been great. Bigoted to antiquated notions the medical science of the old world has stagnated for centuries in prejudices, which have been expelled in the new, where the causes, nature, laws, and treatment of these destructive visitations have been ascertained and systematised. English critics particularly dwell with exultation on their supposed late triumphs over these distempers. Divested of the long prevalent notion of debility and putrescency, they now urge depletion as if the suggestion were their own, whereas thirty years have elapsed since the physicians of this country were in the full employment of it.

The theory and practice of medicine, the fearless and generous resistance of pestilential disease, suggest a recollection of a late medical professor here, whose works are in the libraries of the learned in many countries, and in several languages, whose fascinating manners and eloquent lectures largely contributed to the foundation of a flourishing school, whose zeal, if some times excessive, was characteristic of genius, and the pioneer of success; whose services, let me add, as a patriot, and a philanthropist, shed a divine lustre on his career as a physician. The first leading man to lay down his life in battle in the American revolution, was an eminent physician. The best historian of that period, was also an eminent physician: And in a country, which knows no grade above that of the eminent in learning and usefulness, there have been, and there are, many others of this profession to whom more than professional celebrity belongs. They frequently unite political with professional distinctions. Many of the members of this profession, have filled various stations in every branch of our government. Many of them at this moment, occupy high executive and legislative public offices. The pernicious and degrading system which subdivides labour infinitesimally—a system useful perhaps for pin-makers, but most injurious in all the thinking occupations—has no countenance in America. The American physician practices pharmacy, surgery, midwifery; and is cast on his own resources for success in all he does: The consequence of which is, that he is forced to think more for himself, and of course to excel. In Europe, successful physicians are too often made so by favour or chance. They are, moreover, the luxuries of the metropolis and a few great cities. Throughout the interior of England, generally, the medical attendant is an uneducated apothecary, whose science stops at the compounding of a drug, or the opening of a vein. Even in London, this class is always in reserve to succeed the preliminary and expensive visits of the doctor; whose employment, besides, depends too much on the recommendation of these subordinates. In this country, medical skill is much more generally distributed. Every hamlet, every region abounds with educated physicians, whose qualifications to be sure, ultimately depend much on their opportunities: But who, at least for the most part, begin with the recommendations of diplomas.

Perhaps the most humane discovery in modern medicine is vaccination; to which America has no claim: though superior intelligence here has given it much greater effect, than among the ignorant populace of Europe. The doctrine of non-contagion in pestilential distempers, should it be established, must also enjoy great credit as a triumph for humanity. The most distressing prejudices concerning contagion, are not yet extirpated in Europe. I am not authorised to consider a disbelief in this shocking aggravation of any malady, as a point in which the medical profession of America is quite unanimous with respect to yellow fever: but a foreign physician, who lately collected their opinions, ascertained the ratio of non-contagionists to be 567 to 28 contagionists. A late French ambassador in this country, who was bred a physician, has publicly claimed the merit of the discovery of non-contagion for another French physician, who was in practice in this city in 1793, and is now in the service of the king of France. But in a treatise on the yellow fever by Dr. Hillary, published sixty years ago, its contagion is explicitly denied by the unqualified declaration, that 'it has nothing of a pestilential or contagious nature in it.' That this is not the sentiment prevalent in France, would seem to be inferrible from recent events. A French army was stationed at the foot of the Pyrennees, as a sanitary cordon, to prevent the passage of contagion over those lofty, and frost crowned mountains. Whatever may be the theories or reveries of a few, therefore, it is a remarkable proof of the actual state of the public intelligence on this subject, not only in France, but throughout Europe, that all inquiries concerning the cause of this apparently warlike demonstration were silenced by assurances that its design was to repel contagious disease: under which assertion the wisdom of Europe rested, till the plans thus masked were ripe for execution.

I shall conclude with some views of the American church; which I hope to be able to shew is as justly entitled to that distinctive appellation as the church of Rome, the church of England, the Gallican church, the Greek church, or any others, to theirs respectively.

It is the policy or the prejudice of governments, which use the church as an engine of state, to decry institutions which separate them, and leave religion to self-regulation. They are accused of infidelity and immorality. The want of ecclesiastical respectability is inferred from its want of political protection and influence. These Pagan doctrines have prevailed where ever Christianity has been unknown. They were Egyptian, Grecian, Roman; they are Mahometan. But they cannot endure the light of reason and truth. Whoever reads the text book of Christianity must be convinced that it is the religion of self-government. No European dogma is more unfounded than that republicanism and infidelity are coadjutors. Intelligent men in the United States, with much more unanimity and sincerity than in Europe, believe that without religion humanity would be forlorn and barbarous. And in no country are those ecclesiastical classes and cures, which have formed parts of the institutions of religion, in all times, better established than in this. In estimating the progress and condition of the mind in America, therefore, I have neither disposition nor occasion to deny, that the condition of religion is one of the best tests of the general intellectual state. Independently of their help in the cure of souls, the clergy have always rendered the most important services to the human understanding. Learning and science were long in their exclusive care. In those periods when the mind was most depressed, the church was the chancery of its preservation. To it we owe nearly all the best relics of ancient learning: from it, we still receive much of our education; for here, as elsewhere, most of our teachers are ecclesiastics. It is therefore a very interesting inquiry how the church and its ministers, who are also the ministers of education, fare in any community.

Segregation from political connection and toleration are the cardinal principles of the American church. On the continent of Europe, toleration means, where it is said to exist, catholic supremacy suffering subordinate protestantism. In the united kingdom of Great Britain and Ireland, it means a protestant hierarchy, abetted by dissenters, excluding catholics from political privileges, and subjecting them to double ecclesiastical impositions. France, Italy, Ireland, and Spain, have been desolated by contests between church and state. Toleration has won at least part of these bloody fields. But a segregated church does not appear to have made any advance in Europe. In the United States, both of these principles are not only fundamental political laws, but ancient, deep-seated doctrines, whose bases were laid long before political sovereignty was thought of, when Williams, Penn and Baltimore, by a remarkable coincidence, implanted them in every quarter, and in every creed. American toleration, means the absolute independence and equality of all religious denominations. American segregation, means, that no human authority can in any case whatever control or interfere with the rights of conscience. Adequate trial of these great problems, not less momentous than that of political self-government, has proved their benign solution. Bigotry, intolerance, blood thirsty polemics waste themselves in harmless, if not useful, controversy, when government takes no part. We enjoy a religious calm and harmony, not only unknown, but inconceivable, in Europe. We are continually receiving accessions of their intolerance, which is as constantly disarmed by being let alone. Our schools, families, legislatures, society find no embarrassment from varieties of creed, which in Europe would kindle the deadliest discord.

That these consequences are not the fruits of lukewarmness and disregard to religion, remains to be shewn.

I shall touch but lightly on the dissenting church, as it is called in England; not because its condition in the United States is not worthy of regard, and a great argument for my object, but because its well known prosperity renders it almost unnecessary that I should dwell on any details of it. Always democratic even in Europe, no reason can be imagined why it should not thrive in the aboriginal republicanism of America, the natural and fruitful soil of spontaneous religion. Accordingly, there are upwards of seven hundred congregational churches in the New England States alone, and nearly that number of clergymen of that denomination, including pastors, unsettled ministers, and licensed preachers: from which enumeration I exclude the Baptists of that quarter, who are uniformly of the congregational order in church government. There is a theological seminary at Andover, in Massachusetts, containing about one hundred and fifty students in divinity. At Harvard college, there is a theological professor of the Antitrinitarian faith, with whom several resident graduates commonly study. Of the two hundred and thirty congregational ministers of Massachusetts, about seventy are Anti-trinitarians. In Maine, there is a theological seminary, with two professors, and about forty pupils. Yale college in Connecticut, has a theological department attached to it, in which there are three professors, and a considerable number of students. In Cornwall, in Connecticut, there is also a Heathen mission school, in which, about thirty youths, born in India, on the Pacific ocean, and the western wilds of this continent, or other heathen places, are educated with special reference to ministerial duties in their respective birth places.

The Presbyterian church in the United States, in addition to the congregational, contains about nine hundred ministers, one hundred and thirty five licentiates, one hundred and forty seven candidates, more than fourteen hundred churches, and last year administered the sacrament of the Lord's Supper to an hundred thousand communicants. It has theological seminaries in the States of New Jersey, New York, and Tennessee: And, as is obvious from these indications, is established on broad and flourishing endowments.

I shall also very summarily touch the condition of those enthusiastic, and, for the most part, itinerant churches, which, ever since their first example in the appearance of the Franciscan and Dominican friars of the thirteenth century, in a similar manner and on similar occasions, have, under various titles, interposed their austere and reviving tenets, into the deserted or decaying quarters of Christianity; whose popular and rallying doctrines have a highly beneficial influence on the morals of the community. The Methodist church of America contains three dioceses, eleven hundred itinerant clergy, exclusively clerical, and about three thousand stationary ministers, who attend also to other than ecclesiastical occupations. They reckon twelve conferences, and more than twenty five hundred places of worship. By the report to the Baptist convention, which sat in June last, at Washington, the places of worship of that persuasion are stated at more than two thousand three hundred; and they reckon a very large number of ministers. There are three theological seminaries of the Baptist church, one in New England, one in the interior of the State of New York, and one at the city of Washington. There were likewise two theological seminaries of the Methodist church, of whose services, however, it has been for the present deprived by accidental circumstances. It is a remarkable and most laudable characteristic of all these religious denominations that their means are applied among other beneficial purposes, always liberally to that of education.

The Universalists have one hundred and twenty preachers, two hundred separate societies, and eight periodical publications. The Lutheran, the Dutch Reformed, and Associate Reformed, the Moravians, the Friends, in short, almost an innumerable roll of creeds, have their several seminaries of education, their many places of worship, numerous clergy or preachers, and every other attribute of secular, as well as spiritual, religion in prosperity.

To the clergy of some of these sects, especially the Presbyterian and Congregational, the American revolution is deeply indebted for its origin, progress, and issue. The generous, yet jealous principles of self-government, proclaimed as the motives of that event, have no more steadfast, uniform, or invincible adherents, than their followers. Polemical literature, metaphysical knowledge, pulpit eloquence, philological learning, invigorating the mind, and giving it power over the world, are superadded to the laborious and self-denyed lives and pure ministry of these ecclesiastics. The dissenters in England form, no doubt, a body of learned and zealous divines: but from the time when England first sent her sons to New England to learn and teach theology to the present day, the American dissenting church, is, at least equal to that of the mother country in intelligence and influence, and much superior in eloquence.

But it is on the American church of England and the American church of Rome, that we may dwell with most complacency. Here, where no political predominance, no peculiar, above all, no mysterious, inquisitorial, arbitrary, or occult polity, no tythes, no titles, peerage, crown, or other such appliances sustain the ministry, where the crosier is as plain as the original cross itself, and the mitre does not sparkle with a single brilliant torn from involuntary contribution,—it is here, I venture to say, that within the last century, the church of England and the church of Rome have constructed more places of worship, (relatively speaking,) endowed more dioceses, founded more religious houses, and planted a stronger pastoral influence, than in any other part of the globe. It is in the United States of America, under the power of American religion that the English and Roman Catholic churches are flourishing.

Until the revolution, the church of England was the established church in all the American colonies. In Maryland and Virginia, where it was most firmly seated, a sort of modus or composition for tythes was assessed by law, either on the parishes or by the polls. In Virginia there were moreover glebes annexed to the parish churches. In New York, there was also a fund taken from the public money, appropriated to the few parishes established there. Throughout New England, Pennsylvania, and the other colonies, if I am not misinformed, though the church of England was the national church, yet it languished in great infirmity, having no other support than the pew rents and voluntary assessments which now, under a very different regimen, supply adequate resources for all the occasions of an establishment which has no rich, and no very poor pastorates.

The whole of these vast regions, by a gross ordinance of colonial misrule, were attached to the London diocess. Most of the incumbents, it may be supposed, those especially supported by tythes, at such a distance from the diocesan, were supine and licentious. As soon as the revolution put a stop to their stipends, they generally ceased to officiate: and in Maryland and Virginia, particularly, the Methodists and Baptists stepped in to their deserted places. The crisis for the church of England at this conjuncture, was vital. Several of its ministers at first joined their compatriots for the independence declared. But few endured unto the end of the struggle. When the enemy were in possession of Philadelphia, then the capital of the country, where Congress sat, and that inimitable assembly was driven to resume its deliberations at the village of Yorktown, they elected for their chaplain, a clergyman of the church of England, who had been expelled his home in this city by its capture. Every ingenuous mind will do justice to the predicament in which such an election placed an American pastor of the English church. The cause of independence, to which he was attached was in ruin; the government forced from its seat, the army routed and disheartened, the country prostrate and nearly subdued by a triumphant enemy in undisputed occupation of the capital. The chaplain elected by Congress under such circumstances proved worthy of their confidence. Without other attendant, protection, or encouragement, than the consciousness of a good cause, he repaired to the retreat of his country's abject fortunes, to offer daily prayers from the bosom of that immortal assembly which never despaired of them, to the almighty providence, by which they were preserved and prospered. The chaplain of Congress, at Yorktown, has been rewarded for those days of trial. Already, in the compass of his own life, and ministry, he is at the head of the ten bishoprics into which the American church of England has since then expanded in the United States, with three hundred and fifty clergymen, about seven hundred churches, a theological seminary, and every other assurance of substantial prosperity. Within his life time there was but one, and at the commencement of his ministry but three episcopal churches in Philadelphia, and they in jeopardy of the desecration from which they were saved by his patriotic example and pious influence. It would be an unjust and unacceptable homage, however, to him, not to declare that the intrinsic temperance and resource of popular government mainly contributed to the preservation of the English church in America, where it has since advanced far more than in the mother country, during the same period, and where it is probably destined to flourish greatly beyond the English example. Of this there can be no doubt if it thrives henceforth as it has done heretofore: for under the presidency of a single prelate, still in the effective performance of all the duties of a good bishop, and a good citizen, the American church of England, without a particle of political support, has, as we have seen, extended itself. Within a few years a million of pounds sterling were appropriated by parliament, on the special recommendation of the crown of Great Britain, for the repair and construction of churches; with views doubtless to political as much as to religious consequences. I venture to predict that within the period to elapse from that appropriation to its expenditure, a larger sum of money will have been raised in the United States by voluntary subscription, and expended for similar purposes and to greater effect.

The Roman catholic church grows as vigorously as any other in the soil and atmosphere of America. The late (first) archbishop of that church, likewise adhered with unshaken and zealous constancy to the cause of the American revolution: and indeed, served for it in a public station. His illustrious relative is one of the three signers of a charter, destined to have more influence on mankind than any uninspired writing, who have lived to enjoy its developments during half a century; in which period, all North and South America have been regenerated, and the most intelligent portions of Europe quickened with the spirit of that political scripture. He perilled a million of dollars when he pledged his fortune to the declaration of independence: as to the short sighted, the patriot priest might have seemed to risk his religion when he abjured European allegiance. But neither of them has had reason to regret the effects of self-government on a faith of which they have both, at all times, been the American pillars and ornaments. From a mere mission in 1790, the Roman catholic establishment in the United States, has spread into an extended and imposing hierarchy; consisting of a metropolitan see, and ten bishoprics, containing between eighty and a hundred churches, some of them the most costly and splendid ecclesiastical edifices in the country, superintended by about one hundred and sixty clergymen. The remotest quarters of the U. States are occupied by these flourishing establishments; from the chapels at Damascotti (in Maine) and at Boston, to those of St. Augustine in Florida, and St. Louis in Missouri. There are catholic seminaries at Bardstown and Frankfort in Kentucky, a catholic clerical seminary in Missouri, catholic colleges at St. Louis and New Orleans, where there is likewise a catholic Lancasterian school, two catholic charity schools at Baltimore, two in the District of Columbia, a catholic seminary and college at Baltimore, a catholic college in the District of Columbia, a catholic seminary at Emmitsburg in Maryland, a catholic free school and Orphans' asylum in Philadelphia. These large contributions to education, are not, however, highly respectable and cultivated as many of them are, the most remarkable characteristics of the American Roman catholic church. It is a circumstance pregnant with reflections and results, that the Jesuits, since their suppression in Europe, have been established in this country. In 1801, by a brief of pope Pius the seventh, this society, with the concurrence of the emperor Paul, was established in Russia under a general authorised to resume and follow the rule of St. Ignatius of Loyola; which power was extended in 1806, to the United States of America, with permission to preach, educate youth, administer the sacraments, &c. with the consent and approbation of the ordinary. In 1807, a noviciate was opened at Georgetown college in the District of Columbia, which continued to improve till 1814, when, being deemed sufficiently established, the congregation was formally organised by a papal bull. This society now consists of twenty-six fathers, ten scholastics in theology, seventeen scholarships in philosophy, rhetoric, and belles lettres, fourteen scholastics in the noviciate, twenty-two lay-brothers out of, and four lay-brothers in, the noviciate; some of whom are dispersed throughout the United States, occupied in missionary duties, and the cure of souls. This statement is enough to prove the marvellous radication of the strongest fibres of the Roman Catholic church in our soil. But the argument does not stop here. The oldest catholic literary establishment in this country, is the catholic college just mentioned, which was founded immediately after the revolution, by the incorporated catholic clergy of Maryland, now capable of containing two hundred resident students, furnished with an extensive and choice library, a philosophical and chemical apparatus of the latest improvement, and professorships in the Greek, Latin, French, and English languages, mathematics, moral and natural philosophy, rhetoric, and belles lettres. This institution, I have mentioned, was put in 1805, under the direction of the society of Jesuits: and that nothing might be wanting to the strong relief in which the subject appears, the college thus governed, was by act of Congress of the United States of America, raised to the rank of a University, and empowered to confer degrees in any of the faculties. Thus, since the suppression of the order of Jesuits, about the time of the origin of the American revolution, has that celebrated brotherhood of propagandists been restored in the United States, and its principal and most operative institution organised and elevated by an act of our national Legislature.

In like manner, the Sulpitian monks have been incorporated by act of the legislature of the State of Maryland, in the administration of the flourishing Catholic seminary at Baltimore. Still more remains, however, to be made known: For so silent and unobtrusive is religious progress, when neither announced nor enforced by political power, that it is probable, that many of these curious details may be new to some of those who now hear them mentioned. Those religious houses and retreats, which have been rended from their ancient seats in so many parts of Europe—monasteries and convents—are sprouting up and casting their uncultivated fragrance throughout the kindlier glebes and wilds of America. Even where corruption and abuse had exposed them to destruction, learning turned with sorrow from the abomination of their desolation, and charity wept over the downfall of her ancient fanes. But here, where corruption and abuse can hardly exist in self supported religious institutions—what have we to apprehend from these chaste and pious nurseries of education and alms? What may we not hope, on the contrary, for the mind, from their consecration and extension? In the oldest religious house in America, that of the female Carmelites, near Port Tobacco, in Maryland, the established number of inmates is always complete. The convent of St. Mary's, at Georgetown, in the District of Columbia, contains fifty nuns, having under their care a day school, at which, upwards of a hundred poor girls are educated. The convent of the Sisters of Charity of St. Joseph, incorporated by the Legislature of Maryland, at Emmitsburg in that State, consists of fifty-nine sisters, including novices, with fifty-two young ladies under their tuition, and upwards of forty poor children. A convent of Ursulines, at Boston, is yet in its infancy, consisting of a prioress, six sisters, and two novices, who undertake to instruct those committed to their charge in every polite accomplishment, in addition to the useful branches of female education. The Emmitsburg Sisters of Charity, have a branch of their convent for the benefit of female orphan children, established in the city of New York, where the Roman Catholics are said to have increased in the last twenty years, from 300 to 20,000. The church of St. Augustine, in Philadelphia, belongs to the Augustine monks, by whom it was built. There is also a branch of the Emmitsburg Sisters of Charity in this city, consisting of several pious and well informed ladies, who superintend the education of orphan children. The Daughters of Charity, have another branch in Kentucky, where there are, likewise, a house of the order of Apostolines, lately established by the Pope at Rome, a cloister of Loretto, and another convent. In the State of Missouri, there is a convent of religious ladies at the village of St. Ferdinand, where a noviciate is seated, of five novices and several postulants, with a thriving seminary, largely resorted to by the young ladies of that remote region, and also a day school for the poor. In New Orleans, there is a convent of Ursuline nuns, of ancient and affluent endowment, containing fifteen or sixteen professed nuns, and a number of novices and postulants. The ladies of the Heart of Jesus, are about founding a second establishment for education at Opelousas. I will terminate these curious, I hope not irksome, particulars, by merely adding, that in Maine and Kentucky, there are tribes of Indians attached to the Roman Catholic worship, whose indefatigable ministers have always been successful in reclaiming those aborigines of this continent. Vincennes, the chief town of Indiana, where there is now a Roman Catholic chapel, was once a station of the Jesuits for this purpose.

Upon the whole I do not think that we can reckon less than eight thousand places of worship, and five thousand ecclesiastics in the United States, besides twelve theological seminaries, and many religious houses, containing, the former, about five hundred, and the latter three hundred votaries; all self-erected and sustained by voluntary contribution, and nearly all within the last half century. If this unequalled increase of churches and pastors, and worshippers, attests the prosperity of religion, we may rest assured of its welfare without tythes or political support: and we need not fear its decline from the ascendancy of republicanism.

In proving the existence and magnitude of the American church, I have incidentally, I hope sufficiently, explained its character. For the most part well educated, well informed, and well employed, eloquent, unpensioned, self-sustained, trusting to their own good works, and relying on no court favour or individual interest for advancement, exempt from that parasite worldly-mindedness which the honest Massillon, even when preaching before Louis XIV, denounced as the canker of political religion, the American clergy are necessarily called upon to think, to read, to write, to preach, and officiate more than the European. Accordingly the divinity of the American church, if I am not mistaken, is much more active at this time, and its literature more efficient than that of England. Indeed it is hardly to be accounted for, that with the great inducements, means and opportunities of the dignitaries of the English church, the mind is at present so little benefited by their contributions to its enlargement. I by no means design to speak disrespectfully of personages of whom I know little more than their titles; nor do I call in question their learning, their piety, or even their partial usefulness. But assuredly it is fair to infer some radical defect in the system, when of all the modern English bench of bishops and arch-bishops there are very few, I believe, at present in any way known to literature, not one distinguished for eloquence, and on that noble theatre, the house of peers, who ever heard of their performances? Relying on political protection, they seem to have lost the stimulus which urges their American brethren to incessant labours for the furtherance of religion, by eloquent sermons, by contributions to clerical literature, and by the ardent exercise of all their duties. The Roman Catholics boast of numerous converts from protestantism in Europe. Where is the spirit of Tillotson and Sherlock, the English successors of the Chrysostoms and the Bazils? Not in England at present. The works of the great fathers of the English church, those wells of doctrine as of language undefiled, appear to be much more likely to be replenished and perpetuated in America.

In this review, I have of course abstained from all polemic and various other delicate considerations connected with it: confining myself to the actual progress of religion as indicative of the tendency of the mind on that subject in this country. Anti-trinitarians and jesuits, convents, and quakers, all grow and thrive together. The most imposing Roman catholic cathedral, and a considerable Unitarian church are built within the sound of each others service; and neither the intelligence nor the tranquillity of the community has suffered by their neighbourhood. There may be those who think indeed that the growth is inordinate, that the establishments are on a scale of expense and influence disproportioned to our numbers, our principles, and even our independence. But to all such suggestions the answer is, that while the whole is spontaneous, there can be nothing to apprehend.

My undertaking will be unfinished, if I do not explain the political and physical causes of the results, to which attention has been invited. But that task, I may not attempt on this occasion, if ever. It is said to be the American fault, to expend itself in details, instead of reasoning by generalisation. I am very sensible of this, with many other faults, in this discourse, in which, scarcely any thing more is attempted than the collection of facts. But, however imperfect the performance, my views will be accomplished, if the glimpses thus afforded should induce some qualified person to examine and explain the subject philosophically. The operations of American institutions on the human understanding, are a noble study for the labours of a life. The most intelligent portions of mankind, are animated by their impulses; which already actuate, and, before long, must regulate the destinies of the world. The first settlement of this continent was from England, in a state of revolution, when all minds were exercised with new ideas of religious and political liberty. The associates of Pym and Hampden, and Raleigh, Penn and Locke, founded our institutions. A republican empire, really representative, always as it were, in a state of temperate revolution, has been ever since exciting and evolving the great principles of free agency. Our simple and peaceable, but irresistible, religion and politics, are inoffensively reforming the brilliant abuses, which feudal and chivalric barbarism have rivetted on the nations of Europe. This rouses detraction against the whole elements, moral, physical, and intellectual, as well as political, of our existence. Natural-

ists, and statists, philosophers, historians, ambassadors, poets, priests, nobles, tourists, journalists—I speak with precision to this catalogue— have in vain sentenced this country to degradation. It already ranks with communities highly refined before America was discovered. France and England were enjoying Augustan ages, when the place where we are met to discourse of literature and science, was a wilderness. But one hundred and forty years have elapsed, since the patriarch of Pennsylvania first landed on these shores, and sowed them with the germs of peace, toleration, and self-government. Since when, a main employment has been to reclaim the forests for habitation. It is not yet half a century since the United States were politically emancipated; it is only since the late war that they have begun to be intellectually independent. Colonial habits and reverence still rebuke and counteract intellectual enterprise. Education, the learned professions, the arts, scientific and mechanical, legislation, jurisprudence, literature, society—the mind in a word—require time to be freed from European pupilage.

It was not in a spirit of hostility to any other country, that I undertook to shew what has been already done in this: but by that review to encourage further and keener exertions.

To those who will inquire and reflect, the encouragement of philosophy is as strong as the instinct of patriotism. But the empire of habit and of prejudice is in strong opposition to the supremacy of thought and reason. There was a time when it was not considered disaffection to be ashamed of our country, nor disloyalty to despair of it, when we recolonised ourselves. But within the last ten years, especially, the mind of America, has thought for itself, piercing the veil of European beau ideal.

Still less, however, than national disparagement was national vanity the shrine of my sacrifice. Comparative views are indispensable. I might have compared America now with America forty years ago, which would have presented a striking and enlivening contrast. But I preferred the bolder view of America compared with Europe, disclaiming, however, invidious comparisons, which have been studiously avoided. The cause asserted is of too high respect to be defended by panegyric, or avenged by invective. The truth is an ample vindication. Let us strive to refute discredit by constant improvement. Let our intellectual motto be, that naught is done while aught remains to be done: and our study to prove to the world, that the best patronage of religion, science, literature, and the arts, of whatever the mind can achieve, is SELF—GOVERNMENT.

2

EDWARD EVERETT

1794, born April 11, at Dorchester, Mass.
1811, was graduated from Harvard College
1811–14, student in Harvard Divinity School
1814, received the degree of M.A., Harvard
1814–15, minister of Brattle Street Unitarian Church, Boston
1815–17, study at University of Göttingen
1817, received the degree of Ph.D., Göttingen
1817–19, traveled in Europe
1819–25, professor of Greek literature, Harvard
1819–25, editor of *North American Review*
1824, *The Circumstances Favorable to the Progress of Literature in America*
1825–35, member of U.S. House of Representatives
1836–39, governor of Massachusetts
1841–45, U.S. Minister to Great Britain
1846–49, president of Harvard
1852–53, Secretary of State in Fillmore's cabinet
1853–54, member of the U.S. Senate
1853–68, *Orations and Speeches on Various Occasions*; four volumes
1860, candidate for Vice-president, Constitutional Union Party
1863, address at Gettysburg
1865, died January 15, at Boston

INGERSOLL's oration had stressed the practical aspects of American culture. Although he could not approve of the eclipse of American literature by the British, he felt that this was an area in which no bid for supremacy could be made; because he thought of the temper of America as practical, he did not anticipate the development of a national literature. When William Ellery Channing reviewed Ingersoll's oration in the *Christian Examiner*, in 1830, his comment was entitled "Remarks on National Literature." Channing broadened the term "literature" to include "all the writings of superior minds, be the subjects what they may." There are too many "bonds and analogies" between moral and physical truths to restrict literature only to writings about human nature and human life. He resisted Ingersoll's emphasis on the practical, because he thought that "the great distinction of a country is that it produces superior men. . . . No matter what races of animals a country breeds, the great question is, Does it breed a noble race of men?"

Unfortunately "invention and effort have been expended on matter much more than on mind. . . . The thought of building up a nobler order of intellect and character has hardly crossed the most adventurous statesman." While Channing agreed with Ingersoll that America had no national literature, he dissented by believing that every effort should be made to develop superior minds in order that a national literature might emerge.

Similarly, though without specific reference to Ingersoll's ideas, William Cullen Bryant maintained, in a review of Catherine Sedgwick's *Redwood* in the *North American Review* for 1825, entitled "American Society as a Field for Fiction," that "all civilized countries . . . furnish matter for copies of real life, embodied in works of fiction, which shall be of lasting and general interest. Wherever there are human nature and society there are subjects for the novelist." In any country, however, native genius must write of native scenes. The "delicate shades of manner" would escape a foreign author. "It is only on his native soil that the author of such works can feel himself on safe and firm ground . . . and put forth the whole strength of his powers without risk of failure." The claim has been made that such authors do not and will not exist in the United States because they must come from a leisure class. This Bryant denied; he asserted that members of such a leisure class tend to write only about their own type and thus lose sight of "the wholesome atmosphere of those classes, where the passions and affections have their most salutary and natural play." In short, America is a rich field for the novelist from every point of view.

When we consider all these innumerable differences of character, native and foreign, this infinite variety of pursuits and objects, this endless diversity and change of fortunes, and behold them gathered and grouped into one vast assemblage in our own country, we shall feel little pride in the sagacity or the skill of that native author who asks for a richer or a wider field of observation.

Edward Everett, too, saw promise in American literature. When he returned from his years of study in Germany, his orations took on a fervently nationalistic tone, which he attributed later to his youthful delight at being home. Though twenty-five years later he regretted the overstatement, he found no cause for rejecting the principles he had expressed. He realized that the half-century since the Declaration of Independence had been devoted to the consolidation of American political institutions, but felt that the story of the future would be different.

Hitherto, the political effects of our seclusion behind the mighty veil of waters have been the most important. Now that our political foundations are firmly laid . . . we shall reap in other forms the salutary fruits of our remoteness from the centres of foreign opinion and feeling. . . . That great word Independence . . . comprehends much more than a mere absence of foreign jurisdiction. . . . In every noble, in every true acceptation, it implies, not merely an American government, but an American character, and an American feeling.[1]

What remained to be done, his program for America, he summarized at another time:

No pains should be spared to secure its practical benefits to the whole people; to lessen, if it be not possible wholly to remove, the sad inequalities of condition; to place the advantages of a good education within the reach of every individual; and to add the blessings of social refinement, high civilization, and moral and religious culture, to those of national independence and political equality.[2]

In characteristic Whig fashion, he had every hope for "the people" except absolute economic equality.

His awareness of the people was indeed strong. He thought of the American Revolution as a popular movement. The nineteenth of April, 1775,

was one of those great days, one of those elemental occasions in the world's affairs, when the people rise and act for themselves. . . . It was the people, in their first capacity, as citizens and as freemen, starting from their beds at midnight, from their firesides and from their fields, to take their own cause into their own hands. Such a spectacle is the height of the moral sublime. . . . In the efforts of the people,—of the people struggling for their rights, moving, not in organized disciplined masses, but in their spontaneous action, man for man, and heart for heart,—there is something glorious. . . . The people always conquer. They always must conquer.[3]

Out of this background Everett addressed the Phi Beta Kappa Society of Harvard College on August 26, 1824, less than a year after Ingersoll's speech. He took as his topic for the oration, which is reprinted here, "The Circumstances Favorable to the Progress of Literature in America." In addressing himself to this group, Everett was one of the first, if not actually the first, to distinguish them as "American scholars" and to suggest that the interest and curiosity of each auditor in this topic should be "at once dignified and rendered practical by the connection of the inquiry with the conditions and prospects of his native land." The oration can be considered as an attempt to supply the explanation of "the influence of America on the Mind," which Ingersoll had left vague. Everett points out that "as, in the formation

[1] E. Everett, *Orations and Speeches on Various Occasions*, 4th ed., Boston, 1856, p. 52.

[2] *Ibid.*, p. 97. [3] *Ibid.*, pp. 94–95.

of individual character, there are causes of undisputed and powerful operation, so, in national character, there are causes, equally certain, of growth
and excellence on the one hand, and of degeneracy and ruin on the other."
The interpretation of these causes is the proper function of the philosophy
of history—"to trace physical or political facts into moral and intellectual
consequences, and great historical results."

There are three circumstances favorable to the development of American
literature of which Everett speaks. The first of these, the political structure
of the United States, he conceives as "influencing the progress of letters by
furnishing the motives to intellectual effort among us." The direction of
affairs is in the hands of the vast majority of the people; "whatsoever quickening influence resides in public honors and trusts, and in the cheerful consciousness of individuals, participation in the most momentous political rights
is here, for the first time, exerted, directly, on the largest mass of men, with
the smallest possible deductions." While the immediate impulse is to political
interest, that is only a temporary stage in the development of an active mind
which will ultimately issue in a literary culture. Mind, if not wealth, is
"equally diffused throughout the land, by a sterner leveller than ever marched
in the van of a revolution,—the impartial providence of God," and a like
distribution or diffusion is in the nature of "a free system of constitutional
and representative government." The individual, wherever he may be, stands
out; he has a place, a function, and a social importance which lead him to
"encouragement and hope."

The second great motive to intellectual exertion and, by this fact, circumstance favorable to literary progress, is the "extension of one government,
one language, and, substantially, one character over so vast a space as the
United States of America." This makes possible the exertion of "the favorable effect of free institutions on intellectual progress . . . on a very large
scale." The effect of this circumstance on literature "must eventually be, to
give elevation, dignity, and generous expansion to every species of mental
effort. A nationality at once liberal and great is the parent of great thoughts."

Finally, the unexampled rapidity of American growth and expansion is
an important factor in the progress of literature. "Instead of being shut up,
as it were, in the prison of a stationary, or a slowly progressive community,
the emulation of our countrymen is drawn out and tempted on by an horizon
constantly receding before them." New states which are formed in the
westward march of America are as "new nations of freemen"; the impulse
towards creative expression can only be heightened and excited by this growth
and the consequent intensified range of the creative mind. "The theatre on
which the intellect of America is to appear" is broad as the continent.

For all these reasons, impelled by these motives, Everett calls on his audience of American scholars "to exert our powers, to employ our time, and consecrate our labors, for the honor and service of our native land. . . . It is by the intellect of the country that the mighty mass is to be inspired; that its parts are to communicate and sympathize with each other; its natural progress to be adorned with becoming refinements; its principles asserted and its feelings interpreted to its own children, to other regions, and to after ages."

THE CIRCUMSTANCES FAVORABLE TO THE PROGRESS OF LITERATURE IN AMERICA

IN discharging the honorable trust which you have assigned to me on this occasion, I am anxious that the hour which we pass together should be exclusively occupied with those reflections which belong to us as scholars. Our association in this fraternity is academical; we entered it before our Alma Mater dismissed us from her venerable roof; and we have now come together, in the holidays, from every variety of pursuit, and every part of the country, to meet on common ground, as the brethren of one literary household. The duties and cares of life, like the Grecian states, in time of war, have proclaimed to us a short armistice, that we may come up, in peace, to our Olympia.

On this occasion, it has seemed proper to me that we should turn our thoughts, not merely to some topic of literary interest, but to one which concerns us as American scholars. I have accordingly selected, as the subject of our inquiry, *the circumstances favorable to the progress of literature in the United States of America.* In the discussion of this subject, that curiosity, which every scholar naturally feels, in tracing and comparing the character of the higher civilization of different countries, is at once dignified and rendered practical by the connection of the inquiry with the condition and prospects of his native land.

I am aware that such inquiries are apt to degenerate into fanciful speculations and doubtful refinements. Why Asia has, almost without exception, been the abode of some form of despotism, and Europe more propitious to liberty;—why the civilization of the Egyptians was of a character so melancholy and perishable; that of the Greeks so elegant, versatile, and life-giving; that of the Romans so stern and tardy, till they became the imitators of a people whom they conquered and despised, but never equalled;—why tribes of barbarians, from the north and east, not known to differ, essentially, from each other, at the time of their settlement in Europe, should have laid the foundation of national characters so dissimilar as those of the Spaniards, French, Germans, and English;—are questions to which such answers, only, can be given, as will be just and safe, in proportion as they are general and comprehensive. It is difficult, even in the case of the individual man, to point out precisely the causes, under the operation of which, members of the same community, and even of the same family, grow up, with characters the most diverse. It must, of course, be much more difficult to perform the same analysis on a subject so vast as a nation, composed of communities and individuals, greatly differing from each other; all subjected to innumerable external influences; and working out the final result, often in the lapse of ages, not less by mutual counteraction, than coöperation.

But as, in the formation of individual character, there are causes of undisputed and powerful operation, so, in national character, there are causes, equally certain, of growth and excellence on the one hand, and of degeneracy and ruin on the other. It belongs to the philosophy of history to investigate these causes; and, if possible, to point out the circumstances, which, as furnishing the motives, and giving the direction, to intellectual effort in different nations, have had a chief agency in making them what they were, or are. Where it is done judiciously, it is in the highest degree curious thus to trace physical or political facts into moral and intellectual consequences, and great historical results; and to show how climate, geographical position, local relations, institutions, single events, and the influence of individuals, have fixed the characters and decided the destiny of nations.

In pursuing such inquiries, we may, for instance, be led to the conclusion, that it is the tendency of a tropical climate to enervate a people, and thus fit them to become the subjects of a despotism, though it may render them also, through the medium of a fervid temperament, formidable instruments of desolating but transitory conquest, under the lead of able and daring chiefs. We may find that a broad river, or a lofty chain of mountains, by stopping the inroads of war, or of immigration, becomes the boundary, not merely of governments, but of languages and literature, of institutions and character. We may sometimes think we can trace extraordinary skill in the liberal arts to the existence of quarries of fine marble. We may see popular eloquence springing out of popular institutions, and, in its turn, greatly instrumental in affecting the fortunes of free states. We may behold the spirit of an individual law-giver or reformer perpetuated by codes and institutions, for ages. We may trace a peculiar law of progress in colonial settlements, insular states, tribes fortified within Alpine battlements, or scattered over a smiling region of olive gardens and vineyards,— and deduce the political and historical effects of these physical causes.

These topics of rational curiosity and liberal speculation, as I have already intimated, acquire practical importance, when the land in which we ourselves live is the subject of investigation. When we turn the inquiry to our own country; when we survey its natural features, search its history, and examine its institutions, to see what are the circumstances which are to excite and guide the popular mind; it then becomes an inquiry of the highest interest, and worthy the attention of every patriotic scholar. We then dwell, not on a distant, uncertain, perhaps fabulous, past, but on an impending future, teeming with individual and public fortune; a future, toward which we are daily and rapidly swept forward, and with which we stand in the dearest connection that can bind the generations of men together; a future, which our own characters, actions, and principles, may influence, for good or evil, for lasting glory or shame. We then strive, as far as our poor philosophy can do it, to read the country's reverend auspices; to cast its great horoscope in the national sky, where some stars are waning, and some have set. We endeavor to ascertain whether the soil, which we love as that where our fathers are laid, and we shall presently be laid with them, is likely to be trod, in times to come, by an enlightened, virtuous, and free people.

I. The first circumstance, of which I shall speak, as influencing the progress of letters by furnishing the motives to intellectual effort among us, is the new form of political society established in the United States; viz., a confederacy of republics, in which, however, within the limits of the Constitution, the central government acts upon the individual citizen. It is not my purpose to detain you with so trite a topic as the praises of free political institutions; but to ask your attention to the natural operation of a system like ours on the literary character of a people. I call this a new form of political society. The ancient Grecian republics, indeed, were free enough, within the walls of the single cities, of which many of them were wholly or chiefly composed; while, toward the confederate or tributary states, their governments generally assumed the form of a despotism, more capricious, and not less arbitrary, than that of a single tyrant. Rome was never the abode of well-regulated republican liberty. The remark just made of the Grecian republics, in reference to allied states, applies to the Roman, for the greater portion of its history; while, within the walls of the city, the commonwealth fluctuated between the evils of an oppressive aristocracy and a factious populace. Since the downfall of Rome, the rudiments of a representative legislature are to be found in the *estates* of some of the governments of continental Europe, and far more distinctly and effectually developed in the British Parliament; but a uniform and complete representative system, organized by a written constitution of government and unaccompanied by a powerful hereditary element, is original in this country. Here, for the first time, the whole direction and influence of affairs, and all the great organic functions of the body politic, are subjected, directly or indirectly,—the executive and legislative functions directly,—to free popular choice. Whatsoever quickening influence resides in public honors and trusts, and in the cheerful consciousness of individual participation in the most momentous political rights, is here, for the first time, exerted, directly, on the largest mass of men, with the smallest possible deductions; and as a despotism, like that of Turkey or Persia, is, by all admission, the form of government least favorable to the intellectual progress of a people, it would seem equally certain, that the farther you recede from such a despotism, in the establishment of a system of popular and constitutional liberty, the greater the assurance that the universal mind of the country will be powerfully and genially excited.

I am aware that it is a common notion, that, under an elective government, of very limited powers, like that of the United States, we lose that powerful spring of action which exists in the patronage of strong hereditary governments, and must proceed from the crown. I believe it is a prevalent opinion, abroad, among those who entertain the most

friendly sentiments toward the American system, that we must consent
to dispense with something of the favorable influence of princely and
royal patronage on letters and the arts, and find our consolation in the
political benefits of a republican government. It may be doubted,
however, whether this view be not entirely fallacious. For, in the first
place, it is by no means true that a popular government will be destitute
either of the means or the disposition to exercise a liberal patronage.
No government, as a government, ever did more for the fine arts than
that of Athens. In the next place, it is to be considered, in this connection, that the evils of centralization are as evident, in reference to the
encouragement of the general mind of the people, as they are in regard to a contented acquiescence in political administration. Whatever
is gained, for those who enjoy it, by concentrating a powerful patronage in the capital, and in the central administration, is lost in the neglect
and discouragement of the distant portions of the state, and its subordinate institutions. It must be recollected, that our representative
system extends far beyond the election of the high officers of the national and state governments. It pervades our local and municipal
organizations, and probably exercises, in them, the most efficient and
salutary part of its influence. In the healthful action of this system,
whatever virtue there is in patronage is made to pervade the republic,
like the air; to reach the farthest, and descend to the lowest. It is made
not only to coöperate with the successful, and decorate the prosperous,
but "to remember the forgotten, to attend to the neglected, to visit the
forsaken." Hitherto, for the most part, men in need of patronage have
had but one weary pilgrimage to perform,—to travel up to court. By
an improvement on the Jewish polity, which enjoined a visit, thrice a
year, to the Holy City, the theory of patronage in question requires a
constant residence at the favored spot. *Provincial* has become another
term for inferior and rude; and *unpolite*, which once meant only *rural*,
has been made to signify something little better than barbarous. As it
is, in the nature of things, a small part, only, of the population of a
large state, which can thus bring itself, or by happy chance can fall,
into the sphere of metropolitan favor, it follows, that the mass of the
people are cut off from the operation of those motives to exertion, which
flow from the hope or the possession of patronage.

But the beneficial effect of patronage, properly so called, is probably much overrated. This effect is not, on any system of distribution, to be sought in its direct application to the support of men of genius and learning. Its best operation is in the cheerful effect of kindly notice and intelligent audience. Talent, indeed, desires to earn a support, but not to receive a dole. It is rightfully urged, as the great advantage of our system, that the encouragements of society extend as widely as its burdens, and search out, and bring forward, whatsoever of ability and zeal for improvement are contained in any part of the land. I am persuaded, that, mainly, in this equable diffusion of rights and privileges lies the secret of the astonishing development of intellectual energy in this country. Capacity and opportunity, the twin sisters, who can scarce subsist happily but with each other, are brought together. These little local republics are schools of character and nurseries of mind. The people, who are to choose, and from whose number are to be chosen, by their neighbors, all those who, either in higher or lower stations, are intrusted with the management of affairs, feel the strongest impulse to mental activity. They read, and think, and form judgments on important subjects. In an especial manner, they are moved to make provision for education. With all its deficiencies, our system of public schools—founded, in the infancy of the country, by the colonial legislature, and transmitted to our own days—is superior to any system of public instruction (with possibly a single exception) which has ever been established by the most enlightened states of the Old World. Hasty prejudices, as to the tendencies of representative republics, have been drawn from the disorders of the ill-organized democracies of the ancient world. Terrific examples of license and anarchy, in Greece and Rome, are quoted, to prove that man requires to be protected from himself, forgetting the profound wisdom wrapped up in the well-known formidable inquiry, *Quis custodiet ipsos custodes?* But to reason, in cases like this, from the states of Greece to our constitutions of government, is to be deceived by schoolboy analogies. From the first settlement of New England, and from an early stage of their progress in many of the other states, one of the most prominent traits of the character of our population has been, to provide and to diffuse the means of education. The village school-house and the village church are the monuments of our republicanism; to read, to write, and to discuss grave affairs, in their primary assemblies, are the licentious practices of our democracy.

But, in this acknowledged result of our system of government, another objection is taken to its influence, as far as literary progress is concerned. It is urged, that, though it may be the effect of our system to excite the mind of the people, it excites it too much in a political direction; that the division and subdivision of the country into states and districts, and the equal diffusion of political privileges and powers among the whole population, with the constant recurrence of elections, however favorable to civil liberty, are unfriendly to learning; that they kindle only a political ambition; and particularly, that they seduce the aspiring youth, from the patient and laborious vigils of the student, to plunge prematurely into the conflicts of the forum.

I am inclined to think, that, as far as the alleged facts exist, they are the necessary result of the present stage of our national progress, and not an evil necessarily incident to representative government. Our system is certainly an economical one, both as to the number of persons employed and the compensation of public service. It cannot, therefore, draw more individuals from other pursuits into public life, than would be employed under any other form or system of government. It is obvious, that the administration of the government of a country, whether it be liberal, or absolute, or mixed, is the first thing to be provided for. Some persons must be employed in making and administering the laws, before any other human interest can be attended to. The Fathers of Plymouth organized themselves under a simple compact of government, before they left the Mayflower. This was both natural and wise. Had they, while yet on shipboard, talked of founding learned societies, or engaged in the discussion of philosophical problems, it would have been insipid pedantry. As the organization and administration of the government are, in the order of time, the first of mere human concerns, they must ever retain a paramount importance. Every thing else must come in by *opportunity;* this, of *necessity,* must be provided for: otherwise, life is not safe, property is not secure, and there is no permanence in the social institutions. The first efforts, therefore, of men, in building up a new state, are, of necessity, political. The peculiar relations of the colonies to the parent state, also, called into political action much of the talent of the country, for a century before the revolution. But where else in the world did the foundation of the college ever follow so closely on that of the republic, as in Massachusetts? In the early stages of society, when there is a scanty population, its entire force is required for administration and defence. We are receding from this stage, but have not yet reached, although we are rapidly approaching, that in which a crowded population produces a large amount of cultivated talent, not needed for the service of the state.

As far, then, as the talent and activity of the country are at present called forth, in a political direction, it is fairly to be ascribed, not to any supposed incompatibility of popular institutions with the cultivation of letters, but to the precise point, in its social progress, which the country has reached. A change of government would produce no change in this respect. Can any man suppose, other things remaining the same, that the introduction of an hereditary sovereign, an order of nobility, a national church, a standing army, and a military police, would tend to a more general and more fruitful development of mental energy, or greater leisure, on the part of educated men, to engage in literary pursuits? It is obviously as impossible that any such effect should be produced, as that the supposed producing cause should be put in action, in this country. By the terms of the supposition, if such a change were made, the leading class of the community, the nobles, would be politicians, by birth; as much talent would be required to administer the state; as much physical activity to defend it. If there were a class, as there probably would be, in the horizontal division of society, which exists under such governments, not taking an interest in politics, it would be that, which, under the name of the peasantry, fills, in most other countries, the place of, perhaps, the most substantial, uncorrupted, and intelligent population on earth,—the American Yeomanry. We are not left to theory on this point. There are portions of the American continent, earlier settled than the United States, governed, from the first, by absolute power, and possessing all the advantages which can flow from what is called a strong government. It may be safely left to the impartial judgment of mankind, to compare the progress, either of general intelligence, or of higher literature, in those portions of the continent, and in the United States. Nor would any different conclusion be drawn from the contrast between the colonies and the United States, before and since the revolution.

Again, it cannot be thought a matter of little moment, that, under a purely popular government, the cultivation of letters always has been, and unquestionably always will be, deemed as honorable a pursuit as any to which the attention can be devoted. Under other forms of government, a different standard of respectability exists. Hereditary rank, of necessity, takes precedence; and all the institutions of society are made to regard the accidents of birth, as more important than personal merit. The choicest spirits of Europe, for ten centuries, have been trained up to the feeling, that government and war are the only callings worthy of noble blood. In those foreign countries, as England, where the political institutions have been most improved, and the iron yoke of feudalism most effectually broken,—that is, in other words, where the people have been restored to their natural rights,—we behold, as the invariable consequence, a proportionate intellectual progress. What could be more preposterous, than to attribute this progress to the operation of those remnants of the feudal system, which still remain, rather than to the free principles and popular institutions which have succeeded it; and to deny to such institutions, in their more perfect organization, in this country, a tendency to produce the same happy effects, which their partial introduction has every where else produced?

It cannot but be, that the permanent operation of a free system of constitutional and representative government should be favorable to the culture of mind, because it is in conformity with that law of Nature by which mind itself is distributed. The mental energy of a people, which you propose to call out, the intellectual capacity, which is to be cultivated and improved, has been equally diffused, throughout the land, by a sterner leveller than ever marched in the van of a revolution,—the impartial providence of God. He has planted the germs of intellect alike in the city and the country; by the beaten way-side, and in the secluded valley and solitary hamlet. Sterling native character, strength and quickness of mind, the capacity for brilliant attainment, are not among the distinctions which Nature has given, exclusively, to the higher circles of life. Too often, in quiet times, and in most countries, they perish in the obscurity to which a false organization of society consigns them. And the reason why, in dangerous, convulsed,

and trying times, there generally happens an extraordinary development of talent, unquestionably is, that, in such times, whatever be the
nominal form of the government, necessity, for the moment, proclaims
an intellectual Republic.

What happens in a crisis of national fortune, under all governments, is, in this respect, the steady and natural operation of our political institutions. Their foundation, at last, is in dear Nature. They do
not consign the greater part of the social system to torpidity and
mortification. They send out a vital nerve to every member of the community, however remote, by which it is brought into living conjunction
and strong sympathy with the kindred intellect of the nation. They
thus encourage Nature to perfect her work, on the broadest scale. By
providing systems of universal and cheap education, they multiply,
indefinitely, the numbers of those to whom the path is opened, for
further progress; and thus bring up remote, and otherwise unpatron-
ized, talent into the cheerful field of competition. The practical operation of popular institutions of government provides, in innumerable
ways, a demand for every species of intellectual effort, not merely
within the circle of a capital, but throughout the land. In short, wherever man has been placed by Providence, endowed with rational capacities of improvement, there the genius of the republic visits him,
with a voice of encouragement and hope. Every day he receives, from
the working of the social system, some new assurance that he is not
forgotten in the multitude of the people. He is called to do some act,
to assert some right, and to enjoy some privilege; and he is elevated,
by this consciousness of his social importance, from the condition of
the serf or the peasant, to that of the freeman and the citizen.

In thus maintaining that the tendency of our popular institutions,
at the present stage of our national progress, to excite a diffusive interest in politics, is in no degree unfriendly to the permanent intellectual
improvement of the country, it is not intended to assert that the peculiar
and original character of these institutions will produce no corresponding modification of our literature. The reverse is, unquestionably, the
fact. It may safely be supposed, that, with the growth of the people
in wealth and population, as the various occasions of an enterprising
and prosperous community, placed on the widest theatre of action ever
opened to man, call into strong action and vigorous competition the

cultivated talent of the country, some peculiar tone, form, and proportion will be given to its literature, by the nature of its political institutions, and the social habits founded on them. Literature is but a more
perfect communication of man with man, and mind with mind. It is
the judgment, the memory, the imagination; discoursing, recording,
or musing aloud, upon the materials drawn from the great storehouse
of observation, or fashioned out of them by the creative powers of the
mind. It is the outward expression of the intellectual man; or, if not
this, it is poor imitation. What, therefore, affects the man, affects the
literature; and it may be assumed, as certain, that the peculiarity of our
political institutions will be represented in the character of our intellectual pursuits. Government, war, commerce, manners, and the stage
of social progress, are reflected in the literature of a country. No precedent exists, to teach us what direction the mind will most decidedly
take, under the strong excitements to action above described, unrestrained by the direct power of government, but greatly influenced by
public sentiment, throughout a vastly-extensive and highly-prosperous
country, into which the civilization of older states has been rapidly
transfused.

This condition of things is, evidently, substantially new, and renders
it impossible to foresee what garments our native muses will weave to
themselves. To foretell our literature would be to create it. There was
a time, before an epic poem, a tragedy, an historical composition, or a
forensic harangue, had ever been produced by the wit of man. It was
a time of vast and powerful empires, and of populous and wealthy
cities. We have no reason to think that any work, in either of those departments of literature, (with the exception, perhaps, of some meagre
chronicle, which might be called history,) was produced by the early
Ethiopians, the Egyptians, or the Assyrians. Greece herself had been
settled a thousand years, before the golden age of her literature. At
length, the new and beautiful forms, in which human thought and
passion expressed themselves in that favored region, sprang up, and
under the excitement of free political institutions. Before the epos,
the drama, the oration, the history, appeared, it would, of course, have
been idle for the philosopher to form conjectures as to the paths which
would be struck out by the kindling genius of the age. He who could
form such an anticipation could and would realize it, and it would be

anticipation no longer. The critic is ages behind the poet. Epic poetry was first conceived of, when the gorgeous vision of the Iliad, not, indeed, in its full detail of circumstances, but in the dim fancy of its leading scenes and bolder features, burst upon the soul of Homer.

It would be equally impossible to mark out, beforehand, the probable direction in which the intellect of this country will move, under the influence of institutions as new and peculiar as those of Greece, and so organized as to secure the best blessings of popular government, without the evils of anarchy. But if, as no one will deny, our political system brings more minds into action, on equal terms, and extends the advantages of education, more equally, throughout the community; if it provides a prompter and wider circulation of thought; if, by raising the character of the masses, it swells to tens of thousands and millions those "sons of emulation, who crowd the narrow strait where honor travels," it would seem not too much to anticipate new varieties and peculiar power in the literature, which is but the voice and utterance of all this mental action. The instrument of communication may receive improvement; the written and spoken language acquire new vigor; possibly, forms of address wholly new will be devised. Where great interests are at stake, great concerns rapidly succeeding each other, depending on almost innumerable wills, and yet requiring to be apprehended in a glance, and explained in a word; where movements are to be given to a vast population, not so much by transmitting orders as by diffusing opinions, exciting feelings, and touching the electric chord of sympathy; there language and expression will become intense, and the old processes of communication must put on a vigor and a directness adapted to the condition of things.

Our country is called, as it is, practical; but this is the element for intellectual action. No strongly-marked and high-toned literature, poetry, eloquence, or philosophy, ever appeared, but under the pressure of great interests, great enterprises, perilous risks, and dazzling rewards. Statesmen, and warriors, and poets, and orators, and artists, start up under one and the same excitement. They are all branches of one stock. They form, and cheer, and stimulate, and, what is worth all the rest, understand, each other; and it is as truly the sentiment of the student, in the recesses of his cell, as of the soldier in the ranks, which breathes in the exclamation,

"To all the sons of sense proclaim,
One glorious hour of *crowded life*
Is worth an age without a name;" [1]

crowded with emotion, thought, utterance, and achievement.

Let us now inquire how history and experience confirm the foregoing speculations. Here we shall be met again at the outset, and reminded of the splendid patronage which has been bestowed by strong governments on literature; patronage of a kind which necessarily implies the centralization of the resources of the state, and is consequently inconsistent with a representative system. We shall be told of the rich establishments, and liberal pensions; of museums founded, libraries collected, and learned societies sustained; by Ptolemies, Augustuses, and Louises, of ancient and modern times. Then we shall be directed to observe the fruit of this noble patronage, in the wonders of antiquarian and scientific lore which it has ushered into the world; the Thesauruses and Corpuses, from which the emulous student, who would understand all things, recoils in horror, and in the contemplation of which, meek-eyed Patience folds her hands in despair.

When we have reflected on these things, and turn our thoughts back to our poor republican land; to our frugal state treasuries, and the caution with which they are dispensed; to our modest private fortunes, and the thrift with which they are, of necessity, hoarded; to our scanty public libraries, and proportionably limited private collections,—we may be apt to form gloomy auguries of the influence of free political institutions on letters. Here, then, we may fairly scrutinize the real character of this vaunted patronage, and inquire what it has actually done for the pure original literature of any people. How much was unfruitful pomp and display, and how much mere favoritism; and of the expensive literary enterprises, to which I have alluded, how many may be compared to the Pyramids—stupendous monuments of industry, labor, and power, of little value to the eye of taste, and of no benefit to man?

But let us examine, more carefully, the experience of former ages, and see how far their political institutions, as they have been more or less popular, have been more or less productive of intellectual excel-

---

[1] Scott, *Old Mortality*, Chap. XXXIV.

lence. When we make this examination, we shall be gratified to find, that the clear precedents are all in favor of liberty. The greatest efforts of human genius have been made where the nearest approach to free institutions has taken place. Not one ray of intellectual light shone forth, as far as we know, to cheer the long and gloomy ages of the Memphian and Babylonian despots. Not an historian, not an orator, not a poet, as has been already observed, is heard of in their annals. When we ask what was achieved by the generations of thinking beings,—the millions of men, whose natural genius may have been as bright as that of the Greeks, nay, who forestalled the Greeks in the first invention of many of the arts,—we are told that they built the pyramids of Memphis, the temples of Thebes, the tower of Babylon; and carried Sesostris and Ninus upon their shoulders, from the west of Africa to the Indus. Mark the contrast in Greece. With the first emerging of that country into the light of political liberty, the poems of Homer appear. Some centuries, alike of political confusion and literary darkness, follow, and then the great constellation of their geniuses seems to rise at once. The stormy eloquence and the deep philosophy, the impassioned drama and the grave history, were all produced for the entertainment of the "fierce democratie" of Athens.

Here, then, the genial influence of liberty on letters is strongly put to the test. Athens was certainly a free state; free to licentiousness, free to madness. The rich were arbitrarily pillaged to defray the public expenses; the great were banished to appease the envy of their rivals; the wise sacrificed to the fury of the populace. It was a state, in short, where liberty existed, with most of the imperfections which have sometimes led the desponding to love and praise despotism. Still, however, it was for this lawless, merciless, but free people, that the most chaste and accomplished literature which the world has known, was produced. The philosophy of Plato was the attraction which drew the young men of this factious city to a morning's walk in the olive gardens of the academy. Those tumultuous assemblies of Athens, which rose in their wrath, and to a man, and clamored for the blood of Phocion, required to be addressed in the profoundly studied and exquisitely wrought orations of Demosthenes.

No! the noble and elegant arts of Greece grew up in no Augustan age. Unknown before in the world, strangers on the Nile, and on the

Euphrates, they sprang at once into life, in a region not unlike our own New England,—iron-bound, sterile, but free. The imperial astronomers of Chaldæa went up almost to the stars in their observatories; but it was a Greek who first foretold an eclipse, and measured the year. Some happy genius in the East invented the alphabet, but not a line has reached us of profane literature, in any of their languages; and it is owing to the embalming power of Grecian genius, that the invention itself has been transmitted to the world. The Egyptian architects could erect structures, which, after three thousand years, are still standing in their uncouth, original majesty; but it was only on the barren soil of Attica, that the beautiful columns of the Parthenon and the Theseum could rest, which are standing also.

With the decline of liberty in Greece began the decline of her letters and her arts, though her tumultuous democracies were succeeded by liberal and accomplished princes. Compare the literature of the Alexandrian with that of the Periclean age; how cold, pedantic, and imitative! Compare, I will not say the axes, the eggs, the altars, and the other frigid devices of the pensioned wits in the museum at Alexandria, in a far subsequent age, but compare their best productions with those of independent Greece; Callimachus with Pindar, Lycophron with Sophocles, Aristophanes of Byzantium with Aristotle, and Apollonius the Rhodian with Homer. When we descend to Rome, to the Augustan age, the proverbial era of Mæcenas, we find one uniform work of imitation, often of translation. The choicest spirits seldom rise beyond a happy transfusion of the Grecian masters. Horace translates Alcæus, Terence translates Menander, Lucretius translates Epicurus, Virgil translates Homer, and Cicero, I had almost said, translates Demosthenes and Plato. But the soul of republican liberty did burst forth from the lips of Cicero; her inspiration produced in him the best specimens of a purely original literature, which the Romans have transmitted to us. After him, their literary history is written in one line of Tacitus: *gliscente adulatione, magna ingenia deterrebantur.* The fine arts revived a little, under the princes of the Flavian house, but never rose higher than a successful imitation of the waning excellence of Greece, executed by her fugitive artists. With the princes of this line, the arts of Rome expired, and Constantine the Great was obliged to tear down an arch of Trajan for sculptures, to adorn his own. Finally, a long period of military and barbarous despotism succeeded, which buried letters and arts in one grave with national independence.

In modern times, the question as to the distinct effect of political institutions on learning, has become greatly complicated, in consequence of the large number of separate states, into which the civilized world is divided, and the easy and rapid communication between them. The consequence is, that a powerful impulse, given to mind in one country, under the influence of causes favorable to its progress, may be felt to some extent in other countries, where no such causes exist. Upon the whole, however, the modern history of literature furnishes many illustrious examples, which may well awaken a doubt whether much has been effected by direct patronage, whether of arbitrary or liberal governments, for the encouragement of letters. Dante, Petrarch, and Boccaccio, "the all Etruscan three," were citizens of the Florentine republic, to which they owed nothing but exile, confiscation, and persecution. The Medici rendered important services in promoting the revival of letters, but Machiavelli was pursued for resisting their tyrannical designs; Guicciardini composed his history in exile; and Galileo confessed, in the prisons of the Inquisition, that the earth did not move. Ariosto's princely patron, when presented with a copy of the Orlando, asked, "Where did you pick up this trumpery, Ludovico?" and the "magnanimous Alfonso" confined Tasso in a madhouse, till he became a fitting inmate for it. Cervantes, after he had immortalized himself, in his great work, was obliged to write on, for bread. The whole French Academy was pensioned, to crush the great Corneille. Racine, after living to see his finest pieces derided as cold and worthless, died of a broken heart. The divine genius of Shakespeare found its best patronage in popular favor. It gave him fortune, but it raised him to no higher rank than that of a subaltern actor in his own and Ben Jonson's plays. The immortal Bacon made disastrous wreck of his greatness, in a court, and is said (falsely, I trust) to have begged a cup of beer, in his old age, and begged it in vain. The most valuable of the pieces of Selden were written in that famous resort of great minds, the Tower of London. Milton, surprised by want, in his infirm old age, sold one of the first productions of the human mind for five pounds. The great boast of English philosophy was expelled from his place in Oxford, and kept in banishment, "the king having been given to understand," to use the words of Lord Sunderland, who ordered the expulsion, "that *one Locke* has, upon several occasions, behaved himself very factiously against the government." Dryden presents his translation to his patron, as "the wretched remainder of a sickly age worn out with study and oppressed with fortune, without other support than the constancy and patience of a Christian." Otway was choked with a morsel of bread, too ravenously swallowed after a long fast. Johnson, after the publication of his Dictionary, was released by Richardson from arrest for debt; and Goldsmith, at one period of his career, took refuge from actual starvation among the beggars of London. When we consider these facts, and the innumerable others of which these are a specimen, we may probably be led to the conclusion that the appearance of eminent geniuses, under the forms of government subsisting in Europe, furnishes no decisive proof that they are the most friendly to intellectual progress.

II. The next circumstance, worthy of mention, as peculiarly calculated to promote the progress of improvement, and to furnish motives to intellectual exertion, in this country, is the extension of one government, one language, and, substantially, one character, over so vast a space as the United States of America. Hitherto, in the main, the world has seen but two forms of political government—free governments in small states, and arbitrary governments in large ones. Though various shades of both have appeared, at different times, in the world, yet, on the whole, the political ingenuity of man has never before devised the method of extending purely popular institutions beyond small districts, or of governing large states by any other means than military power. The consequence has been, that the favorable effect of free institutions on intellectual progress, has never been developed, on a very large scale. But, though favorable to the improvement of the mind, under any circumstances, it is evident, that, in order to their full effect, in bringing forth the highest attainable excellence, they must be permanently established, in an extensive region and over a numerous people. Such is the state of things existing in this country, and for the first time in the world, and for which we are indebted to the peculiar nature of our government, as a union of confederated republics. Its effect upon literature must eventually be, to give elevation, dignity, and generous expansion to every species of mental effort. A nationality at once liberal and great is the parent of great thoughts. The extent, the resources, and the destiny of the country are imaged forth in the conception of its leading minds. They are but the organs of the race from which they are descended, the land in which they live, and the patriotic associations under which they have been educated. These prompt their language and elevate their thoughts. Under an impulse like the prophetic enthusiasm of old, they feel and utter the sentiments which are inspired by the system of which they are the members. As the mind goes forth to enter into communion or conflict with millions of kindred spirits, over a mighty realm, it dilates, with a noble consciousness of its vocation. It disdains mean conceptions, and strives to speak a noble word, which will touch the heart of a great people.

This necessary connection between the extent of a country and its intellectual progress, was, it is true, of more importance in antiquity than it is at the present day, because, at that period of the world, owing to political causes, on which we have not time to dwell, there was, upon the whole, but one civilized and cultivated people, at a time, upon the stage; and the mind of one nation found no sympathy, and derived no aid, from the mind of another. Art and refinement followed in the train of political ascendency, from the East to Greece, and from Greece to Rome, declining in one region as they rose in another. In the modern world, a combination of political, intellectual, and even mechanical causes, (for the art of printing is among the most powerful of them,) has produced an extension of the highest civilization over a large family of states, existing contemporaneously in Europe and America. This circumstance might seem to mould the civilized portion of mankind into one republic of letters, and make it, comparatively, a matter of indifference to any individual mind, whether its lot was cast in a small or a large, a weak or a powerful, state. It must be freely admitted, that this is, to some extent, the case; and it is one of the great advantages of the modern over the ancient civilization. And yet a singular fatality immediately presents itself, to neutralize, in a great degree, the beneficial effects of this enlarged and diffused civilization on the progress of letters in any single state. It is true, that, instead of one sole country, as in antiquity, where the arts and refinements find a home, there are, in modern Europe, seven or eight, equally entitled to the general name of cultivated nations, and in each of which some minds of the first order have appeared. And yet, by the *multiplication of languages*, the powerful effect of international sympathy on the progress of letters has been greatly impaired. The muses of Shakspeare and Milton, of Camoens, of Lope de Vega and Calderon, of Corneille and Racine, of Dante and Tasso, of Gœthe and Schiller, are comparative strangers to each other. Certainly it is not intended that these illustrious minds are unknown beyond the limits of the lands in which they were trained, and to which they spoke. But who is ignorant that not one of them finds a full and hearty response from any other people but his own, and that their writings must be, to some extent, a sealed book, except to those who read them in the mother tongue? There are other languages besides those alluded to, in which the works of a great writer would be still more effectually locked up. How few, even of well-educated foreigners, know any thing of the literature of the Hungarian, Sclavonian, or Scandinavian races! to say nothing of the languages of the East.

This evil is so great and obvious, that for nearly two centuries after the revival of letters, the Latin language was adopted, as a matter of course, by the scholars of Europe, in works intended for general circulation. We see men like Luther, Calvin, Erasmus, Bacon, Grotius, and Leibnitz, who could scarce have written a line without exciting the admiration of their countrymen, driven to the use of a tongue which none but the learned could understand. For the sake of addressing the scholars of other countries, these great men, and others like them, in many of their writings, were willing to cut themselves off from all sympathy with the mass of those whom, as patriots, they must have wished most to instruct. In works of pure science and learned criticism, this is of the less consequence; for, being independent of sentiment, it matters less how remote from real life the symbols by which their ideas are conveyed. But, when we see a writer, like Milton, who, as much as any other that ever lived, was a master of the music of his native tongue; who, besides all the beauty of conception and imagery, knew better than most other men how to breathe forth his thoughts and images,

> "In notes with many a winding bout
> Of linked sweetness long drawn out,
> With wanton heed and giddy cunning,
> The melting voice through mazes running,
> Untwisting all the chains that tie
> The hidden soul of harmony;"

when we see a master of English eloquence, thus gifted, choosing a dead language,—the dialect of the closet, a tongue without an echo from the hearts of the people,—as the vehicle of his defence of that people's rights; asserting the cause of Englishmen in the language, as it may be truly called, of Cicero; we can only measure the incongruity, by reflecting what Cicero would himself have thought and felt, if compelled to defend the cause of Roman freedom, not in the language of the Roman citizen, but in that of the Grecian rhetorician, or the Punic merchant. And yet, Milton could not choose but employ this language; for he felt that in this, and this alone, he could speak the word "with which all Europe rang from side to side."

There is little doubt that the prevalence of the Latin language, among modern scholars, was a great cause, not only of the slow progress of letters among the people at large, but of the stiffness and constraint of the vernacular style of most scholars themselves, in the sixteenth and seventeenth centuries. That the reformation in religion advanced with such rapidity is, in no small degree, to be attributed to the translations of the Scriptures and the use of liturgies in the modern tongues. The preservation, in legal acts, in England, of a foreign language,—I will not offend the majesty of Rome by calling it Latin,—down to so late a period as 1730, may be one reason why reform in the law did not keep pace with the progress of reform in some other departments. With the establishment of popular institutions under Cromwell, among various other legal improvements,[2] many of which were speedily adopted by our plain-dealing forefathers, the records of the law were ordered to be kept in English; "a novelty," says the learned commentator on the English laws, "which, at the restoration, was no longer continued, practisers having found it very difficult to express themselves so concisely or significantly in any other language but Latin." [3]

Nor are the other remedies for the evil of a multiplicity of tongues more efficacious. Something, of course, is done by translations, and something by the study of foreign languages. But that no effectual transfusion of the higher literature of a country can take place in the way of translation, need not be urged; and it is a remark of one of the

[2] See a number of them in Lord Somers's *Tracts*, Vol. I.
[3] Blackstone's *Commentaries*, Vol. III. p. 422.

few who could have courage to make such a remark, Madame de Stael, that it is impossible fully to comprehend the literature of a foreign tongue. The general preference, given till lately, to Young's Night Thoughts and Ossian, over all the other English poets, in many parts of the continent of Europe, confirms the justice of this observation. It is unnecessary, however, to repeat, that it is not intended to apply to works of exact science, or merely popular information.

There is, indeed, an influence of exalted genius, coëxtensive with the earth. Something of its power will be felt, in spite of the obstacles of different languages, remote regions, and other times. The minds of Dante and of Shakspeare have, no doubt, by indirect influence, affected thousands who never read a line of either. But the true empire of genius, its sovereign sway, must be at home, and over the hearts of kindred men. A charm, which nothing can borrow, and for which there is no substitute, dwells in the simple sound of our mother tongue. Not analyzed, nor reasoned upon, it unites the simplest recollections of early life with the maturest conceptions of the understanding. The heart is willing to open all its avenues to the language in which its infantile caprices were soothed; and, by the curious efficacy of the principle of association, it is this echo from the faint dawn of intelligence, which gives to eloquence much of its manly power, and to poetry much of its divine charm.

What a noble prospect presents itself, in this way, for the circulation of thought and sentiment in our country! Instead of that multiplicity of dialect, by which mental communication and sympathy between different nations are restrained in the Old World, a continually expanding realm is opened to American intellect, by the extension of one language over so large a portion of the Continent. The enginery of the press is here, for the first time, brought to bear, with all its mighty power, on the minds and hearts of men, in exchanging intelligence, and circulating opinions, unchecked by diversity of language, over an empire more extensive than the whole of Europe.

And this community of language, all important as it is, is but a part of the manifold brotherhood, which already unites the growing millions of America, with a most powerful influence on literary culture. In Europe, the work of international alienation, which begins in diversity of language, is consummated by diversity of race, institutions, and national prejudices. In crossing the principal rivers, channels, and mountains, in that quarter of the world, you are met, not only by new tongues, but by new forms of government, new associations of ancestry, new, and often hostile objects of national pride and attachment. While, on the other hand, throughout the vast regions included within the limits of our republic, not only the same language, but the same national government, the same laws and manners, and common ancestral associations prevail. Mankind will here exist and act in a kindred mass, such as was scarcely ever before congregated on the earth's surface. What would be the effect, on the intellectual state of Europe, at the present day, were all her nations and tribes amalgamated into one vast empire, speaking the same tongue, united into one political system, and that a free one, and opening one broad, unobstructed pathway, for the interchange of thought and feeling, from Lisbon to Archangel? If effects must bear a constant proportion to their causes; if the energy of thought is to be commensurate with the masses which prompt it, and the masses it must penetrate; if eloquence is to grow in fervor with the weight of the interests it is to plead, and the grandeur of the assemblies it addresses; in a word, if the faculties of the human mind are capable of tension and achievement altogether indefinite;

"Nil actum reputans, dum quid superesset agendum;"

then it is not too much to say, that a new era will open on the intellectual world, in the fulfilment of our country's prospects.

If it should be objected, that the permanent and prosperous existence of a commonwealth so extensive is not to be hoped for, I reply, that by the wise and happy partition of powers between the national and state governments, in virtue of which the national government is relieved from all the odium of internal administration, and the state governments are spared the conflicts of foreign politics, all bounds seem removed from the possible extension of our country, but the geographical limits of the continent. Instead of growing cumbrous, as it increases in size, there never was a moment, since the first settlement in Virginia, when the political system of America moved with so firm and bold a step, as at the present day. Should our happy Union continue, this great continent, in no remote futurity, will be filled up with the mightiest kindred people known in history; our language will acquire an extension which no other ever possessed; and the empire of the mind, with nothing to resist its sway, will attain an expansion, of which, as yet, we can but partly conceive. The vision is too magnificent to be fully borne; —a mass of two or three hundred millions, not chained to the oar, like the same number in China, by a stupefying despotism, but held in their several orbits of nation and state, by the grand representative attraction; bringing to bear, on every point, the concentrated energy of such a host; calling into competition so many minds; uniting into one great national feeling the hearts of so many freemen, all to be guided, moved and swayed, by the master spirits of the time!

III. Let me not be told that this is a chimerical imagination of a future indefinitely removed; let me not hear repeated the poor jest of an anticipation of "two thousand years,"—of a vision that requires for its fulfilment a length of ages beyond the grasp of any reasonable computation. It is the last point of peculiarity in our condition, to which I invite your attention, as affecting the progress of intellect, that the country is growing with a *rapidity* hitherto without example in the world. For the two hundred years of our existence, the population has doubled itself in periods of less than a quarter of a century. In the infancy of the country, and while it remained within the limits of a youthful colony, a progress so rapid as this, however important in the principle of growth disclosed, was not yet a circumstance strongly to fix the attention. But, arrived at a population of ten millions, it is a fact of extreme interest, that, within less than twenty-five years, these ten millions will have swelled to twenty; that the younger members of this audience will be citizens of the largest civilized state on earth; that, in a few years more than one century, the American population will equal the fabulous numbers of the Chinese empire. This rate of increase has already produced the most striking phenomena. A few weeks after the opening of the revolutionary drama at Lexington, the momentous intelligence that the first blood was spilt reached a party of hunters beyond the Alleghanies, who had wandered far into the western wilderness. In prophetic commemoration of the glorious event, they gave the name of Lexington to the spot of their encampment in the woods. That spot is now the capital of a state as large as Massachusetts; from which,

in the language of one of her own citizens, one of the brightest ornaments of his country, the tide of emigration still farther westward is
more fully pouring, than from any other in the Union.[4]

I need not say that this astonishing increase of numbers is by no
means the best measure of the country's growth. Arts, letters, agriculture, all the great national interests, all the sources of national wealth,
are growing in a ratio still more rapid. In our cities, the intensest activity is apparent; in the country, every spring of prosperity, from the
smallest improvement in husbandry, to the construction of canals and
railroads across the continent, is in vigorous action. Abroad, our vessels
are beating the pathways of the ocean white; on the inland frontier,
the nation is moving forward with a pace more like romance than
reality.

These facts and influences form one of those peculiarities in our
country's condition, which will have the most powerful effect on the
minds of the people. The population of most of the states of Asia, and
some of Europe, has apparently reached its term. In some it is declining, in some stationary; and in the most prosperous, under the extraordinary impulse of the last part of the eighteenth century, it doubles
itself but about once in seventy-five years. In consequence of this, the
process of social transmission is heavy and slow. Men not adventitiously
favored come forward late in life, and the best years of existence are exhausted in languishing competition. The man grows up, and, in the
stern language of one of their most renowned economists,[5] finds no

[4] Mr Clay's Speech on Internal Improvement. Should the population continue to
double in about twenty-two years, the following will be the result:—

1862	34,126,706
1884	68,253,412
1906	136,506,824
1928	273,013,648

Many persons now in existence will then be alive.

"Il arrivera donc," says M. de Tocqueville, "un tems où l'on pourra voir dans
l'Amérique du Nord 150,000,000 d'hommes, égaux entre eux, qui tous appartiendront
à la même famille, qui auront le même point de départ, la même civilisation, la
même langue, la même religion, les mêmes habitudes, les mêmes mœurs, et à travers
lesquels la pensée circulera sous la même forme et se peindra des mêmes couleurs. Tout
le reste est douteux, mais ceci est certain. Or, voici un fait entièrement nouveau dans
le monde, et dont l'imagination elle-même ne saurait saisir la portée."—De Tocqueville, *De la Démocratie en Amérique,* Tom. II, p. 415, 5me ed.—This work was published in 1834. [These notes were added by Everett in about 1840. Ed.]

[5] Mr Malthus.

cover laid for him at Nature's table. The assurance of the most frugal subsistence commands the brightest talents and the most laborious studies; poor wages pay for the unremitted labor of the most curious hands; and it is a small part of the population only that is within the reach even of these humiliating springs of action.

We need not labor to contrast this state of things with the teeming growth and rapid progress of our own country. Instead of being shut up, as it were, in the prison of a stationary, or a slowly progressive community, the emulation of our countrymen is drawn out and tempted on by an horizon constantly receding before them. New nations of kindred freemen are springing up, in successive periods, shorter even than the active portion of the life of man. "While we spend our time," says Burke, on this topic, "in deliberating on the mode of governing two millions in America, we shall find we have millions more to manage." [6] Many individuals are in this house who were arrived at years of discretion when these words of Burke were uttered; and the two millions which Great Britain was then to manage have grown into ten, exceedingly unmanageable. The most affecting view of this subject is, that it puts it in the power of the wise and good to gather, while they live, the ripest fruits of their labors. Where, in human history, is to be found a contrast like that which the last fifty years have crowded into the lives of those favored men, who, raising their hands or their voices, when the feeble colonies engaged in a perilous conflict with one of the most powerful empires on earth, have lived to be crowned with the highest honors of the republic which they established? Honor to their gray hairs, and peace and serenity to the evening of their eventful days!

Though it may never again be the fortune of our country to bring within the compass of half a century a contrast so dazzling as this, yet, in its grand and steady progress, the career of duty and usefulness will be run by all its children, under a constantly increasing excitement. The voice which, in the morning of life, shall awaken the patriotic sympathy of the land, will be echoed back by a community, vastly swelled in all its proportions, before that voice shall be hushed in death. The writer, by whom the noble features of our scenery shall be sketched with a glowing pencil, the traits of our romantic early history gathered up with filial zeal, and the peculiarities of our character delineated with

---

[6] "Speech on Conciliation with America," March 22, 1775.

delicate perception, cannot mount so rapidly to success, but that ten years will add new millions to the numbers of his readers. The American statesman, the orator, whose voice is already heard in its supremacy from Florida to Maine, whose intellectual empire already extends beyond the limits of Alexander's, has yet new states and new nations starting into being, the willing subjects of his sway.

This rapid march of the population westward has been attended by circumstances in some degree novel in the history of the human mind. It is a fact, somewhat difficult of explanation, that the refinement of the ancient nations seemed comparatively devoid of an elastic and expansive principle. With the exception of the colonies in Asia Minor, the arts of Greece were enchained to her islands and her coasts; they did not penetrate far into the interior, at least not in every direction. The language and literature of Athens were as much unknown to the north of Pindus, at a distance of two hundred miles from the capital of Grecian refinement, as they were in Scythia. Thrace, whose mountain tops may almost be seen from the porch of the temple of Minerva, at Sunium, was the proverbial abode of barbarism. Though the colonies of Greece were scattered on the coasts of Asia, of Italy, of France, of Spain, and of Africa, no extension of their population far inward took place, and the arts did not penetrate beyond the walls of the cities where they were cultivated.

How different is the picture of the diffusion of the arts and improvements of civilization, from the coast to the interior of America! Population advances westward with a rapidity which numbers may describe, indeed, but cannot represent, with any vivacity, to the mind. The wilderness, which one year is impassable, is traversed, the next, by the caravans of industrious emigrants, carrying with them the language, the institutions, and the arts of civilized life. It is not the irruption of wild barbarians, sent to visit the wrath of God on a degenerate empire; it is not the inroad of disciplined banditti, put in motion by reasons of state or court intrigue. It is the human family, led out by Providence to possess its broad patrimony. The states and nations which are springing up in the valley of the Missouri, are bound to us by the dearest ties of a common language, a common government, and a common descent. Before New England can look with coldness on their rising myriads, she must forget that some of the best of her own blood is beat-

ing in their veins; that her hardy children, with their axes on their
shoulders, have been among the pioneers, in this march of humanity;
that, young as she is, she has become the mother of populous states.
What generous mind would sacrifice to a selfish preservation of local
preponderance the delight of beholding civilized nations rising up in
the desert; and the language, the manners, the principles in which he
has been reared, carried, with his household gods, to the foot of the
Rocky Mountains? Who can forget, that this extension of our territorial
limits is the extension of the empire of all we hold dear; of our laws, of
our character, of the memory of our ancestors, of the great achievements in our history? Whithersoever the sons of the thirteen states shall
wander, to southern or western climes, they will send back their hearts
to the rocky shores, the battlefields, the infant settlements of the Atlantic coast. These are placed beyond the reach of vicissitude. They
have become already matter of history, of poetry, of eloquence.

Divisions may spring up, ill blood may burn, parties be formed,
and interests may seem to clash; but the great bonds of the nation are
linked to what is past. The deeds of the great men, to whom this country owes its origin and growth, are a patrimony, I know, of which its
children will never deprive themselves. As long as the Mississippi and
the Missouri shall flow, those men, and those deeds, will be remembered on their banks. The sceptre of government may go where it will;
but that of patriotic feeling can never depart from Judah. In all that
mighty region which is drained by the Missouri and its tributary
streams,—the valley coëxtensive, in this country, with the temperate
zone,—will there be, as long as the name of America shall last, a father
that will not take his children on his knee, and recount to them the
events of the twenty-second of December, the nineteenth of April, the
seventeenth of June, and the fourth of July?

This, then, is the theatre on which the intellect of America is to appear, and such the motives to its exertion; such the mass to be influenced by its energies; such the glory to crown its success. If I err in
this happy vision of my country's fortunes, I thank Heaven for an error
so animating. If this be false, may I never know the truth. Never may
you, my friends, be under any other feeling, than that a great, a growing, an immeasurably expanding country is calling upon you for your
best services. The name and character of our Alma Mater have already

been carried by some of our brethren hundreds of miles from her venerable walls; and thousands of miles still farther westward, the communities of kindred men are fast gathering, whose minds and hearts will act in sympathy with yours.

The most powerful motives call on us, as scholars, for those efforts which our common country demands of all her children. Most of us are of that class who owe whatever of knowledge has shone into our minds to the free and popular institutions of our native land. There are few of us who may not be permitted to boast, that we have been reared in an honest poverty, or a frugal competence, and owe every thing to those means of education which are equally open to all. We are summoned to new energy and zeal, by the high nature of the experiment we are appointed in providence to make, and the grandeur of the theatre on which it is to be performed. At a moment of deep and general agitation in the Old World, it pleased Heaven to open this last refuge of humanity. The attempt has begun, and is going on, far from foreign corruption, on the broadest scale, and under the most benignant prospects; and it certainly rests with us to solve the great problem in human society; to settle, and that forever, the momentous question,—whether mankind can be trusted with a purely popular system of government.

One might almost think, without extravagance, that the departed wise and good, of all places and times, are looking down from their happy seats to witness what shall now be done by us; that they who lavished their treasures and their blood, of old, who spake and wrote, who labored, fought, and perished, in the one great cause of Freedom and Truth, are now hanging from their orbs on high, over the last solemn experiment of humanity. As I have wandered over the spots once the scene of their labors, and mused among the prostrate columns of their senate houses and forums, I have seemed almost to hear a voice from the tombs of departed ages; from the sepulchres of the nations which died before the sight. They exhort us, they adjure us, to be faithful to our trust. They implore us by the long trials of struggling humanity; by the blessed memory of the departed; by the dear faith which has been plighted, by pure hands, to the holy cause of truth and man; by the awful secrets of the prison houses, where the sons of freedom have been immured; by the noble heads which have been brought to the block; by the wrecks of time, by the eloquent ruins of nations, they conjure us not to quench the light which is rising on the world. Greece cries to us by the convulsed lips of her poisoned, dying Demosthenes; and Rome pleads with us in the mute persuasion of her mangled Tully. They address us, each and all, in the glorious appeal which was made by Milton to one who might have canonized his memory in the hearts of the friends of liberty, but who did most shamefully betray the cause: "Reverere tantam de te expectationem, spem patriæ de te unicam. Reverere vultus et vulnera tot fortium virorum, quotquot pro libertate tam strenue decertârunt, manes etiam eorum qui in ipso certamine occubuerunt. Reverere exterarum quoque civitatum existimationem de te atque sermones; quantas res de libertate nostrâ tam fortiter partâ, de nostrâ republicâ tam gloriose exortâ sibi polliceantur; quæ si tam cito quasi aborta evanuerit, profecto nihil æque dedecorosum huic genti atque periculosum fuerit." [7]

Yes, my friends, such is the exhortation which calls on us to exert our powers, to employ our time, and consecrate our labors, for the honor and service of our native land. When we engage in that solemn study, the history of our race; surveying the progress of man, from his cradle in the East to these limits of his wandering; when we behold him forever flying westward from evil and religious thraldom, over mountains and seas, seeking rest and finding none, but still pursuing the flying bow of promise to the glittering hills which it spans in Hesperian climes; we cannot but exclaim, with Bishop Berkeley, the generous prelate, who bestowed his benefactions, as well as blessings, on our country,—

> "Westward the course of Empire takes its way;
> The four first acts already past,
> A fifth shall close the drama with the day;
> Time's noblest offspring is the last."

This exclamation is but the embodiment of a vision, which the ancients, from the earliest period, cherished of some favored land beyond the mountains or the seas; a land of equal laws and happy men. The primitive poets placed it in the Islands of the Blest; the Doric bards dimly beheld it in the Hyperborean region; the mystical sage of the Academy found it in his lost Atlantis; and even the stern spirit of

[7] Milton, *Defensio Secunda*.

Seneca dreamed of the restoration of the golden age in distant worlds, hereafter to be discovered. Can we look back upon these uninspired predictions, and not feel the weight of obligation which they imply? Here must these bright fancies be turned into truth; here must these high visions be realized, in which the seers and sages of the elder world took refuge from the calamities of the days in which they lived. There are no more continents to be revealed; Atlantis hath arisen from the ocean; the farthest Thule is reached; there are no more retreats beyond the sea, no more discoveries, no more hopes.[8]

Here, then, a mighty work is to be performed, or never, by mortals. The *man* who looks with tenderness on the sufferings of good men in other times; the *descendant of the Pilgrims,* who cherishes the memory of his fathers; the *patriot,* who feels an honest glow at the majesty of the system of which he is a member; the *scholar,* who beholds, with rapture, the long-sealed book of truth opened for all to read without prejudice;—these are they, by whom these auspices are to be accomplished. Yes, brethren, it is by the intellect of the country that the mighty mass is to be inspired; that its parts are to communicate and sympathize with each other; its natural progress to be adored with becoming refinements; its principles asserted and its feelings interpreted to its own children, to other regions, and to after ages. . . .

[8] "Now looking anxiously round the world for any new race, which may receive the seed (so to speak) of our present history into a kindly yet vigorous soil, and may reproduce it, the same and yet new, for a future period, we know not where such are to be found. Some appear exhausted, others incapable; and yet the surface of the whole globe is known to us. The Roman colonies along the banks of the Rhine and Danube looked out on the country beyond those rivers, as we look up at the stars, and actually see with our eyes a world of which we know nothing. The Romans knew that there was a vast portion of the earth which they did not know; how vast it might be, was a part of its mysteries. But to us, all is explored; imagination can hope for no new Atlantic island to realize the vision of Plato's Critias; no new continent, peopled by youthful races, the destined restorers of our worn-out generations. Every where the search has been made, and the report has been received; we have the full amount of earth's resources before us, and they seem inadequate to supply life for a third period of human history."—Dr Arnold, (*Inaugural*) *Lecture on Modern History* (1840).

3

GEORGE BANCROFT

1800, born October 3, at Boston
1817, was graduated from Harvard College
1817–18, studied at Harvard Divinity School
1818–20, studied at University of Göttingen
1820, received the degree of Ph.D., Göttingen
1820–21, studied under Schleiermacher and Hegel at Berlin
1821–22, traveled in Europe
1822–23, tutor in Greek at Harvard
1823, *Poems*
1823–31, teacher at Round Hill School, Northampton, Mass.
1826, Fourth of July orator at Springfield, Mass.
1834–74, *History of the United States;* ten volumes
1837–45, Collector of the Port of Boston
1845–46, Secretary of the Navy in Polk's cabinet
1846–49, U.S. Minister to Great Britain
1855, *Literary and Historical Miscellanies*
1867–74, U.S. Minister to Germany
1882, *History of the Formation of the Constitution of the United States*
1883–85, Final revision of *History of the United States in six vols.*
1889, *Martin Van Buren to the End of His Public Career*
1891, died January 17.

JOSEPH STORY, speaking before the Phi Beta Kappa Society of Harvard College in 1826, asserted the need for rigorous self-examination to determine wherein American literature and science fell short of what was desirable for a mature nation. He was speaking in the vein of Ingersoll and Everett in considering intellectual independence as the fulfillment of political independence.

To us, Americans, nothing, indeed, can, or ought to be indifferent, that respects the cause of science and literature. We have taken a stand among the nations of the earth, and have successfully asserted our claim to political equality. . . . But our claims are far more extensive. We assert an equality of voice and vote in the republic of letters, and assume for ourselves the right to decide on the merits of others, as well as to vindicate our own. . . . We ask admission into the temple of fame, as joint heirs of the inheritance, capable in the manhood of our strength of maintaining our title. . . . It is not by a few vain boasts, or vainer self complacency, or rash daring, that we are to win our way to the first literary distinction. . . . We must serve in the hard school of discipline; we must invigorate our powers by the studies of other times. We may not . . . shrink from a rigorous examination of our own deficiencies in science and literature.

This type of approach to the question of American culture continued long. One of its more amusing manifestations came when old Peter S. du Ponceau, who had come from Europe during the Revolution as aide to Baron Steuben, and had remained to become a citizen, a scientist, a lawyer, and an author, and had been under-secretary of foreign affairs in the early confederation and president of the American Philosophical Society, addressed the members of the Pennsylvania Library of Foreign Literature and Science in 1834 on "The Necessity and the Means of Making Our National Literature Independent of That of Great Britain." Du Ponceau produced the choice thought that the proper means to an independent national literature was the reading of continental authors in preference to English, for when the ideas of foreign authors are used as the basis of American works, new expressions are invented, so this borrowing is "imitation," whereas a similar procedure carried out with respect to English works is "plagiarism." Du Ponceau did insist, however, on the need for linguistic conservatism; he opposed neologism in general, and particularly cautioned against the fashionable habit of interlarding foreign phrases into an English context.

A vigorous and novel note in American cultural criticism was struck in the year following Du Ponceau's address by George Bancroft's oration "The Office of the People in Art, Government, and Religion," delivered before the Adelphi Society of Williamstown College, in August, 1835. Whereas Ingersoll and Everett had made the possibility of a distinctive American culture depend upon self-government, whereas Bryant had seen a field for fiction in the structure of American society, and whereas Channing had insisted on the need for the development of a superior group of intellectuals if an American literature was to develop, Bancroft insisted that American culture was a people's culture, that the key to cultural development in America was the development of the "common mind" of the people which was by no means identical with "common sense." Here was the introduction into American cultural speculation of transcendentalism.

When Bancroft delivered this address, he had recently returned from Germany, where, through Goethe and Schleiermacher, he had become familiar with the thought of the romantic followers of Kant. On his return to America he examined his native land through the glass of German transcendentalism and emerged with his romantic concept of the people. The material world, he said, is passive, but man makes progress; the people can enforce change because there is in the people an inherent reason which is the attribute of the race. "We have functions which connect us with heaven, as well as organs which set us in relation with earth. We have not merely the senses opening to us the external world, but an internal sense, which places us in connexion with the world of intelligence and the decrees of God." Reason, judgment, conscience, and a sense of beauty are "the common endowments of the race." Bancroft does not suggest that there is an equality in the degree of development of these powers in different individuals. "I speak for the universal diffusion of human powers, not of human attainments; for the capacity for progress, not for the perfection of undisciplined instincts."

It is worthy of note that the belief in inherent reason was held in common by Bancroft and Emerson. The development from this belief was, however, radically different in these two thinkers. While both saw in it the necessity for a repudiation of authority, and the substitution of "self-reliance," Emerson was concerned with the self-reliant individual. He found in the doctrine of immanent reason the corollary that the reason of each man was competent for any purpose. Bancroft, however, had a more Hegelian cast to his thought. Self-reliance was a characteristic of the collective mind. "Individuals are but shadows, too often engrossed by the pursuit of shadows; the race is immortal: individuals are of limited sagacity; the common mind is infinite in its experience: . . . individuals claim the divine sanction of truth for the deceitful conceptions of their own fancies; the Spirit of God breathes through the combined intelligence of the people." The mind of the individual is not competent for the discovery of truth, which "emerges from the contradictions of personal opinions." "The dictates of pure reason, proclaimed by the general voice of mankind," are the "only faithful interpreter" of truth, because "the people collectively are wiser than the most gifted individual, for all his wisdom constitutes but a part of theirs."

The place assigned by Bancroft to the "common mind" justifies his glorification of the common judgment, the common morality, and the common taste. "If it be true that the gifts of mind and heart are universally diffused, if the sentiment of truth, justice, love and beauty exists in every one, then it follows, as a necessary consequence, that the common judgment in taste, politics, and religion, is the highest authority on earth, and the nearest possible approach to an infallible decision." The judgments and the taste of the public are wiser than those of the wisest critic. "The sentiment of beauty, as it exists in the human mind, is the criterion in works of art, inspires the conceptions of genius, and exercises a final judgment on its productions." For this reason, if the arts are to have a distinguished development in America, "the inspiration must spring from the vigor of the people." This is historically validated by the conclusion that "every beneficent revolution in letters has the character of popularity; every great reform among authors has sprung from the power of the people in its influence on the development and activity of mind."

So, too, "the best government rests on the people and not on the few, on persons and not on property, on the free development of public opinion and not on authority." Property, force, privilege may be dominated; mind alone remains free. "A government of equal rights must, therefore, rest upon mind . . . the sum of the moral intelligence of the community should rule the State." Hitherto, all that has been done in the improvement of the condition of men has been done for the benefit of the few. There is no possibility for further advance by means of exclusive benefits. The time has come to try the alternative; to advance the world "through the culture of the moral and intellectual powers of the people. To accomplish this end by means of the people themselves, is the highest purpose of government. . . . The duty of America is to secure the culture and the happiness of the masses by their reliance on themselves."

Finally, religious advance must rely on the people. "It is only by infusing great principles into the common mind, that revolutions in human society are brought about. . . . Society can be regenerated, the human race can be advanced, only by moral principles diffused through the multitude." Christianity was such a moral revolution, and made its way in Rome by an appeal not to the favored few, but to plebeians and slaves. "When God selected the channel by which Christianity should make its way in the city of Rome . . . he planted truth deep in the common soil." Thus new truths always have become "the common property of the human family." For this reason there is an "irresistible tendency" to progress in the human race; "for absolute power has never succeeded, and can never succeed, in suppressing a single truth. An idea once revealed may find its admission into every living breast and live there. Like God it becomes immortal and omnipresent. . . . Truth is immortal; it cannot be destroyed; it is invincible, it cannot be resisted."

This is rhetorical, and in the light of Bancroft's brahmin background it is easy to question its sincerity. Undoubtedly he espoused the cause of the people as a deliberate maneuver during his later political career; but at the threshold of his public life he had developed a thorough theoretical groundwork for his radical democracy.

THE OFFICE OF THE PEOPLE IN ART,
GOVERNMENT, AND RELIGION

THE material world does not change in its masses or in its powers. The stars shine with no more lustre than when they first sang together in the glory of their birth. The flowers that gemmed the fields and the forests, before America was discovered, now bloom around us in their season. The sun that shone on Homer shines on us in unchanging lustre. The bow that beamed on the patriarch still glitters in the clouds. Nature is the same. For her no new forces are generated; no new capacities are discovered. The earth turns on its axis, and perfects its revolutions, and renews its seasons, without increase or advancement.

But a like passive destiny does not attach to the inhabitants of the earth. For them the expectations of social improvement are no delusion; the hopes of philanthropy are more than a dream. The five senses do not constitute the whole inventory of our sources of knowledge. They are the organs by which thought connects itself with the external universe; but the power of thought is not merged in the exercise of its instruments. We have functions which connect us with heaven, as well as organs which set us in relation with earth. We have not merely the senses opening to us the external world, but an internal sense, which places us in connexion with the world of intelligence and the decrees of God.

There is a *spirit in man:* not in the privileged few; not in those of us only who by the favor of Providence have been nursed in public schools: IT IS IN MAN: it is the attribute of the race. The spirit, which is the guide to truth, is the gracious gift to each member of the human family.

Reason exists within every breast. I mean not that faculty which deduces inferences from the experience of the senses, but that higher faculty, which from the infinite treasures of its own consciousness, originates truth, and assents to it by the force of intuitive evidence; that faculty which raises us beyond the control of time and space, and gives us faith in things eternal and invisible. There is not the difference between one mind and another, which the pride of philosophers might conceive. To them no faculty is conceded, which does not belong to the meanest of their countrymen. In them there can not spring up a truth, which does not equally have its germ in every mind. They have not the power of creation; they can but reveal what God has implanted in every breast.

The intellectual functions, by which relations are perceived, are the common endowments of the race. The differences are apparent, not real. The eye in one person may be dull, in another quick, in one distorted, and in another tranquil and clear; yet the relation of the eye to light is in all men the same. Just so judgment may be liable in individual minds to the bias of passion, and yet its relation to truth is immutable, and is universal.

In questions of practical duty, conscience is God's umpire, whose light illumines every heart. There is nothing in books, which had not first, and has not still its life within us. Religion itself is a dead letter, wherever its truths are not renewed in the soul. Individual conscience may be corrupted by interest, or debauched by pride, yet the rule of morality is distinctly marked; its harmonies are to the mind like music to the ear; and the moral judgment, when carefully analyzed and referred to its principles, is always founded in right. The eastern superstition, which bids its victims prostrate themselves before the advancing car of their idols, springs from a noble root, and is but a melancholy perversion of that self-devotion, which enables the Christian to bear the cross, and subject his personal passions to the will of God. Immorality of itself never won to its support the inward voice; conscience, if questioned, never forgets to curse the guilty with the memory of sin, to cheer the upright with the meek tranquillity of approval. And this admirable power, which is the instinct of Deity, is the attribute of every man; it knocks at the palace gate, it dwells in the meanest hovel. Duty, like death, enters every abode, and delivers its message. Conscience, like reason and judgment, is universal.

That the moral affections are planted every where, needs only to be asserted to be received. The savage mother loves her offspring with all the fondness that a mother can know. Beneath the odorous shade of the boundless forests of Chili, the native youth repeats the story of love as sincerely as it was ever chanted in the valley of Vaucluse. The affections of family are not the growth of civilization. The charities of life are scattered every where; enamelling the vales of human being, as the flowers paint the meadows. They are not the fruit of study, nor the privilege of refinement, but a natural instinct.

Our age has seen a revolution in works of imagination. The poet has sought his theme in common life. Never is the genius of Scott more pathetic, than when, as in the Antiquary, he delineates the sorrows of a poor fisherman, or as in the Heart of Mid Lothian, he takes his heroine from a cottage. And even Wordsworth, the purest and most original poet of the day, in spite of the inveterate character of his political predilections, has thrown the light of genius on the walks of commonest life; he finds a lesson in every grave of the village churchyard; he discloses the boundless treasures of feeling in the peasant, the laborer and the artisan; the strolling peddler becomes, through his genius, a teacher of the sublimest morality; and the solitary wagoner, the lonely shepherd, even the feeble mother of an idiot boy, furnishes lessons in the reverence for Humanity.

If from things relating to truth, justice, and affection, we turn to those relating to the beautiful, we may here still further assert, that the sentiment for the beautiful resides in every breast. The lovely forms of the external world delight us from their adaptation to our powers.

> Yea, what were mighty Nature's self?
> Her features could they win us,
> Unhelped by the poetic voice
> That hourly speaks within us?

The Indian mother, on the borders of Hudson's Bay, decorates her manufactures with ingenious devices and lovely colors, prompted by the same instinct which guided the pencil and mixed the colors of Raphael. The inhabitant of Nootka Sound tattoos his body with the method of harmonious Arabesques. Every form, to which the hands of the artist have ever given birth, sprung first into being as a conception of his mind, from a natural faculty, which belongs not to the artist exclusively, but to man. Beauty, like truth and justice, lives within us; like virtue and like moral law, it is a companion of the soul. The power which leads to the production of beautiful forms, or to the perception of them in the works which God has made, is an attribute of Humanity.

But I am asked if I despise learning? Shall one who has spent much of his life in schools and universities plead the equality of uneducated nature? Is there no difference between the man of refinement and the savage?

"I am a man," said Black Hawk nobly to the chief of the first republic in the world; "I am a man," said the barbarous chieftain, "and you are another."

I speak for the universal diffusion of human powers, not of human attainments; for the capacity for progress, not for the perfection of undisciplined instincts. The fellowship which we should cherish with the race, receives the Comanche warrior and the Caffre within the pale of equality. Their functions may not have been exercised, but they exist. Immure a person in a dungeon; as he comes to the light of day, his vision seems incapable of performing its office. Does that destroy your conviction in the relation between the eye and light? The rioter over his cups resolves to eat and drink and be merry; he forgets his spiritual nature in his obedience to the senses; but does that destroy the relation between conscience and eternity? "What ransom shall we give?" exclaimed the senators of Rome to the savage Attila. "Give," said the barbarian, "all your gold and jewels, your costly furniture and treasures, and set free every slave." "Ah," replied the degenerate Romans, "what then will be left to us?" "I leave you your souls," replied the unlettered invader from the steppes of Asia, who had learnt in the wilderness to value the immortal mind, and to despise the servile herd, that esteemed only their fortunes, and had no true respect for themselves. You cannot discover a tribe of men, but you also find the charities of life, and the proofs of spiritual existence. Behold the ignorant Algonquin deposit a bow and quiver by the side of the departed warrior; and recognise his faith in immortality. See the Comanche chieftain, in the heart of our continent, inflict on himself severest penance; and reverence his confession of the needed atonement for sin. The Barbarian who roams our western prairies has like passions and like endowments with ourselves. He bears within him the instinct of Deity; the consciousness of a spiritual nature; the love of beauty; the rule of morality.

And shall we reverence the dark-skinned Caffre? Shall we respect the brutal Hottentot? You may read the right answer written on every heart. It bids me not despise the sable hunter, that gathers a livelihood in the forests of Southern Africa. All are men. When we know the Hottentot better, we shall despise him less.

II

If it be true, that the gifts of mind and heart are universally diffused, if the sentiment of truth, justice, love, and beauty exists in every one, then it follows, as a necessary consequence, that the common judgment in taste, politics, and religion, is the highest authority on earth, and the nearest possible approach to an infallible decision. From the consideration of individual powers I turn to the action of the human mind in masses.

If reason is a universal faculty, the universal decision is the nearest criterion of truth. The common mind winnows opinions; it is the sieve which separates error from certainty. The exercise by many of the same faculty on the same subject would naturally lead to the same conclusions. But if not, the very differences of opinion that arise prove the supreme judgment of the general mind. Truth is one. It never contradicts itself. One truth cannot contradict another truth. Hence truth is a bond of union. But error not only contradicts truth, but may contradict itself; so that there may be many errors, and each at variance with the rest. Truth is therefore of necessity an element of harmony; error as necessarily an element of discord. Thus there can be no continuing universal judgment but a right one. Men cannot agree in an absurdity; neither can they agree in a falsehood.

If wrong opinions have often been cherished by the masses, the cause always lies in the complexity of the ideas presented. Error finds its way into the soul of a nation, only through the channel of truth. It is to a truth that men listen; and if they accept error also, it is only because the error is for the time so closely interwoven with the truth, that the one cannot readily be separated from the other.

Unmixed error can have no existence in the public mind. Wherever you see men clustering together to form a party, you may be sure that however much error may be there, truth is there also. Apply this principle boldly; for it contains a lesson of candor, and a voice of encouragement. There never was a school of philosophy, nor a clan in the realm of opinion, but carried along with it some important truth. And therefore every sect that has ever flourished has benefited Humanity; for the errors of a sect pass away and are forgotten; its truths are received into the common inheritance. To know the seminal thought of every prophet and leader of a sect, is to gather all the wisdom of mankind.

> "By heaven! there should not be a seer, who left
> The world one doctrine, but I'd task his lore,
> And commune with his spirit. All the truth
> Of all the tongues of earth, I'd have them all,
> Had I the powerful spell to raise their ghosts."

The sentiment of beauty, as it exists in the human mind, is the criterion in works of art, inspires the conceptions of genius, and exercises a final judgment on its productions. For who are the best judges in matters of taste? Do you think the cultivated individual? Undoubtedly not; but the collective mind. The public is wiser than the wisest critic. In Athens, the arts were carried to perfection, when "the fierce democracie" was in the ascendant; the temple of Minerva and the works of Phidias were planned and perfected to please the common people. When Greece yielded to tyrants, her genius for excellence in art expired; or rather, the purity of taste disappeared; because the artist then endeavored to gratify a patron, and therefore, humored his caprice; while before he had endeavored to delight the race.

When, after a long eclipse, the arts again burst into a splendid existence, it was equally under a popular influence. During the rough contests and feudal tyrannies of the middle age, religion had opened in the church an asylum for the people. There the serf and the beggar could kneel; there the pilgrim and the laborer were shrived; and the children of misfortune not less than the prosperous were welcomed to the house of prayer. The church was, consequently, at once the guardian of equality, and the nurse of the arts; and the souls of Giotto, and Perugino, and Raphael, moved by an infinite sympathy with the crowd, kindled into divine conceptions of beautiful forms. Appealing to the sentiment of devotion in the common mind, they dipped their pencils in living colors, to decorate the altars where man adored. By degrees the wealthy nobility desired in like manner to adorn their palaces; but at the attempt, the quick familiarity of the artist with the beautiful declined. Instead of the brilliant works which spoke to the soul, a school arose, who appealed to the senses; and in the land which had produced the most moving pictures, addressed to the religious feeling, and instinct with the purest beauty, the banquet halls were covered with grotesque forms, such as float before the imagination, when excited and bewildered by sensual indulgence. Instead of holy families, the ideal representations of the virgin mother and the godlike child, of the enduring faith of martyrs, of the blessed benevolence of evangelic love, there came the motley group of fawns and satyrs, of Diana stooping to Endymion, of voluptuous beauty, and the forms of licentiousness. Humanity frowned on the desecration of the arts; and painting, no longer vivified by a fellow-feeling with the multitude, lost its greatness in the attempt to adapt itself to personal humors.

If with us the arts are destined to a brilliant career, the inspiration must spring from the vigor of the people. Genius will not create, to flatter patrons or decorate saloons. It yearns for larger influences; it feeds on wider sympathies; and its perfect display can never exist, except in an appeal to the general sentiment for the beautiful.

Again. Italy is famed for its musical compositions, its inimitable operas. It is a well-known fact, that the best critics are often deceived in their judgment of them; while the pit, composed of the throng, does, without fail, render a true verdict.

But the taste for music, it may be said, is favored by natural organization. Precisely a statement that sets in a clearer light the natural capacity of the race; for taste is then not an acquisition, but in part a gift. But let us pass to works of literature.

Who are by way of eminence the poets of all mankind? Surely Homer and Shakspeare. Now Homer formed his taste, as he wandered from door to door, a vagrant minstrel, paying for hospitality by a song; and Shakspeare wrote for an audience, composed in a great measure of the common people.

The little story of Paul and Virginia is a universal favorite. When it was first written, the author read it aloud to a circle in Paris, composed of the wife of the prime minister, and the choicest critics of France. They condemned it, as dull and insipid. The author appealed to the public; and the children of all Europe reversed the decree of the Parisians. The judgment of children, that is, the judgment of the common mind under its most innocent and least imposing form, was more trustworthy than the criticism of the select refinement of the most polished city in the world.

Demosthenes of old formed himself to the perfection of eloquence by means of addresses to the crowd. The great comic poet of Greece, emphatically the poet of the vulgar mob, is distinguished above all others for the incomparable graces of his diction; and it is related of one of the most skilful writers in the Italian, that when inquired of where he had learned the purity and nationality of his style, he replied, from listening to the country people, as they brought their produce to market.

At the revival of letters a distinguishing feature of the rising literature was the employment of the dialect of the vulgar. Dante used the language of the populace and won immortality; Wickliffe, Luther, and at a later day Descartes, each employed his mother tongue, and carried truth directly to all who were familiar with its accents. Every beneficent revolution in letters has the character of popularity; every great reform among authors has sprung from the power of the people in its influence on the development and activity of mind.

The same influence continues unimpaired. Scott, in spite of his reverence for the aristocracy, spurned a drawing-room reputation; the secret of Byron's superiority lay in part in the agreement which existed between his muse and the democratic tendency of the age. German literature is almost entirely a popular creation. It was fostered by no monarch; it was dandled by no aristocracy. It was plebeian in its origin, and therefore manly in its results.

III

In like manner the best government rests on the people and not on the few, on persons and not on property, on the free development of public opinion and not on authority; because the munificent Author of our being has conferred the gifts of mind upon every member of the human race without distinction of outward circumstances. Whatever of other possessions may be engrossed, mind asserts its own independence. Lands, estates, the produce of mines, the prolific abundance of the seas, may be usurped by a privileged class. Avarice, assuming the form of ambitious power, may grasp realm after realm, subdue continents, compass the earth in its schemes of aggrandizement, and sigh after other worlds; but mind eludes the power of appropriation; it exists only in its own individuality; it is a property which cannot be confiscated and cannot be torn away; it laughs at chains; it bursts from imprisonment; it defies monopoly. A government of equal rights must, therefore, rest upon mind; not wealth, not brute force, the sum of the moral intelligence of the community should rule the State. Prescription can no more assume to be a valid plea for political injustice; society studies to eradicate established abuses, and to bring social institutions and laws into harmony with moral right; not dismayed by the natural and necessary imperfections of all human effort, and not giving way to despair, because every hope does not at once ripen into fruit.

The public happiness is the true object of legislation, and can be secured only by the masses of mankind themselves awakening to the knowledge and the care of their own interests. Our free institutions have reversed the false and ignoble distinctions between men; and refusing to gratify the pride of caste, have acknowledged the common mind to be the true material for a commonwealth. Every thing has hitherto been done for the happy few. It is not possible to endow an aristocracy with greater benefits than they have already enjoyed; there is no room to hope that individuals will be more highly gifted or more fully developed than the greatest sages of past times. The world can advance only through the culture of the moral and intellectual powers of the people. To accomplish this end by means of the people themselves is the highest purpose of government. If it be the duty of the individual to strive after a perfection like the perfection of God, how much more ought a nation to be the image of Deity. The common mind is the true Parian marble, fit to be wrought into likeness to a God. The duty of America is to secure the culture and the happiness of the masses by their reliance on themselves.

The absence of the prejudices of the old world leaves us here the opportunity of consulting independent truth; and man is left to apply the instinct of freedom to every social relation and public interest. We have approached so near to nature, that we can hear her gentlest whispers; we have made Humanity our lawgiver and our oracle; and, therefore, the nation receives, vivifies and applies principles, which in Europe the wisest accept with distrust. Freedom of mind and of conscience, freedom of the seas, freedom of industry, equality of franchises, each great truth is firmly grasped, comprehended and enforced; for the multitude is neither rash nor fickle. In truth, it is less fickle than those who profess to be its guides. Its natural dialectics surpass the logic of the schools. Political action has never been so consistent and so unwavering, as when it results from a feeling or a principle, diffused through society. The people is firm and tranquil in its movements, and necessarily acts with moderation, because it becomes but slowly impregnated with new ideas; and effects no changes, except in harmony with the knowledge which it has acquired. Besides, where it is permanently possessed of power, there exists neither the occasion nor the desire for frequent change. It is not the parent of tumult; sedition is bred in the lap of luxury, and its chosen emissaries are the beggared spendthrift and the impoverished libertine. The government by the people is in very truth the strongest government in the world. Discarding the implements of terror, it dares to rule by moral force, and has its citadel in the heart.

Such is the political system which rests on reason, reflection, and the free expression of deliberate choice. There may be those who scoff at the suggestion, that the decision of the whole is to be preferred to the judgment of the enlightened few. They say in their hearts that the masses are ignorant; that farmers know nothing of legislation; that mechanics should not quit their workshops to join in forming public opinion. But true political science does indeed venerate the masses. It maintains, not as has been perversely asserted, that "the people can make right," but that the people can DISCERN right. Individuals are but shadows, too often engrossed by the pursuit of shadows; the race is immortal: individuals are of limited sagacity; the common mind is infinite in its experience: individuals are languid and blind; the many are ever wakeful: individuals are corrupt; the race has been redeemed: individuals are time-serving; the masses are fearless: individuals may be false, the masses are ingenuous and sincere: individuals claim the divine sanction of truth for the deceitful conceptions of their own fancies; the Spirit of God breathes through the combined intelligence of the people. Truth is not to be ascertained by the impulses of an individual; it emerges from the contradictions of personal opinions; it raises itself in majestic serenity above the strifes of parties and the conflict of sects; it acknowledges neither the solitary mind, nor the separate faction as its oracle; but owns as its only faithful interpreter the dictates of pure reason itself, proclaimed by the general voice of mankind. The decrees of the universal conscience are the nearest approach to the presence of God in the soul of man.

Thus the opinion which we respect is, indeed, not the opinion of one or of a few, but the sagacity of the many. It is hard for the pride of cultivated philosophy to put its ear to the ground, and listen reverently to the voice of lowly humanity; yet the people collectively are wiser than the most gifted individual, for all his wisdom constitutes but a part of theirs. When the great sculptor of Greece was endeavoring to fashion the perfect model of beauty, he did not passively imitate the form of the loveliest woman of his age; but he gleaned the several lineaments of his faultless work from the many. And so it is, that a perfect judgment is the result of comparison, when error eliminates error, and truth is established by concurring witnesses. The organ of truth is the invisible decision of the unbiased world; she pleads before no tribunal but public opinion; she owns no safe interpreter but the common mind; she knows no court of appeals but the soul of humanity. It is when the multitude give counsel, that right purposes find safety; theirs is the fixedness that cannot be shaken; theirs is the understanding which exceeds in wisdom; theirs is the heart, of which the largeness is as the sand on the sea-shore.

It is not by vast armies, by immense natural resources, by accumulations of treasure, that the greatest results in modern civilization have been accomplished. The traces of the career of conquest pass away, hardly leaving a scar on the national intelligence. The famous battle grounds of victory are, most of them, comparatively indifferent to the human race; barren fields of blood, the scourges of their times, but affecting the social condition as little as the raging of a pestilence. Not one benevolent institution, not one ameliorating principle in the Roman state, was a voluntary concession of the aristocracy; each useful element was borrowed from the Democracies of Greece, or was a reluctant concession to the demands of the people. The same is true in modern political life. It is the confession of an enemy to Democracy, that "ALL THE GREAT AND NOBLE INSTITUTIONS OF THE WORLD HAVE COME FROM POPULAR EFFORTS."

It is the uniform tendency of the popular element to elevate and bless Humanity. The exact measure of the progress of civilization is the degree in which the intelligence of the common mind has prevailed over wealth and brute force; in other words, the measure of the progress of civilization is the progress of the people. Every great object, connected with the benevolent exertions of the day, has reference to the culture of those powers which are alone the common inheritance. For this the envoys of religion cross seas, and visit remotest isles; for this the press in its freedom teems with the productions of maturest thought; for this the philanthropist plans new schemes of education; for this halls in every city and village are open to the public instructor. Not that we view with indifference the glorious efforts of material industry; the increase in the facility of internal intercourse; the accumulations of thrifty labor; the varied results of concentrated action. But even there it is mind that achieves the triumph. It is the genius of the architect that gives beauty to the work of human hands, and makes the temple, the dwelling, or the public edifice, an outward representation of the spirit of propriety and order. It is science that guides the blind zeal of cupidity to the construction of the vast channels of communication, which are fast binding the world into one family. And it is as a method of moral improvement, that these swifter means of intercourse derive their greatest value. Mind becomes universal property; the poem that is published on the soil of England, finds its response on the shores of lake Erie and the banks of the Missouri, and is admired near the sources of the Ganges. The defence of public liberty in our own halls of legislation penetrates the plains of Poland, is echoed along the mountains of Greece, and pierces the darkest night of eastern despotism.

The universality of the intellectual and moral powers, and the necessity of their development for the progress of the race, proclaim the great doctrine of the natural right of every human being to moral and intellectual culture. It is the glory of our fathers to have established in their laws the equal claims of every child to the public care of its morals and its mind. From this principle we may deduce the universal right to leisure; that is, to time not appropriated to material purposes, but reserved for the culture of the moral affections and the mind. It does not tolerate the exclusive enjoyment of leisure by a privileged class; but defending the rights of labor, would suffer none to sacrifice the higher purposes of existence in unceasing toil for that which is not life. Such is the voice of nature; such the conscious claim of the human mind. The universe opens its pages to every eye; the music of creation resounds in every ear; the glorious lessons of immortal truth, that are written in the sky and on the earth, address themselves to every mind, and claim attention from every human being. God has made man upright, that he might look before and after; and he calls upon every one not merely to labor, but to reflect; not merely to practise the revelations of divine will, but to contemplate the displays of divine power. Nature claims for every man leisure, for she claims every man as a witness to the divine glory, manifested in the created world.

> "Yet evermore, through years renewed
> In undisturbed vicissitude
> Of seasons balancing their flight
> On the swift wings of day and night,
> Kind nature keeps a heavenly door
> Wide open for the scattered poor,
> Where flower-breathed incense to the skies
> Is wafted in mute harmonies;
> And ground fresh cloven by the plough
> Is fragrant with an humbler vow;
> Where birds and brooks from leafy dells
> Chime forth unwearied canticles,
> And vapors magnify and spread
> The glory of the sun's bright head;
> Still constant in her worship, still
> Conforming to the Almighty Will,
> Whether men sow or reap the fields,
> Her admonitions nature yields;
> That not by bread alone we live
> Or what a hand of flesh can give;
> That every day should leave some part
> Free for a sabbath of the heart;
> So shall the seventh be truly blest,
> From morn to eve, with hallowed rest."

The right to universal education being thus acknowledged by our conscience, not less than by our laws, it follows, that the people is the true recipient of truth. Do not seek to conciliate individuals; do not dread the frowns of a sect; do not yield to the proscriptions of a party; but pour out truth into the common mind. Let the waters of intelligence, like the rains of heaven, descend on the whole earth. And be not discouraged by the dread of encountering ignorance. *The prejudices of ignorance are more easily removed than the prejudices of interest; the first are blindly adopted; the second wilfully preferred.* Intelligence must be diffused among the whole people; truth must be scattered among those who have no interest to suppress its growth. The seeds that fall on the exchange, or in the hum of business, may be choked by the thorns that spring up in the hotbed of avarice; the seeds that are let fall in the saloon, may be like those dropped by the wayside, which take no root. Let the young aspirant after glory scatter the seeds of truth broadcast on the wide bosom of Humanity; in the deep, fertile soil of the public mind. There it will strike deep root and spring up, and bear an hundred-fold, and bloom for ages, and ripen fruit through remote generations.

It is alone by infusing great principles into the common mind, that revolutions in human society are brought about. They never have been, they never can be, effected by superior individual excellence. The age of the Antonines is the age of the greatest glory of the Roman empire. Men distinguished by every accomplishment of culture and science, for a century in succession, possessed undisputed sway over more than a hundred millions of men; till at last, in the person of Mark Aurelian, philosophy herself seemed to mount the throne. And did she stay the downward tendencies of the Roman empire? Did she infuse new elements of life into the decaying constitution? Did she commence one great, beneficent reform? Not one permanent amelioration was effected; philosophy was clothed with absolute power; and yet absolute power accomplished nothing for Humanity. It could accomplish nothing. Had it been possible, Aurelian would have wrought a change. Society can be regenerated, the human race can be advanced, only by moral principles diffused through the multitude.

And now let us take an opposite instance; let us see, if amelioration follows, when in despite of tyranny truth finds access to the common people; and Christianity itself shall furnish my example.

When Christianity first made its way into Rome, the imperial city was the seat of wealth, philosophy, and luxury. Absolute government was already established; and had the will of Claudius been gained, or the conscience of Messalina been roused, or the heart of Narcissus, once a slave, then prime minister, been touched by the recollections of his misfortunes, the aid of the sovereign of the civilized world would have been engaged. And did the messenger of divine truth make his appeal to them? Was his mission to the emperor and his minions? to the empress and her flatterers? to servile senators? to wealthy favorites? Paul preserves for us the names of the first converts; the Roman Mary and Junia; Julia and Nerea; and the beloved brethren; all plebeian names, unknown to history. "Greet them," he adds, "that be of the household of Narcissus." Now every Roman household was a community of slaves. Narcissus himself, a freedman, was the chief minister of the Roman empire; his ambition had left him no moments for the envoy from Calvary; the friends of Paul were a freedman's slaves. When God selected the channel by which Christianity should make its way in the city of Rome, and assuredly be carried forward to acknowledged supremacy in the Roman empire, he gave to the Apostle of the Gentiles favor in the household of Narcissus; he planted truth deep in the common soil. Had Christianity been received at court, it would have been stifled or corrupted by the prodigal vices of the age; it lived in the hearts of the common people; it sheltered itself against oppression in the catacombs and among tombs; it made misfortune its convert, and sorrow its companion, and labor its stay. It rested on a rock, for it rested on the people; it was gifted with immortality, for it struck root in the hearts of the million.

So completely was this greatest of all reforms carried forward in the vale of life, that the great moral revolution, the great step of God's Providence in the education of the human race, was not observed by the Roman historians. Once, indeed, at this early period Christians are mentioned; for in the reign of Nero, their purity being hateful to the corrupt, Nero abandoned them to persecution. In the darkness of midnight, they were covered with pitch and set on fire to light the streets of Rome, and this singularity has been recorded. But their system of morals and religion, though it was the new birth of the world, escaped all notice.

Paul, who was a Roman citizen, was beheaded, just outside of the walls of the eternal city; and Peter, who was a plebeian, and could not claim the distinction of the axe and the block, was executed on the cross, with his head downwards to increase the pain and the indignity. Do you think the Roman emperor took notice of the names of these men, when he signed their death-warrant? And yet, as they poured truth into the common mind, what series of kings, what lines of emperors can compare with them, in their influence on the destinies of mankind?

Yes, reforms in society are only effected through the masses of the people, and through them have continually taken place. New truths have been successively developed, and, becoming the common property of the human family, have improved its condition. This progress is advanced by every sect, precisely because each sect, to obtain vitality, does of necessity embody a truth; by every political party, for the conflicts of party are the war of ideas; by every nationality, for a nation cannot exist as such, till humanity makes it a special trustee of some part of its wealth for the ultimate benefit of all. The irresistible tendency of the human race is therefore to advancement, for absolute power has never succeeded, and can never succeed, in suppressing a single truth. An idea once revealed may find its admission into every living breast and live there. Like God it becomes immortal and omnipresent. The movement of the species is upward, irresistibly upward. The individual is often lost; Providence never disowns the race. No principle once promulgated, has ever been forgotten. No "timely tramp" of a despot's foot ever trod out one idea. The world cannot retrograde; the dark ages cannot return. Dynasties perish; cities are buried; nations have been victims to error, or martyrs for right; Humanity has always been on the advance; gaining maturity, universality and power.

Yes, truth is immortal; it cannot be destroyed; it is invincible, it cannot long be resisted. Not every great principle has yet been generated; but when once proclaimed and diffused, it lives without end, in the safe custody of the race. States may pass away; every just principle of legislation which has been once established will endure. Philosophy has sometimes forgotten God; a great people never did. The skepticism of the last century could not uproot Christianity, because it lived in the hearts of the millions. Do you think that infidelity is spreading? Christianity never lived in the hearts of so many millions as at this moment. The forms under which it is professed may decay, for they, like all that is the work of man's hands, are subject to the changes and chances of mortal being; but the spirit of truth is incorruptible; it may be developed, illustrated, and applied; it never can die; it never can decline.

No truth can perish; no truth can pass away. The flame is undying, though generations disappear. Wherever moral truth has started into being, Humanity claims and guards the bequest. Each generation gathers together the imperishable children of the past, and increases them by new sons of light, alike radiant with immortality.

4

GULIAN C. VERPLANCK

1786, born August 6, in New York City
1801, was graduated from Columbia College
1801–7, studied law under Josiah O. Hoffman
1807, was admitted to the bar
1808, one of the founders of the Washington Benevolent Society
1811, participated in riot at Columbia commencement
1815, *A Fable for Statesmen and Politicians*
1815–17, traveled in Europe
1819, *The State Triumvirate; a Political Tale; and The Epistles of Brevet-Major Pindar Puff;* verse satires
1820–23, member of New York State Assembly
1821–24, professor in the General Theological Seminary
1824, *Essays on the Nature and Uses of the Various Evidences of Revealed Religion*
1824–33, member of the U.S. House of Representatives
1826–70, member of the Board of Regents, University of the State of New York
1828–30, one of editors of the *Talisman*
1833, *Discourses and Addresses on Subjects of American History, Arts, and Literature*
1836, *The Advantages and Dangers of the American Scholar*
1838–41, member of the New York State Senate
1847, edited *Shakespeare's Plays; with His Life;* three volumes
1848–70, president of the Board of the Commissioners of Emigration
1870, died March 18, in New York City

DURING the early eighteen thirties the sense of destiny, of national election was very strong in the United States. There were scoffers and doubting Thomases, but the vast majority of Americans had a sense of elevation out of which the country fell sharply in the panic of 1837. Any patriotic occasion was a time of self-glorification of the political advancement of America. Any literary or academic occasion was a time for inflated appraisals of American cultural development.

There were some, however, who resisted the temptation to exaggerate things as they were, and chose, rather, to talk about things as they should be. Others chose objective appraisal and tried to show how the existing cultural situation came to be and what its possibilities were. This was the approach of Gulian C. Verplanck in his address "The Advantages and Dangers of the American Scholar," which is reprinted here.

These are neither the vague speculations of a political theorist, nor the rant of patriotic declamation. They are sober and deliberate opinions, the results of much opportunity of observation . . . formed by one not indifferent to the imperfections of our political or social system, or unwilling to confess them . . . but who has never yet wavered or faltered in his veneration for the sacred cause of republican liberty.

The occasion was the Commencement at Union College in 1836. Verplanck was, perhaps, the outstanding intellectual figure of his time among the descendants of the Dutch settlers of New York. He lectured at the General Theological Seminary, was associated with Bryant and other Democratic writers in the editing of various keepsake annuals, and was a member of the Board of Regents of the State of New York. He befriended Freneau's old age and Bryant's youth. He was, in short, a genuine liberal.

Verplanck's presentation of the advantages of the American scholar, while it is thoughtful and interesting in its manner, is not novel in its matter. The benefits to which he points repeat the ideas of Ingersoll, Everett, and Bryant. His insistence on the uniqueness of the American social, political, and cultural environment gives excellent expression to the typical nationalistic sentiments of the time. "The actual state and the probable future prospects of our country, resemble those of no other land, and are without a parallel in past history." This is his opening sentence; he justifies it with references to the rich fertility of then uncultivated American territory available for development and guaranteeing a reward to labor; to the political system of representative republicanism going far beyond the dreams of any of the great theorists of republicanism; to the extension of the influence of public opinion in affairs as a result of the political system; to the broad range of personal liberty; to the comparative absence of inequalities; to the freedom of religion; and to the rapid spread of European ideas, both good and evil, in America because of the press and emigration. "Circumstances and causes such as these . . . thus pervading the whole mass of the community, cannot fail, in some way or other, to reach and powerfully affect every individual." If these causes affect all in some measure, their influence must be greatest upon the American scholar, "the man of native talent and improved intellect." In proportion to his influence upon the masses will be the influence of the masses upon him.

The first of the American traits influencing the scholar is activity. "Nothing is allowed to remain stagnant or dormant." The American atmosphere induces optimism, buoyancy, mobility, and energy. "Our past is but brief.

We can scarcely be said to have a present—certainly we have none for mere indolent enjoyment. We are all pressing and hastening forward to some better future." This driving, restless ambition carries the scholar along with it. When it is combined with a flexible society, it guarantees a fertile field of application for any talent. When the man of talent and education fails to find his plan for constructive and profitable use of his ability, it must be "from the positive fault of the possessor"; thus Verplanck applies to the American scholar one of the cardinal doctrines of the optimistic economic faith of America. Under the "strong and contagious stimulus" of general activity "the faculties are awakened, the capacity enlarged, the genius roused, excited, inspired. The mind is not suffered to brood undisturbed over its own little stock of favorite thoughts."

The opportunities for public service through applied scholarship are extensive. Genius need not work for selfish objects. The expansion of population and territory in America creates a wider field for extended influence.

We are all of us, in some sort, as waves in the shoreless ocean of human existence. Our own petty agitations soon die away, but they can extend themselves far onward and onward, and there are oftentimes circumstances which may cause those billows to swell as they roll forward, until they rise into a majestic vastness which it could scarce seem possible that our puny efforts could ever have set in motion.

It is thus that "the character, knowledge and happiness of that future and distant multitude, are now in our hands," and the responsibility and the achievements of the American scholar reach forward in time as well as outward in space. The general diffusion of elementary education, inadequate as it is, gives promise of a vast audience for the productions of the scholar, to prevent the sciences from being considered as arcana. "All our experience, our modes of business and ways of life, have a strong tendency to teach us to regard science . . . as an exalted and munificent benefactor, constantly and profusely contributing to our welfare and happiness." All that is required to popularize science is a popularizer; "much indeed of the best science can only be useful, in any high degree, by becoming thus familiar and popular." This is true as well of the physical as of the intellectual sciences.

But is it not true, as it is objected, that this concern with "the useful, the active, and the practical" leads to superficiality and to the restriction of interest? Only to a very limited extent, says Verplanck. Rather, men will make or find applications for their theoretical interests.

The experience of scientific investigation has shown that such application of the test of reality and experiment to theoretic truth, has not only often thrown a clearer light on that theory . . . but has also evolved new combinations, suggested new inferences, and manifested higher laws. . . . Contemplations, apparently the most shadowy, have often operated with the greatest efficiency upon the most engrossing cares of daily life.

He would approve neither of art for art's sake nor of science for science's. All of art and all of science must relate to the on-going affairs of the practical world of men.

So, too, the tradition of independence, with its value of "habituating men to the free use of their judgment, and the manly, direct avowal of their thoughts." His own security provided for by the economic opportunities in the country, the American scholar need fear no one, need curry favor with no individual patron, with no ruling caste. The "ardent, restless spirit ruling our whole people, can have little communion with that abject prostration of intellect that makes man crouch before his fellow, submitting his reason and conscience to another's will."

These are the advantages of the American scholar; their number and variety indicate that his dangers are those of prosperity, not of adversity. The most obvious is the danger of falling into superficiality. The way of avoiding this pitfall is the thorough mastery of one branch of knowledge, meantime keeping curiosity alive with respect to other branches. Then, too, the occasional acquisition of great fortune by gambling, by accident, or by other sudden means has led too many Americans, educated and uneducated, to develop an "impatience of continuous systematic labor," a love of the short-cut, the easy way. To offset this tendency it is necessary for the young scholar to have his regular profession, and, if an attractive speculative opportunity arises, to take advantage of that possibility without abandoning his profession, upon which he may fall back if the speculation fails. A third danger is that emphasis upon the practical will lead to the adoption of a criterion of utility, and finally to "paring down utility to mere selfishness" of material interests. This is a danger which is avoided by the sense of interdependence. "The prosperity of each man depends upon the prosperity of all. Every active citizen feels that he partakes largely of the practical and real, as well as of the theoretical sovereignty." There exists the possibility that the young scholar will set his ambitions beyond his powers, and will fail; this failure will breed in him cynicism, disappointment, and disgust with republican institutions, for he blames his country rather than himself for his failure. This is a mental disease to which literary men are particularly subject. A final danger to which American scholars are prone to fall victims is that of subserviency to party or to faction. Parties, when they serve their legitimate purpose of giving political expression to a variety of opinions, are beneficial; but the literary man who becomes a party hack sacrifices his independence and becomes a slave to the many rather than to the few.

These, according to Verplanck, are the dangers to be avoided by the American scholar. What, finally, is his duty? It is to stop the incipient plague of intolerance and dictation, which, taking its rise in the political parties, is passing over from political to social and religious life. Young scholars must not

think to keep themselves pure by holding themselves aloof from action. Let them take their stand manfully as their own best judgment may dictate in the political and religious divisions of our people; but let them feel for those who honestly differ from them as for erring brethren. . . . Never sacrifice your own honor, and still less, the cause of religion or freedom, to the subsidiary means used to promote them, or the external forms in which they may be invested. . . . Profane not those high gifts, disappoint not the just expectations of the friends of learning and liberty. Be true to yourselves and your country.

THE ADVANTAGES AND DANGERS OF THE AMERICAN SCHOLAR

THE actual state and the probable future prospects of our country, resemble those of no other land, and are without a parallel in past history. Our immense extent of fertile territory opening an inexhaustible field for successful enterprise, thus assuring to industry a certain reward for its labors, and preserving the land, for centuries to come, from the manifold evils of an overcrowded, and consequently degraded population—our magnificent system of federated republics, carrying out and applying the principles of representative democracy to an extent never hoped or imagined in the boldest theories of the old speculative republican philosophers, the Harringtons, Sydneys and Lockes of former times—the re-action of our political system upon our social and domestic concerns, bringing the influence of popular feeling and public opinion to bear upon all the affairs of life in a degree hitherto wholly unprecedented—the unconstrained range of freedom of opinion, of speech, and of the press, and the habitual and daring exercise of that liberty upon the highest subjects—the absence of all serious inequality of fortune and rank in the condition of our citizens—our divisions into innumerable religious sects, and the consequent co-existence, never before regarded as possible, of intense religious zeal, with a great degree of toleration in feeling and perfect equality of rights—our intimate connexion with that elder world beyond the Atlantic, communicating to us, through the press and emigration, much of good and much of evil not our own, high science, refined art, and the best knowledge of old experience, as well as prejudices and luxuries, vices and crimes, such as could not have been expected to spring up in our soil for ages— all these, combined with numerous other peculiarities in the institutions and in the moral, civil and social condition of the American people, have given to our society, through all its relations, a character exclusively its own, peculiar and unexampled.

Circumstances and causes such as these, wide, general and incessantly operative, thus pervading the whole mass of the community, cannot fail, in some way or other, to reach and powerfully affect every individual. Any American citizen who will look about him with an attentive eye, and then turn his contemplation inward upon himself, and examine his own breast and his own life, will readily perceive how sovereignly some or other of these external causes control his fortunes, direct his destinies, and mould his habits and his conduct, swaying or guiding his tastes, his reason, his feelings, or his affections. But if these can thus reach the humblest citizen, how much more decided must be their effect upon the man of native talent and improved intellect! As his mind expands itself more largely on the surface of society, as it enters with a bolder ambition or a keener relish into the concerns of men, the pursuits of fame, of power, or of knowledge, just so in proportion must he sympathize more readily with the surrounding world, and in acting upon many, must feel more sensibly the reciprocal action of the greater mass upon himself. Hence, all that is singular and peculiar in our country, her people or her institutions, will be in some sort imaged in his mind, and will operate upon his mental constitution as silently but as certainly as his physical frame is affected by the food that sustains him, or the air that he breathes.

It is, therefore, gentlemen, that I have thought that I could not more usefully discharge the duty assigned to me by your kind partiality, or select a theme more appropriate to the annual academic celebration of a college, which already boasting among its alumni so large a proportion of the active talent of our state, continues annually to swell that number by a numerous body of our most promising youth, than to call your attention to the consideration of the blessings and advantages resulting from the political and social conditions of our republic, to the American scholar—not merely in common to him with the rest of his fellow-citizens, but to him especially and above others, as an educated and intellectual man.

These are blessings and advantages, in themselves peculiar, unrivalled, inestimable; still, like all other temporal goods, they are not unmixed with evil, not unaccompanied by dangers, always liable to abuse. Like, too, to the other gifts of the Most High, intrusted to man for the use of his fellow men, they impose upon their possessor weighty, solemn and holy duties.

It is then of these blessings and advantages of the American scholar, their accompanying dangers and their attendant duties, that I now purpose to speak to you.

The subject ought certainly to interest those whom I am called to address, for it is of themselves that I must speak. From the lips of wisdom and genius, the theme could not fail to be fruitful of the deepest and most precious instruction. For myself, and the very imperfect views I am about to lay before you, I can claim no other weight or authority, than what may arise from the fact, that these are neither the vague speculations of a political theorist, nor the rant of patriotic declamation. They are sober and deliberate opinions, the results of much opportunity of observation, and that by no means careless or hasty, and formed by one not indifferent to the imperfections of our political or social system, or unwilling to confess them—not blind to the faults and errors of his country or his countrymen, but who has yet never wavered or faltered in his veneration for the sacred cause of republican liberty, or in his confidence of the ultimate and certain tendency of our free institutions to promote truth and justice, to diffuse happiness and virtue.

First of all then—We all know and feel that every thing in the condition and prospects of our country tends to excite and maintain a bold and stirring activity of thought and action throughout the whole community. Nothing is allowed to remain stagnant or dormant. Every mind is compelled, sometimes in despite of its own inclinations, to partake of the buoyant spirit, the restless mobility, the irrepressible energy of youth and hope.

In most other lands society moves with steady regularity, in one slow, sure and accustomed round. Each ascending step in the scale of wealth and distinction is completely filled up, and the vast majority, doomed to hereditary ignorance and privation, must be content to pass their whole lives where birth or accident has first placed them. Feeling no stimulus to exertion, besides that of daily want, their desires and their hopes conform themselves to the narrow scale of their regular toils and their humble enjoyments. But with us, commerce, arts, agriculture, enterprise, adventure, ambition, are crowding and hurrying every man forward. Our past is but brief. We can scarcely be said to have a present—certainly we have none for mere indolent enjoyment. We are all pressing and hastening forward to some better future. No single mind can well resist the general impulse. The momentum of the whole mass of society, composed of myriads of living forces, is upon each individual, and he flies forward with accelerated velocity, without any other power over his own motion than that of the direction of its course. The universal ardor is contagious, and we all rush into the throng of life, and are swept along by its broad, resistless current.

Least of all can the mind, formed to liberal studies, habituated from early youth to the employment of its most vigorous faculties, resist the wide spread sympathy. "The clear spirit," to use Milton's phrase, "nursed up with brighter influences and with a soul enlarged to the dimensions of spacious and high knowledge," sees in every direction careers of honor, or of usefulness open to its exertions, and tasking its noblest powers. For with us talent cannot well slumber; knowledge may always find some fit application.

Travel elsewhere, and where is it that you may not find talent chilled and withered by penury, or profound learning wasted on the drudgery of elementary instruction, or else "lost in a convent's solitary gloom?" With us this need never be. In fact, it is seldom long so, unless from the positive fault of the possessor. Excepting those melancholy cases, where some unavoidable calamity has weighed down the spirits and extinguished joy and hope for ever, knowledge and ability cannot well run here to waste without their voluntary degradation by gross vice or the maddest imprudence. But I do not now speak of the varied opportunities for the successful exertion of matured, cultivated talent, or the substantial rewards that its exercise may win, so much as of the still greater advantage which that talent may derive to itself from the prevailing activity and energy that animate the whole community. Under that strong and contagious stimulus, the faculties are awakened, the capacity enlarged, the genius roused, excited, inspired. The mind is not suffered to brood undisturbed over its own little stock of favorite thoughts, treading the same unceasing round of habitual associations, until it becomes quite incapable of fixing its attention upon any new object, and its whole existence is but a dull, drowsy dream. On the contrary, it is forced to sympathize with the living world around, to enter into the concerns of others and of the public, and to partake, more or less, of the cares and the hopes of men. Thus every hour it imbibes, unconsciously, new and strange knowledge, quite out of the sphere of its own personal experience. Thus it receives, and in its turn spontaneously communicates that bright electric current that darts its rapid course throughout our whole body politic, removing every sluggish obstruction, and bracing every languid muscle to vigorous toil. As compared with the more torpid state of society exhibited elsewhere, to live in one such as this, is like emerging from the fogs of the lowland fens heavy with chilling pestilence.

> "——the dull pacific air
> Where mountain zephyr never blew,
> The marshy level dank and bare,
> That Pan, that Ceres never knew—"

and ascending to inhale the exhilarating mountain atmosphere, where the breeze is keen and pure, and the springs gush bright from their native rock, bestowing on the children of the hills the bounding step, the strong arm, the far seeing eye, and the stout heart. It is much then to breathe such a mental air from earliest youth. It is much to be educated and formed under such potent and perpetual stimulants to intellectual development. But for a mind thus formed and framed for vigorous and effective action, it is not less necessary that fitting occupations may be found for its nobler qualities and powers. This is much for worldly success. It is every thing for honor, for conscience, for content, for beneficence. Let genius, however brilliant, however gifted with rare, or copious, or varied acquirements, be but doomed to labor for selfish objects, for personal necessities and sensual gratifications, and for those only—and its aspirations too will become low, its desires sordid, and its powers (adroit, doubtless, and very effective as to their accustomed occupations) will dwindle and become enfeebled, until they are quite incapable of any generous and magnanimous undertaking.

But with us the man of intellectual endowment is not so "cabined, cribbed, bound in" to his own puny cares. Far otherwise; his generous ambition, his large philanthropy, his zeal for the service of his God or his country, may spread themselves abroad "as wide and general as the casing air," without finding any check or barrier to their farthest range.

In the eternal order of Providence, minds act and re-act, and become the transcripts and reflections of each other, thus multiplying and perpetuating the evils or the excellence of our short being upon this globe. It is not the exclusive prerogative of the great, the eloquent, the chosen sons of genius or of power, who can speak trumpet-tongued to millions of their fellow creatures from the high summits of fame or authority, thus to be able to extend themselves in the production of good or evil far around and forward. We are all of us, in some sort, as waves in the shoreless ocean of human existence. Our own petty agitations soon die away, but they can extend themselves far onward and onward, and there are oftentimes circumstances which may cause those billows to swell as they roll forward, until they rise into a majestic vastness which it could scarce seem possible that our puny efforts could have ever set in motion. Such favoring circumstances, in other nations comparatively rare, are here the common blessings of our land. We have a population doubling and re-doubling with a steady velocity so unexampled in former history, as to have utterly confounded the speculations of all older political philosophy. We have a territory, which rapidly as that population subdues the forest and covers the desert, has still ample room for coming generations. These things alone are enormous elements in the mighty process of social melioration. Whatever is effected in removing any of the evils that afflict those about us, must, ere long, reach far beyond us and beyond them, to other and more numerous generations, to distant fields, as yet silent and desolate, but destined soon to swarm with a busy multitude. The character, knowledge and happiness of that future and distant multitude, are now in our hands. They are to be moulded by our beneficent labors, our example, our studies, our philanthropic enterprise. Thus the "spirit of our deeds," long after those deeds have passed away, will continue to walk the earth, from one ocean-beat shore of our continent to the other, scattering blessings or curses upon after-times.

Consider too the general elementary instruction of this nation—too slight, meagre and superficial indeed to content the patriot as an ultimate end wherewith to rest satisfied, but admirable as the means of spreading information and pouring a bright flood of light and truth over our whole continent. Books, newspapers, periodicals, are scattered profusely through the land, and present to a large proportion of our population their favorite and most unfailing relaxation from business and toil. Our people are daily, hourly habituated to discussions of the most interesting nature, sometimes upon the most abstruse, frequently upon the most important subjects of human interest. All our experience, our modes of business and ways of life, have a strong tendency to teach us to regard science, not as a thing mysterious and solitary, never to be mixed with common life and its ordinary thoughts and concerns, but as an exalted and munificent benefactor, constantly and profusely contributing to our welfare and happiness. Hence it requires nothing but the steady and well-directed efforts of enlightened and liberal minds to make a very large part, and that in many respects too, the best part of science, familiar and popular to a degree which the recluse scholar of former days could never imagine. Much indeed of the best science can only be useful, in any high degree, by becoming thus familiar and popular; for unless it be so, it must remain a barren theory, dry and useless.

This is eminently and self-evidently true in all political and economical science. It is equally so of all ethical truth: and as it is the beautiful characteristic of the loftiest and most perfect science, most rapidly to simplify and generalize its knowledge as it increases its stores, it is not easy to conjecture any assignable limit beyond which the grand conclusions (at least) of sound scientific investigation, and the results of learned labor, may not be laid open to the liberal curiosity of the humblest artisan. In the same or some similar way, the choicest refinements of classical taste, and the congenial study of the remains of ancient genius, which beautify and enrich the scholar's mind, may be made through him to enlarge, to elevate, and ennoble the general mind of his country.

But these are not the only facilities we enjoy for making the acquisitions of learning profitable to all, and for bringing intellectual force to bear upon its appropriate objects. The quick and keen sense of self-interest, that gives such sagacity and energy to the business operations of this country, is equally propitious to the success of every art, every discovery, invention, undertaking, and science, that involves in it any amount of practical improvement or power. Hence, whatever of theoretical science, inventive skill, ingenious speculation, or reasoning eloquence, can be made to tell upon any of the multitudinous affairs making up the business of life, or to minister in any way to the increased power or enjoyment of man, will soon find ready attention for their claims. Here no prejudices in favor of time-honored usages are strong enough long to resist the advance of scientific improvement or wise innovation. Society is not divided into castes, each one of them watching with jealous vigilance against any encroachment of their several exclusive walks by any rude intruder from another class, themselves clinging to the settled usages and old forms of their own clan, with the steady pertinacity of men whose unexamined prejudices are interwoven with their earliest habits and their most valuable personal interests. If Science, descending from her starry throne in the heavens, light the student to any discovery or invention in any manner applicable to the wants of his fellow creatures—if Genius prompts the lofty thought —if love of God or of man inspire the generous design, no matter how the novelty may astonish for the moment, no matter what prejudices may be shocked, no matter what interests may be alarmed and band themselves against the innovator, let him go on undismayed. He advances to certain victory.

But it has often been objected that this all-absorbing gravitation towards the useful, the active, and the practical, in our country, propels every student from his most favorite studies into the struggles, the competition, and tumult of life, and is thus fatal at once to all recondite and curious learning, to deep attainment in pure science or polished excellence in elegant art and literature. There is certainly some portion of truth in this objection, and yet but a portion only. Where the demands for competent ability are so pressing, and the temptations to employ that ability in such occupations as bring with them instant rewards are so great, it is quite certain that but few will be found inclined to spend their lives in studies which have no interest for others, and no perceptible bearing on private or public good. When, however, we consider the wonderful connexion and inter-dependence of all knowledge, made more and more manifest by every day's advance in science, so as almost to prove by an accumulation of particular examples the sublime hypothesis of the old philosophy, "that by circuit of deduction, all truth out of any truth may be concluded;" when we reflect how singularly adapted the various parts of knowledge are to the individual tastes and character of different men, so as to seize and draw them as with an irresistible mental magnetism to their several studies, we cannot, I think, doubt that all that is most valuable in science or literature, will find votaries among us, who, not content to make such studies the amusements of their leisure or to devote a life of monastic gloom to their solitary worship, will make or find for them a fit application. The experience of scientific investigation has shown that such application of the test of reality and experiment to theoretic truth, has not only often thrown a clearer light on that theory, at once limiting its generalities and confirming its evidence, but has also evolved new combinations, suggested new inferences, and manifested higher laws. Art more than repays its obligations to science. The large processes of manufactures have proved the best school of chemical discovery. Natural knowledge has contributed largely to medical skill, and it has in turn received its most precious accessions from the observation of the physician. The abstrusest speculations of the metaphysician, have found their place in those controversies of theologians that rend the religious world, as well as in questions of political discussion, of legislation, and of jurisprudence. Thus contemplations, apparently the most shadowy, have often operated with the greatest efficiency upon the most engrossing concerns of daily life.

Nevertheless, it may well be that there are some meditations so subtile and unreal, some branches of learning so remote from use, some laborious arts of refinement requiring for their successful cultivation such silent abstraction and unremitting, undivided labor for years, that they can find no room amid the strife and bustle, the *fumum, strepitumque*,—the rail-road noise and rapidity of this work-day world of America. Be it so. We would not willingly lose them. For nothing that has filled the thoughts of the good and wise, or weaned men from sensual pleasure by the better attractions of art, taste or learning, can be without value and dignity. But if we must lose them, let us be content, and the more so, because their deprivation, if such be of necessity the case, is more than compensated by countervailing benefits resulting from the same causes. Such acquirements or accomplishments cannot flourish here, because they require the devotion of the whole man to their service, whilst the American man of letters is incessantly called off from any single inquiry, and allured or compelled to try his ability in every variety of human occupation.

Though he may be laboriously devoted to the duties of a particular calling, or, on the other hand, exempted from the pressure of regular professional labor, no man of informed mind can with us exclude the surrounding world. The *Quidquid agunt homines,* familiarity with men and their business is forced upon him, and it is a rare thing indeed if he can remain a cool looker-on. It may be patriotism, it may be humanity, that animates him—it may be personal pride, or political zeal, or ambition, or perhaps merely the mysterious sympathy of universal example; but whatever may be the special motive in the individual, no scholar, no professional student or practitioner can well remain the mere man of books. If in this acquaintance with many other matters, something is lost as to particular skill and minute accuracy of knowledge, assuredly much more is gained in the healthful development of the faculties, the enlargement of the understanding, the more equable poise of the judgment, and the richness, variety, and originality of the materials for reflection, combination, or invention thus stored in the memory.

If awed by that veneration the scholar naturally feels for those who consecrate their days and nights to learning, alternating only between books and the pen, you hesitate to allow the superiority conferred by this variety and versatility over the man of one solitary study, let me appeal to the unvarying testimony of literary history for the proof. The great men of antiquity, the models of eloquence, the fathers of poetry, the teachers of ethical wisdom, the founders of that ancient jurisprudence, that still rules the greater part of the civilized world, were none of them solitary scholars; none of them were contented with the "half wisdom of books" alone. They performed well all the duties of war and peace; and their immortal works, beautiful in the severe simplicity of truth and nature, still remain "eternal monuments"—as

Thucydides, in the calm consciousness of genius, has said of his own majestic history—eternal monuments for the good of after ages, of things which they had themselves seen and done. There was scarce one of them who could not, like Cicero, look back, with proud satisfaction, to his labors in the forum, the senate, and the field, disastrous ofttimes, but full of glory—*"summi labores nostri, magnâ compensati gloriâ, mitigantur"* [1] and then turn to those studies which were the grace and crown of their prosperity, and the sure consolation of their misfortunes, *"non modo sedatis molestiis jucundâ, sed etiam hærentibus salutaria."*

The self-same lesson is taught in the history of the philosophy and literature of our own mother tongue. Whose are the venerated and enduring names—whose the volumes that we turn to, with reverent affection, as the oracles of just thought, or the ever fresh springing fountains of delight? Who were they from Bacon to our own Franklin—from Spenser and Shakspeare to Walter Scott, but men of those mixed pursuits, that multifarious instruction, that familiar intercourse with actual life, which narrow-minded learning would brand as the bane of philosophy, the destruction of letters. Compare their works with those of men devoted to literature alone, and who looked at nothing beyond its precincts—the plodding compiler, the laborious collector of scientific trifles, valuable only as materials for some wiser mind to use, the herd of dealers in light literature, either the servile imitators of past excellence, or the echoes of the follies of their day, or baser yet, the pandars to its vices. How short and fleeting has been their popularity! Here and there one among the number has deserved the gratitude of posterity by moral worth and well directed labor. His works keep an honored place in our libraries, but they rarely exercise a living sway over the opinions and tastes of nations.

> A mortal born he meets the general doom,
> But leaves, like Egypt's kings, a lasting tomb.

Such is also the experience of the arts of taste and design. The father of the Italian arts, Leonardo da Vinci, was a scholar, a politician, a poet, a musician. Michael Angelo, the sublime and the holy, was still more universal. Sculptor, painter, poet, architect, engineer—we find him now painting his grand frescos, now modelling his gigantic statues, now

[1] *De Oratore,* Lib. II.

heaving the dome of St. Peter's into the air, and now fortifying his loved Florence, the city of his affections, with a humble diligence and a patriot's zeal. There are no such artists now in Italy. The painters and sculptors with which it swarms, are devoted to painting and sculpture exclusively; but how do they compare as artists with their great predecessors? Could any authority whatever add weight to the facts I have just referred to, such would be found in the opinion of Milton himself. In a well known passage of one of those fervid and brilliant prose tracts of his youth, which (to use the noble metaphor of an eloquent critic) announced the Paradise Lost as plainly as ever the bright purple clouds in the east announced the rising of the sun; Milton, with a sublime and determined confidence in his own genius, covenanted—for that is his remarkable expression—in some few years thereafter, to produce "a work not to be raised from the heats of youth or the vapors of wine, like that which flows at will from the pen of some vulgar amorist, nor by invocation of Memory and her syren sisters, but by devout prayer to that Eternal Spirit which can enrich with all utterance and knowledge, and send out his seraphim with the hallowed fire of his altar to touch and purify the lips of whom he pleases." "To this," he subjoins in a lower strain of eloquence, but with the same decision of tone—"to this must be added industrious and select readings, steady observation, and an insight into all seemly and generous arts and affairs." Had Milton confined himself to the studies of his library, or the halls of his university—had he not thrown himself into the hottest conflicts of the day—had he not stood forth the terrible champion of freedom of opinion and of republican liberty, raising on high his spirit-stirring voice in their defence in worst extremes, and "on the perilous verge of battle where it raged;" had he not participated in counsel, in act, and in suffering with England's boldest spirits—had he not thus felt in himself, and seen in others, the "might of the unconquerable will," the unshaken, unseduced, unterrified constancy of faithful zeal and love, he would not have gained that insight into seemly and generous arts and affairs, that intimate acquaintance with the nobler parts of human nature that made him the greatest of poets. Had Milton lived always a recluse student, his learned fancy would undoubtedly have enriched his country's literature with Lycidas and Comus, but the world would have wanted the Paradise Lost.

But the American literary man has yet other reasons to be grateful for having been born in this age and country; and they are reasons such as a mind cast in the grand antique mould of Milton's, would prize as most worthy of fervent thanksgiving. Every thing here is propitious to honest independence of thought. Such an independence is the presiding genius of all our institutions; it is the vital spirit that gives life to the whole. Without this, our constitutions and laws, our external forms of equality, our elections, our representation, our boasted liberty of speech and of conscience, are but poor and beggarly elements, shadows without substance, dead and worthless carcasses, from which the living soul, the grace, the glory, the strength, have for ever fled. It is not the parchment record of our constitutions, the bills of right, the trial by jury, the elective franchise, nor all the securities provided by the jealous wisdom of our fathers for the unrestrained exercise of liberty, that can call back this living spirit when once it has fled—no, nor the unrestrained press scattering its millions of daily sheets over the land, nor the representative halls echoing with their never-ending discussions. These cannot repair its loss, but they are all admirable agents in its production and preservation; and there are besides other circumstances in our condition not less favorable to this temper, than our political institutions. The numberless shades of opinions upon the doctrines of revelation, as well as upon other momentous concerns and duties, coming to us from the various stocks whence we descend, or the different influences under which our citizens grow up, with all the creeds, all the prejudices, and all the knowledge of the old world pouring in upon them, though involving or producing dangerous errors, have yet a healthful efficacy in habituating men to the free use of their judgment, and the manly, direct avowal of their thoughts. Here there is no apparently general agreement of society to awe the mind from investigation of what claims to be certain and established truth. And when examination on any subject brings conviction, the inquirer is seldom compelled to meet that hardest trial of human fortitude, the renunciation of old associations and long cherished doctrines in the face of universal scorn and indignation, and without the solace of human sympathy. More than this:—that restlessness of enterprise, which alike nerves the frontier settler to the toils and adventures of the wilderness, and kindles the young dreams of the political aspirant, which whitens the ocean with our canvass, drives the rail-road through the desert, and startles the moose at his watering-place, or scares the eagle from his high solitary perch with the sudden beat of the steam-boat's wheels—that one and the same ardent, restless spirit ruling our whole people, can have little communion with that abject prostration of intellect, that makes man crouch before his fellow, submitting his reason and his conscience to another's will. It is thus that the adventurous ardor, so efficient in external and material matters, naturally extends its energies to the moral and intellectual. Here are at once provided facilities for the propagation of truth, and securities for some portion, at least, of respect for conscientious error.

It is not easy to realize the full value of the blessings made familiar to us by daily enjoyment, without some experience of their opposite evils. It is our happy fate to know nothing personally of the severer tyranny of power over the conscience. History can alone teach us what this is, and how to estimate duly our political advantages in this respect. What then is the history of human opinions but a long record of martyrdom for truth, for religion, for private conscience, for public liberty? Every monument of antiquity in the old world, like that one of "London's lasting shame,"

The *Traitor's Gate*, miscalled, through which of yore
Past Raleigh, Cranmer, Russel, Sydney, More,—[2]

every vestige of the past recalls some remembrance of the "lifted axe, the agonizing wheel," the scaffold, the stake, and the fagot, on which the patriot poured out his life's blood, and where the martyr breathed forth in torture his last prayer of triumphant forgiving faith. But, traveller, stop not there to mourn. Rejoice rather—for these are the monuments of the victories of truth—of the triumph of the self-sustaining, immortal mind, over the impotence of transient power. The martyrs have conquered. Their sentence is reversed. Their tyrants have passed away with names blackened and branded by universal scorn. The cause for which they died has now mounted the seat of worldly empire, or else is enthroned still more regally in the hearts of millions. Mourn not for the martyrs. Mourn rather for truth suppressed by fear, for genius shrinking from the torture or the dungeon; or, more

[2] These lines are quoted from memory, I believe from Rogers, and slightly varied.

melancholy still, deeming ease and wealth cheaply bought by the sacrifice of honor, of conscience, of faith, and of truth. Mourn for Galileo and Beranger, and a crowd of others as wise, and as good, and as weak as they were. Pity, but despise them not. Look to your own age, and then compare it with theirs. Look to your own country and her laws, and then look to theirs. Be thankful for your happier lot, yet fear—lest you yourselves should some time yield up your integrity under trials that, weighed with theirs, are as light as air.

Well has a philosophical poet [3] of our own age enforced the deep moral to be drawn from such examples.

> "Ye who secure midst trophies not your own,
> Judge him who won them, when he stood alone,
> And proudly talk of '*Galileo's fall.*'
> Oh, first the age and then the man compare,
> That age how dark, congenial minds how rare;
> No host of friends, with kindred zeal did burn,
> No throbbing hearts awaited his return.
> Prostrate alike, when prince and peasant fell,
> He only, disenchanted from the spell,
> Like the weak worm that gems the starless night,
> Moved in the scanty circlet of his light.
> And was it strange that he withdrew the ray
> That did but guide the night birds to their prey?"

But whilst there are great political and public causes to shield the American mind from exposure to the stern tyranny of power, there are others less conspicuous and prominent, equally protecting it from more degrading tendencies. I do not count as the least among these the absence of marked difference of hereditary or permanent rank. It is impossible for any one, who has not personally witnessed it, to comprehend the strange reverence to worse and inferior men than themselves, the submission of the understanding to the vices and caprices of those they deem the higher orders, which beginning with early youth, and confirmed by education, clings throughout life to thousands of the well-instructed and the good. I well remember the astonishment expressed to me, some years ago, by several learned and respectable ministers of the gospel in Great Britain, at the ease with which an eloquent divine

[3] Coleridge.

of our country (the late Dr. Mason) conversed and argued with, and even contradicted, a royal duke who had honored an anniversary charity festival with his presence. They accounted for this phenomenon not by ascribing it to its right cause, the temper and education of his country, but by attributing it to his presumed habits of familiar association with the political dignitaries of his own land. This feeling struck me as the more remarkable, because these worthy men (several of whom enjoyed an honorable distinction in the religious literary world) were themselves dissenters from the national established church, and almost republican opposers of the then administration of the state. It requires a very strong effort of mind, and often too as great an excitement of feeling, to throw off this prejudice; and when it is thus thrown off, the danger is that it either runs into wild insubordination of just authority, or else lasts but for a time, till the fervor of youthful zeal is over, and the suggestions of interested prudence concur with early opinions; and then the half obliterated impressions of youth reappear.

Now the obvious tendency of all this is to bow down the intellect before authority, making the soul crouch and crawl before place, rank and dignity. I say that such is its *tendency*—for I should do foul wrong and insult to the deep serious thought of England and her native sturdy manliness, as well as to the enthusiastic intellectual daring of the continental scholars, were I to say that such were the constant and necessary consequences of any external and artificial condition of social order whatsoever—still less so of a mixed government like theirs. It is, however, an influence deeply deleterious to the right feeling of mental independence, and it is therefore happy that it in no degree threatens us. But in other lands, pecuniary dependence is too often connected with this reverence for rank, so that they produce together the most complete vassalage. The market for intellectual labor is overstocked. Nature's rich banquet is crowded with titled and hereditary guests, "the table is full." To emerge from the crowd of menials, and obtain some share of the feast, the unbidden scholar must attach himself to the train of a patron, and feed on the alms his niggard bounty may bestow. Such has been the degrading history of literary men, poets, authors, and, I blush to add, philosophers, throughout the world, for many centuries. And if in our own times the literature of France and of England have, in a good degree, freed themselves from that ignoble thraldom, this is mainly to be attributed to the growth of principles similar to our own, to the diffusion of knowledge amongst the people, to the rapid increase of commercial and manufacturing riches, all combining to build up the sovereignty of public opinion, and to make the patronage of aristocratic wealth more and more insignificant in comparison with the unpretending munificence of an educated people. Yet the causes which originally led to this degradation of the literary character remain, and much of the best talent of Europe still wears (as nearly the whole of it did for centuries) the galling though gilded chain of patronage.

> Yet think what ills the scholar's life assail,
> Toil, envy, want, the *patron* and the gaol,—

said the indignant Johnson, filled as he was with habitual reverence for rank, yet resenting, with manly contempt, the wrongs of genius and the disgrace of letters.

At a later period of his life, the same veteran author recorded in his great English Dictionary the bitter result of his long and sad experience and that of his literary associates, by sarcastically defining the *patron* as being "commonly a wretch, who protects with insolence and is paid by flattery." The same sad story is told more in detail in the precarious dependant lives of the wits and poets of London and Paris during the reigns of Louis XIV., Charles II., and the first and second Georges. It is written at large in their shameless flatteries, addressed to venal statesmen and ribald courtiers, embodied in servile dedications, or embalmed in works where taste and fancy struggle in vain to rise under the load of baseness and pollution imposed upon the unhappy literary slave by his equally unhappy patron. The facility with which a sure and comfortable subsistence may be obtained in this country, and the certainty with which educated talent, directed by ordinary discretion and industry, may obtain to a decent competency, are such as to exclude all temptation, much more all necessity, to follow in this respect the humiliating example of European learning. To such evils "the lack of means need never drive us." If dazzled by the false glitter of office, if bribed by the doles of political patronage, or by such paltry boons as private interest can bestow, the American scholar is ever weak enough to sell his conscience, or bow down his independence before a master, he falls a voluntary victim. The sin is his own—his own be the shame. Let him not seek to divide it with his country. Is it not then a glorious privilege to be wholly free from the necessity of such dependence, never to be forced by the tyrannous compulsion of need to man-worship, the meanest of all idolatries? Far nobler, far happier, than kings can make him, is the lot of him who dedicates his life and his intellect to instruct and delight the people—who looks to them not for alms or bounty, but for a just compensation in honor and in profit, for the pleasure or the instruction he affords them—who seeks to serve them as a friend, not to fawn on them as a flatterer—to please them or to teach them, yet as having a higher master and knowing the solemn responsibility of one who acts upon the happiness or the morals of many. Happy he who, in the discharge of such duties, leads none into dangerous error, lulls none into careless or contemptuous negligence of right, nor ever sullies the whiteness of an innocent mind. Happier—still happier, he who has scattered abroad into many hearts those moral seeds whence benevolent and heroic actions spring up, who has "given ardor to virtue and confidence to truth," or, in more sacred language, "has turned many unto righteousness." Such genius, fired from heaven's own light, will continue to the end of time to burn and spread, kindling congenial flames far and wide, until they lift up their broad united blaze on high, enlightening, cheering, and gladdening the nations of the earth.

Nevertheless, sad experience has sometimes proved that he who draws his subsistence or his fame from the taste of a corrupted people, may debase and dishonor himself in ministering to the corrupted tastes of the million, as well as he who pandars to that of the corrupt aristocratic few.

> "The drama's laws, the drama's patrons give,
> For they who live to please, must please to live;"

And what is true of the drama, holds equally good of all the literature and the arts that minister to pleasure and entertainment. Yet the lure to evil from serving the many is far less than from serving the few. To one entire half of the great domain of mind it reaches not at all. The cultivator of mathematical and physical science, more fortunate in this than the man of letters, is wholly beyond such danger. All of his labors, in order to bring honor or advantage to himself, must be felt in the increased comforts of thousands, or the augmented power of his species. What a magnificent accompaniment is this thought to the other worldly rewards of his successful toils! What a moral dignity does it give to the exploits of art and science, in themselves the most purely physical and mechanical!

But the man who aspires to guide or to please the minds of others by eloquence or literature, will soon find that, in proportion as he addresses himself to enduring public interests or universal natural feelings in preference to those which are local or personal, artificial or temporary, so his own genius will be elevated, and the ethical character of his thoughts and works ennobled and purified. For in order to advance those large public interests, he must look to the grand laws, political or moral, that govern human happiness. In order to touch the universal natural sensibilities, he must stir up the generous sympathies, that in individuals are entangled or choked with their peculiar vices, but still are common to human nature. He must rouse up the virtues that sleep in most hearts, but are dead in none. So only can he gain and keep a firm hold upon the public mind. Now in the very effort of so doing, his own littleness is insensibly lost in the greatness of a common humanity. He tasks himself to high purposes, and in that exertion brings forth powers he dreamt not of in himself. The author rises above the man. He becomes unto himself, his own "exceeding great reward."

I was much struck, years ago, with an admirable application made by a veteran statesman of this general truth to a sound doctrine of political ethics. It is contained in that beautiful historical fragment left by the late Charles Fox—a work that, I know not why, has never obtained that reputation of which it seems to me to be eminently worthy. Whilst it vies in sober dignity with the best remains of classical antiquity, it breathes throughout every page the same generous and manly benevolence that (whatever might have been his public or his private faults) marked the whole character of that frank and kind-hearted statesman. In relating the secret negotiation of James II. with the French court, by which the English king was to be furnished by Louis XIV. with pecuniary aid for the enslaving of his people, one of the very meanest and most criminal transactions recorded by modern history, the historian stops to wonder and regret, that in company with several far inferior men, no unfit agents for such a business, are found named the able and eminent Lord Godolphin, and Lord Churchill, afterwards better known as the celebrated Duke of Marlborough. "It is with difficulty," says he, "that the reader can persuade himself that the Godolphin and Churchill here named are the same persons who were afterwards, one in the cabinet and one in the field, the great conductors of the war of the succession. How little do they appear in one instance! how great in the other! And the investigation of the cause to which this excessive difference is owing, will produce a most useful lesson. In the one case they were the tools of a king plotting against his people; in the other, the ministers of a free government acting upon enlarged principles, and with energies which no state that is not in some degree republican, can supply. How forcibly must the contemplation of these men, in such opposite situations, teach persons engaged in political life, that a free and popular government is desirable, not only for the public good, but for their own greatness and consideration, for every object of generous ambition."

Every good citizen of our republic will readily acquiesce in the soundness of this political conclusion of the English statesman. But I do not hesitate to give the doctrine a much wider application, and to say that a state of society, free and popular, is eminently conducive to exalted principles of thought and action, and the best energies of intellectual men in every liberal and generous pursuit, and is therefore desirable to them, not only for the public welfare, "but for their own greatness and consideration, for every object of generous ambition." In such a state, Poetry and Painting may perhaps look around in vain for Mæcenases. They need not despair if they find them not in individuals—for they will find them in the multitude.

> "Unbroken spirits cheer! still, still remains,
> The *eternal patron* Liberty, whose flame,
> While she protects, inspires the noblest strains;
> The best and sweetest far are toil-created gains."

So many historical and biographical illustrations in the belles lettres, in jurisprudence, in the arts of taste and design, in the numberless applications of science, all strongly corroborating the views I have just stated, are crowding upon my memory, that were I to recapitulate them in detail, I should weary your patience with a string of names and incidents already familiar to every reading man; whilst I should be compelled to leave the remaining parts of my subject wholly untouched. To them I must hurry, and I can speak of them but briefly.

It is of the intellectual dangers, growing out of circumstances otherwise thus fruitful in blessings, that I purposed also to speak. The dangers of prosperity, more insidious than those of adversity, are often more fatal, and these are of that class.

One of the most obvious of them, is the danger of falling into a conceited, smattering superficiality in consequence of that very universality of occupation and inquiry which seems, in other respects, so propitious to the formation of a sound, comprehensive understanding, so useful to the man of books, so graceful to the man of business. Such superficiality is undeniably one of the besetting sins of our reading men. It shows itself in the capacity of talking fluently upon all things, and of doing every thing; and in the habit of talking inaccurately upon all things, and of doing every thing badly. It nourishes and sustains itself upon compends, abridgments, extracts, and all the other convenient subsidia of improved education; excellent things in their way, but like other great improvements of our day, wheeling you to the object of your journey, without permitting you to know much of the country you pass through. You may trace it by the small pedantry that commonly accompanies half knowledge. You may track it in legislative speeches and reports, in public documents and legal arguments, and even in judicial opinions, where facts, and numbers, and grave statements of argument and collations of authorities are all that is wanted; but where their place is filled by puerile rhetoric, by common-place instances of Greek and Roman history, or by mouldy scraps of thumb-worn schoolboy Latin—shabby finery at the best, and all of it out of place. Yet the temptation to the commission of such folly is not great, and the remedy is easy. No man can hope to know every thing within the knowledge of his whole race. Let him then study with diligent accuracy that single branch of knowledge which it happens to be most his duty to know well, and he will have time and opportunity left to learn much more. Let him keep his curiosity awake, and his affections alive to whatever concerns the welfare of his neighbor, his country, or his kind. He cannot then fail to learn much, and he will know how to use all he learns well. His understanding will be tempered by use to that right medium that best brings the scattered and broken rays of light from all quarters, to converge upon any object on which the mind is called to fix its attention.

This impatience of continuous systematic labor, and the hope of reaching by some new and short road those objects of human desire which the Creator has not less beneficently than wisely decreed, should be gained only by the sweat of the brow or the toil of the mind—

—————————— Pater ipse colendi
Haud facilem esse viam voluit,—

this same impatience of slow study that engenders the parading superficiality which I have just described, is often seen to produce still more serious effects upon the character and the whole course of life. Such effects are peculiarly apparent at the present time in our own country.

In the wonderful and accelerated progress of this nation to wealth and greatness, the public mind is continually surprised by the sudden apparition of enormous riches gained as it were in a moment, sometimes seemingly by accident, sometimes the hasty fruit of a quick-eyed and bold sagacity. Then again in our political contentions, the unexpected mutation of popular favor frequently raises an individual at once to eminence from some humble professional walk, where he leaves his former superiors to toil on far beneath him. Under the strong excitements of such examples, it is but natural that the ardent youth of acquirement and ability should be often tempted to look with disgust upon the slow returns of regular labor, whether in study or in business. He closes his books, or he flies from his office or counting-room, and rushes to the field of gambling speculation, or it may be of equally gambling politics, trusting to become immediately rich or great, by the favor of fortune, as others have become before him.

Unquestionably in such a republic as ours, the rewards of public favor are legitimate objects of honorable ambition. So too in a country where population and capital are so rapidly augmenting, to neglect the means of securing to ourselves some share of that general prosperity, which long-sighted sagacity assures us must be the natural effect of causes already in action, would be to reject the goods which Providence tenders to our acceptance. But the great danger in this country, and especially at the present time, and peculiarly to the well-educated young man, is that he is most strongly tempted to stake at once his whole chance of success and of happiness upon such uncertain contingencies and upon them alone; turning with scorn from the sober certainties of life, as being worthy the attention of none but dull, plodding spirits.

Now viewing this subject as a mere question of prudent calculation, we are met with the striking and certain fact, that the whole aggregate profits of mere speculative gain among us (throwing aside all account of the perhaps equal losses) are utterly insignificant in comparison with those of regular commerce, or well directed industry in other pursuits. In the same way, and for precisely the same reasons, the highest honors and rewards of the mere political adventurer are just as paltry, when placed by the side of those of Marshall, and Wirt, and Dwight, of Wistar, or of White, and, I might add, many living names scarcely less honored than those of the venerated dead—whose long, steady, successful course of professional or of learned labor, was crowned by the universal and affectionate veneration of their countrymen. But if turning our view from external circumstances of wealth or of respect, we look to the influence of such a temper upon character and happiness, the contrast is still more striking. On the one side are domestic quiet, calm content, cheerful industry, well employed days and peaceful nights, and above all, a steady reliance on your own exertions—under the care of Heaven, the true security of independence and the best guarantee of virtue. Yet all this our youth are seen throwing aside to take in exchange the feverish excitement of the gambler, now elated into wild exultation, now harassed by doubt and fears, now weighed down by mortification, disappointment, and sorrow of heart—ay, and to take the gambler's hazardous, precarious fortunes too, his frequent, sudden and dreadful fluctuations from wealth to poverty, from power and splendor to beggary, a state of mind and of fortune leaving no room for domestic happiness, little for personal independence, hardly any for steady, straight-forward honesty. Nor let the young man flatter himself with the false hope, that all this is but for a time, and that when his fortunes are made, he will rest in safety. If he starts into life, risking every thing upon hazards like these, he is a doomed man. He must go on to the end of life as he begun. His early habits are incongruous with the calm, unexciting details of ordinary life, and render his mind eventually incompetent for the ordinary duties of society.

Against this danger there is but one sure safe-guard of intellectual discipline. Religious and moral duty may indicate others. I am far from advising a timid abstinence from any creditable or honest undertaking that may offer strong inducements to enter upon it. Such advice would be idle and ineffectual, if it were in other respects wise, and it is not wise in the times and country in which we live. The intellectual safe-guard I would recommend is simply this:—to form your permanent habits and tastes to some study, some business, some profession, of common and constant utility: to become masters of this, familiar with it, fond of it. If afterwards more exciting avocations call you off for a time, to this you may always look as the agreeable and respectable employ-ment of your prosperous leisure, and upon this you may fall back in adversity, with the certainty of finding a sure protection for your honor, your independence, and your virtue.

There is another fault with which our country has been sometimes reproached, and this reproach, to which I have already alluded, much exaggerated as it is, is not without some foundation in reality. This degree of reality is again another of the evils that may befal the Ameri-can scholar, and against which it most behooves him to guard. It has been said by shrewd though unfriendly observers, that in America the practical and the profitable swallow up every other thought. There, say they, fancy withers, art languishes, taste expires; there the mind looks only to the material and the mechanical, and loses its capacity for the ideal and the abstract; the sensuous understanding is vigorous, the pure reason is torpid and blind. It might seem that there were very little reason to complain of our lot, if our nation effects every thing it at-tempts in the useful and practical; and that the ideal and the abstract might well be left to others who have less of solid and material con-solation. Yet I think not exactly so; and, first wholly protesting against the sweeping broadness of the change—am willing to confess, that the American mind is peculiarly exposed to suffer in this very way. The demands upon talent for active service are so numerous and imperative, the compensation and rewards for such service are so immediate and tempting, that the educated man is induced naturally to value the worth of knowledge by its direct utility. This is not amiss in itself, if it stop there, but he is often led on to take another step, and measure the degree of that utility by its value to his own interests—thus paring down utility to mere selfishness, and that too most commonly the selfishness of the coarsest and meanest material interests. To this, there are, it must be confessed, stronger temptations here than in other countries. On the other hand, there are here also stronger inducements to a more liberal habit of thought and a more generous course of action. If the facilities of advancing our personal interests are here numerous and absorbing, so again those interests will here be found to be peculiarly bound up and interwoven with those of our country and our neighbor. The prosperity of each man depends upon the prosperity of all. Every active citizen feels that he partakes largely of the practical and real, as well as of the theoretical sovereignty, and may make his own character and influence felt far and near. For the same reason, in all the operations of private enterprise, and in our public concerns, as the laws and principles regulating their action are evolved and manifested, even enlightened self-interest is constantly called to look to something loftier and more lasting than its own direct and immediate objects. Thus whilst the intelligent American citizen is surrounded by the strongest temptations to devote himself solely to selfish pursuits, he is at the same time every where invited to conform his own spirit to that of our liberal institutions, and instructed to uplift his mind to the consideration of large principles, and to regard himself as being but a small part of the vast whole which claims his best affections.

With such a choice before him, pitiable indeed is the lot of him who turns from the nobler and manlier side, to think, to live, and to drudge for himself alone. He cuts himself off from the best delights of the heart—its endearing charities and its elevating sympathies. He paralyzes his own intellect by suffering it to become half dead through inaction, and that in its nobler parts. The mighty ladder of thought and reason, reaching from the visible to the invisible—from the crude knowledge gained through the senses to the sublimest inferences of the pure reason—from the earth to the very footstool of God's own throne—is before him and invites his ascent. But he bends his eyes obstinately downwards upon the glittering ores at his feet, until he loses the wish or the hope for any thing better.

This, however, is but an extreme case, to be pointed out as a beacon to mark the covert peril. That such grovelling materiality, such mean selfishness, is not the necessary, nor the constant, no, nor the frequent result of our ardent industry in the affairs of life, let the discoveries of Franklin, and the magnificent far-drawn speculations of Edwards— let the grand philosophy, and the poetic thought, flashing quick and thick through the cloudy atmosphere of political discussion in our senate-house—let the open-handed charity, the more than princely munificence, the untiring personal labors of benevolence, exhibited by our most devoted and successful men of business, bear splendid testimony.

There is yet a danger of quite another sort, that with us sometimes besets and misleads the literary man. Familiarized from youth with the glories and beauties of European literature, his ambition is early fired to imitate or to rival its excellence. He forms to himself grand plans of intellectual exploits, all of them probably incongruous with the state and taste of his country, and most of them doubtless beyond his own ability. The embryo author projects epic poems, and in the mean while executes sonnets in quantities; the artist feeds his imagination with ideal historical compositions on the scale and above the excellence of those of Raphael; the young orator dreams of rivalling the younger Pitt, and of ruling the nation by his eloquence, at the age of four-and-twenty. These enthusiasts enter the living world, and soon find that their expectations are but a dream. They discover either that the world rates their talent very differently from their own estimate of it, or else that the state of society about them is wholly adverse to its exercise in the direction or on the scale their ambitious fancy had anticipated. The coarse matter-of-fact character of our world begins to disgust them. They see duller school-fellows outstrip them in worldly success. They see the honors and profits of public office bestowed upon some whom they know to be unworthy. The profits of trade and speculation are gathered before their eyes by the unlettered.

Disappointed and disgusted, they are now tempted to ascribe their disappointment to the republican institutions of their country; not reflecting that it is impossible to enjoy all kinds of good at the same time; that whatever is administered by men must be subject to abuse; and that to be happy and successful, every man must some how or other conform himself to the sphere where Providence has placed him.

If the scholar gives way to this temptation, he becomes a discordant, jarring thing in society, harmonizing with nothing near or around him. He dwells with a sort of complacent disgust upon every imperfection of our social state. He gradually becomes a rebel in heart to our glorious institutions. His affections and secret allegiance transfer themselves to some other form of government and state of society, such as he dreams to have formed the illustrious men and admirable things of his favorite studies—forms of government or states of society, such as he knows only by their accidental advantages without a glimpse of their real and terrible evils.

When this mental disease, for so it may be called without a metaphor, seizes irrecoverably upon the thoughts of the retiring, the sensitive, and timid lover of books and meditation, his capacity for useful exertion is ended; he is thenceforward doomed to lead a life of fretful restlessness alternated with querulous dejection. On the other hand, should he be naturally a man of firmer temperament and sounder discretion, time and experience will sober down his fancies, and make him join in the labors of life with cool submission. Still he is in danger of being a soured and discontented man, occasionally compelled to feign what he does not feel, and always unsustained by that glad confidence, that eager zeal and gay hope, which ever cheer him who loves and honors his country, feels her manifold blessings, and is grateful for all of them.

As various bodily diseases are observed to be specially incident to their several particular arts, trades, and professions, so the malady I have just described seems in this country to be that to which men of purely literary cultivation are specially predisposed. The men of daily toil seem happily to live quite below the level of its agency, those of abstract inquiry, of mathematical study, physical observation and high science, as much above it.

The early history of American literature affords a distinguished example of this influence upon a most elegant, accomplished and brilliant mind. So modern are our American antiquities, that much of this early history is within the memory of men not beyond the middle of life, and such it happens to be in this instance. It is that of one once called the American Addison, and still justly regarded as a father of our native literature, the late Joseph Dennie. Nature had endowed him with the quickest taste for beauty, the keenest sensibility for all intellectual excellence. A scholar from his cradle, he became very soon, by practice, "a ripe and good one." His ready memory was stored to a degree unequalled by any one on this side the Atlantic, and surpassed by none on the other, except his contemporary, the celebrated Porson. It was filled, crowded, bursting with the choicest beauties of thought, the rarest gems of expression that refined taste could select from the most extensive range of reading. He united to this reading much originality of thought, a gay and sportive fancy, and an unsurpassed power of brilliant expression. He was a genuine enthusiast in his love of literature, and he made it the pleasure and the business of his life to propagate the same taste among his countrymen. In this he achieved much, but he would have accomplished very far more, had he not yielded to a strange, unwise and unhappy morbid dislike for the institutions and social order of his own country. This discolored his views and distorted his judgment. It enabled inferior, every-day men, to vex and thwart him in his best and most favorite designs. It abridged the influence of his opinions and of his taste, and broke down the authority of his criticism and his example. Worst of all, it identified in the minds of the unlettered, the cause of elegant literature with that of attachment to foreign principles and establishments, and contempt for our own. Honest men reasoned, and correctly too, though from false premises, that if literature could be gained only at the expense of patriotic feeling, it is best that we should go without it. It lessened too the merit and value of his writings as literary compositions; for it tended to strip them of the original American air they would otherwise have had, and to give them the common cast of mere English literature. Hence, instead of ranking with those of Irving, at the head of our literature, both in time and in merit, his works are already passing into oblivion. The same perverse prejudice had also, I fear, an unhappy effect upon the regular activity of his intellect and the course of his life. Peace to his spirit, and gratitude for his services to our commonwealth of letters at a time when most it wanted aid. But let the student take warning from his great and single error.

I would not now have called forth his frailties from the tomb, did I not consider them as affording a most salutary and impressive lesson to the youthful enthusiast. More especially on a literary occasion like this, I could not have brought myself to speak thus publicly of the weakness of one whom I esteemed and honored, did I not firmly believe that it was for a purpose which his own gentle spirit, could he know of it, would approve, and could I not, at the same time, pay a cordial, heart-felt tribute to his many amiable and generous qualities, his worth, his accomplishment, and his genius.

It is the happy privilege of Americans to be free from the necessity of miserable dependance upon the caprice of other men for their daily subsistence or enjoyments. An honorable pride of character is native to our soil. Our reason and our conscience are our own. No man need to seek for himself a master, no man need to fawn upon a patron. Yet another danger, similar in effect to that from which we are thus exempt, yet quite opposite in its cause, threatens our mental liberty. It is that of slavery, not to one but to many, not to a patron but to a party. In our popular form of government, the existence of organized parties for the promotion of any system of policy, for the success of any principles of administration on which opinions are divided, and even for local objects and questions that must be decided ultimately by the ballot-boxes and legislative action, seems to be unavoidable, and when confined to their legitimate sphere, not only harmless but salutary. They keep up a more constant and exciting interest in public affairs through the whole community. They lead to a more vigilant watchfulness of those intrusted with power. They give greater stability and regularity to the action of government, and preserve it from becoming the sport of accident and caprice. But no dispassionate man, who examines the character of all our political parties for the last few years, can fail to perceive that there is something in their organization threatening to defeat the primary object of their own formation, and injurious to personal honor and independence.

The rule of a majority of the people is the fundamental law of our institutions, and the will of the people has a right to be expressed on every question. But the modern doctrine loses sight of the people as a whole, and substitutes for loyalty to the people, fealty to party. It teaches the true liege-men of faction to move together with the discipline and blind obedience of a regular army, and to regard those who do not act with them, not as republican fellow-citizens who differ from them in opinion on some secondary though important points, but as aliens and enemies, persons not entitled to any weight in the nation, whose approval of the course of one of our friends is a good ground of suspecting his fidelity, and to act with whom, though on an insulated question and for obvious public good, is treason and desertion. We must add to this, that by the decision of party, is meant that of a bare majority of the party only, or more commonly that of its prominent leaders, assisted by a few active professional partisan politicians. Thus the preferences of the rest, corresponding perhaps with a very large majority of the whole people numerically, are swallowed up in party allegiance. The result of all this is, that in a land of professed equal rights, one large portion of the citizens is politically disfranchised, until they can by the same discipline acquire power, and then disfranchise their opponents. Under a constitution professing the will of the majority to be the supreme law, the most vital questions are settled by an active bold minority. Connected with all this, and as a most essential ingredient in the system, a bitter spirit of intolerance is nursed up, unjust to the motives of adversaries, degrading to public men, and engendering narrow jealousies among the people. The public man is taught in his official character to look not to the welfare or the judgment of the people as a whole, but (what should be wholly subordinate) to the success and approbation of his party. Thus, means usurp the place of ends. The first who suffer the just punishment of this moral treason, for such it is, against republican principles, are the successful leaders themselves. They deprive themselves at once of the honest enthusiasm, the cheerful confidence that ever accompany the zealous support of principles. They become the timid, temporizing slaves of expediency, looking at every step, not to its justice or wisdom, but to its probable popularity. Their own policy prevents them from relying for respect and support upon the broad judgment of all honest and enlightened men, and when age or adversity arrives, when "interest calls off all her sneaking train," they are left helpless and contemptible. Such being the pitiable condition of the Magnates of faction, what must be that of him who follows at their heels as a hireling—above all, of the educated and literary hireling? He has sold his manhood for a little pelf; he must revile, and he must glorify; he must shout huzzas, or whisper calumnies, just as he is bidden. His time is not his own. His thoughts are not his own. His soul is not his own.

Strange thing it is, but true, that in this our republic, the land of abundance, the native soil of independence, there may be found some Americans of talent and information as abject in the submission of their understanding and will to the dictation of another, as was ever the most awe-struck courtier of Louis XIV. or the Czar, and who can fawn upon the dispensers of office with a cringing servility that would have mantled with shame the cheek of the worst hireling of Walpole, or the most profligate parasite of Dubois, the scandal of the church, or of Jefferies, the reproach of the law.

I have before said that I looked with undoubting confidence to the ultimate tendency of our free institutions, to elevate and purify the general mind. Nor do these things shake me in that conviction. They are but for a time. These dark clouds will pass away. They cannot quench the glorious sun of our republic. To-morrow—

> To-morrow, he repairs his golden beams,
> And floods the nation with redoubled ray.

But their time is now. The evils are present. They are confined to no individuals, to no one party or faction. I have even feared that this spirit of intolerance and dictation was extending itself from the political into the social and the religious world. Even before the altars of the Most High, strange and unhallowed fires have been lighted up in the priest's censers. It is for our generous, educated, high-minded youth to stay this plague. Let them not think to keep themselves pure, by holding themselves aloof from action. Let them take their stand manfully as their own best judgment may dictate, in the political and religious divisions of our people; but let them feel for those who honestly differ from them as for erring brethren. Be your zeal as fervent as it may, still temper it with a kind-hearted tolerance for the sincere and the honest. Reserve your warmest indignation for the narrow and bitter Pharisee, whether for you or against you, for the hypocrite, the impostor, and the persecutor. Above all, reverence yourself, your country, and the principles for which you contend. Never sacrifice your own honor, and still less, the cause of religion or freedom, to the subsidiary means designed to promote them, or the external forms in which they may be invested.

Go forth then, gentlemen, to your exalted duties. Go—sustain and elevate the high privileges of the American scholar. Shrink not from the dangers, yield not to the temptations that await you.

The father of epic poetry, when Diomed rushes to the field, describes the goddess of wisdom as nerving her champion's arm with strength, filling his breast with courage, and circling his shield and spear and helmed head, with her own living fires. Even so—the Minerva of your distinguished college has armed you in the bright panoply of science, and fired your souls with a holier inspiration, than pagan antiquity could feign. Profane not those high gifts, disappoint not the just expectations of the friends of learning and liberty. Be true to yourselves and your country.

5

RALPH WALDO EMERSON [1]

VERPLANCK advised the young men of Union College to "be true to yourself and your country." How they were to follow advice such as this is the central idea of Emerson's "American Scholar," delivered as a Phi Beta Kappa address at Harvard in 1837. This address has been called by Oliver Wendell Holmes "our intellectual Declaration of Independence." Previous selections in this volume show that in a strict chronological sense it was not so. In terms of its general effect, in its own time and throughout the years, as well as of its particular effect upon Holmes, Lowell, and Thoreau, it wears the title deservedly. The stirring words "We have listened too long to the courtly muses of Europe . . . We will walk on our own feet; we will work with our own hands; we will speak our own minds" ushered in the era of which one critic has written as "the golden day."

The America of the "American Scholar," is, however, a visionary land that never was and never will be. It is "a nation of men . . . because each believes himself inspired by the Divine Soul which also inspires all men." Although the everyday life and language of the common man is to make one of the resources of the scholar, "if it were only for a vocabulary," although Emerson momentarily was led to say "I embrace the common, I explore and sit at the feet of the familiar, the low," it is not for itself that he would do so. It is for "the sublime presence of the highest spiritual cause lurking, as it always does lurk, in these suburbs and extremities of nature." He is not concerned with the farmer as farmer, but as "Man on the farm."

Emerson's Swedenborgian view of the unity of Man is at the heart of this address and of his conception of the scholar.

There is One Man—present to all particular men only partially, or through one faculty . . . you must take the whole society to find the whole man. Man is not a farmer or a professor or an engineer, but he is all. . . . In the *divided* or social state these functions are parceled out to individuals. . . . In this distribution of functions, the scholar is the delegated intellect. In the right state he is *Man Thinking.*

In any other state, the farmer is only a farmer, the soldier a soldier, the scholar "a mere thinker, or still worse, the parrot of other men's thoughts."

---

[1] For biographical sketch of Emerson see page 586.

The main influences upon the mind of the scholar are three: nature, books, and action. Nature is not to be known for itself. To the scholar "Nature becomes . . . the measure of his attainments," because he finds in the study of nature, by processes of classification, the perception of relationships among apparently chaotic facts, that they "are not chaotic and are not foreign, but have a law which is also a law of the human mind." Nature and man are the symmetrical parts of one whole; "nature is the opposite of the soul, answering to it part for part."

Books are no more than nature to be studied for their own sakes. They are the "best type of the influence of the past," but there is the danger in their use that young men will "grow up in libraries, believing it their duty to accept the views which Cicero, which Locke, which Bacon, have given; forgetful that Cicero, Locke, and Bacon were only young men in libraries when they wrote these books." The purpose of a book, well-used, is to inspire the active soul of man not to accept another's truth, but to see and to create truth for itself. In valuing books as such "instead of Man Thinking, we have the bookworm . . . the restorers of readings, the emendators, the bibliomaniacs of all degrees." "Books are for the scholar's idle times"; when his well of inspiration has ceased to flow, books can prime the pump.

The world of action also is a major formative influence on the mind of the scholar; again, however, not for what it is, but for what it is converted into. "The true scholar grudges every opportunity of action passed by as a loss of power. It is the raw material out of which the intellect molds her splendid products. A strange process too, this, by which experience is converted into thought as a mulberry leaf is converted into satin." Emerson believed that the process of conversion was unconscious in origin, that "in some contemplative hour it detaches itself from the life like a ripe fruit, to become a thought of the mind. Instantly it is raised, transfigured; the corruptible has put on incorruption. Henceforth it is an object of beauty, however base its origin and neighborhood. . . . So is there no fact, no event, in our private history, which shall not, sooner or later, lose its adhesive, inert form and astonish us by soaring from our body into the empyrean." So "the final value of action . . . is that it is a resource."

The duties of the scholar are all contained in the idea of self-reliance. He thinks and speaks for all men. He must value his judgment of the relative importance of things and "defer never to the popular cry. . . . Let him not quit his belief that a popgun is a popgun, though the ancient and honorable of the earth affirm it to be the crack of doom." He must not accept for himself, and must labor to prevent the acceptance of false standards by others. "Wake them and they shall quit the false good and leap to the true, and leave government to clerks and desks. This revolution is to be wrought by the gradual domestication of the idea of Culture." The greatest, most splendid, most extensive "enterprise of the world" is the development of a real man, "for a man, rightly viewed, comprehendeth the particular natures of all men."

Hope for the achievement of developed manhood he finds in the romantic movement in literature and art, with its exploration of the commonplace for qualities of beauty and meaning, and in the social and political movements of individualism. "Everything that tends to insulate the individual—to surround him with barriers of natural respect, so that each man shall feel the world is his, and man shall treat with man as a sovereign state with a sovereign state—tends to true union as well as greatness." These are the trends of the times which the scholar must take up into his thought, and it is in America that such a promise of future greatness for mankind can be fulfilled in man.

THE AMERICAN SCHOLAR

I GREET you on the recommencement of our literary year. Our anniversary is one of hope and, perhaps, not enough of labor. We do not meet for games of strength or skill, for the recitation of histories, tragedies, and odes, like the ancient Greeks; for parliaments of love and poesy, like the Troubadours; nor for the advancement of science, like our contemporaries in the British and European capitals. Thus far, our holiday has been simply a friendly sign of the survival of the love of letters amongst a people too busy to give to letters any more. As such it is precious as the sign of an indestructible instinct. Perhaps the time is already come when it ought to be, and will be, something else; when the sluggard intellect of this continent will look from under its iron lids and fill the postponed expectation of the world with something better than the exertions of mechanical skill. Our day of dependence, our long apprenticeship to the learning of other lands, draws to a close. The millions that around us are rushing into life cannot always be fed on the sere remains of foreign harvests. Events, actions arise that must be sung, that will sing themselves. Who can doubt that poetry will revive and lead in a new age, as the star in the constellation Harp, which now flames in our zenith, astronomers announce, shall one day be the polestar for a thousand years?

In this hope I accept the topic which not only usage but the nature of our association seem to prescribe to this day—the AMERICAN SCHOLAR. Year by year we come up hither to read one more chapter of his biography. Let us inquire what light new days and events have thrown on his character and his hopes.

It is one of those fables which out of an unknown antiquity convey an unlooked-for wisdom, that the gods, in the beginning, divided Man into men, that he might be more helpful to himself; just as the hand was divided into fingers, the better to answer its end.

The old fable covers a doctrine ever new and sublime; that there is One Man—present to all particular men only partially, or through one faculty; and that you must take the whole society to find the whole man. Man is not a farmer or a professor or an engineer, but he is all. Man is priest and scholar and statesman and producer and soldier. In the *divided* or social state these functions are parceled out to individuals, each of whom aims to do his stint of the joint work, whilst each other performs his. The fable implies that the individual, to possess himself, must sometimes return from his own labor to embrace all the other laborers. But, unfortunately, this original unit, this fountain of power, has been so distributed to multitudes, has been so minutely subdivided and peddled out, that it is spilled into drops and cannot be gathered. The state of society is one in which the members have suffered amputation from the trunk, and strut about, so many walking monsters—a good finger, a neck, a stomach, an elbow, but never a man.

Man is thus metamorphosed into a thing, into many things. The planter, who is Man sent out into the field to gather food, is seldom cheered by any idea of the true dignity of his ministry. He sees his bushel and his cart and nothing beyond, and sinks into the farmer, instead of Man on the farm. The tradesman scarcely ever gives an ideal worth to his work, but is ridden by the routine of his craft, and the soul is subject to dollars. The priest becomes a form; the attorney, a statute book; the mechanic, a machine; the sailor, a rope of the ship.

In this distribution of functions the scholar is the delegated intellect. In the right state he is *Man Thinking*. In the degenerate state, when the victim of society, he tends to become a mere thinker, or still worse, the parrot of other men's thinking.

In this view of him, as Man Thinking, the theory of his office is contained. Him nature solicits with all her placid, all her monitory pictures; him the past instructs; him the future invites. Is not indeed every man a student, and do not all things exist for the student's behoof? And, finally, is not the true scholar the only true master? But the old oracle said, "All things have two handles: beware of the wrong one." In life, too often, the scholar errs with mankind and forfeits his privilege. Let us see him in his school, and consider him in reference to the main influences he receives.

I. The first in time and the first in importance of the influences upon the mind is that of nature. Every day, the sun; and, after sunset, Night and her stars. Ever the winds blow; ever the grass grows. Every day, men and women, conversing—beholding and beholden. The scholar is he of all men whom this spectacle most engages. He must settle its value in his mind. What is nature to him? There is never a beginning, there is never an end, to the inexplicable continuity of this web of God, but always circular power returning into itself. Therein it resembles his own spirit, whose beginning, whose ending, he never can find—so entire, so boundless. Far too as her splendors shine, system on system shooting like rays, upward, downward, without center, without circumference—in the mass and in the particle, nature hastens to render account of herself to the mind. Classification begins. To the young mind everything is individual, stands by itself. By and by, it finds how to join two things and see in them one nature; then three, then three thousand; and so, tyrannized over by its own unifying instinct, it goes on tying things together, diminishing anomalies, discovering roots running under ground whereby contrary and remote things cohere and flower out from one stem. It presently learns that since the dawn of history there has been a constant accumulation and classifying of facts. But what is classification but the perceiving that these objects are not chaotic and are not foreign, but have a law which is also a law of the human mind? The astronomer discovers that geometry, a pure abstraction of the human mind, is the measure of planetary motion. The chemist finds proportions and intelligible method throughout matter; and science is nothing but the finding of analogy, identity, in the most remote parts. The ambitious soul sits down before each refractory fact; one after another reduces all strange constitutions, all new powers, to their class and their law and goes on forever to animate the last fiber of organization, the outskirts of nature, by insight.

Thus to him, to this schoolboy under the bending dome of day, is suggested that he and it proceed from one root; one is leaf and one is flower; relation, sympathy, stirring in every vein. And what is that Root? Is not that the soul of his soul? A thought too bold; a dream too wild. Yet when this spiritual light shall have revealed the law of more earthly natures—when he has learned to worship the soul and to see that the natural philosophy that now is, is only the first gropings of its gigantic hand—he shall look forward to an ever-expanding knowledge as to a becoming creator. He shall see that nature is the opposite of the soul, answering to it part for part. One is seal and one is print. Its beauty is the beauty of his own mind. Its laws are the laws of his own mind. Nature then becomes to him the measure of his attainments. So much of nature as he is ignorant of, so much of his own mind does he not yet possess. And, in fine, the ancient precept, "Know thyself" and the modern precept, "Study nature," become at last one maxim.

II. The next great influence into the spirit of the scholar is the mind of the Past, in whatever form, whether of literature, of art, of institutions, that mind is inscribed. Books are the best type of the influence of the past, and perhaps we shall get at the truth—learn the amount of this influence more conveniently—by considering their value alone.

The theory of books is noble. The scholar of the first age received into him the world around; brooded thereon; gave it the new arrangement of his own mind and uttered it again. It came into him life; it went out from him truth. It came to him short-lived actions; it went out from him immortal thoughts. It came to him business; it went from him poetry. It was dead fact; now, it is quick thought. It can stand and it can go. It now endures, it now flies, it now inspires. Precisely in proportion to the depth of mind from which it issued, so high does it soar, so long does it sing.

Or, I might say, it depends on how far the process had gone, of transmuting life into truth. In proportion to the completeness of the distillation, so will the purity and imperishableness of the product be. But none is quite perfect. As no air-pump can by any means make a perfect vacuum, so neither can any artist entirely exclude the conventional, the local, the perishable from his book, or write a book of pure thought that shall be as efficient, in all respects, to a remote posterity as to contemporaries, or rather to the second age. Each age, it is found, must write its own books; or rather, each generation for the next succeeding. The books of an older period will not fit this.

Yet hence arises a grave mischief. The sacredness which attaches to the act of creation, the act of thought, is transferred to the record. The poet chanting was felt to be a divine man: henceforth the chant is divine also. The writer was a just and wise spirit: henceforward it is settled the book is perfect; as love of the hero corrupts into worship of his statue. Instantly the book becomes noxious: the guide is a tyrant. The sluggish and perverted mind of the multitude, slow to open to the incursions of Reason, having once so opened, having once received this book, stands upon it and makes an outcry if it is disparaged. Colleges are built on it. Books are written on it by thinkers, not by Man Thinking; by men of talent, that is, who start wrong, who set out from accepted dogmas, not from their own sight of principles. Meek young men grow up in libraries, believing it their duty to accept the views which Cicero, which Locke, which Bacon, have given; forgetful that Cicero, Locke, and Bacon were only young men in libraries when they wrote these books.

Hence, instead of Man Thinking, we have the bookworm. Hence the book-learned class, who value books, as such; not as related to nature and the human constitution but as making a sort of Third Estate with the world and the soul. Hence the restorers of readings, the emendators, the bibliomaniacs of all degrees.

Books are the best of things, well used; abused, among the worst. What is the right use? What is the one end which all means go to effect? They are for nothing but to inspire. I had better never see a book than to be warped by its attraction clean out of my own orbit and made a satellite instead of a system. The one thing in the world of value is the active soul. This every man is entitled to; this every man contains within him, although in almost all men obstructed and as yet unborn. The soul active sees absolute truth and utters truth, or creates. In this action it is genius; not the privilege of here and there a favorite, but the sound estate of every man. In its essence it is progressive. The book, the college, the school of art, the institution of any kind, stop with some past utterance of genius. This is good, say they—let us hold by this. They pin me down. They look backward and not forward. But genius looks forward; the eyes of man are set in his forehead, not in his hindhead; man hopes; genius creates. Whatever talents may be, if the man create not, the pure efflux of the Deity is not his; cinders and smoke there may be, but not yet flame. There are creative manners, there are creative actions and creative words; manners, actions, words, that is, indicative of no custom or authority but springing spontaneous from the mind's own sense of good and fair.

On the other part, instead of being its own seer, let it receive from another mind its truth, though it were in torrents of light, without periods of solitude inquest, and self-recovery, and a fatal disservice is done. Genius is always sufficiently the enemy of genius by over-influence. The literature of every nation bears me witness. The English dramatic poets have Shakspearized now for two hundred years.

Undoubtedly there is a right way of reading, so it be sternly subordinated. Man Thinking must not be subdued by his instruments. Books are for the scholar's idle times. When he can read God directly, the hour is too precious to be wasted in other men's transcripts of their readings. But when the intervals of darkness come, as come they must—when the sun is hid and the stars withdraw their shining—we repair to the lamps which were kindled by their ray, to guide our steps to the East again, where the dawn is. We hear, that we may speak. The Arabian proverb says, "A fig tree, looking on a fig tree, becometh fruitful."

It is remarkable, the character of the pleasure we derive from the best books. They impress us with the conviction that one nature wrote and the same reads. We read the verses of one of the great English poets, of Chaucer, of Marvell, of Dryden, with the most modern joy—with a pleasure, I mean, which is in great part caused by the abstraction of all *time* from their verses. There is some awe mixed with the joy of our surprise, when this poet, who lived in some past world, two or three hundred years ago, says that which lies close to my own soul, that which I also had well-nigh thought and said. But for the evidence thence afforded to the philosophical doctrine of the identity of all minds, we should suppose some pre-established harmony, some foresight of souls that were to be, and some preparation of stores for their future wants, like the fact observed in insects, who lay up food before death for the young grub they shall never see.

I would not be hurried by any love of system, by any exaggeration of instincts, to underrate the Book. We all know that as the human body can be nourished on any food, though it were boiled grass and the broth of shoes, so the human mind can be fed by any knowledge. And great and heroic men have existed who had almost no other information than by the printed page. I only would say that it needs a strong head to bear that diet. One must be an inventor to read well. As the proverb says, "He that would bring home the wealth of the Indies must carry out the wealth of the Indies." There is then creative reading as well as creative writing. When the mind is braced by labor and invention, the page of whatever book we read becomes luminous with manifold allusion. Every sentence is doubly significant, and the sense of our author is as broad as the world. We then see, what is always true, that as the seer's hour of vision is short and rare among heavy days and months, so is its record, perchance, the least part of his volume. The discerning will read, in his Plato or Shakspeare, only that least part— only the authentic utterances of the oracle; all the rest he rejects, were it never so many times Plato's and Shakspeare's.

Of course there is a portion of reading quite indispensable to a wise man. History and exact science he must learn by laborious reading. Colleges, in like manner, have their indispensable office—to teach elements. But they can only highly serve us when they aim not to drill, but to create; when they gather from far every ray of various genius to their hospitable halls and by the concentrated fires set the hearts of their youth on flame. Thought and knowledge are natures in which apparatus and pretension avail nothing. Gowns and pecuniary foundations, though of towns of gold, can never countervail the least sentence or syllable of wit. Forget this, and our American colleges will recede in their public importance, whilst they grow richer every year.

III. There goes in the world a notion that the scholar should be a recluse, a valetudinarian—as unfit for any handiwork or public labor as a penknife for an axe. The so-called "practical men" sneer at speculative men as if, because they speculate or *see*, they could do nothing. I have heard it said that the clergy—who are always, more universally than any other class, the scholars of their day—are addressed as women; that the rough, spontaneous conversation of men they do not hear but only a mincing and diluted speech. They are often virtually disfranchised; and indeed there are advocates for their celibacy. As far as this is true of the studious classes, it is not just and wise. Action is with the scholar subordinate, but it is essential. Without it he is not yet man. Without it thought can never ripen into truth. Whilst the world hangs before the eye as a cloud of beauty, we cannot even see its beauty. Inaction is cowardice, but there can be no scholar without the heroic mind. The preamble of thought, the transition through which it passes from the unconscious to the conscious, is action. Only so much do I know as I have lived. Instantly we know whose words are loaded with life and whose not.

The world—this shadow of the soul, or *other me*—lies wide around. Its attractions are the keys which unlock my thoughts and make me acquainted with myself. I run eagerly into this resounding tumult, I grasp the hands of those next me, and take my place in the ring to suffer and to work, taught by an instinct that so shall the dumb abyss be vocal with speech. I pierce its order; I dissipate its fear; I dispose of it within the circuit of my expanding life. So much only of life as I know by experience, so much of the wilderness have I vanquished and planted, or so far have I extended my being, my dominion. I do not see how any man can afford, for the sake of his nerves and his nap, to spare any action in which he can partake. It is pearls and rubies to his discourse. Drudgery, calamity, exasperation, want, are instructors in eloquence and wisdom. The true scholar grudges every opportunity of action passed by as a loss of power. It is the raw material out of which the intellect molds her splendid products. A strange process too, this, by which experience is converted into thought as a mulberry leaf is converted into satin. The manufacture goes forward at all hours.

The actions and events of our childhood and youth are now matters of calmest observation. They lie like fair pictures in the air. Not so with our recent actions, with the business which we now have in hand. On this we are quite unable to speculate. Our affections as yet circulate through it. We no more feel or know it than we feel the feet, or the hand, or the brain of our body. The new deed is yet a part of life—

remains for a time immersed in our unconscious life. In some contemplative hour it detaches itself from the life like a ripe fruit to become a thought of the mind. Instantly it is raised, transfigured; the corruptible has put on incorruption. Henceforth it is an object of beauty, however base its origin and neighborhood. Observe too the impossibility of antedating this act. In its grub state, it cannot fly, it cannot shine, it is a dull grub. But suddenly, without observation, the selfsame thing unfurls beautiful wings and is an angel of wisdom. So is there no fact, no event, in our private history, which shall not, sooner or later, lose its adhesive, inert form and astonish us by soaring from our body into the empyrean. Cradle and infancy, school and playground, the fear of boys, and dogs, and ferules, the love of little maids and berries, and many another fact that once filled the whole sky, are gone already; friend and relative, profession and party, town and country, nation and world, must also soar and sing.

Of course, he who has put forth his total strength in fit actions has the richest return of wisdom. I will not shut myself out of this globe of action, and transplant an oak into a flowerpot, there to hunger and pine; nor trust the revenue of some single faculty and exhaust one vein of thought, much like those Savoyards, who, getting their livelihood by carving shepherds, shepherdesses, and smoking Dutchmen for all Europe, went out one day to the mountain to find stock and discovered that they had whittled up the last of their pine trees. Authors we have, in numbers, who have written out their vein and who, moved by a commendable prudence, sail for Greece or Palestine, follow the trapper into the prairie, or ramble around Algiers, to replenish their merchantable stock.

If it were only for a vocabulary, the scholar would be covetous of action. Life is our dictionary. Years are well spent in country labors; in town; in the insight into trades and manufactures; in frank intercourse with many men and women; in science; in art; to the one end of mastering in all their facts a language by which to illustrate and embody our perceptions. I learn immediately from any speaker how much he has already lived, through the poverty or the splendor of his speech. Life lies behind us as the quarry from whence we get tiles and copestones for the masonry of today. This is the way to learn grammar.

Colleges and books only copy the language which the field and the work-yard made.

But the final value of action, like that of books, and better than books, is that it is a resource. That great principle of Undulation in nature that shows itself in the inspiring and expiring of the breath; in desire and satiety; in the ebb and flow of the sea; in day and night; in heat and cold; and, as yet more deeply ingrained in every atom and every fluid, is known to us under the name of Polarity—these "fits of easy transmission and reflection," as Newton called them, and are the law of nature because they are the law of spirit.

The mind now thinks, now acts, and each fit reproduces the other. When the artist has exhausted his materials, when the fancy no longer paints, when thoughts are no longer apprehended and books are a weariness—he has always the resource *to live*. Character is higher than intellect. Thinking is the function. Living is the functionary. The stream retreats to its source. A great soul will be strong to live, as well as strong to think. Does he lack organ or medium to impart his truths? He can still fall back on this elemental force of living them. This is a total act. Thinking is a partial act. Let the grandeur of justice shine in his affairs. Let the beauty of affection cheer his lowly roof. Those "far from fame," who dwell and act with him, will feel the force of his constitution in the doings and passages of the day better than it can be measured by any public and designed display. Time shall teach him that the scholar loses no hour which the man lives. Herein he unfolds the sacred germ of his instinct, screened from influence. What is lost in seemliness is gained in strength. Not out of those on whom systems of education have exhausted their culture comes the helpful giant to destroy the old or to build the new, but out of unhandseled savage nature; out of terrible Druids and Berserkers come at last Alfred and Shakspeare.

I hear therefore with joy whatever is beginning to be said of the dignity and necessity of labor to every citizen. There is virtue yet in the hoe and the spade for learned as well as for unlearned hands. And labor is everywhere welcome; always we are invited to work; only be this limitation observed, that a man shall not for the sake of wider activity sacrifice any opinion to the popular judgments and modes of action.

I have now spoken of the education of the scholar by nature, by books, and by action. It remains to say somewhat of his duties.

They are such as become Man Thinking. They may all be comprised in self-trust. The office of the scholar is to cheer, to raise, and to guide men by showing them facts amidst appearances. He plies the slow, unhonored, and unpaid task of observation. Flamsteed and Herschel, in their glazed observatories, may catalogue the stars with the praise of all men, and the results being splendid and useful, honor is sure. But he, in his private observatory, cataloguing obscure and nebulous stars of the human mind, which as yet no man has thought of as such—watching days and months sometimes for a few facts, correcting still his old records—must relinquish display and immediate fame. In the long period of his preparation he must betray often an ignorance and shiftlessness in popular arts, incurring the disdain of the able who shoulder him aside. Long he must stammer in his speech; often forego the living for the dead. Worse yet, he must accept—how often!—poverty and solitude. For the ease and pleasure of treading the old road, accepting the fashions, the education, the religion of society, he takes the cross of making his own, and, of course, the self-accusation, the faint heart, the frequent uncertainty and loss of time, which are the nettles and tangling vines in the way of the self-relying and self-directed; and the state of virtual hostility in which he seems to stand to society, and especially to educated society. For all this loss and scorn, what offset? He is to find consolation in exercising the highest functions of human nature. He is one who raises himself from private considerations and breathes and lives on public and illustrious thoughts. He is the world's eye. He is the world's heart. He is to resist the vulgar prosperity that retrogrades ever to barbarism, by preserving and communicating heroic sentiments, noble biographies, melodious verse, and the conclusions of history. Whatsoever oracles the human heart, in all emergencies, in all solemn hours, has uttered as its commentary on the world of actions—these he shall receive and impart. And whatsoever new verdict Reason from her inviolable seat pronounces on the passing men and events of today—this he shall hear and promulgate.

These being his functions, it becomes him to feel all confidence in himself and to defer never to the popular cry. He and he only knows the world. The world of any moment is the merest appearance. Some great decorum, some fetish of a government, some ephemeral trade, or war, or man, is cried up by half mankind and cried down by the other half, as if all depended on this particular up or down. The odds are that the whole question is not worth the poorest thought which the scholar has lost in listening to the controversy. Let him not quit his belief that a popgun is a popgun, though the ancient and honorable of the earth affirm it to be the crack of doom. In silence, in steadiness, in severe abstraction, let him hold by himself; add observation to observation, patient of neglect, patient of reproach, and bide his own time— happy enough if he can satisfy himself alone that this day he has seen something truly. Success treads on every right step. For the instinct is sure that prompts him to tell his brother what he thinks. He then learns that in going down into the secrets of his own mind he has descended into the secrets of all minds. He learns that he who has mastered any law in his private thoughts is master to that extent of all men whose language he speaks and of all into whose language his own can be translated. The poet, in utter solitude remembering his spontaneous thoughts and recording them, is found to have recorded that which men in crowded cities find true for them also. The orator distrusts at first the fitness of his frank confessions, his want of knowledge of the persons he addresses, until he finds that he is the complement of his hearers; that they drink his words because he fulfills for them their own nature; the deeper he dives into his privatest, secretest presentiment, to his wonder he finds this is the most acceptable, most public, and universally true. The people delight in it; the better part of every man feels, This is my music; this is myself.

In self-trust all the virtues are comprehended. Free should the scholar be—free and brave. Free even to the definition of freedom, "without any hindrance that does not arise out of his own constitution." Brave; for fear is a thing which a scholar by his very function puts behind him. Fear always springs from ignorance. It is a shame to him if his tranquillity, amid dangerous times, arise from the presumption that, like children and women, his is a protected class; or if he seek a temporary peace by the diversion of his thoughts from politics or vexed questions, hiding his head like an ostrich in the flowering bushes, peeping into microscopes, and turning rhymes, as a boy whistles to keep his courage up. So is the danger a danger still; so is the fear worse.

Manlike let him turn and face it. Let him look into its eye and search its nature, inspect its origin—see the whelping of this lion—which lies no great way back; he will then find in himself a perfect comprehension of its nature and extent; he will have made his hands meet on the other side and can henceforth defy it and pass on superior. The world is his who can see through its pretension. What deafness, what stone-blind custom, what overgrown error you behold is there only by sufferance—by your sufferance. See it to be a lie, and you have already dealt it its mortal blow.

Yes, we are the cowed—we the trustless. It is a mischievous notion that we are come late into nature; that the world was finished a long time ago. As the world was plastic and fluid in the hands of God, so it is ever to so much of his attributes as we bring to it. To ignorance and sin it is flint. They adapt themselves to it as they may; but in proportion as a man has anything in him divine, the firmament flows before him and takes his signet and form. Not he is great who can alter matter, but he who can alter my state of mind. They are the kings of the world who give the color of their present thought to all nature and all art and persuade men by the cheerful serenity of their carrying the matter that this thing which they do is the apple which the ages have desired to pluck, now at last ripe and inviting nations to the harvest. The great man makes the great thing. Wherever Macdonald sits, there is the head of the table. Linnæus makes botany the most alluring of studies, and wins it from the farmer and the herbwoman; Davy, chemistry; and Cuvier, fossils. The day is always his who works in it with serenity and great aims. The unstable estimates of men crowd to him whose mind is filled with a truth, as the heaped waves of the Atlantic follow the moon.

For this self-trust, the reason is deeper than can be fathomed— darker than can be enlightened. I might not carry with me the feeling of my audience in stating my own belief. But I have already shown the ground of my hope, in adverting to the doctrine that man is one. I believe man has been wronged; he has wronged himself. He has almost lost the light that can lead him back to his prerogatives. Men are become of no account. Men in history, men in the world of today, are bugs, are spawn, and are called "the mass" and "the herd." In a century, in a millennium, one or two men; that is to say, one or two approximations to the right state of every man. All the rest behold in the hero or the poet their own green and crude being—ripened; yes, and are content to be less, so *that* may attain to its full stature. What a testimony, full of grandeur, full of pity, is borne to the demands of his own nature by the poor clansman, the poor partisan, who rejoices in the glory of his chief. The poor and the low find some amends to their immense moral capacity for their acquiescence in a political and social inferiority. They are content to be brushed like flies from the path of a great person, so that justice shall be done by him to that common nature which it is the dearest desire of all to see enlarged and glorified. They sun themselves in the great man's light and feel it to be their own element. They cast the dignity of man from their downtrod selves upon the shoulders of a hero, and will perish to add one drop of blood to make that great heart beat, those giant sinews combat and conquer. He lives for us, and we live in him.

Men, such as they are, very naturally seek money or power; and power because it is as good as money—the "spoils," so called, "of office." And why not? for they aspire to the highest, and this, in their sleep-walking, they dream is highest. Wake them and they shall quit the false good and leap to the true, and leave governments to clerks and desks. This revolution is to be wrought by the gradual domestication of the idea of Culture. The main enterprise of the world for splendor, for extent, is the upbuilding of a man. Here are the materials strewn along the ground. The private life of one man shall be a more illustrious monarchy, more formidable to its enemy, more sweet and serene in its influence to its friend, than any kingdom in history. For a man, rightly viewed, comprehendeth the particular natures of all men. Each philosopher, each bard, each actor, has only done for me, as by a delegate, what one day I can do for myself. The books which once we valued more than the apple of the eye we have quite exhausted. What is that but saying that we have come up with the point of view which the universal mind took through the eyes of one scribe; we have been that man and have passed on. First one, then another, we drain all cisterns and, waxing greater by all these supplies, we crave a better and more abundant food. The man has never lived that can feed us ever. The human mind cannot be enshrined in a person who shall set a barrier on any one side to this unbounded, unboundable empire. It is one central fire, which, flaming now out of the lips of Etna, lightens the capes of Sicily, and now out of the throat of Vesuvius, illuminates the towers and vineyards of Naples. It is one light which beams out of a thousand stars. It is one soul which animates all men.

But I have dwelt perhaps tediously upon this abstraction of the Scholar. I ought not to delay longer to add what I have to say of nearer reference to the time and to this country.

Historically, there is thought to be a difference in the ideas which predominate over successive epochs, and there are data for marking the genius of the Classic, of the Romantic, and now of the Reflective or Philosophical age. With the views I have intimated of the oneness or the identity of the mind through all individuals, I do not much dwell on these differences. In fact, I believe each individual passes through all three. The boy is a Greek; the youth, romantic; the adult, reflective. I deny not, however, that a revolution in the leading idea may be distinctly enough traced.

Our age is bewailed as the age of Introversion. Must that needs be evil? We, it seems, are critical; we are embarrassed with second thoughts; we cannot enjoy anything for hankering to know whereof the pleasure consists; we are lined with eyes; we see with our feet; the time is infected with Hamlet's unhappiness—"Sicklied o'er with the pale cast of thought." It is so bad then? Sight is the last thing to be pitied. Would we be blind? Do we fear lest we should outsee nature and God, and drink truth dry? I look upon the discontent of the literary class as a mere announcement of the fact that they find themselves not in the state of mind of their fathers, and regret the coming state as untried; as a boy dreads the water before he has learned that he can swim. If there is any period one would desire to be born in, is it not the age of Revolution; when the old and the new stand side by side and admit of being compared; when the energies of all men are searched by fear and by hope; when the historic glories of the old can be compensated by the rich possibilities of the new era? This time, like all times, is a very good one, if we but know what to do with it.

I read with some joy of the auspicious signs of the coming days, as they glimmer already through poetry and art, through philosophy and science, through church and state.

One of these signs is the fact that the same movement which effected the elevation of what was called the lowest class in the state assumed in literature a very marked and as benign an aspect. Instead of the sublime and beautiful, the near, the low, the common, was explored and poetized. That which had been negligently trodden under foot by those who were harnessing and provisioning themselves for long journeys into far countries is suddenly found to be richer than all foreign parts. The literature of the poor, the feelings of the child, the philosophy of the street, the meaning of household life, are the topics of the time. It is a great stride. It is a sign—is it not?—of new vigor when the extremities are made active, when currents of warm life run into the hands and the feet. I ask not for the great, the remote, the romantic; what is doing in Italy or Arabia; what is Greek art, or Provençal minstrelsy; I embrace the common, I explore and sit at the feet of the familiar, the low. Give me insight into today, and you may have the antique and future worlds. What would we really know the meaning of? The meal in the firkin; the milk in the pan; the ballad in the street; the news of the boat; the glance of the eye; the form and the gait of the body—show me the ultimate reason of these matters; show me the sublime presence of the highest spiritual cause lurking, as always it does lurk, in these suburbs and extremities of nature; let me see every trifle bristling with the polarity that ranges it instantly on an eternal law; and the shop, the plough, and the ledger referred to the like cause by which light undulates and poets sing—and the world lies no longer a dull miscellany and lumber-room, but has form and order; there is no trifle, there is no puzzle, but one design unites and animates the farthest pinnacle and the lowest trench.

This idea has inspired the genius of Goldsmith, Burns, Cowper, and, in a newer time, of Goethe, Wordsworth, and Carlyle. This idea they have differently followed and with various success. In contrast with their writing, the style of Pope, of Johnson, of Gibbons, looks cold and pedantic. This writing is blood-warm. Man is surprised to find that things near are not less beautiful and wondrous than things remote. The near explains the far. The drop is a small ocean. A man is related to all nature. This perception of the worth of the vulgar is fruitful in discoveries. Goethe, in this very thing the most modern of the moderns, has shown us, as none ever did, the genius of the ancients.

There is one man of genius who has done much for this philosophy of life, whose literary value has never yet been rightly estimated—I mean Emanuel Swedenborg. The most imaginative of men, yet writing with the precision of a mathematician, he endeavored to engraft a purely philosophical Ethics on the popular Christianity of his time. Such an attempt, of course, must have difficulty which no genius could surmount. But he saw and showed the connection between nature and the affections of the soul. He pierced the emblematic or spiritual character of the visible, audible, tangible world. Especially did his shade-loving muse hover over and interpret the lower parts of nature; he showed the mysterious bond that allies moral evil to the foul material forms, and has given in epical parables a theory of insanity, of beasts, of unclean and fearful things.

Another sign of our times, also marked by an analogous political movement, is the new importance given to the single person. Everything that tends to insulate the individual—to surround him with barriers of natural respect, so that each man shall feel the world is his, and man shall treat with man as a sovereign state with a sovereign state—tends to true union as well as greatness. "I learned," said the melancholy Pestalozzi, "that no man in God's wide earth is either willing or able to help any other man." Help must come from the bosom alone. The scholar is that man who must take up into himself all the ability of the time, all the contributions of the past, all the hopes of the future. He must be a university of knowledges. If there be one lesson more than another which should pierce his ear, it is, The world is nothing, the man is all; in yourself is the law of all nature, and you know not yet how a globule of sap ascends; in yourself slumbers the whole of Reason; it is for you to know all; it is for you to dare all. Mr. President and Gentlemen, this confidence in the unsearched might of man belongs, by all motives, by all prophecy, by all preparation, to the American Scholar. We have listened too long to the courtly muses of Europe. The spirit of the American freeman is already suspected to be timid, imitative, tame. Public and private avarice make the air we breathe thick and fat. The scholar is decent, indolent, complaisant. See already the tragic consequence. The mind of this country, taught to aim at low objects, eats upon itself. There is no work for any but the decorous and the complaisant. Young men of the fairest promise, who begin life upon our shores, inflated by the mountain winds, shined upon by all the stars of God, find the earth below not in unison with these, but are hindered from action by the disgust which the principles on which business is managed inspire, and turn drudges, or die of disgust, some of them suicides. What is the remedy? They did not yet see, and thousands of young men as hopeful now crowding to the barriers for the career do not yet see that if the single man plant himself indomitably on his instincts and there abide, the huge world will come round to him. Patience, patience; with the shades of all the good and great for company; and for solace the perspective of your own infinite life; and for work the study and the communication of principles, the making those instincts prevalent, the conversion of the world. Is it not the chief disgrace in the world, not to be a unit—not to be reckoned one character—not to yield that peculiar fruit which each man was created to bear, but to be reckoned in the gross, in the hundred, or the thousand, of the party, the section, to which we belong; and our opinion predicted geographically, as the north, or the south? Not so, brothers and friends— please God, ours shall not be so. We will walk on our own feet; we will work with our own hands; we will speak our own minds. The study of letters shall be no longer a name for pity, for doubt, and for sensual indulgence. The dread of man and the love of man shall be a wall of defense and a wreath of joy around all. A nation of men will for the first time exist, because each believes himself inspired by the Divine Soul which also inspires all men.

—6—

ORESTES AUGUSTUS BROWNSON

1803, born September 16, at Stockbridge, Vt.
1822, became a Presbyterian
1824, became a Universalist
1826, was ordained a Universalist minister
1829–30, editor of the *Gospel Advocate*, Auburn, N.Y.
1830–32, associate editor of the *Free Enquirer* (with Frances Wright and Robert Dale Owen)
1832–36, Unitarian minister at Walpole, N.H., and Canton, Mass.
1836–44, founder of the Society for Christian Union and Progress
1836, *New Views of Christianity, Society and the Church*
1838–42, founder and editor of the *Boston Quarterly Review*
1840, *Charles Elwood; or, The Infidel Converted*
1842, *The Mediatorial Life of Jesus*
1842–43, the *Boston Quarterly Review* was merged with the *Democratic Review*
1844, became a Roman Catholic
1844–65, edited *Brownson's Quarterly Review*
1854, *The Spirit Rapper; an Autobiography*
1857, *The Convert; or, Leaves from My Experience*
1865, *The American Republic; Its Constitution, Tendencies, and Destiny*
1876, died April 17, at Detroit, Mich.

FRANCES WRIGHT lectured at Utica in the fall of 1829 and repeated her four lectures at Auburn, New York, a week or so later. In her audience in both towns was young Orestes Augustus Brownson, who became one of the stormy petrels of American intellectual life in the nineteenth century. At this time Brownson was a Universalist, editor of the *Gospel Advocate*. Under Miss Wright's spell he became contributing editor and agent for Auburn of the *Free Enquirer*. Some more conservative Universalists thought his free thought activities unsuitable; Brownson resigned from the *Gospel Advocate* and became for a time actively associated with Miss Wright and Robert Dale Owen. His particular interest in their work stemmed from their belief in the equality of all men. Still under the influence of Owen and Miss Wright, he became an organizer for the Working Man's Party, then about a year old and not a very radical organization.

Brownson's connection with this group occurred during the period when

Miss Wright and Owen were attempting to make of it a political vehicle for the attainment of their educational objectives. Less than a year later, when his friends had been defeated in their purposes, he severed his relations with the Working Man's Party. He was careful to explain, in retrospect, that his sympathy with labor had not changed. "I abandoned, indeed, after a year's devotion to it, the Working-Men's Party, but not the working-men's cause." He became convinced that he was on the wrong tack, and, characteristically, he became an immediate convert to another idea. As he tells his life story, this new view was that the laboring class could not achieve its ends save by the co-operation of all classes. "I could effect nothing by appealing to them as a separate class. My policy must not be a working-man's party, but to induce all classes of society to co-operate in efforts for the working-men's cause."

His brief flirtation with this labor organization over, Brownson soon ended his connection with the "free enquirers" and took the path of Unitarianism back into Christianity, possibly under the influence of Cousin's version of the transcendental philosophy of Kant. In one of his autobiographical works, *The Convert*, he speaks of himself as having become during his association with Miss Wright and Owen a philosophic skeptic who by following his reason had lost the Bible, the Savior, Providence, and reason itself and had left but his five animal senses. Another autobiographical work, *Charles Elwood*, describes its infidel hero as converted to Unitarianism through Cousin. Whether these autobiographical suggestions are to be taken literally or not, he did become a Unitarian and he did associate for a time with the transcendentalists.

In 1836, at the instigation of William Ellery Channing and George Ripley, Brownson went to Boston to combat the free enquirers there, one of the strongest of the free-thought groups, under the leadership of Abner Kneeland, who like Brownson, had come to free enquiry from Universalism. In Boston, Brownson organized the "Society for Christian Union and Progress" and edited the *Boston Quarterly*, which was later called *Brownson's Quarterly*. Both organ and organization were founded to advance their founder's belief that free thinking did not necessarily end in free thought and that his brand of Christianity provided an adequate social philosophy through which the cause of labor could be advanced.

A departure from the pattern of this collection is being made here in order to reprint one of the most interesting and important statements of Brownson's point of view at this period, his controversial article "The Laboring Classes," from his *Boston Quarterly Review*. In this article, which used Carlyle's pamphlet on *Chartism* as a stepping-off place, Brownson discussed the problem of adequate economic and social returns to the ultimate producers, the laboring men of the world. The opposition, he pointed out, is greatest among the members of the middle class, "always a firm champion of equality, when it concerns humbling a class above it; but . . . its inveterate foe, when it concerns, elevating a class below it." To the power of the middle class he ascribed the defeat of "nearly all the practical benefit of the French Revolution."

Carlyle's two solutions for the problem, universal education and general emigration, Brownson found unsatisfactory. Emigration he saw as a temporary expedient rather than a solution. In his comment on education as a method of solving the labor problem Brownson revealed how far he had come from his Owenite days. "We have little faith in the power of education to elevate a people compelled to labor from twelve to sixteen hours a day. . . . Give your starving boy a breakfast before you send him to school." The solution will come, he assured his readers, only at the end of a long and bloody class struggle. He felt sure that his era was witnessing the beginning of that struggle.

He discussed slave labor and free labor and asserted that the slave was better off than the free industrial worker—this despite his opposition to slavery. He came to the heart of his theme when he pointed out the clergy as the allies of employer groups. He decried all attempts to solve the problem on an individualistic basis and declared that "the evil we speak of is inherent in all our social arrangements, and cannot be cured without a radical change of those arrangements."

When Brownson began to discuss the solution which was satisfactory to him, his belief in equality of rights, his radical anticlericalism, and his faith in Christianity as a gospel of social justice were very clearly set forth. He defined the task of the age as "the emancipation of the proletaries," the realization "in the actual condition of all men" of a God-given equality of rights. The fount of inequality he found in religion, as administered by the priestly class in every age and in every clime. On this basis he explained the hostility of the social reformer to the priestly guardians of prerogative. He did not deny that "priests are the first civilizers of the race"; he asserted only that "for the wild freedom of the savage, they substitute the iron despotism of the theocrat." The first step in restoring man to freedom is the destruction of the priest.

In calling for this radically anticlerical step, Brownson considered that he was being true to the historic mission of Jesus and the original character of Christianity, "the sublimest protest against the priesthood ever uttered." To this original character of Christianity he applied the title "Christianity of Christ," as opposed to the "Christianity of the Church." The gospel of Jesus, he insisted, is a gospel of social justice and equality.

Finally, after the road has been cleared by disposing of "sacerdotal corporations" and the "pseudo-gospel" of the churches, recourse must be had to governmental action, especially for the purpose of freeing the worker from the incubus of financial control, in his day represented by the Whig Party and the banks. All privilege, especially the inheritance of property, must be driven out of existence. Brownson insisted that this could be achieved only by revolution, "by the strong arm of physical force," probably at the end of a terrible war.

Not so very long after taking this extreme position, Brownson came to despair of democracy and became a convert to Catholicism. He accepted, in theory, the principle of authority. His acceptance was only in theory; as a Catholic he was a thorn in the side of the Catholic hierarchy. He retained much of his independence of mind. His greatest and most lasting work, *The American Republic*, was produced, however, under the influence of the organismic political theory of the Catholic Church and serves as a precursor of the organismic theories of American Hegelians.

In his early days Brownson seems to have been a late survival of the liberal thought of the Enlightenment; in his later life, he accepted authoritarianism as a principle and anticipated the conservatism of idealist political theory, after passing briefly through the orbits of free thought and transcendentalism. His thought is a cross-section of the history of thought in his day.

THE LABORING CLASSES

THOMAS CARLYLE [1] unquestionably ranks among the ablest writers of the day. His acquaintance with literature seems to be almost universal, and there is apparently no art or science with which he is not familiar. He possesses an unrivalled mastery over the resources of the English tongue, a remarkably keen insight into the mysteries of human nature, and a large share of genuine poetic feeling. His works are characterized by freshness and power, as well as by strangeness and singularity, and must be read with interest, even when they cannot be with approbation.

The little work, named at the head of this article, is a fair sample of his peculiar excellencies, and also of his peculiar defects. As a work intended to excite attention and lead the mind to an investigation of a great

[1] *Chartism.* By Thomas Carlyle.

subject, it possesses no ordinary value; but as a work intended to throw light on a difficult question, and to afford some positive directions to the statesman and the philanthropist, it is not worth much. Carlyle, like his imitators in this country, though he declaims against the destructives, possesses in no sense a constructive genius. He is good as a demolisher, but pitiable enough as a builder. No man sees more clearly that the present is defective and unworthy to be retained; he is a brave and successful warrior against it, whether reference be had to its literature, its politics, its philosophy, or its religion; but when the question comes up concerning what ought to be, what should take the place of what is, we regret to say, he affords us no essential aid, scarcely a useful hint. He has fine spiritual instincts, has outgrown materialism, loathes skepticism, sees clearly the absolute necessity of faith in both God and man, and insists upon it with due sincerity and earnestness; but with feelings very nearly akin to despair. He does not appear to have found as yet a faith for himself, and his writings have almost invariably a skeptical tendency. He has doubtless a sort of faith in God, or an overwhelming Necessity, but we cannot perceive that he has any faith in man or in man's efforts. Society is wrong, but he mocks at our sincerest and best directed efforts to right it. It cannot subsist as it is; that is clear: but what shall be done to make it what it ought to be, that he saith not. Of all writers we are acquainted with, he is the least satisfactory. He is dissatisfied with every thing himself, and he leaves his readers dissatisfied with every thing. Hopeless himself, he makes them also hopeless, especially if they have strong social tendencies, and are hungering and thirsting to work out the regeneration of their race.

Mr. Carlyle's admirers, we presume, will demur to this criticism. We have heard some of them speak of him as a sort of soul-quickener, and profess to derive from his writings fresh life and courage. We know not how this may be. It may be that they derive advantage from him on the homeopathic principle, and that he cures their diseases by exaggerating them; but for ourselves we must say, that we have found him anything but a skilful physician. He disheartens and enfeebles us; and while he emancipates us from the errors of tradition, he leaves us without strength or courage to engage in the inquiry after truth. We rise from his writings with the weariness and exhaustion one does from the embraces of the Witch Mara. It is but slowly that our blood begins to circulate again, and it is long before we recover the use of our powers. Whether his writings produce this effect on others or not, we are unable to say; but this effect they do produce on us. We almost dread to encounter them.

Mr. Carlyle would seem to have great sympathy with man. He certainly is not wanting in the sentiment of Humanity; nor is he deceived by external position, or dazzled by factitious glare. He can see worth in the socially low as well as in the socially high; in the artisan as well as the noble. This is something, but no great merit in one who can read the New Testament. Still it is something, and we are glad to meet it. But after all, he has no true reverence for Humanity. He may offer incense to a Goethe, a Jean Paul, a Mirabeau, a Danton, a Napoleon, but he nevertheless looks down upon his fellows, and sneers at the mass. He looks down upon man as one of his admirers has said, "as if man were a mouse." But we do not wish to look upon man in that light. We would look upon him as a brother, an equal, entitled to our love and sympathy. We would feel ourselves neither above him nor below him, but standing up by his side, with our feet on the same level with his. We would also love and respect the common-place mass, not merely heroes and sages, prophets and priests.

We are moreover no warm admirers of Carlyle's style of writing. We acknowledge his command over the resources of our language, and we enjoy the freshness, and occasional strength, beauty, and felicity of his style and expression, but he does not satisfy us. He wants clearness and precision, and that too when writing on topics where clearness and precision are all but indispensable. We have no patience with his mistiness, vagueness, and singularity. If a man must needs write and publish his thoughts to the world, let him do it in as clear and as intelligible language as possible. We are not aware of any subject worth writing on at all, that is already so plain that it needs to be rendered obscure. Carlyle can write well if he chooses; no man better. He is not necessarily misty, vague, nor fantastic. The antic tricks he has been latterly playing do not spring from the constitution of his mind, and we must say do by no means become him. We are disposed ourselves to assume considerable latitude in both thought and expression; but we believe every scholar should aim to keep within the general current of his language. Every language receives certain laws from the genius of the people who use it, and it is no mark of wisdom to transgress them; nor is genuine literary excellence to be attained but by obeying them. An Englishman, if he would profit Englishmen, must write English, not French nor German. If he wishes his writings to become an integral part of the literature of his language, he must keep within the steady current of what has ever been regarded as classical English style, and deny himself the momentary eclat he might gain by affectation and singularity.

We can, however, pardon Carlyle altogether more easily than we can his American imitators. Notwithstanding his manner of writing, when continued for any considerable length, becomes monotonous and wearisome, as in his History of the French Revolution,—a work which, with all its brilliant wit, inimitable humor, deep pathos, and graphic skill, can scarcely be read without yawning,—yet in his case it is redeemed by rare beauties, and marks a mind of the highest order, and of vast attainments. But in the hands of his American imitators, it becomes puerile and disgusting; and what is worthy of note is, that it is adopted and most servilely followed by the men among us who are loudest in their boasts of originality, and the most intolerant to its absence. But enough of this. For our consolation, the race of imitators is feeble and shortlived.

The subject of the little work before us, is one of the weightiest which can engage the attention of the statesman or the philanthropist. It is indeed, here, discussed only in relation to the working classes of England, but it in reality involves the condition of the working classes throughout the world,—a great subject, and one never yet worthily treated. Chartism, properly speaking is no local or temporary phenomenon. Its germ may be found in every nation in Christendom; indeed wherever man has approximated a state of civilization, wherever there is inequality in social condition, and in the distribution of the products of industry. And where does not this inequality obtain? Where is the spot on earth, in which the actual producer of wealth is not one of the lower class, shut out from what are looked upon as the main advantages of the social state?

Mr. Carlyle, though he gives us few facts, yet shows us that the condition of the workingmen in England is deplorable, and every day growing worse. It has already become intolerable, and hence the outbreak of the Chartists. Chartism is the protest of the working classes against the injustice of the present social organization of the British community, and a loud demand for a new organization which shall respect the rights and well-being of the laborer.

The movements of the Chartists have excited considerable alarm in the higher classes of English society, and some hope in the friends of Humanity among ourselves. We do not feel competent to speak with any decision on the extent or importance of these movements. If our voice could reach the Chartists we would bid them be bold and determined; we would bid them persevere even unto death; for their cause is that of justice, and in fighting for it they will be fighting the battles of God and man. But we look for no important results from their movements. We have little faith in a John Bull mob. It will bluster, and swagger, and threaten much; but give it plenty of porter and roast-beef, and it will sink back to its kennel, as quiet and as harmless as a lamb. The lower classes in England have made many a move since the days of Wat Tyler for the betterment of their condition, but we cannot perceive that they have ever effected much. They are doubtless nearer the day of their emancipation, than they were, but their actual condition is scarcely superior to what it was in the days of Richard the Second.

There is no country in Europe, in which the condition of the laboring classes seems to us so hopeless as in that of England. This is not owing to the fact, that the aristocracy is less enlightened, more powerful, or more oppressive in England than elsewhere. The English laborer does not find his worst enemy in the nobility, but in the middling class. The middle class is much more numerous and powerful in England than in any other European country, and is of a higher character. It has always been powerful; for by means of the Norman Conquest it received large accessions from the old Saxon nobility. The Conquest established a new aristocracy, and degraded the old to the condition of Commoners. The superiority of the English Commons is, we suppose, chiefly owing to this fact.

The middle class is always a firm champion of equality, when it concerns humbling a class above it; but it is its inveterate foe, when it concerns elevating a class below it. Manfully have the British Commoners struggled against the old feudal aristocracy, and so successfully that they now constitute the dominant power in the state. To their struggles against the throne and the nobility is the English nation indebted for the liberty it so loudly boasts, and which, during the last half of the last century, so enraptured the friends of Humanity throughout Europe.

But this class has done nothing for the laboring population, the real *proletarii*. It has humbled the aristocracy; it has raised itself to dominion, and it is now conservative,—conservative in fact, whether it call itself Whig or Radical. From its near relation to the workingmen, its kindred pursuits with them, it is altogether more hostile to them than the nobility ever were or ever can be. This was seen in the conduct of England towards the French Revolution. So long as that Revolution was in the hands of the middle class, and threatened merely to humble monarchy and nobility, the English nation applauded it; but as soon as it descended to the mass of people, and promised to elevate the laboring classes, so soon as the starving workman began to flatter himself, that there was to be a revolution for him too as well as for his employer, the English nation armed itself and poured out its blood and treasure to suppress it. Everybody knows that Great Britain, boasting of her freedom and of her love of freedom, was the life and soul of the opposition to the French Revolution; and on her head almost alone should fall the curses of Humanity for the sad failure of that glorious uprising of the people in behalf of their imprescriptible, and inalienable rights. Yet it was not the English monarchy, nor the English nobility, that was alone in fault. Monarchy and nobility would have been powerless, had they not had with them the great body of the English Commoners. England fought in the ranks, nay, at the head of the allies, not for monarchy, not for nobility, nor yet for religion; but for trade and manufactures, for her middle class, against the rights and well-being of the workingman; and her strength and efficiency consisted in the strength and efficiency of this class.

Now this middle class, which was strong enough to defeat nearly all the practical benefit of the French Revolution, is the natural enemy of the Chartists. It will unite with the monarchy and nobility against them; and spare neither blood nor treasure to defeat them. Our despair for the poor Chartists arises from the number and power of the middle class. We dread for them neither monarchy nor nobility. Nor should they. Their only real enemy is in the employer. In all countries is it the same. The only enemy of the laborer is your employer, whether appearing in the shape of the master mechanic, or in the owner of a factory. A Duke of Wellington is much more likely to vindicate the rights of labor than an Abbot Lawrence, although the latter may be a very kind-hearted man, and liberal citizen, as we always find Blackwood's Magazine more true to the interests of the poor, than we do the Edinburgh Review, or even the London and Westminster.

Mr. Carlyle, contrary to his wont, in the pamphlet we have named, commends two projects for the relief of the workingmen, which he finds others have suggested,—universal education, and general emigration. Universal education we shall not be thought likely to depreciate; but we confess that we are unable to see in it that sovereign remedy for the evils of the social state as it is, which some of our friends do, or say they do. We have little faith in the power of education to elevate a people compelled to labor from twelve to sixteen hours a day, and to experience for no mean portion of the time a paucity of even the necessaries of life, let alone its comforts. Give your starving boy a breakfast before you send him to school, and your tattered beggar a cloak before you attempt his moral and intellectual elevation. A swarm of naked and starving urchins crowded into a school-room will make little proficiency in the "Humanities." Indeed, it seems to us most bitter mockery for the well-dressed, and well-fed to send the schoolmaster and priest to the wretched hovels of squalid poverty,—a mockery at which devils may laugh, but over which angels must weep. Educate the working classes of England; and what then? Will they require less food and less clothing when educated than they do now? Will they be more contented or more happy in their condition? For God's sake beware how you kindle within them the intellectual spark, and make them aware that they too are men, with powers of thought and feeling which ally them by the bonds of brotherhood to their betters. If you will doom them to the external condition of brutes, do in common charity keep their minds and hearts brutish. Render them as insensible as possible, that they may feel the less acutely their degradation, and see the less clearly the monstrous injustice which is done them.

General emigration can at best afford only a temporary relief, for the colony will soon become an empire, and reproduce all the injustice and wretchedness of the mother country. Nor is general emigration necessary. England, if she would be just, could support a larger population than she now numbers. The evil is not from over population, but from the unequal repartition of the fruits of industry. She suffers from over production, and from over production, because her workmen produce not for themselves but for their employers. What then is the remedy? As it concerns England, we shall leave the English statesman to answer. Be it what it may, it will not be obtained without war and bloodshed. It will be found only at the end of one of the longest and severest struggles the human race has ever been engaged in, only by that most dreaded of all wars, the war of the poor against the rich, a war which, however long it may be delayed, will come, and come with all its horrors. The day of vengeance is sure; for the world after all is under the dominion of a Just Providence.

No one can observe the signs of the times with much care, without perceiving that a crisis as to the relation of wealth and labor is approaching. It is useless to shut our eyes to the fact, and like the ostrich fancy ourselves secure because we have so concealed our heads that we see not the danger. We or our children will have to meet this crisis. The old war between the King and the Barons is well nigh ended, and so is that between the Barons and the Merchants and Manufacturers,— landed capital and commercial capital. The business man has become the peer of my Lord. And now commences the new struggle between the operative and his employer, between wealth and labor. Every day does this struggle extend further and wax stronger and fiercer; what or when the end will be God only knows.

In this coming contest there is a deeper question at issue than is commonly imagined; a question which is but remotely touched in your controversies about United States Banks and Sub-Treasuries, chartered Banking and free Banking, free trade and corporations, although these controversies may be paving the way for it to come up. We have discovered no presentiment of it in any king's or queen's speech, nor in any president's message. It is embraced in no popular political creed of the day, whether christened Whig or Tory, *Juste-milieu* or Democratic. No popular senator, or deputy, or peer seems to have any glimpse of it; but it is working in the hearts of the million, is struggling to shape itself, and one day it will be uttered, and in thunder tones. Well will it be for him, who, on that day, shall be found ready to answer it.

What we would ask is, throughout the Christian world, the actual condition of the laboring classes, viewed simply and exclusively in their capacity of laborers? They constitute at least a moiety of the human race. We exclude the nobility, we exclude also the middle class, and include only actual laborers, who are laborers and not proprietors, owners of none of the funds of production, neither houses, shops, nor lands, nor implements of labor, being therefore solely dependent on their hands. We have no means of ascertaining their precise proportion to the whole number of the race; but we think we may estimate them at one half. In any contest they will be as two to one, because the large class of proprietors who are not employers, but laborers on their own lands or in their own shops will make common cause with them.

Now we will not so belie our acquaintance with political economy, as to allege that these alone perform all that is necessary to the production of wealth. We are not ignorant of the fact, that the merchant, who is literally the common carrier and exchange dealer, performs a useful service, and is therefore entitled to a portion of the proceeds of labor. But make all necessary deductions on his account, and then ask what portion of the remainder is retained, either in kind or in its equivalent, in the hands of the original producer, the workingman? All over the world this fact stares us in the face, the workingman is poor and depressed, while a large portion of the non-workingmen, in the sense we now use the term, are wealthy. It may be laid down as a general rule, with but few exceptions, that men are rewarded in an inverse ratio to the amount of actual service they perform. Under every government on earth the largest salaries are annexed to those offices, which demand of their incumbents the least amount of actual labor either mental or manual. And this is in perfect harmony with the whole system of repartition of the fruits of industry, which obtains in every department of society. Now here is the system which prevails, and here is its result. The whole class of simple laborers are poor, and in general unable to procure any thing beyond the bare necessaries of life.

In regard to labor two systems obtain; one that of slave labor, the other that of free labor. Of the two, the first is, in our judgment, except so far as the feelings are concerned, decidedly the least oppressive. If the slave has never been a free man, we think, as a general rule, his sufferings are less than those of the free laborer at wages. As to actual freedom one has just about as much as the other. The laborer at wages has all the disadvantages of freedom and none of its blessings, while the slave, if denied the blessings, is freed from the disadvantages. We are no advocates of slavery, we are as heartily opposed to it as any modern abolitionist can be; but we say frankly that, if there must always be a laboring population distinct from proprietors and employers, we regard the slave system as decidedly preferable to the system at wages. It is no pleasant thing to go days without food, to lie idle for weeks, seeking work and finding none, to rise in the morning with a wife and children you love, and know not where to procure them a breakfast, and to see constantly before you no brighter prospect than the almshouse. Yet these are no unfrequent incidents in the lives of our laboring population. Even in seasons of general prosperity, when there was only the ordinary cry of "hard times," we have seen hundreds of people in a not very populous village, in a wealthy portion of our common country, suffering for the want of the necessaries of life, willing to work, and yet finding no work to do. Many and many is the application of a poor man for work, merely for his food, we have seen rejected. These things are little thought of, for the applicants are poor; they fill no conspicuous place in society, and they have no biographers. But their wrongs are chronicled in heaven. It is said there is no want in this country. There may be less than in some other countries. But death by actual starvation in this country is we apprehend no uncommon occurrence. The sufferings of a quiet, unassuming but useful class of females in our cities, in general sempstresses, too proud to beg or to apply to the almshouse, are not easily told. They are industrious; they do all that they can find to do; but yet the little there is for them to do, and the miserable pittance they receive for it, is hardly sufficient to keep soul and body together. And yet there is a man who employs them to make shirts, trousers, &c., and grows rich on their labors. He is one of our respectable citizens, perhaps is praised in the newspapers for his liberal donations to some charitable institution. He passes among us as a pattern of morality, and is honored as a worthy Christian. And why should he not be, since our *Christian* community is made up of such as he, and since our clergy would not dare question his piety, lest they should incur the reproach of infidelity, and lose their standing, and their salaries? Nay, since our clergy are raised up, educated, fashioned, and sustained by such as he? Not a few of our churches rest on Mammon for their foundation. The basement is a trader's shop.

We pass through our manufacturing villages; most of them appear neat and flourishing. The operatives are well dressed, and we are told, well paid. They are said to be healthy, contented, and happy. This is the fair side of the picture; the side exhibited to distinguished visitors. There is a dark side, moral as well as physical. Of the common operatives, few, if any, by their wages, acquire a competence. A few of what Carlyle terms not inaptly the *body-servants* are well paid, and now and then an agent or an overseer rides in his coach. But the great mass wear out their health, spirits, and morals, without becoming one whit better off than when they commenced labor. The bills of mortality in these factory villages are not striking, we admit, for the poor girls when they can toil no longer go home to die. The average life, working life we mean, of the girls that come to Lowell, for instance, from Maine, New Hampshire, and Vermont, we have been assured, is only about three years. What becomes of them then? Few of them ever marry; fewer still ever return to their native places with reputations unimpaired. "She has worked in a Factory," is almost enough to damn to infamy the most worthy and virtuous girl. We know no sadder sight on earth than one of our factory villages presents, when the bell at break of day, or at the hour of breakfast, or dinner, calls out its hundreds or thousands of operatives. We stand and look at these hard working men and women hurrying in all directions, and ask ourselves, where go the proceeds of their labors? The man who employs them, and for whom they are toiling as so many slaves, is one of our city nabobs, revelling in luxury; or he is a member of our legislature, enacting laws to put money in his own pocket; or he is a member of Congress, contending for a high Tariff to tax the poor for the benefit of the rich; or in these times he is shedding crocodile tears over the deplorable condition of the poor laborer, while he docks his wages twenty-five per cent.; building miniature log cabins, shouting Harrison and "hard cider." And this man too would fain pass for a Christian and a republican. He shouts for liberty, stickles for equality, and is horrified at a Southern planter who keeps slaves.

One thing is certain; that of the amount actually produced by the operative, he retains a less proportion than it costs the master to feed, clothe, and lodge his slave. Wages is a cunning device of the devil, for the benefit of tender consciences, who would retain all the advantages of the slave system, without the expense, trouble, and odium of being slave-holders.

Messrs. Thome and Kimball, in their account of the emancipation of slavery in the West Indies, establish the fact that the employer may have the same amount of labor done 25 per ct. cheaper than the master. What does this fact prove, if not that wages is a more successful method of taxing labor than slavery? We really believe our Northern system of labor is more oppressive, and even more mischievous to morals, than the Southern. We, however, war against both. We have no toleration for either system. We would see a slave a man, but a free man, not a mere operative at wages. This he would not be were he now emancipated. Could the abolitionists effect all they propose, they would do the slave no service. Should emancipation work as well as they say, still it would do the slave no good. He would be a slave still, although with the title and cares of a freeman. If then we had no constitutional objections to abolitionism, we could not, for the reason here implied, be abolitionists.

The slave system, however, in name and form, is gradually disappearing from Christendom. It will not subsist much longer. But its place is taken by the system of labor at wages, and this system, we hold, is no improvement upon the one it supplants. Nevertheless the system of wages will triumph. It is the system which in name sounds honester than slavery, and in substance is more profitable to the master. It yields the wages of iniquity, without its opprobium. It will therefore supplant slavery, and be sustained—for a time.

Now, what is the prospect of those who fall under the operation of this system? We ask, is there a reasonable chance that any considerable portion of the present generation of laborers, shall ever become owners of a sufficient portion of the funds of production, to be able to sustain themselves by laboring on their own capital, that is, as independent laborers? We need not ask this question, for everybody knows there is not. Well, is the condition of a laborer at wages the best that the great mass of the working people ought to be able to aspire to? Is it a condition,—nay can it be made a condition,—with which a man should be satisfied; in which he should be contented to live and die?

In our own country this condition has existed under its most favorable aspects, and has been made as good as it can be. It has reached all the excellence of which it is susceptible. It is now not improving but growing worse. The actual condition of the working-man to-day, viewed in all its bearings, is not so good as it was fifty years ago. If we have not been altogether misinformed, fifty years ago, health and industrious habits, constituted no mean stock in trade, and with them almost any man might aspire to competence and independence. But it is so no longer. The wilderness has receded, and already the new lands are beyond the reach of the mere laborer, and the employer has him at his mercy. If the present relation subsist, we see nothing better for him in reserve than what he now possesses, but something altogether worse.

We are not ignorant of the fact that men born poor become wealthy, and that men born to wealth become poor; but this fact does not necessarily diminish the numbers of the poor, nor augment the numbers of the rich. The relative numbers of the two classes remain, or may remain, the same. But be this as it may; one fact is certain, no man born poor has ever by his wages, as a simple operative, risen to the class of the wealthy. Rich he may have become, but it has not been by his own manual labor. He has in some way contrived to tax for his benefit the labor of others. He may have accumulated a few dollars which he has placed at usury, or invested in trade; or he may, as a master workman, obtain a premium on his journeymen; or he may have from a clerk passed to a partner, or from a workman to an overseer. The simple market wages for ordinary labor, has never been adequate to raise him from poverty to wealth. This fact is decisive of the whole controversy, and proves that the system of wages must be supplanted by some other system, or else one half of the human race must forever be the virtual slaves of the other.

Now the great work for this age and the coming, is to raise up the laborer, and to realize in our own social arrangements and in the actual condition of all men, that equality between man and man, which God has established between the rights of one and those of another. In other words, our business is to emancipate the proletaries, as the past has emancipated the slaves. This is our work. There must be no class of our fellow men doomed to toil through life as mere workmen at wages. If wages are tolerated it must be, in the case of the individual operative, only under such conditions that by the time he is of a proper age to settle in life, he shall have accumulated enough to be an independent laborer on his own capital,—on his own farm, or in his own shop. Here is our work. How is it to be done?

Reformers in general answer this question, or what they deem its equivalent, in a manner which we cannot but regard as very unsatisfactory. They would have all men wise, good, and happy; but in order to make them so, they tell us that we want not external changes, but internal; and therefore instead of declaiming against society and seeking to disturb existing social arrangements, we should confine ourselves to the individual reason and conscience; seek merely to lead the individual to repentance, and to reformation of life; make the individual a practical, a truly religious man, and all evils will either disappear, or be sanctified to the spiritual growth of the soul.

This is doubtless a capital theory, and has the advantage that kings, hierarchies, nobilities,—in a word, all who fatten on the toil and blood of their fellows, will feel no difficulty in supporting it. Nicholas of Russia, the Grand Turk, his Holiness the Pope, will hold us their especial friends for advocating a theory, which secures to them the odor of sanctity even while they are sustaining by their anathemas or their armed legions, a system of things of which the great mass are and must be the victims. If you will only allow me to keep thousands toiling for my pleasure or my profit, I will even aid you in your pious efforts to convert their souls. I am not cruel; I do not wish either to cause, or to see suffering; I am therefore disposed to encourage your labors for the souls of the workingman, providing you will secure to me the products of his bodily toil. So far as the salvation of his soul will not interfere with my income. I hold it worthy of being sought; and if a few thousand dollars will aid you, Mr. Priest, in reconciling him to God, and making fair weather for him hereafter, they are at your service. I shall not want him to work for me in the world to come, and I can indemnify myself for what your salary costs me, by paying him less wages. A capital theory this, which one may advocate without incurring the reproach of a disorganizer, a jacobin, a leveller, and without losing the friendship of the rankest aristocrat in the land.

This theory, however, is exposed to one slight objection, that of being condemned by something like six thousand years' experience. For six thousand years its beauty has been extolled, its praises sung and its blessings sought, under every advantage which learning, fashion, wealth, and power can secure; and yet under its practical operations, we are assured, that mankind, though totally depraved at first, have been growing worse and worse ever since.

For our part, we yield to none in our reverence for science and religion; but we confess that we look not for the regeneration of the race from priests and pedagogues. They have had a fair trial. They cannot construct the temple of God. They cannot conceive its plan, and they know not how to build. They daub with untempered mortar, and the walls they erect tumble down if so much as a fox attempt to go up thereon. In a word they always league with the people's masters, and seek to reform without disturbing the social arrangements which render reform necessary. They would change the consequents without changing the antecedents, secure to men the rewards of holiness, while they continue their allegiance to the devil. We have no faith in priests and pedagogues. They merely cry peace, peace, and that too when there is no peace, and can be none.

We admit the importance of what Dr Channing in his lectures on the subject we are treating recommends as "self-culture." Self-culture is a good thing, but it cannot abolish inequality, nor restore men to their rights. As a means of quickening moral and intellectual energy, exalting the sentiments, and preparing the laborer to contend manfully for his rights, we admit its importance, and insist as strenuously as any one on making it as universal as possible; but as constituting in itself a remedy for the vices of the social state, we have no faith in it. As a means it is well, as the end it is nothing.

The truth is, the evil we have pointed out is not merely individual in its character. It is not, in the case of any single individual, of any one man's procuring, nor can the efforts of any one man, directed solely to his own moral and religious perfection, do aught to remove it. What is purely individual in its nature, efforts of individuals to perfect themselves, may remove. But the evil we speak of is inherent in all our social arrangements, and cannot be cured without a radical change of those arrangements. Could we convert all men to Christianity in both theory and practice, as held by the most enlightened sect of Christians among us, the evils of the social state would remain untouched. Continue our present system of trade, and all its present evil consequences will follow, whether it be carried on by your best men or your worst. Put your best men, your wisest, most moral, and most religious men, at the head of your paper money banks, and the evils of the present banking system will remain scarcely diminished. The only way to get rid of its evils is to change the system, not its managers. The evils of slavery do not result from the personal characters of slave masters. They are inseparable from the system, let who will be masters. Make all your rich men good Christians, and you have lessened not the evils of existing inequality in wealth. The mischievous effects of this inequality do not result from the personal characters of either rich or poor, but from itself, and they will continue, just so long as there are rich men and poor men in the same community. You must abolish the system or accept its consequences. No man can serve both God and Mammon. If you will serve the devil, you must look to the devil for your wages, we know no other way.

Let us not be misinterpreted. We deny not the power of Christianity. Should all men become good Christians, we deny not that all social evils would be cured. But we deny in the outset that a man, who seeks merely to save his own soul, merely to perfect his own individual nature, can be a good Christian. The Christian forgets himself, buckles on his armor, and goes forth to war against principalities and powers, and against spiritual wickedness in high places. No man can be a Christian who does not begin his career by making war on the mischievous social arrangements from which his brethren suffer. He who thinks he can be a Christian and save his soul, without seeking their radical change, has no reason to applaud himself for his proficiency in Christian science, nor for his progress towards the kingdom of God. Understand Christianity, and we will admit, that should all men become good Christians, there would be nothing to complain of. But one might as well undertake to dip the ocean dry with a clam-shell, as to undertake to cure the evils of the social state by converting men to the Christianity of the Church.

The evil we have pointed out, we have said, is not of individual creation, and it is not to be removed by individual effort, saving so far as individual effort induces the combined effort of the mass. But whence has this evil originated? How comes it that all over the world the working classes are depressed, are the low and vulgar, and virtually the slaves of the non-working classes? This is an inquiry which has not yet received the attention it deserves. It is not enough to answer, that it has originated entirely in the inferiority by nature of the working classes; that they have less skill and foresight, and are less able than the upper classes, to provide for themselves, or less susceptible of the highest moral and intellectual cultivation. Nor is it sufficient for our purpose to be told, that Providence has decreed that some shall be poor and wretched, ignorant and vulgar; and that others shall be rich and vicious, learned and polite, oppressive and miserable. We do not choose to charge this matter to the will of God. "The foolishness of man perverteth his way, and his heart fretteth against the Lord." God has made of one blood all the nations of men to dwell on all the face of the earth, and to dwell there as brothers, as members of one and the same family; and although he has made them with a diversity of powers, it would perhaps, after all, be a bold assertion to say that he has made them with an inequality of powers. There is nothing in the actual difference of the powers of individuals, which accounts for the striking inequalities we everywhere discover in their condition. The child of the plebeian, if placed early in the proper circumstances, grows up not less beautiful, active, intelligent, and refined, than the child of the patrician; and the child of the patrician may become as coarse, as brutish as the child of any slave. So far as observation on the original capacities of individuals goes, nothing is discovered to throw much light on social inequalities.

The cause of the inequality we speak of must be sought in history, and be regarded as having its root in Providence, or in human nature, only in that sense in which all historical facts have their origin in these. We may perhaps trace it in the first instance to conquest, but not to conquest as the ultimate cause. The Romans in conquering Italy no doubt reduced many to the condition of slaves, but they also found the great mass of the laboring population already slaves. There is every where a class distinct from the reigning class, bearing the same relation to it, that the Gibeonites did to the Jews. They are principally *colons*, the cultivators for foreign masters, of a soil which they seemed to have been dispossessed. Who has dispossessed them? Who has reduced them to their present condition,—a condition which under the Roman dominion is perhaps even ameliorated? Who were this race? Whence came they? They appear to be distinct from the reigning race, as were the Helotæ from the Doric-Spartan. Were they the aborigines of the territory? Had they once been free? By what concurrence of events have they been reduced to their present condition? By a prior conquest? But mere conquest does not so reduce a population. It may make slaves of the prisoners taken in actual combat, and reduce the whole to tributaries, but it leaves the mass of the population free, except in its political relations. Were they originally savages, subjugated by a civilized tribe? Savages may be exterminated, but they never, so far as we can ascertain, become to any considerable extent "the hewers of wood and drawers of water" to their conquerors. For our part we are disposed to seek the cause of the inequality of conditions of which we speak, in religion, and to charge it to the priesthood. And we are confirmed in this, by what appears to be the instinctive tendency of every, or almost every, social reformer. Men's instincts, in a matter of this kind, are worthier of reliance than their reasonings. Rarely do we find in any age or country, a man feeling himself commissioned to labor for a social reform, who does not feel that he must begin it by making war upon the priesthood. This was the case with the old Hebrew reformers, who are to us the prophets of God; with Jesus, the Apostles, and the early Fathers of the Church; with the French democrats of the last century; and is the case with the Young Germans, and the Socialists, as they call themselves in England, at the present moment. Indeed it is felt at once that no reform can be effected without resisting the priests and emancipating the people from their power.

Historical research, we apprehend, will be found to justify this instinct, and to authorize the eternal hostility of the reformer, the advocate of social progress, to the priesthood. How is it we ask, that man comes out of the savage state? In the savage state, properly so called, there is no inequality of the kind of which we speak. The individual system obtains there. Each man is his own centre, and is a whole in himself. There is no community, there are no members of society; for society is not. This individuality, which, if combined with the highest possible moral and intellectual cultivation, would be the perfection of man's earthly condition, must be broken down before the human race can enter into the path of civilization, or commence its career of progress. But it cannot be broken down by material force. It resists by its own nature the combination of individuals necessary to subdue it. It can be successfully attacked only by a spiritual power, and subjugated only by the representatives of that power, that is to say, the priests.

Man is naturally a religious being, and disposed to stand in awe of invisible powers. This makes, undoubtedly, under certain relations, his glory; but when coupled with his ignorance, it becomes the chief source of his degradation and misery. He feels within the workings of a mysterious nature, and is conscious that hidden and superior powers are at work all around him, and perpetually influencing his destiny; now wafting him onward with a prosperous gale, or now resisting his course, driving him back, defeating his plans, blasting his hopes, and wounding his heart. What are his relations to these hidden, mysterious, and yet all-influencing forces? Can their anger be appeased? Can their favor be secured? Thus he asks himself. Unable to answer, he goes to the more aged and experienced of his tribe, and asks them the same questions. They answer as best they can. What is done by one is done by another, and what is done once is done again. The necessity of instruction, which each one feels in consequence of his own feebleness and inexperience, renders the recurrence to those best capable of giving it, or supposed to be the best capable of giving it, frequent and uniform. Hence the priest. He who is consulted prepares himself to answer, and therefore devotes himself to the study of man's relations to these invisible powers, and the nature of these invisible powers themselves. Hence religion becomes a special object of study, and the study of it a profession. Individuals whom a thunder-storm, an earthquake, an eruption of a volcano, an eclipse of the sun or moon, any unusual appearance in the heavens or earth, has frightened, or whom some unforeseen disaster has afflicted, go to the wise-man for explanation, to know what it means, or what they shall do in order to appease the offended powers. When reassured they naturally feel grateful to this wise-man; they load him with honors, and in the access of their gratitude raise him far above the common level, and spare him the common burdens of life. Once thus distinguished, he becomes an object of envy. His condition is looked upon as superior to that of the mass. Hence a multitude aspire to possess themselves of it. When once the class has become somewhat numerous, it labors to secure to itself the distinction it has received, its honors and its emoluments, and to increase them. Hence the establishment of priesthoods or sacerdotal corporations, such as the Egyptians, the Braminical, the Ethiopian, the Jewish, the Scandinavian, the Druidical, the Mexican, and Peruvian.

The germ of these sacerdotal corporations is found in the savage state, and exists there in that formidable personage called a *jongleur*, juggler, or conjurer. But as the tribe or people advances, the juggler becomes a priest and the member of a corporation. These sacerdotal corporations are variously organized, but everywhere organized for the purpose, as that arch rebel, Thomas Paine, says, "of monopolizing power and profit." The effort is unceasing to elevate them as far above the people as possible, to enable them to exert the greatest possible control over the people, and to derive the greatest possible profit from the people.

Now if we glance over the history of the world, we shall find, that at the epoch of coming out of the savage state, these corporations are universally instituted. We find them among every people; and among every people, at this epoch, they are the dominant power, ruling with an iron despotism. The real idea at the bottom of these institutions, is the control of individual freedom by moral laws, the assertion of the supremacy of moral power over physical force,—a great truth, and one which can never be too strenuously insisted on; but a truth which at this epoch can only enslave the mass of the people to its professed representatives, the priests. Through awe of the gods, through fear of divine displeasure, and dread of the unforeseen chastisements that displeasure may inflict, and by pretending, honestly or not, to possess the secret of averting it, and of rendering the gods propitious, the priests are able to reduce the people to the most wretched subjection, and to keep them there; at least for a time.

But these institutions must naturally be jealous of power and ambitious of confining it to as few hands as possible. If the sacerdotal corporations were thrown open to all the world, all the world would rush into them, and then there would be no advantage in being a priest. Hence the number who may be priests must be limited. Hence again a distinction of clean and unclean is introduced. Men can be admitted into these corporations only as they descend from the priestly race. As in India, no man can aspire to the priesthood unless of Braminical descent, and among the Jews unless he be of the tribe of Levi. The priestly race was the ruling race; it dealt with science, it held communion with the Gods, and therefore was the purer race. The races excluded from the priesthood were not only regarded as inferior, but as unclean. The Gibeonite to a Jew was both an inferior and an impure. The operation of the principles involved in these considerations, has, in our judgment, begun and effected the slavery of the great mass of the people. It has introduced distinctions of blood or race, founded privileged orders, and secured the rewards of industry to the few, while it has reduced the mass to the most degrading and hopeless bondage.

Now the great mass enslaved by the sacerdotal corporations are not emancipated by the victories which follow by the warrior caste, even when those victories are said to be in behalf of freedom. The military order succeeds the priestly; but in establishing, as it does in Greece and Rome, the supremacy of the state over the church, it leaves the great mass in the bondage in which it finds them. The Normans conquer England, but they scarcely touch the condition of the old Saxon bondmen. The Polish serf lost his freedom, before began the Russian dominion, and he would have recovered none of it, had Poland regained, in her late struggle, her former political independence. The subjection of a nation is in general merely depriving one class of its population of its exclusive right to enslave the people; and the recovery of political independence, is little else than the recovery of this right. The Germans call their rising against Napoleon a rising for liberty, and so it was, liberty for German princes and German nobles; but the German people were more free under Napoleon's supremacy than they are now, or will be very soon. Conquest may undoubtedly increase the number of slaves; but in general it merely adds to the number and power of the middle class. It institutes a new nobility, and degrades the old to the rank of commoners. This is its general effect. We cannot therefore ascribe to conquest, as we did in a former number of this journal, the condition in which the working classes are universally found. They have been reduced to their condition by the priest, not by the military chieftain.

Mankind came out of the savage state by means of the priests. Priests are the first civilizers of the race. For the wild freedom of the savage, they substitute the iron despotism of the theocrat. This is the first step in civilization, in man's career of progress. It is not strange then that some should prefer the savage state to the civilized. Who would not rather roam the forest with a free step and unshackled limb, though exposed to hunger, cold, and nakedness, than crouch an abject slave beneath the whip of the master? As yet civilization has done little but break and subdue man's natural love of freedom; but tame his wild and eagle spirit. In what a world does man even now find himself, when he first awakes and feels some of the workings of his manly nature? He is in a cold, damp, dark dungeon, and loaded all over with chains, with the iron entering into his very soul. He cannot make one single free movement. The priest holds his conscience, fashion controls his tastes, and society with her forces invades the very sanctuary of his heart, and takes command of his love, that which is purest and best in his nature, which alone gives reality to his existence, and from which proceeds the only ray which pierces the gloom of his prison house. Even that he cannot enjoy in peace and quietness, nor scarcely at all. He is wounded on every side, in every part of his being, in every relation in life, in every idea of his mind, in every sentiment of his heart. O, it is a sad world, a sad world to the young soul just awakening to its diviner instincts! A sad world to him who is not gifted with the only blessing which seems compatible with life as it is—absolute insensibility. But no matter. A wise man never murmurs. He never kicks against the pricks. What is is, and there is an end of it; what can be may be, and we will do what we can to make life what it ought to be. Though man's first step in civilization is slavery, his last step shall be freedom. The free soul can never be wholly subdued; the ethereal fire in man's nature may be smothered, but it cannot be extinguished. Down, down deep in the centre of his heart it burns inextinguishable and forever, glowing intenser with the accumulating heat of centuries; and one day the whole mass of Humanity shall become ignited, and be full of fire within and all over, as a live coal; and then—slavery, and whatever is foreign to the soul itself, shall be consumed.

But, having traced the inequality we complain of to its origin, we proceed to ask again what is the remedy? The remedy is first to be sought in the destruction of the priest. We are not mere destructives. We delight not in pulling down; but the bad must be removed before the good can be introduced. Conviction and repentance precede re-generation. Moreover we are Christians, and it is only by following out the Christian law, and the example of the early Christians, that we can hope to effect anything. Christianity is the sublimest protest against the priesthood ever uttered, and a protest uttered by both God and man; for he who uttered it was God-Man. In the person of Jesus both God and Man protest against the priesthood. What was the mission of Jesus but a solemn summons of every priesthood on earth to judgment, and of the human race to freedom? He discomfited the learned doctors, and with whips of small cords drove the priests, degenerated into mere money changers, from the temple of God. He instituted himself no priesthood, no form of religious worship. He recognized no priest but a holy life, and commanded the construction of no temple but that of the pure heart. He preached no formal religion, enjoined no creed, set apart no day for religious worship. He preached fraternal love, peace on earth, and good will to men. He came to the soul enslaved, "cabined, cribbed, confined," to the poor child of mortality, bound hand and foot, unable to move, and said in the tones of a God, "Be free; be enlarged; be there room for thee to grow, expand, and overflow with the love thou wast made to overflow with."

In the name of Jesus we admit there has been a priesthood instituted, and considering how the world went, a priesthood could not but be instituted; but the religion of Jesus repudiates it. It recognizes no mediator between God and man but him who dies on the cross to redeem man; no propitiation for sin but a pure love, which rises in a living flame to all that is beautiful and good, and spreads out in light and warmth for all the chilled and benighted sons of mortality. In calling every man to be a priest, it virtually condemns every possible priesthood, and in recognising the religion of the new covenant, the religion written on the heart, of a law put within the soul, it abolishes all formal worship.

The priest is universally a tyrant, universally the enslaver of his brethren, and therefore it is Christianity condemns him. It could not prevent the re-establishment of a hierarchy, but it prepared for its ultimate destruction, by denying the inequality of blood, by representing all men as equal before God, and by insisting on the celibacy of the clergy. The best feature of the Church was in its denial to the clergy of the right to marry. By this it prevented the new hierarchy from becoming hereditary, as were the old sacerdotal corporations of India and Judea.

We object to no religious instruction; we object not to the gathering together of the people on one day in seven, to sing and pray, and listen to a discourse from a religious teacher; but we object to every thing like an outward, visible church; to everything that in the remotest degree partakes of the priest. A priest is one who stands as a sort of mediator between God and man; but we have one mediator, Jesus Christ, who gave himself a ransom for all, and that is enough. It may be supposed that we, protestants, have no priests; but for ourselves we know no fundamental difference between a catholic priest and a protestant clergyman, as we know no difference of any magnitude, in relation to the principles on which they are based, between a protestant church and the catholic church. Both are based on the principle of authority; both deny in fact, however it may be in manner, the authority of reason, and war against freedom of mind; both substitute dead works for true righteousness, a vain show for the reality of piety, and are sustained as the means of reconciling us to God without requiring us to become godlike. Both therefore ought to go by the board.

We may offend in what we say, but we cannot help that. We insist upon it, that the complete and final destruction of the priestly order, in every practical sense of the word priest, is the first step to be taken towards elevating the laboring classes. Priests are, in their capacity of priests, necessarily enemies to freedom and equality. All reasoning demonstrates this, and all history proves it. There must be no class of men set apart and authorized, either by law or fashion, to speak to us in the name of God, or to be the interpreters of the word of God.. The word of God never drops from the priest's lips. He who redeemed man did not spring from the priestly class, for it is evident that our Lord sprang out of Judea, of which tribe Moses spake nothing concerning the priesthood. Who in fact were the authors of the Bible, the book which Christendom professes to receive as the word of God? The priests? Nay, they were the inveterate foes of the priests. No man ever berated the priests more soundly than did Jeremiah and Ezekiel. And who were they who heard Jesus the most gladly? The priests? The chief priests were at the head of those who demanded his crucifixion.

In every age the priests, the authorized teachers of religion, are the first to oppose the true prophet of God, and to condemn his prophecies as blasphemies. They are always a let and a hindrance to the spread of truth. Why then retain them? Why not abolish the priestly office? Why continue to sustain what the whole history of man condemns as the greatest of all obstacles to intellectual and social progress.

We say again, we have no objection to teachers of religion, as such; but let us have no class of men whose profession it is to minister at the altar. Let us leave this matter to Providence. When God raises up a prophet, let that prophet prophesy as God gives him utterance. Let every man speak out of his own full heart, as he is moved by the Holy Ghost, but let us have none to prophesy for hire, to make preaching a profession, a means of gaining a livelihood. Whoever has a word pressing upon his heart for utterance, let him utter it, in the stable, the market-place, the street, in the grove, under the open canopy of heaven, in the lowly cottage, or the lordly hall. No matter who or what he is, whether a graduate of a college, a shepherd from the hill sides, or a rustic from the plough. If he feels himself called to go forth in the name of God, he will speak words of truth and power, for which Humanity shall fare the better. But none of your hireling priests, your "dumb dogs" that will not bark. What are the priests of Christendom as they now are? Miserable panders to the prejudices of the age, loud in condemning sins nobody is guilty of, but silent as the grave when it concerns the crying sin of the times; bold as bold can be when there is no danger, but miserable cowards when it is necessary to speak out for God and outraged Humanity. As a body they never preach a truth till there is none whom it will indict. Never do they as a body venture to condemn sin in the concrete, and make each sinner feel "thou art the man." When the prophets of God have risen up and proclaimed the word of God, and, after persecution and death, led the people to acknowledge it to be the word of God, then your drivelling priest comes forward, and owns it to be a truth, and cries, "cursed of God and man is he who believes it not." But enough. The imbecility of an organized priesthood, of a hireling clergy, for all good, and its power only to demoralize the people and misdirect their energies, is beginning to be seen, and will one day be acknowledged. Men are beginning to speak out on this subject, and the day of reckoning is approaching. The people are rising up and asking of these priests whom they have fed, clothed, honored, and followed, What have ye done for the poor and friend-less, to destroy oppression, and establish the kingdom of God on earth? A fearful question for you, O ye priests, which we leave you to answer as best ye may.

The next step in this work of elevating the working classes will be to resuscitate the Christianity of Christ. The Christianity of the Church has done its work. We have had enough of that Christianity. It is powerless for good, but by no means powerless for evil. It now unmans us and hinders the growth of God's kingdom. The moral energy which is awakened it misdirects, and makes its deluded disciples believe that they have done their duty to God when they have joined the church, offered a prayer, sung a psalm, and contributed of their means to send out a missionary to preach unintelligible dogmas to the poor heathen, who, God knows, have unintelligible dogmas enough already, and more than enough. All this must be abandoned, and Christianity, as it came from Christ, be taken up, and preached, and preached in simplicity and in power.

According to the Christianity of Christ no man can enter the kingdom of God who does not labor with all zeal and diligence to establish the kingdom of God on the earth; who does not labor to bring down the high, and bring up the low; to break the fetters of the bound and set the captive free; to destroy all oppression, establish the reign of justice, which is the reign of equality, between man and man; to introduce new heavens and a new earth, wherein dwelleth righteousness, wherein all shall be as brothers, loving one another, and no one possessing what another lacketh. No man can be a Christian who does not labor to re-form society, to mould it according to the will of God and the nature of man; so that free scope shall be given to every man to unfold himself in all beauty and power, and to grow up into the stature of a perfect man in Christ Jesus. No man can be a Christian who does not refrain from all practices by which the rich grow richer and the poor poorer, and who does not do all in his power to elevate the laboring classes, so that one man shall not be doomed to toil while another enjoys the fruits; so that each man shall be free and independent, sitting under "his own vine and figtree with none to molest or to make afraid." We grant the power of Christianity in working out the reform we demand;

we agree that one of the most efficient means of elevating the working-men is to christianize the community. But you must christianize it. It is the gospel of Jesus you must preach, and not the gospel of the priests. Preach the Gospel of Jesus, and that will turn every man's attention to the crying evil we have designated, and will arm every Christian with power to effect those changes in social arrangements, which shall secure to all men the equality of position and condition, which it is already acknowledged they possess in relation to their rights. But let it be the genuine Gospel that you preach, and not that pseudo-gospel, which lulls the conscience asleep, and permits men to feel that they may be servants of God while they are slaves to the world, the flesh, and the devil; and while they ride roughshod over the hearts of their prostrate brethren. We must preach no Gospel that permits men to feel that they are honorable men and good Christians, although rich and with eyes standing out with fatness, while the great mass of their brethren are suffering from iniquitous laws, from mischievous social arrangements, and pining away for the want of the refinements and even the neces-saries of life.

We speak strongly and pointedly on this subject, because we are desirous of arresting attention. We would draw the public attention to the striking contrast which actually exists between the Christianity of Christ, and the Christianity of the Church. That moral and intellectual energy which exists in our country, indeed throughout Christendom, and which would, if rightly directed transform this wilderness world into a blooming paradise of God, is now by the pseudo-gospel, which is preached, rendered wholly inefficient, by being wasted on that which, even if effected, would leave all the crying evils of the times un-touched. Under the influence of the Church, our efforts are not directed to the reorganization of society, to the introduction of equality be-tween man and man, to the removal of the corruptions of the rich, and the wretchedness of the poor. We think only of saving our own souls, as if a man must not put himself so out of the case, as to be willing to be damned before he can be saved. Paul was willing to be accursed from Christ, to save his brethren from the vengeance which hung over them. But nevertheless we think only of saving our own souls; or if perchance our benevolence is awakened, and we think it desirable to labor for the salvation of others, it is merely to save them from imaginary sins and the tortures of an imaginary hell. The redemption of the world is understood to mean simply the restoration of mankind to the favor of God in the world to come. Their redemption from the evils of inequality, of factitious distinctions, and iniquitous social institutions, counts for nothing in the eyes of the Church. And this is its condemnation.

We cannot proceed a single step, with the least safety, in the great work of elevating the laboring classes, without the exaltation of sentiment, the generous sympathy and the moral courage which Christianity alone is fitted to produce or quicken. But it is lamentable to see how, by means of the mistakes of the Church, the moral courage, the generous sympathy, the exaltation of sentiment, Christianity does actually produce or quicken, is perverted, and made efficient only in producing evil, or hindering the growth of good. Here is wherefore it is necessary on the one hand to condemn in the most pointed terms the Christianity of the Church, and to bring out on the other hand in all its clearness, brilliancy, and glory the Christianity of Christ.

Having, by breaking down the power of the priesthood and the Christianity of the priests, obtained an open field and freedom for our operations, and by preaching the true Gospel of Jesus, directed all minds to the great social reform needed, and quickened in all souls the moral power to live for it or to die for it; our next resort must be to government, to legislative enactments. Government is instituted to be the agent of society, or more properly the organ through which society may perform its legitimate functions. It is not the master of society; its business is not to control society, but to be the organ through which society effects its will. Society has never to petition government; government is its servant, and subject to its commands.

Now the evils of which we have complained are of a social nature. That is, they have their root in the constitution of society as it is, and they have attained to their present growth by means of social influences, the action of government, of laws, and of systems and institutions upheld by society, and of which individuals are the slaves. This being the case, it is evident that they are to be removed only by the action of society, that is, by government, for the action of society is government.

But what shall government do? Its first doing must be an *un*doing.

There has been thus far quite too much government, as well as government of the wrong kind. The first act of government we want, is a still further limitation of itself. It must begin by circumscribing within narrower limits its powers. And then it must proceed to repeal all laws which bear against the laboring classes, and then to enact such laws as are necessary to enable them to maintain their equality. We have no faith in those systems of elevating the working classes, which propose to elevate them without calling in the aid of government. We must have government, and legislation expressly directed to this end.

But again what legislation do we want so far as this country is concerned? We want first the legislation which shall free the government, whether State or Federal, from the control of the Banks. The Banks represent the interest of the employer, and therefore of necessity interests adverse to those of the employed; that is, they represent the interests of the business community in opposition to the laboring community. So long as the government remains under the control of the Banks, so long it must be in the hands of the natural enemies of the laboring classes, and may be made, nay, will be made, an instrument of depressing them yet lower. It is obvious then that, if our object be the elevation of the laboring classes, we must destroy the power of the Banks over the government, and place the government in the hands of the laboring classes themselves, or in the hands of those, if such there be, who have an identity of interest with them. But this cannot be done so long as the Banks exist. Such is the subtle influence of credit, and such the power of capital, that a banking system like ours, if sustained, necessarily and inevitably becomes the real and efficient government of the country. We have been struggling for ten years in this country against the power of the banks, struggling to free merely the Federal government from their grasp, but with humiliating success. At this moment, the contest is almost doubtful,—not indeed in our mind, but in the minds of no small portion of our countrymen. The partizans of the Banks count on certain victory. The Banks discount freely to build "log cabins," to purchase "hard cider," and to defray the expense of manufacturing enthusiasm for a cause which is at war with the interests of the people. That they will succeed, we do not for one moment believe; but that they could maintain the struggle so long, and be as strong as they now are, at the end of ten years constant hostility, proves but all too well the power of the Banks, and their fatal influence on the political action of the community. The present character, standing, and resources of the Bank party, prove to a demonstration that the Banks must be destroyed, or the laborer not elevated. Uncompromising hostility to the whole banking system should therefore be the motto of every working man, and of every friend of humanity. The system must be destroyed. On this point there must be no misgiving, no subterfuge, no palliation. The system is at war with the rights and interest of labor, and it must go. Every friend of the system must be marked as an enemy to his race, to his country, and especially to the laborer. No matter who he is, in what party he is found, or what name he bears, he is, in our judgment, no true democrat, as he can be no true Christian.

Following the destruction of the Banks, must come that of all monopolies, of all PRIVILEGE. There are many of these. We cannot specify them all: we therefore select only one, the greatest of them all, the privilege which some have of being born rich while others are born poor. It will be seen at once that we allude to the hereditary descent of property, an anomaly in our American system, which must be removed, or the system itself will be destroyed. We cannot now go into a discussion of this subject, but we promise to resume it at our earliest opportunity. We only say now, that as we have abolished hereditary monarchy and hereditary nobility, we must complete the work by abolishing hereditary property. A man shall have all he honestly acquires, so long as he himself belongs to the world in which he acquires it. But his power over his property must cease with his life, and his property must then become the property of the state, to be disposed of by some equitable law for the use of the generation which takes his place. Here is the principle without any of its details, and this is the grand legislative measure to which we look forward. We see no means of elevating the laboring classes which can be effectual without this. And is this a measure to be easily carried? Not at all. It will cost infinitely more than it cost to abolish either hereditary monarchy or hereditary nobility. It is a great measure, and a startling. The rich, the business community, will never voluntarily consent to it, and we think we know too much of human nature to believe that it will ever be effected peaceably. It will be effected only by the strong arm of physical force. It will come, if it ever come at all, only at the conclusion of war, the like of which the world as yet has never witnessed, and from which, however inevitable it may seem to the eye of philosophy, the heart of Humanity recoils with horror.

We are not ready for this measure yet. There is much previous work to be done, and we should be the last to bring it before the legislature. The time, however, has come for its free and full discussion. It must be canvassed in the public mind, and society prepared for acting on it. No doubt they who broach it, and especially they who support it, will experience a due share of contumely and abuse. They will be regarded by the part of the community they oppose, or may be thought to oppose, as "graceless varlets," against whom every man of substance should set his face. But this is not, after all, a thing to disturb a wise man, nor to deter a true man from telling his whole thought. He who is worthy of the name of man, speaks what he honestly believes the interests of his race demand, and seldom disquiets himself about what may be the consequences to himself. Men have, for what they believed the cause of God or man, endured the dungeon, the scaffold, the stake, the cross, and they can do it again, if need be. This subject must be freely, boldly, and fully discussed, whatever may be the fate of those who discuss it.

7

WILLIS HALL

1801, born April 1, Granville, N.Y.
1824, was graduated from Yale College
1824–27, studied law in New York City and in Litchfield, Conn.
1827–31, practiced law in Mobile, Ala.
1831–38, practiced law in New York City
1837, member of New York State Assembly
1838–39, attorney general of New York State
1839–41, lectured in Law School at Saratoga, N.Y.
1842, member of New York State Assembly
1843, suffered a paralytic stroke
1848–68, lived in retirement
1868, died July 14

THE emphasis which Ingersoll had placed, at the very beginning of the trend of cultural discussion which has been presented, on the superiority of the American culture in technological and practical advance had become disturbing to many of the less democratic analysts of American culture. The defense of "liberal studies," of the humanities, was the point at which the attack on the practical, the useful, and the popular started. So, for example, William Goddard, in addressing the Phi Beta Kappa Society of Rhode Island in 1836, in defense of liberal studies, epitomized the whole argument thus:

Society every where seems to be running mad after what it deems the exclusively practical and useful. Every object of pursuit or of contemplation is subjected to some gross popular test, and if it fail to yield a coarse visible product, it may despair of any enthusiastic general favor. In estimating our social tendencies, this influence deserves particular attention; because the peculiar conditions of society under which we, as a people, are placed, seem to make a regard to utility almost a part of our religion.[1]

So, too, Tayler Lewis, in discussing the need for more emphasis on the religious implications of knowledge, in 1838, declared that

Immediate practical utility is becoming one of the cant phrases of the day. The spirit which gave rise to it, leaving its native sphere in the low region of modern

[1] William Goddard, *An Address*, Boston, 1837, p. 22.

politics and political economy, is found invading the higher departments of science, and endeavoring to subject them to its groveling standard. We are told of the time wasted in the abstract or theoretical sciences, in the acquisition of mere words, or in exploded theological speculations which are behind the spirit of the age. It is lamented that years should be thus squandered, which might be devoted to branches of *immediate practical utility* having direct bearing upon the wants and business of life.

Analyze what is meant by this phrase, and you will invariably find it to terminate in something which has relation to the mere physical constitution of man, using the term in its lowest sense. The advocates of this course, 'tis true, profess to cultivate the mind, but ever as the means to something else. . . . The soul is to be disciplined, and treated physiologically, for the sake of the body; the immortal for the sake of the mortal part.[2]

N. C. Brooks made a similar point at Gettysburg in 1840, but expressed it as a broader social criticism.

The genius of the present age is utilitarian. The inventive faculty is taxed to the utmost for the applications of science to the different mechanic arts; commercial enterprise seeks to open new avenues of trade; manual labor is abridged; hidden sources of wealth are evolved; the physical wants of man are supplied, and his bodily comfort promoted.

But while the acquisition of wealth is thus rendered easy, and time and resources are provided for a more extensive cultivation and refinement of the intellectual faculties, it is to be regretted that opulence is regarded as an end, rather than a means, of happiness; and accordingly all the energies of the mind are absorbed in a base passion for wealth—ambitious luxury, and vulgar display. The discoveries of science—the investigations of philosophy, the power and pathos of oratory, and the inspirations of song, are all valued in proportion as they minister to lucre, and are converted into gold by the alchymy of the times.[3]

Thus, Caleb Sprague Henry was not alone in his criticisms, though his suggestion of a "learned order" to stand outside of these general trends was unusual.

Just as in the contemporary controversy over the very same issue, a variety of intermediate positions were taken by contributors to the discussion a century ago. A typical middle-of-the-road position was that taken by Albert Hopkins, professor of mathematics and natural philosophy at Williams College, in 1838. Hopkins did not believe that any educational plan

[2] Tayler Lewis, *Faith the Life of Science; an address delivered before the Pi Beta Phi Society of Union College, Schenectady, N.Y., July 1838*, Albany, 1838, p. 7.

[3] N. C. Brooks, *The Utility of Classical Studies; an address; pronounced before the Philomathaean Society of Pennsylvania College, at Gettysburg, Pa., on the anniversary February 14, 1840*, Baltimore, 1840, p. 5.

should "discard utility altogether as an object." He felt, however, that the United States stood in danger of developing "a species of empiricism favorable to any thing rather than the promotion of sound science." His general point he expressed thus:

The epithet practical, as applied to our times, is descriptive of them; not because we have less theory now than formerly—the world was never so speculative—but because the theoretical is made subordinate and valued only as subservient to its applications. These applications . . . respect, for the most part, and centre in the achievement of a good which has little or nothing moral in its elements. . . . The remark so often made and so currently received, that the age is one of dogmatical empiricism and visionary speculation . . . in general appears not to be well founded. The wildness of conjecture is tempered by a turn for the useful, and the subordination of the practical to just theoretical principles is better understood than formerly. It must be confessed, however . . . that selfishness has given too much prominence to the question "cui bono." Intellect has thus become tainted with a secularizing spirit, a spirit which as usual has found its way through into the heart, and which would fain measure and gauge the affections by the rules of a sordid and calculating self-interest.[4]

For reproduction here, as typical of the extreme statement of a practical, utilitarian point of view, Willis Hall's Yale Phi Beta Kappa address of 1844 has been chosen. Hall's emphasis on the principle of utility, "the greatest good of the greatest number," allies him with Richard Hildreth, whose *Theory of Morals* was published in the same year as this address, among the few Benthamites in American intellectual life. Hall examines the entire history of philosophy in a rapid sketch designed to show the "barren waste" left by philosophy before Bacon. "She has been the guide and controller of mind, from the time of Aristotle to that of Bacon. . . . But where is her patent office? What has she done for the physical advancement of man?"

Hall also defends with ardor the motive of self-interest in morals, and is unique in America in this respect. He describes self-interest as the form which the principle of utility takes in questions relating solely to the individual. Finally, he applies the whole development of utility to proving that democracy is the only acceptable form of government, and advocates an open and direct appeal to utility in education. "It is upon a generation of generous youths refined and elevated in this manner, and habituated in every thing they do to look upon it in the light of the most enlarged and liberal utility, that our government, built up out of the fragments of a thousand states, will rest and be perpetuated."

[4] Albert Hopkins, *An Address, Delivered at the Opening of the Observatory of Williams College, June 12, 1838*, Pittsfield, no date, p. 5.

ADDRESS

Delivered August 14, 1844 before the Society of Phi Beta Kappa in Yale College

BY the recent report of the Commissioner of Patents, it appears that the whole number of patents issued by the United States, from the establishment of the office, to January 8, 1844, scarce half a century, amounts to the incredible sum of thirteen thousand five hundred and twenty three. How have the elements been put to the question, and racked, and tortured, to extort their secrets for the benefit of man! Bacon declared at his day "there remained a world of sciences and inventions unknown;" and research has ever since been verifying the truth of this assertion, and developing the wonders which he foretold.

There is no limit to the career of improvement—from the humblest agency to the highest—from the patent razor-strop to the power-loom —from the improved churn, which curtails the painful labors of the housewife, to the applications of galvanism; its range is as wide as the elements. Look at galvanism alone; it already propels the car, it plates the wire, it writes upon steel, it has superseded the pains of lithotomy. It has robbed Jason of his honors; the golden fleece is no longer a fable.

The island of Great Britain, by means of its machinery, now performs more labor than the empire of China. The United States, by the application of new discoveries to arts and to agriculture, now accumulates more capital annually, than seventy millions would have accomplished two centuries ago. The powers of nature are inexhaustible, the discovery of one principle facilitates that of another, and multiplies the chances of some new invention—something, which like the application of steam, shall revolutionize society.

Hitherto the patents granted have been on the gradual increase, amounting to an average of two hundred and fifty per annum. Last year the number allowed amounted to five hundred. The spacious and beautiful edifice of the Patent Office is already crowded; the spectator is lost amidst the confused mass of improved ploughs, fanning mills, furnaces, chronometers, philosophical instruments, water wheels, and printing presses, to say nothing of the innumerable improvements in the various processes of the arts, as in the preparation of leather, glass, building materials, and wearing apparel.

This too, it will be observed, is the result of but a few years in an obscure quarter of the world. All Europe, with her two hundred and fifty millions of inhabitants, has been engaged in this career for two hundred years, and is now pursuing it with increased ardor and success.

The prize held out is splendid beyond the dreams of antiquity. The fame of Fulton, the wealth of Watt, dazzle the eyes of the projector. Whatever is most prized or sought for among men is given without measure and without stint to successful ingenuity. It is a well ascertained law, that the increase of the human family is limited to a supply of the means of support. Wherever new channels of industry are opened, nature's children seem to rush in to feast on her exuberance. What philanthropist will not rejoice at the masses thus added to the great sum of human enjoyment!—at the millions that thus become participants of the joys of this living and breathing world! What Christian will not thank God for the added myriads who will swell the chorus of his praise! What man but will exclaim with Bacon, "all knowledge, limited by religion, is to be referred to *use* and action!"

The world is now nearly six thousand years old. Strike from the transmitted wealth of the past the accumulation of the last three centuries, and what have we left! Little besides the ground we stand upon. Go back but a few years, and all beyond is a barren waste. Proud philosophy! She has been the guide and controller of mind, from the time of Aristotle to that of Bacon, a period of more than two thousand years. But where is her patent office? What has she done for the physical advancement of man? The same mental labor which has been expended, if properly directed, would have filled the world with the comforts and conveniences of life, abrogated that vast portion of crime which springs from poverty, and elevated the moral condition of man far above its present standard.

I will, with your permission, dwell a moment upon this ancient barrenness, and the vicious tendency of the schools, and ascertain their cause and contrast them with the productiveness of recent times, and close with a few remarks upon *utility* as a motive and a rule of human conduct. The wisdom gathered from a perpetual recurrence to the errors of the past, is the surest guide to future improvement.

The *discipline* and *methods* of instruction of the ancients, were in many respects mischievous. They made a mystery of knowledge. Plato declares that "it is a difficult thing to discover the Creator of the universe, and being discovered it is impossible and would even be impious to expose the discovery to vulgar understanding." He did not indeed close the door of his school, nor exact an oath of secrecy from his pupils, like Pythagoras; but he, as well as Aristotle and most of the philosophers, had his esoteric and exoteric doctrines. The first of these they taught only to the select few; the second were the doctrines which they promulgated to the world. In teaching their students to love philosophy, they made them esteem themselves; in training them to aspire to an elevated object, they led them to look with scornful pride upon the mass beneath, for whom they professed to have no regard, and with whom it was their highest boast to have no sympathy. All this tended to create unworthy distinctions among men, and to secure the sway of arbitrary power. Plato, Aristotle, and other ancient teachers, are said to have dressed themselves splendidly, and with as much regard to scenic effect upon their schools, as stage-players upon their audience.

This affectation of peculiarity in dress and manners, has tinged the habits of the studious world even to the present day. The costume of all professions until recently, was invariably the flowing gown; the professions of divinity and law, in Europe, still retain the dress of Aristotle, and it is feared, cling to many other vanities of his school, more puerile and degrading.

Thus much for the mere habits and discipline of their schools. Their *doctrines* exercised a still more important influence; many of them were radically wrong, and tended only to increase the superstition of the age. All believed that matter was eternal, and most that it was sentient. Pythagoras believed in a soul of the world—that all matter was animated with a *spirit*—that there was but one soul in the universe, which was all-pervasive, and of which the souls of individuals were parts.

Plato is said by some of his followers to have taught, that every object possessed an unconscious soul. Thales and some of the earlier philosophers, did not separate mind from motion; they taught that the magnet was animated with a spirit. This was fostering the deepest source of vulgar superstition—that matter, especially such as moves, feels. Hence the bleeding bush of Virgil, from which issued the voice of Polydorus. Hence the enchanted forest of Tasso; Rinaldo sees his beloved Chlorinda start from every pine, and every myrtle is embraced by the beautiful and imploring Armida. No wonder that the unreasoning but sympathetic multitude, should people every grove with hamadryads, every brook with nymphs, and that every breeze should be laden with the wailings of spirits. No wonder that such men, with such instructions, should become, like the Athenians, "in all things too superstitious."

If poets are to be literally considered as *creators,* the true poets of antiquity were their philosophers. Their grave theories of the formation of the universe, surpassed any thing ancient or modern in wildness of invention. Considered as intended for sober truth, the fairies and the genii of the Arabian Nights Entertainment, do not make such draughts upon credulity.

Plato, and after him his pupil Aristotle, imagined the universe to consist of ten spheres, like ten concave globes, one within the other; in the outward, an infinite circle of *cerulean,* silent, motionless and self-willed, they placed the Omnipotent; next came the *crystalline* sphere, or *primum mobile,* which receiving its motion from the motionless First Cause, communicates it through the universe. It is thus described by the Portuguese poet:

> "Within its shining frame,
> In motion swifter than the lightning's flame,
> Swifter than sight the moving parts may spy,
> Another sphere whirls round its rapid sky;
> Hence motion darts,—its force impulsive draws,
> And on the other orbs impresses laws."

The eighth sphere in the system of these philosophers, is called the starry heavens; this is the spangled vault which presents itself to the naked eye. The seven planets were supposed to revolve in the seven subordinate spheres, to which they gave names.

It is strange that a theory so fanciful and so puerile, should have gained the credence of mankind, during a period commencing four centuries before Christ, and terminating with the general adoption of the Christian religion, about four centuries after; but it is obvious, that this theory, as well as most of the speculations of these philosophers, such as the numbers of Pythagoras, and the ideas or plastic forms of Plato, were more calculated to cultivate and strengthen the imagination than the reason.

But bad as were the *doctrines* of the ancient schools, the utter *perversion* of the *true object* of study, was the capital error of the ancient philosophy. They attempted to invert the order of acquisition; they uniformly endeavored to abstract the soul from the body, and educate it separately, instead of considering it as God made it, and educating them together. They constantly aimed to make men love *virtue*, or immutable truth, or some other abstract and metaphysical name, while they should have striven to make them love labor. The last was humble, but practicable; the first lofty, but incomprehensible and impossible. By saying that they inverted the order of acquisition, I mean to affirm, that virtue is merely an inference—that, by inculcating a love of labor, the advantages of the arts, the love of our fellow men, the excellency of contributing to the enjoyments of human life, the love of virtue would have followed. Seneca says, "It is not the office of philosophy to teach men how to use their hands; the object of her lessons is to form the soul." But the only way to teach men how to form the soul, is to teach them first how most judiciously to use the hands.

Thus we see, that while their discipline and doctrines served to swell the pride of man, inflame the imagination, widen the gulf between the different classes of the human family, pamper power by inculcating authority, their visionary, speculative and fruitless object brought the blight of barrenness upon two thousand years of human thought.

Let it not be supposed, that it is a part of my plan to enter upon a crusade against the learning of the ancients. No man can appreciate more highly than I do, their contributions to geometry, and the almost perfect models which they have bequeathed us in every department of belles-lettres. Their perfection only renders regret the more poignant, that their efforts in the physical and moral sciences had not received a more useful and practical direction. The most enthusiastic apologist sees not more clearly, that it is unfair to judge them by a modern standard. Their books were few, and obtained by great labor or expense; men of thought were rare; there was no interchange of the intellectual and moral wealth of nations,—all was at first confined to the Greek, afterwards to the Greek and Latin. The progress of science had been continually interrupted by wars and commotions, and at last it was engulfed by one universal uprising of the elements of savagery. Besides, the depositories of their limited learning have been from time to time annihilated. The first library, that of Pisistratus, was destroyed by Xerxes; the celebrated collection of Aristotle was scattered soon after his death,—most of it went into that of the Ptolemies at Alexander, which was consumed by the rash and ignorant soldiers of Julius Cæsar. The library of the Roman empire, preserved in the temple of Apollo, was destroyed by lightning. In later times the fire of Omar will be remembered, the bigotry of Pope Gregory, and the vanity of Almaman, to each of which the most precious remains of antiquity fell a sacrifice. Still, abundance remains to show the character and direction of the ancient philosophy. Much that was valuable, though it has now become superseded by modern discoveries, has remained to recent times as a monument of the extraordinary genius of those sages, who could so indelibly stamp their own minds on the great current of human thought. We can not forget that the astronomical theory of Pythagoras differs little from that of Copernicus, or that the atomic theory of Epicurus seems to be demonstrated by modern chemistry. Recent experiments have also proved the truth of Plato's theory, that bodies are combined in numerical proportion.

In process of time, the ancient schools were swallowed up in the modern professions. The theories of Epicurus and Aristotle on physics, were especially regarded by physicians, although the authority of this latter writer was paramount on almost every subject of human investigation. In the church, although at first denounced, his writings were at length admitted as a commentary on the Bible, and the commentary was read with more zeal, and deemed of more weight than the text.

The doctrines of the Academy harmonized more with the principles of the Christian religion. Indeed the gospel of St. John opens with an expression which can not fail to be recognized as the language of the Academy, by all who remember the λόγος of Plato. The professors of jurisprudence may be said to be the descendants of Zeno, —at least the subtle disquisitions of the Stoics had this practical effect, that they furnished the lawyers with maxims, definitions and distinctions, on which they have erected a noble and far-extending science. It is right however to say, that their definitions were never intended for any such practical purpose; they pursued no such contemptible object; they disdained to be useful. They never sought the forum,—they would not tarnish their dignity with the dust of the courts; but the lawyers sought *them*. Jurisprudence was formerly called philosophy, and its professors, divided into Πράκτοι and Ἄπρακτοι, were called philosophers. No one was thought qualified to practice law, who had not spent years in studying philosophy; that is, the wordy, subtle, quibbling philosophy of the Stoics. Their language was noble; it was the language of the gods. Their promises were more magnificent than Golconda,—their performance "as poor as winter." To the followers of Zeno we are indebted for that great maxim, which lies at the corner of our republican edifice, that "all men are born free and equal." It is a truth of world-wide importance, and while we express our boundless gratitude to them, we must admit that, in *practice*, they were the most subservient and basest sycophants of arbitrary power,—proclaiming the natural liberty of man, and at the same time kneeling to Tiberius, justifying the cruelties of Nero, and flattering every despot that ever sat on a Roman or barbarian throne.

They too were the first to discover and proclaim the absurdity of human *bondage*. "That man," they exclaimed, "to whom all other things were given as property, should be *himself* the subject of property, is monstrous. Man the slave of man,—the Anthropophagi, with heads beneath their shoulders, were not so gross a violation of the nature of things." Noble language! The whole world listened; the poor slave erected himself,—bright hope beamed once more in his haggard eye. But the Stoic speaks again: "*Slaves* are *things*, and *things* are justly under the dominion of man." The slave again bent beneath his burthen, and his hopes vanished forever! This is a fair specimen of the fruitlessness, verbiage and equivocation of their proud philosophy. So with reference to utility, they held, according to Cicero, that "from birth the animal, human and brute, directs his attention to conciliating or procuring those things which are preservative of himself." But, though they admitted the truth of the utilitarian doctrine, they were the most useless and trifling of men; they soared infinitely above its practical application. They were constantly haunted by a spectre which they called the "*dignity* of human nature," which frightened them from every thing useful, and gave them a strained and stilted morality. Bacon says, that "it is no less true in this human kingdom of knowledge, than in God's kingdom of heaven, that no man shall enter into it except that first he become as a little child." Their foundation was right; had they built upon it they would have constructed a refuge from sorrow and from shame; but their pride ruined all. Theirs was a philosophy of great swelling worlds, but of paltry results.

Two great misfortunes befell the Christian religion; the first and the minor one was its early union with philosophy. The most distinguished of modern philosophers has said, that "the prejudice hath been infinite that both divine and human knowledge have received by the intermingling and tempering the one with the other—as that which hath filled the one full of heresies, and the other full of speculative fictions and vanities." The one threw its robe of pride over the coarse garment of the fisherman. The other subjected to the vain fallibility of human reason what was intended only for the eye of faith, and gave up its sacred mysteries and revelations to be mingled with the vagaries of philosophy.

The second, and by far the greater evil, was the union of temporal and spiritual authority. The conversion of Constantine, and the consequent elevation of the humble religion of the cross to the divided throne of the world—the union of church and state—although at the time deemed an event glorious in itself, has been proved by the experience of several centuries of a world sunk in darkness and in slavery, to have been most baleful to human happiness, and most disastrous to the Christian religion. Had Constantine continued to persecute and oppress, religion would have continued as at first, humble and useful, full of sympathy for the multitude, dispensing its hopes and consolations to those who most require them. Its progress would have been that of the flood, first covering the humble valleys of the poor, and at last completing the work of universal charity by embracing the high places of power. It would then have taken possession of temporal thrones as a conqueror to be obeyed, and as the friend of man to be loved; not as a jealous equal to be conciliated, or a *particeps criminis* to be watched and feared.

But this ill-omened alliance was now complete, the church of Christ, civil government, and the philosophy of the schools.

Self-conceited *philosophy*, bloated with her vain-glorious pride, and black with hatred of the ignoble vulgar, proclaimed that the mass of men were born to be slaves.

The *church*, under the insidious maxim that the command of God *makes* right, and that the decrees of the church are his voice, erected the monstrous fallacy of the infallibility of Rome.

Civil *government*, borrowing the pregnant maxims of her obsequious allies, stamped with a divine sanction the power of the worst of rulers, and enforced with a divine command the slavery of the people.

I will not advert to the darkness of the middle ages, consequent upon this conspiracy against human rights. Never was the intellect so poor, and never so vain of its achievements. The mind was doomed for centuries to describe the same idle and never ending circle. All minds were drawn into these magic vortices; all thought was employed in physics, in ascertaining the nature and extent of stellar influence, casting nativities, seeking for the stone of transmutation, or the elixir of immortality; and in metaphysics, in solving the grave questions—Whether "spirit has essence, independent of existence?" Whether an angel can see in darkness? Whether God loves the greatest possible non-existing angel better than the smallest existing insect? Abelard on his return to the University of Paris, after an absence of two years, says that "he found the students still discussing the same old questions—whether spirit has extension? whether it can be in two places at the same time?" and such idle puerilities, the decision of which is utterly impossible, and as immaterial as it is impossible. It was not through apathy, that the mind retrograded from its natural onward march of improvement. At no period have the colleges and schools of Europe been more thronged; two or three thousand are said to have crowded to hear the lectures of Abelard, and several equally popular schools of law and philosophy are said to have existed at the same time in England. What then was the cause of the extreme paucity or the utter absence of results from so much mental labor? It was the utter neglect of that immutable law of our moral and physical nature, that man seeks his own preservation. This was considered and treated as a deformity to be concealed, not as a principle to be educated as destined to give complexion to all our conduct. Men refused to glide forward easily on the current of nature, but chose rather to offer a useless opposition; hence all the barrenness, all the absurdities, all the mysteries and the mischiefs which we have described, from the curious imaginings of Pythagoras to the senseless jargon of the scholastics. They were blinded by their pride. Philosophy disdained to be useful! Science scorned an alliance with the arts!

The first faint effort of common sense to throw off some portion of the incubus which the schools had heaped upon her, was made by the *nominalists* in the eleventh century. The dispute between them and the *realists* was not, as has been supposed, some vain question of scholastic discussion,—it was a struggle against the materialism of thought. Plato and Aristotle maintained, that the ideas of genera and species were impressed or daguerreotyped upon matter at its creation. The nominalists contended, that these universal ideas had neither form nor essence, and were no more than mere terms and nominal representations.

Long and eventful was the contest; all Europe was disturbed for centuries with the noise of the conflict. On the part of the realists were enlisted the three great allies, the church, the state, and the schools of the philosophers. On the part of the nominalists the more distinguished names were John the sophist, Robert of Paris, Rosaline of Compagne, Abelard, Porphyry, Occam, Gerson, and Luther. But, after bloody persecutions, martyrdoms, even wars among the nations, the nominalists triumphed; and their triumph maimed, if it did not destroy, one of the tripartite alliance. The dead weight of philosophy was gone, the mind became more buoyant; one of the chains was broken; it became more free. What was left unfinished by this contest was completed by Luther at the Reformation. He grappled with another of the allies, and strove to restore religion to its original simplicity, purity, and humility. He separated it in a great measure from its disastrous connection with temporal power. It no longer pressed with crushing weight upon human rights, but became, as it was first intended, the corner-stone of the fabric of human liberty. Reformers sprung up every where, responsive to his voice. Men of distant nations, who were unacquainted with each other, who spoke not the same language,—Zuinglius of Switzerland, Melancthon and Erasmus of Germany, Latimer and Coverdale of England, Farel and Lefevre in France,—heard and understood. They were the mountain-tops watching over the silent and mist-covered valleys beneath; and the vividness and rapidity of the work of the Reformation, reminds us of the poet's description of a thunder storm among the Alps:

> "From peak to peak leaps the live thunder"—

not from one lone cloud, but

> —"every mountain now hath found a tongue,
> And Jura answers from her misty shroud,
> Back to the joyous Alps, which cry to her aloud."

Thus the other of the great oppressors of human thought was removed, or rather converted into a friend. The disastrous alliance was broken up, the mind stood forth disembarrassed but uncultivated; untaught, but at the same time unbiassed. Thus far it was not advanced, but only disincumbered; stripped for the race, but no steps taken in its career;—prepared for any direction that might be given to it.

At this time the immortal Bacon arose. We can not sufficiently express our admiration at the perfect preparation which was made for his appearance; no character of the drama ever entered upon the stage more apropos to the development of the plot. A few years sooner and his voice would have been drowned in the clamor of the schools; a few years later, and the mind would again have received a false direction from which the powers of Verulam would have been inadequate to recall it.

He commenced, not so much by establishing a new philosophy, as by divesting the mind of *all* philosophy,—by planting it firmly upon the rocks of *common sense* (called by a distinguished writer the "*genius of humanity*") and *common experience*. Although he calls his method the Novum Organum, to distinguish it from the old Organon of Aristotle, it might with equal propriety be called the *nullum organum*, that is, no "*artificial method*"— "the way of nature," or those ordinary teachings of experience pursued equally in the highest investigations of science, and by the brutes themselves in seeking shelter from the peltings of "the pitiless storm."

His predecessors, as we have seen, were too proud to be useful; their shot, elevated above mortality, but too weak to reach the stars, spent its force upon the idle air. He, on the other hand, in his own quaint language declares, that "the access to his work has been by that port or passage which the divine Majesty doth infallibly continue and observe; that is the felicity wherewith he hath blessed a *humility* of mind, such as rather laboreth to spell and so by degrees to read the volumes of his creatures, than to solicit and urge, and as it were to invocate a man's own spirit, to divine and give oracles unto him." Their love of abstract speculation led them to make even physics metaphysical. He utterly disregarded metaphysics, except so far as they contributed to some practical and useful end.

No wonder that these opposite courses should produce the most opposite results. Theirs it has been the object of this digression to illustrate. His are before and around us. Utility found no place in their vocabulary; he inculcates it in every sentence as the only proper guide and object in all our pursuits.

Already have the *commoda vitæ* accumulated immensely under his system, which is destined ultimately to enrich the whole human family, and go far to eradicate poverty and crime.

I do not mean to confound mere *practical* philosophy with utilitarianism. It is admitted that in our own time Bentham has gone farther than Bacon, and has considered utility not only as a guide and an end, but as a motive of action, and as a law of our nature. Whether his theory be true or false, it must be admitted that his reasonings from this law of our nature have been wonderfully successful in pointing out right qualities in governments and legislation.

The most distinguished philosopher of modern times has facetiously intimated that the fall of our first parents was caused by the too earnest discussion of the metaphysical question of the constitution of good and evil. Thus warned, I shall be careful not to commit so great a sin.

The utmost apparent diversity has prevailed among modern philosophers, as to the essential quality which enters into all right action. Cumberland calls it practical *reason;* Grotius, the preservation of human *society;* Cudworth follows Plato and his school in supposing it *virtue;* Clark, the *fitness of things;* Wollaston, *truth;* More, the *boniform faculty.* This quaint name gave rise to what Shaftsbury and his followers to the present day have called the *moral sense;* Malebranche calls this quality the love of *universal order;* Butler, *conscience;* Adam Smith, *sympathy;* Hartley, *association of ideas;* Tucker, *translation of ideas;* Brown, *suggestion of ideas.* But this diversity is only apparent. They may all, with sufficient precision, be thrown into two great classes—viz. those who suppose that all our notions have an intellectual origin, and those who believe that some of them at least spring from emotion; those who suppose that all action arises from instinctive and intellectual nature, having reference solely to our self-preservation, modified by our relations and guided by experience, and those who suppose that all action, or so much at least as relates to right and wrong, springs from some involuntary emotion, or separate moral nature superior to the intellect, which acts not in reference to self, but to some abstract and perfect rule of right and wrong.

To this last theory there seem to be three objections—it is *unproved* —it is *unnecessary.*

"Nec Deus intessit
Nisi sit dignus vindice nodus,"

is a maxim as true in metaphysical philosophy as in the art of poetry. Even Stuart, Mackintosh and others, the great champions of a moral sense, admit that it may have been an after growth. They insist that there is an apparent disinterestedness, whether it arise from an original cause or a subsequent result. This is admitting the whole question. The utilitarians contend for no more. They do not deny the existence of liberality, of benevolence, of charity, of heroism, and of magnanimity, and that they all spring apparently in some instances from a disinterested impulse. So the unreflecting suppose, that they see the distance and shape of objects, although it is certain that these are only the result of judgment from their appearance. The utilitarians define charity, for instance, the rejection of a little present indulgence in favor of a great future happiness.

Another objection to this theory is, that it confounds the distinction between a motive and a criterion. All acknowledge the existence of a moral taste as well as a natural one, and that it is equally liable to be depraved; but it no more originates moral action, than natural taste can be said to originate a breakfast.

Again, this theory was constructed to obviate a supposed difficulty of predicating guilt or innocence of human action; but it is obvious that there is as much merit in obeying a necessity of our nature called self-love, as in obeying one dignified with the title of a moral sense; nor is there any more sin in violating the laws of a moral sense, than in violating those laws of self-preservation which our all-wise Creator has impressed upon our nature.

On the whole perhaps the simplest, the safest, and the truest principle, is that all action, whether good or bad, voluntary or involuntary, springs from the laws of nature, reason and instinct, directed to *self-preservation*, as the motive and the end. It is at least a safe criterion. Sir James Mackintosh, although an ardent advocate of disinterested emotions, declares that "the whole sagacity of the wisdom of the world, may be safely challenged to point a case in which virtuous dispositions, habits and feelings, are not conducive in the highest degree to the happiness of the individual." So that even by the confession of its enemies, utility is always a *safe guide* to virtuous conduct.

In favor of self-preservation, as a law of our nature, universal analogy may be adduced; the form of every vegetable that grows, the unerring instinct of every animal, point to their self-preservation. Natural religion deduces the conclusion of an omniscient architect, from these evidences of design. All the functions of our bodies, on which life depends, the beating of our hearts, the breathing of our lungs, are placed beyond the reach of our volition, but are conducted exclusively with reference to our preservation. All our instincts, all our propensities, all our passions, although often perverted from this purpose, have an obvious reference to the same object. The same divine architect, who contrived the involuntary, made also the voluntary part of our natures, and analogy would incline us to the belief, that he pursued the same object in both cases.

I am aware of the scorn with which this doctrine has been spurned by distinguished men; they have deemed it unworthy a good man, to be governed by no higher motive than his own greatest happiness. It does not make the gulf which separates the learned from the ignorant, wide enough to suit their pride; they wish not to be better than, but to be different from the vulgar mass; they labor to escape the disgrace of a community with mankind; they run upon the tops of their toes and would fain persuade the world that they fly; they would build up a sort of hero-worship. The only faculties of the vulgar herd which they would cultivate, are those of wonder, reverence and admiration.

But if utility is denounced on account of its humility, the charge will avail little with those who think with Bacon, that this is the only door of entrance into the kingdom of knowledge, and who remember that the same charge was made from the same source against the religion of Christ. If it raises what is humble and prostrates what is elevated, it only assimilates the more to the divine command "to love our neighbor as ourself." But it may truly be said, if it is low, it is at least intelligible; if we have a humble, we certainly have a safe guide,—if it does not conduct us to an impossible virtue, it will never lead to crime,—if it does not make us gods, it will surely make us better men.

Much of this opposition to utility, has doubtless arisen from increasing admiration of German transcendentalism. The influence of that philosophy is yet limited, but it is all employed to sap the foundations of laws, government and religion. However pure may be some of its professors, they are destined to share the fate of poor Epicurus and his philosophy. Abandoned men perverted his doctrines to sanction every thing most debasing and profligate. The name of the most abstemious of men, the anchorite of philosophers, became synonymous with indulgence. These men are struggling to bring back the mysteries, the folly and the fruitlessness of the old philosophy. They are imitating the miserable pride of the disciples of Zeno, by preferring form to substance, seeking rather to excite astonishment, by clothing old truths in new paradoxes, than by discovering new truths and explaining them to the world in plain language; they prefer the surprise excited by the slight of hand of the mountebank, or the tricks of a juggler, to the honest praise of a good mechanic.

It is with no ordinary pride, that I turn to this celebrated seat of the muses, and find its professors still foremost among the champions of sound learning and far reaching utility. They still inculcate in their lessons, that the only object of science is to enrich the world; the final use of all learning, but to strengthen the judgment, and to enable it more certainly to secure the ultimate good.

This new philosophy, uprooting and prostrating with blind hostility, the bulwarks as well as the abuses of society, solicits them in vain. This monstrous creation of a foreign soil has no place here; this misshapen production of vanity, fermenting with the admitted wrongs of foreign institutions, dares not approach these sacred portals.

The space allowed me will barely permit of illustrating the principle of utility in some of the more ordinary relations of life.

This philosophy beholds man with hopes, with longings, with thoughts, stretching far beyond this world, which nothing but the revelations of religion can satisfy. In the various misfortunes and sorrows incident to this life, she discovers that the more stately preachings of philosophy about fortitude—the superiority of mind to physical ills—are empty mouthings, and that nothing but the soothing hopes of religion have been found to alleviate the distress of mental suffering; consequently she leads man to religion. Other philosophies, proud, conceited, self-sufficient, would be themselves the physicians, she only the handmaid; they aspire to be the rivals, she the humble follower; and when her temporal task is done, she resigns her charge to the fruition of an immortality she has given her humble aid to inculcate throughout life.

Again, the simple maxim of the pursuit of individual good, becomes in society the pursuit of the good of the greatest number. No additional element whatever intermingles with this fundamental maxim of voluntary society; it is simply the pursuit of individual good modified by each man's social relations. When individualism, says Guizot, is absolute, society is impossible; society is necessary for protection, and government necessary for society. The individual is compelled by his nature and the circumstances which surround him to become a member of society, and the only condition on which he can be admitted is to pursue the greatest good of the greatest number. The same principle which leads to the formation of governments, dictates also, when undisturbed, that these governments shall be popular in their form. This appears by the following illustration; the whole world has concurred in the remark of Montesquieu, which I shall therefore assume—that "honesty is the principle of republics, honor of monarchies, and fear of despotisms." It can not be for the greatest happiness that all should be governed by fear; despotism must therefore be rejected.

Honor is defined, the distinction of one above many; it can not be for the greatest happiness of the greatest number, that the majority should be oppressed by the elevation of a few at their expense; monarchy and every species of aristocracy must therefore be rejected. As there is no other kind of government but that of the many, it follows that this species of government alone meets the terms of this proposition. The same thing may be demonstrated in various ways. That the dictates of utility require that government be administered on this principle, appears from the fact that such a government is more likely to be *right* than any other.

The idiosyncrasy of every man leads him to take his own particular view of every subject presented for his decision. Almost all the differences in life arise from viewing the same thing from different points. The more numerous the voters in any community, the more numerous the points of view of any given subject, and the less the probability that any circumstance will escape the observation of those who are required by law to decide upon its adoption or rejection.

Utility dictates such a form of government for another reason,—that it is more likely to be safe and enduring, because the government, being influenced by practical men of every pursuit, will be less likely to come in collision with any great interest. Such a collision often produces revolts and revolutions in other governments. But even if a disturbance should occur, there is no danger of overthrowing the government, for it is built upon the maxim of the greatest good to the greatest number. They can not enjoy more, and they will voluntarily accept of no form of government which gives less.

Utility suggests still another reason for this form of government, which is indeed but a branch or corollary of the last. It is capable of indefinite improvement. In other governments, admitted salutary reforms are rejected through fear of innovation. "Monarchs are perplexed through fear of change." When one or a few are conscious of having arrogated to themselves advantages which belong to the body at large, they are naturally solicitous to retain them. The foundation of such a government is narrow and weak. It stands like an inverted pyramid. Improvement in any one particular may lead to the overthrow of the whole edifice. But in a government founded upon this principle, which we have seen can not in the nature of things be overthrown, experiment may follow experiment like the waves; innovation has no terrors; novelties are invited and freely examined, and improvements even in fundamental law adopted without injury. There is no limit to this law but the injury which arises from change itself. Enough has been said to show that this maxim lies at the foundation of democratic government. Modern improvement in representation has obviated the principal objection, and rendered it accessible even to the most extended nations. Nor is it a sanguine anticipation, that this principle of the greatest good will ultimately prevail throughout the world. It is a law of human nature, as much as gravity is a law of matter; and in the chances and changes of human affairs, as men and nations are placed in favorable circumstances for its action, it will surely develop itself. Thus much for the application of this principle to the *forms* of government.

Its adaptations to the *administration* of government, are equally familiar to every American; but the illustration of the wide application of the principle of utility, and the repeated injunction to recur often to first principles, must excuse its triteness. A government conducted on this principle, requires that all its functions should be discharged by the people themselves. By the people themselves I mean, in contradistinction from a class salaried, educated and set apart for any particular duty. Every citizen becomes in turn a magistrate, a soldier or a juryman. To say nothing of the faithful, honest and economical discharge of these functions, secured by such a system, its indirect benefits, by educating the people, by accustoming them to the exercise of power, by identifying them occasionally with the government itself, are incalculable. In this point of view, who can estimate the advantages arising from *jury duty*. I venture to say it does more towards disseminating among the people a practical knowledge of their rights and duties, than our schools, academies, and every other means of instruction. The accustoming the citizen to command as well as obey, tends to elevate the lowest, by filling them with a sense of their importance and responsibility; while on the other hand, it effects a comparative depression in the more elevated, and constantly teaches them a practical lesson,—to honor the law which is above them all.

Another inference which arises from the application of this principle is, that all should take an active interest in public affairs. All have a voice either by themselves, their husbands, their brothers, or their fathers; it is their duty to express it, and whatever is duty can not with propriety be called disreputable. I refer not merely to the act of voting, but to the preliminary discussions and the acquisition of all the necessary means of influence. An active interest in the public measures of the day is often and generally denounced as discreditable. The thought is of foreign birth, and most truly it is alien to the institutions of this country. In those nations where the citizens have *no* voice, and can only influence public measures through sycophancy and flattery of the great, politics are indeed idle if not disgraceful. Formerly it was considered disreputable to take a part in religion; all theological discussion was left to the priest. Even many of the Doctors of the Reformation thought it dangerous to put the Bible in the hands of the people. More enlightened views have prevailed in modern times; every man, whether priest or layman, is responsible on his own account; no man can answer for another in matters of conscience; neither can he in matters of state, —the responsibility may differ in degree, but not in kind. As I love my country, I earnestly pray that she may never cease to be agitated by political discussion. While men think and speak freely, they will be divided in opinion; and parties will never give way but to the torpor which precedes death.

Many suppose that the powers of government should always be restricted to their direct object, that is, to the protection of persons and of property. Others suppose that they may also be advantageously employed in securing *collateral* benefits to their respective nations. In every government there is always a large mass of power conferred upon its organs ordinarily inert, to be used only in the event of war or some extraordinary emergency. The great problem which has entered more or less into the political discussions of ancient and modern times, is, shall this great unused reservoir of public power remain idle, or be employed to feed the conduits of private affairs.

We will refrain from giving examples of these two theories reduced to practice among modern nations; but among the ancients, Sparta with her black broth, and iron money, and her utter contempt for all the decencies, moralities and comforts of life, is an eminent example of the first. She struggled only for existence, and continued five or six centuries. A straight line upon the map of history, contains all that is worth remembering of her story. Athens is an illustration of the other theory; that republic facilitated in some degree the private pursuits of her citizens. She has sunk also, but has left a long train of brilliant and undying light behind her, in the glorious achievements of her sons.

Among modern political philosophers, Rousseau is a conspicuous advocate of the first school. He was not only opposed to any aid from government in advancing the arts of civilized life, but rather recommended all men to become "unsophisticated" again, like crazy Lear and poor Tom, and seek the independence of their original forests. Adam Smith is an equally illustrious example of the other school. He first reduced the economy of nations to a science, and taught the art of so using their powers as to enrich themselves and their subjects.

The views of those who disapprove of any collateral exercise of the powers of government, are derived exclusively from foreign institutions, and have no application to our own. A reference to the principle of the *greatest good*, to which we have so often had occasion to advert, will satisfactorily solve this most vexed question. In governments founded and conducted upon this principle, such an interference is not only safe, but generally in the highest degree beneficial. In this case the benefits and the burthens are equally divided; and if any given measure is not found to the advantage of the majority, it is sure to be repealed before material injury can accrue. On the other hand, in a government administered for the benefit of a few, where the advantages are monopolized by the rulers and their sycophants, and the burthens thrown upon the nation at large, the exercise of this privilege is dangerous in the extreme. It is sure to be abused—to add strength to oppression, and accumulate new afflictions upon humble industry.

It is but very recently that commerce, manufactures and the arts have been considered of sufficient importance to attract the notice and the care of government. In whatever government attention to these interests is found, it is a *democratic* feature; it is a partial, and as experience has proved a most salutary application of the utilitarian principle. About the middle of the seventeenth century, the celebrated John De Witte induced the republic of Holland to pass a law regulating its traffick with foreign nations. At the same time Oliver Cromwell procured the passage of the Navigation act. At this time Holland was a republic, and England a commonwealth. These were the first serious attempts to draw the private occupations of men into the policy of nations, and each of these acts in its turn, as it had an opportunity of being felt, made its respective nation master of the wealth of the world.

The establishment of the Patent Office is another pregnant illustration of the application of this principle to the administration of the affairs of government. The Patent Office is no part of the state; it is not necessary to the protection of person or property; and if improvements were now made under the patronage and for the exclusive benefit of a few great people, who conduct the government and monopolize trade, it would unquestionably be unjust to tax the people for the purpose of rewarding these favorites. But if, as with us, the benefits as well as the burthens are equally distributed among all, it becomes another example of those collateral advantages which government, administered upon this principle, may safely secure to the people.

It is remarkable that this admirable institution for the encouragement of the arts, should spring from that old and vicious system of monopolies with which government formerly encumbered and well nigh extinguished trade. In its history two opposites meet: the first half springs from a government administered for the benefit of a few; the second, for the many. It had its origin in a clause in one of King James the First's laws regulating monopolies. Bacon was then Lord Chancellor of England, and probably inserted this admirable provision, which without the suspicion of his ignorant associates, completely reversed the character of the law. It seems contrived expressly to encourage and reward those anticipated inventions, which his Novum Organum had taught the world the art of making. The last pointed out the course; the first gave the impulse. The age felt the power, and darted forward in the race of improvement like the boat of Cloanthus; and like that too, cautiously avoided the rock on which its predecessors had been wrecked, or delayed in their career. The fable of the mystery-men in the house of Solomon, has become reality. The government provides at its own expense an inquisition over the whole world. All that is new in discovery or production, is collected and disseminated through the country,—mulicole rye from France, Gama grass from the West Indies, tea from China. It is thus that for the past few years, the whole earth has become the garden of the botanist, the school of the engineer, and the laboratory of the alchemist.

The age of *philosophy* has passed, and left few memorials of its existence. That of *glory* has vanished, and nothing but a painful tradition of human suffering remains. That of *utility* has commenced, and it requires little warmth of imagination to anticipate for it a reign lasting as time, and radiant with the wonders of unveiled nature.

These applications of the principle of utility to the various relations of life enable us to see it, not only in its simple form as it leads to aversion or attachment, but in its various combinations and results, and to trace all actions, however apparently disinterested or dissimilar, to this one motive. It has indeed a wonderful variety of applications. But let it be remembered that half a dozen postulates and self-evident truths are the foundation for the whole superstructure of pure geometry, and if to this be added the application of these truths to physics, the world would hardly contain the books that could be written. There is little resemblance between the definition of a straight line and the celebrated Pythagorean demonstration that the square of the hypothenuse of a right-angled triangle is equal to the sum of the squares of the two sides, so we may be able to trace but little resemblance between the great law that men will be governed by a desire of happiness, and the conduct of Regulus in tearing himself from his weeping friends at Rome, after advising a continuance of the war, and rushing to certain death among his foes at Carthage to preserve inviolate the promises given to his captors; yet in the one case as well as the other, if these first truths did not exist, these very important but remote and apparently disconnected results could not have been.

The unreasoning observer sees only the nebulæ of brilliant light, but the stars from which they proceed are sunk far into the depths of heaven beyond the reach of the eye or the telescope.

Locke, and many wise and good men since his time, have declared that there is no difference between virtue and enlightened self-love.

If therefore there are yet to be found in our schools any remains of the fopperies and disguises of the old philosophy about abstract good and the love of virtue, away with them! and let our youths be taught to refer every action public or private to an enlarged utility. Knowledge is virtue—that is, a clear and distinct perception that a given act is for our benefit will insure its performance; and to suppose that that act must not necessarily be virtuous, is blasphemy against the Creator of the universe.

Let then the whole end of education be to enlighten that perception. Let every appeal be openly and directly made to utility. Let the student be taught to feel, that, properly viewed, it becomes an elevating not a debasing motive. The appeal must be effective, for it coincides with all the instincts and impulses of our nature. It is in this way that knowledge may finally secure its object and triumph over the perversity of our moral as well as physical nature. It is upon a generation of generous youths refined and elevated in this manner, and habituated in every thing they do to look upon it in the light of the most enlarged and liberal utility, that our government, built up out of the fragments of a thousand states, will rest and be perpetuated.

8

HENRY JAMES, SR.

1811, born June 3, at Albany, N.Y.
1830, was graduated from Union College, Schenectady, N.Y.
1835–37, student at Princeton Theological Seminary
1837, visited England, came under the influence of Robert Sandeman
1838, edited Sandeman's *Letters on Theron and Aspasio*
1852, *Lectures and Miscellanies*
1854, *The Church of Christ Not an Ecclesiasticism*
1857, *Christianity the Logic of Creation*
1861, *The Social Significance of Our Institutions*
1863, *Substance and Shadow*
1869, *The Secret of Swedenborg*
1879, *Society the Redeemed Form of Man*
1882, died December 18, at Newport, R.I.
1885, posthumous, *The Literary Remains of the Late Henry James*, edited by
    William James

EMERSON called Emanuel Swedenborg's genius, "the genius which was to penetrate the science of the age with a far more subtle science; to pass the bounds of space and time; venture into the dim, spirit-realm, and attempt to establish a new religion in the world." Swedenborg was "a rich discoverer" whose "thought dwells in essential resemblances. . . . He saw things in their law, in likeness of function, not of structure. There is an invariable method and order in his delivery of his truth, the habitual proceeding of the mind from inmost to outmost." In spite of this appreciation of Swedenborg and his mystic insights, there was for Emerson one factor which detracted from the value of the man and his work. Swedenborg had little sense of the individual; for this reason, thought Emerson, "Swedenborg's system of the world wants central spontaneity; it is dynamic, not vital, and lacks power to generate life. . . . What seems an individual and a will, is none. There is an immense chain of intermediation, extending from centre to extremes, which bereaves every agency of all freedom and character." [1]

The very factor in Swedenborg's thinking to which Emerson took exception was central in the acceptance of Swedenborg by Henry James, Sr. For

---

[1] Emerson, *Representative Men*, "Swedenborg; or the Mystic," in *The Works of Ralph Waldo Emerson*, Boston, The Jefferson Press, no date, pp. 289, 304, 310–11.

James, as for Swedenborg, selfhood was the sin of sins. James had reached Swedenborg after an apprentice training in Calvinism at Union College and Princeton and a journeyman's acceptance of Sandemanianism. His knowledge of Swedenborg came through J. J. Garth Wilkinson, the most distinguished English Swedenborgian of the nineteenth century. James did not, however, become a Swedenborgian. He was unable to accept any revelation as ultimate. Yet many of his own religious insights were akin to those of Swedenborg. This relationship was recognized by Wilkinson, who wrote to James in 1879,

You would be better, not as a man, but as a consistency, if you were detached from Swedenborg. Your theory has been suggested by his collision with your mind; he has struck you hard; and in the tenderness and generosity of your constitution, you have accepted his heavy blow as polite intercourse; and founded, on your own side, not his, a friendship with his works, instead of recognizing his opposition as the main fact between you.[2]

If Swedenborg, in this highly un-Swedenborgian way, was the source of James's mature religious insights, François Marie Charles Fourier was the source of his social insights. There were, as Perry has pointed out, both methodological and doctrinal similarities between Fourier and Swedenborg, and the movements which stemmed from these two men "seemed predestined to marriage." Parke Godwin, Horace Greeley, and Albert Brisbane came to Swedenborg after they had accepted Fourier. Having accepted a program of social reform, they found in Swedenborg a complementary religious basis. Henry James and Emerson knew Swedenborg first; and James's acceptance of Fourier came because of his need for a social science that would fit his religious beliefs, by emphasizing social solidarity and innocent individual "spontaneities," and reinforce his Sandemanian democratic views. Community organization has as its purpose the avoidance of maladjustment, so that misconduct, which was conceived as the result of maladjustment, might be prevented.

For James, democracy was such an organization, in which institutional control could be reduced to a minimum without individual misconduct.

Democracy [he said] is not so much a new form of political life, as a dissolution or disorganization of the old forms. . . . Democracy everywhere proclaims the superiority of man to institutions, allowing the latter no respect, however consecrated by past worth, save in so far as they also reflect the present interests of humanity. . . . The positive or constructive results . . . which I anticipate from Democracy, are of a moral or social character, rather than political. . . . I

[2] Ralph Barton Perry, *The Thought and Character of William James*, Boston, 1936, I, 26–27.

look upon Democracy as heralding the moral perfection of man, as inaugurating the existence of perfectly just relations between man and man, and as consequently preparing the way for the reign of infinite Love. . . . It supposes that men are capable of so adjusting their relations to each other, as that they will need no police or external force to control them, but will spontaneously do the right thing in all places and at all times.[8]

The theme of social solidarity is the keynote of James's Fourth of July address at Newport in 1861, entitled "The Social Significance of Our Institutions." The address is an unhesitating affirmation of the creed of the Declaration of Independence and an equally firm denial of the individualism which was then regarded as the dominant principle of American life. It is certainly one of the wisest of patriotic speeches; wise alike in what it praises and what it condemns in American life. "As Americans, we love our country, we are proud to belong to it, because it is the country of all mankind, because she opens her teeming lap to the exile of every land, and bares her hospitable breast. to whatsoever wears the human form." Americans are born to the belief that what is important is men, not persons; this is their great distinction and the reason for the superiority not only of their political institutions, but also of their social life and even of their manners. The "social sentiment," "every man's joint and equal dependence with every other man upon the association of his kind for all that he himself is or enjoys," dominates the "moral sentiment," "what is exceptionally due to this, that, or the other *person*." James admits, and even insists, that human freedom in America expresses itself in forms which are open to criticism; "but he who sees the uncouth form alone, and has no feeling for the beautiful human substance within it, for the soul of fellowship that animates and redeems it of all malignity, would despise the shapeless embryo because it is not yet the branching oak." The highest points of European life are Protestantism and constitutional liberty; both have been improved and reached fruition in America. "Protestantism vacates the priestly pretension, by turning religion into an affair of the congregation. We applaud this, but go further, in making religion an affair of the individual conscience exclusively, with which neither priest nor congregation has the least right to intermeddle." Constitutional liberty supersedes the divine right of kings, "but the liberty which we assert, or which constitutes our ideal . . . is identical with the God-made constitution of the human mind itself, and . . . consists in the inalienable right of every man to believe according to the unbribed inspiration of his own heart, and to act according to the unperverted dictates of his own

[8] Henry James, Sr., *Lectures and Miscellanies*, New York, 1852; Lecture I, "Democracy and Its Issues."

understanding." In short, in this speech James suggests a combination of social and religious beliefs which appears in the title of another of his works, that society is the redeemed form of man.

THE SOCIAL SIGNIFICANCE OF
OUR INSTITUTIONS

A FRIEND observed to me a few days since, as I accepted the invitation with which your Committee of Arrangements has honored me, to officiate as your orator on this occasion, that I could hardly expect, under the circumstances, to regale my auditors with the usual amount of spread-eagleism. I replied, that that depended upon what he meant by spread-eagleism. If he meant what was commonly meant by it, namely, so clearly defined a Providential destiny for our Union, that, do what we please, we shall never fall short of it, I could never, under any circumstances, the most opposed even to existing ones, consent to flatter my hearers with that unscrupulous rubbish. No doubt many men, whose consciences have been drugged by our past political prosperity, do fancy some such inevitable destiny as this before us,— do fancy that we may become so besotted with the lust of gain as to permit the greatest rapacity on the part of our public servants, the most undisguised and persistent corruption on the part of our municipal and private agents, without forfeiting the Providential favor. From that sort of spread-eagleism I told my friend that I hoped we were now undergoing a timely and permanent deliverance. But if he meant by that uncouth word an undiminished, yea, a heightened confidence in our political sanity and vigor, and in the fresh and glowing manhood which is to be in yet larger measure than ever the legitimate fruit of our institutions, I could assure him that my soul was full of it, and it would be wholly my fault if my auditors did not feelingly respond to it.

I never felt proud of my country for what many seem to consider her prime distinction, namely, her ability to foster the rapid accumulation of private wealth. It does not seem to me a particularly creditable thing, that a greater number of people annually grow richer under our institutions than they do anywhere else. It is a fact, no doubt, and like all facts has its proper amiable signification when exposed to the rectifying light of Truth. But it is not the fact which in a foreign land, for example, has made my heart to throb and my cheeks to glow when I remembered the great and happy people beyond the sea, when I thought of the vast and fertile land that lay blossoming and beckoning to all mankind beyond the setting sun. For there in Europe one sees this same private wealth, in less diffused form, it is true, concentrated in greatly fewer hands, but at the same time associated in many cases with things that go every way to dignify it or give it a lustre not its own,—associated with traditional family refinement, with inoffensive unostentatious manners, with the practice of art and science and literature, and sometimes with the pursuit of toilsome and honorable personal adventure. Every one knows, on the other hand, how little *we* exact from our rich men; how meagre and mean and creeping a race we permit our rich men to be, if their meanness is only flavored with profusion. I have not been favored with a great many rich acquaintance, but still I have known a not inconsiderable number, and I have never found them the persons to whom one would spontaneously resort in his least personal moments, or communicate with the most naturally in his hours of the purest intellectual elation or despondency. Of course I have known exceptions to this rule, men whose money only serves to illustrate their superior human sweetness, men of whose friendship everybody is proud. But as a general thing, nevertheless, one likes best to introduce one's foreign acquaintance, not to our commercial nabobs, who aggravate the price of house-rent and butcher's meat so awfully to us poor Newporters; not to our fast financiers and bank cashiers, who on a salary of three thousand a year contrive to support in luxury, beside their proper wife and offspring, a dozen domestic servants and as many horses; but to our, in the main, upright, self-respecting, and, if you please, untutored, but at the same time unsophisticated, children of toil, who are the real fathers and mothers of our future distinctive manhood.

No; what makes one's pulse to bound when he remembers his own home under foreign skies, is never the rich man, nor the learned man, nor the distinguished man of any sort who illustrates its history, for in all these petty products almost every country may favorably, at all events tediously, compete with our own; but it is all simply the abstract manhood itself of the country, man himself unqualified by convention, the man to whom all these conventional men have been simply introductory, the man who—let me say it—for the first time in human history finding himself in his own right erect under God's sky, and feeling himself in his own right the peer of every other man, spontaneously aspires and attains to a far freer and profounder culture of his nature than has ever yet illustrated humanity.

Shallow people call this pretension of ours the offspring of national vanity, and stigmatize it as implying the greatest immodesty in every one who asserts it. Is it not the same as saying, they ask, that ignorance is as good as experience, weakness as good as skill, nature as good as culture, the crude ore as good as the polished metal which is extracted from it? I will show you the absurdity of this criticism in a few moments, when I show you the peculiar foundation which the sentiment in question, the sentiment of human equality, claims in our historic evolution and growth. For the present, I have a word more to say in regard to the contrasts of European and American thought and aspiration.

No American, who is not immersed in abject spread-eagleism,— that is to say, no American who has had the least glimpse of the rich social promise of our institutions, or of the free play they accord to the spiritual activities of our nature,—values the mere political prestige of his nation, or the repute it enjoys with other nations, as the true ground of its glory. Much less, of course, does he esteem the mere *personnel* of his government as conferring any distinction upon him. Loyalty, which is a strictly personal sentiment, has long given place even in the English bosom where it was native, to patriotism, which is a much more rational sentiment. Loyalty bears to patriotism the same relation that superstition bears to religion. The zealot worships God, not as an infinite Spirit of Love, but as a finite person: not for what He is inwardly in himself, but for what He may outwardly be to the worshipper. He adores him, not for what alone renders him worthy of adoration, namely, his essential humanity, that infinitely tender sympathy with his infirm creature which leads him forever to humble himself that the latter may be exalted, but simply because he is eminent in place and power above all beings, and so is able to do all manner of kindness to those who please him, and all manner of unkindness to those who displease him. Exactly so the loyalist worships his king or his queen,—not for their radiant human worth; not for the uses their great dignity promotes to the common or associated life; in short, not from any rational perception of their inward adjustment to the place they occupy; but simply because they do occupy that eminent place, simply because they happen to be crowned king and crowned queen, traditional sources of honor and dishonor to their subjects. In both cases alike, the homage is purely blind or instinctive, and, though befitting children, is unworthy of adult men. Religion, on the contrary, clothes the Divine supremacy with essentially spiritual attributes, makes His perfection the perfection of character, the perfection of love and wisdom, and of power thence alone energized, so that no religious man worships God from choice or voluntarily, but spontaneously, or because he cannot help himself, so much does the overpowering loveliness constrain him. That is to say, every man truly worships God in the exact measure of his own unaffected goodness, purity, and truth. And it is thus precisely that the patriot loves his king or queen,—not for their traditional sanctity, not for their exalted privilege, not for their conventional remoteness, in short, from other men,—but for their willing nearness to them, that is, for their positive human use or worth, and consequent fitness to lead the great honest hearts they represent. In one word, what the patriot sees and loves in his king is his country and his country only; and he serves him, therefore, as the spiritually enlightened man serves God, not with a ceremonial or ritual devotion, but with a cordial or living one, with a service which only exalts, instead of any longer degrading, either of the parties to it.

No wonder, then, that the sentiment of loyalty should have utterly died out of our blood, when even that higher sentiment of country, to which alone it ministered in the bosom of our English ancestry, has in its turn given place in *our* bosoms to a sentiment still higher, that of humanity. We are the descendants, not of English loyalists by any means, but of English patriots exclusively; that is, of men who valued royalty only so long as it served the common life, and when it grew tired of that service, and claimed only to be served in its turn, unhesitatingly suspended it by the neck, and sent its descendants skipping. And this English patriotism, which was itself a regenerate loyalty, or a love of country purified of all personal allegiance, has itself become glorified in our veins into a still grander sentiment,—that is, from a love of country has become exalted into a love of humanity. It is the truest glory any nation may boast, that the love it enkindles in the bosom of its children is the love of man himself; that the respect it engenders there for themselves is identical with the respect which is due to all men. As Americans, we love our country, it is true, but not because it is *ours* simply; on the contrary, we are proud to belong to it, because it is the country of all mankind, because she opens her teeming lap to the exile of every land, and bares her hospitable breast to whatsoever wears the human form. This is where the ordinary European mind inevitably fails to do us any justice. The purblind piddling mercenaries of literature, like Dickens, and the ominous scribes and Pharisees of the Saturday Review, have just enough of cheap wit to see and caricature the cordial complacency we feel in our virgin and beautiful mother; but it takes an acumen bred of no London police-courts, and an education of the heart which all the studies of Oxford will never yield, to see the rich human soul that vivifies that complacency, that burns away all its dross, and makes it laughable only to literary louts and flunkies who live by pandering to the prejudices of the average human understanding.

The American misses in European countries and institutions this exquisite human savor, this exquisite honor which is due to man alone, and this exquisite indifference which is due to persons. In European institutions,—I do not say in existing European *sentiment*, for that, no doubt, is greatly in advance of the institutions,—but in European institutions persons are everything and man comparatively nothing. It is always the skilled man, or the learned man, or the mighty man, or the noble man, in short the propertied or qualified man of some sort, that is had in reverence; never our common humanity itself, which, on the contrary, is starved in garrets in order that the man of quality may live in plenty, is ground to powder by toil in order to keep up his iniquitous state, is butchered in crowds to maintain his peace, and rots in prisons to avouch his purity. Abroad every American sees, of course and accordingly, any amount of merely political energy and efficiency, sees governments flourishing by the permanent demoralization of their people. He sees every appliance of luxurious art, all manner of imposing edifices, of elaborate gardens and pleasure-places, the deadliest arsenals of war, armies innumerable, and natives disciplined with infernal force, all consecrated to the sole purpose of keeping up the purely *political* status of the country, or aggrandizing its own selfish aims and repute to the eyes of other nations and its own people. And he cries aloud to his own heart, May America perish out of all remembrance, before what men blasphemously call public order finds itself promoted there by this costly human degradation! Disguise it as you will in your own weak, wilful way, in no country in Europe has the citizen as yet consciously risen into the man. In no country of Europe does the government consciously represent, or even so much as affect to represent, the unqualified manhood of the country, its lustrous human worth, the honest unadulterate blood of its myriad beautiful and loving bosoms, its fathers and mothers, its brothers and sisters, its sons and daughters, its husbands and wives, its lovers and friends, every throb of whose life is sacred with God's sole inspiration; but only the adulterate streams which course through the veins of some insignificant conventional aristocracy. Take England itself for an example of the perfect truth of my allegations. We may easily do injustice to England just now; may easily forget the shining and proud pre-eminence which belongs to her political development among all the polities of the earth. Another nation so great, so vowed in its political form to freedom, so renowned for arms, for art, for industry, for the intelligence of its scholars, for its public and private morality, does not illustrate human annals; and yet, because she now thinks of herself before she thinks of us, because she listens to the prayer of her starving operatives before she listens to the demands of our betrayed nationality, we are ready to forget her glorious past, and pronounce her a miracle of selfishness. But no truly human virtue is compatible with an empty stomach; and England, like everybody else, must be allowed first of all to secure her own subsistence before she bestows a thought upon other people. I will not blame England, then, for her present timidity. I will never forget the inappreciable services she has rendered to the cause of political progress. But just as little can I be blind to the immense limitations she exhibits when measured by American humanitary ideas. She claims to be the freest of European nations; and so she is, as I have already admitted, so far as her public or political life is concerned. But viewed internally, viewed as to her *social* condition, you observe such a destitution of personal freedom and ease and courtesy among her children as distinguishes no other people, and absolutely shocks an American. Conventional routine, a wholly artificial morality, has so bitten itself into the life of the people, into the national manners and countenance even, that the kindly human heart within is never allowed to come to the surface, and what accordingly is meant among them for civility to each other is so coldly and grudgingly rendered as to strike the stranger like insult. The intensely artificial structure of society in England renders it inevitable in fact, that her people should be simply the worst-mannered people in Christendom. Indeed, I venture to say that no average American resides a year in England without getting a sense so acute and stifling of its hideous class-distinctions, and of the consequent awkwardness and *brusquerie* of its upper classes, and the consequent abject snobbery or inbred and ineradicable servility of its lower classes, as makes the manners of Choctaws and Potawatamies sweet and christian, and gives to a log-cabin in Oregon the charm of comparative dignity and peace.

For, after all, what do we prize in men? Is it their selfish or social worth? Is it their personal or their human significance? Unquestionably, only the latter. All the refinement, all the accomplishment, all the power, all the genius under heaven, is only a nuisance to us if it minister to individual vanity, or be associated with a sentiment of aloofness to the common life, to the great race which bears us upon her spotless bosom and nourishes us with the milk of her own immortality. What is the joy we feel when we see the gifted man, the man of genius, the man of high conventional place of whatever sort, come down to the recognition of the lowliest social obligations,—what is it but a testimony that the purest personal worth is then most pure when it denies itself, when it leaps over the privileged interval which separates it from the common life, and comes down to identify itself with the commonest? This sentiment of human unity, of the sole original sacredness of man and the purely derivative sanctity of persons, no matter who they are, *is what we are born to,* and what we must not fail to assert with an emphasis and good-will which may, if need be, make the world resound. For it is our very life, the absolute breath of our nostrils, which alone qualifies us to exist. I lived, recently, nearly a year in St. John's Wood in London, and was daily in the habit of riding down to the city in the omnibus along with my immediate neighbors, men of business and professional men, who resided in that healthy suburb, and fared forth from it every morning to lay up honest, toilsome bread for the

buxom domestic angels who sanctified their homes, and the fair-haired
cherubs who sweetened them. Very nice men, to use their own lingo,
they were, for the most part; tidy, unpretending, irreproachable in
dress and deportment; men in whose truth and honesty you would confide at a glance; and yet, after eight months' assiduous bosom solicita-
tion of their hardened stolid visages, I never was favored with the
slightest overture to human intercourse from one of them. I never
once caught the eye of one of them. If ever I came nigh doing so, an
instant film would surge up from their more vital parts, if such parts
there were, just as a Newport fog suddenly surges up from the cold remorseless sea, and wrap the organ in the dullest, fishiest, most disheartening of stares. They took such extreme pains never to look at
one another, that I knew they must be living men, devoutly intent each
on disowning the other's life; otherwise I could well have believed
them so many sad well-seasoned immortals, revisiting their old London
haunts by way of a nudge to their present less carnal satisfactions. I
had myself many cherished observations to make upon the weather,
upon the lingering green of the autumn fields, upon the pretty suburban
cottages we caught a passing glimpse of, upon the endless growth of
London, and other equally conservative topics; but I got no chance to
ventilate them, and the poor things died at last of hope deferred. The
honest truth is what Dr. Johnson told Boswell, that the nation is deficient in the human sentiment. "Dr. Johnson," says Boswell, "though
himself *a stern, true-born* Englishman, and fully prejudiced against
all other nations, had yet discernment enough to see, and candor enough
to censure, the cold reserve among Englishmen toward strangers (of
their own nation). 'Sir,' said he, 'two men of any other nation who are
shown into a room together, at a house where they are both visitors,
will immediately find some conversation. But two Englishmen will
probably go each to a different window and remain in obstinate silence.
Sir, we do not, as yet,' proceeded the Doctor, 'understand the common
rights of humanity.'"

These common rights of humanity of which Dr. Johnson speaks are
all summed up in the truth of man's social equality; that is, every
man's joint and equal dependence with every other man upon the association of his kind for all that he himself is or enjoys. These common
rights of humanity have got political ratification in England, as they

have got it nowhere else in Europe out of Switzerland; but the private life of England, as Dr. Johnson charges, is shockingly indifferent to them. The moral sentiment, the sentiment of what is exceptionally due to this, that, or the other *person*, utterly dominates in that sphere the social sentiment, the sentiment of what is habitually due to every man as man. It is this unchallenged primacy of the moral life over the social life of England, this intense sensibility among her scholars to personal claims over human claims, which so exalts her Pharisaic pride and abases her true spirituality, which leaves her outwardly the greatest and inwardly the poorest of peoples, and makes the homesick because better-nurtured foreigner feel, when exposed to it, how dismal and dingy the very heaven of heavens would become if once these odiously correct and lifeless white-cravatted and black-coated respectabilities should get the run of it.

You see at a glance that this penury of England in all spiritual regards is owing to the simple fact that not *man*, but *English*-man, is the key-note of her aspirations. European thought generally and at best is peninsular,—that is, *almost* insular,—in that it regards European culture as constituting the probable limits of the human mind. But English thought is absolutely insular, in that it makes England the actual measure of human development. Every Englishman who lives and dies an Englishman, that is to say, who has not been made by God's grace a partaker in heart of the *common*-wealth of mankind, or a spiritual alien from the mother that bore him, believes that no Europe, but England itself, one of the smallest corners of Europe, as Judæa was one of the smallest corners of Asia, furnishes the real *Ultima Thule* of human progress. This being the key-note of English thought, the pitch to which all its tunes are set, you are not surprised to see the sentiment dominating the whole strain of English character, till at last you find the Englishman not only isolating himself from the general European man, but each individual Englishman becoming a bristling independent unapproachable little islet to every other Englishman, ready, as Dr. Johnson describes them, to leap out of the windows rather than hold that safe and salutary parley with each other which God and nature urge them to; so that probably a huger amount of painful plethoric silence becomes annually accumulated under English ribs than befalls the whole world beside, and an amount of spiritual numbness and imbecility generated which is not to be paralleled by anything this side of old Judæa. And it is exactly the rebound of his thought from all this social obstruction and poverty which causes the American wayfarer's heart to dance with glee when he remembers his own incorrect and exceptionable Nazareth, his own benighted but comfortable and unsuspecting fellow-sinners, who are said to sit sometimes with their tired feet as high as their head, who light their innocent unconscious pipes at everybody's fire, and who occasionally, when the sentiment of human brotherhood is at a white heat in their bosom, ask you, as a gentleman from Cape Cod once asked me at the Astor House table, the favor of being allowed to put his superfluous fat upon your plate, provided, that is, the fat is in no way offensive to you. That the forms in which human freedom expresses itself in these latitudes are open to just criticism in many respects, I cordially admit, and even insist; but he who sees the uncouth form alone, and has no feeling for the beautiful human substance within it, for the soul of fellowship that animates and redeems it of all malignity, would despise the shapeless embryo because it is not the full-formed man, and burn up the humble acorn because it is not yet the branching oak. But the letter is nothing, the spirit everything. The letter kills, the spirit alone gives life; and it is exclusively to this undeniable spiritual difference between Europe and America, as organized and expressed in our own constitutional polity, that all our formal differences are owing. Our very Constitution binds us, that is to say, the very breath of our political nostrils binds us, to disown all distinctions among men, to disregard persons, to disallow privilege the most established and sacred, to legislate only for the common good, no longer for those accidents of birth or wealth or culture which spiritually individualize man from his kind, but only for those great common features of social want and dependence which naturally unite him with his kind, and inexorably demand the organization of such unity. It is this immense constitutional life and inspiration we are under which not only separate us from Europe, but also perfectly explain by antagonism that rabid hostility which the South has always shown towards the admission of the North to a fair share of government patronage, and which now provokes her to the dirty and diabolic struggle she is making to give human slavery the sanction of God's appointment.

When I said awhile ago that an American, as such, felt himself the peer of every man of woman born, I represented my hearers as asking me whether that claim was a righteous one; whether, in fact, he whose conscience should practically ratify it in application to himself would not thereby avouch his own immodesty,—confess himself devoid of that humility which is the life of true manhood. To this question I reply promptly, No! for this excellent reason,—that the claim in question is by no means a distinctive personal claim, but a claim in behalf of every man. When, by virtue of our national genesis and genius, I claim before God and man a rightful equality with every other man, what precisely is it that I do? Do I claim for myself an equality of wit, of learning, of talent, of benevolence, with this, that, or the other special person whom you may name as remarkable for those endowments? Do I mean to allege my private personal equality with all other persons; my equal claim, for example, to the admiring or sympathetic homage of mankind, with Shakespeare, with Washington, with Franklin? No man who is not an ass can believe this; and yet you perpetually hear the paid scribes of old-fogyism repeating the slander throughout the world, as if it were the most indisputable of truths. Nothing is more common than to hear persons who are disaffected to the humane temper of our polity affecting to quote the Declaration of Independence as saying that all men are *born* equal, and under cover of that audacious forgery exposing it to ridicule. The Declaration is guilty of no such absurdity. It does not say that all men are born equal, for it is notorious that they are born under the greatest conceivable inequalities,—inequalities of heart and head and hand,—inequalities even of physical form and structure; but it says that, notwithstanding these inequalities, they are all *created* equal,—that is, are all equal before God, or can claim no superior merit one to another in his sight, being all alike dependent upon his power, and possessing a precisely equal claim, therefore, each with the other, to the blessings of his impartial providence. The inequalities under which men are born, or which they inherit from their forefathers, are the needful condition of their individuality, of their various personal identity. The framers of the Declaration saw this as well as anybody, but they also saw, and so in effect said, that however much men may differ among themselves, it was yet not these personal differences which commend them to each other's true respect, but rather that common human want which identifies them all in the Divine regard by making them all equal retainers of His sovereign bounty. No man not a fool can gainsay this, and no man not a fool, consequently, can pretend that when I urge this constitutional doctrine of human equality I have anything whatever to say of myself personally regarded, or *as discriminated from other persons,* but only as SOCIALLY regarded,—that is, as *united* with all other persons. In short, it is not a claim urged on my own behalf alone, but in behalf of every other man who is too ignorant or too debased by convention to assert it for himself.

Our political Constitution, like every other great providential stride in human affairs, was intentionally educative; was designed to gather us together under the discipline of well-disposed but often sorely tried and disheartened political guides, in order finally to draw us fully forth out of the land of darkness and the house of bondage. The sole great aim of our political Constitution has been gradually to induct us out of errors and evils, which no Pagan Jew was ever more slow and reluctant to suspect than we are, into a new and far more grandly human consciousness, into a land of everlasting righteousness and peace. Not one of its literal framers ever had the faintest foresight of its ultimate scientific destination, any more than Moses had of the Messiah whom he prefigured; any more than Isaiah or Jeremiah had of the tremendous spiritual scope of the prophecies which uttered themselves through their rapt and dizzy imaginations. The scientific promise of our polity is only to be understood by watching its practical unfolding, by observing the expansive influence it has hitherto exerted, and is now more than ever exerting, upon the popular mind and upon the popular heart. View it either positively or negatively, its influence is the same. In its negative aspect,—its aspect toward Egypt, which is the European conception of man's true state on earth,—it denies all absoluteness both to persons and institutions, by boldly resolving what is the highest of personalities, namely, the king, and what is the most sacred of institutions, namely, the Church, both alike from a power into the servant of a power, from a righteousness into the symbol of a righteousness, from a substance into the shadow of a substance; this substance itself being those great disregarded instincts of human unity or fraternity which all along the course of history have been patiently soliciting scientific recognition, in order to put on organic form and cover the

earth with holiness and peace. In its positive aspect,—the aspect it
bears toward Canaan,—which means the supremacy of man's associated
life over his individual one, it makes my private righteousness, or that
which inwardly relates me to God, utterly posterior to, and dependent
upon, my public righteousnes, or that which relates me to my fellow-
man. How is it possible, therefore, that its practical effect should be
otherwise than educative,—educative, too, in the very profoundest
manner, that is, out of all evil into all good? Its direct influence is to
modify or enlarge my private conscience, the consciousness I have of
myself as a moral being, a being independent of my kind and capable
of all manner of arrogant presumptuous private hope toward God, into
a public conscience, into a consciousness of myself as above all things a
social being most intimately and indissolubly one with my kind, and
incapable therefore of any blessing which they do not legitimately
share. It laughs at the pretensions of any person however reputable,
and of any institution however venerable, to claim an absolute divine
sanctity,—that is, a sanctity irrespective of his or its unaffected human
worth; and it gradually so inflames the mind with its own august
spiritual meaning, so quickens it with its own vivid and palpitating
divine substance, that the conscience which is governed by it of necessity finds itself regenerating, finds itself expanding from a petty drivelling and squeaking witness of one's own righteousness, into the clear
and ringing and melodious testimony of God's sole righteousness in
universal man.

The European priest and king were at best only theoretically perfect,
both alike having always been actually below the spirit of their great
office. Their office was purely ministerial and typical, while they themselves had always the stupidity to regard it as magisterial and final, as
constituting in fact its own end. The office of the Christian priesthood
has always been to typify the spotless inward purity, the office of the
Christian royalty to typify the boundless outward power, which, by
virtue of the Incarnation, or of God's personal indwelling in human nature, shall one day characterize universal man. Every man's heart and
mind, by reason of their infinite source, insatiably crave, the one that
perfect righteousness which is peace towards God, the other that perfect
knowledge which is command over Nature. And the priest and the
king have existed only to authenticate this insatiate longing, and

formally prefigure its eventual exact fulfilment. European culture accordingly was established upon this typical and transitory basis of Church and State, the one representing the infinite Divine righteousness which is incarnated in universal man; the other the infinite Divine power which is engendered of such righteousness. But no actual churchman and no actual statesman ever grasped the grand humanitary prophecy of his office. Each supposed his office to be absolutely, not representatively, sacred; supposed it to be valid in itself, and not solely for its uses to the social development of the race. The priest claimed for the Church an absolute divine sanctity, a sanctity irrespective of the education it ministered to the popular heart; and the king claimed for the State an absolute divine authority, an authority underived from the elevation it afforded to the popular thought: so that the sum of European culture in a religious way has scarcely amounted to anything more than a practical desecration of the priestly office, or a secularizing of the Church by a diffusion of the priestly prerogative among the laity; as the sum of its political progress has consisted in limiting the royal prerogative, or democratizing the government, by diffusing it among the people. In short, Protestantism and constitutional liberty are the topmost waves of European progress, the bound beyond which European thought cannot legitimately go,—the one denying the Church as an absolute Divine substance, the other denying the State as an absolute Divine form. No overt aim is there practised towards a positive realization of the idea embodied in our institutions, which is that of a perfect human society or fellowship, in which every member shall be alike sacred before God and alike privileged before man. The ingrained inveterate Pharisaism of the English mind is so frankly obtuse to the conception of a Divine or universal righteousness on the earth, and the complacent Sadduceeism of Continental thought begets such an indifference to that great expectation, that one can see no hope for Europe socially but in the absorption of her effete nationalities by a new Northern invasion, and the consequent infusion of a ruddier blood into the veins of her languid populations.

But however this may be, we in this hemisphere, at all events, have no European problems to solve, and are not called upon in any manner to repeat the European experience. We *inherit* the solution which Europe has already given to her own peculiar problems, and start upon our distinctive career from the basis of her most approved experience. Europe has made religion an affair of the laity as much as of the clergy; government, an affair of the people as much as of the aristocracy. *We inherit her ripest culture in both of these particulars.* We inherit Protestantism and constitutional liberty; but there is this vast difference between us and them, *we begin where they leave off.* Like all heirs, we enter upon a full fruition of the estate which it cost them their best blood to found and mature. Thus Protestantism is not to us the bright expansive heaven to which all *their* religious aspiration ascends. It is rather the solid, compact, somewhat dingy and disagreeable earth upon which our feet are planted, only in order to survey entirely new and infinitely more inviting heavens. And constitutional liberty is not the welcome haven to us it has ever been to them, is not to us the same broad protective anchorage to which, over weary wastes of ocean and through alternate sickening calm and driving tempest, their political bark has been always steering. It is, on the contrary, our port of departure, whence with swelling sails we confidently voyage forth to tempt unknown seas, and lay open lands as yet untrodden by human feet. Protestantism vacates the priestly pretension, by turning religion into an affair of the congregation. We applaud this, but go further, in making religion an affair of the individual conscience exclusively, with which neither priest nor congregation has the least right to intermeddle. So constitutional liberty, which is the European ideal of liberty, vacates the divine right of kings, by complicating the royal power with numerous cunning constitutional checks and balances. But the liberty we assert, or which constitutes our ideal, does not flow from any man-made constitution under heaven, but is one on the contrary which all such constitutions are bound under fatal penalties simply and servilely to reflect, being the liberty which is identical with the God-made constitution of the human mind itself, and which consists in the inalienable right of every man to believe according to the unbribed inspiration of his own heart, and to act according to the unperverted dictates of his own understanding. In short, they affirm the inalienable sanctity and freedom of the nation as against other nations; we, the inalienable sanctity and freedom of the subject as against the nation. They say that every nation is sacred by virtue of its nationality, or has an inviolable

title to the respect and homage of all other nations. We say that every
man is similarly sacred by virtue of his humanity, and has an inviolable
title to the love and respect of all other men. Thus they truly assert
the Divine Incarnation in humanity; but they limit it to the public
sphere of life, to the national will and the national intelligence. We
do this, but we do much more also, for we practically ratify the Incarnation as a private no less than a public truth, as sanctifying the individual life indeed far more profoundly than the common one. They
laugh at us because we set the pulpit to the tune of the streets, and expect our governors to reflect the wisdom of the farm-yard and the
factory. But this is because they do not know that we, unlike themselves,
are without ecclesiastical and political conscience, our very Church and
State being themselves exclusively human and social. We are no mere
civil polity, designed, like those of the Old World, to lead men out of
barbarism into civilization. On the contrary, we find them citizens, and
out of citizens aspire to make them men. We are at bottom nothing
more and nothing less than a broad human society or brotherhood, of
which every man is in full membership by right of manhood alone; and
what we seek to do is to turn our nominal Church and State into the
unlimited service of this society. In fact, we declare the childhood of
the race forever fairly past, and its manhood at least entered upon. We
deny the ability of any church, Catholic or Protestant, to sanctify any
human being, or even enhance the sanctity he derives from his creative
source. We deny the ability of any government, arbitrary or constitutional, to enfranchise the human mind, or even enhance the freedom
which inheres in its God-given constitution. We maintain, on the contrary, that the Church can only and at best *develop* the righteousness
which every man derives in infinite measure from God; and that the
State can only and at best *promote* the freedom which Divinely inheres in his very form as man: so leaving every man's religion to the
sole inspiration of the Divine Good in his own heart, every man's freedom to the sole arbitrament of the Divine Truth in his own understanding. In short, we practically affirm the literal verity of the Divine
Incarnation in every form of human nature, the unlimited indwelling
of the infinite Godhead in every man of woman born; so turning every
man by the sheer pith of his manhood into mitred priest and crowned

king, or avouching ourselves finally to our own consciousness and the world's willing recognition as a faultless human society, instinct with God's unspeakable delight and approbation.

Such, my friends, I conceive to be our undeniable inward significance as a nation. Such the bright consummate flower of manhood, which is spiritually disengaging itself from the coarse obscuring husks of our literal Democracy, consisting in the gradual but complete subjugation of the selfish instinct in our bosoms to the service of the social instinct. Such is the great and righteous temper of mind to which we are Divinely begotten; such the paternal animating spirit that shapes our constitutional polity, that originally gave us birth as a nation, and that even now, in this day of seeming adversity, gives us a conscience of rectitude and invincible might which is itself incomparably richer than all prosperity. It is idle to talk,—as silly people, however, will talk, as all people will talk whose gross grovelling hearts go back *to the flesh-pots of Egypt, when they eat bread to the full,*—it is idle to talk of our political troubles as springing up out of the ground, as having no graver origin than party fanaticism or folly. These troubles, on the contrary, are the inevitable fruit of our very best growth, the sure harbingers, I am persuaded, of that rising Sun of Righteousness whose beams shall never again know eclipse. They are merely an evidence, on a larger scale and in a public sphere, of the discord which every righteous man perceives at some time or other to exist between his essential human spirit and his perishable animal flesh. For every nation is in human form, is in fact but an aggregate or composite form of manhood, greatly grander and more complex than the simple forms of which it is made up, but having precisely the same intense unity within itself, and claiming, like each of them, a quickening controlling spirit, and an obedient servile body. This animating controlling spirit of our national polity, like that of our own private souls, is Divine, comes from God exclusively, and is only revealed never exhausted, only embodied or empowered never belittled or enfeebled, by the literal symbols in which human wisdom contrives to house it. That part of the letter of our Constitution which best reveals the majestic human spirit that animates our polity is of course its preamble. But the real divinity of the nation, its vital imperishable holiness, resides not in any dead parchment, but only in the righteous unselfish lives of those who see in any constitution but the luminous letter of their inward spiritual faith, but the visible altar of their invisible worship, and rally around it therefore with the joyous unshrinking devotion not of slaves but of men.

Now, such being the undoubted spirit of our polity, what taint was there in its material constitution, in our literal maternal inheritance, to affront this righteous paternal spirit and balk its rich promise, by turning us its children from an erect sincere hopeful and loving brotherhood of men intent upon universal aims, into a herd of greedy luxurious swine, into a band of unscrupulous political adventurers and sharpers, the stink of whose corruption pervades the blue spaces of ocean, penetrates Europe, and sickens every struggling nascent human hope with despair?

The answer leaps at the ears; it is Slavery, and Slavery only. This is the poison which lurked almost harmless at first in our body politic, and to which its righteous soul is an utter stranger; this is the curse we inherited from the maternal English Eve out of whose somewhat loose lascivious lap we sprung. But of late years the poison has grown so rank and pervasive, making its citadel, indeed, the very heart of the commonwealth, or those judicial and legislative chambers whence all the tides of its activity proceed, that each successive political administration of the country proves more recreant to humanity than its predecessor, until at last we find shameless God-forsaken men, holding high place in the government, become so rabid with its virus as to mistake its slimy purulent ooze for the ruddy tide of life, and commend its foul and fetid miasm to us as the fragrant breath of assured health. It is easy enough to falsify the divinity which is shaping our constitutional action, wherever a will exists to do so. Men whose most cherished treasure can be buttoned up in their breeches pocket, and whose heart, of course, is with their treasure, are doubtless panting to convince the country that we have already done enough for honor, and the sooner a sham peace is hurried up the better. It only needs a wily wolf of this sort to endue himself here and there in sheep's clothing, and bleat forth a cunning pathetic lament over the causeless misfortunes which have befallen our bread-and-butter interests, to see dozens of stupid sheep taking up in their turn the sneaking hypocritical bleat, and preparing their innocent fleece for his dishonest remorseless shears. The friends of Mammon are numerous in every community; but, blessed be God,

they nowhere rule in the long run. They are numerous enough to give
an odious flavor to the broth; but they never constitute its body. It is
impossible that we should err in this great crisis of our destiny, a crisis
to which that of our national birth or independence yields in dignity
and importance, as much as body yields to soul, flesh to spirit, childhood to manhood. For this is the exact crisis we are in; the transition
from youth to manhood, from appearance to reality, from passing
shadow to deathless substance. Every man and every nation of men encounters somewhere in its progress a critical hour, big with all its future
fate; and woe be to the man, woe be to the nation, who believes that this
sacred responsibility can be trifled with. To every man and to every
nation it means eternal life or eternal death; eternal liberty or eternal
law; the heaven of free spontaneous order, or the hell of enforced pru-
dential obedience. There is no man who hears me who does not know
something of this bitter sweat and agony; whose petty trivial cares
have not been dignified and exalted by some glimpse of this hidden inward fight; who has not at times heard the still small voice of truth on
the one hand counselling him to do the right thing though ruin yawn
upon his hopes,—counselling him *to force himself* to do the honest thing
though it cost him tears of blood,—and the earthquake voice of hell
on the other, or the fiery breath of passion infuriated by long starvation,
doing its best to drown and devour it. Our national life, believe me, is
at that exact pass in this awful moment, and nowhere else. It is the
hour of our endless rise into all beautiful human proportions, into all
celestial vigor and beatitude, or of our endless decline into all in-
fernality and uncleanness, and into the inevitable torments which
alone discipline such uncleanness. And we must not hesitate for a moment to fight it manfully out to its smiling blissful end, feeling that it is
not our own battle alone, that we are not fighting for our own country
only, for our own altars and firesides as men have fought hitherto, but
for the altars and firesides of universal man, for the ineradicable rights
of human nature itself. Let bloated European aristocracies rejoice in
our calamities; let the mutton-headed hereditary legislators of England raise a shout of insult and exultation over our anticipated downfall; the honest, unsophisticated masses everywhere will do us justice,
for they will soon see, spite of all efforts to blind them, that we occupy
in this supreme moment no petty Thermopylæ guarding some paltry

Greece, but the broad majestic pass that commands the deathless wealth and worth of human nature itself, the Thermopylæ of the human mind; they will soon see, in fact, that our flags are waving, our trumpets sounding, our cannon showering their deathful hail, not merely to avenge men's outraged political faith and honor, but to vindicate the inviolable sanctity of the human form itself, which for the first time in history is Divinely bound up with that faith and honor.

This is the exact truth of the case. The political tumble-down we have met with is no accident, as unprincipled politicians would represent it. It is the fruit of an inevitable expansion of the human mind itself, of an advancing social consciousness in the race, an ever-widening sense of human unity, which will no longer be content with the old channels of thought, the old used-up clothes of the mind, but irresistibly demands larger fields of speculation, freer bonds of intercourse and fellowship. We have only frankly to acknowledge this great truth in order to find the perturbation and anxiety which now invade our unbelieving bosoms dispelled; in order to hear henceforth, in every tone of the swelling turbulence that fills our borders, no longer forebodings of disease, despair, and death, but prophecies of the highest health, of kindling hope, of exuberant righteousness, and endless felicity for every man of woman born. "I was once," says an old writer, "I was once in a numerous crowd of spirits, in which everything appeared at sixes and sevens: they complained, saying that now a total destruction was at hand, for in that crowd nothing appeared in consociation, but everything loose and confused, and this made them fear destruction, which they supposed also would be total. But in the midst of their confusion and disquiet, I perceived a soft sound, angelically sweet, in which was nothing but what was orderly. The angelic choirs thus present were within or at the centre, and the crowd of persons to whom appertained what was disorderly were without or at the circumference. This flowing angelic melody continued a long time, and it was told me that hereby was signified how the Lord rules confused and disorderly things which are upon the surface, namely, *by virtue of a pacific principle in the depths or at the centre; whereby the disorderly things upon the surface are reduced to order, each being restored from the error of its nature.*" The pacific and restorative principle which in the same way underlies all our political confusion and disorder, and which will irresistibly shape our national life to its own righteous and orderly issues, is the rising sentiment of human society or fellowship, the grand, invincible faith of man's essential unity and brotherhood. The social conscience, the conscience of what is due to every man as man, having the same divine origin and the same divine destiny with all other men, is becoming preternaturally quickened in our bosoms, and woe betide the church, woe betide the state, that ventures to say to that conscience, Thus far shalt thou go, and no further!

Slavery has this incredible audacity. Slavery, which is the only institution of our European inheritance we have left unmodified, confronts and spits upon this rising tide of God's righteousness in the soul of man. Slavery boldly denies what all our specific culture affirms, namely, the inviolable sanctity of human affection in every form, the inviolable freedom of human thought in every direction. The cultivated intelligence of the race abhors the claim of any human being to possess an *absolute* property in any other being, that is, a property unvivified by the other's unforced, spontaneous gift. Slavery affirms this diabolic pretension,—affirms the *unqualified* title of the master to outrage, if need be, the sacredest instincts of natural affection in the slave, and to stifle at need his feeblest intellectual expansion. Accordingly, the heart of man, inspired by God and undepraved by Mammon, pronounces slavery with no misgiving an unmitigated infamy; and the intelligence of man, thence enlightened, declares that its empire shall not be extended. We have no right to say that evil shall not exist where it already does exist without our privity; but we have not only all manner of right, both human and divine, to say that its existence shall not be promoted by our active connivance; it is our paramount wisdom as men, and our paramount obligation as citizens, to say so. Such, at all events, is our exact social attitude with respect to slavery. Every unsophisticated soul of man feels it to be what it actually is, namely, the ultimate or most general form and hence the king of all the evil pent up in human nature; so that when *it* once disappears by the clear indignant refusal of the human mind any longer actively to co-operate with it, all those interior and subtler shapes of evil which now infest us, and are held together by it as the viscera of the body are held together by the skin, will be dissipated along with it. We know not when the hour of this great salvation shall strike. We only know that as God is just and sovereign it must strike erelong, and that when it does strike the morning stars of a richer creation than has yet been seen on earth will sing together, and all the sons of God in every subtlest ineffable realm of his dominion shout for joy. Our government itself is waking up from its long trance; is beginning to perceive that there is something sacreder than commerce on earth,—that the interests of this very commerce, in fact, will best be promoted by first of all recognizing that there are depths in the human soul, demands of immaculate righteousness and assured peace, which all the pecuniary prosperity of the world can never satisfy. In short, the government is fast coming, let us hope, to a consciousness of its distinctively social or human function, by practically confessing that its supreme responsibility is due only to man, and no longer to persons, or infuriated sectional exactions. Of course, in pursuing this career, it will become gradually converted from the mere tool it has hitherto been for adroit political knaves to do what they please with, into a grandly social force, reflecting every honest human want, fulfilling every upright human aspiration. What matters it, then, if we forfeit the empty political prestige we have hitherto enjoyed with European *statesmen?* Let us only go on overtly to inaugurate that promised perfect society on earth, all whose officers shall be *peace,* and its sole exactors *righteousness,* by practically acknowledging on all occasions the infinite Divine Good enshrined in man's heart, the infinite Divine Truth enthroned in his understanding, and we shall fast attain to a social standing in the eyes of European *peoples* which shall grandly compensate our mere political disasters, and do more to modify the practice of European statesmen themselves than anything else we could possibly do.

In this state of things, how jealously should we watch the Congress to-day assembling at Washington! How clear should be the watchword we telegraph to guide their deliberations! Have *we* indeed no higher monition for our legislature than old heathen Rome supplied to hers, namely, *to see that the Republic suffer no damage?* The body is much, but it is not the soul. The Republic is much, but it is not all. It is much as a means, but nothing as an end. It is much as a means to human advancement, but nothing as its consummation. It is much as an onward march of the race, it is nothing whatever as its final victory and rest. Let us be sure that, so far as we are concerned, our legislators understand this. Let them know that we value the Republic so much, only because we value man more; that we value peace, prosperity, and wealth not as ends, but as means to an end, which is justice, truth, and mercy, in which alone man's real peace, his true prosperity, and his abiding wealth reside, and which will be ours so long as we are faithful to the gospel of human freedom and equality. For my part, if I thought that our rulers were going to betray in this agonizing hour the deathless interest confided to them,—if I thought that Mr. Lincoln and Mr. Seward were going at last to palter with the sublime instincts of peace and righteousness that elevated them to power and give them all their personal prestige, by making the least conceivable further concession to the obscene demon of Slavery,—then I could joyfully see Mr. Lincoln and Mr. Seward scourged from the sacred eminence they defile, yea more, could joyfully see our boasted political house itself laid low in the dust forever, because in that case its stainless stars and stripes would have sunk from a banner of freemen into a dishonored badge of the most contemptible people on earth; a people that bartered away the fairest spiritual birthright any people ever yet were born to, for the foulest mess of material pottage ever concocted of shameless lust and triumphant fraud.

9

WENDELL PHILLIPS

1811, born November 29, at Boston
1831, was graduated from Harvard College
1831–34, studied at Harvard Law School
1835–37, practiced law in Boston
1837, began activity in anti-slavery movement
1840, Massachusetts delegate to World's Anti-Slavery Convention in London
1863, *Speeches, Lectures, and Letters*
1865, president of American Anti-Slavery Society
1870, defeated as labor and prohibition candidate for governor of Massachusetts
1871, presided over Labor Reform Convention at Worcester, Mass., and wrote
    its platform
1881, *The Scholar in a Republic*
1884, died February 2, at Boston

A LIVING faith is always many steps ahead of the achievements of any society. Although the society may move ahead, may even come up to the
faith of an earlier period, the faith itself is progressive. Like a will o' the
wisp, it is glimpsed by a few men in every generation, who are doomed to
follow its tantalizing, remote flickering wherever it may lead. For the man
whose fate it is to follow the faith, no labor is too great, no hardship too
extreme. Every decent belief has its martyrs in every generation. Years later,
those upon whom obloquy was heaped in their own time come into their full
stature, because the spirit and the practice of the time have caught up with
them. At the same time, new martyrs are coming forward in their turn to
assault the reactionaries of their day and to lead the way into the future.

The martyrs of the democratic faith may come from any part of society.
Thomas Paine came from the work bench; Henry Wallace from the farm;
Wendell Phillips from the Boston brahmins and Harvard. From such
diverse places they have come, each in his own generation, to speak for the
oppressed of earth and against the oppression. They have given the voiceless
of the world a voice in the councils of the world. Their reward? Neither
gratitude nor respect, but only their own sense that they did right and the
unknown devotion and sympathy of future generations. Phillips believed
that the duty of the democratic leader is to initiate, to "act without casting

his eyes over his shoulder to see how far the people will support him." Paine wrote from virtual exile a stinging criticism of the reactionary tendencies of George Washington, as President. Wallace insists that justice to be democratic must be world-wide. Such men have a mission; there is no power which can shake their faith. Democratic practice, however, is far behind them. Only in recent years has Paine's service to the democratic ideal in America been granted any recognition; after more than a century the United States of America, which he named, has begun to regard him as an ancestor to be proud of. The early work of Wendell Phillips in the abolitionist movement is now respected; many of his later ideas, if they are remembered at all, are remembered only to be flouted. Henry Wallace lives through today what they lived through in their own times. When, in the future, Wallace, too, is accepted, there will be others rejected in their own times, to keep alive the progressive ideal of the democratic faith.

In 1837, but recently graduated from Harvard Law School, Wendell Phillips became one of the major voices of the abolition movement. He toured the country lecturing for this cause until the Civil War had come and gone. Originally he had been, like Garrison, in favor of destroying the Union to save his country from the guilt of slavery. Where Garrison, the man of one idea, never changed, Phillips, for whom the anti-slavery movement had come to be the most important, but not the only problem of squaring democratic practice with democratic faith, decided, on the eve of the war, to support the Union and enfranchisement of the liberated slaves.

I did prefer purity to peace,—I acknowledge it. The child of six generations of Puritans, knowing well the value of Union, I did prefer disunion to being the accomplice of tyrants. But now—when I see what the Union must mean in order to last, when I see that you cannot have union without meaning justice, and when I see twenty millions of people . . . determined that this Union shall mean justice, why should I object to it? . . . Do you suppose I am not Yankee enough to buy Union when I can have it at a fair price? [1]

Even after the war had ended, when Garrison wished to disband the American Anti-Slavery Society, Phillips insisted that the society had to continue until the negro had won civil rights. Garrison's approach was negative, merely humanitarian; Phillips's was positive, aggressive, militantly democratic.

After the Civil War, Phillips was reinstated into respectability; true, he had been an agitator, but his agitation had been successful, and it had been directed against the South. His passion for social justice, however, led him to causes which again made his name anathema to the brahmins. Such

[1] Wendell Phillips, *Speeches, Lectures, and Letters,* Boston, 1894, I, 440.

themes as women's suffrage, the temperance crusade, British oppression of Ireland, and especially the labor movement called forth his energies as did the slavery crusade in earlier years.

His work in the labor movement merits more than casual notice. In a sense it was an extension of his anti-slavery activity. Then he had fought the institution of chattel slavery; now it was wage slavery he opposed. This was hitting very close to home; he was regarded by his neighbors, whose fortunes came from industry, as a renegade, a traitor to his class. There are two related aspects of his labor theory which should be mentioned. The first is his economic argument, which was socialistic. He drafted and presented a platform to a Labor Reform Convention in 1871 which set forth his fundamental views. Some sections of it are worthy of preservation:

We affirm, as a fundamental principle, that labor, the creator of wealth, is entitled to all it creates.

Affirming this, we avow ourselves willing to accept the final results of the operation of a principle so radical,—such as the overthrow of the whole profit-making system, the extinction of all monopolies, the abolition of privileged classes, universal education and fraternity, perfect freedom of exchange, and, best and grandest of all, the final obliteration of that foul stigma upon our so-called Christian civilization,—the poverty of the masses. . . .

Resolved,—That we declare war with the wages system, which demoralizes alike the hirer and the hired, cheats both, and enslaves the working-man; war with the present system of finance, which robs labor, and gorges capital, makes the rich richer, and the poor poorer, and turns a republic into an aristocracy of capital. . . . We demand that every facility, and all encouragement, shall be given by law to co-operation in all branches of industry and trade, and that the same aid be given to co-operative efforts that has heretofore been given to railroads and other enterprises. We demand a ten-hour day for factory-work, as a first step, and that eight hours be the working-day of all persons thus employed hereafter. We demand that, whenever women are employed at public expense to do the same kind and amount of work as men perform, they shall receive the same wages.[2]

To achieve any such program, he realized, entailed political organization and agitation. This is the second important point in his program for labor. As early as 1865, in a speech before a labor meeting in Faneuil Hall, he declared that "a political movement, saying, 'We will have our rights,' is a mass meeting in perpetual session. Filtered through the ballot-box comes the will of the people, and statesmen bow to it." [3] In 1870, in accepting the nomination of the Labor Party for governor of Massachusetts, he wrote:

[2] *Ibid.*, II, 152–53.
[3] *Ibid.*, II, 144.

I feel sure that the readiest way to turn public thought and effort into this channel, is for the workingmen to organize a political party. No social question ever gets fearlessly treated here till we make politics turn on it. The real American college is the ballot-box. On questions like these, a political party is the surest and readiest, if not the only, way to stir discussion, and secure improvement.[4]

With such strong views as these, Phillips conceived it to be the duty of the scholars of America to serve as he had done, to lead the agitation on important issues of the day. The centennial address before the Phi Beta Kappa Society of Harvard, "The Scholar in a Republic," which is reprinted here, was not his only academic address. In 1852 he spoke before the Adelphi Society of Williams College on "The Duty of a Christian Scholar in a Republic." In 1855, at Dartmouth, it was "The Duties of Thoughtful Men to the Republic." In 1857, in a Phi Beta Kappa address at Yale, his topic was "The Republican Scholar of Necessity an Agitator." These earlier speeches have not been preserved except in brief summaries made by his auditors. In "The Scholar in a Republic" he sums up the wisdom of a life-time on this theme. The greatest weakness of the American scholar is servility to vested interest. The scholar has not taken his proper place in the vanguard of advancing democracy in any of the major crusades of the era. The proper function of the scholar is to educate the people, to develop the intelligence and moral sense the absence of which spells failure to repub-lican institutions. In this sense education does not mean book-learning, but participating constructively in popular agitations. College men fail in their duty to the republic "when they allow others to lead in the agitation of the great social questions which stir and educate the age." "Agitation is the only peaceful method of progress."

Naturally, the scholar in a republic should espouse the people's side of every cause. Phillips speaks with approval of George Bancroft, and there can be no doubt that he inherited Bancroft's faith in the essential rightness of the people. The scholar in the people's service can prevent any evil being mixed with the good of the cause. God provides the "agitations" of the day as texts for refining the taste, molding the character, lifting the purpose, and educat-ing the moral sense of the masses.

In this speech Phillips, near the end of his life, presented a stirring *apologia* for the way he had taken. He believed sincerely that "God means that un-just power shall be insecure." He thought that every scholar should serve as he had served to promote that insecurity. It embodies his conviction that he had chosen the right way, that he had lived the true life of the scholar in a republic.

[4] Charles E. Russell, *The Story of Wendell Phillips*, Chicago, 1914, p. 140.

THE SCHOLAR IN A REPUBLIC

A HUNDRED years ago our society was planted—a slip from the older root in Virginia. The parent seed, tradition says, was French,—part of that conspiracy for free speech whose leaders prated democracy in the *salons*, while they carefully held on to the flesh-pots of society by crouching low to kings and their mistresses, and whose final object of assault was Christianity itself. Voltaire gave the watchword,—

"Crush the wretch."
"*Écrasez l'infame.*"

No matter how much or how little truth there may be in the tradition: no matter what was the origin or what was the object of our society, if it had any special one, both are long since forgotten. We stand now simply a representative of free, brave, American scholarship. I emphasize *American* scholarship.

In one of those glowing, and as yet unequalled pictures which Everett drew for us, here and elsewhere, of Revolutionary scenes, I remember his saying, that the independence we then won, if taken in its literal and narrow sense, was of no interest and little value; but, construed in the fulness of its real meaning, it bound us to a distinctive American character and purpose, to a keen sense of large responsibility, and to a generous self-devotion. It is under the shadow of such unquestioned authority that I use the term "American scholarship."

Our society was, no doubt, to some extent, a protest against the sombre theology of New England, where, a hundred years ago, the atmosphere was black with sermons, and where religious speculation beat uselessly against the narrowest limits.

The first generation of Puritans—though Lowell does let Cromwell call them "a small colony of pinched fanatics"—included some men, indeed not a few, worthy to walk close to Roger Williams and Sir Harry Vane, the two men deepest in thought and bravest in speech of all who spoke English in their day, and equal to any in practical statesmanship. Sir Harry Vane was in my judgment the noblest human being who ever walked the streets of yonder city—I do not forget Franklin or Sam Adams, Washington or Fayette, Garrison or John Brown.

But Vane dwells an arrow's flight above them all, and his touch consecrated the continent to measureless toleration of opinion and entire equality of rights. We are told we can find in Plato "all the intellectual life of Europe for two thousand years": so you can find in Vane the pure gold of two hundred and fifty years of American civilization, with no particle of its dross. Plato would have welcomed him to the Academy, and Fénelon kneeled with him at the altar. He made Somers and John Marshall possible; like Carnot, he organized victory; and Milton pales before him in the stainlessness of his record. He stands among English statesmen preëminently the representative, in practice and in theory, of serene faith in the safety of trusting truth wholly to her own defence. For other men we walk backward, and throw over their memories the mantle of charity and excuse, saying reverently, "Remember the temptation and the age." But Vane's ermine has no stain; no act of his needs explanation or apology; and in thought he stands abreast of our age,—like pure intellect, belongs to all time.

Carlyle said, in years when his words were worth heeding, "Young men, close your Byron, and open your Goethe." If my counsel had weight in these halls, I should say, "Young men, close your John Winthrop and Washington, your Jefferson and Webster, and open Sir Harry Vane." The generation that knew Vane gave to our Alma Mater for a seal the simple pledge,—*Veritas.*

But the narrowness and poverty of colonial life soon starved out this element. Harvard was rededicated *Christo et Ecclesiae;* and, up to the middle of the last century, free thought in religion meant Charles Chauncy and the Brattle Street Church protest, while free thought hardly existed anywhere else. But a single generation changed all this. A hundred years ago there were pulpits that led the popular movement; while outside of religion and of what called itself literature, industry and a jealous sense of personal freedom obeyed, in their rapid growth, the law of their natures. English common sense and those municipal institutions born of the common law, and which had saved and sheltered it, grew inevitably too large for the eggshell of English dependence, and allowed it to drop off as naturally as the chick does when she is ready. There was no change of law,—nothing that could properly be called revolution,—only noiseless growth, the seed bursting into flower, infancy becoming manhood. It was life, in its omnipotence, rending whatever dead matter confined it. So have I seen the tiny weeds of a luxuriant Italian spring upheave the colossal foundations of the Cæsars' palace, and leave it a mass of ruins.

But when the veil was withdrawn, what stood revealed astonished the world. It showed the undreamt power, the serene strength, of simple manhood, free from the burden and restraint of absurd institutions in Church and State. The grandeur of this new Western constellation gave courage to Europe, resulting in the French Revolution, the greatest, the most unmixed, the most unstained and wholly perfect blessing Europe has had in modern times, unless we may possibly except the Reformation, and the invention of printing.

What precise effect that giant wave had when it struck our shore we can only guess. History is, for the most part, an idle amusement, the day-dream of pedants and triflers. The details of events, the actors' motives, and their relation to each other, are buried with them. How impossible to learn the exact truth of what took place yesterday under your next neighbor's roof! Yet we complacently argue and speculate about matters a thousand miles off, and a thousand years ago, as if we knew them. When I was a student here, my favorite study was history. The world and affairs have shown me that one half of history is loose conjecture, and much of the rest is the writer's opinion. But most men see facts, not with their eyes, but with their prejudices. Any one familiar with courts will testify how rare it is for an honest man to give a perfectly correct account of a transaction. We are tempted to see facts as we think they ought to be, or wish they were. And yet journals are the favorite original sources of history. Tremble, my good friend, if your sixpenny neighbor keeps a journal. "It adds a new terror to death." You shall go down to your children not in your fair lineaments and proportions, but with the smirks, elbows, and angles he sees you with. Journals are excellent to record the depth of the last snow and the date when the Mayflower opens; but when you come to men's motives and characters, journals are the magnets that get near the chronometer of history and make all its records worthless. You can count on the fingers of your two hands all the robust minds that ever kept journals. Only milksops and fribbles indulge in that amusement, except now and then a respectable mediocrity. One such journal nightmares New England annals, emptied into history by respectable middle-aged gentlemen, who fancy that narrowness and spleen, like poor wine, mellow into truth when they get to be a century old. But you might as well cite the *Daily Advertiser* of 1850 as authority on one of Garrison's actions.

And, after all, of what value are these minutiæ? Whether Luther's zeal was partly kindled by lack of gain from the sale of indulgences, whether Boston rebels were half smugglers and half patriots, what matters it now? Enough that he meant to wrench the gag from Europe's lips, and that they were content to suffer keenly, that we might have an untrammelled career. We can only hope to discover the great currents and massive forces which have shaped our lives: all else is trying to solve a problem of whose elements we know nothing. As the poet historian of the last generation says so plaintively, "History comes like a beggarly gleaner in the field, after Death, the great lord of the domain, has gathered the harvest, and lodged it in his garner, which no man may open."

But we may safely infer that French debate and experience broadened and encouraged our fathers. To that we undoubtedly owe, in some degree, the theoretical perfection, ingrafted on English practical sense and old forms, which marks the foundation of our republic. English civil life, up to that time, grew largely out of custom, rested almost wholly on precedent. For our model there was no authority in the record, no precedent on the file; unless you find it, perhaps, partially, in that Long Parliament bill with which Sir Harry Vane would have outgeneralled Cromwell, if the shameless soldier had not crushed it with his muskets.

Standing on Saxon foundations, and inspired, perhaps, in some degree, by Latin example, we have done what no race, no nation, no age, had before dared even to try. We have founded a republic on the unlimited suffrage of the millions. We have actually worked out the problem that man, as God created him, may be trusted with self-government. We have shown the world that a church without a bishop, and a state without a king, is an actual, real, every-day possibility. Look back over the history of the race: where will you find a chapter that precedes us in that achievement? Greece had her republics, but they were the republics of a few freemen and subjects and many slaves; and "the battle of Marathon was fought by slaves, unchained from the doorposts of their masters' houses." Italy had her republics: they were the republics of wealth and skill and family, limited and aristocratic. The Swiss republics were groups of cousins. Holland had her republic,—a republic of guilds and landholders, trusting the helm of state to property and education. And all these, which, at their best, held but a million or two within their narrow limits, have gone down in the ocean of time.

A hundred years ago our fathers announced this sublime, and, as it seemed then, foolhardy declaration, that God intended all men to be free and equal,—all men, without restriction, without qualification, without limit. A hundred years have rolled away since that venturous declaration; and to-day, with a territory that joins ocean to ocean, with fifty millions of people, with two wars behind her, with the grand achievement of having grappled with the fearful disease that threatened her central life, and broken four millions of fetters, the great republic, stronger than ever, launches into the second century of her existence. The history of the world has no such chapter in its breadth, its depth, its significance, or its bearing on future history.

What Wycliffe did for religion, Jefferson and Sam Adams did for the state,—they trusted it to the people. He gave the masses the Bible, the right to think. Jefferson and Sam Adams gave them the ballot, the right to rule. His intrepid advance contemplated theirs as its natural, inevitable result. Their serene faith completed the gift which the Anglo-Saxon race makes to humanity. We have not only established a new measure of the possibilities of the race: we have laid on strength, wisdom, and skill a new responsibility. Grant that each man's relations to God and his neighbor are exclusively his own concern, and that he is entitled to all the aid that will make him the best judge of these relations; that the people are the source of all power, and their measureless capacity the lever of all progress; their sense of right the court of final appeal in civil affairs; the institutions they create the only ones any power has a right to impose; that the attempt of one class to prescribe the law, the religion, the morals, or the trade of another is both unjust and harmful,—and the Wycliffe and Jefferson of history mean this if they mean anything,—then, when, in 1867, Parliament doubled the English franchise, Robert Lowe was right in affirming amid the cheers of the House, "Now the first interest and duty of every Englishman is to educate the masses—our masters." Then, whoever sees farther than his neighbor is that neighbor's servant to lift him to such higher level.

Then, power, ability, influence, character, virtue, are only trusts with which to serve our time.

We all agree in the duty of scholars to help those less favored in life, and that this duty of scholars to educate the mass is still more imperative in a republic, since a republic trusts the state wholly to the intelligence and moral sense of the people. The experience of the last forty years shows every man that law has no atom of strength, either in Boston or New Orleans, unless, and only so far as, public opinion indorses it, and that your life, goods, and good name rest on the moral sense, self-respect, and law-abiding mood of the men that walk the streets, and hardly a whit on the provisions of the statute-book. Come, any one of you, outside of the ranks of popular men, and you will not fail to find it so. Easy men dream that we live under a government of law. Absurd mistake! we live under a government of men and newspapers. Your first attempt to stem dominant and keenly-cherished opinions will reveal this to you.

But what is education? Of course it is not book-learning. Book-learning does not make five per cent of that mass of common sense that "runs" the world, transacts its business, secures its progress, trebles its power over nature, works out in the long run a rough average justice, wears away the world's restraints, and lifts off its burdens. The ideal Yankee, who "has more brains in his hand than others have in their skulls," is not a scholar; and two-thirds of the inventions that enable France to double the world's sunshine, and make Old and New England the workshops of the world, did not come from colleges or from minds trained in the schools of science, but struggled up, forcing their way against giant obstacles, from the irrepressible instinct of untrained natural power. Her workshops, not her colleges, made England, for a while, the mistress of the world; and the hardest job her workman had was to make Oxford willing he should work his wonders.

So of moral gains. As shrewd an observer as Governor Marcy of New York often said he cared nothing for the whole press of the seaboard, representing wealth and education (he meant book-learning), if it set itself against the instincts of the people. Lord Brougham, in a remarkable comment on the life of Romilly, enlarges on the fact that the great reformer of the penal law found all the legislative and all the judicial power of England, its colleges and its bar, marshalled against him, and owed his success, *as all such reforms do*, says his lordship, to public meetings and popular instinct. It would be no exaggeration to say that government itself began in usurpation, in the feudalism of the soldier and the bigotry of the priest; that liberty and civilization are only fragments of rights wrung from the strong hands of wealth and book-learning. Almost all the great truths relating to society were not the result of scholarly meditation, "hiving up wisdom with each curious year," but have been first heard in the solemn protests of martyred patriotism and the loud cries of crushed and starving labor. When common sense and the common people have stereotyped a principle into a statute, then bookmen come to explain how it was discovered and on what ground it rests. The world makes history, and scholars write it, one half truly, the other half as their prejudices blur and distort it.

New England learned more of the principles of toleration from a lyceum committee doubting the dicta of editors and bishops when they forbade it to put Theodore Parker on its platform; more from a debate whether the Anti-Slavery cause should be so far countenanced as to invite one of its advocates to lecture; from Sumner and Emerson, George William Curtis, and Edwin Whipple, refusing to speak unless a negro could buy his way into their halls as freely as any other,—New England has learned more from these lessons than she has or could have done from all the treatises on free printing from Milton and Roger Williams, through Locke, down to Stuart Mill.

Selden, the profoundest scholar of his day, affirmed, "No man is wiser for his learning"; and that was only an echo of the Saxon proverb, "No fool is a perfect fool until he learns Latin." Bancroft says of our fathers, that "the wildest theories of the human reason were reduced to practice by a community so humble that no statesman condescended to notice it, and a legislation without precedent was produced off-hand by the instincts of the people." And Wordsworth testifies that, while German schools might well blush for their subserviency,—

"A few strong instincts and a few plain rules,
    Among the herdsmen of the Alps, have wrought
  More for mankind at this unhappy day
    Than all the pride of intellect and thought."

Wycliffe was, no doubt, a learned man. But the learning of his day would have burned him, had it dared, as it did burn his dead body afterward. Luther and Melanchthon were scholars, but were repudiated by the scholarship of their time, which followed Erasmus, trying "all his life to tread on eggs without breaking them"; he who proclaimed that "peaceful error was better than tempestuous truth." What would college-graduate Seward weigh, in any scale, against Lincoln bred in affairs?

Hence I do not think the greatest things have been done for the world by its bookmen. Education is not the chips of arithmetic and grammar,—nouns, verbs, and the multiplication table; neither is it that last year's almanac of dates, or series of lies agreed upon, which we so often mistake for history. Education is not Greek and Latin and the air-pump. Still, I rate at its full value the training we get in these walls. Though what we actually carry away is little enough, we do get some training of our powers, as the gymnast or the fencer does of his muscles: we go hence also with such general knowledge of what mankind has agreed to consider proved and settled, that we know where to reach for the weapon when we need it.

I have often thought the motto prefixed to his college library catalogue by the father of the late Professor Peirce,—Professor Peirce, the largest natural genius, the man of the deepest reach and finest grasp and widest sympathy, that God has given to Harvard in our day,— whose presence made you the loftiest peak and farthest outpost of more than mere scientific thought,—the magnet who, with his twin Agassiz, made Harvard for forty years the intellectual Mecca of forty States,—his father's catalogue bore for a motto, "*Scire ubi aliquid invenias magna pars eruditionis est;*" and that always seemed to me to gauge very nearly all we acquired at college, except facility in the use of our powers. Our influence in the community does not really spring from superior attainments, but from this thorough training of faculties, and more even, perhaps, from the deference men accord to us.

Gibbon says we have two educations, one from teachers, and the other we give ourselves. This last is the real and only education of the masses,—one gotten from life, from affairs, from earning one's bread; necessity, the mother of invention; responsibility, that teaches prudence, and inspires respect for right. Mark the critic out of office: how reckless in assertion, how careless of consequences; and then the caution, forethought, and fair play of the same man charged with administration. See that young, thoughtless wife suddenly widowed; how wary and skilful! what ingenuity in guarding her child and saving his rights! Any one who studied Europe forty or fifty years ago could not but have marked the level of talk there, far below that of our masses. It was of crops and rents, markets and marriages, scandal and fun. Watch men here, and how often you listen to the keenest discussions of right and wrong, this leader's honesty, that party's justice, the fairness of this law, the impolicy of that measure;—lofty, broad topics, training morals, widening views. Niebuhr said of Italy, sixty years ago, "No one feels himself a citizen. Not only are the people destitute of hope, but they have not even wishes touching the world's affairs; and hence all the springs of great and noble thoughts are choked up."

In this sense the Frémont campaign of 1856 taught Americans more than a hundred colleges; and John Brown's pulpit at Harper's Ferry was equal to any ten thousand ordinary chairs. God lifted a million hearts to his gibbet, as the Roman cross lifted a world to itself in that divine sacrifice of two thousand years ago. As much as statesmanship had taught in our previous eighty years, that one week of intellectual watching and weighing and dividing truth taught twenty millions of people. Yet how little, brothers, can we claim for bookmen in that uprising and growth of 1856! And while the first of American scholars could hardly find, in the rich vocabulary of Saxon scorn, words enough to express, amid the plaudits of his class, his loathing and contempt for John Brown, Europe thrilled to him as proof that our institutions had not lost all their native and distinctive life. She had grown tired of our parrot note and cold moonlight reflection of older civilizations. Lansdowne and Brougham could confess to Sumner that they had never read a page of their contemporary, Daniel Webster; and you spoke to vacant eyes when you named Prescott, fifty years ago, to average Europeans; while Vienna asked, with careless indifference, "Seward, who is he?" But long before our ranks marched up State Street to the John Brown song, the banks of the Seine and of the Danube hailed the new life which had given us another and nobler Washington. Lowell foresaw him when forty years ago he sang of,—

"Truth forever on the scaffold,
   Wrong forever on the throne;
Yet that scaffold sways the future:
   And behind the dim unknown
Standeth God, within the shadow,
   Keeping watch above His own."

And yet the bookmen, as a class, have not yet acknowledged him.

It is here that letters betray their lack of distinctive American character. Fifty million of men God gives us to mould; burning questions, keen debate, great interests trying to vindicate their right to be, sad wrongs brought to the bar of public judgment,—these are the people's schools. Timid scholarship either shrinks from sharing in these agitations, or denounces them as vulgar and dangerous interference by incompetent hands with matters above them. A chronic distrust of the people pervades the book-educated class of the North; they shrink from that free speech which is God's normal school for educating men, throwing upon them the grave responsibility of deciding great questions, and so lifting them to a higher level of intellectual and moral life. Trust the people—the wise and the ignorant, the good and the bad—with the gravest questions, and in the end you educate the race. At the same time you secure, not perfect institutions, not necessarily good ones, but the best institutions possible while human nature is the basis and the only material to build with. Men are educated and the state uplifted by allowing all—every one—to broach all their mistakes and advocate all their errors. The community that will not protect its most ignorant and unpopular member in the free utterance of his opinions, no matter how false or hateful, is only a gang of slaves!

Anacharsis went into the Archon's court at Athens, heard a case argued by the great men of that city, and saw the vote by five hundred men. Walking in the streets, some one asked him, "What do you think of Athenian liberty?" "I think," said he, "wise men argue cases, and fools decide them." Just what that timid scholar, two thousand years ago, said in the streets of Athens, that which calls itself scholarship here says to-day of popular agitation,—that it lets wise men argue questions and fools decide them. But that Athens where fools decided the gravest questions of policy and of right and wrong, where property you had gathered wearily to-day might be wrung from you by the caprice of the mob to-morrow,—that very Athens probably secured, for its era, the greatest amount of human happiness and nobleness; invented art, and sounded for us the depths of philosophy. God lent to it the largest intellects, and it flashes to-day the torch that gilds yet the mountain peaks of the Old World: while Egypt, the hunker conservative of antiquity, where nobody dared to differ from the priest or to be wiser than his grandfather; where men pretended to be alive, though swaddled in the grave-clothes of creed and custom as close as their mummies were in linen,—that Egypt is hid in the tomb it inhabited, and the intellect Athens has trained for us digs to-day those ashes to find out how buried and forgotten hunkerism lived and acted.

I knew a signal instance of this disease of scholar's distrust, and the cure was as remarkable. In boyhood and early life I was honored with the friendship of Lothrop Motley. He grew up in the thin air of Boston provincialism, and pined on such weak diet. I remember sitting with him once in the State House when he was a member of our Legislature. With biting words and a keen crayon he sketched the ludicrous points in the minds and persons of his fellow-members, and, tearing up the pictures, said scornfully, "What can become of a country with such fellows as these making its laws? No safe investments; your good name lied away any hour, and little worth keeping if it were not." In vain I combated the folly. He went to Europe,—spent four or five years. I met him the day he landed, on his return. As if our laughing talk in the State House had that moment ended, he took my hand with the sudden exclamation, "You were all right: I was all wrong! It *is* a country worth dying for; better still, worth living and working for, to make it all it can be!" Europe made him one of the most American of all Americans. Some five years later, when he sounded that bugle-note in his letter to the London *Times,* some critics who knew his early mood, but not its change, suspected there might be a taint of ambition in what they thought so sudden a conversion. I could testify that the mood was five years old: years before the slightest shadow of political expectation had dusked the clear mirror of his scholar life.

This distrust shows itself in the growing dislike of universal suffrage, and the efforts to destroy it made of late by all our easy classes. The white South hates universal suffrage; the so-called cultivated North distrusts it. Journal and college, social-science convention and the pulpit,- discuss the propriety of restraining it. Timid scholars tell their dread of it. Carlyle, that bundle of sour prejudices, flouts universal suffrage with a blasphemy that almost equals its ignorance. See his words: "Democracy will prevail when men believe the vote of Judas as good as that of Jesus Christ." No democracy ever claimed that the vote of ignorance and crime was as good in any sense as that of wisdom and virtue. It only asserts that crime and ignorance have the same right to vote that virtue has. Only by allowing that right, and so appealing to their sense of justice, and throwing upon them the burden of their full responsibility, can we hope ever to raise crime and ignorance to the level of self-respect. The right to choose your governor rests on precisely the same foundation as the right to choose your religion; and no more arrogant or ignorant arraignment of all that is noble in the civil and religious Europe of the last five hundred years ever came from the triple crown on the Seven Hills than this sneer of the bigot Scotsman. Protestantism holds up its hands in holy horror, and tells us that the Pope scoops out the brains of his churchmen, saying, "I'll think for you: you need only obey." But the danger is, you meet such popes far away from the Seven Hills; and it is sometimes difficult at first to recognize them, for they do not by any means always wear the triple crown.

Evarts and his committee, appointed to inquire why the New York City government is a failure, were not wise enough, or did not dare, to point out the real cause, the tyranny of that tool of the demagogue, the corner grog-shop; but they advised taking away the ballot from the poor citizen. But this provision would not reach the evil. Corruption does not so much rot the masses: it poisons Congress. Credit Mobilier and money rings are not housed under thatched roofs: they flaunt at the Capitol. As usual in chemistry, the scum floats uppermost. The railway king disdained canvassing for voters: "It is cheaper," he said, "to buy legislatures."

It is not the masses who have most disgraced our political annals. I have seen many mobs between the seaboard and the Mississippi. I never saw or heard of any but well-dressed mobs, assembled and countenanced, if not always led in person, by respectability and what called itself education. That unrivalled scholar, the first and greatest New England ever lent to Congress, signalled his advent by quoting the original Greek of the New Testament in support of slavery, and offering to shoulder his musket in its defence; and forty years later the last professor who went to quicken and lift the moral mood of those halls is found advising a plain, blunt, honest witness to forge and lie, that this scholarly reputation might be saved from wreck. Singular comment on Landor's sneer, that there is a spice of the scoundrel in most of our literary men. But no exacting level of property qualification for a vote would have saved those stains. In those cases Judas did not come from the unlearned class.

Grown gray over history, Macaulay prophesied twenty years ago that soon in these States the poor, worse than another inroad of Goths and Vandals, would begin a general plunder of the rich. It is enough to say that our national funds sell as well in Europe as English consols; and the universal-suffrage Union can borrow money as cheaply as Great Britain, ruled, one half by Tories, and the other half by men not certain that they dare call themselves Whigs. Some men affected to scoff at democracy as no sound basis for national debt, doubting the payment of ours. Europe not only wonders at its rapid payment, but the only taint of fraud that touches even the hem of our garment is the fraud of the capitalist cunningly adding to its burdens, and increasing unfairly the value of his bonds; not the first hint from the people of repudiating an iota even of its unjust additions.

Yet the poor and the unlearned class is the one they propose to punish by disfranchisement.

No wonder the humbler class looks on the whole scene with alarm. They see their dearest right in peril. When the easy class conspires to steal, what wonder the humbler class draws together to defend itself? True, universal suffrage is a terrible power; and, with all the great cities brought into subjection to the dangerous classes by grog, and Congress sitting to register the decrees of capital, both sides may well dread the next move. Experience proves that popular governments are the best protectors of life and property. But suppose they were not, Bancroft allows that "the fears of one class are no measure of the rights of another."

Suppose that universal suffrage endangered peace and threatened property. There is something more valuable than wealth, there is something more sacred than peace. As Humboldt says, "The finest fruit earth holds up to its Maker is a man." To ripen, lift, and educate a man is the first duty. Trade, law, learning, science, and religion are only the scaffolding wherewith to build a man. Despotism looks down into the poor man's cradle, and knows it can crush resistance and curb ill-will. Democracy sees the ballot in that baby-hand; and selfishness bids her put integrity on one side of those baby footsteps and intelligence on the other, lest her own hearth be in peril. Thank God for His method of taking bonds of wealth and culture to share all their blessings with the humblest soul He gives to their keeping! The American should cherish as serene a faith as his fathers had. Instead of seeking a coward safety by battening down the hatches and putting men back into chains, he should recognize that God places him in this peril that he may work out a noble security by concentrating all moral forces to lift this weak, rotting, and dangerous mass into sunlight and health. The fathers touched their highest level when, with stout-hearted and serene faith, they trusted God that it was safe to leave men with all the rights He gave them. Let us be worthy of their blood, and save this sheet-anchor of the race,—universal suffrage,—God's church, God's school, God's method of gently binding men into commonwealths in order that they may at last melt into brothers.

I urge on college-bred men that, as a class, they fail in republican duty when they allow others to lead in the agitation of the great social questions which stir and educate the age. Agitation is an old word with a new meaning. Sir Robert Peel, the first English leader who felt himself its tool, defined it to be "marshalling the conscience of a nation to mould its laws." Its means are reason and argument,—no appeal to arms. Wait patiently for the growth of public opinion. That secured, then every step taken is taken forever. An abuse once removed never reappears in history. The freer a nation becomes, the more utterly democratic in its form, the more need of this outside agitation. Parties and sects laden with the burden of securing their own success cannot afford to risk new ideas. "Predominant opinions," said Disraeli, "are the opinions of a class that is vanishing." The agitator must stand outside of organizations, with no bread to earn, no candidate to elect, no party to save, no object but truth,—to tear a question open and riddle it with light.

In all modern constitutional governments, agitation is the only peaceful method of progress. Wilberforce and Clarkson, Rowland Hill and Romilly, Cobden and John Bright, Garrison and O'Connell, have been the master spirits in this new form of crusade. Rarely in this country have scholarly men joined, as a class, in these great popular schools, in these social movements which make the great interests of society "crash and jostle against each other like frigates in a storm."

It is not so much that the people need us, or will feel any lack from our absence. They can do without us. By sovereign and superabundant strength they can crush their way through all obstacles.

> "They will march prospering,—not through our presence;
> Songs will inspirit them,—not from our lyre;
> Deeds will be done—while we boast our quiescence;
> Still bidding crouch whom the rest bid aspire."

The misfortune is, we lose a God-given opportunity of making the change an unmixed good, or with the slightest possible share of evil, and are recreant beside to a special duty. These "agitations" are the opportunities and the means God offers us to refine the taste, mould the character, lift the purpose, and educate the moral sense of the masses, on whose intelligence and self-respect rests the state. God furnishes these texts. He gathers for us this audience, and only asks of our coward lips to preach the sermons.

There have been four or five of these great opportunities. The crusade against slavery—that grand hypocrisy which poisoned the national life of two generations—was one,—a conflict between two civilizations which threatened to rend the Union. Almost every element among us was stirred to take a part in the battle. Every great issue, civil and moral, was involved,—toleration of opinion, limits of authority, relation of citizen to law, place of the Bible, priest and layman, sphere of woman, question of race, State rights and nationality; and Channing testified that free speech and free printing owed their preservation to the struggle. But the pulpit flung the Bible at the reformer; law visited him with its penalties; society spewed him out of its mouth; bishops expurgated the pictures of their Common Prayer-books; and editors omitted pages in republishing English history; even Pierpont emasculated his class-book; Bancroft remodelled his chapters; and Everett carried Washington through thirty States, remembering to forget the brave words the wise Virginian had left on record warning his country-men of this evil. Amid this battle of the giants, scholarship sat dumb for thirty years until imminent deadly peril convulsed it into action, and colleges, in their despair, gave to the army that help they had re-fused to the market-place and the rostrum.

There was here and there an exception. That earthquake scholar at Concord, whose serene word, like a whisper among the avalanches, topples down superstitions and prejudices, was at his post, and, with half a score of others, made the exception that proved the rule. Pulpits, just so far as they could not boast of culture, and nestled closest down among the masses, were infinitely braver than the "spires and antique towers" of stately collegiate institutions.

Then came reform of penal legislation,—the effort to make law mean justice, and substitute for its barbarism Christianity and civiliza-tion. In Massachusetts Rantoul represents Beccaria and Livingston, Mackintosh and Romilly. I doubt if he ever had one word of encourage-ment from Massachusetts letters; and, with a single exception, I have never seen, till within a dozen years, one that could be called a scholar active in moving the Legislature to reform its code.

The London *Times* proclaimed, twenty years ago, that intemperance produced more idleness, crime, disease, want, and misery, than all other causes put together; and the *Westminster Review* calls it a "curse that far eclipses every other calamity under which we suffer." Glad-stone, speaking as Prime Minister, admitted that "greater calamities are inflicted on mankind by intemperance than by the three great his-torical scourges,—war, pestilence, and famine." De Quincey says, "The most remarkable instance of a combined movement in society which history, perhaps, will be summoned to notice, is that which, in our day, has applied itself to the abatement of intemperance. Two vast move-ments are hurrying into action by velocities continually accelerated,—the great revolutionary movement from *political* causes concurring with the great *physical* movement in locomotion and social intercourse from the gigantic power of steam. At the opening of such a crisis, had no *third movement arisen of resistance to intemperate habits,* there would have been ground of despondency as to the melioration of the human race." These are English testimonies, where the state rests more than half on bayonets. Here we are trying to rest the ballot-box on a drunken people. "We can rule a great city," said Sir Robert Peel, "America cannot;" and he cited the mobs of New York as sufficient proof of his assertion.

Thoughtful men see that up to this hour the government of great cities has been with us a failure; that worse than the dry-rot of legislative corruption, than the rancor of party spirit, than Southern barbarism, than even the tyranny of incorporated wealth, is the giant burden of intemperance, making universal suffrage a failure and a curse in every great city. Scholars who play statesmen, and editors who masquerade as scholars, can waste much excellent anxiety that clerks shall get no office until they know the exact date of Cæsar's assassination, as well as the latitude of Pekin, and the Rule of Three. But while this crusade—the temperance movement—has been, for sixty years, gathering its facts and marshalling its arguments, rallying parties, besieging legislatures and putting great States on the witness-stand as evidence of the soundness of its methods, scholars have given it nothing but a sneer. But if universal suffrage ever fails here for a time,—permanently it cannot fail,—it will not be incapable civil service, nor an ambitious soldier, nor Southern vandals, nor venal legislatures, nor the greed of wealth, nor boy statesmen rotten before they are ripe, that will put universal suffrage into eclipse: it will be rum intrenched in great cities and commanding every vantage-ground.

Social science affirms that woman's place in society marks the level of civilization. From its twilight in Greece, through the Italian worship of the Virgin, the dreams of chivalry, the justice of the civil law, and the equality of French society, we trace her gradual recognition; while our common law, as Lord Brougham confessed, was, with relation to women, the opprobrium of the age and of Christianity. For forty years, plain men and women, working noiselessly, have washed away that opprobrium; the statute books of thirty States have been re-modelled, and woman stands to-day almost face to face with her last claim,—the ballot. It has been a weary and thankless, though successful, struggle. But if there be any refuge from that ghastly curse, the vice of great cities,—before which social science stands palsied and dumb,—it is in this more equal recognition of woman. If, in this critical battle for universal suffrage,—our fathers' noblest legacy to us, and the greatest trust God leaves in our hands,—there be any weapon, which, once taken from the armory, will make victory certain, it will be, as it has been in art, literature, and society, summoning woman into the political arena.

But, at any rate, up to this point, putting suffrage aside, there can be no difference of opinion: everything born of Christianity, or allied to Grecian culture or Saxon law, must rejoice in the gain. The literary class, until half a dozen years, has taken note of this great uprising only to fling every obstacle in its way. The first glimpse we get of Saxon blood in history is that line of Tacitus in his *Germany*, which reads, "In all grave matters they consult their women." Years hence, when robust Saxon sense has flung away Jewish superstition and Eastern prejudice, and put under its foot fastidious scholarship and squeamish fashion, some second Tacitus, from the Valley of the Mississippi, will answer to him of the Seven Hills, "In all grave questions we consult our women."

I used to think that then we could say to letters as Henry of Navarre wrote to the Sir Philip Sidney of his realm, Crillon, "the bravest of the brave," "We have conquered at Arques, *et tu n'y étais pas, Crillon*" (You were not there, my Crillon). But a second thought reminds me that what claims to be literature has been always present in that battle-field, and always in the ranks of the foe.

Ireland is another touchstone which reveals to us how absurdly we masquerade in democratic trappings while we have gone to seed in tory distrust of the people; false to every duty, which, as eldest-born of democratic institutions, we owe to the oppressed, and careless of the lesson every such movement may be made in keeping public thought clear, keen, and fresh as to principles which are the essence of our civilization, the groundwork of all education in republics.

Sydney Smith said, "The moment Ireland is mentioned the English seem to bid adieu to common sense, and to act with the barbarity of tyrants and the fatuity of idiots." "As long as the patient will suffer, the cruel will kick. . . . If the Irish go on withholding and forbearing, and hesitating whether this is the time for discussion or that is the time, they will be laughed at another century as fools, and kicked for another century as slaves." Byron called England's union with Ireland "the union of the shark with his prey." Bentham's conclusion, from a survey of five hundred years of European history, was, "Only by making the ruling few uneasy can the oppressed many obtain a particle of relief." Edmund Burke—Burke, the noblest figure in the Parliamentary history of the last hundred years, greater than Cicero in the senate and almost Plato in the academy—Burke affirmed, a century ago, "Ireland has learned at last that justice is to be had from England, only when demanded at the sword's point." And a century later, only last year, Gladstone himself proclaimed in a public address in Scotland, "England never concedes anything to Ireland except when moved to do so by fear."

When we remember these admissions, we ought to clap our hands at every fresh Irish "outrage," as a parrot-press styles it; aware that it is only a far-off echo of the musket-shots that rattled against the Old State House on March 5th, 1770, and of the warwhoop that made the tiny spire of the "Old South" tremble when Boston rioters emptied the three India tea-ships into the sea,—welcome evidence of living force and rare intelligence in the victim, and a sign that the day of deliverance draws each hour nearer. Cease ringing endless changes of eulogy on the men who made North's Boston port-bill a failure while every leading journal sends daily over the water wishes for the success of Gladstone's copy of the bill for Ireland. If all rightful government rests on consent,—if, as the French say, you "can do almost anything with a bayonet except sit on it,"—be at least consistent, and denounce the man who covers Ireland with regiments to hold up a despotism which, within twenty months, he has confessed rests wholly upon fear.

Then note the scorn and disgust with which we gather up our garments about us and disown the Sam Adams and William Prescott, the George Washington and John Brown, of St. Petersburg, the spiritual descendants, the living representatives, of those who make our history worth anything in the world's annals,—the Nihilists.

Nihilism is the righteous and honorable resistance of a people crushed under an iron rule. Nihilism is evidence of life. When "order reigns in Warsaw," it is spiritual death. Nihilism is the last weapon of victims choked and manacled beyond all other resistance. It is crushed humanity's only means of making the oppressor tremble. God means that unjust power shall be insecure; and every move of the giant, prostrate in chains, whether it be to lift a single dagger or stir a city's revolt, is a lesson in justice. One might well tremble for the future of the race if such a despotism could exist without provoking the bloodiest resistance. I honor Nihilism; since it redeems human nature from the suspicion of being utterly vile, made up only of heartless oppressors and contented slaves. Every line in our history, every interest of civilization, bids us rejoice when the tyrant grows pale and the slave rebellious. We cannot but pity the suffering of any human being, however richly deserved; but such pity must not confuse our moral sense. Humanity gains. Chatham rejoiced when our fathers rebelled. For every single reason they alleged, Russia counts a hundred, each one ten times bitterer than any Hancock or Adams could give. Sam Johnson's standing toast in Oxford port was, "Success to the first insurrection of slaves in Jamaica," a sentiment Southey echoed. "Eschew cant," said that old moralist. But of all the cants that are canted in this canting world, though the cant of piety may be the worst, the cant of Americans bewailing Russian Nihilism is the most disgusting.

I know what reform needs, and all it needs, in a land where discussion is free, the press untrammelled, and where public halls protect debate. There, as Emerson says, "What the tender and poetic youth dreams to-day, and conjures up with inarticulate speech, is to-morrow the vociferated result of public opinion, and the day after is the charter of nations." Lieber said, in 1870, "Bismarck proclaims to-day in the Diet the very principles for which we were hunted and exiled fifty years ago." Submit to risk your daily bread, expect social ostracism, count on a mob now and then, "be in earnest, don't equivocate, don't excuse, don't retreat a single inch," and you will finally be heard. No matter how long and weary the waiting, at last,—

"Ever the truth comes uppermost,
    And ever is justice done.
For Humanity sweeps onward:
    Where to-day the martyr stands,
On the morrow crouches Judas
    With the silver in his hands;

"Far in front the cross stands ready,
    And the crackling fagots burn,
While the hooting mob of yesterday
    In silent awe return

To glean up the scattered ashes
Into History's golden urn."

In such a land he is doubly and trebly guilty who, except in some most extreme case, disturbs the sober rule of law and order.

But such is not Russia. In Russia there is no press, no debate, no explanation of what Government does, no remonstrance allowed, no agitation of public issues. Dead silence, like that which reigns at the summit of Mont Blanc, freezes the whole empire, long ago described as "a despotism tempered by assassination." Meanwhile, such despotism has unsettled the brains of the ruling family, as unbridled power doubtless made some of the twelve Cæsars insane: a madman, sporting with the lives and comfort of a hundred million of men. The young girl whispers in her mother's ear, under a ceiled roof, her pity for a brother knouted and dragged half dead into exile for his opinions. The next week she is stripped naked, and flogged to death in the public square. No inquiry, no explanation, no trial, no protest, one dead uniform silence, the law of the tyrant. Where is there ground for any hope of peaceful change? Where the fulcrum upon which you can plant any possible lever?

Macchiavelli's sorry picture of poor human nature would be fulsome flattery if men could keep still under such oppression. No, no! in such a land dynamite and the dagger are the necessary and proper substitutes for Faneuil Hall and the *Daily Advertiser*. Anything that will make the madman quake in his bedchamber, and rouse his victims into reckless and desperate resistance. This is the only view an American, the child of 1620 and 1776, can take of Nihilism. Any other unsettles and perplexes the ethics of our civilization.

Born within sight of Bunker Hill, in a commonwealth which adopts the motto of Algernon Sidney, *sub libertate quietem* (accept no peace without liberty),—son of Harvard, whose first pledge was "Truth," citizen of a republic based on the claim that no government is rightful unless resting on the consent of the people, and which assumes to lead in asserting the rights of humanity,—I at least can say nothing else and nothing less—no, not if every tile on Cambridge roofs were a devil hooting my words!

I shall bow to any rebuke from those who hold Christianity to command entire non-resistance. But criticism from any other quarter is only that nauseous hypocrisy, which, stung by three-penny tea-tax, piles Bunker Hill with granite and statues, prating all the time of patriotism and broadswords, while, like another Pecksniff, it recommends a century of dumb submission and entire non-resistance to the Russians, who, for a hundred years, have seen their sons by thousands dragged to death or exile, no one knows which, in this worse than Venetian mystery of police, and their maidens flogged to death in the market-place, and who share the same fate if they presume to ask the reason why.

"It is unfortunate," says Jefferson, "that the efforts of mankind to secure the freedom of which they have been deprived should be accompanied with violence and even with crime. But while we weep over the means, we must pray for the end." Pray fearlessly for such ends: there is no risk! "Men are all tories by nature," says Arnold, "when tolerably well off: only monstrous injustice and atrocious cruelty can rouse them." Some talk of the rashness of the uneducated classes. Alas! ignorance is far oftener obstinate than rash. Against one French Revolution—that scarecrow of the ages—weigh Asia, "carved in stone," and a thousand years of Europe, with her half-dozen nations meted out and trodden down to be the dull and contented footstools of priests and kings. The customs of a thousand years ago are the sheet-anchor of the passing generation, so deeply buried, so fixed, that the most violent efforts of the maddest fanatic can drag it but a hand's-breadth.

Before the war Americans were like the crowd in that terrible hall of Eblis which Beckford painted for us,—each man with his hand pressed on the incurable sore in his bosom, and pledged not to speak of it: compared with other lands, we were intellectually and morally a nation of cowards.

When I first entered the Roman States, a custom-house official seized all my French books. In vain I held up to him a treatise by Fénelon, and explained that it was by a Catholic archbishop of Cambray. Gruffly he answered, "It makes no difference: *it is French*." As I surrendered the volume to his remorseless grasp, I could not but honor the nation which had made its revolutionary purpose so definite that despotism feared its very language. I only wished that injustice and despotism everywhere might one day have as good cause to hate and to fear everything American.

At last that disgraceful seal of slave complicity is broken. Let us inaugurate a new departure, recognize that we are afloat on the current of Niagara,—eternal vigilance the condition of our safety,—that we are irrevocably pledged to the world not to go back to bolts and bars,—could not if we would, and would not if we could. Never again be ours the fastidious scholarship that shrinks from rude contact with the masses. Very pleasant it is to sit high up in the world's theatre and criticise the ungraceful struggles of the gladiators, shrug one's shoulders at the actors' harsh cries, and let every one know that but for "this villainous saltpetre you would yourself have been a soldier." But Bacon says, "In the theatre of man's life, God and His angels only should be lookers-on." "Sin is not taken out of man as Eve was out of Adam, by putting him to sleep." "Very beautiful," says Richter, "is the eagle when he floats with out-stretched wings aloft in the clear blue; but sublime when he plunges down through the tempest to his eyry on the cliff, where his unfledged young ones dwell and are starving." Accept proudly the analysis of Fisher Ames: "A monarchy is a man-of-war, stanch, iron-ribbed, and resistless when under full sail; yet a single hidden rock sends her to the bottom. Our republic is a raft, hard to steer, and your feet always wet; but nothing can sink her." If the Alps, piled in cold and silence, be the emblem of despotism, we joyfully take the ever-restless ocean for ours,—only pure because never still.

Journalism must have more self-respect. Now it praises good and bad men so indiscriminately that a good word from nine-tenths of our journals is worthless. In burying our Aaron Burrs, both political parties —in order to get the credit of magnanimity—exhaust the vocabulary of eulogy so thoroughly that there is nothing left with which to distinguish our John Jays. The love of a good name in life and a fair reputation to survive us—that strong bond to well-doing—is lost where every career, however stained, is covered with the same fulsome flattery, and where what men say in the streets is the exact opposite of what they say to each other. *De mortuis nil nisi bonum* most men translate, "Speak only good of the dead." I prefer to construe it, "Of the dead say nothing unless you can tell something good." And if the sin and the recreancy have been marked and far-reaching in their evil, even the charity of silence is not permissible.

To be as good as our fathers we must be better. They silenced their fears and subdued their prejudices, inaugurating free speech and equality with no precedent on the file. Europe shouted "Madmen!" and gave us forty years for the shipwreck. With serene faith they persevered. Let us rise to their level. Crush appetite and prohibit temptation if it rots great cities. Intrench labor in sufficient bulwarks against that wealth, which, without the tenfold strength of modern incorporation, wrecked the Grecian and Roman States; and, with a sterner effort still, summon women into civil life as reënforcement to our laboring ranks in the effort to make our civilization a success.

Sit not, like the figure on our silver coin, looking ever backward.

"New occasions teach new duties;
Time makes ancient good uncouth;
They must upward still, and onward,
Who would keep abreast of Truth.
Lo! before us gleam her camp-fires!
We ourselves must Pilgrims be,
Launch our Mayflower, and steer boldly
Through the desperate winter sea,
Nor attempt the Future's portal
With the Past's blood-rusted key."

— II —

PHILOSOPHY OF SCIENCE

10

CADWALLADER COLDEN

1688, born February 7 (N.S.), in Ireland of Scotish parents
1705, received the degree of A.B., University of Edinburgh
1705–10, studied medicine in London
1710, emigrated to America
1710–18, medical practice and commercial career in Philadelphia
1718, moved to New York
1720, surveyor general of New York
1721, appointed member of Governor's Council, New York
1727, *History of the Five Indian Nations Depending on the Province of New York*
1745, *An Explication of the First Causes of Action in Matter*
1751, *The Principles of Action in Matter, the Gravitation of Bodies, and the Motion of the Planets Explained from These Principles*
1761–76, Lieutenant-Governor of the Province of New York
1776, died September 28, in New York

THE Newtonian world-view was the unified statement of nearly two hundred years of scientific and mathematical thinking. Many of the ideas which were incorporated into Newton's synthesis were widely prevalent among men of science at the close of the seventeenth century. Newton's mechanistic natural philosophy, which provided the philosophical orientation of scientists for almost two centuries after his time, was itself the end-term of the Copernican and Cartesian "revolutions." With Locke's empirical science of human nature, Newton's mechanistic system of physical nature was the fountainhead of the Enlightenment both in Europe and in America.

The ground for the study, criticism, and acceptance of Newtonianism had been prepared in Harvard, at least, by the teaching of the discoveries and ideas of Copernicus, Galileo, Gilbert, and Kepler. Some part of the material used by Newton was supplied by a series of observations upon comets made by a Harvard graduate, Thomas Brattle, in 1680. Until 1727, however, the only work by Newton which was studied at Harvard was the *Opticks*. Most of the American knowledge of Newton came by way of secondary sources. Yale was more fortunate; Newton himself gave the Connecticut colonial agent J. Dummer a copy of the 1713 second edition of the *Principia*, as well as a copy of the *Opticks*. From 1714, then, Yale was in a position to teach the Newtonian philosophy and did so, despite the theological preoccupations of most of the faculty. It was at Yale that Samuel Johnson, later president of Kings College (Columbia) in New York first learned Newtonian thought.

New York produced the most competent American Newtonian of his age in the person of Cadwallader Colden. Colden made the attempt to criticize and to apply practically both the theory of fluxions and the theory of gravitation, Newtonian mathematics and physics. He had received his academic training at Edinburgh University, where he had been granted his medical degree. Edinburgh was in his time a center of antischolasticism, and Colden seems to have imbibed a fair and lasting share of this opposition.

Colden's elaborations of Newtonian physics in his *First Causes of Action in Matter and the Cause of Gravitation* (1746), in *The Principles of Action in Matter* (1751), and in various manuscript notes and treatises center in the criticism of the cause of gravitation. Newton had suggested that the mutual attraction of bodies was only apparent; that it was an effect rather than a cause. Colden tried to define that cause as the joint action of the moving, resisting, and elastic powers. He maintained that matter could not be inactive, for were it so, we could in no way perceive it. Thus, matter is dynamic; it is a combination of forces or energies.

From this view he was led to differ from the prevailing Lockean psychology. Knowledge could not be the cognition of inactive objects passively received by the senses. On the contrary, he asserted that all our primary ideas of external objects arise from the actions of the objects on our senses; that our knowledge of things is our perception of their actions; that thinking is a particular and unique kind of action. Thus, bodies and minds act jointly in perception. All knowledge is of action and its effects; passivity is cognitive nonexistence.

Faced with the question of the cause of the actions in matter which affect our senses, he could not fall into the occasionalism of Samuel Johnson in attributing all action immediately to God.[1] Such a solution would eliminate secondary causation and, with it, the uniformity of nature. He reached the solution that matter acts to the extent of its created powers and that we have no ideas of substances, but only of the actions of substances.

About 1760 Colden wrote a brief introductory statement of his views on natural philosophy for the benefit of young Peter Delancey and sent a copy to his son Alexander Colden for the use of other young members of the family. He accompanied the treatise with the following letter:

[1] See the correspondence between Johnson and Colden in H. W. Schneider and C. Schneider, *Samuel Johnson, President of King's College: His Career and Writings*, New York, 1929, II, 286–305.

To my son Alexander

Coldengham July 10th 1760

DEAR SON,

While your nephew, Peter De Lancey, was a few weeks with me, I wrote, for his use, the principal part of what I now send you. You cannot doubt of my having as great affection for your children, as for any of my grandchildren; but their age does not admit of my showing it to them, in the manner I did to him. It is probable, that by the time they come to the age proper for receiving instruction of this sort, I may not be capable of giving it. I have therefore gone over the papers which I wrote for your nephew; I have enlarged them in several places, for the use of your children. I now send them to you, as I write them, that you may preserve them for your children; and that they may be some memorial to them of their grandfather. I have no copy, and therefore must desire you to set one of your clerks to make out a copy for me which I design for another use.

You may allow Dr. Midletone or any other of my friends, who have been desirous to know my thoughts on the subject of these papers, to read them; but be careful that they be not lost; for, as I said before I have not another copy. You know some are very careless of papers put into their hands.

Your affectionate father

CADWALLADER COLDEN

Tell Dr. Midleton I shall receive any remarks on them as a favour.

To

Alexander Colden Esq.

New York

The treatise, which has never before been published, is printed here as a general indication of the views of a "natural philosopher," a type of scholar who perished with the Enlightenment. It will be noted that this brief work reveals both anticlericalism and opposition to scholasticism, both probably the heritage of Colden's Edinburgh student days, an account of Colden's doctrine of action in matter accompanied by a brief critique of Berkeley's position, and Colden's doctrine of the three types of action in matter, *vis inertiae*, or resistance, motion like light, and ether. It will be found by the reader to be an interesting and, though simplified, well-reasoned account of Colden's viewpoint.

AN INTRODUCTION TO THE STUDY OF PHYLOSOPHY WROTE IN AMERICA FOR THE USE OF A YOUNG GENTLEMAN

SECT. I

YOU are now, my ———, going to the college, in order to learn those principles, which may be of use to you in all your future inquiries; and to acquire that knowledge, by which you may be enabled to

distinguish yourself in every part of your life, either in public employments, or in private life, or that you may become an useful member of
the commonwealth and of a private family. But the common methods
of teaching, hitherto generally in use in the public Schools, is so far
from answering these good purposes, that it serves only to fill young
people's heads with useless notions and prejudices, which unfit them
for the acquiring of real and useful knowledge. The design of my present writing is to guard you against these common errors, and to instruct
you how to avoid them. In doing this I have supposed that you have
a general notion of the sciences, which are usually taught. I could not
do otherwise, within the limits I have set to myself, and therefore be not
discouraged, if at present you do not comprehend the full scope and
view of what I write. When you come to read on any of the sciences I
hope you will then find it of use to you.

History informs us, that the Egyptian priests, the Chald[ee] and
Persian magi had acquired great knowledge in physics, before the
Christian era, such as exceeds the knowledge of th[e] most learned
of the moderns. It is certain that they had carr[ied] Geometry,
Ast[r]onomy and Mechanics to a great perfection. The Greeks were
only meer Scholars of the Egyptians. It may be questioned whether
they made any discovery absolutely their own: and it is not improbable, that, like meer Scholars, they did not perfectly understand
the principles of the Egyptian philosophy; and yet it is from the
Greeks only that we have any knowledge of the learning of these ancients. Pythagoras was the best instructed of any of the Greeks in the
Egyptian learning. It appears from the little which remains of his
doctrine, that the Egyptians knew what of late times has been called
the Copernican System, and that he knew the general apparent attraction between bodies, which has been rediscovered in the last century by
Sr Isaac Newton. But as we have nothing remaining of the Pythagorean
philosophy, except what is found in a few abstracts in much later
writers, we know very little of what were the true principles of that
philosophy. It may be that we are now regaining the Principles of
Physics, which were known many ages before the beginning of the
Christian era. Wars, and the irruption of barbarous nations into the
countries where learning flourished, have been the destruction of
knowledge in those countries. But nothing so much prevented the
propagation of knowledge as the Craft of the pagan priests, who, in

order to secure their influence over the people, confined learning to their own order, and communicated their knowledge only to the *Initiated*, to such only of whose taciturnity and fidelity, after a severe trial, they were well assured. Whoever attempted to put mankind on a free inquiry into the truth of popularly received opinions, certainly suffered under a cruel persecution of the heathen priests. Socrates was persecuted and condemned to death, as a corrupter of youth, as an enemy to the Gods, and of the orthodox religion of his country; and yet Socrates, in all after ages, has been deemed the wisest man, and the man of the greatest probity that ever appeared among the pagans.

Nothing, in later ages, so much obstructed the advancement of knowledge as the craft of the popish priests, when they, in imitation of the pagan priests, founded the power of their dominion on the ignorance and credulity of the laity: by which they established a Tyranny in the Pope and the Clergy over Kings and Princes as well as over private persons, under pretence of their being intrusted with the keys of heaven and hell, and exerted their power more absolutely than ever had been done by any potentate before that time. To serve these purposes, all books, which might propagate real and useful knowledge, and thereby detect this priestcraft, were proscribed: they were, under the severest penalties, ordered to be brought in and burnt, and it became an unpardonable sin to read them. For the same purposes, the clergy assumed the sole power of licensing books; that is, without their consent no book could be published or was permitted to be read. By these means the best books of antiquity are lost, or curtailed, while the lascivious poets are transmitted to us entire. Copernicus durst not publish his system, till he was near his death, when he thought himself out of the reach of their persecution. He lived to see only one printed copy of it. Galileo was the first who applied the telescope to astronomical observations, and thereby absolutely confirmed the Copernican system. The nobility of Italy flocked to his house to view the planets. They saw clearly that the planets are really globular bodies, similar to our earth: and they saw the satellites of Jupiter, like so many moons, moving round the body of that planet. The priests could not bear that they should be convicted of teaching errors in philosophy, or that any knowledge can be obtained otherwise than from them. Galileo was clapt into the inquisition, and to free himself from the rack and a cruel death, he was forced to recant, and to give himself the lie publicly, he was forced to deny the truth of what he and many others had seen distinctly. Had not the reformation in religion taken place about that time, and several nations thrown off the authority of the Pope, the learning and knowledge of the present age had been nipt in the bud, and we should at this day have been in barbarous ignorance.

Nothing was so effectual in establishing the dominion of the priests as the education of youth, which they assumed solely to themselves. All the professors and teachers in the public Schools and universities were priests, none others were allowed to teach, nor are any others allowed at this day in popish countries. They know well how easy it is to instill strong prejudices into young minds, and of what force these prejudices are in the whole course of life.

To divert inquisitive minds (for such there are in all ages) from applying their thoughts and inquiries after real knowledge, the priests introduced into their schools a kind of learning of things, which, like dreams, exist nowhere but in the imagination: Abstracted notions, a multiplicity of terms or hard words, which have no meaning but to cover ignorance, perplexed definitions, Distinctions without real difference, from which were introduced endless disputes about mysterious trifles, of no real use, either to the advancement of knowledge or conduct in life; but served well to divert the inquisitive mind from inquiring into any kind of knowledge, which may be prejudicial to the dominion of the priests.

This kind of learning, at first introduced into the popish schools, has of late obtained the name of *school learning,* in opposition to the real knowledge of things. The *School Logic* is the art of continuing an argument or dispute without end, and without convincing or being convinced, without design to discover truth, but to cover ignorance, and defend error: and therefore well fitted to the chicanery of the law, or for perpetuating religious controversies, for it equally serves to defend the opinions of all sects.

The school learning is now expelled from the sciences. You'll find nothing of it in the modern astronomy, or in any of the mathematical sciences: the best writers in medicine are ashamed to make use of it; but it is to be found plentifully in books of Theology and Law. It is really surprising, that wherever the clergy, even among protestants, have the direction of the schools, that the youth are obliged to waste so much time in the study of this useless learning, or rather hurtful learning: for it really unfits them for the acquiring of real and useful knowledge. It must not be supposed that the protestant clergy do this, with a view to blindfold the laity, that they may have the leading of them: I rather suppose, that the first of the protestant clergy having been educated in the popish schools, they were not able to divest themselves of the prejudices which they received there, and by continuing their successors in the same studies, the same prejudices continue. But surely that kind of learning, by which only enthusiasm and superstition can be defended and propagated, cannot be the proper method to extirpate them. I hope therefore, that either the protestant clergy will expel this kind of learning from their schools, or that they no longer shall be suffered to have the direction of the schools of learning.

As to the Law, it is not to be expected that any reformation can come from the lawyers. No number of men will act contrary to their private interest, when they are too powerful in the state to be easily reduced to order. It can only be done by such a prince as the King of Prussia. I think it appears evidently from history, that when the people become generally uneasy under any great abuse, they throw the Society into confusion; but they are never able to give proper redress, by setting things on a proper and lasting foundation. This, at all times, has been done by the uncommon abilities of some single person. Is there anything in popery, or in the grossest idolatry more absurd than this, that to know how a man is to act in the common affairs of life, without endangering his liberty, property, or life, it should be necessary to study several years in the inns of court, and to have 2 or 300 books? Such are the mischievous effects of school learning; for without it such abuses could never have prevailed among mankind. Unless the understandings of mankind had been greatly depraved, the defending of fraud and villainy, and perverting of Justice must allwise have been held in abhorrence: and yet there is no rogue or villain (if he have money) who cannot find a lawyer to defend him, and to endeavour knowingly to pervert or at least to delay Justice, in favour of the rogue, and to the prejudice of the innocent, and this lawyer still preserves among his neighbours the character of a good lawyer, tho' in all cases, even in defence of right, he be a sort of licensed pickpocket. Ought not the truly good lawyers to spurn such men from among them, as the disgrace of their profession?

It may be now proper to give you some more particular knowledge of the school learning by informing you of the principles of the Schools in Physiology.

SECT. II

The Schoolmen tell us, that everything is either a Substance, a Quality, an Accident or a Mode.

A *Substance* is defined to be, something we conceive to subsist of it-self, independently of any created being, or any particular mode or accident.

A *Quality* is that affection of a thing, whence it is denominated such: or that which occasions a thing to affect our senses, in this or that manner.

A *Mode* is a manner of being: or a quality or attribute of a substance or subject, which we conceive as necessarily depending on the subject, and incapable of subsisting without it. An *Accident* is something ad-ditional, or superadded to substance: or not essentially belonging thereto, but capable indifferently either of being or not being in it, without the destruction thereof.

Definitions ought to give clear and distinct ideas or conceptions of the things defined, especially when they are introductory to every-thing we learn afterwards: and are the foundations of our knowledge as these definitions are designed to be. You can judge, whether you have received from them any clearer conceptions of the real differ-ences of things, than you had before you read them: or whether your conceptions be not rather more perplexed thereby than enlightened. These, however, have been received generally in all the universities and Schools of Europe, and have been delivered out by the learned Doc-tors, to their Scholars, as the Foundation of all knowledge.

Let us try what we can make of them, in discovering the nature of things. For example, let us try to find out what the substance of the candle now before us, is.

It is round; but this is only a mode, it might have been channelled, or square, or triangular, and still a candle.

It is white, this is a quality; it might have been yellow, or green, and it is of no colour in the dark.

It is greasy and of a certain stiffness. These likewise are only qualities, and the substance of the candle may subsist without them.

It may be set on fire, and it will burn and give light. This is only an accident, for it is as much a candle when it does not burn, as when it does.

Now to find out the substance of the candle, or to discover what the candle really is, we must remove all these qualities, modes, and accidents, which are only outside coverings and meer appearances, that we may come at the substance. But after you have removed the shape, the colour, the greasiness and stiffness, and its being capable of burning, what idea of the candle have you remaining? Have you any kind of conception of the substance? We are told by these learned doctors, that what we know of things by our senses are only qualities, only appearances or sensations, which often deceive us, and exist nowhere but in our own brains: for they have no existence but while they are felt or perceived. To know, therefore, what things really are, we must divest them of all their qualities, and throw aside our own sensations. Try to do this, and then tell me what the candle is. If, by this kind of learning, you can neither form any notion or conception of things to yourself, nor talk intelligibly to others, of what use is it? Why must two or three years of the best time of life be thrown away in acquiring it? Truly I think it will be difficult to assign any other reason, than what has been already mentioned, viz: to divert the inquisitive mind from all real and useful knowledge.

However a popish priest may show you some use of it in a remarkable instance. All the sensible qualities of bread, its colour, taste, smell, and consistence may be removed, without destroying the substance of the bread. So all the appearances, to the senses, of Flesh may be taken away, without destroying the substance of the Flesh. Then if the Substance of Flesh be substituted under the qualities of bread, there is no absurdity in conceiving transubstantiation, with a small degree of Faith or credulity in the divine power of the priesthood, after the disciple is well instructed in school learning; but if the disciple be defective in this learning, it must require much more credulity to be able to swallow either transubstantiation or consubstantiation.

In short, the most part of the logic and metaphysics, taught not only in the popish and church of England schools, but likewise in the Schools of the dissenters is of the kind of stuff, which I have just now shewn you. They have served the purposes of Robert Barclay, as well as the purposes of Cardinal Bellarmine, and of both with equal success.

SECT. III

The Schoolmen continued dictators in the republic of literature. *The Master or the Doctor said it* was an irresistible argument, 'till about the year 1640, when Rene Descartes, a Frenchman, published his philosophy. He, in opposition to them, boldly asserted, that we must receive nothing in philosophy on meer authority. We must doubt the truth of every proposition, 'till we have sufficient evidence of its truth. He has the honour of asserting the liberty of philosophising, and of thereby introducing all the discoveries which have been since made in physics. He carried the humour of doubting a little too far. The only, or rather first, self evident proposition, which he allowed, was *I think, therefore I am;* but surely I can as little doubt of your existence, who sit by me, as I can of my own. His physics are founded on ingenious hypotheses by which he attempts to explain the phenomena of nature; but, as in forming these hypotheses, he had not the advantage of the accurate observations, and numerous experiments, which have been since made, and many phenomena have been discovered, of which in his time they had no knowledge, it is no wonder that he should have failed in many things, and that his system of physics is rather an amusing philosophic romance than a true natural history. However he had the honour of exciting that passion for new discoveries, which, from his time to the present, has so much advanced real and useful knowledge: and he was the first among the moderns who made use of Geometry in physical researches.

This liberty in philosophising, which Descartes assumed, alarmed all the Doctors of the Schools. They, whose assertions had passed uncontested on their single authority, could not bear such freedom of doubting and inquiring. As they could not withstand the force of Descartes' arguments, they took that course of silencing him which a Quaker, after their example, lately took with a gentleman's dog, that had been disorderly among his sheep. When the gentleman did not give the Quaker the redress which he expected, he told the gentleman, that he would give his dog an ill-name: and accordingly the next time the dog appeared in the street, the Quaker bawl'd out, a mad dog, a mad dog, on which the neighbours dispatched him with stones. The Doctors published every where that Descartes is an atheist but at that time the priests had in a great measure lost their influence in France, and their exclamations had not the effect they expected. They applied therefore to the Parliament of Paris to have Descartes' books suppressed: and, it is said, they would have succeeded, had not the parliament been diverted by a burlesque petition. Ridicule often is of more force than a serious argument. You may generally observe that when any use scurrility in argument they are sensible of the want of other force.

My present purpose does not allow me to give you a particular account of Descartes' system. I shall only mention his general distinction of Matter and Spirit. The essence of matter, he says, consists in extension, that it cannot be conceived but of some length, breadth, and thickness: and the essence of Spirit in thinking. But supposing that a spirit is not united to body, in the manner the soul is, it is difficult, if not impossible to shew, that it thinks, or that it has any kind of action similar to what we call thinking. Extension cannot distinguish any one being from another: for can any thing be conceived to exist, or to be any where, or in any part of space, and to be of no length, breadth, or thickness? I cannot conceive anything to exist, but either by an universal extension or expansion through all space, or by a limited extension in some part of space, otherwise it exists nowhere, which to me is to say that it does not exist. Extension, therefore, can make no distinction between matter and spirit, unless it be said, that Spirit is universally extended, and matter confined within limits. Again the properties of everything depends on its essence, and may be evidently deduced from it; but I think, none have attempted to deduce the properties and phenomena of matter from meer extension, and it is impossible to do it: for meer extension gives no idea of any power by which any effect or phenomenon can be produced.

To avoid these difficulties and just exceptions, the present teachers in the Schools tell us, that the essential difference between matter and spirit is in *Inactivity* and *Activity*. Matter, they say, is an absolutely passive substance, which can do nothing of itself: it receives all action from the active substance or from spirit.

May I ask, what idea or conception can I have of a thing which does nothing? A definition which consists wholly of negatives is a definition of nothing. An absolute negation is a denial of existence. Something must be positively affirmed of a thing before I can receive any conception of it. We have no idea or perception of any thing external to us but in consequence of some impression on our senses, if any thing can exist, which has no kind of power, action, or force, we can by no means discover that it exists. A being absolutely inactive can produce no one phenomenon; it is absolutely useless, and no reason of the least probability can be given for its existence.

For these reasons Dr. Berkeley denied the existence of Matter, and affirmed, that everything which we call matter exists nowhere but in our own mind. That neither our thoughts, passions, nor ideas formed by Imagination exist without the mind, he says, is evident; nor is it less evident that the various ideas or sensations imprinted on the sense, however blended or combined (that is whatever objects they compose) cannot exist otherwise, than as in a mind perceiving them. What are hills and trees etc., but things perceived by sense; and what do we perceive but our own ideas and sensations: and can any one of these, or any combination of them exist unperceived? Thus your body, head, hands, etc. are only the ideas of body, head, hands, etc. which exist only in my mind; and my body is only an idea which exists in your mind and in the mind of others who perceive it. You will hardly believe, I suppose, that he was in earnest when he wrote these things. Yes he was, he wrote a large and learned treatise in proof of this doctrine: and he has obtained disciples, who have formed a sect in philosophy called *Idealists*, which has extended to America, where you will find men of sense advocates for it. In truth, if matter be really and absolutely inactive, that it does nothing, Dr. Berkeley's arguments are unanswerable; but if it be said, that all these ideas, which we have of bodies, are excited in consequence of some action of matter, they are of no force.

From what proceeds it is a necessary consequence, that matter, if there be any such thing, must have some power or force. Our next inquiry shall be what power or force this is, which distinguishes matter from all other beings.

Matter or body (which is some certain quantity of matter) in some degree or other resists our touch, and thereby excites the sense of feeling. This is so general an observation that if we can feel nothing in any place we conclude there is no body there.

When a body is at rest it requires some force to move it. If it require a certain degree of force to make a body move one foot in a second, it requires double that force to make it move two feet in a second, and thrice the force to make it move three feet in the same time. Again if it require a certain force to move a certain quantity of matter one foot in a second, it requires a double force to move a double quantity of the same matter the same distance in the same time, and thrice the force to move a treble quantity of matter. From these observations, which may be made every day, it is evident, that there is some power or force in matter, by which it persists in its present state, and resists any change of its state. It cannot be by meer inactivity, or by doing nothing; because one absolute want of any thing cannot be greater or less than any other absolute want. It is nonsense to say, one thing does nothing, and another thing does twice as much nothing.

If a body swimming in water, receive any degree of motion, it from time to time loses its motion gradually, till at last it rests. If the same body receive the same degree of motion in the air, it loses its motion at last, but continues it to a greater distance and longer time. If the same body be put in motion in a place void of air it continues its motion longer than it did in air. From these observations it is concluded, that a body once put in motion, would continue to move with the same degree of velocity, if it meet with no resistance from some other body, or from the medium in which it moves. And if any quantity of matter, moving with a certain velocity, require a certain degree of force to stop it, double the quantity of matter, moving with the same velocity, requires double the force to stop it, and so on. From these observations equally true, at all times and in all places, it is concluded, that there is a power or force in matter, by which it persists in its present state, whether it be in motion or at rest. When two bodies move with the same degree of motion, and have different force, and this difference is constantly observed to be in proportion to the quantity of matter in each, it cannot arise from the motion; for it is equal in both; and therefore can only arise from the quantity of matter, to which it is allwise in proportion.

When you take a ball in your hand, and put your hand and the ball in motion, and then suddenly withdraw your hand from the ball, the ball continues to move after your hand, which gave it motion, is withdrawn from it. So likewise when a ball receives motion, from the explosion of gunpowder within a gun barrel, the ball continues its motion with great velocity to a great distance, after the gunpowder has entirely ceased to act upon it. What is it, which continues this motion in the ball, after your hand is withdrawn and the gunpowder ceases to act? Not your hand, nor the gunpowder: for nothing can act where it is not, nor after it has ceased to act. If you attend to the proper conception of cause and effect, anything can as little act at the distance of one hair's breadth, as it can at the distance of one thousand miles, without something passing from it to the other thing on which it acts, or without some middle thing or medium, by which the action is continued from the one to the other: for nothing can act where it is not, or produce any effect after it has ceased to act, more than it can after it has ceased to be or to exist. Therefore the continuance of motion in the ball is by some power in the ball itself, that is, by that power by which matter resists all change in its present state, whether it be in motion or at rest.

You have, my ———, thrown many a stone, without imagining that there was any difficulty in conceiving how the stone moved of itself, after it was gone from your hand. You may hence learn, how the powers of things may be discovered, from the most common and trivial effects, when properly and attentively considered: and that a truly philosophic turn of mind can never want opportunities of improving in knowledge, without the expense of any apparatus for experiments.

Sʳ Isaac was the first who observed this power in matter, that it is essential to it and distinguishes it from all other beings. Is it not wonderful, that where the means of discovery are so easy and obvious, that the discovery was not made before his time: tho' it be a power every where to be observed, from its effects, and without which none of the phenomena of matter can be explained, and the understanding of it be of the greatest use in the arts and sciences? Can any other reason be given, than that the inquisitive mind was diverted by the vain sub-tilities of the schools, and the prejudices early received there?

Sr Isaac Newton called this power in matter *Vis inertia*. It is difficult to find an English word to convey a proper idea of this power. It has been commonly turned into the word *Inactivity*, and this was done, I suppose, in favour of the prevailing opinion, that matter is absolutely passive and unactive. But this can never express Sr Isaac Newton's meaning: for to talk of a power or force which does nothing, can only serve to make people laugh. It is as plain a contradiction to say force without action as to say force without force. Power without force, and force without action, or which does nothing is as unintelligible as any absurdity can be. This power is more properly called the power of re-sisting any change in its present state, whether it be in motion or at rest, as Sr Isaac defines it; for resistance carries the idea of force and of action with it, or of doing something.

Some cannot conceive any action without motion. This arises from a faulty connection of ideas, by joining motion to all kind of action: for which no kind of reason can be given. Thinking is certainly doing something, or is a kind of action; but we conceive no kind of motion in thinking. Some likewise expect that we shall tell them in what manner the resisting power acts. To this it is answered, that we cannot explain the manner of acting of any simple power otherwise than by its effects. Motion can no otherwise be explained than by change of place; but change of place is only the effect of motion: and the effects of the re-sisting power can be as clearly shewn, as the effects of motion can be.

I told you before that the school learning is really a misapplication of time, in learning of things which exist nowhere but in the imagina-tions of idle, monkish, useless men, and serves no good purpose in life. It is otherwise in acquiring knowledge of the powers and force of those things on which our well-being depends. Our life and health, our pleas-ures and pain all depend on the powers of those beings, which con-stitute the human system, and on the powers of other things, which are continually acting upon it. Not only the speculative sciences, the ex-plaining of all the phenomena which strike our senses, depend on the knowledge of these powers; but likewise all the practical arts depend on them. This knowledge is useful to us in every circumstance of life, whether as individuals and private persons, or as members of Society: as will very evidently appear to you, when you shall apply your thoughts to any particular art or science.

From the resisting power of matter we form a clear conception of its impenetrability, or that no quantity of matter can occupy the same space, which any other quantity of matter does: for if it could, we lose the idea of its resisting power, this power must be supposed to be destroyed, and with it we lose every conception we have of matter. We cannot conceive two quantities of matter in the same space, without losing any idea we have at least of one of them: all ideas which distinguish them are lost. In short, take away the idea of resistance from matter and we have no idea of matter remaining. Its essence, therefore, consists in its power of resisting all change of its present state, from which all the phenomena or properties of matter are deduced, as the effects of this power, and without it none of them can be understood.

SECT. V

Nothing so much prevents the advancement of knowledge, as false maxims, when received on the authority of great names, as the test and evidence of truth. They are, in our progress to knowledge, like shackles on our legs in walking, they are not only a continual hindrance to our advancing, but frequently throw us down in the dirt. It may be of use to discover such, and to expose them, especially when supported by venerable names, which otherwise have great respect due to them.

In consequence of the maxim, that activity is peculiar to spiritual substances, and that the material are entirely passive, it is said that God, in the beginning, created a certain quantity of motion, and distributed it, in certain proportions, through the universe: that the same quantity in the whole allwise remains; but that the distribution of it in the several parts is continually changing, some bodies are losing all or part of their motion, while others are acquiring or increasing motion. It is said, God created motion, because it is not to be imagined, that he communicates motion by impulse, or by projecting: for thereby we should reduce our conceptions of God, to that of some finite material being. So far in a proper sense is true, but then they add, that when God created motion, he did not create any being, or real thing: for then there must be some active being besides spirit. He created, they say, only a quality or an action, which he distributed through the universe. Can any thing be more ridiculous in all the exploded School learning than this? God created a certain quantity of no real thing, or he created no being, but only a certain quantity of a mode or an action. May we not with the same propriety say God in the beginning created a certain quantity of colours and sounds, of darkness and silence? or, that he created a certain quantity of round, square, triangular, and other figures or forms, and distributed them over the universe, which are continually changing from one part of the universe to another. And thus we may receive any kind of learned jargon that can enter the most disordered imagination.

On this supposition, that the same quantity of motion remains allwise, when anything acquires motion some other thing must lose as much motion, and nothing can communicate more motion than it had and loses. A single spark of fire gradually sets a large city all in fire, or a single spark sets fire to a quantity of gunpowder, which with immense force throws rocks and castles up into the air. Can it be imagined that all that motion, which appears while a whole city is in flames, was really in the little spark which began the fire, or that the whole force of motion, produced by the gunpowder, was in the little spark, which set fire to it? Is it not more reasonable to think that some active being, which has in itself the power of moving, is included in the materials of the city, or in the gunpowder, which, in the one case, was gradually set at liberty to act, and in the other case suddenly all in one instant?

It is therefore more natural, or consistent with common sense, to say: God in the beginning created a certain being, to which he gave the power of motion; and distributed this being, in certain proportions, in the several parts of the universe. The granting of this is no negative to the existence of spirits; they may, and undoubtedly both exist, without including any contradiction.

It is not difficult to discover a being evidently distinct both from matter and spirit, as I think may clearly appear from what follows. We cannot open our eyes in daylight without discovering it, and the effects produced by it. Wherever we discover light we discover motion. Take away motion from light, and every conception we have of it ceases; that is, we cannot conceive any effect from light, without conceiving it to be in motion: and from motion alone, and from the different velocities of the several rays of light, all the phenomena of light can be explained, without supposing that it has any other power or property; and without supposing that the parts of light are of any magnitude or of any shape. By the increase of the sun's light, in the several parts of the earth, motion is everywhere increased in summer: and by the lessening the degree of light in winter, motion is lessened; as is evident in vegetables, animals, and fluids. Generally light either precedes or attends all violent motions, and our not seeing it, wherever we perceive motion, is no proof of its absence; but only that there is not sufficient light to affect our senses. Cats, owls, bats, etc., see clearly with a degree of light by which we can discover nothing. The motion of the planets seems to put it beyond dispute, that their motion proceeds from the light of the sun: for their velocities is precisely as the density or force of light at their several distances from the sun; that is in a ratio reciprocal to the squares of their distances from the sun.

However it is to be carefully observed, that tho' bodies originally receive their motion from light, yet they very generally continue that motion by their resisting power only: and by this same power communicate motion from one to another. This is very different from simple motion or light, as the effects of it likewise are. It is a compound effect or action of the moving and resisting powers united: for it is allwise in a compound ratio of the degree of motion or velocity and the quantity of matter in the body which moves. For this reason, Sr Isaac Newton has distinguished this compound force by a peculiar name; he calls it *Momentum*. None of our teachers, so far as I know, have distinguished the moving power from this compound effect of the moving and resisting powers. The whole doctrine or laws of motion, which you'll find in books, is only of bodies in motion, and of their effects on other bodies, either in motion or at rest. For this reason you'll often find strange perplexity in their writings, by distinguishing velocity from motion, as if velocity were something else than a greater or less degree of motion.

The natural simple powers can only be distinguished by their effects, or by the phenomena which they produce; some very obvious appearances, which every man may observe, lead us to such knowledge of light, as will sufficiently distinguish it from every other being. As rays of light pass from every visible point of an illuminated room, to every other point of that room, to which a straight line can be drawn: for this point can be seen by an eye placed in any of the other points. Then every ray of light, moving from any one point of the room, meets with another ray moving in a direct opposite direction; yet the motion of no one ray is stopt by their meeting in opposite directions, nor are they in the least turned aside. Again, the ray which moves from any one point, in the corner of the room, to the opposite corner of the room, is crossed in every point of that line, by rays from every point in the room: for every point of the room can be seen by eyes placed in every point of that line. And yet the motion of the ray from corner to corner is in no manner obstructed or its direction diverted, by these innumerable rays which cross it. The like is to be observed in the rays from the fixed stars; they pass through an immense distance, and everywhere in that immense space cross the rays from the sun, from other fixed stars, and from the planets, yet nowhere are they stopt or diverted from their course in a straight line.

From these and innumerable other phenomena, it is evident, that the rays of light are mutually penetrable: and that light has no power of resisting; consequently that light and resisting matter are essentially different beings or substances. Tho' this be so very obvious, how few, if any, have made this reflexion. The reason of it can only be, from a prejudice we have received from our infancy, that there are no other beings except matter and spirit: and yet I know no one reason for this assertion, if the authority of venerable names be excepted.

Since light has no power of resisting, and its parts are mutually penetrable, it follows that any quantity of light may be contained in any space: that the smallest quantity in bulk or extension may be so expanded as to fill the largest space, without leaving any vacuity between its parts: and the largest quantity may be condensed into the smallest space. No doubt, this appears to be a paradox to you; but if I can shew that in fact it is so, there can be no absurdity in asserting it. Consider how prodigiously light is expanded by the explosion of gunpowder, by the distance at which it can be seen in every direction: and consider what small space this light occupied, in the gunpowder, before explosion, after the space occupied by the resisting matter of the gunpowder is deducted. A candle may be seen at the distance of one mile at least, in a clear serene air and a dark night. Sailors will inform you, that a ship at sea has been discovered at a much greater distance, by the light of a candle on board. Light is emitted by momentary vibrations, and the light emitted, from a candle, in every one of these momentary vibrations fills at least a spherical space of two miles diameter; because no point within that space can be assigned, which is not in that moment illuminated. Now if it be considered what a small quantity of a candle is dissolved, in that instant of one emission of light, and the resisting matter of the candle be deducted from that quantity, the light, which filled the sphere of two miles diameter, must have been contained in a less space than can be imagined. Sr Isaac Newton has shewn in his Optics that the vibrations of light are in less time than in the thirds or fourths of time, none of which can be distinguished by our senses.

Consider the vast expansion of light which is emitted from the surface of the sun, the vast expansion of the same light when reflected from the surface of the moon, and lastly its vast expansion when reflected from every point of any body on the earth, which is seen either by the naked eye or by the help of a microscope, and it must appear that this expansion exceeds anything which we can conceive by imagination; and after all this vast expansion, not the least vacuity or distance between the parts of light can, by any means, be discovered.

When what precedes is well considered, you cannot doubt of light's being a distinct substance from matter, and that they have nothing in common between them, except that they both may be considered as of some quantity, that there may be a greater and a less quantity of light, and that it may be confined within certain limits, by some other power. It is easy to conceive from what precedes that light is the moving power or the principle of motion: and you will find this confirmed by every observation you shall make of the great and small phenomena in nature.

The contemplation of the wonderful power of light, and of its universal influence in every part of the world, especially on animals and vegetables, led the ancient Persians into a kind of enthusiasm, which made them deify the sun, the source of light. Their descendants to this day continue to worship the sun and fire, as the fountains of light and life. It cannot be a doubt, that they conceived light as a real being distinct from all others.

SECT. VI

The occult qualities have been long exploded and excluded from the republic of learning, as only artful coverings of ignorance, by which pretenders to knowledge would make others believe that they know things of which they are absolutely ignorant. This they do by imposing words, which have no meaning, in place of real knowledge. When you ask one of these learned Doctors, who is unwilling to be thought ignorant of any thing, by what means amber draws a straw, or a feather to it, they gravely tell you it is by an occult quality in the amber. Why a stone falls to the earth? It is by an occult quality in the stone, by which it allwise tends to the center of the earth. Put these answers into plain English and they are no other than this. Amber attracts a feather or a straw; but I know not how. A stone allwise falls to the ground; but I know not why. Such plain and direct answers are inconsistent with the pretensions of the learned professor: and, which is worse, would not please the Scholar. Mankind in general are better pleased to be duped, with the unmeaning appearance of knowledge, than to allow that their teachers are ignorant or deceitful.

Notwithstanding that in this enlightened age, no maxims in philosophy are admitted, but what are self evident, and which the unlearned as well as the learned clearly perceive to be true: and no theorem or conclusions are received, but what are demonstratively deduced from these maxims; yet we find many, of great reputation for their knowledge in physics, asserting, that all bodies attract each other, while at a distance from each other, without supposing any thing between these bodies, or passing from the one to the other, by which any kind of action can pass from the one to the other; but by some inherent quality or power in the bodies themselves. Can anything in the occult qualities of the Schools be more absurd than this? If it be supposed, that a body can act on another at the least distance from where it is, without something passing or some medium between them, by which the action is continued, it may in the like manner act at the greatest distance with equal force: for where nothing passes and nothing is between the bodies, no reason can be given for its acting with less force at any distance. It supposes that bodies act where they are not, and with equal reason they may be supposed to act after they have ceased to be. I can see no reason why a man who admits of this mutual attraction in bodies should be shocked at Transubstantiation, or at any other fashionable absurdity.

Innumerable phenomena shew that all bodies tend to each other, by some force or other; but no phenomenon can shew, that it is done by an attractive quality in themselves: nor can it be done by any of emission from themselves, for no motion from a body can give motion to the same body. It seems, then, necessary to conclude, that this mutual tendency and motion of bodies to each other is by the action of some medium, surrounding all bodies, or in which all bodies are placed. The knowledge of the nature or power of this medium can only be obtained, as the knowledge of all other powers is, by an accurate observation of the effects or phenomena produced by it. I suppose none will affirm, that nothing exists, but what we either feel, see, hear, smell, or taste. The existence of some things may be as evident by reflexion on the phenomena, or on the effects produced by them, or by reasoning, as the existence of others is by immediate perception. Where effects are evidently perceived, it is with the greatest certainty concluded, that something exists which has sufficient power to produce these effects. In truth we have no other method to discover the existence of anything, but by its effects either mediately, or immediately on the senses. Neither can I conceive any necessity to think that this medium consists either of resisting matter or of light, or of both united. Its effects shew it to be something different from either of them, some being which has a power peculiar to itself, the nature of which is to be discovered by its effects, as the powers of matter and light are, by an accurate observation of the effects produced by them.

From an accurate observation of the effects between bodies at a distance from each other, I conclude, that the parts of the medium in which they are placed are all, in every respect, contiguous; and therefore it cannot be conceived as consisting of particles, of any shape or dimensions. Nevertheless, it may be conceived as of different quantities, or as occupying a smaller or larger quantity of space, in the same manner as space is considered as of different quantities. From the same observation I conclude that this medium receives equally the action of resisting from any contiguous body, or of motion from light which passes through it: and that the parts or quantity of the medium contiguous to the body receives the action immediately from the body and communicates the same to the next contiguous parts or quantity and so on to a great distance. This communication to the greatest distance is done in one instant, because there is no distance between the parts of the medium, in the same manner as any motion is communicated from one end of a rod, however long it be, in the same instant to the other end. Immediately after any quantity of this medium has received the action, either of resisting or of moving, it reacts the same with the same force which it received. This alternate action and reaction is made evident in Sr Isaac Newton's Optics, by the alternate transmission and stopping of light on passing through pellucid bodies. You may imagine this reaction as something similar to what you feel, when taking one end of a rod in your hand, you push the other end against a wall, you feel the wall react or push the rod against your hand, with the same force with which you pushed the rod. In the next place it is constantly observed, that the resisting power in matter, is opposite, or a negative power to motion: it allwise either destroys, or stops, or lessens the action of motion.

These observations being premised, call this medium Ether, for it is proper to give it a name, suppose the Ether, surrounding any spherical body of resisting matter, be divided into equidistant concentric spherical surfaces, it is evident that these spherical surfaces increase the farther they are from the center of the spherical body. Geometers demonstrate that this increase is in the ratio of the squares of their diameters or of the distance of the surface from the common center. Again it is observed that if any certain force communicate a degree of force to any certain quantity, it communicates half the degree of force to double the quantity, or that the degree of action communicated is reciprocal to the quantity of the thing which receives the action. Then it follows that the quantity of the action of resisting, which is communicated to the several parts of Ether surrounding a spherical body, decreases continually from the body, in a ratio reciprocal to the square of their distance from the body. Since the action of resistance is negative to motion, if motion be communicated by light to the Ether the reaction of motion will be more lessened the nearer the parts of the Ether are to the body: consequently the reaction will be allwise stronger on the side of any small body farther distant from the other large spherical body than on the side nearest to it and the little body will be moved toward the great body. Thus I have indeavoured to give you some conception how one body may appear to be attracted by another at a distance from it, tho' the effect be really that of a third thing acting upon it.

Since it is impossible, that anything can act where it is not, we may safely conclude that it is done in the manner and by such powers as are sufficient to produce all the phenomena of apparent mutual attraction. We have no other method of discovering the powers which produce the phenomena, and when they appear evidently sufficient, we cannot doubt of their existence. My present purpose does not allow me to go through all the phenomena of mutual apparent attraction, and of gravitation, and to shew how clearly they are deduced from a reacting medium as before described; the understanding of it requires more skill in Geometry, than you have as yet obtained. What I have now wrote may be of use to you, when you come to read what has been wrote on this subject, with the assistance of your Master of Mathematics.

After what you have read in the preceding pages, I must imagine, that you will be surprised afterwards to find that men who pretend to receive nothing but what is self-evident, or demonstratively deduced from such, at this time teach that bodies mutually attract each other at a distance by an inherent quality in themselves: and they teach this, they say, on the authority of Sr Isaac Newton. No authority is sufficient to establish an absurdity; but in the present case Sr Isaac takes care to guard against this absurdity. He tells that bodies in appearance only attract each other at a distance from each other, and that this apparent attraction is reciprocal to the squares of their distances. He says this must be done by the power of some medium, of which, he candidly confesses, he has not obtained sufficient knowledge; but he nowhere asserts that it is by any power inherent in matter: on the contrary he asserts that such a supposition is so great an absurdity, that he believes, no man, who has a competent faculty of thinking in philosophical matters, can fall into it. You will find many late writers in physics, who pretend to deduce their theorems from mathematical principles; and yet, notwithstanding of these high pretensions, and geometrical figures, and algebraical calculations, are often falling into gross errors in physics. You will find some of them assuming geometrical figures as physical causes. It is necessary, therefore, to guard you against such high pretenders.

No doubt, the method of geometrical demonstration, and algebraical investigation is the best Logic: and may be of the greatest use, in accustoming young people to a regular method of reasoning. But to be perpetually poring [on lines] and figures, and jumbling together algebraical characters, cramps the imagination; they become like the dog in a wheel, perpetually running the same round, and is good for nothing else. You will find some of these high mathematicians as ignorant of the true principles of knowledge, as any pretenders whatsoever, and as little fitted for the most useful parts of life, or for common conversation.

The gentleman, who proposes to be generally useful in society, ought not to fix his thoughts singly on any one branch of science, but to have a competent knowledge of the principles of every branch, which he may obtain without fatiguing his imagination, by too continued an application. While he reads and thinks by turns, he should, in the intervals, cultivate his intellectual faculties by general conversation, where he may obtain more useful knowledge, than can be learned from books. The mere Scholar, the mere Physician, the mere Lawyer, Musician or painter, take them out of their own way, and they are often more insipid, than the mere plowman.

BENJAMIN RUSH

1745, born December 24 (O.S.) in Byberry, Pa.
1760, received the degree of A.B., College of New Jersey (Princeton)
1761–66, studied medicine under Dr. John Redman
1766–68, completed medical education, University of Edinburgh
1768–69, St. Thomas's Hospital, London; beginning of intimacy with Franklin
1769, entered medical practice at Philadelphia, Pa.
1769, professor of chemistry, College of Philadelphia
1770, *A Syllabus of a Course of Lectures on Chemistry*
1772, *Sermons to Gentlemen upon Temperance and Exercise*
1773, *An Address to the Inhabitants of the British Settlements in America, upon Slave Keeping*
1774, one of the organizers of the Pennsylvania Society for Promoting the Abolition of Slavery (President, 1803)
1776, June, elected to Provincial Conference
1776, July, elected to Continental Congress
1777, surgeon general at Armies of the Middle Department
1780, lecturer at University of State of Pennsylvania
1783, trustee of Dickinson College
1783, staff member of Pennsylvania Hospital
1786, established first free dispensary in the United States
1787, elected to Pennsylvania Ratifying Convention
1787, one of the organizers of Philadelphia College of Physicians
1789, with James Wilson, led move for new liberal state constitution
1789, professor of medical theory and practice, College of Philadelphia
1792, professor of institutes of medicine and clinical practice in newly formed University of Pennsylvania
1796, professor of medical theory and practice, University of Pennsylvania
1797–1813, treasurer of the U.S. Mint
1798, *Essays, Literary, Moral, and Philosophical*
1799, *Three Lecturers upon Animal Life*
1812, *Medical Inquiries and Observations upon the Diseases of the Mind*
1813, died April 19, at Philadelphia, Pa.

THE political results of the Enlightenment in the Declaration of Independence, the Jeffersonian tradition, and in general the theory of democratic republicanism are especially noteworthy and have become a focus for the thought of liberals of today who seek a positive ground for their thinking. No less important in the eighteenth and early nineteenth centuries was the impulse to scientific speculation which derived from the philosophy of the Enlightenment. That much of this scientific speculation is today no more than a curiosity of intellectual history is in itself a tribute to the development of the scientific habit of mind on a wide basis during this period.

The primary impetus to scientific investigation came from the belief in natural law which was characteristic of thought in that period. Newtonian mechanism had a marked effect in the colonies; one recent writer finds in Newtonianism one of the chief sources of the thought of Tom Paine, while another dignifies the pre-Revolutionary period by the title "the Newtonian epoch in the American colonies." The study of Newton led to the search for regularities in nature, and, among some more liberal thinkers, to a religion of nature, in the extreme form of which, in such thinkers as Elihu Palmer and Joseph Buchanan, nature was apotheosized. The progress of science was intimately allied with natural religion and democratic political thought and therefore with the weakening of authoritarian beliefs.

One such authoritarian belief whose influence was on the wane was the belief in revelation. The Scriptural account of man and his environment could be questioned in this period as it had not been for centuries. The sciences of the Enlightenment were physiology, anthropology, and geology. Thomas Jefferson communicated to the American Philosophical Society (organized in 1744) descriptions of fossil remains which he had unearthed; he challenged Buffon's theory that the American continents produced animals of a size inferior to those of Europe and defended the contrary by statistical tables. Even the relatively orthodox Samuel Stanhope Smith, son-in-law of John Witherspoon and president of Princeton, entered the lists with an anthropological pamphlet explaining environmentally the causes of variety in human figure and complexion.

The men of the Enlightenment held in common a belief in the powers of the human mind to comprehend the laws of the natural environment for the benefit of mankind. This positive faith was nowhere better stated than in Joel Barlow's *Columbiad*:

> And lo, my son, that other sapient band
> The torch of science flaming in their hand!
>
> . . .
>
> Fixt in sublimest thought, behold them rise
> World after world unfolding to their eyes,
> Lead, light, allure them thro the total plan
> And give new guidance to the paths of man.

Benjamin Rush, by no means the least distinguished of the early scientists in the United States, was politically active during the Revolution, and was one of the signers of the Declaration of Independence. His major scientific work was in the field of physiology. His professorship of chemistry at the College of Philadelphia was the first such chair in the American colonies. He held chairs of medicine in the College of Philadelphia, and the University of Pennsylvania. His physiological researches led him to speculate upon the theme of the relation between physiology and morals, to move toward the development of a materialistic ethics. He presented this view in an address before the American Philosophical Society in 1786. This address, which is here reprinted, was the source of Joseph Buchanan's theory of the "unity of excitement," and, through the attention it received from George Combe, it became one of the vital documents in the development of the "science" of phrenology.

Rush borrowed the term "moral faculty" from Dr. Beattie and thus indicated the continuity of the American and the Scottish enlightenment. He presents, however, a most important limitation of the moral faculty. "As I consider virtue and vice to consist in *action*, and not in opinion, and as this action has its seat in the *will*, and not in the conscience, I shall confine my inquiries chiefly to the influence of physical causes upon that moral power of the mind, which is connected with volition." The state of the conscience Rush considered beyond investigation, because it is invisible, whereas the state of the moral faculty, or will, "is visible in actions, which affect the well-being of society." Thus, again, Rush's ethical theory was in accord with the trend of Scottish and American thought in virtually equating virtue and benevolence.

Recognizing that his theory of the influence of the physical on the moral might be supposed by its opponents to favor materialism, he asserted its neutrality on this question, with the addition of the remark that "the writers in favour of the immortality of the soul have done that truth great injury, by connecting it necessarily with its immateriality,"—a remark which makes it evident that Rush was himself not far from materialism. In fact he declared that "matter is in its own nature as immortal as spirit." The trend of his thought is further revealed in a later passage, where he maintained "that the operations of the divine government are carried on in the moral, as in the natural world, by the instrumentality of second causes."

If, as Rush believed, physical causes influence the moral faculty, then the conditions of education become a matter of vital importance. These matters were frequently discussed by Rush; in 1786, he proposed "a plan for establishing public schools in Pennsylvania, and for conducting education agreeably to a republican form of government"; again, in discussing "the mode of education proper in a republic," he remarks of physical discipline that "the influence of these physical causes will be powerful upon the intellects, as well as upon the principles and morals of young people." Education became one of the foci of his thought.

It is true, too, that if physical causes influence the moral faculties, there is no unregenerable criminal. Criminality can be eradicated by alteration of the physical conditions which produced it and the substitution of physical conditions which produce benevolence. Such was the theme of Rush's writings on crime and punishment which together with many of his earlier writings on education were collected and published at Philadelphia in 1798.

In sum, then, Rush's mechanistic philosophy approached materialism. With a mild nod in the direction of a First Cause, he ascribed all actual changes in the world and in man to secondary causes. His address reprinted here provides an excellent introduction to the fuller discussion in his *Three Lectures upon Animal Life* (Philadelphia, 1799), with its three general propositions: (1) every part of the human body is endowed with sensibility or excitability or both; (2) the human body is a unit and impressions made on one part excite motion or sensation or both in every other part; (3) life is the effect of stimuli acting upon the body, and with its thoroughly behaviorist summary:

The action of the brain, the diastole and systole of the heart, the pulsation of the arteries, the contraction of the muscles, the peristaltic motion of the bowels, the absorbing power of the lymphatics, secretion, excretion, hearing, seeing, smelling, taste, and the sense of touch, nay more, thought itself, are all the effects of stimuli acting upon the organs of sense and motion.

THE INFLUENCE OF PHYSICAL CAUSES
ON THE MORAL FACULTY

IT was for the laudable purpose of exciting a spirit of emulation and inquiry among the members of our body, that the founders of our society instituted an annual oration. The task of preparing, and delivering this exercise, hath devolved, once more, upon me. I have submitted to it, not because I thought myself capable of fulfilling your intentions, but because I wished, by a testimony of my obedience to your requests, to atone for my long absence from the temple of science.

The subject, upon which I am to have the honour of addressing you this evening, is on the influence of physical causes upon the moral faculty.

By the moral faculty I mean a capacity in the human mind of distinguishing and choosing good and evil, or, in other words, virtue and vice. It is a native principle, and though it be capable of improvement by experience and reflection, it is not derived from either of them. St. Paul and Cicero give us the most perfect account of it that is to be found in modern or ancient authors. "For when the Gentiles (says St. Paul,) which have not the law, do by nature the things contained in the law, *these*, having not the law, are a *law* unto themselves; which show the works of the law written in their hearts, their consciences also, bearing witness, and their thoughts the mean while accusing, or else excusing, another." [1]

The words of Cicero are as follow: "Est igitur hæc, judices, non scripta, sed nata lex, quam non didicimus, accepimus, legimus, verum ex natura ipsa arripuimus, hausimus, expréssimus, ad quam non docti, sed facti, non instituti, sed imbuti sumus." [2] This faculty is often confounded with conscience, which is a distinct and independent capacity of the mind. This is evident from the passage quoted from the writings of St. Paul, in which conscience is said to be the witness that accuses or excuses us, of a breach of the law written in our hearts. The moral faculty is what the schoolmen call the "regula regulans;" the conscience is their "regula regulata;" or, to speak in more modern terms, the moral faculty performs the office of a lawgiver, while the business of conscience is to perform the duty of a judge. The moral faculty is to the conscience, what taste is to the judgment, and sensation to perception. It is quick in its operations, and like the sensitive plant, acts without reflection, while conscience follows with deliberate steps, and measures all her actions by the unerring square of right and wrong. The moral faculty exercises itself upon the actions of others. It approves, even in books, of the virtues of a Trajan, and disapproves of the vices of a Marius, while conscience confines its operations only to its own actions. These two capacities of the mind are generally in an exact ratio to each other, but they sometimes exist in different degrees in the same person. Hence we often find conscience in its full vigour, with a diminished tone, or total absence of the moral faculty.

[1] *Rom.* i. 14, 15.   [2] *Oratio pro Milone.*

It has long been a question among metaphysicians, whether the conscience be seated in the will or in the understanding. The controversy can only be settled by admitting the will to be the seat of the moral faculty, and the understanding to be the seat of the conscience. The mysterious nature of the union of those two moral principles with the will and understanding is a subject foreign to the business of the present inquiry.

As I consider virtue and vice to consist in *action*, and not in opinion, and as this action has its seat in the *will*, and not in the conscience, I shall confine my inquiries chiefly to the influence of physical causes upon that moral power of the mind, which is connected with volition, although many of these causes act likewise upon the conscience, as I shall show hereafter. The state of the moral faculty is visible in actions, which affect the well-being of society. The state of the conscience is invisible, and therefore removed beyond our investigation.

The moral faculty has received different names from different authors. It is the "moral sense" of Dr. Hutchison; "the sympathy" of Dr. Adam Smith; the "moral instinct" of Rousseau; and "the light that lighteth every man that cometh into the world" of St. John. I have adopted the term of moral faculty from Dr. Beattie, because I conceive it conveys, with the most perspicuity, the idea of a capacity in the mind of choosing good and evil.

Our books of medicine contain many records of the effects of physical causes upon the memory, the imagination, and the judgment. In some instances we behold their operation only on one, in others on two, and in many cases, upon the whole of these faculties. Their derangement has received different names, according to the number or nature of the faculties that are affected. The loss of memory has been called "amnesia;" false judgment upon one subject has been called "melancholia;" false judgment upon all subjects has been called "mania;" and a defect of all the three intellectual faculties that have been mentioned has received the name of "amentia." Persons who labour under the derangement, or want, of these faculties of the mind, are considered, very properly, as subjects of medicine; and there are many cases upon record, that prove that their diseases have yielded to the healing art.

In order to illustrate the effects of physical causes upon the moral faculty, it will be necessary *first* to show their effects upon the memory, the imagination, and the judgment; and at the same time to point out the analogy between their operation upon the intellectual faculties of the mind and the moral faculty.

1. Do we observe a connection between the intellectual faculties and the degrees of consistency and firmness of the brain in infancy and childhood? The same connection has been observed between the strength, as well as the progress, of the moral faculty in children.

2. Do we observe a certain size of the brain, and a peculiar cast of features, such as the prominent eye, and the acquiline nose, to be connected with extraordinary portions of genius? We observe a similar connection between the figure and temperament of the body and certain moral qualities. Hence we often ascribe good temper and benevolence to corpulency, and irascibility to sanguineous habits. Cæsar thought himself safe in the friendship of the "sleek-headed" Anthony and Dolabella, but was afraid to trust to the professions of the slender Cassius.

3. Do we observe certain degrees of the intellectual faculties to be hereditary in certain families? The same observation has been frequently extended to moral qualities. Hence we often find certain virtues and vices as peculiar to families, through all their degrees of consanguinity and duration, as a peculiarity of voice, complexion, or shape.

4. Do we observe instances of a total want of memory, imagination, and judgment, either from an original defect in the stamina of the brain, or from the influence of physical causes? The same unnatural defect is sometimes observed, and probably from the same causes, of a moral faculty. The celebrated Servin, whose character is drawn by the Duke of Sully, in his Memoirs, appears to be an instance of the total absence of the moral faculty, while the chasm produced by this defect, seems to have been filled up by a more than common extension of every other power of his mind. I beg leave to repeat the history of this prodigy of vice and knowledge. "Let the reader represent to himself a man of a genius so lively, and of an understanding so extensive, as rendered him scarce ignorant of any thing that could be known; of so vast and ready a comprehension, that he immediately made himself master of whatever he attempted; and of so prodigious a memory, that he never forgot what he once learned. He possessed all parts of philosophy, and

the mathematics, particularly fortification and drawing. Even in theology he was so well skilled, that he was an excellent preacher, whenever he had a mind to exert that talent, and an able disputant for and against the reformed religion, indifferently. He not only understood Greek, Hebrew, and all the languages which we call learned, but also all the different jargons, or modern dialects. He accented and pronounced them so naturally, and so perfectly imitated the gestures and manners both of the several nations of Europe, and the particular provinces of France, that he might have been taken for a native of all, or any, of these countries: and this quality he applied to counterfeit all sorts of persons, wherein he succeeded wonderfully. He was, moreover, the best comedian, and the greatest droll that perhaps ever appeared. He had a genius for poetry, and had wrote many verses. He played upon almost all instruments, was a perfect master of music, and sang most agreeably and justly. He likewise could say mass, for he was of a disposition to do, as well as to know, all things. His body was perfectly well suited to his mind. He was light, nimble, and dexterous, and fit for all exercises. He could ride well, and in dancing, wrestling, and leaping, he was admired. There are not any recreative games that he did not know, and he was skilled in almost all mechanic arts. But now for the reverse of the medal. Here it appeared, that he was treacherous, cruel, cowardly, deceitful, a liar, a cheat, a drunkard, and a glutton, a sharper in play, immersed in every species of vice, a blasphemer, an atheist. In a word, in him might be found all the vices that are contrary to nature, honour, religion, and society, the truth of which he himself evinced with his latest breath; for he died in the flower of his age, in a common brothel, perfectly corrupted by his debaucheries, and expired with the glass in his hand, cursing and denying God." [3]

It was probably a state of the human mind such as has been described, that our Saviour alluded to in the disciple who was about to betray him, when he called him "a devil." Perhaps the essence of depravity, in infernal spirits, consists in their being wholly devoid of a moral faculty. In them the will has probably lost the power of choosing,[4] as well as

---

[3] Vol. iii. pp. 216, 217.

[4] Milton seems to have been of this opinion. Hence, after ascribing repentance to Satan, he makes him declare,

> "Farewell remorse; all good to me is lost,
> *Evil*, be thou my *good*."————
> *Paradise Lost*, Book IV.

the capacity of enjoying moral good. It is true, we read of their trembling in a belief of the existence of a God, and of their anticipating future punishment, by asking whether they were to be tormented before their time: but this is the effect of conscience, and hence arises another argument in favour of this judicial power of the mind being distinct from the moral faculty. It would seem as if the Supreme Being had preserved the moral faculty in man from the ruins of his fall, on purpose to guide him back again to Paradise, and at the same time had constituted the conscience, both in men and fallen spirits, a kind of royalty in his moral empire, on purpose to show his property in all intelligent creatures, and their original resemblance to himself. Perhaps the essence of moral depravity in man consists in a total, but temporary, suspension of the power of conscience. Persons in this situation are emphatically said in the Scriptures to "be past feeling," and to have their consciences seared with a "hot iron;" they are likewise said to be "twice dead," that is, the same torpor, or moral insensibility, has seized both the moral faculty and the conscience.

5. Do we ever observe instances of the existence of only *one* of the three intellectual powers of the mind that have been named, in the absence of the other two? We observe something of the same kind with respect to the moral faculty. I once knew a man, who discovered no one mark of reason, who possessed the moral sense or faculty in so high a degree, that he spent his whole life in acts of benevolence. He was not only inoffensive (which is not always the case with idiots), but he was kind and affectionate to every body. He had no ideas of time, but what were suggested to him by the returns of the stated periods for public worship, in which he appeared to take great delight. He spent several hours of every day in devotion, in which he was so careful to be private, that he was once found in the most improbable place in the world for that purpose, viz. in an oven.

6. Do we observe the memory, the imagination, and the judgment to be affected by diseases, particularly by madness? Where is the physician, who has not seen the moral faculty affected from the same causes! How often do we see the temper wholly changed by a fit of sickness! And how often do we hear persons of the most delicate virtue utter speeches, in the delirium of a fever, that are offensive to decency or good manners! I have heard a well-attested history of a clergyman of

the most exemplary moral character, who spent the last moments of a fever, which deprived him both of his reason and his life, in profane cursing and swearing. I once attended a young woman in a nervous fever, who discovered, after her recovery, a loss of her former habit of veracity. Her memory (a defect of which might be suspected of being the cause of this vice), was in every respect as perfect as it was before the attack of the fever.[5] The instances of immorality in maniacs, who were formerly distinguished for the opposite character, are so numerous, and well known, that it will not be necessary to select any cases, to establish the truth of the proposition contained under this head.

7. Do we observe any of the three intellectual faculties that have been named enlarged by diseases? Patients in the delirium of a fever, often discover extraordinary flights of imagination, and madmen often astonish us with their wonderful acts of memory. The same enlargement, sometimes, appears in the operations of the moral faculty. I have more than once heard the most sublime discourses of morality in the cell of a hospital, and who has not seen instances of patients in acute diseases discovering degrees of benevolence and integrity, that were not natural to them in the ordinary course of their lives? [6]

8. Do we ever observe a partial insanity, or false perception on one subject, while the judgment is sound and correct, upon all others? We perceive, in some instances, a similar defect in the moral faculty. There are persons who are moral in the highest degree as to certain duties, who nevertheless live under the influence of some one vice. I knew an instance of a woman, who was exemplary in her obedience to every command of the moral law, except one. She could not refrain from stealing. What made this vice the more remarkable was, that she was in easy circumstances, and not addicted to extravagance in any thing. Such was her propensity to this vice, than when she could lay her hands upon nothing more valuable, she would often, at the table of a friend, fill her pockets secretly with bread. As a proof that her judgment was not affected by this defect in her moral faculty, she would both confess and lament her crime, when detected in it.

[5] I have selected this case from many others which have come under my notice, in which the moral faculty appeared to be impaired by diseases, particularly by the typhus of Dr. Cullen, and by those species of palsy which affect the brain.

[6] Xenophon makes Cyrus declare, in his last moments, "That the soul of man, at the hour of death, appears *most divine*, and then foresees something of future events."

9. Do we observe the imagination in many instances to be affected with apprehensions of dangers that have no existence? In like manner we observe the moral faculty to discover a sensibility to vice, that is by no means proportioned to its degrees of depravity. How often do we see persons labouring under this morbid sensibility of the moral faculty refuse to give a direct answer to a plain question, that related perhaps only to the weather, or to the hour of the day, lest they should wound the peace of their minds by telling a falsehood!

10. Do dreams affect the memory, the imagination, and the judgment? Dreams are nothing but incoherent ideas, occasioned by partial or imperfect sleep. There is a variety in the suspension of the faculties and operations of the mind in this state of the system. In some cases the imagination only is deranged in dreams, in others the memory is affected, and in others the judgment. But there are cases in which the change that is produced in the state of the brain, by means of sleep, affects the moral faculty likewise; hence we sometimes dream of doing and saying things, when asleep, which we shudder at, as soon as we awake. This supposed defection from virtue exists frequently in dreams, where the memory and judgment are scarcely impaired. It cannot therefore be ascribed to an absence of the exercises of those two powers of the mind.

11. Do we read, in the accounts of travellers, of men, who, in respect of intellectual capacity and enjoyments, are but a few degrees above brutes? We read likewise of a similar degradation of our species, in respect to moral capacity and feeling. Here it will be necessary to remark, that the low degrees of moral perception, that have been discovered in certain African and Russian tribes of men, no more invalidate our proposition of the universal and essential existence of a moral faculty in the human mind, than the low state of their intellects prove, that reason is not natural to man. Their perceptions of good and evil are in an exact proportion to their intellectual faculties. But I will go further, and admit, with Mr. Locke,[7] that some savage nations are totally devoid of the moral faculty, yet it will by no means follow, that this was the original constitution of their minds. The appetite for certain aliments is uniform among all mankind. Where is the nation and the individual, in their primitive state of health, to whom bread is

[7] *Essay concerning the Human Understanding*, Book I. chap. 3.

not agreeable? But if we should find savages, or individuals, whose stomachs have been so disordered by intemperance as to refuse this simple and wholesome article of diet, shall we assert that this was the original constitution of their appetites? By no means. As well might we assert, because savages destroy their beauty by painting and cutting their faces, that the principles of taste do not exist naturally in the human mind. It is with virtue as with fire. It exists in the mind, as fire does in certain bodies, in a latent or quiescent state. As collision renders the one sensible, so education renders the other visible. It would be as absurd to maintain, because olives become agreeable to many people from habit, that we have no natural appetites for any other kind of food, as to assert that any part of the human species exist without a moral principle, because in some of them it has wanted causes to excite it into action, or has been perverted by example. There are appetites that are wholly artificial. There are tastes so entirely vitiated, as to perceive beauty in deformity. There are torpid and unnatural passions. Why, under certain unfavourable circumstances, may there not exist also a moral faculty, in a state of sleep, or subject to mistakes?

The only apology I shall make, for presuming to differ from that justly celebrated oracle,[8] who first unfolded to us a map of the intel-. lectual world, shall be, that the eagle eye of genius often darts its views beyond the notice of facts, which are accommodated to the slender organs of perception of men, who possess no other talent than that of observation.

It is not surprising, that Mr. Locke has confounded this moral principle with *reason*, or that Lord Shaftsbury has confounded it with *taste*, since all three of these faculties agree in the objects of their approbation, notwithstanding they exist in the mind independently of each other. The favourable influence, which the progress of science and taste has had upon the morals, can be ascribed to nothing else, but to the perfect union that subsists in nature between the dictates of reason, of taste, and of the moral faculty. Why has the spirit of humanity made such rapid progress for some years past in the courts of Europe? It is because kings and their ministers have been taught to *reason* upon philosophical subjects. Why have indecency and profanity been banished from the stage in London and Paris? It is because immorality is an of-

[8] Mr. Locke.

fence against the highly cultivated *taste* of the French and English nations.

It must afford great pleasure to the lovers of virtue, to behold the depth and extent of this moral principle in the human mind. Happily for the human race, the intimations of duty and the road to happiness are not left to the slow operations or doubtful inductions of reason, nor to the precarious decisions of taste. Hence we often find the moral faculty in a state of vigour in persons, in whom reason and taste exist in a weak, or in an uncultivated state. It is worthy of notice, likewise, that while *second* thoughts are best in matters of judgment, *first* thoughts are always to be preferred in matters that relate to morality. *Second* thoughts, in these cases, are generally parlies between duty and corrupted inclinations. Hence Rousseau has justly said, that "a well regulated moral instinct is the surest guide to happiness."

It must afford equal pleasure to the lovers of virtue to behold, that our moral conduct and happiness are not committed to the determination of a single legislative power. The conscience, like a wise and faithful legislative council, performs the office of a check upon the moral faculty, and thus prevents the fatal consequences of immoral actions.

An objection, I foresee, will arise to the doctrine of the influence of physical causes upon the moral faculty, from its being supposed to favour the opinion of the *materiality* of the soul. But I do not see that this doctrine obliges us to decide upon the question of the nature of the soul, any more than the facts which prove the influence of physical causes upon the memory, the imagination, or the judgment. I shall, however, remark upon this subject, that the writers in favour of the *immortality* of the soul have done that truth great injury, by connecting it necessarily with its *immateriality*. The immortality of the soul depends upon the *will* of the Deity, and not upon the supposed properties of spirit. Matter is in its own nature as immortal as spirit. It is resolvable by heat and mixture into a variety of forms; but it requires the same Almighty hand to annihilate it, that it did to create it. I know of no arguments to prove the immortality of the soul, but such as are derived from the Christian revelation.[9] It would be as reasonable to assert that the basin of the ocean is immortal, from the greatness of its capacity

---

[9] "Life and immortality *are* brought to light *only* through the gospel."

2 Tim. i. 10.

to hold water; or that we are to live for ever in this world, because we are afraid of dying; as to maintain the immortality of the soul, from the greatness of its capacity for knowledge and happiness, or from its dread of annihilation.

I remarked, in the beginning of this discourse, that persons who are deprived of the just exercise of memory, imagination, or judgment, were proper subjects of medicine; and that there are many cases upon record which prove, that the diseases from the derangement of these faculties have yielded to the healing art.

It is perhaps only because the diseases of the moral faculty have not been traced to a connection with physical causes, that medical writers have neglected to give them a place in their systems of nosology, and that so few attempts have been hitherto made to lessen or remove them, by physical as well as rational and moral remedies.

I shall not attempt to derive any support to my opinions, from the analogy of the influence of physical causes upon the temper and conduct of brute animals. The facts which I shall produce in favour of the action of these causes upon morals in the human species, will, I hope, render unnecessary the arguments that might be drawn from that quarter.

I am aware, that in venturing upon this subject I step upon untrodden ground. I feel as Æneas did, when he was about to enter the gates of Avernus, but without a sybil to instruct me in the mysteries that are before me. I foresee, that men who have been educated in the mechanical habits of adopting popular or established opinions will revolt at the doctrine I am about to deliver, while men of sense and genius will hear my propositions with candour, and if they do not adopt them, will commend that boldness of inquiry, that prompted me to broach them.

I shall begin with an attempt to supply the defects of nosological writers, by naming the partial or weakened action of the moral faculty, MICRONOMIA. The total absence of this faculty I shall call ANOMIA. By the law, referred to in these new genera of vesaniæ, I mean the law of nature written in the human heart, and which I formerly quoted from the writings of St. Paul.

In treating of the effects of physical causes upon the moral faculty, it might help to extend our ideas upon this subject, to reduce virtues and vices to certain species, and to point out the effects of particular species of virtue and vice; but this would lead us into a field too extensive for the limits of the present inquiry. I shall only hint at a few cases, and have no doubt but the ingenuity of my auditors will supply my silence, by applying the rest.

It is immaterial, whether the physical causes that are to be enumerated act upon the moral faculty through the medium of the senses, the passions, the memory, or the imagination. Their influence is equally certain, whether they act as remote, predisposing, or occasional causes.

1. The effects of CLIMATE upon the moral faculty claim our first attention. Not only individuals, but nations, derive a considerable part of their moral, as well as intellectual character, from the different portions they enjoy of the rays of the sun. Irascibility, levity, timidity, and indolence, tempered with occasional emotions of benevolence, are the moral qualities of the inhabitants of warm climates, while selfishness, tempered with sincerity and integrity, form the moral character of the inhabitants of cold countries. The state of the weather, and the seasons of the year also, have a visible effect upon moral sensibility. The month of November, in Great Britain, rendered gloomy by constant fogs and rains, has been thought to favour the perpetration of the worst species of murder, while the vernal sun, in middle latitudes, has been as generally remarked for producing gentleness and benevolence.

2. The effects of DIET upon the moral faculty are more certain, though less attended to, than the effects of climate. "Fullness of bread," we are told, was one of the predisposing causes of the vices of the Cities of the Plain. The fasts so often inculcated among the Jews were intended to lessen the incentives to vice; for pride, cruelty, and sensuality, are as much the natural consequences of luxury, as apoplexies and palsies. But the *quality* as well as the quantity of aliment has an influence upon morals; hence we find the moral diseases that have been mentioned are most frequently the offspring of animal food. The prophet Isaiah seems to have been sensible of this, when he ascribes such salutary effects to a temperate and vegetable diet. "Butter and honey shall he eat," says he, "*that* he may know to refuse the evil, and to choose the good." But we have many facts which prove the efficacy of a vegetable diet upon the passions. Dr. Arbuthnot assures us, that he cured several patients of irascible tempers, by nothing but a prescription of this simple and temperate regimen.

3. The effects of CERTAIN DRINKS upon the moral faculty are not less observable, than upon the intellectual powers of the mind. Fermented liquors, of a good quality, and taken in a moderate quantity, are favourable to the virtues of candour, benevolence, and generosity; but when they are taken in excess, or when they are of a bad quality, and taken even in a moderate quantity, they seldom fail of rousing every latent spark of vice into action. The last of these facts is so notorious, that when a man is observed to be ill-natured or quarrelsome in Portugal, after drinking, it is common in that country to say, that "he has drunken bad wine." While occasional fits of intoxication produce ill-temper in many people, habitual drunkenness (which is generally produced by distilled spirits) never fails to eradicate veracity and integrity from the human mind. Perhaps this may be the reason why the Spaniards, in ancient times, never admitted a man's evidence in a court of justice, who had been convicted of drunkenness. Water is the universal sedative of turbulent passions; it not only promotes a general equanimity of temper, but it composes anger. I have heard several well-attested cases, of a draught of cold water having suddenly composed this violent passion, after the usual remedies of reason had been applied to no purpose.

4. EXTREME HUNGER produces the most unfriendly effects upon moral sensibility. It is immaterial, whether it act by inducing a relaxation of the solids, or an acrimony of the fluids, or by the combined operations of both those physical causes. The Indians in this country whet their appetites for that savage species of war, which is peculiar to them, by the stimulus of hunger; hence, we are told, they always return meagre and emaciated from their military excursions. In civilized life we often behold this sensation to overbalance the restraints of moral feeling; and perhaps this may be the reason why poverty, which is the most frequent parent of hunger, disposes so generally to theft; for the character of hunger is taken from that vice; it belongs to it "to break through stone walls." So much does this sensation predominate over reason and moral feeling, that cardinal de Retz suggests to politicians, never to risk a motion in a popular assembly, however wise or just it may be, immediately before dinner. That temper must be uncommonly guarded, which is not disturbed by long abstinence from food. One of the worthiest men I ever knew, who made his breakfast his principal

meal, was peevish and disagreeable to his friends and family, from the time he left his bed till he sat down to his morning repast; after which, cheerfulness sparkled in his countenance, and he became the delight of all around him.

5. I hinted formerly, in proving the analogy between the effects of DISEASES upon the intellects, and upon the moral faculty, that the latter was frequently impaired by fevers and madness. I beg leave to add further upon this head, that not only madness, but the hysteria and hypochondriasis, as well as all those states of the body, whether idiopathic or symptomatic, which are accompanied with preternatural irritability—sensibility—torpor—stupor or mobility of the nervous system, dispose to vice, either of the body or of the mind. It is in vain to attack these vices with lectures upon morality. They are only to be cured by medicine,—particularly by exercise,—the cold bath,—and by a cold or warm atmosphere. The young woman, whose case I mentioned formerly, that lost her habit of veracity by a nervous fever, recovered this virtue, as soon as her system recovered its natural tone, from the cold weather which happily succeeded her fever.[10]

6. Idleness is the parent of every vice. It is mentioned in the Old Testament as another of the predisposing causes of the vices of the Cities of the Plain. Labor of all kinds favors and facilitates the practice of virtue. The country life is happy, chiefly because its laborious employments are favourable to virtue, and unfriendly to vice. It is a common practice, I have been told, for the planters in the southern states, to consign a house slave, who has become vicious from idleness, to the drudgery of the field, in order to reform him. The bridewells and

---

[10] There is a morbid state of excitability in the body during the convalescence from fever, which is intimately connected with an undue propensity to venereal pleasures. I have met with several instances of it. The marriage of the celebrated Mr. Howard to a woman who was twice as old as himself, and very sickly, has been ascribed by his biographer, Dr. Aiken, to *gratitude* for her great attention to him in a fit of sickness. I am disposed to ascribe it to a sudden paroxysm of another passion, which as a religious man, he could not gratify in any other, than in a lawful way. I have heard of two young clergymen who married the women who had nursed them in fits of sickness. In both cases there was great inequality in their years, and condition in life. Their motive was, probably, the same as that which I have attributed to Mr. Howard. Dr. Patrick Russel takes notice of an uncommon degree of venereal excitability which followed attacks of the plague at Messina, in 1743, in all ranks of people. Marriages, he says, were more frequent after it than usual, and virgins were, in some instances, violated, who died of that disease, by persons who had just recovered from it.

workhouses of all civilized countries prove, that LABOR is not only a very severe, but the most benevolent of all punishments, in as much as it is one of the most suitable means of reformation. Mr. Howard tells us in his History of Prisons, that in Holland it is a common saying, "Make men work and you will make them honest." And over the rasp and spin-house at Grœningen, this sentiment is expressed (he tells us) by a happy motto:

"Vitiorum semina—otium—labore exhauriendum."

The effects of steady labour in early life, in creating virtuous habits, is still more remarkable. The late Anthony Benezet of this city, whose benevolence was the sentinel of the virtue, as well as of the happiness of his country, made it a constant rule in binding out poor children, to avoid putting them into wealthy families, but always preferred masters for them who worked themselves, and who obliged these children to work in their presence. If the habits of virtue, contracted by means of this apprenticeship to labour, are purely mechanical, their effects are, nevertheless, the same upon the happiness of society, as if they flowed from principle. The mind, moreover, when preserved by these means from weeds, becomes a more mellow soil afterwards, for moral and rational improvement.

7. The effects of EXCESSIVE SLEEP are intimately connected with the effects of idleness upon the moral faculty; hence we find that moderate, and even scanty portions of sleep, in every part of the world, have been found to be friendly, not only to health and long life, but in many instances to morality. The practice of the monks, who often sleep upon a floor, and who generally rise with the sun, for the sake of mortifying their sensual appetites, is certainly founded in wisdom, and has often produced the most salutary moral effects.

8. The effects of BODILY PAIN upon the moral, are not less remarkable than upon the intellectual powers of the mind. The late Dr. Gregory, of the University of Edinburgh, used to tell his pupils, that he always found his perceptions quicker in a fit of the gout, than at any other time. The pangs which attend the dissolution of the body, are often accompanied with conceptions and expressions upon the most ordinary subjects, that discover an uncommon elevation of the intellectual powers. The effects of bodily pain are exactly the same in rousing and direct-

ing the moral faculty. Bodily pain, we find was one of the remedies employed in the Old Testament, for extirpating vice and promoting virtue: and Mr. Howard tells us, that he saw it employed successfully as a means of reformation, in one of the prisons which he visited. If pain has a physical tendency to cure vice, I submit it to the consideration of parents and legislators, whether moderate degrees of corporal punishments, inflicted for a great length of time, would not be more medicinal in their effects, than the violent degrees of them, which are of short duration.

9. Too much cannot be said in favour of CLEANLINESS, as a physical means of promoting virtue. The writings of Moses have been called, by military men, the best "orderly book" in the world. In every part of them we find cleanliness inculcated with as much zeal, as if it was part of the moral, instead of the Levitical law. Now, it is well-known, that the principal design of every precept and rite of the ceremonial parts of the Jewish religion, was to prevent vice, and to promote virtue. All writers upon the leprosy, take notice of its connection with a certain vice. To this disease gross animal food, particularly swine's flesh, and a dirty skin, have been thought to be predisposing causes—hence the reason, probably, why pork was forbidden, and why ablutions of the body and limbs were so frequently inculcated by the Jewish law. Sir John Pringle's remarks, in his oration upon Captain Cook's Voyage, delivered before the Royal Society in London, are very pertinent to this part of our subject:—"Cleanliness (says he) is conducive to health, but is it not obvious, that it also tends to good order and other virtues? Such (meaning the ship's crew) as were made more cleanly, became more sober, more orderly, and more attentive to duty." The benefit to be derived by parents and schoolmasters from attending to these facts, is too obvious to be mentioned.

10. I hope I shall be excused in placing SOLITUDE among the physical causes which influence the moral faculty, when I add, that I confine its effects to persons who are irreclaimable by rational or moral remedies. Mr. Howard informs us, that the chaplain of the prison at Liege in Germany assured him, "that the most refractory and turbulent spirits, became tractable and submissive, by being closely confined for four or five days." In bodies that are predisposed to vice, the stimulus of

cheerful, but much more of profane society and conversation, upon the animal spirits, becomes an exciting cause, and like the stroke of the flint upon the steel, renders the sparks of vice both active and visible. By removing men out of the reach of this exciting cause, they are often reformed, especially if they are confined long enough to produce a sufficient chasm in their habits of vice. Where the benefit of reflection, and instruction from books, can be added to solitude and confinement, their good effects are still more certain. To this philosophers and poets in every age have assented, by describing the life of a hermit as a life of passive virtue.

11. Connected with solitude, as a mechanical means of promoting virtue, SILENCE deserves to be mentioned in this place. The late Dr. Fothergill, in his plan of education for that benevolent institution at Ackworth, which was the last care of his useful life, says every thing that can be said in favour of this necessary discipline, in the following words: "To habituate children from their early infancy, to silence and attention, is of the greatest advantage to them, not only as a preparative to their advancement in a religious life, but as the groundwork of a well-cultivated understanding. To have the active minds of children put under a kind of restraint—to be accustomed to turn their attention from external objects, and habituated to a degree of abstracted quiet, is a matter of great consequence, and lasting benefit to them. Although it cannot be supposed, that young and active minds are always engaged in silence as they ought to be, yet to be accustomed thus to quietness, is no small point gained towards fixing a habit of patience, and recollection, which seldom forsakes those who have been properly instructed in this entrance of the school of wisdom, during the residue of their days."

For the purpose of acquiring this branch of education, children cannot associate too early, nor too often with their parents, or with their superiors in age, rank, and wisdom.

12. The effects of MUSIC upon the moral faculty, have been felt and recorded in every country. Hence we are able to discover the virtues and vices of different nations, by their tunes, as certainly as by their laws. The effects of music, when simply mechanical, upon the passions, are powerful and extensive. But it remains yet to determine

the degrees of moral ecstasy, that may be produced by an attack upon the ear, the reason, and the moral principle, at the same time, by the combined powers of music and eloquence.

13. The ELOQUENCE of the PULPIT is nearly allied to music in its effects upon the moral faculty. It is true, there can be no permanent change in the temper and moral conduct of a man, that is not derived from the understanding and the will; but we must remember that these two powers of the mind are most assailable, when they are attacked through the avenue of the passions; and these, we know, when agitated by the powers of eloquence, exert a mechanical action upon every power of the soul. Hence we find, in every age and country where Christianity has been propagated, the most accomplished orators have generally been the most successful reformers of mankind. There must be a defect of eloquence in a preacher, who, with the resources for oratory which are contained in the Old and New Testaments, does not produce in every man who hears him at least a temporary love of virtue. I grant that the eloquence of the pulpit alone cannot change men into Christians, but it certainly possesses the power of changing brutes into men. Could the eloquence of the stage be properly directed, it is impossible to conceive the extent of its mechanical effects upon morals. The language and imagery of a Shakspeare, upon moral and religious subjects, poured upon the passions and the senses, in all the beauty and variety of dramatic representation, who could resist, or describe their effects?

14. ODOURS of various kinds have been observed to act in the most sensible manner upon the moral faculty. Brydone tells us, upon the authority of a celebrated philosopher in Italy, that the peculiar wickedness of the people who live in the neighbourhood of Ætna and Vesuvius is occasioned chiefly by the smell of the sulphur, and of the hot exhalations which are constantly discharged from those volcanoes. Agreeable odours seldom fail to inspire serenity, and to compose the angry spirits. Hence the pleasure, and one of the advantages, of a flower-garden. The smoke of tobacco is likewise of a composing nature, and tends not only to produce what is called a train in perception, but to hush the agitated passions into silence and order. Hence the practice of connecting the pipe or cigar and the bottle together, in public company.

15. It will be sufficient only to mention LIGHT and DARKNESS, to sug-

gest facts in favour of the influence of each of them upon moral sensibility. How often do the peevish complaints of the night, in sickness, give way to the composing rays of the light of the morning? Othello cannot murder Desdemona by candle-light, and who has not felt the effects of a blazing fire upon the gentle passions? [11]

16. It is to be lamented, that no experiments have as yet been made, to determine the effects of all the different species of AIRS, which chemistry has lately discovered, upon the moral faculty. I have authority, from actual experiments, only to declare, that dephlogisticated air, when taken into the lungs, produces cheerfulness, gentleness, and serenity of mind.

17. What shall we say of the effects of MEDICINES upon the moral faculty? That many substances in the materia medica act upon the intellects is well known to physicians. Why should it be thought impossible for medicines to act in like manner upon the moral faculty? May not the earth contain, in its bowels, or upon its surface, antidotes? But I will not blend facts with conjectures. Clouds and darkness still hang upon this part of my subject.

Let it not be suspected, from any thing that I have delivered, that I suppose the influence of physical causes upon the moral faculty renders the agency of divine influence unnecessary to our moral happiness. I only maintain, that the operations of the divine government are carried on in the moral, as in the natural world, by the instrumentality of second causes. I have only trodden in the footsteps of the inspired writers; for most of the physical causes I have enumerated are connected with moral precepts, or have been used as the means of reformation from vice, in the Old and New Testaments. To the cases that have been mentioned, I shall only add, that Nebuchadnezzar was cured of his pride, by means of solitude and a vegetable diet. Saul was cured of his evil spirit, by means of David's harp, and St. Paul expressly says, "I keep my body under, and bring it into subjection, lest that by any means, when I have preached to others, I myself should be a cast-away." But I will go one step further, and add, in favour of divine influence upon the

[11] The temperature of the air has a considerable influence upon moral feeling. Henry the Third of France was always ill-humoured, and sometimes cruel, in cold weather. There is a damp air which comes from the sea in Northumberland county in England, which is known by the name of the *seafret*, from its inducing fretfulness in the temper.

moral principle, that in those extraordinary cases, where bad men are suddenly reformed, without the instrumentality of physical, moral or rational causes, I believe that the organization of those parts of the body, in which the faculties of the mind are seated, undergoes a physical change; [12] and hence the expression of a "new creature," which is made use of in the Scriptures to denote this change, is proper in a literal, as well as a figurative sense. It is probably the beginning of that perfect renovation of the human body, which is predicted by St. Paul in the following words: "For our conversation is in heaven, from whence we look for the Saviour, who shall change our vile bodies, that they may be fashioned according to his own glorious body." I shall not pause to defend myself against the charge of enthusiasm in this place; for the age is at length arrived, so devoutly wished for by Dr. Cheyne, in which men will not be deterred in their researches after truth, by the terror of odious or unpopular names.

I cannot help remarking under this head, that if the conditions of those parts of the human body which are connected with the human soul influence morals, the same reason may be given for a virtuous education, that has been admitted for teaching music, and the pronunciation of foreign languages, in the early and yielding state of those organs which form the voice and speech. Such is the effect of a moral education, that we often see its fruits in advanced stages of life, after the religious principles which were connected with it have been renounced; just as we perceive the same care in a surgeon in his attendance upon patients, after the sympathy which first produced this care has ceased to operate upon his mind. The boasted morality of the deists is, I believe, in most cases, the offspring of habits, produced originally by the principles and precepts of Christianity. Hence appears the wisdom of Solomon's advice, "Train up a child in the way he should go, and when he is old he will not," I had almost said, he cannot, "depart from it."

Thus have I enumerated the principal causes which act mechanically upon morals. If, from the combined action of physical powers that are

---

[12] St. Paul was suddenly transformed from a persecutor into a man of a gentle and amiable spirit. The manner in which this change was effected upon his mind, he tells us in the following words: "Neither circumcision availeth any thing, nor uncircumcision, but a new creature. From henceforth let no man trouble me; for I bear in *my body* the *marks* of our Lord Jesus." Galatians vi. 15, 17.

opposed to each other, the moral faculty should become stationary, or if the virtue or vice produced by them should form a neutral quality, composed of both of them, I hope it will not call in question the truth of our general propositions. I have only mentioned the effects of physical causes in a simple state.[13]

It might help to enlarge our ideas upon this subject, to take notice of the influence of the different stages of society, of agriculture and commerce, of soil and situation, of the different degrees of cultivation of taste, and of the intellectual powers, of the different forms of government, and, lastly, of the different professions and occupations of mankind, upon the moral faculty; but as these act indirectly only, and by the intervention of causes that are unconnected with matter, I conceive they are foreign to the business of the present inquiry. If they should vary the action of the simple physical causes in any degree, I hope it will not call in question the truth of our general propositions, any more than the compound action of physical powers that are opposed to each other. There remain but a few more causes which are of a compound nature, but they are so nearly related to those which are purely mechanical, that I should beg leave to trespass upon your patience, by giving them a place in my oration.

The effects of imitation, habit, and association, upon morals, would furnish ample matter for investigation. Considering how much the shape, texture, and conditions of the human body influence morals, I submit it to the consideration of the ingenious, whether, in our endeavours to imitate moral examples, some advantage may not be derived, from our copying the features and external manners of the originals. What makes the success of this experiment probable is, that we generally find men, whose faces resemble each other, have the same manners and dispositions. I infer the possibility of success in an attempt to imitate originals in a manner that has been mentioned, from the facility with which domestics acquire a resemblance to their masters and mistresses, not only in manners, but in countenance, in those cases where they are tied to them by respect and affection. Husbands and wives also, where they possess the same species of face, under cir-

[13] The doctrine of the influence of physical causes on morals is happily calculated to beget charity towards the failings of our fellow-creatures. Our duty to practise this virtue is enforced by motives drawn from science, as well as from the precepts of Christianity.

cumstances of mutual attachment often acquire a resemblance to each other.

From the general detestation in which hypocrisy is held, both by good and bad men, the mechanical effects of habit upon virtue have not been sufficiently explored. There are, I am persuaded, many instances, where virtues have been assumed by accident or necessity, which have become real from habit, and afterwards derived their nourishment from the heart. Hence the propriety of Hamlet's advice to his Mother:

> "Assume a virtue, if you have it not.
> That monster, Custom, who all sense doth eat
> Of habits evil, is angel yet in this,
> That to the use of actions fair and good
> He likewise gives a frock or livery,
> That aptly is put on. Refrain to-night,
> And that shall lend a kind of easiness
> To the next abstinence; the next more easy:
> For use can almost change the stamp of nature,
> And master even the devil, or throw him out,
> With wondrous potency."

The influence of ASSOCIATION upon morals opens an ample field for inquiry. It is from this principle, that we explain the reformation from theft and drunkenness in servants, which we sometimes see produced by a draught of spirits, in which tartar emetic had been secretly dissolved. The recollection of the pain and sickness excited by the emetic, naturally associates itself with the spirits, so as to render them both equally the objects of aversion. It is by calling in this principle only, that we can account for the conduct of Moses, in grinding the golden calf into a powder, and afterwards dissolving it (probably by means of hepar sulphuris,) in water, and compelling the children of Israel to drink of it, as a punishment for their idolatry. This mixture is bitter and nauseating in the highest degree. An inclination to idolatry, therefore, could not be felt, without being associated with the remembrance of this disagreeable mixture, and of course being rejected, with equal abhorrence. The benefit of corporal punishments, when they are of a short duration, depends in part upon their being connected, by time and place, with the crimes for which they are inflicted. Quick as the thunder follows the lightning, if it were possible, should punishments follow the crimes, and the advantage of association would be more certain, if the spot where they were committed were made the theatre of their expiation. It is from the effects of this association, probably, that the change of place and company, produced by exile and transportation, has so often reclaimed bad men, after moral, rational, and physical means of reformation had been used to no purpose.

As SENSIBILITY is the avenue to the moral faculty, every thing which tends to diminish it tends also to injure morals. The Romans owed much of their corruption to the sights of the contests of their gladiators, and of criminals, with wild beasts. For these reasons, executions should never be public. Indeed, I believe there are no public punishments of any kind, that do not harden the hearts of spectators, and thereby lessen the natural horror which all crimes at first excite in the human mind.

CRUELTY to brute animals is another means of destroying moral sensibility. The ferocity of savages has been ascribed in part to their peculiar mode of subsistence. Mr. Hogarth points out, in his ingenious prints, the connection between cruelty to brute animals in youth, and murder in manhood. The emperor Domitian prepared his mind, by the amusement of killing flies, for all those bloody crimes which afterwards disgraced his reign. I am so perfectly satisfied of the truth of a connection between morals and humanity to brutes, that I shall find it difficult to restrain my idolatry for that legislature, that shall first establish a system of laws to defend them from outrage and oppression.

In order to preserve the vigour of the moral faculty, it is of the utmost consequence to keep young people as ignorant as possible of those crimes that are generally thought most disgraceful to human nature. Suicide, I believe, is often propagated by means of newspapers. For this reason, I should be glad to see the proceedings of our courts kept from the public eye, when they expose or punish monstrous vices.

The last mechanical method of promoting morality that I shall mention, is to keep sensibility alive, by a familiarity with scenes of distress from poverty and disease. Compassion never awakens in the human bosom, without being accompanied by a train of sister virtues. Hence the wise man justly remarks, that "By the sadness of the countenance, the heart is made better."

A late French writer in his prediction of events that are to happen in the year 4000, says, "That mankind in that era shall be so far improved by religion and government, that the sick and the dying shall no longer be thrown, together with the dead, into splendid houses, but shall be relieved and protected in a connection with their families and society." For the honour of humanity, an institution,[14] destined for that distant period, has lately been founded in this city, that shall perpetuate the year 1786 in the history of Pennsylvania. Here the feeling heart, the tearful eye, and the charitable hand, may always be connected together, and the flame of sympathy, instead of being extinguished in taxes, or expiring in a solitary blaze by a single contribution, may be kept alive by constant exercise. There is a necessary connection between animal sympathy and good morals. The priest and the Levite, in the New Testament, would probably have relieved the poor man who fell among thieves, had accident brought them near enough to his wounds. The unfortunate Mrs. Bellamy was rescued from the dreadful purpose of drowning herself, by nothing but the distress of a child, rending the air with its cries for bread. It is probably owing, in some measure, to the connection between good morals and sympathy, that the fair sex, in every age and country, have been more distinguished for virtue than men; for how seldom do we hear of a woman devoid of humanity?

Lastly, ATTRACTION, COMPOSITION, and DECOMPOSITION, belong to the passions as well as to matter. Vices of the same species attract each other with the most force—hence the bad consequences of crowding young men (whose propensities are generally the same) under one roof, in our modern plans of education. The effects of composition and decomposition upon vices, appear in the meanness of the school boy, being often cured by the prodigality of a military life, and by the precipitation of avarice, which is often produced by ambition and love.[15]

If physical causes influence morals in the manner we have described, may they not also influence religious principles and opinions?—I answer in the affirmative; and I have authority, from the records of

---

[14] A public dispensary.

[15] A citizen of Philadelphia had made many unsuccessful attempts to cure his wife of drinking ardent spirits. At length, despairing of her reformation, he purchased a hogshead of rum, and after tapping it, left the key in the door where he had placed it, as if he had forgotten it. His design was to give her an opportunity of destroying herself, by drinking as much as she pleased. The woman suspected this to be his design— and suddenly left off drinking. Anger here became the antidote of intemperance.

physic, as well as from my own observations, to declare, that religious melancholy and madness, in all their variety of species, yield with more facility to medicine, than simply to polemical discourses, or to casuistical advice. But this subject is foreign to the business of the present inquiry.

From a review of our subject, we are led to contemplate with admiration, the curious structure of the human mind. How distinct are the number, and yet how united! How subordinate and yet how coequal are all its faculties! How wonderful is the action of the mind upon the body! Of the body upon the mind!—And of the divine spirit upon both! What a mystery is the mind of man to itself!——O! nature!—— Or to speak more properly, ——O! THOU GOD OF NATURE!—— In vain do we attempt to scan THY immensity, or to comprehend THY various modes of existence, when a single particle of light issued from THYSELF, and kindled into intelligence in the bosom of man, thus dazzles and confounds our understandings!

The extent of the moral powers and habits in man is unknown. It is not improbable, but the human mind contains principles of virtue, which have never yet been excited into action. We behold with surprise the versatility of the human body in the exploits of tumblers and rope-dancers. Even the agility of a wild beast has been demonstrated in a girl of France, and an amphibious nature has been discovered in the human species, in a young man in Spain. We listen with astonishment to the accounts of the *memories* of Mithridates, Cyrus, and Servin. We feel a veneration bordering upon divine homage, in contemplating the stupendous *understandings* of Lord Verulam and Sir Isaac Newton; and our eyes grow dim, in attempting to pursue Shakspeare and Milton in their immeasurable flights of *imagination*. And if the history of mankind does not furnish similar instances of the versatility and perfection of our species in virtue, it is because the moral faculty has been the subject of less culture and fewer experiments than the body, and the intellectual powers of the mind. From what has been said, the reason of this is obvious. Hitherto the cultivation of the moral faculty has been the business of parents, schoolmasters and divines.[16] But if the prin-

[16] The people commonly called Quakers, and the Methodists, make use of the greatest number of physical remedies in their religious and moral discipline, of any sects of Christians; and hence we find them every where distinguished for their good morals.

ciples we have laid down be just, the improvement and extension of this principle should be equally the business of the legislator—the natural philosopher—and the physician; and a physical regimen should as necessarily accompany a moral precept, as directions with respect to the air—exercise—and diet, generally accompany prescriptions for the consumption and the gout. To encourage us to undertake experiments for the improvement of morals, let us recollect the success of philosophy in lessening the number, and mitigating the violence of incurable diseases. The intermitting fever, which proved fatal to two of the monarchs of Britain, is now under absolute subjection to medicine. Continual fevers are much less fatal than formerly. The small-pox is disarmed of its mortality by inoculation, and even the tetanus and the cancer have lately received a check in their ravages upon mankind. But medicine has done more. It has penetrated the deep and gloomy abyss of death, and acquired fresh honours in his cold embraces.—Witness the many hundred people who have lately been brought back to life, by the successful efforts of the humane societies, which are now established in many parts of Europe, and in some parts of America. Should the same industry and ingenuity, which have produced these triumphs of medicine over diseases and death, be applied to the moral science, it is highly probable, that most of those baneful vices, which deform the human breast, and convulse the nations of the earth, might be banished from the world. I am not so sanguine as to suppose, that it is possible for man to acquire so much perfection from science, religion, liberty and good government, as to cease to be mortal; but I am fully persuaded, that from the combined action of causes, which operate at once upon the reason, the moral faculty, the passions, the senses, the brain, the nerves, the blood and the heart, it is possible to produce such a change in his moral character, as shall raise him to a resemblance of angels—nay more, to the likeness of GOD himself. The state of Pennsylvania still deplores the loss of a man, in whom not only reason and revelation, but many of the physical causes that have been enumerated, concurred to produce such attainments in moral excellency, as have seldom ap-

---

There are several excellent *physical* institutions in other churches; and if they do not produce the same moral effects that we observe from physical institutions among those two modern sects, it must be ascribed to their being more neglected by the members of those churches.

peared in a human being. This amiable citizen, considered his fellow-creature, man, as God's extract, from his own works; and, whether this image of himself, was cut out from ebony or copper—whether he spoke his own or a foreign language—or whether he worshipped his Maker with ceremonies, or without them, he still considered him as a brother, and equally the object of his benevolence. Poets and historians, who are to live hereafter, to you I commit his panegyric; and when you hear of a law for abolishing slavery in each of the American states, such as was passed in Pennsylvania, in the year 1780—when you hear of the kings and queens of Europe, publishing edicts for abolishing the trade in human souls—and lastly, when you hear of schools and churches with all the arts of civilized life, being established among the nations of Africa, then remember and record, that this revolution in favour of human happiness, was the effect of the labours—the publications—the private letters—and the prayers of ANTHONY BENEZET.[17]

I return from this digression, to address myself in a particular manner to you, VENERABLE SAGES and FELLOW-CITIZENS in the REPUBLIC OF LETTERS. The influence of Philosophy, we have been told, has already been felt in course. To increase, and complete, this influence, there is nothing more necessary, than for the numerous literary societies in Europe and America to add the SCIENCE OF MORALS to their experiments and inquiries. The godlike scheme of Henry IV. of France, and of the illustrious queen Elizabeth, of England, for establishing a perpetual peace in Europe, may be accomplished without a system of

[17] This worthy man was descended from an ancient and honourable family that flourished in the court of Louis XIV. With liberal prospects in life, he early devoted himself to teaching an English school; in which, for industry, capacity, and attention to the morals and principles of the youth committed to his care, he was without an equal. He published many excellent tracts against the African trade, against war, and the use of spirituous liquors, and one in favour of civilizing and christianizing the Indians. He wrote to the queen of Great Britain, and the queen of Portugal, to use their influence in their respective courts to abolish the African trade. He also wrote an affectionate letter to the king of Prussia, to dissuade him from making war. The history of his life affords a remarkable instance, how much it is possible for an individual to accomplish in the world; and that the most humble stations do not preclude good men from the most extensive usefulness. He bequeathed his estate (after the death of his widow), to the support of a school for the education of negro children, which he had founded and taught for several years before he died. He departed this life in May, 1784, in the seventy-first year of his age, in the meridian of his usefulness, universally lamented by persons of all ranks and denominations.

jurisprudence, by a confederation of learned men and learned societies. It is in their power, by multiplying the objects of human reason, to bring the monarchs and rulers of the world under the subjection, and thereby to extirpate war, slavery, and capital punishments, from the list of human evils. Let it not be suspected that I detract, by this declaration, from the honour of the Christian religion. It is true, Christianity was propagated without the aid of human learning; but this was one of those miracles, which was necessary to establish it, and which, by repetition, would cease to be a miracle. They misrepresent the Christian religion, who suppose it to be wholly an internal revelation, and addressed only to the moral faculties of the mind. The truths of Christianity afford the greatest scope for the human understanding, and they will become intelligible to us, only in proportion as the human genius is stretched, by means of philosophy, to its utmost dimensions. Errors may be opposed to errors; but truths, upon all subjects, mutually support each other. And perhaps one reason why some parts of the Christian revelation are still involved in obscurity, may be occasioned by our imperfect knowledge of the phenomena and laws of nature. The truths of philosophy and Christianity dwell alike in the mind of the Deity, and reason and religion are equally the offspring of his goodness. They must, therefore, stand and fall together. By reason, in the present instance, I mean the power of judging of truth, as well as the power of comprehending it. Happy era! when the divine and the philosopher shall embrace each other, and unite their labours for the reformation and happiness of mankind!

ILLUSTRIOUS COUNSELLORS and SENATORS of Pennsylvania! [18] I anticipate your candid reception of this feeble effort to increase the quantity of virtue in our republic. It is not my business to remind you of the immense resources for greatness, which nature and Providence have bestowed upon our state. Every advantage which France has derived from being placed in the centre of Europe, and which Britain has derived from her mixture of nations, Pennsylvania has opened to her. But my business, at present, is to suggest the means of promoting the happiness, not the greatness, of the state. For this purpose, it is

[18] The president and supreme executive council, and the members of the general assembly of Pennsylvania, attended the delivery of the oration, in the hall of the University, by invitation from the Philosophical Society.

absolutely necessary that our government, which unites into one all
the minds of the state, should possess, in an eminent degree, not only
the understanding, the passions, and the will, but, above all, the moral
faculty and the conscience of an individual. Nothing can be politically
right, that is morally wrong; and no necessity can ever sanctify a law,
that is contrary to equity. VIRTUE is the soul of a republic. To promote
this, laws for the suppression of vice and immorality will be as ineffectual, as the increase and enlargement of jails. There is but one method
of preventing crimes, and of rendering a republican form of government durable, and that is, by disseminating the seeds of virtue and
knowledge through every part of the state, by means of proper modes
and places of education, and this can be done effectually only by the
interference and aid of the legislature. I am so deeply impressed with
the truth of this opinion, that were this evening to be the last of my life,
I would not only say to the asylum of my ancestors, and my beloved
native country, with the patriot of Venice, "Esto perpetua," but I
would add, as the last proof of my affection for her, my parting advice
to the guardians of her liberties, "To establish and support PUBLIC
SCHOOLS in every part of the state."

12

FRANCIS WAYLAND

1796, born March 11, in New York City
1813, was graduated from Union College, Schenectady
1813–15, studied medicine in Troy, New York, and in New York City
1816, attended Andover Theological Seminary; was influenced by Moses Stuart
1817–21, tutor at Union College
1821–26, pastor of the First Baptist Church in Boston
1823, *The Moral Dignity of the Missionary Enterprise, a sermon*
1825, *The Duties of an American Citizen*, two fast-day sermons
1826, professor of mathematics and natural philosophy, Union College
1827–55, fourth president of Brown University
1831, *A Discourse on the Philosophy of Analogy;* an address
1835, *The Elements of Moral Science*
1837, *Elements of Political Economy*
1837, *The Moral Law of Accumulation*
1837, *The Limitations of Human Responsibility*
1842, *Thoughts on the Present Collegiate System in the United States*
1845, *Domestic Slavery Considered as a Scriptural Institution*
1847, *The Duty of Obedience to the Civil Magistrate*
1850, *Report on the Condition of Brown University*
1854, *The Elements of Intellectual Philosophy*
1865, died, September 30

THE nineteenth century witnessed the development of systematic instruction in philosophy in the American colleges. The system of thought which was generally accepted for instructional purposes was that of the Scottish "common sense" realists, with greater or lesser admixture of compatible Kantian elements. This choice was dictated primarily by the need for a system which did not come into conflict with the teachings of religion, for, after all, a majority of the American colleges of the time were organized and supported by religious groups. To the extent that college courses were instruction in a system of thought, the materials of instruction had to be reduced to teachable form. This meant that textbooks in philosophy had to be invented. The need was met, and it was met chiefly by the presidents of the colleges, who were in Schmidt's apt phrase, "bearers of the old tradition." G. S. Hall's incomplete listing of textbooks used in the teaching of various branches of philosophy covers twelve closely printed pages. Thomas C. Upham, of Bowdoin College, was the first of the textbook writers. Francis Wayland, of Brown, Noah Porter, of Yale, Mark Hopkins, of Williams, and Francis Bowen, of Harvard, were outstanding among his rivals. In addition, there were a host of minor imitators. By making of philosophy a teachable system, finally, this group of writers succeeded in making philosophy an orthodoxy rather than the search for and love of wisdom.

One of the earliest contributors to this movement was Francis Wayland, whose *Elements of Moral Science*, 1835, *Elements of Political Economy*, 1837, and *Elements of Intellectual Philosophy*, 1854, were among the most widely used textbooks. Even before the first of these texts, however, Wayland made a little-known contribution to the cause of Scottish realism in America in his *Discourse on the Philosophy of Analogy*, which was delivered before the Phi Beta Kappa Society of Rhode Island, September 7, 1831, and is here reprinted. Essentially what Wayland did in this address was to attempt the creation of a logic of science in terms of his philosophic background. Such a statement had not been made before his time, yet analogical reasoning, the nature of which he explored, was one of the primary methods used by the scientists of his day. Much of the reasoning in Rush's "Inquiry into the Influence of Physical Causes on the Moral Faculty," for example, is based upon "analogy." Wayland was especially qualified for such a task because of his studies in medicine and his briefly held professorship of mathematics and natural philosophy.

Starting with a *tabula rasa* theory of the human mind, Wayland postulates in man a "universal appetite for knowledge, which, by a law of his nature, grows by what it feeds on." The universe, by beneficent Providence, is admirably adapted to serve both as fodder and as appetizer for the human mind. This external universe corresponds to the mental appetite in all respects; but neither the appetite itself nor the relation of correspondence can be the source of knowledge. This epistemological hurdle is leaped by the faculties of the mind "by the exercise of which he is able to discover that truth by which his desires are gratified and his intellectual happiness created."

The steps in the progress of knowledge are: (1) observation of facts, that is, of the existence of things and of the changes taking place in things, (2) the perception of succession in the changes, with increasing detail, until "a nearer and nearer approximation is made to pure and unchangeable truth," and (3) the discovery of points of coincidence between the laws of succession of various phenomenal changes, which are thus subsumed under more and more general laws. This process of generalizing the laws of nature has not yet reached its ultimate.

Demonstration, or deduction, and induction are recognized as the two processes of thought by means of which knowledge of the laws of the universe may be acquired. Demonstration is limited in its use to the sphere of quantity; induction is the process used in all except the mathematical sciences, and to some extent even in these. Nature's answer to our questioning must be "deciphered by the exercise of the faculties which she herself hath given us. In the forms of demonstration and induction alone can these faculties be used to decypher it."

Nature's answer, after deciphering, has several significant characteristics. The answer is always limited by the question; it is always confined to the predication of existence or nonexistence, and never concerned with the "how"; negative answers are as difficult of interpretation as affirmative. Therefore, skill in interpreting the answer of nature, skill in the use of the instruments of proof, can never insure the progress of discovery. There must also be skill in asking the right questions. This skill is what Wayland means by the philosophy of analogy. "There is needed a science, which standing on the confines of what is known, shall point out the direction in which truth probably lies, in the region that is unknown. This, when it has assumed a definite form, will be the *science of analogy*." This science does not exist; when it is created, Wayland feels sure that it will rest on two "self-evident" principles: that a part of a system created by an intelligent agent is similar in principle to the whole system, and that the work of an intelligent agent will reveal intelligence. The best user of analogy will therefore be the one who most thoroughly understands the system of the universe and who is "most deeply penetrated with a conviction of the attributes of the first Cause of all things." Thus, infidel scientists are distinguished in the use of the sciences, but Christian scientists are most successful in foretelling the direction of discovery.

When a science of analogy is created, it will guarantee progress not only in physical sciences, but also in morals and taste, which will thereby become areas of positive and determinate knowledge. Thus, there will truly be a moral science and a science of beauty. Furthermore, in the light of the "self-evident" principles mentioned before, not only will each successful application of the science of analogy increase our knowledge of the entire system, and thereby hasten the next application of the science, but also every increase in our knowledge of God, as the author of the system, will better our chances of understanding the system, and thereby learning to ask the right questions and interpret the answers.

Wayland, in this address, built very well. The "natural philosophers" of the Enlightenment tended to be less concerned with matters of religion than was thought desirable by the more orthodox thinkers of Wayland's time. By making knowledge of God one of the bases of scientific advance, Wayland tried to break down this separation between natural philosophy and teleology. At the same time, he did not yield a jot of the inductive, empirical approach of his school. He conserved both orthodoxy and realistic empiricism while making the optimistic belief in progress the dogmatic keynote of his thought.

THE PHILOSOPHY OF ANALOGY

IT was not without unfeigned reluctance, that I complied with the request to appear before you on the present occasion. Do not, however, suppose that I for a moment distrusted either your candor or your forbearance. Full well was I assured, that you would look with indulgence upon the humblest attempt to advance the science or to adorn the literature of our country. My reluctance proceeded from a different source. Accustomed to the investigation of abstract truth, I feared lest the train of my reflections should seem too far removed from the ordinary walks of literary life. I however remembered that general truth is, in its nature, abstracted, and nowhere could I expect that such truth would meet with more devoted admirers than in a society, whose only object is the cultivation of letters. Besides, I have thought that, by giving to these annual discourses the tinge of our different professional pursuits, we shall enlarge the field from which subjects for discussion may be selected, and secure as great a degree of variety as the occasion may demand.

Influenced by these considerations, I venture to request your attention to some remarks which I shall offer upon THE PHILOSOPHY OF ANALOGY; a subject, which, so far as I have been able to discover, has not yet attracted the notice of any writer in our language. This neglect is at least somewhat remarkable, for I know of none which stands more intimately connected, both with the improvement of science, and the progress of discovery. May we not, then, hope that by exploring a field, which has been so long overlooked, we may find something to reward our search which has thus far eluded notice of more able inquirers.

The most obvious thought that meets us, when we reflect upon the intellectual relation which man sustains to the universe around him, is, that he commences his existence entirely destitute of knowledge. He is, however, so constituted, that knowledge must inevitably result from the elements of which his intellectual character is composed, and the circumstances under which those elements are placed. Thus, we find him endowed with an universal appetite for knowledge, which, by a law of his nature, grows by what it feeds on. Again, we find man surrounded by an universe, in all respects corresponding to this mental appetite, and adapted, at the same moment, both to gratify and stimulate inquiry. Knowledge, however, is acquired, neither by this appetite, nor by its relation to this universe. Man is, therefore, endowed also with faculties, by the exercise of which he is able to discover that truth by which his desires are gratified and his intellectual happiness created.

If we consider the subject somewhat more attentively, we not only perceive that the universe is spread around us to stimulate our love of truth, but we may also discover the mode in which the successive developments of truth are addressed to the ever-growing faculties of an immortal spirit. It may not be unprofitable to occupy a few moments in illustrating this position.

The first step in the progress of knowledge is the observation of facts, that is, that *certain things exist,* and that certain changes are taking place in them. This information we derive at first entirely from the senses.

But, it is found that these changes, or, as they are technically called, phenomena, do not take place at random, but in the order of a succession, at first, dimly, but, by close inspection, more clearly, seen. The order of this succession is next noted, and this forms the first conception of a law of nature. Subsequent observation and more accurate experiments determine more of the circumstances actually connected with this law of succession, disengage from it that which is accidental, extend its dominion to other changes placed by the Author of nature under its control, and thus a nearer and nearer approximation is made to pure and unchangeable truth. Thus, in mechanics, we learn, first, the fact that bodies, under certain circumstances, without any impulse change their place. Pursuing our investigations further, we learn under what circumstances and in what direction alone this motion or change of place occurs, we ascertain the various facts or laws which pertain to the motion itself, and extend, as far as we are able, our knowledge of the objects to which these laws apply. Thus also, by knowing the laws which govern any particular class of objects, we preclude the necessity of innumerable experiments, and are enabled to predict, under given circumstances, what, throughout the material universe, will be the certain result.

Again, between the laws which govern different classes of objects, there are found to exist various points of coincidence. These points of coincidence, and the circumstances under which they occur, are also objects of knowledge. They form laws of a higher class, or *more general laws* by which the less general laws themselves are governed. Thus, I mentioned that the law by which the attraction of gravity operates, is discovered. The laws by which the attraction of magnetism, and that of electricity operate, have also been discovered, and these laws are found to coincide, and hence we derive a *general law* of attraction, applying to gravity, magnetism, electricity, and probably to all kinds of attraction throughout the universe.

But it is evident that the progress of human knowledge is not here arrested. These *general laws* may be subject to others yet more general. Again, correspondences may be discovered between these and others yet more general. Thus, at every step of our progress, we are enabled to predict not only an infinity of changes, but also an infinity of laws by which those changes are governed. Thus, I have spoken of the general law of attraction governing the laws of gravitation, electricity, and magnetism. This law of attraction may yet be found subject to some more general law which governs both attraction and repulsion, and every species of motion. Again, these more general laws of motion may be connected with those of light, and a multitude of other classes of laws not yet discovered. And so on to infinity.

But it is still to be observed that not only is human knowledge thus continually extending, it is moreover evident that *a tendency* to universal extension has been impressed upon it by its Creator. For we find that a law, when legitimately established, is never known to vary. Some unexplained deviation is however frequently discovered in the mode of its operation. This, by the constitution of the human mind, leads to more extensive investigation. Investigation shows that the language of nature had been misinterpreted, and that every discrepancy vanishes, by adopting a wider generalization and admitting a more universal philosophical principle. Thus, to refer to the case of gravity, it was at first found that some bodies *rose* instead of falling in the air, and hence there seemed an exception to the law which before appeared established. More accurate experiment, however, proved that the air itself gravitated to the earth, and thus not only the exception was explained, but a wider universality was given to the general law than had been before conceded to it. Thus, also, in chemistry, Lavoisier considered oxygen the only supporter of combustion. To this law there seemed some curious anomalies. It was reserved for the genius of Sir Humphrey Davy to discover another supporter, and thus not only to arrive at a principle of wider application, but also to unfold the universal truth that the whole matter of our earth is composed of but two classes of substances, combustibles and supporters of combustion. Thus, the tendency of mind is, in its very nature, upward. Thus, that intellect, which, at the beginning the Almighty formed in his own image, was made to soar with untiring wing towards the Author of her being, while with an eye that never blenches, she gazes without ceasing upon that holy uncreated light in which He sits pavilioned.

Such then is the nature of that love of knowledge which the Creator hath made an element of our intellectual being, and such the objects which He hath spread around to employ and to ennoble it.

But you will at once perceive that this desire, and these objects, might exist in connexion forever, and that, were there no other elements in our intellectual constitution, no knowledge would ever be the result. The simple desire to know never discovers truth, and of course never produces knowledge. Truth, the most valuable of treasures, is to be attained only by labor. The pearl may be had, but the price must be paid for it. Like every other acquisition it is also the result of the employment of means. And, unless the means be employed, the result must not be expected.

To illustrate this by a single consideration. All the various laws which I have mentioned as the objects of knowledge, evidently exist. But they are not visible, simply by inspection. They do not lie every where on the surface. The changes of the universe are every where going on; but they are seen only as *results*. The laws which regulate them can be known only by patient analysis and careful generalization. Thus also the relations of quantity have always existed; but how many ages of research have been required to develop them as they are now displayed in the science of mathematics. The same is true of mechanics, of astronomy, of chemistry, and of all the other sciences.

There are two processes of thought by which this knowledge may be acquired; the one demonstration, the other induction. Demonstration proceeds from self-evident principles to the most complicated relations. Its sphere is the science of quantity, and, within that sphere, its dominion is absolute. To quantity, and whatever may be brought within the grasp of quantity, its empire is however limited. It is by the use of this instrument that the mathematicians have shed so resplendent a flood of light upon mechanics, optics, astronomy, and motion.

The other instrument is induction. By means of this, we commence with individual instances, and, by comparison and classification, arrive at laws more and more general. This instrument is used in all the sciences not within the province of the mathematics, and even for many of these it forms the basis for their reasonings. The difference between these two processes is this. The one proceeds from self-evident truth to its necessary results; the other from known effects to their actual antecedents. Such are the modes of intellectual labor by which alone human knowledge is extended. The whole universe is spread out before us, we are constituted with an irrepressible desire to know the laws by which it is regulated. The means are placed in our power, by the exercise of which, this desire is gratified. When we ask of nature a question, she points us to this beauteous earth, that heaving ocean, and yon measureless expanse, and, in the living characters which are there inscribed, bids us read her answer. But that answer must be deciphered by the exercise of the faculties which she herself hath given us. In the forms of demonstration and induction alone can these faculties be used to decypher it.

If now we consider the answer which is thus obtained, we shall observe in it several things well worthy of our attention.

And first. The answer is always strictly limited to the question proposed. We interrogate nature, and she replies *to that interrogation* alone. I do not mean to assert, that accidental discoveries are not frequently made. But the very mode in which they are made confirms the truth of my remark. Suppose a man wished to know the nature of colors, and he pursued a course of experiment which taught the gravity of the air, the result of his experiment would be the answer to the question, has the air weight? This, therefore, would be the real question which he was asking, and to this question the answer would be definite. But as the inquirer had another question in his mind, the chances are almost infinite to one that he would not understand the answer which he received.

Second. The answer of nature in every case is confined to either an affirmative or a negative. The inquirer asks, and she simply replies, *it is*, or, *it is not*. If he inquires *how*, she is invariably silent. He must put the particular case, and then, when he has interpreted her answer, he will find it always *positive and determinate*. It, however, as I have said, never goes beyond a simple yea or nay. This is the case with the longest and most complicated as well as with the simplest and most expeditious processes of investigation.

Third. The negative characters of nature's language are as difficult to interpret as the affirmative. Both also are alike destitute of meaning until the answer is decyphered. Hence the collected sagacity of the world might toil for ages to interpret a single answer of nature, and find at last that it contained nothing else than the monosyllable no.

From a comparison of these obvious facts, it is evident that were we possessed of no other means of discovery than the strict exercise of the reasoning faculties, the progress of knowledge would be merely accidental. To speak with exactness, demonstration and induction never discover a law of nature; they only show whether a law has or has not been discovered. And as truth is one, and error infinite, it is manifest, that were we in possession of no other means of advancement, we might weary ourselves forever in interpreting the answers of nature, and find, in the end, that we had only taken a few from an infinity of possibilities of error.

That all this is true will, I think, be evident from facts within the knowledge of all of us. A cursory survey of the history of the human mind will convince us that progress in discovery of the laws of nature has not been in proportion to the improvement of our skill in the use of the instruments of investigation. The Hindoos are said to have been acquainted with algebra, in a very remote age, and even in an early period of their history to have discovered the Binomial Theorem; but what achievements over nature have they transmitted to us? The

Arabians learned algebra probably from the Hindoos, but how have the Arabians enlarged the sphere of human knowledge? The Greeks made distinguished progress in geometry, their processes in this science may even now be used with advantage, Sir Isaac Newton himself acknowledges them his masters, but their processes are almost all that has come down to us. Their applications of these processes to the advancement of truth were rare and trivial. The ages emphatically denominated dark were distinguished for a subtilty of logic which has never been surpassed, and yet they carried human knowledge backward. Skill in the use of the instruments of proof can never therefore, of itself, insure the progress of discovery.

Besides skill in interpreting the answer of nature, man must also then acquire skill in asking of her the question. There is needed a science, which, standing on the confines of what is known, shall point out the direction in which truth probably lies, in the region that is unknown. This, when it has assumed a definite form, will be the *science of analogy*.

You observe that I speak of the science of analogy, as something which is yet to be. It does not now exist, but it must exist soon. He who shall create it will descend to posterity with a glory in nowise inferior to that of Bacon or of Newton. He who would complete such a work must be acquainted with the whole circle of the sciences, and be familiar with their history; he must examine and analyze all the circumstances of every important discovery, and, from the facts thus developed, point out the laws by which is governed the yet unexplained process of original investigation. When God shall have sent that Genius upon earth who was born to accomplish this mighty labor, then, one of the greatest obstacles will have been removed to our acquiring an unlimited control over all the agents of nature.

But passing this part of the subject, I remark that, whenever the laws of such a science shall have been discovered, I think that they will be found to rest upon the two following self-evident principles.

First. A part of any system which is the work of an intelligent agent, is similar, so far as the principles which it involves are concerned, to the whole of that system.

And, secondly. The work of an intelligent and moral being must bear, in all its lineaments, the traces of the character of its Author.

And, hence, he will use analogy the most skilfully who is most thoroughly imbued with the spirit of the system, and at the same time most deeply penetrated with a conviction of the attributes of the first Cause of all things.

To illustrate this by a single remark. Suppose I should present before you one of the paintings of Raphael, and, covering by far the greater part of it with a screen, ask you to proceed with the work and designate where the next lines should be drawn. It is evident that no one but a painter need even make the attempt; and of painters, he would be the most likely to succeed, who had become best acquainted with the genius of Raphael and had most thoroughly meditated upon the manner in which that genius had displayed itself in the work before him. So, of the system of the universe we see but a part. All the rest is hidden from our view. He will, however, most readily discover *where the next lines are drawn*, who is most thoroughly acquainted with the character of the Author, and who has observed, with the greatest accuracy, the manner in which that character is displayed, in that portion of the system which he has condescended to reveal to us.

All this is confirmed by the successive efforts of mind which resulted in the greatest of Sir Isaac Newton's discoveries. "As he sat alone in his garden," says Dr. Pemberton, "he fell into a speculation on the power of gravity. That, as this power sensibly diminished at the remotest distances from the centre of the earth to which we can rise, it appeared to him reasonable, to conclude that this power must extend much farther than was usually thought. Why not as high as the moon, said he to himself, and if so, her motion must be influenced by it; perhaps she is retained in her orbit thereby. And if the moon be retained in her orbit by the force of gravity, no doubt the primary planets are carried round the sun by the like power." [1] I think it self-evident, that this first germ of the system of the universe would never have been suggested to any man whose mind had not been filled with exalted views of the greatness of the Creator, and who had not diligently contemplated the mode in which those attributes were displayed in that part of his works which science had already discovered to us.

And if this distinction be just, it will lead us to divide philosophers

[1] Preface to *Account of Sir I. Newton's Discoveries.*

into, those who have been eminent for attainment in those sciences which are instruments of investigation; and those, who, to their acquisitions, have added unusual skill in foretelling where these instruments could with the greatest success be applied. Among the ancients, probably Aristotle belonged to the former, and Pythagoras and Archimedes to the latter class. Among the moderns, I think that infidel philosophers generally will be found to have distinguished themselves by accurate use of the sciences, and Christian philosophers by the additional glory of foretelling when and how the sciences may be used. I am not aware that infidelity hath presented to the world any discoveries to compare with those of Boyle and Pascal, and Bacon and Newton, or of Locke, and Milton, and Butler.

And here I may be allowed to suggest that, often as the character of Newton has been the theme of admiration, it has seemed to me that the most distinctive element of his greatness has commonly escaped the notice of his eulogists. It was neither in mathematical skill nor in mathematical invention, that he so far surpassed his contemporaries; for in both these respects, he divided the palm with Huygens, and Kepler, and Leibnitz. It is in the wide sweep of his far-reaching analogy, distinguished alike by its humility and its boldness, that he has left the philosophers of all previous and all subsequent ages so immeasurably behind him. Delighted with his modesty and reciprocating his confidence, nature held communion with him as with a favorite son; to him she unveiled her most recondite mysteries; to him she revealed the secret of her most subtle transformations, and then taking him by the hand she walked with him abroad over the wide expanse of universal being.

Thus much concerning the *nature* of analogy. I come next to speak of its *practical applications* and the *sources* of its improvement.

The applications of analogy to the sciences have been already in part considered. Some additional illustrations of this part of the subject may, however, be worthy of our attention.

I have already shown that the use of analogy, in extending the dominion of knowledge, is to teach us in what direction we should apply the instruments of discovery. I have alluded to the skill with which it was employed by Newton, and how wonderfully it contributed to the unparalleled result which crowned his indefatigable labor. Every one must, I think, be persuaded that without it, his success would have been in no manner distinguished from that of the other eminent men by whom he was surrounded. And hence we see that, just in proportion as the science of analogy is perfected, will the useless intellectual labor of the human race be diminished. Discovery will cease to be the creature of accident, and, like the other operations of the human soul, bow submissively to the dominion of Law.

Besides teaching us how to interrogate nature, analogy will also instruct us in the best method of interpreting her answer. I have said that the instruments used by the understanding for the eviction of truth are demonstration and induction. But the forms in which these instruments may be used are various. Demonstration may be conducted by different processes, and the modes of induction in chemistry, optics, and philosophy, already numerous, are multiplying with unexampled rapidity. Now it is evidently in the power of analogy, to select that process which is most likely to furnish the particular solution of which the philosopher is in search. Thus every one must perceive how greatly a judicious classification of the modes of proof in the various sciences, and of the results which have emanated from each, would tend to facilitate the progress of discovery.

Again analogy may be used with great success to rebuke erroneous reasonings from either correct or incorrect general principles. Human pride and human indolence have always been strongly averse to the sure but tardy process of reasoning by induction. Hence men have been much more prone to tell how a phenomenon must be, than to find out how it is. At the head of this sect, stands Descartes who supposed himself capable of proving the existence and qualities of all things from the simple proposition, I think, therefore, I exist. The reasonings of the ancient philosophers proceeded very much upon the same principles. Now it is evident that demonstrations of this kind, if they are true, must be in their nature universal. They are otherwise entirely nugatory. They attempt to show, not that the fact in question *does*, but that it *must*, or, not that it *does not*, but that it *cannot exist*. Here then they are met at the outset by the analogical reasoner. He presents a case from actual existence, in which the same principles are involved as in the case in dispute, and asks the unanswerable question, why should not the range of these principles be universal. Thus supposing an Atheist to assert that there is no God and therefore there can be neither future existence nor any state of rewards and punishments; the argument from analogy would be sufficient of itself, to overwhelm him with confusion. For, granting his assertion that there is no God, yet it is evident that we now exist, and he can show no reason why we should not in another state, continue to do so; and still more if, as is evidently the case, we are rewarded and punished for our actions now, while, as he asserts there is no God, there is no reason why we should not be so rewarded and punished, although there were no God, to all eternity.

And, once more, the argument from analogy is not only capable of answering objections, on moral subjects, it is sufficient moreover to establish a very definite probability. Moral truth is in its nature immutable, for it stands in unchangeable relation to the attributes of the Eternal God. If, therefore, it can be shown that He has ever admitted, in his dealings with any race of his creatures a given moral principle, it is at once proved that that principle is right, and that there is no moral reason why it should not be admitted in the dealings of God with that race of beings at any other time. And yet more, I think that a pledge is hereby given to the universe that that principle will never be retracted, but that it will remain forever unchangeable. Were it otherwise, the Divine Government would be a Government not of law but of caprice. And thus the whole moral constitution in our present state, so far as it has been illustrated, is found to bear its willing testimony to the antecedent probability of revelation. It is upon these indisputable truths, that Butler has reared his immortal work, a work which has done more to promote the discovery and establish the truth of ethical philosophy, than any uninspired treatise in any age or language.

The applications of analogy to the fine arts must already have suggested themselves to you; they will therefore require only a passing illustration.

The intellectual exertion on which the fine arts depend consists of a combined effort of imagination and taste. How closely connected are the analogies of science with those of the imagination will easily be seen. In the analogies of science, we commence with a single *cause*, and search throughout the universe for effects which may be brought under its dominion. In the analogies of the imagination, we commence with an *effect*, and range throughout all that the mind hath conceived in quest of *causes* which produce a *similar effect*. It is thus that we are enabled to enrobe the deductions of the understanding with aught that creation can present of beauty or of grandeur.

> The poet's eye, in a fine frenzy rolling,
> Glances from heaven to earth, from earth to heaven,
> And, as Imagination pictures forth
> The forms of things unknown, the poet's pen
> Turns them to shape, and gives to airy nothings
> A local habitation and a name.

Thus we perceive that the effort of Newton, carrying out by analogy the principle of gravitation to the utmost verge of the material creation, was strikingly analogous to that of Milton in his Allegro or Penseroso, looking through all that the eye hath seen or the heart imagined, in search of images of gaiety or of sadness.

Nor is the philosophy of taste substantially dissimilar. Taste is the sensibility of our nature to the various forms of beauty which the Creator hath spread with such profusion around us. He who made the mind for beauty, made beauty also for the mind. He hath penciled it upon the spangled meadow and on the burnished cloud. He hath chiseled it in the gigantic majesty of the cedar of Lebanon and in the trembling loveliness of the tendril which twines around its branches. In obedience to its laws, He hath taught the linnet to flutter in the grove and the planets to revolve in their pathway through the heavens. We hear it in the purling brook and in the thundering cataract, and we perceive it yet more legibly inscribed upon all those social and moral qualities in the exercise of which our Maker hath intended that we should be forever approaching nearer and nearer to the exhaustless source of uncreated excellence. These are the models which nature presents for the contemplation of the Artist; and, just in proportion to his power of detecting among her complicated forms the simple elements of loveliness, and of combining them according to the examples which she herself has set before him, will he fill the vacant canvass with images of beauty and animate the dull cold marble with breathing intelligence. It is this communion with nature which confers upon the artist what Lord Chatham has so well denominated the prophetic eye of taste, and which has left the Belvidere Apollo and the Medicean

Venus, the temple on the Ilyssus and the temple of Minerva, to illustrate to all coming generations what genius can accomplish. We see thus that in taste, as in all the original operations of the human mind, it is the sublimest attribute of intelligence to see things as they are.

Allow me, in the last place, to direct your attention to the *sources* from which may be expected the improvement of analogy.

We may expect the science of analogy to improve from the greater *accuracy of human knowledge.* I have already alluded to the fact, that discovery proceeds by observing a particular law in an individual instance, and then by analogy extending the dominion of that law to the infinitely greater instances within the reach of our observation.

It is evident, therefore, that the elements with which we commence must be strictly and purely true, or our seemingly just anticipations will be invariably disappointed. This may be exemplified by an incident which occurred in the progress of Sir I. Newton's discoveries. "In his investigation of the question, whether the force of gravity were sufficient to keep the moon in her orbit, he used as the basis of his calculations, the then common estimate, that sixty English miles were contained in one degree of the latitude of the earth. But as this is a very faulty supposition, his computation did not answer expectation, whence he concluded that some other cause must at least join with the action of the power of gravity on the moon. On this account he laid aside for that time any thoughts on that matter. It was not until some years had elapsed and a more accurate admeasurement of the earth had been effected, that he resumed the subject; and, as soon as he introduced the true estimate into the element of his reasonings, he immediately ascertained, what he had formerly anticipated, that the moon is held in her orbit by the power of gravitation alone." [2] Of so great importance is pure and unadulterated truth, in every thing which claims to be elementary in our knowledge.

How greatly the science of analogy must be improved by increasing *the extent* of human knowledge, I scarcely need remind you. It is manifest that every new law which is discovered throws light upon some other law, and also points to some more general principle, by which, it, and the class to which it belongs, are governed. That this is true, is evident from the fact, that in those periods, in which science

[2] Dr. Pemberton's Preface to *Account of Sir I. Newton's Discoveries.*

has advanced with the greatest rapidity, the same discovery has frequently been made, by several individuals, at the same time. This teaches us that the laws then discovered had pointed out the next step in discovery, and thus that talent common to many was able to accomplish what the highest endowments in intellect had previously found to be impossible.

And yet more. I have alluded to a knowledge of the spirit of the system, as far as it has been investigated, as of the greatest importance in promoting the science of analogy. But it is evident that this knowledge can only be perfected in proportion as the system itself in its various relations is discovered. Every step in our progress gives us a wider range of observation and enables us to induce our general principles from a more extensive comparison of facts. It is thus also, that from an attentive contemplation of the progress of the system, we are enabled to perceive the result to which the whole is tending, the modes of operation by which that result is produced, and the various circumstances, physical, intellectual, and moral, by which the advancement of knowledge is either accelerated or retarded. Thus, if you will allow me to allude to an illustration which I have used before, if a painting was placed before you, of which the larger portion was covered, and you were requested to complete the work of a Titian, or a Raphael, it is evident that no one would be able to succeed, unless he had attentively studied the nature of the work and the character of the artist. But it is evident also, that just in proportion as the work advanced, and portion after portion of the screen was removed, just in that proportion would the difficulty of completing the whole diminish. We should see, more and more clearly, the end which the artist had in view, and we should learn the modes of expression which he was accustomed to employ, until the sight of a single feature would enable us to delineate the entire countenance of which it formed a part, and a single prominent figure would suggest to us the expression and design of an animated group.

Again, it is evident that, in attempting to delineate such a painting as I have described, it would be natural for us to acquire, by all the means in our power, as accurate an acquaintance as was possible of the character of its author. If a history of his life, or a delineation of his habits could be obtained, we should derive the greatest advantage from contemplating it with the profoundest attention. And specially if there could be obtained a specimen of his work on a more exalted subject, on which he had expended his profoundest skill, and which he had finished with extraordinary care, of the advantage of meditating on such a picture, we should be insane if we did not incessantly avail ourselves.

This leads me to observe that we may anticipate the greatest improvement in the science of analogy from the progress of our race in the knowledge of the character of God. Beside the works which he has created for our instruction, he has condescended to make himself known to us in a written revelation. Here he has taught us the infinity of his power, the unsearchableness of his wisdom, the boundlessness of his omnipresence, the tenderness of his compassion, and the purity of his holiness. Now, it is evident that the system of things around us must all have been constructed in accordance with the conceptions of so ineffably glorious an intelligence. But to such a being as this we are infinitely dissimilar. Compared with the attributes of the Eternal, our knowledge, and power, and goodness are but the shadow of a name. As the heavens are higher than the earth, so are His ways higher than our ways, and his thoughts than our thoughts. So long, then, as we measure his works by our conceptions, is it wonderful if we are lost in inextricable darkness, and weary ourselves in asking of nature questions to which the indignant answer is invariably no! It is only when, in the profoundest humility, we acknowledge our own ignorance and look to the Father of light for wisdom, it is only when, bursting loose from the littleness of our own limited conceptions, we lose ourselves in the vastness of the Creator's infinity, that we can rise to the height of this great argument and point out the path of discovery to coming generations. While men, measuring the universe by the standard of their own narrow conceptions, and surveying all things through the distempered medium of their own puerile vanity, placed the earth in the centre of the system, and supposed sun, moon and stars to revolve daily around it, the science of astronomy stood still, and age after age groped about in almost rayless darkness. It was only when humility had taught us how small a space we occupied in the boundlessness of creation, and raised us to a conception of the plan of the Eternal, that light broke in like the morning star upon our midnight, and a beauteous universe rose out of void and formless chaos.

And, yet more, the Book of Revelation contains the only delineation which we possess of the commencement, prosecution, and completion of one of the designs of Deity. It is the work of man's restoration to purity and happiness. We here may detect the benevolence which actuates the Almighty, the modes which he adopts to carry that benevolence into effect, the manner in which his infinite wisdom directs all things to the accomplishment of his merciful purposes, and how, in despite of apparently insurmountable obstacles, he by the simplest means makes all events conspire to a perfect and triumphant consummation.

Now, when we compare the system of man's redemption with the system of the material universe, we shall find them, in many respects, analogous. Both are the conceptions of the same infinite Deity. Both are designed to promote the happiness of man. They differ only in this, that the one is adapted to his physical, the other to his moral wants. It would, therefore, be totally unlike any of the other works of God, if that system, of which the outline of the whole is known, did not shed abundant light upon those portions of the other system which yet remain unknown. And to this must be added another consideration. It cannot have escaped the attention of any thinking mind, that the progress of every science, since the revival of letters, has served to shed new light upon the Book of Revelation. Geography has borne witness to the truth of its delineations, the discovery and interpretation of ancient writings have illustrated its antiquities, political economy has confirmed the truth of its ethics, while intellectual philosophy is establishing the science of testimony, and fixing the principles of interpretation. And all this is evidently but in its very commencement. Who can foresee the glory of the result, when the full blaze of every science shall be concentrated upon the page of everlasting Truth, and thence reflected, with undiminished effulgence, upon the upward path of baptized philosophy.

And lastly. As the constitution under which we are placed is a moral government, God bestows his richest blessings in strict accordance with the moral character of his creatures. May we not hope, then, that with the improvement of our race in piety, he will invigorate our powers of discovery; and specially, that that "spirit, who above all temples does prefer the upright heart and pure," will be sent to instruct us; that "what is dark in us he will illumine, what is low raise and support." Then, at last, every obstacle to our progress in knowledge and virtue having been removed, we shall enter upon that career of improvement for which we were originally designed by our Creator. Then, as at the beginning, shall God look upon all the works which he has made, and behold all will be again good. Then shall the morning stars sing together, and all the sons of God shout aloud for joy.

13

JOHN NEAL

1793, born August 25, at Falmouth (i.e., Portland), Maine
1815, began study of law and editorial activities in Baltimore, Md.
1817, *Keep Cool*
1818, *Battle of Niagara . . . and Goldau*
1819, *Otho*
1819, collaborated with others under the group pseudonym Paul Allen, in writing
  A History of the American Revolution, 2 volumes
1822, *Logan; a Family History*
1823, *Errata; or The Works of Will Adams*
1823, *Seventy Six*
1823, *Randolph*
1823–27, lived in England
1824–25, "American Writers," a series of articles in *Blackwood's Magazine*
1825, *Brother Jonathan*
1827–76, legal practice and editorial and civic activities in Portland, Maine
1828, *Rachel Dyer*
1828–29 edited the *Yankee*
1830, translated Bentham's *Principles of Legislation* from the French version
  of Dumont
1830, *Authorship*
1833, *The Down-Easters*
1836, received the degree (honorary) of M.A. Bowdoin College
1838, *Man*
1843, edited *Brother Jonathan*; a weekly
1854, *One Word More*
1859, *True Womanhood*
1863, *The White Faced Pacer*
1864, *The Moose Hunter*
1866, *Little Moccasin; or, Along the Madawaska*
1869, *Wandering Recollections of a Somewhat Busy Life*
1870, *Great Mysteries and Little Plagues*
1874, *Portland Illustrated*
1876, died June 20, at Portland, Maine

THE first half of the nineteenth century witnessed the development of a
marked increase of interest in the science of mind, or what we would today

call psychology. In part, at least, this was the result of the shift of attention in the Enlightenment from divinity to humanity; in part it was a continuation of the empirical movement in philosophy, which was sharply challenged by the question How can the mind know the external world? Therefore men had to learn more about the mind. While experimental psychology in something like the form we know it today did not exist in America until the establishment of the first psychological laboratory at Johns Hopkins University, Baltimore, in 1881, the roots of experimentalism go much farther back in this country, to the work of Benjamin Rush.

In Europe, at the beginning of the century, F. J. Gall and his pupils J. K. Spurzheim and G. Combe attempted to restore on a more modern, scientific basis a system of empirical psychology whose antecedents reached back into early medieval thought. This science, to which the name "phrenology" was given, had many followers and much appeal in the United States. As it lost the respect of men of scientific temper, it developed as a secular faith, akin to mesmerism, animal magnetism, and other such fads, and also as a popular pseudo-science, much like graphology and astrology today. Men and women visited the phrenologist to learn whether they were likely to be successful in business or in love and to find out the outlines of their future from the "bumps" on their heads. Even today a phrenologist is likely to be one of the sideshow attractions at a rural fair.

For a time, however, until its underlying principles were proved to be false, phrenology was one of the sciences and by no means the least of them. There are five principles of progressive dubiety on which this science was based. The first of these was that the brain is the organ of mind. The second was that the mental powers of man are analyzable into a number of innate faculties, independent of each other. Third, each of these faculties has its seat in a definite area of the surface of the brain; this is the theory of localization, of which more recent physiological psychologists have spoken favorably. The fourth principle is that the size of the area of brain-surface assigned as the seat of a specific faculty is the measure of the degree to which that faculty is present in the make-up of any individual. Fifth, and of all the least supportable, is the belief that there is a sufficiently close correspondence between the contour of the outer surface of the skull and that of the brain-surface beneath it to enable a trained observer to recognize the relative sizes of the different brain areas, and thereby to interpret the relative intensities of the faculties by an examination of the outside of the head. As a hypothesis, this is simple and neat, and it had a vast attraction for an uncritical public. More critical men were apt to point out that the hypothesis of correspondence was based upon too few cases to have any real foundation. Later, the investigation of a greater number of cases proved the hypothesis completely erroneous.

While phrenology was still a plausible theory, it attracted the attention of John Neal, who was for about a decade the *enfant terrible* of American letters. Uneducated, almost unlettered, he hurtled across the literary sky in 1816, when at the age of twenty-three he reviewed the works of Byron in six issues of the *Portico*. Seven years later, he went to England; during those years he had qualified as a lawyer and established a fair practice in Baltimore, published five novels, a tragedy, a volume of poems, and supported himself by literary hack work and editorial work on the Baltimore *Telegraph*. Along with the energy, the unchecked exuberance, akin to genius, which led his fellow law students to nickname him Jehu O'Cataract, there was a lack of discipline which led him to publish extravagant and ill-timed criticism of William Pinkney in his *Randolph*, despite the fact that Pinkney had died while the manuscript was being written, and to include in his *Errata* stories offensive to people in his boyhood home, Portland, Maine.

In 1823 Neal, on impulse, sailed for England, where he wrote a number of articles for the magazines, including the recently republished series of five articles in *Blackwood's*, entitled "American Writers." In these papers he lost whatever popularity he had left in the United States. In addition, he became for eighteen months after November, 1825, the intimate pupil and secretarial assistant to the aged Jeremy Bentham. One of Neal's most delightful pieces of work is his biographical sketch of Bentham, prefaced to his Boston, 1830, edition of Bentham's *Principles of Legislation*.

In 1827 Neal returned home and settled down to his legal career in Portland, and in 1828 he established a literary weekly, *The Yankee*, which he edited for years. He lost some of the ebullience of his earlier years, save for occasional flashes; for this loss he compensated by his service to causes such as woman suffrage, in which he was an early and active worker, and the restoration and beautification of his native city. He also became interested in spiritualism, mesmerism, and phrenology.

On September 4, 1838, Neal went to Brown University to deliver the annual address before the United Brothers Society, one of the two literary groups which, in those democratic days before the introduction of Greek-letter fraternities, divided the student body—and if accounts of the rushing of freshmen are true, the students' bodies—between them. He took for his theme the potentialities of man and delivered the rhapsodical address which is reprinted here. Neal divided the history of man into five eras. In the first, that of brute man, the physical hero held undisputed sway. The second, the era of intellectual man, saw the orator, the poet, the lawgiver, and the statesman utilize the force of the brute for their own ends. The third era was that of spiritual man, the age of darkness, superstition, and priesthood. In the fourth era, that of Neal's own times, the artificial man, "the man of neglected or perverted faculties," the powerless, chattering, idle, "emasculated gossips," led without power or rule. The fifth age, he declared, was yet to be. It was to be the age of the perfect man, the phrenological man, the natural man, fashioned in the image of God, commanded to increase and multiply, to subdue and have dominion over the earth. The superiority of the phrenological man is that of the perfect blending of man's threefold nature, "a corporeal nature, an intellectual nature, and a religious or moral nature."

In the four past eras the leaders of mankind have been "one-idead," surely as much of a handicap as being one-armed, or one-legged. In the era to come, nothing less than the possession of "all the faculties of a Man in their highest perfection," faculties of body, mind, and heart, will be taken as a type. This era might, he thought, be near; "it may be for this generation to decide: it may be for *you*. . . . Some of us may yet live to see the day when . . . the very *possession* of a faculty will be held to involve an obligation to *employ* and *strengthen* it. . . . We may hear it acknowledged before we die, that MAN is a creature worth studying even in our colleges and universities."

Thus, Neal made phrenology more than an empirical psychology to be used for purposes of analysis; he made of it a normative science setting forth an ideal towards the achievement of which mankind was to bend its fullest efforts.

MAN

MAN, the great aboriginal Man, was fashioned, we are told, in the image of his Maker. Being so fashioned, he was permitted to increase and multiply. Being so fashioned, he was commanded to replenish the earth, *and subdue it—and have dominion over it!*

But under this command, who are they, that, from the first, have presumed to increase and multiply?—to replenish the earth—*and subdue it—and have dominion over it?* In what have they resembled their great original archetype? In what are they the undegenerate issue of that majestic and astonishing creature, the aboriginal Man, as he leaped forth from the dust at the command of his Father, and stood, face to face with Jehovah, 'haughty and high and beautiful,' and *worthy* to have dominion over the earth, and to perpetuate his image forever?

For nearly three thousand years, it was the *Brute man* that bore sway, with his blood-thirsty and tyrannous strength, over the goodliest part of our broad heritage. It was the giant and the hero that lorded it over the degenerate children of God—the base multitude bowing down before them in terror and consternation, if a shadow but crossed their path:

And then, after awhile, and over a large portion of the earth, it was the *Intellectual man,* the orator, the poet, the magician, the lawgiver, and the statesman, that bore sway—carrying no outward symbol of power, not even a 'barren sceptre'—wearing no 'purple robe nor diadem of gold'—but working the subjugation of the whole world afar off, by the help of the brute man, and with a stillness like that which holds the planets to their courses.

And then, after another thousand years, behold the *Spiritual man!* the cowled and sceptred sovereign, the hermit and the monk, the warrior-prophet, the reformer, the martyr, the anchorite, and the palmer—the Priesthood of Superstition—oversweeping the whole earth, and laying waste her treasuries and her sanctuaries; tumbling her thrones into the dust, and tearing up all the foundations of established power.

Age after age, the *Spiritual* man sat in darkness, administering the law in darkness. But to him there were no thousand years appointed. The decree went forth—the power of the Spiritual man passed away— the very throne whereon he sat, vanished in earthquake and in thunder, and when the darkness cleared away, lo! the *Artificial man!* the man of neglected or perverted faculties, the man of the *present generation,* standing face to face with the *Ancient of Days,* and claiming relationship with God's own image—*the Natural man!* And this, while the storm is yet raging afar off—the battle undecided—that the Darkness roaring for its prey: This!

> '———— while the midnight air
> With bright commotion burns—
> Thronging, with giant shape,
> Banner and spear by turns.'

But who is the *Natural* man? And what is he that we should glory in our relationship to him? Is he the naked or painted barbarian, with crushed and stinted affections, and long-smothered appetites?—every yearning and every prompting of his godlike and original nature trampled under foot, or dishonored by a dreary and brutal selfishness? —every fierce passion imprisoned and concentrated, and burning with inextinguishable energy—his proudest faculties unexercised, and there-fore unstrengthened, and therefore unfelt—his mind a desert, where no green thing flourisheth, and the very waters are the waters of bitter-ness—lifeless and motionless—and stagnant with the foul atmosphere that broods there—his heart a sepulchre, where all that distinguisheth or ennobleth man lies buried in the smouldering ashes of human passion —and the glorious instincts of his original nature, the divine image of his Creator, lie festering with rottenness and corruption!

Is *he* the Natural man? Was it to such as *he,* that God gave dominion over the earth? bidding him increase and multiply—and *replenish* the earth, and *subdue* it?

Was it to the Arab or the Scythian?—or to the learned idolaters of Egypt?—to the builders of Babylon the great?—to the Medes and the Persians?—to the faithless Hebrew?—to the warrior Greek, or the turbulent and imperious Roman? Were these, or any of these, the com-missioned of God, while overshadowing the nations and wasting their heritage?—Were they *subduing the earth,* or only subduing the proud-est hopes of man, treading whole empires under foot, and quelling, to their utmost, every grand, every lofty and every glorious instinct of Man's nature, every exulting aspiration, and every luminous hope? And how did they fulfil that other and greater command—to *replenish* the earth?—By replenishing the graveyards and the charnel-houses, by firing cities, and overpeopling the desert and the solitude with frantic women and famished children!—by covering earth and sea with the wreck of nations!—Were these *Natural* men? Were they but faithful copies of the great original archetype?

But if these were not, who were? Were they the short-sighted, miserable drudges that followed after them—their flatterers and their slaves—reciting their histories in public—chanting their praises with poetry and song—building temples to them, and ministering, age after age, in their utter self-abasement, to all their brutish appetites, and all their dangerous and detestable passions, without remorse or shame —lavishing the frankincense of poetry, the splendors of painting and of sculpture, the wonders of architecture, and all the burning and tempestuous glory of eloquence, upon the destroyers of their race!— And for what?

Let the history of the World answer. For centuries the Intellectual bore sway. Their wisdom controlled the councils of the mighty—kings bowed to the earth before them—the living and the dead were alike dependent upon them for that which men most value—enduring reputation. And yet, with all this power—unquestioned and unquestionable power—what did these intellectual men for their wretched brethren, the rest of mankind? What did they, I should say, in comparison with what they might have done, had they rightly understood their own accountableness, or the dignity and worth of Man?

But no! As the earlier barbarians, with their trumpets' 'dread hour-rah' sounding forever and ever among the frozen solitudes and glittering deserts, like the natural voice of the wind or the sea, looked only at the animal nature of Man—reverencing only his outward shape, or his strength and swiftness, or his capability of enduring hunger and thirst, and watchfulness and bodily suffering—so these, the later and more polished barbarians of our race, could see nothing in that god-like creature, Man, worthy of man's homage, beyond the power of learning by rote, of saying over, for the ten thousandth time, what had been said ten thousand times before, without being heeded or cared for—of thinking as others had thought, of reasoning as others had reasoned—nothing, in short, but the combined advantages of a chart, a tread-mill and 'calculating-machine.'

To such, Man was a pure abstraction. He was *all mind,* without body or soul, heart or human affections. What wonder, therefore, that they failed to subdue the earth to any good purpose; and how lucky for us that they never seriously undertook to replenish it! Had their dominion spread, as it threatened to spread at the revival of letters— had it been established, with what sort of men would the earth now be peopled? A race of pure abstractions, dwarfs and pigmies, the skeletons and shadows of men. With their *all-minds,* what would have become of all the great business of life? Our very market-places and thorough-fares would have been thronged with starved poets and orators, mathematicians and metaphysicians, alike helpless and hopeless, and altogether dependent upon the *no-minded,* or the brute man, for the wherewithal to cover their nakedness or to satisfy their hunger.

Was it to such as these, that God gave, or intended to give, dominion over the earth?—to such as these! the starved and miserable shadows of what they should be, that God said, Go forth! increase and multiply! and replenish the earth, and *subdue* it?

Was it to the learned, the scholar, the monk, or the churchman—to the *Spiritual* man, whether he bear sway as a sovereign pontiff, before whose projecting shadow victorious banners are bowed, and armies halted in battle array:—whether he go about as a reformer, waging a war of extermination against whatever he may happen to regard as heresy or superstition:—or, combining the two characters of warrior and prophet, pushes forward to the consummation of his gigantic hope, without rest or pause, thrusting people after people aside from his triumphant path, and scattering the nations like a whirlwind—or cowering and creeping his life away, amid the dark and solitary breeding places of spiritual men, forgetting his chief duties, and suffering his heart's best blood, with all its original affections to stagnate, until his very nature grows loathsome to itself—the great globe a penal orb for trial and punishment and suffering—the 'brave o'erhanging firmament a congregation of pestilent vapors'—and Man, the image of God, a monster and a beast; and he is ready to lie down forever in his uncomfortable and abject selfishness, and wish he had been created a drivelling idiot, or numbered with the beasts that perish:

Was it to such as these, or any of these, that God meant to give dominion over the earth; or the power to increase and multiply? Or shall we stand up and acknowledge the truth, saying with a loud voice, that if all such were smitten with perpetual barrenness, as most are—that if the 'organs of increase' were dried up within them, and sweet Nature made unfaithful to her holy trust, until

'——upon their heads they wore a fruitless crown,
And held a barren sceptre in their gripe'—

or at least *until* some one of their number appeared, breathing the 'still, sad music of humanity,' anxious to 'minister to a mind diseased'—ever watchful and ever ready to 'pluck from the breast a rooted sorrow;' and,

> '————with sweet oblivious antidote,
> To cleanse the foul bosom of the perilous stuff
> That *weighs upon the heart*'—

making of Man, proud, generous Man! a troublesome and profitless abstraction—a vain-glorious, unproductive, and idle spirituality—a discontented, moping, cheerless, and worthless generality—in short, a shadowless, unsubstantial image of the *Natural Man*.

But if not to these, to whom then? If dominion and power and might and majesty, on earth, were not vouchsafed to the *Intellectual man*, nor to the *Spiritual man*, was it to the *Artificial man*? to the man of abused and perverted instincts? or of neglected and dishonored faculties? Was the great world to be subdued and replenished—*subjugated* and *peopled*, that is—by the wretched offspring of the world? by chatterers and idlers; emasculated gossips, and creatures 'half made up,'

> 'So withered, and so *strange* in their attire,
> They look not like the inhabitants of the earth,
> And yet are on't?'

Forbid it Heaven! forbid it Manhood! forbid it Womanhood! Let not such have dominion over the blessed earth! Let *them* never presume to *replenish* the earth, much less to *subdue* it! What knows the Artificial man? what can he ever hope to know, fashioned as he is, *diluted* as he is, of the strong and gentle and obedient yearnings of unadulterate manhood? of the deep and affectionate mysteries that abide in the human heart, so long as it continues unsullied and healthy —no matter how passionless it may appear, no matter how cold and serene—for, say what you will,

> 'The deepest ice that ever froze,
> Can only o'er the surface close,
> The living stream runs quick below,
> And flows, and ne'er can cease to flow.'

What can the *Artificial* man ever hope to understand of such mysteries? of hushed passions and trembling hopes, like half-opened flowers,

'*Violets dim*,
And sweeter than the lids of Juno's eyes,
Or Cytherea's breath?'

But if to none of these, to whom then? If the *Brute* man be still un-worthy, occupying though he does the goodliest portion of the whole earth; if the *Intellectual* man be unfitted, as he claims to be, and most undoubtedly is, 'the self-torturing sophist!' if the *Spiritual* man, the 'apostle of affliction,' he who draws from 'woe o'erwhelming elo-quence,' be, for that very reason, utterly disqualified; and if the *Artifi-cial* man be powerless, to whom *shall* the dominion of the earth be granted? Who shall be clôthed with power to subdue and replenish it?

I answer,—the original or natural man: in other words, the perfect man: or, in still other and better words, the *Phrenological Man!* And why? Simply because the perfect and the phrenological Man are one; they are both Man in his three-fold nature: Man with body, mind, and heart—Man with a corporeal nature, an intellectual nature, and a reli-gious or moral nature. And this! the lordly and august creature of our hope, was the *Original Man!*

Are we to persuade ourselves that he, the Original Man, was of in-ferior mind, or heart, or bodily shape? And, if not, how fearfully have we degenerated! We, the inhabitants of the earth, how lamentably!— when looking abroad over all nations and kindreds and tongues, not a Man is to be found—not so much as one single Man—alike wonder-ful for bodily shape, and mental strength, and moral beauty!

To state the argument another way. From the first, Man's three-fold nature appears to have been lost sight of; to have been always and every where overlooked, or misunderstood. Where most attention has been bestowed upon the body, there the mind, or the heart, or both, have been most cruelly neglected, or most wretchedly betrayed. Where the mind has been cherished most faithfully and reverentially, with scholarship, and learning, and wisdom, and knowledge, or with all the blandishments of life, there the body has been looked upon as utterly worthless, and the human heart, that sea-deep treasury of wealth and power, of glorious hope and obedient faith, of lowly and devout affec-tion, as a treacherous and detestable thing. And where, in the progress of change, that human heart has come to be understood, or interrogated with solemnity or earnestness; why, even there, it has been from the first, and still is, to the comparative neglect of the body, or of the mind, or both. As if it were enough to satisfy the cravings of an immortal Teacher, to find only a third part of heaven—that heaven of the human heart, drawn after him, and obedient to his will! As if, when God created man, he never intended that more than one third part of his whole nature should be in fashion at a time!

As it has been from the beginning, so is it now. Our men of learning, our men of mind, are bodiless, and too often heartless. Afflicted all their lives long with feeble constitutions and wretched health, what are they good for, but to read books, or make them? They have little or no fellowship with the *present;* all their sympathies are with the *past,* all their hopes with a remote *future.* Our men of shape and stature, our men of great bodily strength, are they not *mindless,* to a proverb? And as for men of cultivated affections, men of heart, good-natured men—the gentle and the yielding—how few of them all have either body or mind to boast of! Would you know if they are fitted for a world like this? Go to the poor debtor's apartment, or to the alms-house, and ask to be left alone for a few minutes with the most amiable men to be found there. Hear their story—look at their pale faces, and affectionate eyes, and patient mouths—and judge for yourself. They are the men whose hearts only have been dealt with.

And now if we would know what Man should be, and what he is by nature, let us look at him for a few moments in another light; after which it may be profitable for us to compare ourselves with him, in the silence of our own hearts.

And first, of the physical man—of his bodily strength, and capability of endurance: in other words, of his animal nature.

As a mere animal, notwithstanding all that has been said in his disparagement, notwithstanding his utter helplessness for a long time after birth; and notwithstanding the greater perfection of sense, or the greater bulk, or the greater strength, to be found in others, still Man is, by nature, the most perfect animal upon the face of the earth; more than a match for any in his natural, unassisted strength and swiftness, and uniting in himself greater powers, and a greater variety of powers for self-preservation or annoyance, and a more astonishing combination of bodily endowments than any other animal. He bears up under a pressure that would crush the elephant, were the elephant loaded in like proportion to his bulk; that is, he can preserve himself erect under the pressure of two thousand pounds, properly distributed, which would give to the horse fourteen thousand pounds, were he loaded in proportion to his bulk, and to the elephant ninety-eight thousand pounds, or nearly fifty tons! So astonishing in fact is man's bodily strength, that, in some cases, as in that of Topham, a man of moderate size, it equals that of seven or eight ordinary men. He lifts with his hands a round, smooth stone, weighing eight hundred pounds; he lies down flat upon the earth, and suffers large masses of stone to be laid upon his abdomen, and broken to pieces with a sledge-hammer, or arches his broad chest and allows a blacksmith's anvil to be placed upon it, and iron to be forged there, without flinching; he bears up a cannon weighing between two and three thousand pounds, pulls against two horses, and breaks large ropes, with a single effort, in stretching himself, by the mere strength of his loins; in fact, so far as the legs and thighs are concerned, and the double arch of the pelvis, a man of ordinary strength is capable of bearing up under a weight of between four and five thousand pounds, which would give to the elephant more than one hundred tons; yet four thousand pounds, or two tons, are a load for the largest elephant.

Nor should we stop here. His wind and swiftness are equal to his strength. He tires out the fleetest horses of the desert, keeping up with them all day long, and beating them at full speed; he runs down the ostrich and the antelope; he endures extremes of heat and cold, and changes of temperature, not only without injury, but without suffering, which would be fatal to any other animal; even the walrus and the polar bear have been found no match for him in their capability of enduring cold, though he was a stranger, and they *at home,* in the frozen regions of the north. Man is found where mercury freezes in the bulb of the thermometer, maintaining his vital heat, and upholding his god-like supremacy by nothing but exercise. You find him flourishing where that same thermometer shows a heat of from one hundred and twenty-five, to one hundred and forty degrees Fahrenheit, in the sun, and going about bareheaded in the perpetual furnace of that region; and you see him exposed to a heat which boils water and roasts flesh, and still maintaining the equable temperature of his blood, and the steady beating of his pulse; dependent wholly upon perspiration for relief.

Upon the earth you find him capable of enduring the steady pressure of the atmosphere, which is equal to thirty-two thousand four hundred and forty pounds—diving into the sea to a depth where he has to support the pressure of many atmospheres, or ascending mountains, or sailing about the sky in balloons, where that pressure is diminished to such a degree, that the blood oozes from every pore of his body—and yet he lives on! The immortal spirit of the machine upholds it forever, and it cannot be crushed nor extinguished. Add to all this, Man is, by nature, *omnivorous*. All food and all climates are alike to him, so far at least as this, that he thrives upon all sorts of food, whether animal or vegetable, cooked or raw, and flourishes in all sorts of climates, from the torrid to the frozen zone.

Such is the *Natural Man;* and unless we are ready to believe that the first Man was inferior to his degenerate offspring in bodily power, in swiftness and strength, and the capability of enduring toil and hunger and thirst, and of establishing his dominion over the beasts of the field and the fowls of the air, such must have been the great original archetype of that superb animal, Man.

As with the body, so with the mind of the first Man; and so with his heart; as with his animal nature, so with his intellectual and moral nature. As a model, he stood the impersonation of Man's threefold nature. Instead of being at best but one third of a Man, as the wisest and best of men are now, he was a complete and perfect Man—every inch a Man.

Though he might understand little or nothing of geology, or mineral, or chemistry, or navigation; of steam power, or balloon sailing, or animal magnetism; and might know as little of hydraulics, as the Romans did when they built their aqueducts; still, if we would not dishonor his Maker, in whose image he was made, we must believe that he was at least the perfection of human nature, and therefore capable of whatever Man has ever shown himself to be capable of since. Though he carried no burthens, and, peradventure, underwent no trials of strength or swiftness; although he might know nothing of metaphysics or theology, and as little of the difference between the head and the heart of man, or between morality and religion; although he may never have indulged in audible poetry, or song, or eloquence; and may have been ignorant alike of the terrors and the splendors, the glory and the gloom of the imagination,—still, as a perfect Man, as a creature fashioned in the likeness of his Creator, he must have been of a lordly stature and a glorious bearing, shapely and magnificent; with a mind capable of the mightiest things, and a heart overflowing with devout and exalted affections—with unwearied prayer and thankfulness and worship. To deny this, would be to deny that the Original Man was the type and model of the species; yet more, it would be denying either the goodness, or the wisdom and the power of God.

Without being an orator, a poet, a lawgiver, a statesman, or a mathematician, the Original Man, having all the faculties of a Man in their highest perfection, must have been capable of being all these; of being indeed whatever any other Man has been since, or may hereafter be. He may not have waged war; he may not have struggled for dominion; he may not have hymned forth his tumultuous thanksgivings, with the 'pomp and prodigality of phrase' that we, as men of a later growth, are so familiar with; but his heart swelled with a generous, undoubting faith, and his head was bravely uplifted, and his arms outstretched— of all that we may be sure,—when 'earth, sky and ocean' burst upon him, whithersoever he turned his unabashed, untrembling look; seeing above and below, and on every side of him, the unquestioned, the unquestionable evidence of a Father's love and a Father's anxious watchfulness; the same lavish expenditure of wisdom and power and contrivance, alike in the most perishable and the most enduring of his labors; in the more delicate and unperceived, as in the grander and mightier and more awful manifestations of his nature; the glory of the firmament itself, set thick with blazing constellations, or burning with the unutterable splendors of sunset, being altogether of a piece with the glories of the insect and the flower, the plumage of birds, the delicate armor of fishes, the gorgeous tinting of shells, the flashing of gems, whether of earth or sea, and the vast machinery of the empyrean, with all—

'its adamantine spheres
Wheeling unshaken through the void immense,'

and no whit more wonderful than the exquisite adaptation of means to ends in the structure of the smallest mite that breathes, nor better contrived for the promotion of earthly happiness.

To a mind so constituted, there would be no littleness nor unworthiness in these manifestations. To such a mind, the sarcasm upon Man's nature which Man has long received for truth, implied in the saying, that 'he who can carve heads upon cherry-stones,' cannot, for that very reason, be expected to 'cut a colossus from a rock,' would be a miserable flourish of words, without meaning. To such a mind, there would be nothing little, which tended to the promotion of happiness; nothing beneath the mightiest, provided it were an employment of our faculties. It is so with GOD—why should it not be so with MAN?

To such a mind, the great original mind of Man, as it sprang forth, like a sun, from the boundless and fathomless ocean of Man's being, there would be neither mystery nor littleness in the devotion of an immortal creature's whole life to the study of flowers, or insects, or shells, or earths; nor would such a mind feel a thousandth part of the amazement that we do, to find an exalted nature busying itself, year after year, with the habits of a grub or a butterfly—the stars or the seas—provided there were no sacrifice of higher duties; the highest of which is the diligent cultivation of every faculty, whether bodily, mental, or moral, wherewith we are endowed by our Creator.

To such a mind, the gymnasia of Greece, where the body was worshipped and ministered unto—the schools of Greece, where the mind alone was dealt with, as of itself constituting the Man—the religious associations and monastic establishments of the middle ages—and the schools of modern Europe, her colleges, her universities, and her sanctuaries, where the mind alone is thought worthy of being nourished or exercised, are all alike but signs and vestiges of the rudest barbarism—badges of servitude, of pitiable blindness, of most melancholy and alarming infatuation.

To such a mind, the simple fact, that not more than two thirds of the machinery wherewith Man is endowed for bodily purposes—not more than two thirds of his muscles—are ever exercised by the great mass of mankind, the unreasoning multitude—while the 'enlightened few' are satisfied with the exercise of two or three, at most, of their distinguishing mental or moral faculties, to the utter destruction of all the rest, and the entire neglect of the *body*, and the generous *duties* of the body!—to such a mind, so constituted, proud of its integrity or *wholeness*, and glorying in its relationship to God, such lamentable errors and perversions, would be altogether as pitiable, as if the men and women of our earth were to agree in using but one half, or one third part of their bodily powers or natural senses at a time—stopping their ears in one part of the world, and bandaging their eyes in another—at one time refusing to walk, as unworthy of their exalted lineage—at another, to use their hands or arms, or never more than one at a time, lest they should be overlooked in the world's warp and woof—and all trying to persuade themselves and others, and living and dying in the belief, that it is never worth any human creature's while, to think of using eyes and ears, hands and feet, or any other of their neglected surplus faculties at one and the same time.

Yet such is the doctrine of the world with regard not only to the body of Man, but to all his diviner faculties. There are whole nations that hear not, whole nations that see not; and the mightiest of the sons of men have been, from the first, either blind, or halt, or lame, or deaf—satisfied to go through this world with one leg, or one arm apiece; thereby dishonoring alike themselves and their Creator, and laboring to no purpose but the degradation or extinction of his image; filling the whole earth, not with men and women, but with the fragments of both, helpless, worthless, and degenerate—with the lame, and the blind, and the halt—bodies without souls, and souls without bodies.

Have not these frightful superstitions prevailed long enough? Are we never to see a system of education established, whereby Man shall be recognized as a creature of more than half a dozen faculties worth cherishing?—as endowed with a three-fold nature, each seeking its own appropriate stimulus? Are the one-armed, or the one-eyed, to subdue the earth, and replenish it, and have dominion over it? And why not, as rightfully as the *one-idead*—the Brute Man, the Spiritual Man, the Intellectual Man, or the Artificial Man, if these, like the one-eyed, or the one-armed, are, as they certainly are, but Men of abused, or neglected, or perverted, or extinguished faculties? Or shall we insist upon having the whole or perfect Man—the original or phrenological Man—for a type hereafter? It may be for this generation to decide: it may be for *you*. And the day may not be far off, when the mathematics shall cease to be a standard of perfection for man's immortal nature at one college, Aristotle at another, and the dead languages at another. Courage! and some of us may yet live to see the day when the bed of Procrustes will be no longer in fashion; and the stretching and lopping of God's image be abandoned throughout the world: when the very *possession* of a faculty will be held to involve a correspondent obligation to *employ* and *strengthen* it; as a gift of our Heavenly Father; as a talent, for the use of which Man must be answerable.

'Once more into the breach, dear friends!—*Once more!*'

And we may hear it acknowledged before we die, that MAN is a creature worth studying even in our colleges and universities; and that, peradventure, he may have something in him which delighteth not in geometry or logic; neither in polemics nor in ethics; neither in Cicero nor Demosthenes, and yet be capable of immortalizing itself, of contributing largely to the happiness of mankind, and of propagating a diviner image of Man's original nature than is now to be found upon the face of the earth. And, therefore,

'Once more into the breach, dear friends!—*Once more!*'

14

JOB DURFEE

1790, born September 20, Tiverton, R.I.

1813, graduated from Brown University

1813, Fourth of July address, later published

1813–14, studied law under his father, who was chief justice of Rhode Island
Court of Common Pleas

1814, *The Vision of Petrarch*; a poem

1814–20, Republican representative to Rhode Island legislature

1820–24, member of Congress from Rhode Island

1826–29, Rhode Island legislature; part of time Speaker

1832, *Whatcheer*; a long poem about Roger Williams

1833–35, associate justice of Rhode Island Supreme Court

1835–47, chief justice of Rhode Island Supreme Court

1838, two lectures on aboriginal history

1839, *Idea of the Supernatural among the Indians*

1843, *Influence of Scientific Discovery and Invention on Social and Political
Progress*

1846, *Pan-Idea*

1847, *Discourse on the Rhode Island Idea of Government*

1847, died July 26

CONSERVATIVE thinkers of the nineteenth century developed many variations of the antidemocratic argument. The subject matter of many fields
of knowledge was explored to find ways and means of combating popular
sovereignty. In many respects the most interesting of these developments
is the use of the weapons of the Enlightenment to reach conclusions opposed
to the general trends of the Enlightenment. This type of thinking began
early; John Adams, for example, found inequality rooted in nature where
Thomas Jefferson had found equality. Where Madison had found the
independent individual in nature, Calhoun found civil society. In general,
the content of nature was a variable.

Joel Barlow, in the pattern of the left-wing of the Enlightenment, found
in the progress of science an earnest of the perfectibility of mankind, and
hence an argument for free democratic institutions, not in one country only,
but in every part of the world. Job Durfee, chief justice of Rhode Island,
earlier in his career an elected Republican representative to the State legisla-

ture, author of *Whatcheer,* an epic poem glorifying Roger Williams, found in the advancement of science an eternal law of progress, which came from God, and which invalidated the claims of perfectibilists.

Durfee examined history and found that social and political progress followed scientific discovery and invention by necessary law. The efforts of reformers are inconsequential; if the reformers happen to live when scientific progress has made the steps necessary to social or political progress the efforts of the reformers will appear to be successful; if the times are not right, the efforts of the reformers will appear to be unsuccessful. Actually the scientific progress is the determining factor.

The great truth that human progress is the result of an ever-active law, manifesting itself chiefly in scientific discovery and invention, and thereby controlling legislation, and giving enduring improvement to all social and political institutions . . . is a law as palpable in the history of the social mind, as the law of gravitation in the movement of matter.

This deterministic philosophy of history is used by Durfee in two ways. The first and less important of these is to assert that men of science are the actual powers in a society, regardless of who its nominal rulers may be. "Where there is progress, the highest order of intellect must lead." The second and more important use to which it is put is to demolish the idea "that there is an absolute, undefinable popular sovereignty, which can, in a manner its own, and at any moment, carry a certain supposed natural equality into social and political life, and thereby elevate poor human nature, however rude and degraded its condition, at once, as by a sort of magic, into a state of supreme and absolute perfection." Legislation is not the means toward the achievement of human progress. Historical necessity can make nonsense out of the program of any legislative group. This point Durfee illustrates by referring to the then recent invention of the steam engine. "There can be," said he, "little danger in predicting too much for the progress of this invention," and yet, at the time, his predictions must have sounded far-fetched and extravagant to many of his auditors. He asserted that steam is a power stronger than democracy, to which our democracy must adapt itself, "to radiate our country with communications for its defence," for the Atlantic in the age of steam "has become a narrow frith over which armies may be ferried in twelve to fifteen days." The will of the people to resist this change, to resist centralization of authority in the Federal Government is irrelevant; "no matter what government first applies this invention to all its practical naval and military uses, other governments must follow, however reluctantly, or cease to exist." The states rights program of the Southern leaders is disposed of in a single parenthetic expression; the armies ferried across the Atlantic may "land in slave or non-slaveholding States, at option." Durfee's analysis is of particular interest and should receive consideration today in the light of the changes in international relations which are compelled by the atomic bomb.

Durfee considered this address as a special application of the theme of his *Pan-Idea*, which was published three years later, in 1846. The *Pan-Idea* introduced the concept of a universal mind, which in the *Influence of Scientific Discovery and Invention on Social and Political Progress* is seen to operate in history as the universal law of progress. The doctrine shows signs of having developed partly under the influence of the German transcendentalists, whom Durfee, according to his son, knew through the works of Coleridge and Cousin. These writers, with Emanuel Swedenborg, deeply colored Durfee's thinking and helped him to develop his individual interpretation of the facts of history and the history of science.

THE INFLUENCE OF SCIENTIFIC DISCOVERY AND INVENTION ON SOCIAL AND POLITICAL PROGRESS

THE influence of discovery in science, and of invention in art, on social and political progress, may certainly form an appropriate theme for an occasion like the present; and if, during the short time which has been left to us by the preceding exercises of the day, I should endeavor to draw your attention to this subject, rest assured that the attempt will not be prompted by a confidence in any peculiar qualification of mine for the task, but from a desire, in some manner, to fulfil a duty which, perhaps with too little caution, I undertook to perform.

We are disposed, I think, to ascribe too much of human progress to particular forms of government—to particular political institutions, arbitrarily established by the will of the ruler, or wills of the masses, in accordance with some theoretic abstraction. And this is natural enough in a country where popular opinion makes the law. But, to the mind that has formed the habit of penetrating beyond effects into the region of causes, it may, I think, appear that the will of the one, or the wills of the many, equally are under the dominion of a higher law than any that they may ordain; and that political and social institutions are, in the end, drawn or constrained to all their *substantial* improvements, by an order of mind still in advance of that which rules in politics, and flatters itself that dominion is all its own.

If it be true that knowledge is power, then it would seem to follow that any change in the arts or sciences, favorable or unfavorable, must be followed by corresponding changes in society. And such, in fact, we find to be the result. When the arts and sciences become stationary, all social and political institutions become stationary; when the arts and sciences become progressive, all social and political institutions become progressive. The universality of this fact clearly demonstrates the necessary connection of cause and effect between scientific and social progress. And if the form in which this statement is made be correct, it does as clearly show which is the cause, and which the effect, and that we are not to seek for the causative energy of human progress in the wisdom of the political, but in that of the scientific and inventive mind. Let it moreover be recollected, that, at least in these our times, the scientific and inventive genius has a universality which elevates it above all human jurisdictions; that it belongs to the whole humanity; can be monopolized by no government; and that its discoveries and inventions walk the earth with the freedom of God's own messengers.

This is an important position, which I shall presently endeavor further to confirm by some brief references to history.

But though we may find the cause of human progress in the scientific and inventive genius of the race, still we may question the extent of its power over those institutions that are created and sustained by the social or political will. I shall ascribe to it, on the present occasion, none but the power of ordaining for those institutions their only true law of progress. It prescribes to them no particular form of government; but requires that every government, whether in theory despotic or liberal, should be so administered as to enable the human mind to put forth, in a manner consistent with order, all its powers for the benefit of humanity. It forces upon government, whatever be its form, the necessity of extending practical freedom to all. It requires it, upon the penalty of ceasing to exist, to carry out to the utmost extent, both in the social and political spheres, every important discovery or invention, and thus coerces, by a process its own, obedience to its supreme authority.

But what is this progress? It may be a short, but it is a sufficient answer for the occasion, to say, that it is the elevation of mind over matter; in the material universe it is the extension of the dominion of man over the powers and forces of nature; in humanity it is the orderly elevation of the high moral and intellectual energies over the brute force of passion, prejudice, and ignorance.

In the realm of science and art, the most exalted geniuses and the brightest intellects that it contains are ever at the head of affairs. They are there, not by the appointment of government, nor by the election of the masses, but by a decree of the supreme Intelligence. And, if it be true, as I hope to demonstrate, that their discoveries and inventions rule in the grand course of events, it will afford some consolation to reflect, that, whether government falls into the hands of demagogue or despot (and it suffers equally from either), this high order of intellect doth, after all, by setting limits to their follies, guide and govern in the main. To it we bow with deferential awe—to it we willingly own allegiance, and are proud to confess ourselves its subjects.

Time, indeed, was, when this order of mind formed a union with government, and was itself despotic, or was ruled by despotism. Such seems to have been its condition in ancient Egypt—such may be its condition still, under those oriental governments, where every change must operate a social disorganization; but such, from the earliest date of Grecian freedom, has never been its condition in the sphere of western civilization. It has been subject to restraint, it has suffered persecution, but it has formed no necessary part of any local government. It has been under no necessity of limiting its discoveries, or shaping its inventions to suit particular political or social organizations. At that early date it cut its connection with these, and, by so doing, found the Archimedean standpoint and lever, by which it is enabled to move the world.

But where and what is this point on which the scientific intellect takes this commanding stand? It is not to be found in that space which can be measured by a glance of the eye, or a movement of the hand. It is to be found only in the world of mind; and even there, only in that perfect reason which is at once a law to humanity and the revealer of all truth. It is a point which lies even beyond the extravagant wish of Archimedes. Perhaps he had unwittingly found it, when engaged in the solution of that mathematical problem which cost him his life;

when, whilst the streets of Syracuse were thronged with bands of military plunderers, and the Roman soldier, amid shouts of triumph, entering his study, placed the sword at his throat, he exclaimed, "Hold, friend, one moment, and my demonstration will be finished." Far elevated above local interests, far above the petty strife and confusion of the day, it is a point from whose Olympian height all humanity is seen dwindled to a unit. It is in this elevation, above the world and its turmoils, that the scientific philosopher interrogates the deity of truth, and communicates its oracles to the whole nether humanity; confident, that as they are true, whatever may be their present effect, they will ultimately promote the progress of the race.

Nor is he at liberty to abstain from interrogating this deity; to refrain from the efforts to discover, and consequently to invent, whenever a discovery is to be actualized by invention. That law which prompts the mind spontaneously to search for the cause of every effect, and for the most effectual means for the accomplishment of the end, is not superinduced by education. It comes from a source above man; it is constitutional, therefore irresistible; and he makes his discoveries and inventions because he must make them.

Now the sciences and arts, comprehending not merely the liberal and fine, but the physical and useful, consist of a logical series of discoveries and inventions, commenced at the earliest date of human progress and continued down to the present time, the last grand result being the sum of all the labors that have gone before it; nay, not unfrequently the sum of the blood and sufferings of the ignoble masses, as well as of the labors of the exalted philosophic mind. I mean not to say that this law of reason, which impels man to discover and invent, conducts him from step to step, from truth to truth, in a direct line to the far result; for he has his liberty, and he often deviates, not for a day merely, but for a generation; nay, sometimes for a whole epoch. But, however widely he may err, he at last discovers the error of the first false step that he has made; his false premise is brought to its *reductio ad absurdum;* and, with the benefit of all the experience, discipline, and knowledge that he has acquired by pursuing it to this result, he returns to the point of departure, and, with redoubled energy, follows out the demonstration direct, to its *quod erat demonstrandum.*

Gentlemen, excuse me, whilst on an occasion so purely literary, I draw an illustration of this idea from a thought suggested by an invention in a branch of mechanic art.

I lately visited an establishment, perhaps in some respects the first of the kind in our country, for the manufacture of iron into bars. I stood by, and for the time, witnessed the operation of its enginery. I saw the large misshapen mass of crude metal taken blazing from the furnace, and passed through the illumined air to the appropriate machine. I saw it there undergo the designed transformation. It was made to pass repeatedly between two grooved revolving iron cylinders, of immense weight. At every turn of the wheel it took new form; it lengthened, stretched, approximating still its intended shape, till at the end of the operation it came forth a well-fashioned fifteen or twenty foot bar of iron, ready for the hand of the artizan, or the machine that was to resolve it into forms for ultimate use.

When I had witnessed this process, I thought I did not want to go to the banks of the Nile to be assured either of the antiquity or the progress of the race. An older than the pyramids was before me; one which, though voiceless, told a tale that commenced before the Pharaohs, before the Memnon, before the Thebes. Here was a material which had been common to the historical portion of the human family for the space of five or six thousand years. Millions on millions of minds had been tasked to improve the process of its manufacture. I went back, in imagination, to that primitive age, when the first unskilful hand—some fur-clad barbarian or savage—drew a mass of the raw material from the side of some volcanic mountain. He constructed a vessel of clay for its reception, and, somewhat in imitation of the process he had witnessed, he placed it over a heap of blazing combustibles. With long and patient labor and care, he reduced it to a liquid mass; and then cast it into the shape of some rude implement of husbandry or war. Exulting in his success, he brandished the instrument in triumph, and deemed it the *ne plus ultra* of human improvement.

He disappeared; but he left a successor. I followed him, in imagination, and saw him take the art at the point at which his predecessor had left it. He had discovered that the material was not only fusible, but ductile; and with sweat and toil that knew no fatigue, he gradually beat the heated mass into the shape of something like a hatchet, or a sword. At this point he also disappeared; but his successor came, and still improved on the labors of his predecessor. Generation thus followed generation of apt apprentices in the art; they formed a community of masters skilful to direct, and of servants prompt to obey. They fashioned new implements as their numbers increased, and the wants of advancing civilization varied and multiplied. The masterminds studied, and studied successfully, all the various qualities and susceptibilities of the metal. They became skilful in all its various uses, in agriculture, commerce, manufactures and war. Yes, ye philanthropists! in war! For humanity actually armed herself against humanity to draw out and discipline the faculties of the human mind, and bring the art to perfection. She instituted a school of her own, and was herself its stern and unyielding preceptress. She chastened her laggard and truant children as with a rod of iron. I saw her force her sons into bondage by thousands—aye, by millions. I saw them sweat and toil at the anvil like so many living machines. They were once free barbarians; but they were now in the school of civilization. They were learning something of the arts. They would not labor from the love of labor, but only from constraint and fear. Their willing task-masters grew strong and powerful in the labors of the barbarous masses, that superior knowledge and power had subjected to their will. They took counsel together, and still went forth to conquer and enslave. Ages, centuries, epochs passed away, and still the same process was going on. They built up for themselves a bright and glorious intellectual civilization, that extended far and wide over the earth; yet it was but the gilding of the surface; for it had its deep and dark foundations upon mind in bondage, upon masses in slavery; and their power grew feeble from expansion. The numbers of the free would not suffice to sustain their dominion. And they sought for aid, but could conceive of none, save in the enslaved masses beneath them. And now came, improved by long ages of civilization, the scientific and inventive genius to their aid. She glanced back upon the past; she discovered the point of departure from the progress direct, and the source of the errors whence this appalling result. She sought, and sought not in vain, to substitute the brute forces of nature for the labor of human hands. Then began the water-wheel to turn at the falls, and the trip-hammer to sound upon the anvil, and the manacles of the slave to fall off, as improvement was built upon improvement, in regular consecutive order, till the burning bar shot from the perfected machinery almost unaided by human strength.

This brought me to the process which I had just witnessed, and I thought I saw in it the grand result of the discipline and labor of the race for thousands of years. I thought I saw in it, not only the reality of a progress in the race, but the unquestionable proof of the existence of a law of progress, carrying on its grand process through the whole humanity by a logical series of causes and effects, from its earliest premises, in far distant antiquity, to its latest result; and that the law which rules in discovery and invention, is one and identical with that which governs in the progress of the race.

I speak not here of particular communities or nations—for nations, like men, decay and die—but of the whole humanity, which is as immortal as the spirit of man, or, perhaps, as the divinity that rules it; which feeds and grows in one branch of its existence upon the decaying energies of another, and which is thus ever renovating its vital and intellectual energies out of the past, and, amid unceasing decay, enjoying a perpetual rejuvenescence. On such an existence doth this law of progress ever act; constantly forming and energizing the individual intellect by the unceasingly accumulating wisdom of the past, and by appropriating the forces of nature to the uses of social man, it is, at this day, carrying on in the world of mind that work of creation which the Divine Author of humanity did but commence in the garden of Eden.

There may be limits to man's capacities, but to the energies of nature which those capacities, acting under this law, may put in requisition, there are no limits. Each new discovery in science suggests the existence of something yet undiscovered; each new combination in art, on trial, suggests combinations yet untried; thus revealing, on the one hand, a law of suggestion, which, from the nature of mind, must ever act; and, on the other, objects and subjects of action which are as boundless and as inexhaustible as the universe.

Now if this be, and must continue to be the true process of discovery and invention; and if, in its progress, as I hope to prove, it must constantly reflect itself into all social and political organizations, we have an assurance of progress, not dependent, thank Heaven, upon carrying to their results any political abstractions, or any idea of popular sovereignty drawn from the perversions of revolutionary France; but upon a law of progress, which God has ordained for the government of humanity, and which is as certain and eternal in its operations as any law which governs the material universe.

But let us see, by a brief glance at the page of history, whether this law of progressive discovery and invention, doth, or doth not, rule in social and political progress.

And here let me premise, that the sciences and the arts, considered with reference to social and political progress, may be divided into two classes; first, those which are necessary or useful as aids or instruments of thought and sentiment; as among the sciences, grammar, rhetoric, logic, geometry; and among the arts, music, poetry, painting, sculpture, architecture, and the art of writing, or preserving the memory of the past. Second, those whose immediate object it is to enlarge our knowledge of nature, and improve the physical condition of man. These are the physical sciences, and useful arts improved by science. In the progress of the race, the first class is necessarily brought earliest to perfection. Man must be disciplined to think logically, and to communicate and preserve his thoughts and sentiments, before he can make any considerable progress in the physical sciences and useful arts. Hence it is, that, among the ancient nations of the earth, we find this high order of mind almost exclusively engaged in carrying the first class to perfection, whilst it devoted comparatively little attention to the physical sciences and useful arts. Indeed the useful arts seem to have been abandoned almost entirely to slaves. They were carried on by manual labor. Invention had not yet subjected the forces of nature to the human will, and that vast amount of toil, which is required to support a splendid civilization, was urged on by an immense mass of people in bondage.

I would further observe, that as the scientific and inventive order of mind subsists, generally, independent of any necessary connection with any particular government, so its influence is not to be traced in the history of this or that people or community merely, but rather in that of a common civilization; such as that of classical antiquity, or modern christendom, consisting of a community of nations, in which one government or society acts upon another, and from which, through this very diversity, that order of mind derives its power to coerce. It acts through one government on another, through one society on another, through society on government, and through government on society; its discoveries and inventions everywhere inviting the appropriate change, at first from policy, but if not adopted from policy, compelling its adoption, at last, by force of the principle of self-preservation.

History enables us to show, in but a few instances, the effects which each succeeding discovery or invention produced on society in the infancy of the race; but it does enable us to see their combined results in the form which society took under their dominion.

In Egypt, the sacerdotal order was the depository of all the science and learning of the age; and that order, in fact, seems to have been the governing power. Now what were its sciences, real or pretended? Geometry, astronomy, astrology, and a mystic theology. These were studied as the great sciences of ancient Egypt, and carried out into their respective arts; and, to say nothing about their geometry and astronomy, have not the two last left the distinctive impress of their mysticism upon everything that remains of this ancient civilization? It appears in the labyrinth, the pyramid, the temple, and the hieroglyphics with which they were blazoned; and in the statuary, the sphinx, the veiled Isis, and mute Harpocrates, with which each entrance was sanctified. Society divided itself, spontaneously, into castes. Where there is progress, the highest order of intellect must lead, and the priesthood of Egypt, with the king at their head, necessarily stood first. Next to them the warrior caste, by which all was defended or preserved. Beneath them, the mass consisting chiefly of slaves, or those who were elevated little above the condition of bondmen. These were again divided into castes, corresponding to the laborious arts which they followed, with, probably, each its tutelary deity. The son followed the occupation of his father, and society underwent a sort of petrifaction, from the arts which admitted of no change without destruction. This arrangement could not have resulted from the designs of a cunning priesthood, establishing and ordaining the organization for their particular benefit. It must have grown up with the progress of the sciences and arts. Each art, newly invented or introduced, had its artisans, who transmitted, like the sacerdotal order, their peculiar mystery to their particular posterity. The governing power, since it embodied within itself all science, and took its constitution from it, might, after the arts had reflected themselves into society, have very naturally interfered to protect that social organization, into which, as mysteries, they spontaneously fell.

But let us pass to Greece. No one doubts that Greece owed her civilization to her literature and arts. But to what was she indebted for the successful cultivation of these? It has been ascribed to the freedom of her political institutions. But, again it may be asked, to what were *they* indebted for that freedom? Is it not plain that they were indebted for it to the fact that her literature and arts early took root in the vigorous barbarism of distinct and independent communities, and that as her political institutions settled down into definite and fixed forms, they took their complexion and shape necessarily from the arts and literature cultivated by society? In Lacedæmon, the art of war alone was cultivated, and she was, for long, exclusively a martial State, but was finally obliged to give way to the influences operating around and within her. As to all the rest of Greece, it was under the dominion of the fluctuating wills of the many, or the few, and there was nothing permanent to give regular progression and tendency to political and social institutions, but the arts and sciences cultivated.

Greece commenced her civilization with colonies from Egypt and Phœnicia. They brought with them the arts and sciences, and something of the wealth of the parent countries, and ingrafted all on her active barbarism. And here, again, the immediate influence of the newly introduced sciences and arts, or of any particular discovery or invention, rarely appears in history, and is but dimly shadowed forth in the myths of the golden and heroic ages. But until they were introduced, Greece was peopled by bands of roving savages. Piracy was an honorable profession; the coast could not be safely inhabited; one savage band was continually driven back upon another. Attica was spared for its poverty. The Corinthians made the first great improvement in naval architecture. They invented the war galley of three banks of oars; they constructed a navy of like craft. This was followed by great results; they cleared the Grecian seas of pirates; nations settled on the coast, and by like means kept them clear. The Mediterranean was laid open to honest traffic; commerce flourished; the arts flourished. The Grecian communities took the longest stride in the infancy of their progress from this simple improvement in naval architecture—the long-est with the exception of that made by the Trojan war. That war did for the Greeks what the crusades in modern times did for the nations of Europe—it made them known to each other; disciplined them in a common art of war; made them acquainted with a higher civilization and its arts, and restored them to their country with a common history, and themes for their bards of all time.

Greece, it is believed, presents the first instance of a civilized people in which the exercise of the powers of government and the almost ex-clusive cultivation of the sciences are not to be found in the same hands. The sacerdotal corporation in Greece did not embrace all learning, as in Egypt, and did not, as there, control the state. Science and art, ab-solved from political connection, stood then and there, on the same independent ground, as in our own age and country. Philosophy, it is true, was held in check by superstition; but government did not assume to restrain, control, or direct improvement in art and science. And now, what was the result of this independent and isolated existence of the scientific mind upon the social and political organizations of Greece? It seems to me to have been immense. Whatever of art or science was introduced from Egypt found no corresponding social organization in Greece, and the bondage of caste there never appeared—and for this reason it is that of all the races of men the Grecian is the first to present us with an intellectual people; a people intellectual and progressive by force of its own internal and all-pervasive action. Science was no mys-tery, and each Greek was at liberty to cultivate whatever branch of knowledge or art it to him seemed meet; and therefore it was that the Grecian society necessarily became free to the extent to which this cultivation could be carried, and *there* freedom stopped—*there* slavery commenced. Those who were consigned to the labors of the industrial arts, if it had been permitted, had neither the means nor the power to cultivate the sciences; and they were slaves.

Every free Greek did or might cultivate grammar, logic, rhetoric, music, and geometry. And what was the product of these sciences? The fine arts. They improved language; they improved the power of ex-pressing thought and sentiment; and they produced philosophers, poets, historians, orators, sculptors, painters, and architects. These pro-duced an ever-enduring literature, and specimens in the fine arts destined to become models for all time. The sciences and arts of Greece became the sciences and arts of Rome and the Roman empire, and were diffused to the full extent of Roman conquest.

I will not indulge in any common-place rhetoric about Grecian civilization. You know what it was. The only point to which I would here call your attention is, that the arts and sciences of classical antiquity were not effects of the improved character of the social and political institutions of the epoch; but, on the contrary, that their improved character was the result of the scientific progress of the common mind, which progress went on in obedience to no law, save that which God has ordained for its government.

But it was the liberal sciences and the fine arts that were mainly cultivated in this ancient civilization. Man had not learned to go abroad out of himself into nature to search for facts. He found the elements of the sciences and arts, which he almost exclusively cultivated, within his own mind, or within his immediate social sphere. He was preparing the necessary means, the instruments, by which he was in after times to explore the universe, and extend the sphere of social improvement by the physical sciences and useful arts.

And now what was the consequence of this perhaps necessary restriction of discovery and invention? A superficial civilization, grand and imposing it is true, but still a civilization that went no further than the practically free cultivation of the predominant arts and sciences of the epoch; a civilization that did not penetrate the great mass of human society. The laborious industry by which it was supported, was carried on by an immense mass of unintellectual bondmen, who were to be employed by their masters, lest they should find employment for themselves. The useful arts became mysteries, and the secrets of nature remained secrets still.

Everywhere, throughout this ancient civilization, whether Grecian or Roman, the same horizontal division of society prevailed, and in portions of like ratio. A portion of the social mind, large, it is true, if compared with anything in preceding history, was cultivated; but still a very small portion, if compared with the masses in bondage. In Attica, the proportion of the freemen to the whole enslaved population, was as two to forty; in the Roman empire, at one time, as seven to sixty; and the bondmen subsequently so far increased, that armies sufficient for the defence of the State could not be enlisted from the freemen.

Beneath this bright covering of civilization, what a vast amount of intellectual susceptibility lay slumbering in the night of ignorance and bondage!

The predominant arts and sciences of this epoch were at last brought to their perfection. They ceased to advance, and society became stationary. The mind of Asia and the south of Europe could go no further. It was the hardy vigor of the north, alone, that was competent successfully to use the instruments which this ancient civilization had perfected; to go out of the sphere of social man into nature; to regenerate and multiply the useful arts and sciences, and, by their means, to elevate the masses from the condition of bondage to the freedom of intellectual life. Northern barbarism, therefore, came; and it conquered, for this simple reason, that the arts and sciences of antiquity had not made the civilization of the epoch sufficiently strong to resist it.

Gentlemen, we are not dealing with a history of events, but with the causes which produce them, and especially those changes which add permanently to the improvement of the social and political condition of man. I know you may follow these changes in the history of events, civil, religious, and military; but I am endeavoring to point out their origin in those causes which gave the institutions they produced shape, consistency, and duration; and to demonstrate, that they are not to be found in accident, or in the arbitrary dictates of the human will, but in an eternal law of mind, which especially manifests itself in the arts and sciences. For this reason it is not necessary to cite all history, but merely a number of its facts, sufficient to establish the position.

And now, lest I should exhaust your patience, I pass the gulf of the middle ages with this single observation, that it was a season during which Christianity was engaged in humanizing and softening the heart of barbarism, and thus qualifying its mind to take form under the influence of modern art and science; and landing on the margin of our present civilization, I proceed to discuss the social and political effects of scientific discovery and invention in modern times. And here we have an opportunity of tracing those effects with historical certainty to their causes, and of proving, as I hope, to minds the most skeptical, the truth of our position.

But, before doing this, I must speak of the social condition of the mass of society on which early modern discoveries produced their effects. Time will permit me to state it only in the most general terms; and perhaps, on an occasion like the present, and to such an audience, this is all that is necessary, or even proper.

Guizot, in his admirable history of the civilization of modern Europe, dates the commencement of modern society in the sixteenth century. But modern society came out of a pre-existent state of things, which state of things first manifested itself and became general in the tenth century, when Europe rose out of the bosom of a chaotic barbarism, and took distinct form in the feudal system. This remark, however, applies more particularly to the north and west of Europe. It was whilst this was the predominant system that she commenced and carried on the crusades, and not only made herself acquainted with herself, but with the remnants of civilization in the east and south of Europe. It was not until the thirteenth century that she manifested a decided tendency to her present political and social organization. And it is to a mere glance at her condition at this period, that I would now invite your attention.

In the east was the Greek, the remnant of the ancient Roman empire, still consisting of the same elements which distinguished it at the time of Constantine, a master class and a servant class. Those of the first class, eclipsed though they were, "had not yet lost all their original brightness." They were still imbued with something of the philosophy and literature of ancient Greece; and, in point of numbers, they bore perhaps about the same ratio as the progenitors to the immense mass of slaves beneath them. In Italy, were the Italian republics, exhibiting remnants of the ancient Roman municipal institutions. They cultivated the Latin literature, and were soon to be engaged in renovating the fine arts of classical antiquity, and were already, for the era, extensively employed in commercial enterprise. The ratio of the free to the bond was probably about the same as it had been during the Roman empire. Subject to these exceptions, all Europe fell under the feudal system, and certain corporations, called free cities, which, situated within the fief of some baron, wrested or wrung from him whatever privilege they could, by force or compact. There were no nations—no governments on a large scale. Europe was dotted all over with baronies and these free cities. Each barony, whatever it might be in theory, was a little sovereignty. Each baron, with his retainers, under a load of armor, and armed with sword and lance, and other offensive weapons of the times, occupied his castle in the country. He willingly submitted to no law, save that of superior force. His kingdom was his fief, and his subjects were his vassals, who followed him in war, or tilled his land, or performed for him other laborious service. The free cities were walled; the dwelling of the burgher was not merely in law, but in fact, his castle, protected by tower and parapet; and the burgher himself, when he ventured abroad to thread the narrow lanes and crooked streets of his city, went armed with lance, and often under cover of armor. The Romish church presented the only element which pervaded all these little sovereignties and cities. Except among the clergy and the civilians, there were no scholars; and, to say nothing about their vassals, perhaps not one in a hundred of the noble barons themselves could either read or write. Nay, they were proud of their ignorance of those accomplishments. The author of *Marmion* means to give them their true character, at a much later period, when he represents the Douglas as exclaiming—

> "Thanks to St. Botham! son of mine,
> Save Gawain, ne'er could pen a line;
> I swore it once, I swear it still—
> Let my boy-bishop fret his fill."

It is true, that when the crusades ceased, something of that zeal which had originated and carried them on began to pass into new channels. Those immense masses that had passed out of the north and west of Europe, had made themselves acquainted with the advancing civilization of the Italian republics, and with the remnant of ancient civilization in the Greek empire. They had penetrated into Asia, and had heard and credited all the fables that oriental imagination could invent, of the wealth and splendor of the gorgeous east, who with

> "richest hand
> Showered on her kings barbaric pearl and gold."

And they returned to their respective countries with these fables, and stimulated a thirst for further knowledge; but above all, they excited the love of adventure and discovery, a yearning for the yet unexplored and unknown; breeding a vague but confident faith in a something vast, boundless, mysterious, that was yet in reserve for daring enterprise, or unyielding perseverance—haply a true augury this of the discovery yet to be made on this side the Atlantic—yet, however fertile their imaginations, the most ardent of them had not conceived the possibility of the existence of this continent. Here it lay, secreted in the western skies, beyond an ocean whose westward rolling billow, it was then deemed, broke on no shore toward the setting sun, awaiting, in all the grandeur of waving forest, towering mountain, and majestically winding stream, the further discoveries of science, and the future wants of a progressive civilization.

Now let us for one moment contemplate this condition of affairs throughout Europe—this vast number of scattered petty sovereignties and municipal communities—this general pervasive ignorance—this enormous mass of vassals, serfs, and slaves, which underlaid and gave foundation to all; and then ask ourselves, what process of legislation or compact, originating merely in the human will, could have resolved this jumble of conflicting materials into those organized nations and communities of nations, which now constitute the civilization of all christendom. We can conceive of no process so originating, that could possibly have brought about this grand result. Yet human legislation and compact were the secondary causes by which it was accomplished. But what, humanly speaking, was the primary cause? That is the subject of our inquiry. I find it in a necessary result of that law of scientific progress, which I have already pointed out; I find it in the grand revolution which at this time took place in the science and art of war; in one word, I find it in the invention of gunpowder. Start not with incredulity and aversion at the annunciation; the cause of causes is there. Tell me not of wars domestic and foreign, of treaties, of parliaments, of councils of state and church. They were the mere external symptoms of the action of the all-sufficient internal cause. Yes, the first cannon that projected the ball of stone or iron, announced, in its own voice of thunder, the final doom of the feudal system, the centralization of nations, the ultimate emancipation of the enthralled, and the establishment of a Christian civilization on a basis never more to be perilled by the inroad of barbarian, or the invasion of Turk. The revival of ancient learning might have done much toward again plating over society with the civilization of classical antiquity; but neither that nor mere human legislation could have overthrown the feudal system, centralized nations, penetrated, and finally emancipated the nether mass of bondmen, and forever shut out the inundations of barbarism.

Feudalism gave way either immediately, in anticipation of the results of the discovery, or finally, under the direct operation of its physical force. What availed the Herculean arm, or giant muscular force? What availed the panoply of helmet, and shield, and coat of mail? Nay, what availed tower and trench, parapet and battlement, whether of baronial castle, walled city, or burgher's armed abode? They all crumbled into atoms, or stood scathed and powerless before the blast of this tremendous invention.

Gunpowder, in the material world, is a most terrible leveller; it makes no distinction between the strong man and the weak. But in the world of mind, it is a most determined aristocrat. It establishes "in times that try men's souls," none but the aristocracy of intellect. Nay, in the long run, it goes still further; for, since to command its service it requires national wealth, it perpetuates power in the hands of those only who know how best to use it for the benefit of all.

The barons abandoned their castles for the court of the sovereign suzerain or lord; and that lord became the most powerful whose resources were the most abundant. Immense wealth, such only as a people at least practically free can create, became necessary in order to carry on a war of offence or defence. The suzerain, or king, was thus at once converted into the friend, and became the liberator of bondmen. Vassals and burghers became subjects and citizens; practically free. And their freedom was guarantied to them by no plighted faith of kings; by no lettered scroll of parchment; but by an irreversible law of necessity, enacted by this sovereign invention. What it did for individuals, it did for nations; armies could no longer carry on war in a foreign country without keeping up a communication with their own; and to conquer a new country, was to establish a new base for military operations against others; and thus, from necessity, was established a community of nations, in which the safety of all found a guaranty only in the independence and freedom of each. Hence comes that law of nations which is recognized by all christendom, and that sleepless vigilance which guards and preserves the balance of power.

Gentlemen: After considering these consequences, permit me to ask you whether christendom be indebted for her progress, thus far stated, to human legislation, guided by some abstract theory merely, or to the sovereign law imposed upon her by this all-controlling invention? When one nation had adopted this invention, all were obliged to adopt it, and christendom having thus necessarily received this power into her bosom, shaped her policy by the necessities which it imposed. Indeed, she owed her then, and owes her present condition, not to the foresight of her counsels guided by the speculations of her theorists, but to this law of human progress, which has overruled her follies and sustained her wisdom.

I have been considering an invention which begins its influence in the world of matter and reflects it inward to the world of mind. I now pass to another discovery or invention, that belongs to the same century, but which begins its influence in the world of mind, and reflects it outward to the world of matter. You will at once understand me to refer to the art of printing.

Were human progress a mere result of fortuitous events, and not the necessary operation of a law of mind, proceeding from a designing reason, these two discoveries, made about the same time, might be inscribed in the list of remarkable coincidences. But they belong to no such list. The invention of printing, like every other, may be traced from its first rude essays down through a logical series of discoveries and improvements, urged on by the conspiring action of the whole humanity, to its last grand result, as the necessary consequence of all that has preceded it. It was necessary that a large portion of the human race should be educated to the use of letters; that the art of reading and writing should become widely diffused; the materials for copying cheap, and the demand for copies beyond the capacity of the penman to supply. You may accordingly trace the growth, which produced this invention, from the first symbolic painting of thought on rock or tree, by roving savage, to the mnemonic hieroglyphics inscribed on pyramid and temple; then to characters representing words; then to those representing syllables; till the very elements of the human voice at last take representative form in the alphabet. In this form it branches forth beyond the sacerdotal caste, and, like the banyan tree, repeats itself by striking its far-reaching branches into fresh soil. It passes from the Egyptian into the Phœnician, thence into the stronger intellectual soil of Greece; it multiplies itself throughout the Roman empire, at every repetition making still further demand upon the labors of the hand; it survives the middle ages, that its far-extending root and branch might draw increased vigor from the northern mind, and that nether mass of humanity, which is at length thrown open to more genial influences; and then it is, that this stupendous growth of all time puts forth, as its last fruit, this wonder-working art of printing. Readers had multiplied with the revival of ancient learning, with the progress of emancipation, with the love of the marvellous in romance, and the mysterious in religion, and demands for copies of great works, and especially for such as were sacred, or were so esteemed, could be satisfied in no way but by the labor-saving machinery of the press.

Now the military art must date its rude origin at the same distant epoch. It must have grown by force of the same law of suggestion, and therefore must have almost necessarily produced its corresponding invention of gunpowder, during the same century. Thus it was that one and the same law of progress conspired to perfect these two grand inventions at about the same time. Twin sovereigns, the one to commence its labors in the world of mind, the other in the world of matter.

And what were the effects of the art of printing, on social and political institutions? Did it take law from the human legislator, or give him law? Let us see.

It created, for the first time in history, what may be called a public mind. Cabined and cribbed though it was, within the forms of an age of despotism and bigotry, that mind grew and expanded, till it felt the pressure of those forms as obstructions to its growth. It then reformed the legislator himself, and through him cast off its obstructions, and thereupon expanded, with a broader liberty, into a mightier stature.

This mind thus shaped itself, not upon general speculating ideas, but upon natural tendencies and habits of thought, coming from the hoary past, and common to all, and to which the inspiring influence of the press now gave an all-pervasive life. Society was thus made to feel its existence through its organized entirety through all its institutions and interests; and on this regenerated feeling, common to all, was established a true sovereignty of public opinion. Do not misunderstand me. When I speak of public opinion, I do not mean the wild impulse of minority or majority; I do not mean popular agitation or effervescence.

I do not mean a state of mind indicated by mass meetings, barbecues, and the like. These may indicate a feverish state of the public mind, but they indicate no public opinion. On the contrary, they show that public opinion on the given subject is not yet formed. But I mean that opinion which is a natural, spontaneous growth, or proceeding from the organized whole; which is therefore in accordance with the political institutions, established interests, and the general moral and religious sense of a community. Until these are endangered, threatened or disturbed, public opinion rests unmoved, and heeds not the angry discussions that are going on among the overheated partizans of the day.

If, therefore, you would know what public opinion is, do not look to a party press that is doing what it can to draw forth an opinion favorable to the cause which it advocates, but look to the established interests, the intellectual character, and the moral and religious sense of the people, which the whole press, in all the variety of its departments, has contributed to form, and from them estimate what the common judgment, in the last result, must be.

Public opinion, in our country, indulges in no abstract speculations: it leaves them to the dreams of the theorist. In the full enjoyment of its own unobstructed freedom, it is never clamorous, it is never violent. It moves only on great occasions, and under the pressure of some stern necessity; but, when it does move, it is irresistible; it bears down all opposition before it. The demagogue frequently attempts to imitate the incipient stages of this movement, by an artificial agitation of the masses. Yet his imposture is sure to be detected in the end, by the fraudful expedients to which he resorts in order to sustain that continued excitement in which alone he can live. Public opinion neither countenances such expedients, nor desires the agitation which they provoke. To it, all agitation is incidental, and results from extraneous causes, or from its partial manifestations. Sovereign in itself, it seeks not the aid of violently excited feeling, and when it unequivocally manifests itself, all agitation ceases, and the stream of events rolls quietly on.

It is when the course of the waters is obstructed, and they are accumulating behind the obstruction, that this artificial, this counterfeit agitation begins. It is then that every monstrous thing, little and great, which peoples the flood, swells into unnatural dimensions, and each, from the small fry to the leviathan,

"Hugest that swims the ocean stream,"

creates for itself its particular whirlpool and circle of bubble and foam, deceiving the inconsiderate spectator into the belief that all this is the agitation of the onward rolling flood, the indication of the natural tendency and pressure of the mighty mass. Yet let but the master-mind, which alone is competent to view the entirety *ab extra*, open the sluice-way, or the accumulating wave break the obstruction down, and the tide rolls tranquilly on, swallowing up in its prevailing current, whirlpool, bubble, and foam, and little monster and great, and bearing them all quietly off to the ocean of eternal oblivion.

This is public opinion; the gravitation of the general mass of mind through all its institutions and interest towards its eternal centre; and when it so gravitates, it is always right; but this *artificial* agitation is generally wholly individual, and when it is such, it is always wrong; since its object, whatever may be the pretext, is wholly selfish. It is only when the agitation is natural, spontaneous, and comes from an effort to express the common wants and desires of a people, and is conducted with a religious reverence for public morals, for good order, and all truth, that it is ever the true harbinger of a genuine and enduring public opinion. A public opinion, based upon the generally received ideas of morality, religion, and law, doth in fact constitute the common conscience of a people; and it is this conscience which in every great and trying emergency makes heroes or cowards of us all, as we may chance to be right or wrong.

It was a deep religious and moral feeling of this sort, for the first time brought into general activity by the diffusion of the Scriptures through the agency of the Press, which in the sixteenth century commenced and carried on the great work of religious reformation. The obstructions to its efforts were mountainous, and a deep and wide searching agitation went before it, often mingling error with truth. It touched, it moved that principle which lies beneath the deepest foundations of all that is human, and at once all social institutions were agitated as by an earthquake. It taught the human to give place to the divine. It dashed government against government, institution against institution, man against man; and urged on that series of religious revolutions, which for ages shook all Europe to its centre. It passed from religion into philosophy; it took form in politics; it produced its consequences in this country; it exploded, with most murderous effect, the combustible monarchy of France, and is to this day, with almost undiminished energy, passing down its tremulous agitations through the present into the boundless future. It changed the aspect of christendom; it established Protestantism and Protestant states, and reformed Romanism itself.

Nobody can doubt that all these changes were the necessary results of the discovery of the art of printing. They date from the commencement of the reformation; but the reformation could not have succeeded except by the aid of this art. Before this discovery, it had been repeatedly attempted both in church and out of church, and the attempts had failed; but after this discovery, it was attempted by a poor obscure monk in Germany, and the attempt did not fail. It began in the social mind, and extended itself, after much agitation, by a regular and orderly process, through the legitimate legislation of each community, out into state and church.

The creation of means by which the common mind, in every country of christendom, may in an orderly manner produce every desirable and necessary change in government, is one of the important results of this discovery; but its general social results have been no less important.

Let us go back, if we can, to the middle of the fourteenth century. Let us place ourselves in the bosom of that country whence all our political and social institutions are directly or indirectly derived; nay, from which all our ideas of legal right and duty, of liberty and law, proceed; and now, as in the midst of that century, let us see what the condition of the common mind is without the aid of this art. The first thing, then, that must strike our attention, is the general apathy and indifference of the mass around us, as to all matters of general, social and political importance. There is no press, there are no newspapers, no periodicals, political, religious, literary or scientific. In the place of the light which should come from these sources on the common mind, a profound darkness prevails, beneath which, all thought and action still rest in primeval slumber. But this is not all; there are no books in circulation or use, save those few that are transcribed on parchment by the slow and tedious operations of the pen. If we enter their public libraries, the precious manuscripts are chained to the tables, or are guarded with the vigilance of armed sentinels. If we enter their schools, the child is learning his alphabet from a written scroll furnished him by his master. What a mass of ignorance; aye, and of necessary bondage! How eagerly the million multitudes look up to the learned few for light and guidance! With what intensity of attention do they hang on the utterance of their lips, and how carefully do they treasure up, in their memories of iron, the oracles that fall on their ears! Ah! these are days when it well behoves the learned to take heed what they say. They are rulers of necessity, if not of choice, and their words are law; and well may they subject themselves to some general rules of thought and speech, and become a corporate community, sacerdotal or other, that the masses may take organization beneath them. Well is it for humanity and human progress that they have this absolute masterdom, and can hold, in unqualified subjection, the blind passions and terrible energies that are slumbering under them! Now let us return to this our day and generation, and—

What a change! The press is pouring forth its torrents of truth or falsehood; the land is whitened with its daily sheets; the labors of a whole literary life may be purchased by an hour's labor of the mechanic; reading is the pastime of man, woman, and child, of prince and peasant; and strange voices, laden with strange thoughts, come thick on the classic ear, from cottage, and garret, and cellar. Where is that awful intensity of attention, that necessary and salutary subjection of the masses to the learned few? Gone! gone never to return! Every individual has become an original centre of thought; and thought is everywhere tending to clash with thought, and action with action. What is it that preserves order in the midst of all this tendency to anarchy? Why, it is done by that public opinion which subsists from the organized whole, and which the press itself has created. It is that public opinion, which, by its mere *vis inertiæ*, sustains the law, and holds the struggling demon of discord down. It takes the place of the learned of old; and how important it is that its genuine authority should be sustained, and that no demagogue or insane enthusiast should be permitted to impose on the world its counterfeit!

This invention came not from legislation, but on the contrary, from the independent progress of science and art. Unaided by human policy, it organized for itself an empire within the privacy of the human mind; and, gradually extending its dominion from spirit outward into matter, brought human legislation, at last, to follow reluctantly in the steps of its progress. And when, at length, the old world became too limited for the intellectual growth which it had generated, or ancient institutions so incorporated with the life of nations as not to admit of that change which its irrepressible expansion required, it was then that the excess of this growth sought for and found in the newly discovered western world, an ample theatre for its enlargement.

A world newly discovered! and how? Why, by the progressive improvement of the art of navigation, aided by the then recent discovery or application of the virtues of the magnet; an art which had taken its birth at the first stage of the progressive humanity, and which has proceeded, *pari passu*, with other arts, under a common law of progress, and which consequently had its corresponding discovery at this very juncture of affairs. Under the government of Divine Providence, all is order and law; and notwithstanding the occasional outbreaks of human passion, and the perversity of the human will, that government compels its own puny creatures, whatever may be their motives, or however widely they may err, to shape their actions, at last, to its own grand train of events, and to carry out and fulfil its own great designs.

All three of those wonderful inventions, gunpowder, printing, and the compass, were necessary to the successful establishment of the Anglo-Saxon colonies on these shores. A number of tempest-driven Northmen doubtless discovered and colonized them in the beginning of the eleventh century; but their discovery was premature. It came not in the logical order of progress. The colonists necessarily failed to effect a permanent establishment. Their intercourse with the mother country was fraught with every peril of uncertainty; for, over fog-wrapt surge, or beneath cloud-invested sky, they wandered without compass or guide. The shores themselves were occupied by ferocious savages, and fire-arms were wanting to subdue them. And then, what availed it to add the forest and barbarism of the new world to the forest and semi-barbarism of the old? The invention of printing was yet wanting to reform the general mind of Europe, and to generate that spirit which in after times was to go forth to establish its emancipation on these shores, under the auspices of institutions to be formed from all that was select and glorious in the past. The establishment and development of the institutions under which we live, are due to no arbitrary enactments, suggested by abstract speculations, but are the necessary re-sults of the operations of these discoveries and inventions, on the free growth of the Anglo-Saxon idea of liberty and law.

Thus the state of the arts and sciences, in the beginning of the eleventh century, was not such as to enable the progressive humanity to discover these shores, and to establish permanent dominion on this side the Atlantic. Their accidental discovery, at that time, yielded no useful results. But the progress of the arts and sciences in the fifteenth century had been such as to furnish all the necessary means for the purpose; and the discovery and colonization of this continent followed as a necessary consequence in the consecutive order of events. Its dis-covery *then* took its place, as a logical result of the grand series of discoveries and inventions that had preceded it, and thus became a new premise, or broader basis for the progressive action of the race.

I might here dwell on the consequences of the discovery of America, and its settlement by civilized communities. I might show how those consequences reacted on the arts and sciences themselves, on the rela-tions of nations, on their internal polities, their domestic habits, and social enjoyments; shaping their institutions and controlling their legislation. But I deem further historical illustrations unnecessary. The great truth that human progress is the result of an ever-active law, manifesting itself chiefly in scientific discovery and invention, and thereby controlling legislation, and giving enduring improvement to all social and political institutions, cannot be a subject of historical ques-tion or doubt. It is a law as palpable in the history of the social mind, as the law of gravitation in the movement of matter. Indeed, I should feel that I owed a serious apology to my hearers for having detained them so long on this point, were it not for certain extravagant ideas which seem to be rife in the land. The advocates of those ideas would teach us that there is an absolute, undefinable popular sovereignty, which can, in a manner its own, and at any moment, carry a certain supposed natural equality into social and political life, and *thereby* ele-vate poor human nature, however rude and degraded its condition, at once, as by a sort of magic, into a state of supreme and absolute per-fection. When this sovereignty does not itself act to this end, it invokes the legislature, which is supposed to be competent to do nearly as much. No doubt government can do much; it can suppress insurrection, it can repel invasion, it can enforce contracts, preserve the peace, concentrate and protect the existing arts; but all this is to organize, and sustain organization, and not to establish the *natural* equality. Yet this is all that government can do to promote human improvement; but in doing this, it does but act in obedience to that law, by which God governs in the progress of the race.

The idea that legislation necessarily acts an inferior part in human progress, that this progress is governed by a law that overrules and controls political sovereignty, may be humbling indeed to the demagogue, who would make everything bend to the popular will. But there this law is, an undoubted and incontrovertible reality, which will bear with no paltering, but demands the obedience of all, on the penalty of degradation or ruin. The true statesman, the real promoter of human progress, at once recognizes, and feels proud to obey it. He feels that in so doing, he is performing the most elevated and dignified of duties. For though by legislation he cannot advance the entire humanity a single step, yet he may by legislation materially advance the nation for which he legislates. You may be able to add nothing to the light of the sun, yet you may concentrate his rays in a focus, and thus make a particular point as bright as the source from which they emanate. The statesman can concentrate the scattered arts; he may carry out each discovery and invention to all its available uses, and thus elevate the nation which he serves, to the head of the progressive humanity. Yet if he would do this, he must not wait to be driven to the task, like a galley slave, by the rival and threatening policy of foreign governments. For the very fact that they coerce him, shows that they are already in his advance.

Supposing that a people has already adopted the common arts and sciences, as far as they are available, there will still remain certain discoveries and inventions of more recent date, which are not fully applied, or carried to their necessary consequences. Among these, in modern times, there has always been some one susceptible of such universality of application, as would seem to merit the particular consideration of statesmen. Take, for instance, at the present time, the steam engine. What is susceptible of more universal application? What, bringing out all its powers, can add greater energy and vigor to the arm of government? What has, or can perform greater wonders? Not gunpowder, not the compass, nay, not even the press. It may be made to toil in the field, and supplant the labor of the slave. It already works at the spindle, and the loom, and the forge, and the mine. It is even now, whilst I am speaking, moving over earth with the speed of wings, walking up the downward torrent, and triumphantly striding over the roaring billows of the Atlantic. Already, where in use, has it reduced the distance one half between man and man, nation and nation, of extreme islands and continents of the habitable globe. It has brought civilization into immediate contact with barbarism, and Christianity with heathenism.

Unless all history be false, and the eternal laws of matter and mind nothing but a dream, there can be little danger in predicting too much for the progress of this invention. Indeed, the danger is, that the most extravagant predictions will fall short of the reality. No matter what government first applies this invention to all its practical naval and military uses, other governments must follow, however reluctantly, or cease to exist. Nay, should an unwonted apathy seize on all civilized governments, society would, at length, do the work to a great extent at their hands. The progress of this invention is ever onward, and will not cease until it has filled the world with its consequences.

Already has it coasted the shores of India, penetrated its interior by river or road, invaded the empire of China, and roused the Chinese mind by its appalling apparition, from the long slumber of centuries past. Ere long it shall bind subject Asia to Europe by bands of iron, and the Cossack and the Tartar, whilst feeding their herds on the banks of the Don and the steppes of southern Russia, shall start with amazement at the shrill whistle of the locomotive, and the thunder of the railroad car, as it sweeps on toward the confines of China. Can the monarchies of Europe slumber in security, whilst the immense Russian empire is thus centralizing and condensing its vast military resources and population at their backs? Never; their very existence must depend upon their resort to like means of defence or annoyance. And, from the heart of every monarchy of Europe, must diverge railroads to every assailable extreme; that when danger comes, and come it must, the whole war force of the nation may move, at a moment's warning, with the speed of wings, to the extreme point of peril.

The governments of Europe must become stronger internally and externally; more secure within and more formidable without, maugre the democratic tendencies by which they are threatened. Democracy is strong, but here is a power still stronger, that *will* have its course. It is a power with which governments will and must organize themselves, at their peril, whatever may be their form. And when thus organized, their endurance must be as that of adamant. Organized on like basis, our representative democracy itself may be secure; but if not thus organized, it can only wait, with as much quietude as it may, to be gradually absorbed, and finally swallowed up by the strong organizations that may be brought to bear upon it. Think ye that the military progress of this invention in the old world is to produce no effect on the new; that the breadth of the Atlantic is to set bounds to its effects? The breadth of the Atlantic! Why, it has become a narrow frith, over which armies may be ferried in twelve or fifteen days, to land in slave or non-slaveholding States, at option; and that power, "whose home is on the deep," already transports over her watery empire, on the wings of this invention, her victorious cannon. Other governments are little behind her in the application of this power. Thus menaced, have we strength to do our duty with dignity? Can we much longer be governed by factions?

I am not suggesting a course of policy; I am simply carrying our premises to their necessary consequences; and to *that* end I ask: If we continue a free and independent people, must we not organize ourselves on the basis which this invention affords? Can we avoid it? Have we any choice but to radiate our country with communications for its defence, that the whole war force of the nation may be thrown with railroad speed on any point of danger? This system of defence may not be adopted till the shock of some foreign invasion, or some terrible internal convulsion, forces upon the government the necessity of adopting it; and then, if it be the will of God that we continue one people, it will, and must be adopted. When it is done, this union will be complete; its duration will depend on no written scroll of parchment; on no variable popular breath; its strength on no constitutional constructions changing to suit the temper of the times, but the constitution itself, resolved by the law of progress, shall take form, over the whole face of the land, in bands of iron.

Such must be the political progress of this invention. Government, in this country, has as yet done nothing, but society has done much. True to itself and its highest interests, it has been prompt in obedience to the law of progress. It has already extended, and still continues to extend the application of this sovereign invention. It has contracted, as it were, this country within half its former space. It has made a sparse population dense, and if a dense population has its evils, as in large cities it certainly has, the same invention offers an antidote. It can, without disadvantage, render those populations sparse. It can combine the morality and the occupation of a rural with the intellectual activity of an urban population. It will and must proceed on its mission, by force of the very law which gave it existence, till the civilization of christendom, on the basis which it affords, has been fully accomplished, and then, by force of the same law, will it bear that civilization into the bosom of barbarism, christianize the nations, and establish the dominion of the arts over the broad face of earth and ocean.

Such is the nature of the law of progress. Ever adding to the triumphs of intellect, ever expanding the sphere of civilization, ever enlarging the domain of liberty and law, it began its political and social manifestations, as from a central point, in the sacerdotal caste of Egypt. It continued them in Greece, and there, with the fine arts and liberal sciences, expanded its influence over a wider compass. It reflected its action thence into the yet barbarous Latium. It created the civilization of Rome; Rome carried that civilization abroad among the nations of the earth, and enstamped her image wherever she set down the foot of her power. Barbarism came to receive the teachings of this civilization, at length christianized, and to open a sphere of action for the physical sciences and useful arts in the nether masses. Then came the era for deepening as well as widening the action of this law, by the aid of physical discovery and invention. Fire-arms resolved the feudal system into a community of nations. The press inspired that community with a common soul. The compass revealed this western world, and pioneered to these shores the select mind and choicest institutions of Europe. It still urged on its discoveries; it has nearly completed the exploration of the globe. And now comes this invention of Watt to perfect what these discoveries have begun, and then to penetrate into every part of the world, and to carry a Christian civilization wherever it penetrates. Springing, armed for its mission, from the head of the progressive humanity, it cometh forth the genuine offspring of that one Eternal Reason which hath ruled through all ages past. It embraceth within itself, struggling for utterance, the history of millenniums to come. It standeth before the portals of the future, but as no veiled Isis, as no mute and motionless Harpocrates. It hath a language its own; and as it moveth to its task, it talketh freely of its mission. Thou unambiguous prophet! what a voice for the future speaketh from the expanding volume of thy force! What a·tale to the future is foretokened in the movements of thy demon strength! Great fashioner of the destinies of nations! Thou has hardly commenced thy career of victory; but when it is finished, all lands and all seas shall lie beneath thy feet, at once conquered and glorified by thy conquest!

And now, gentlemen, if such be the law of human progress, if it must thus ever operate from the past into the present, and through the present to the future, and as by a sort of logical process, what becomes of those doctrines of social and political reform, with which our land is now so rife, and with which the public ear is so incessantly abused? What becomes of those ideas of a natural, absolute, unlimited and uncontrollable popular sovereignty, which is at once to bring humanity to perfection by establishing a *natural* liberty and a *natural* equality in *social* and *political* life? There may be a dire clashing among some of the ideas that are thus brought forcibly together; but the wise advocates of these doctrines see it not, feel it not. They have sundry naked abstractions, which they have created for themselves, or others for them, upon which, by their own unassisted wisdom, they hope to build up society anew, on an improved plan. They would cut clear from the past; they would establish a new theory of human nature, and base a human progress upon ideas and laws their own. Well! let them do it; but let them do it, as they must, with material their own. Let them create their world, and their man and woman, after their own image, and then, on their principles, run their course of events in rivalry with that of Divine Providence. But let them not lay their hands on those whom God has created after his image, and who are moving on to their high destiny under his divine guidance. Let them not undertake to substitute their will for His, their laws for His, over any except their own, and we shall then know what that progress is about which they are now so abundantly eloquent.

In their estimation, all social and political institutions can be removed, by their sovereign wills, with the same ease that you take the glove from your hand, and any of their own imaginings substituted in their place. Their abstractions have no reference to the influence of the past on the present; no reference to the existing social or political organizations which have grown out of by-gone centuries; and it is not strange that they are utterly astonished to find, when they attempt to carry them into effect, that they are entering into conflict with all that the past has done for us. And then it is very natural for them to proceed, from lauding their own principles, to the abuse of the past; to the abuse of all our ancestral institutions and social and political ideas, as antiquated, and as obstructions to human progress.

Gentlemen, the present state of human progress is a child, of which the hoary past is the venerable father. And the child bears the image and feels the pulsating blood, and enjoys the patrimony of its sepulchred parent. There is not an institution, or science, or art, of any practical value, nothing of the good or true, in social or political life, that has not come down to us as a creation, or as a result of the labors and achievements of the venerated dead; the dead, not of modern times merely, but of far-distant antiquity. The blood of Thermopylæ, of Marathon, and Platea, flowed not in vain for us. Homer sung, Plato mused, and Socrates moralized, for our benefit. For us Rome went forth in her invincible legion to conquer and humanize; for us Roman wisdom planned and Roman valor fought, and laid broad and deep the foundations of christendom. Aye, something even of our nearer selves appears in the action of the distant past. That blood, which now circulates warm through the Anglo-American heart, may be traced through centuries of light and shadow, of triumph and trial, in the Anglo-Saxon line. For us it struggled under the Norman rule, and created *our* idea of liberty and law; for us it struck the harp of heaven in Milton, of nature in Shakespeare, and proclaimed the laws of the universe in the philosophy of Newton. O! let us build monuments to the past. Let them tower on mound and mountain; let them rise from the corners of our streets, and in our public squares, that childhood may sport its marbles at their basements, and lisp the names of the commemorated dead, as it lisps the letters of its alphabet. Thus shall the past be made to stand out in a monumental history, that may be seen by the eye, and touched by the hand. Thus shall it be made to subsist to the senses, as it still lives in the organization of the social mind; an organization from which its errors have died out, or are dying, and in which nothing but its Herculean labors do, or are to endure. Yes, let us sanctify the past, and let no hand, with sacrilegious violence, dare mar its venerable aspect. Change indeed must come, but then let it come by force of the necessary law of progress. So shall the present still ever build and improve on a patrimony formed by the deeds of heroic virtue, and the labors of exalted intellect. So shall the great and glorious be added to the great and glorious, and the labors of the illustrious dead still be made fruitful by the labors of the illustrious living, time without end.

Such is the nature of that inheritance which has come down to us from the past, worthy to be honored by every philanthropic feeling for the present, and cherished by every hope for the future. And now do these theorists expect us to renounce this patrimony, and go and build on their barren abstractions?—commence a new progress on their empty expectations? And shall we do it? No, never, never, whilst humanity, through her grand organization of nations, yields a necessary obedience to the laws of the Supreme Reason, or Nature, through her universal frame of worlds, stands fast in the laws of her God!

15

OLIVER WENDELL HOLMES, SR.

1809, born August 29, at Cambridge, Mass.
1829, was graduated from Harvard College
1836, completed medical course at Harvard
1836, *Poems*
1836, Boylston prize winner
1837, Boylston prize winner
1838–40, professor of anatomy, Dartmouth College
1842, *Homeopathy and Its Kindred Delusions*
1843, *The Contagiousness of Puerperal Fever*
1847–82, Parkman professor of anatomy and physiology at Harvard Medical School
1847–53, dean of Harvard Medical School
1853, Lowell Institute lectures on the English poets
1858, *The Autocrat of the Breakfast Table*
1860, *The Professor at the Breakfast Table*
1861, *Elsie Venner*
1867, *The Guardian Angel*
1872, *The Poet at the Breakfast Table*
1885, *A Mortal Antipathy*
1891, *Over the Teacups*
1894, died October 7, at Boston

OLIVER WENDELL HOLMES the elder was not just a funny little man. At his funniest, in "The Deacon's Masterpiece," he was writing not of a "one-hoss shay," but of the New England theology, which did not break down piece by piece, but held together as a usable system until it crumbled into dust. However little he was physically, he was big enough to crusade successfully for his correct theory of the transmission of puerperal fever, big enough to write novels whose psychological analysis is of interest today, big enough to be a leader in the outstanding literary culture of his day. The depreciation of the father by a recent biographer of his son was an unfortunate disservice to both.

Holmes knew the medical science of his time thoroughly. He wrote, as he could not help writing, with a too-charming preciosity; this need not blind the reader to the scientific and speculative values of what he said. His ideas were fresh in his day, and some retain their freshness today.

This is especially true of his address on "Mechanism in Thought and Morals," delivered before the Phi Beta Kappa Society of Harvard University on June 29, 1870, and here reprinted. This address was a two-edged sword, whose incisive insistence was on a more mechanistic approach to thought and a less mechanical approach to morals than orthodoxy had previously allowed. In the first part of the address Holmes turns to the main stream of physiological psychology, neatly sidestepping the phrenological pit. He continues and develops the psychological mechanism of Rush and Buchanan and cleverly avoids the imputation of materialism which in his day would have been fatal. The second part is a polemic against the Calvinistic doctrine of transmissible responsibility and against any morality which considers the consequences of an act rather than its intention.

The combination of these apparently diverse themes in a single address comes about through Holmes's definition of the mechanical aspect of life as that part "which is independent of our volition." He devotes much care to proving that there is such an aspect of our intellectual life, which is revealed by the unconscious operation of the brain, in sleep, in the solution of problems which have been pushed aside temporarily or given up completely, and in similar situations. Volition is not apparent in these activities; they are, therefore, mechanical.

It is noteworthy that even in 1870 Holmes found it necessary to justify the study of the brain. We must study "the conditions of the thinking organ in connection with thought, just as we study the eye in its relation to sight." Whether mind directs the brain, as the "spiritualists" hold, or is a force developed by the brain, as "materialists" maintain, "the instrument must be studied by the one as much as by the other." He adds that he is giving this explanation as "a concession to the timidity" of those who think the study of the brain necessarily binds them to the belief that changes in the material conditions of thinking constitute thought. "All that is held may be, that they accompany thought." Let no one charge him with materialism.

As for phrenology, by Holmes's time, it was a dead issue, except for the location of the various faculties of the brain. Holmes makes some tentative suggestions to what he calls "our knowledge of the relations existing between mental action and space," which are of no particular interest and are based upon our "rudimentary consciousness" of processes of thought. He has really shifted over to a neurological analysis of the brain and discarded all but the word phrenology.

When Holmes introduces the question of morals, he makes it clear that this is an area where nothing is independent of volition. "What we can help and what we cannot help are on two sides of a line which separates the sphere of human responsibility from that of the Being who has arranged and controls the order of things." The sins of our fathers are on the wrong side of the line; we cannot be considered responsible for them and should not be punished for them. In a note in the published version of the address, commenting on the "Romanists' fear for the future welfare of babes that perish unborn," and Michael Wigglesworth's handing "the infants over to the official tormentor, only assigning them the least uncomfortable of the torture-chambers," and similar manifestations of the doctrine of transmissible responsibility, Holmes remarked, "However these doctrines may be softened in the belief of many, the primary barbarism on which they rest—that is, the transfer of mechanical ideas into the world of morals, with which they are in no sense homologous—is almost universally prevalent, and like to be at present." Similarly, it is mechanism in morals to apply a calculus of gravity to "mal-volitions" on the basis of their consequences. It is mechanism in morals to measure human culpability on the scale of the Infinite, rather than on "that of the total moral capacity of the finite agent." It is moral materialism to punish perverse moral choice by physical suffering on the basis of an arbitrary scale of equivalents, or to consider moral evil as a separate entity rather than as a condition of the moral agent. Finally it is mechanism and materialism in morals to work out formal methods of avoiding the consequences of immorality—prayers, ritual observances, rites, and penances, instead of "perpetual and ever-renewed acts of moral self-determination."

MECHANISM IN THOUGHT AND MORALS

AS the midnight train rolls into an intermediate station, the conductor's voice is heard announcing, "Cars stop ten minutes for refreshments." The passengers snatch a brief repast, and go back, refreshed, we will hope, to their places. But, while they are at the tables, one may be seen going round among the cars with a lantern and a hammer, intent upon a graver business. He is clinking the wheels to try if they are sound. His task is a humble and simple one: he is no machinist, very probably; but he can cast a ray of light from his lantern, and bring out the ring of iron with a tap of his hammer.

Our literary train is stopping for a very brief time at its annual station; and I doubt not it will be refreshed by my youthful colleague before it moves on. It is not unlikely that the passengers may stand much in need of refreshment before I have done with them: for I am the one with the hammer and the lantern; and I am going to clink some of the wheels of this intellectual machinery, on the soundness of which we all depend. The slenderest glimmer I can lend, the lightest blow I can strike, may at least call the attention of abler and better-equipped inspectors.

I ask your attention to some considerations on the true mechanical relations of the thinking principle, and to a few hints as to the false mechanical relations which have intruded themselves into the sphere of moral self-determination.

I call that part of mental and bodily life mechanical which is independent of our volition. The beating of our hearts and the secretions of our internal organs will go on, without and in spite of any voluntary effort of ours, as long as we live. Respiration is partially under our control: we can change the rate and special mode of breathing, and even hold our breath for a time; but the most determined suicide cannot strangle himself without the aid of a noose or other contrivance which shall effect what his mere will cannot do. The flow of thought is, like breathing, essentially mechanical and necessary, but incidentally capable of being modified to a greater or less extent by conscious effort. Our natural instincts and tastes have a basis which can no more be reached by the will than the sense of light and darkness, or that of heat and cold. All these things we feel justified in referring to the great First Cause: they belong to the "laws of Nature," as we call them, for which we are not accountable.

Whatever may be our opinions as to the relations between "mind" and "matter," our observation only extends to thought and emotion as connected with the living body, and, according to the general verdict of consciousness, more especially with certain parts of the body; namely, the central organs of the nervous system. The bold language of certain speculative men of science has frightened some more cautious persons away from a subject as much belonging to natural history as the study of any other function in connection with its special organ. If Mr. Huxley maintains that his thoughts and ours are "the expression of molecular changes in that matter of life which is the source of our other vital phenomena;"[1] if the Rev. Prof. Haughton suggests, though in the most guarded way, that "our successors may even dare to speculate on the changes that converted a crust of bread, or a bottle of wine, in the brain of Swift, Molière, or Shakespeare, into the conception of the gentle Glumdalclitch, the rascally Sganarelle, or the immortal Falstaff,"[2]—all this need not frighten us from studying the conditions of the thinking organ in connection with thought, just as we study the eye in its relations to sight. The brain is an instrument, necessary, so far as our direct observation extends, to thought. The "materialist" believes it to be wound up by the ordinary cosmic forces, and to give them out again as mental products:[3] the "spiritualist" believes in a conscious entity, not interchangeable with motive force, which plays upon this instrument. But the instrument must be studied by the one as much as by the other: the piano which the master touches must be as thoroughly understood as the musical box or clock which goes of itself by a spring or weight. A slight congestion or softening of the brain shows the least materialistic of philosophers that he must recognize the strict dependence of mind upon its organ in the only condition of life with which we are experimentally acquainted. And what all recognize as soon as disease forces it upon their attention, all thinkers should recognize, without waiting for such an irresistible demonstration. They should see that the study of the organ of thought, microscopically, chemically, experimentally, on the lower animals, in individuals and races, in health and in disease, in every aspect of external observation, as well as by internal consciousness, is just as necessary as if mind were known to be nothing more than a function of the brain, in the same way as digestion is of the stomach.

These explanations are simply a concession to the timidity of those who assume that they who study the material conditions of the thinking centre necessarily confine the sphere of intelligence to the changes in those conditions; that they consider these changes constitute thought;

---

[1] *On the Physical Basis of Life.* New Haven, 1870, p. 261.

[2] *Medicine in Modern Times.* London, 1869, p. 107.

[3] "It is by no means generally admitted that the brain is governed by the mind. On the contrary, the view entertained by the best cerebral physiologists is, that the mind is a force developed by the action of the brain."—*Journal of Psychological Medicine,* July, 1870, Editor's (W. A. Hammond) Note, p. 535.

whereas all that is held may be, that they accompany thought. It is a well-ascertained fact, for instance, that certain sulphates and phosphates are separated from the blood that goes to the brain in increased quantity after severe mental labor. But this chemical change may be only one of the factors of intellectual action. So, also, it *may* be true that the brain is inscribed with material records of thought; but what that is which reads any such records, remains still an open question. I have meant to leave absolutely untouched the endless discussion as to the distinctions between "mind" and "matter," [4] and confine myself chiefly to some results of observation in the sphere of thought, and some suggestions as to the mental confusion which seems to me a common fact in the sphere of morals.

The central thinking organ is made up of a vast number of little starlike bodies embedded in fine granular matter, connected with each other by ray-like branches in the form of pellucid threads; the same which, wrapped in bundles, become nerves,—the telegraphic cords of the system. The brain proper is a double organ, like that of vision; its two halves being connected by a strong transverse band, which unites them like the Siamese twins. The most fastidious lover of knowledge may study its general aspect as an after-dinner amusement upon an English walnut, splitting it through its natural suture, and examining either half. The resemblance is a curious freak of Nature's, which Cowley has followed out, in his ingenious, whimsical way, in his fifth "Book of Plants;" thus rendered in the old translation from his original Latin:—

> "Nor can this head-like nut, shaped like the brain
> Within, be said that form by chance to gain:
> For membranes soft as silk her kernel bind,
> Whereof the inmost is of tenderest kind,
> Like those which on the brain of man we find;
> All which are in a seam-joined shell inclosed,
> Which of this brain the skull may be supposed."

The brain must be fed, or it cannot work. Four great vessels flood every part of it with hot scarlet blood, which carries at once fire and

---

[4] Matter itself has been called "frozen force," and, as Boscovich has said, is only known to us as localized points of attraction and repulsion.

fuel to each of its atoms. Stop this supply, and we drop senseless. Inhale a few whiffs of ether, and we cross over into the unknown world
of death with a return ticket; or we prefer chloroform, and perhaps
get no return ticket. Infuse a few drachms of another fluid into the
system, and, when it mounts from the stomach to the brain, the pes-
simist becomes an optimist; the despairing wretch finds a new heaven
and a new earth, and laughs and weeps by turns in his brief ecstasy. But,
so long as a sound brain is supplied with fresh blood, it perceives, thinks,
wills.[5] The father of Eugène Sue, the novelist, in a former generation,
and M. Pinel in this, and very recently, have advocated doing away
with the guillotine, on the ground that the man, or the nobler section
of him, might be conscious for a time after the axe had fallen. We
need not believe it, nor the story of Charlotte Corday; still less that
one of Sir Everard Digby, that when the executioner held up his heart
to the gaze of the multitude, saying, "This is the heart of a traitor!"
the severed head exclaimed, "Thou liest!" These stories show, however, the sense we have that our personality is seated in the great
nervous centre; and, if physiologists could experiment on human beings
as some of them have done on animals, I will content myself with
hinting that they would have tales to relate which would almost
rival the legend of St. Denis.[6]

An abundant supply of blood to a part implies a great activity in its
functions. The oxygen of the blood keeps the brain in a continual state
of spontaneous combustion. The waste of the organ implies as constant
a repair. "Every meal is a rescue from one death, and lays up for another; and while we think a thought, we die," says Jeremy Taylor. It
is true of the brain as of other organs: it can only live by dying. We

[5] That is, acts as the immediate instrument through which these phenomena are manifested. So a good watch, in good order and wound up, tells us the time of day. The
making and winding-up forces remain to be accounted for.

[6] There is a ghastly literature of the axe and block, of which the stories above referred to are specimens. All the express trials made on the spot after executions in 1803,
in 1853, and more recently at Beauvais, have afforded only negative results, as might
be anticipated from the fact that the circulation through the brain is instantly arrested;
and Père Duchesne's *éternuer dans le sac* must pass as a frightful pleasantry. But a distinguished physiological experimenter informed me that the separated head of a dog,
on being injected with fresh blood, manifested signs of life and intelligence.—See *London Quarterly Review*, Vol. LXXIII. p. 273 *et seq.*; also *N. Y. Medical Gazette* for
April 9, 1870. The reader who would compare Dr. Johnson's opinion of vivisection
with Mr. Huxley's recent defence of it may consult the *Idler*, No. 17.

must all be born again, atom by atom, from hour to hour, or perish all at once beyond repair.[7]

Such is the aspect, seen in a brief glance, of the great nervous centre. It is constantly receiving messages from the senses, and transmitting orders to the different organs by the "up and down trains" of the nervous influence. It is traversed by continuous lines of thought, linked together in sequences which are classified under the name of "laws of association." The movement of these successions of thought is so far a result of mechanism that, though we may modify them by an exertion of will, we cannot stop them, and remain vacant of all ideas.

My bucolic friends tell me that our horned cattle always keep a cud in their mouths: when they swallow one, another immediately replaces it. If the creature happens to lose its cud, it must have an artificial one given it, or, they assure me, it will pine, and perhaps die. Without committing myself to the exactness or the interpretation of the statement, I may use it as an illustration. Just in the same way, one thought replaces another; and in the same way the mental cud is sometimes lost while one is talking, and he must ask his companion to supply its place. "What was I saying?" we ask; and our friend furnishes us with the lost word or its equivalent, and the jaws of conversation begin grinding again.

The brain being a double organ, like the eye, we naturally ask whether we can think with one side of it, as we can see with one eye; whether the two sides commonly work together; whether one side may not be stronger than the other; whether one side may not be healthy, and the other diseased; and what consequences may follow from these various conditions. This is the subject ingeniously treated by Dr. Wigan in his work on the duality of the mind. He maintains and illustrates by striking facts the independence of the two sides; which, so far as headache is concerned, many of my audience must know from their own experience. The left half of the brain, which controls the right half

---

[7] It is proper to say here, that the waste occurring in an organ is by no means necessarily confined to its stationary elements. The blood itself in the organ, and for the time constituting a part of it, appears to furnish the larger portion of the fuel, if we may call it so, which is acted on by its own oxygen. This, at least, is the case with muscle, and is probably so elsewhere.

of the body, is, he believes, the strongest in all but left-handed persons.[8]

The resemblance of the act of intelligence to that of vision is remarkably shown in the terms we borrow from one to describe the other. We *see* a truth; we *throw light* on a subject; we *elucidate* a proposition; we *darken* counsel; we are *blinded* by prejudice; we take a *narrow view* of things; we look at our neighbor with a *jaundiced eye*. These are familiar expressions; but we can go much farther. We have intellectual myopes, near-sighted specialists, and philosophers who are purblind to all but the distant abstract. We have judicial intellects as nearly achromatic as the organ of vision, eyes that are color-blind, and minds that seem hardly to have the sense of beauty. The old brain thinks the world grows worse, as the old retina thinks the eyes of needles and the fractions in the printed sales of stocks grow smaller. Just as the eye seeks to refresh itself by resting on neutral tints after looking at brilliant colors, the mind turns from the glare of intellectual brilliancy to the solace of gentle dullness; the tranquillizing green of the sweet human qualities, which do not make us shade our eyes like the spangles of conversational gymnasts and *figurantes*.

We have a field of vision: have we a field of thought? Before referring to some matters of individual experience, I would avail myself of Sir John Herschel's apology, that the nature of the subject renders such reference inevitable, as it is one that can be elucidated only by the individual's putting on record his own personal contribution to the stock of facts accumulating.

Our conscious mental action, aside from immediate impressions on the senses, is mainly pictured, worded, or modulated, as in remembered music; all, more or less, under the influence of the will. In a general way, we refer the seat of thinking to the anterior part of the head. *Pictured* thought is in relation with the field of vision, which I perceive —as others do, no doubt—as a transverse ellipse; its vertical to its hori-

[8] Gratiolet states that the left frontal convolutions are developed earlier than the right. Baillarger attributes right-handedness to the better nutrition of the left hemisphere, in consequence of the disposition of the arteries; Hyrtl, to the larger current of blood to the right arm, etc.—See an essay on "Right and Left Handedness," in the *Journal of Psychological Medicine* for July, 1870, by Thomas Dwight, Jr., M.D.; also "Aphasia and the Physiology of Speech," by T. W. Fisher, in the *Boston Medical and Surgical Journal* for September 22, 1870.

zontal diameter about as one to three. We shut our eyes to recall a visible object: we see visions by night. The bright ellipse becomes a black ground, on which ideal images show more distinctly than on the illuminated one. The form of the mental field of vision is illustrated by the fact that we can follow in our idea a ship sailing, or a horse running, much farther, without a sense of effort, than we can a balloon rising. In seeing persons, this field of mental vision seems to be a little in front of the eyes. Dr. Howe kindly answers a letter of inquiry as follows:—

"Most congenitally-blind persons, when asked with what part of the brain they think, answer, that they are not conscious of having any brain.

"I have asked several of the most thoughtful and intelligent among our pupils to designate, as nearly as they can, the seat of sensation in thought; and they do so by placing the hand upon the *anterior* and *upper* part of the cranium."

Worded thought is attended with a distinct impulse towards the organs of speech: in fact, the effort often goes so far, that we "think aloud," as we say.[9] The seat of this form of mental action seems to me to be beneath that of pictured thought; indeed, to follow certain nerves downward: so that, as we say, "My heart was in my mouth," we could almost say, "My brain is in my mouth." A particular spot has been of late pointed out by pathologists, not phrenologists, as the seat of the faculty of speech.[10] I do know that our sensations ever point to it.

[9] The greater number of readers are probably in the habit of articulating the words mentally. Beginners read syllable by syllable.

"A man must be a poor beast," said Dr. Johnson, "that should read no more in quantity than he could utter aloud." There are books of which we can exhaust a page of its meaning at a glance; but a man cannot do justice to a poem like Gray's Elegy except by the distinct mental articulation of every word. Some persons read sentences and paragraphs as children read syllables, taking their sense in block, as it were. All instructors who have had occasion to consult a text-book at the last moment before entering the lecture-room know that *clairvoyant* state well enough in which a page prints itself on their perception as the form of types stamped itself on the page.

We can read aloud, or mentally articulate, and keep up a distinct train of pictured thought,—not so easily two currents of worded thought simultaneously: though this can be done to some extent; as, for instance, one may be reading aloud, and internally articulating some well-known passage.

[10] A part of the left anterior lobe.—See Dr. Fisher's elaborate paper before referred to.

Modulated or musical consciousness is to pictured and worded thought as algebra is to geometry and arithmetic. Music has an absolute sensuous significance—the woodchuck which used to listen to my friend playing the piano I suppose stopped at that; [11] but for human beings it does not cause a mere sensation, nor an emotion, nor a definable intellectual state, though it may excite many various emotions and trains of worded or pictured thought. But words cannot truly define it: we might as well give a man a fiddle, and tell him to play the Ten Commandments, as give him a dictionary, and tell him to describe the music of "Don Giovanni."

The nerves of hearing clasp the roots of the brain as a creeping vine clings to the bole of an elm. The primary seat of musical consciousness seems to be behind and below that of worded thought; but it radiates in all directions, calling up pictures and words, as I have said, in endless variety. Indeed, the various mental conditions I have described are so frequently combined that it takes some trouble to determine the locality of each.

The seat of the *will* seems to vary with the organ through which it is manifested; to transport itself to different parts of the brain, as we may wish to recall a picture, a phrase, or a melody; to throw its force on the muscles or the intellectual processes. Like the general-in-chief, its place is anywhere in the field of action. It is the least like an instrument of any of our faculties; the farthest removed from our conceptions of mechanism and matter, as we commonly define them.

This is my parsimonious contribution to our knowledge of the relations existing between mental action and space. Others may have had a different experience; the great apostle did not know at one time whether he was in the body or out of the body: but my system of phrenology extends little beyond this rudimentary testimony of consciousness.

When it comes to the relation of mental action and *time*, we can say with Leibnitz, *"Calculemus;"* for here we can reach quantitative results. The "personal equation," or difference in rapidity of recording the same occurrence, has been recognized in astronomical records since

[11] For various alleged instances of the power of music over different lower animals,—the cow, the stag, mice, serpents, spiders,—see Dwight's *Journal of Music* for October 26, 1861.

the time of Maskelyne, the royal astronomer; and is allowed for with the greatest nicety, as may be seen, for instance, in Dr. Gould's recent report on Transatlantic Longitude. More recently, the time required in mental processes and in the transmission of sensation and the motor impulse along nerves has been carefully studied by Helmholtz, Fizeau, Marey, Donders, and others.[12] From forty to eighty, a hundred or more feet a second are estimates of different observers: so that, as the newspapers have been repeating, it would take a whale a second, more or less, to feel the stroke of a harpoon in his tail.[13] Compare this with the velocity of galvanic signals, which Dr. Gould has found to be from fourteen to eighteen thousand miles a second through iron wire on poles, and about sixty-seven hundred miles a second through the submarine cable. The brain, according to Fizeau, takes one tenth of a second to transmit an order to the muscles; and the muscles take one hundredth of a second in getting into motion. These results, such as they are, have been arrived at by experiments on single individuals with a very delicate chronometric apparatus. I have myself instituted a good many experiments with a more extensive and expensive machinery than I think has ever been employed,—namely, two classes, each of ten intelligent students, who with joined hands represented a nervous circle of about sixty-six feet: so that a hand-pressure transmitted ten times round the circle traversed six hundred and sixty feet, besides involving one hundred perceptions and volitions. My chronometer was a "horse-timer," marking quarter-seconds. After some practice, my second class gradually reduced the time of transmission ten times round, which, like that of the first class, had stood at fourteen and fifteen seconds, down to ten seconds; that is, one tenth of a second for the passage through the nerves and brain of each individual,—less than the least time I have ever seen assigned for the whole operation; no more than Fizeau had assigned to the action of the

---

[12] See *Annual of Scientific Discovery* for 1851, 1858, 1863, 1866; *Journal of Anatomy and Physiology*, 2d Series, No. 1, for November, 1867; Marey, *Du Mouvement dans les Fonctions de la Vie*, p. 430 *et seq.*

[13] Mr. W. F. Barrett calculates, that as the mind requires one tenth of a second to form a conception and act accordingly, and as a rifle-bullet would require no more than one thousandth of a second to pass through the brain, it could not be felt (*An. Sc. Discov.* 1866–7, p. 278). When Charles XII. was struck dead by the cannon-ball, he clapped his hand on his sword. This, however, may have probably been an unconscious reflex action.

brain alone. The mental process of judgment between colors (red, white, and green counters), between rough and smooth (common paper and sand-paper), between smells (camphor, cloves, and assafœtida), took about three and a half tenths of a second each; taste, twice or three times as long, on account of the time required to reach the true sentient portion of the tongue.[14] These few results of my numerous experiments show the rate of working of the different parts of the machinery of consciousness. Nothing could be easier than to calculate the whole number of perceptions and ideas a man could have in the course of a life-time.[15] But as we think the same thing over many millions of times, and as many persons keep up their social relations by the aid of a vocabulary of only a few hundred words, or, in the case of some very fashionable people, a few scores only, a very limited amount of thinking material may correspond to a full set of organs of sense, and a good development of the muscular system.[16]

[14] Some of these results assign a longer time than other observers have found to be required. A little practice would materially shorten the time, as it did in the other experiment.

[15] "The sensible points of the retina, according to Weber and Smith, measure no more than the ⅛₀₀₀ inch in diameter. If, adopting the views of Mr. Solly, we consider the convolutions of the brain as made up of an extensive surface of cineritious neurine, we may estimate the number of ideas, the substrata of which may be contained in a square inch, as not certainly less than 8,000; and, as there must be an immense number of square inches of surface in the gray matter extended through the cerebro-spinal axis of man, there is space sufficient for millions."—*On the Reflex Function of the Brain,* by T. M. Laycock, M.D. *Brit. and For. Med. Review* for January, 1845.

Dr. Hooke, the famous English mathematician and philosopher, made a calculation of the number of separate ideas the mind is capable of entertaining, which he estimated as 3,155,760,000.—Haller, *Elementa Physiologiæ,* vol. v. p. 547. The nerve-cells of the brain vary in size from ⅓₀₀₀ to ⅓₀₀ of an inch in diameter (Marshall's *Physiology,* i. 77); and the surface of the convolutions is reckoned by Baillarger at about 670 square inches (*Ibid.* p. 302); which, with a depth of one fifth of an inch, would give 134 cubic inches of cortical substance, and, if the cells average ⅟₁₀₀₀ of an inch, would allow room in the convolutions for 134,000,000,000 cells. But they are mingled with white nerve-fibres and granules. While these calculations illustrate the extreme complexity of the brain-substance, they are amusing rather than explanatory of mental phenomena, and belong to the province of *Science mousseuse,* to use the lively expression of a French academician at a recent session.

[16] The use of *slang,* or cheap generic terms, as a substitute for differentiated specific expressions, is at once a sign and a cause of mental atrophy. It is the way in which a lazy adult shifts the trouble of finding any exact meaning in his (or her) conversation on the other party. If both talkers are indolent, all their talk lapses into the vague generalities of early childhood, with the disadvantage of a vulgar phraseology. It is a prevalent social vice of the time, as it has been of times that are past.

The time-relation of the sense of vision was illustrated by Newton by the familiar experiment of whirling a burning brand, which appears as a circle of fire. The duration of *associated* impressions on the memory differs vastly, as we all know, in different individuals. But, in uttering distinctly a series of unconnected numbers or letters before a succession of careful listeners, I have been surprised to find how generally they break down, in trying to repeat them, between seven and ten figures or letters; though here and there an individual may be depended on for a larger number. Pepys mentions a person who could repeat sixty unconnected words, forwards or backwards, and perform other wonderful feats of memory; but this was a prodigy.[17] I suspect we have in this and similar trials a very simple mental dynamometer which may yet find its place in education.

Do we ever think without knowing that we are thinking? The question may be disguised so as to look a little less paradoxical. Are there any mental processes of which we are unconscious at the time, but which we recognize as having taken place by finding certain results in our minds? [18]

That there are such unconscious mental actions is laid down in the strongest terms by Leibnitz, whose doctrine reverses the axiom of Descartes into *sum, ergo cogito*. The existence of unconscious thought is

---

"Thus has he (and many more of the same breed, that, I know, the drossy age dotes on) only got the tune of the time, and outward habit of encounter; a kind of yesty collection, which carries them through and through the most fond and winnowed opinions; and do but blow them to their trial, the bubbles are out."—*Hamlet*, act v. sc. 2.

Swift says (in the character of Simon Wagstaff, Esq.), speaking of "witty sentences," "For, as long as my memory reaches, I do not recollect one new phrase of importance to have been added; which defect in us moderns I take to have been occasioned by the introduction of cant-words in the reign of King CHARLES the Second."—*A Complete Collection of Genteel and Ingenious Conversation, etc.* Introduction.

"English is an expressive language," said Mr. Pinto, "but not difficult to master. Its range is limited. It consists, as far as I can observe, of four words,—'nice,' 'jolly,' 'charming,' and 'bore;' and some grammarians add 'fond.' "—*Lothair*, chap. xxviii.

[17] This is nothing to the story told by Seneca of himself, and still more of a friend of his, one Portius *Latro* (*Mendax*, it might be suggested) ; or to that other relation of Muretus about a certain young Corsican.—See Rees's *Cyclopædia*, art. "Memory," also Haller's *Elem. Phys.* V. 548, etc.

[18] "Such a process of reasoning is more or less implicit, and *without the direct and full advertence of the mind exercising it.*"—J. H. Newman, *Essay in Aid of a Grammar of Assent.*

maintained by him in terms we might fairly call audacious, and illustrated by some of the most striking facts bearing upon it. The "insensible perceptions," he says, are as important in pneumatology as
corpuscles are in physics.—It does not follow, he says again, that, because we do not perceive thought, it does not exist.—Something goes
on in the mind which answers to the circulation of the blood and all
the internal movements of the viscera.—In one word, it is a great source
of error to believe that there is no perception in the mind but those of
which it is conscious.

This is surely a sufficiently explicit and peremptory statement of the
doctrine, which, under the names of "latent consciousness," "obscure
perceptions," "the hidden soul," "unconscious cerebration," "reflex action of the brain," has been of late years emerging into general recognition in treatises of psychology and physiology.

His allusion to the circulation of the blood and the movements of the
viscera, as illustrating his paradox of thinking without knowing it,
shows that he saw the whole analogy of the mysterious intellectual
movement with that series of reflex actions so fully described half a
century later by Hartley, whose observations, obscured by wrong interpretation of the cerebral structure, and an insufficient theory of vibrations which he borrowed from Newton, are yet a remarkable anticipation of many of the ideas of modern physiology, for which credit has
been given so liberally to Unzer and Prochaska. Unconscious activity
is the rule with the actions most important to life. The lout who lies
stretched on the tavern-bench, with just mental activity enough to keep
his pipe from going out, is the unconscious tenant of a laboratory
where such combinations are being constantly made as never Wöhler or
Berthelot could put together; where such fabrics are woven, such
colors dyed, such problems of mechanism solved, such a commerce
carried on with the elements and forces of the outer universe, that the
industries of all the factories and trading establishments in the world
are mere indolence and awkwardness and unproductiveness compared
to the miraculous activities of which his lazy bulk is the unheeding
centre. All these unconscious or reflex actions take place by a mechanism
never more simply stated than in the words of Hartley, as *"vibrations*
which ascend up the sensory nerves first, and then are detached down
the motory nerves, which communicate with these by some common

trunk, plexus, or ganglion." [19] The doctrine of Leibnitz, that the brain may sometimes act without our taking cognizance of it, as the heart commonly does, as many internal organs always do, seems almost to belong to our time. The readers of Hamilton and Mill, of Abercrombie, Laycock, and Maudsley, of Sir John Herschel, of Carpenter, of Lecky, of Dallas, will find many variations on the text of Leibnitz, some new illustrations, a new classification and nomenclature of the facts; but the root of the matter is all to be found in his writings.

I will give some instances of work done in the underground workshop of thought,—some of them familiar to the readers of the authors just mentioned.

We wish to remember something in the course of conversation. No effort of the will can reach it; but we say, "Wait a minute, and it will come to me," and go on talking. Presently, perhaps some minutes later, the idea we are in search of comes all at once into the mind, delivered like a prepaid bundle, laid at the door of consciousness like a foundling in a basket. How it came there we know not. The mind must have been at work groping and feeling for it in the dark: it cannot have come of itself. Yet, all the while, our consciousness, so far as we are conscious of our consciousness, was busy with other thoughts.

In old persons, there is sometimes a long interval of obscure mental action before the answer to a question is evolved. I remember making an inquiry, of an ancient man whom I met on the road in a wagon with his daughter, about a certain old burial-ground which I was visiting. He seemed to listen attentively; but I got no answer. "Wait half a minute, or so," the daughter said, "and he will tell you." And sure enough, after a little time, he answered me, and to the point. The de-

---

[19] He goes on to draw the distinction between "automatic motions of the secondary kind" and those which were originally automatic. "The fingers of young children bend upon almost every impression which is made upon the palm of the hand; thus performing the action of grasping in the original automatic manner." ("He rastled with my finger, the blank little etc.!" says the hard-swearing but tender-hearted "Kentuck," speaking of the new-born babe whose story Mr. Harte has told so touchingly in "The Luck of Roaring Camp.") Hartley traces this familiar nursery experience onwards, until the original automatic action becomes associated with sensations and ideas, and by and by subject to the will; and shows still further how this and similar actions, by innumerable repetitions, reach another stage, "repassing through the same degrees in an inverted order, till they become secondarily automatic on many occasions, though still perfectly voluntary on some; viz., whensoever an express act of the will is exerted."—*Obs. on Man*, Propositions xix, xxi.

lay here, probably, corresponded to what machinists call "lost time," or "back lash," in turning an old screw, the thread of which is worn. But within a fortnight, I examined a young man for his degree, in whom I noticed a certain regular interval, and a pretty long one, between every question and its answer. Yet the answer was, in almost every instance, correct, when at last it did come. It was an idiosyncrasy, I found, which his previous instructors had noticed. I do not think the mind knows what it is doing in the interval, in such cases. This latent period, during which the brain is obscurely at work, may, perhaps, belong to mathematicians more than others. Swift said of Sir Isaac Newton, that if one were to ask him a question, "he would revolve it in a circle in his brain, round and round and round" (the narrator here describing a circle on his own forehead), "before he could produce an answer." [20]

I have often spoken of the same trait in a distinguished friend of my own, remarkable for his mathematical genius, and compared his sometimes long-deferred answer to a question, with half a dozen others stratified over it, to the thawing-out of the frozen words as told of by Baron Munchausen and Rabelais, and nobody knows how many others before them.

I was told, within a week, of a business-man in Boston, who, having an important question under consideration, had given it up for the time as too much for him. But he was conscious of an action going on in his brain which was so unusual and painful as to excite his apprehensions that he was threatened with palsy, or something of that sort. After some hours of this uneasiness, his perplexity was all at once cleared up by the natural solution of his doubt coming to him,—worked out, as he believed, in that obscure and troubled interval.

The cases are numerous where questions have been answered, or problems solved, in dreams, or during unconscious sleep. Two of our most distinguished professors in this institution have had such an experience, as they tell me; and one of them has often assured me that he never dreams. Somnambulism and double-consciousness offer another series of illustrations. Many of my audience remember a murder case, where the accused was successfully defended, on the ground of somnambulism, by one of the most brilliant of American lawyers. In

[20] Note to *A Voyage to Laputa*.

the year 1686 a brother of Lord Culpeper was indicted at the Old Bailey for shooting one of the guards, and acquitted on the same ground of somnambulism; that is, an unconscious, and therefore irresponsible, state of activity.[21]

A more familiar instance of unconscious action is to be found in what we call "absent" persons,—those who, while wide awake, act with an apparent purpose, but without really knowing what they are doing; as in La Bruyère's character, who threw his glass of wine into the backgammon-board, and swallowed the dice.

There are a vast number of movements which we perform with perfect regularity while we are thinking of something quite different,—"automatic actions of the secondary kind," as Hartley calls them, and of which he gives various examples. The old woman knits; the young woman stitches, or perhaps plays her piano, and yet talks away as if nothing but her tongue was busy. Two lovers stroll along side by side, just born into the rosy morning of their new life, prattling the sweet follies worth all the wisdom that years will ever bring them. How much do they think about that wonderful problem of balanced progression which they solve anew at every step?

We are constantly finding results of unperceived mental processes in our consciousness. Here is a striking instance, which I borrow from a recent number of an English journal. It relates to what is considered the most interesting period of incubation in Sir William Rowan Hamilton's discovery of quaternions. The time was the 15th of October, 1843. On that day, he says in a letter to a friend, he was walking from his observatory to Dublin with Lady Hamilton, when, on reaching Brougham Bridge, he "felt the galvanic circle of thought close; and the sparks that fell from it were the fundamental relations between i, j, k," just as he used them ever afterwards.[22]

Still another instance of the spontaneous evolution of thought we may find in the experience of a great poet. When Goethe shut his eyes, and pictured a flower to himself, he says that it developed itself before him in leaves and blossoms.[23] The result of the mental process appeared as pictured thought, but the process itself was automatic and imperceptible.

---

[21] Dallas, *The Gay Science*, I. 324.

[22] *Nature*, February 7, 1870, p. 407; *North British Review*, September, 1866, p. 57.

[23] Muller's *Physiology* (Baly's translation), Vol. II. p. 1364.

There are thoughts that never emerge into consciousness, which yet make their influence felt among the perceptible mental currents, just as the unseen planets sway the movements of those which are watched and mapped by the astronomer. Old prejudices, that are ashamed to confess themselves, nudge our talking thought to utter their magisterial veto. In hours of languor, as Mr. Lecky has remarked, the beliefs and fancies of obsolete conditions are apt to take advantage of us.[24] We know very little of the contents of our minds until some sudden jar brings them to light, as an earthquake that shakes down a miser's house brings out the old stockings full of gold, and all the hoards that have hid away in holes and crannies.

We not rarely find our personality doubled in our dreams, and do battle with ourselves, unconscious that we are our own antagonists. Dr. Johnson dreamed that he had a contest of wit with an opponent, and got the worst of it: of course, he furnished the wit for both. Tartini heard the Devil play a wonderful sonata, and set it down on awaking. Who was the Devil but Tartini himself? I remember, in my youth, reading verses in a dream, written, as I thought, by a rival fledgling of the Muse. They were so far beyond my powers, that I despaired of equalling them; yet I must have made them unconsciously as I read them. Could I only have remembered them waking!

But I must here add another personal experience, of which I will say beforehand,—somewhat as honest Izaak Walton said of his pike, "This dish of meat is too good for any but anglers or very honest men," —this story is good only for philosophers and very small children. I will merely hint to the former class of thinkers, that its moral bears on two points: first, the value of our self-estimate, sleeping,—possibly, also, waking; secondly, the significance of general formulæ when looked at in certain exalted mental conditions.

I once inhaled a pretty full dose of ether, with the determination to put on record, at the earliest moment of regaining consciousness, the thought I should find uppermost in my mind. The mighty music of the triumphal march into nothingness reverberated through my brain, and filled me with a sense of infinite possibilities which made me an archangel for the moment. The veil of eternity was lifted. The one great truth which underlies all human experience, and is the key to all the

[24] *History of Rationalism*, II. 96, note.

mysteries that philosophy has sought in vain to solve, flashed upon me in a sudden revelation. Henceforth all was clear: a few words had lifted my intelligence to the level of the knowledge of the cherubim. As my natural condition returned, I remembered my resolution; and, staggering to my desk, I wrote, in ill-shaped, straggling characters, the all-embracing truth still glimmering in my consciousness. The words were these (children may smile; the wise will ponder): "*A strong smell of turpentine prevails throughout.*" [25]

My digression has served at least to illustrate the radical change which a slight material cause may produce in our thoughts, and the way we think about them. If the state just described were prolonged, it would be called insanity.[26] I have no doubt that there are many ill-organized, perhaps over-organized, human brains, to which the common air is what the vapor of ether was to mine: it is madness to them to drink in this terrible burning oxygen at every breath; and the atmosphere that enfolds them is like the flaming shirt of Nessus.

The more we examine the mechanism of thought, the more we shall see that the automatic, unconscious action of the mind enters largely into all its processes. Our definite ideas are stepping-stones; how we get from one to the other, we do not know: something carries us; we do not take the step. A creating and informing spirit which is with us, and not of us, is recognized everywhere in real and in storied life. It is the Zeus that kindled the rage of Achilles; it is the Muse of Homer; it is the Daimon of Socrates; it is the inspiration of the seer; it

[25] Sir Humphrey Davy has related an experience, which I had forgotten when I recorded my own. After inhaling nitrous-oxide gas, he says, "With the most intense belief and prophetic manner, I exclaimed to Dr. Kingslake, 'Nothing exists but thoughts. The universe is composed of impressions, ideas, pleasures, and pains.' "— *Works*, London, 1839, Vol. III. p. 290.

[26] We are often insane at the moment of awaking from sleep. " 'I have desired Apronia to be always careful, especially about the legs.' Pray, do you see any such great wit in that sentence? I must freely own that I do not. Pray, read it over again, and consider it. Why—ay—you must know that I dreamed it just now, and waked with it in my mouth. Are you bit, or are you not, sirrahs?"—Swift's *Journal to Stella*, letter xv.

Even when wide awake, so keen and robust a mind as Swift's was capable of a strange momentary aberration in the days of its full vigor. "I have my mouth full of water, and was going to spit it out, because I reasoned with myself, 'How could I write when my mouth was full?' Have you not done things like that,—reasoned wrong at first thinking?"—*Ibid.*, letter viii.

All of us must have had similar experiences.

is the mocking devil that whispers to Margaret as she kneels at the altar; and the hobgoblin that cried, "Sell him, sell him!" in the ear of John Bunyan: it shaped the forms that filled the soul of Michael Angelo when he saw the figure of the great Lawgiver in the yet unhewn marble, and the dome of the world's yet unbuilt basilica against the blank horizon; it comes to the least of us, as a voice that will be heard; it tells us what we must believe; it frames our sentences; it lends a sudden gleam of sense or eloquence to the dullest of us all, so that, like Katterfelto with his hair on end, we wonder at ourselves, or rather not at ourselves, but at this divine visitor, who chooses our brain as his dwelling-place, and invests our naked thought with the purple of the kings of speech or song.

After all, the mystery of unconscious mental action is exemplified, as I have said, in every act of mental association. What happens when one idea brings up another? Some internal movement, of which we are wholly unconscious, and which we only know by its effect. What is this action, which in Dame Quickly agglutinates contiguous circumstances by their surfaces; in men of wit and fancy, connects remote ideas by partial resemblances; in men of imagination, by the vital identity which underlies phenomenal diversity; in the man of science, groups the objects of thought in sequences of maximum resemblance? Not one of them can answer. There is a Delphi and a Pythoness in every human breast.

The poet sits down to his desk with an odd conceit in his brain; and presently his eyes fill with tears, his thought slides into the minor key, and his heart is full of sad and plaintive melodies. Or he goes to his work, saying, "To-night I would have tears;" and, before he rises from his table he has written a burlesque, such as he might think fit to send to one of the comic papers, if these were not so commonly cemeteries of hilarity interspersed with cenotaphs of wit and humor. These strange hysterics of the intelligence, which make us pass from weeping to laughter, and from laughter back again to weeping, must be familiar to every impressible nature; and all is as automatic, involuntary, as entirely self-evolved by a hidden organic process, as are the changing moods of the laughing and crying woman. The poet always recognizes a dictation *ab extra;* and we hardly think it a figure of speech when we talk of his inspiration.

The mental attitude of the poet while writing, if I may venture to define it, is that of the "nun breathless with adoration." Mental stillness is the first condition of the listening state; and I think my friends the poets will recognize that the sense of effort, which is often felt, accompanies the mental spasm by which the mind is maintained in a state at once passive to the influx from without, and active in seizing only that which will serve its purpose.[27] It is not strange that remembered ideas should often take advantage of the crowd of thoughts, and smuggle themselves in as original. Honest thinkers are always stealing unconsciously from each other. Our minds are full of waifs and estrays which we think are our own. Innocent plagiarism turns up everywhere. Our best musical critic tells me that a few notes of the air of "Shoo Fly" are borrowed from a movement in one of the magnificent harmonies of Beethoven.[28]

[27] Burns tells us how he composed verses for a given tune:—

"My way is, I consider the poetic sentiment correspondent to my idea of the musical expression; then choose my theme; begin one stanza. When that is composed, which is generally the most difficult part of the business, I walk out, sit down now and then, look out for objects in Nature that are in unison or harmony with the cogitations of my fancy, and workings of my bosom; humming every now and then the air with the verses I have framed. When I feel my Muse beginning to jade, I retire to the solitary fireside of my study, and there commit my effusions to paper; swinging at intervals on the hind-legs of my elbow-chair, by way of calling forth my own critical strictures, as my pen goes on."—*Letters to G. Thomson*, No. xxxvii.

[28] One or two instances where the same idea is found in different authors may be worth mentioning in illustration of the remark just made. We are familiar with the saying, that the latest days are the old age of the world.

Mr. Lewes finds this in Lord Bacon's writings, in Roger Bacon's also, and traces it back as far as Seneca. I find it in Pascal (*Préface sur le Traité du Vide*); and Hobbes says, "If we will reverence the ages, the present is the oldest." So, too, Tennyson:—

> "For we are ancients of the earth,
> And in the morning of the times."
> *The Day-Dream: L'Envoi.*

Here are several forms of another familiar thought:—

> "And what if all of animated nature
> Be but organic harps diversely framed,
> That tremble into thought as o'er them sweeps,
> Plastic and vast, one intellectual breeze,
> At once the soul of each, and God of all?"
> Coleridge, *The Æolian Harp.*

"Are we a piece of machinery, which, like the Æolian harp, passive, takes the impression of the passing accident?"—Burns to Mrs. Dunlop, letter 148.

"Un seul esprit, qui est universel et qui anime tout l'univers,—comme un même

And so the orator,—I do not mean the poor slave of a manuscript, who takes his thought chilled and stiffened from its mould, but the impassioned speaker who pours it forth as it flows coruscating from the furnace,—the orator only becomes our master at the moment when he himself is surprised, captured, taken possession of, by a sudden rush of fresh inspiration. How well we know the flash of the eye, the thrill of the voice, which are the signature and symbol of nascent thought,— thought just emerging into consciousness, in which condition, as is the case with the chemist's elements, it has a combining force at other times wholly unknown!

But we are all more or less improvisators. We all have a double, who is wiser and better than we are, and who puts thoughts into our heads, and words into our mouths. Do we not all commune with our own hearts upon our beds? Do we not all divide ourselves, and go to buffets on questions of right or wrong, of wisdom or folly? Who or what is it that resolves the stately parliament of the day, with all its forms and conventionalities and pretences, and the great Me presiding, into the committee of the whole, with Conscience in the chair, that holds its solemn session through the watches of the night?

Persons who talk most do not always think most. I question whether persons who think most—that is, have most conscious thought pass through their minds—necessarily do most mental work. The tree you are sticking in "will be growing when you are sleeping." So with every new idea that is planted in a real thinker's mind: it will be growing

---

souffle de vent fait sonner differemment divers tuyaux d'orgue."—Leibnitz, *Considérations sur la Doctrine d'un Esprit Universel.*

Literature is full of such coincidences, which some love to believe plagiarisms. There are thoughts always abroad in the air, which it takes more wit to avoid than to hit upon, as the solitary "Address without a Phœnix" may remind those critical ant-eaters whose aggressive feature is drawn to too fine a point.

Old stories reproduce themselves in a singular way,—not only in such authors as Mr. Joseph Miller, but among those whom we cannot for a moment suspect of conscious misappropriation. Here is an instance forced upon my attention. In the preface to *The Guardian Angel,* I quoted a story from Sprague's "Annals of the American Pulpit," which is there spoken of as being told, by Jonathan Edwards the younger, of a brutal fellow in New Haven. Some one found a similar story in a German novel, and mentioned the coincidence. The true original, to which I was directed by Dr. Elam's book, *A Physician's Problems,* is to be found in the seventh chapter of the seventh book of Aristotle's Ethics. My Latin version renders it thus: "Et qui a filio trahebatur trahendi finem jubebat ad foreis, nam a se quoque ad hunc locum patrem suum tractum esse."

when he is least conscious of it. An idea in the brain is not a legend carved on a marble slab: it is an impression made on a living tissue, which is the seat of active nutritive processes. Shall the initials I carved in bark increase from year to year with the tree? and shall not my recorded thought develop into new forms and relations with my growing brain? Mr. Webster told one of our greatest scholars that he had to change the size of his hat every few years. His head grew larger as his intellect expanded. Illustrations of this same fact were shown me many years ago by Mr. Deville, the famous phrenologist, in London. But organic mental changes may take place in shorter spaces of time. A single night of sleep has often brought a sober second-thought, which was a surprise to the hasty conclusion of the day before. Lord Polkommet's description of the way he prepared himself for a judicial decision is in point, except for the alcoholic fertilizer he employed in planting his ideas: "Ye see, I first read a' the pleadings; and then, after letting them wamble in my wame wi' the toddy two or three days, I gie my ain interlocutor." [29]

The counterpart of this slow process is found in the ready, spontaneous, automatic, self-sustaining, continuous flow of thought, well illustrated in a certain form of dialogue, which seems to be in a measure peculiar to the female sex. The sternest of our sisters will, I hope, forgive me for telling the way in which this curious fact was forced upon my notice.

I was passing through a somewhat obscure street at the west end of our city a year or two since, when my attention was attracted to a narrow court by a sound of voices and a small crowd of listeners. From two open windows on the opposite sides of the court projected the heads, and a considerable portion of the persons, of two of the sex in question,—natives, both of them, apparently, of the green isle famous for shamrocks and shillalahs. They were engaged in argument, if that is argument in which each of the two parties develops his proposition without the least regard to what the other is at the same time saying. The question involved was the personal, social, moral, and, in short, total standing and merit of the two controversialists and their respective families. But the strange phenomenon was this: The two women, as if by preconcerted agreement, like two instruments playing

[29] Dean Ramsay's *Reminiscences of Scottish Life and Character*, p. 126.

a tune in unison, were pouring forth simultaneously a calm, steady, smooth-flowing stream of mutual undervaluation, to apply a mild phrase to it; never stopping for punctuation, and barely giving themselves time to get breath between its long-drawn clauses. The dialogue included every conceivable taunt which might rouse the fury of a sensitive mother of a family, whose allegiance to her lord, and pride in her offspring, were points which it displeased her to have lightly handled. I stood and listened like the quiet groups in the more immediate neighborhood. I looked for some explosion of violence, for a screaming volley of oaths, for an hysteric burst of tears, perhaps for a missile of more questionable character than an epithet aimed at the head and shoulders projecting opposite. "At any rate," I thought, "their tongues will soon run down; for it is not in human nature that such a flow of scalding rhetoric can be kept up very long." But I stood waiting until I was tired; and, with *labitur et labetur* on my lips, I left them pursuing the even tenor, or treble, of their way in a duet which seemed as if it might go on until nightfall.

I came away thinking I had discovered a new national custom, as peculiar, and probably as limited, as the Corsican vendetta. But I have since found that the same scolding duets take place between the women in an African kraal. A couple of them will thrust their bodies half out of their huts, and exhaust the vocabulary of the native Worcester and Webster to each other's detriment, while the bystanders listen with a sympathy which often leads to a general disturbance.[30] And I find that Homer was before us all in noticing this curious logomachy of the unwarlike sex. Æneas says to Achilles after an immensely long-winded discourse, which Creüsa could hardly have outdone,—

> "But why in wordy and contentious strife
> Need we each other scold, as women use,
> Who, with some heart-consuming anger wroth,
> Stand in the street, and call each other names,
> Some true, some false; for so their rage commands?"[31]

[30] *Uncivilized Races of Men,* by Rev. J. G. Wood, Vol. I. p. 213.
[31] *Iliad,* xx. 251–255. And Tennyson speaks of
> "Those detestable
> That let the bantling scald at home, and brawl
> Their rights or wrongs like pot-herbs in the street."
> *The Princess,* 323.

I confess that the recollection of the two women, drifting upon their vocabularies as on a shoreless ocean, filled me at first with apprehension as to the possible future of our legislative assemblies. But, in view of what our own sex accomplishes in the line of mutual vituperation, perhaps the feminine arrangement, by which the two save time by speaking at once, and it is alike impossible for either to hear the other, and for the audience to hear them both, might be considered an improvement.

The automatic flow of thought is often singularly favored by the fact of listening to a weak, continuous discourse, with just enough ideas in it to keep the mind busy on something else. The *induced current* of thought is often rapid and brilliant in the inverse ratio of the force of the inducing current.

The vast amount of blood sent to the brain implies a corresponding amount of material activity in the organ. In point of fact, numerous experiments have shown (and I may refer particularly to those of our own countrymen,—Professors Flint, Hammond, and Lombard) that the brain is the seat of constant nutritive changes, which are greatly increased by mental exertion.

The mechanical co-efficient of mental action may be therefore considered a molecular movement in the nervous centres, attended with waste of material conveyed thither in the form of blood,—not a mere tremor like the quiver of a bell, but a process more like combustion; the blood carrying off the oxidated particles, and bringing in fresh matter to take their place.

This part of the complex process must, of course, enter into the category of the correlated forces. The brain must be fed in order to work; and according to the amount of waste of material will be that of the food required to repair losses. So much logic, so much beef; so much poetry, so much pudding: and, as we all know that all growing things are but sponges soaked full of old sunshine, Apollo becomes as important in the world of letters as ever.[32]

But the intellectual product does not belong to the category of force at all, as defined by physicists. It does not answer their definition as

[32] It is curious to compare the Laputan idea of extracting sunbeams from cucumbers with George Stephenson's famous saying about coal.

"that which is expended in producing or resisting motion." It is not reconvertible into other forms of force. One cannot lift a weight with a logical demonstration, or make a tea-kettle boil by writing an ode to it. A given amount of molecular action in two brains represents a certain equivalent of food, but by no means an equivalent of intellectual product. Bavius and Mævius were very probably as good feeders as Virgil and Horace, and wasted as much brain-tissue in producing their *carmina* as the two great masters wasted in producing theirs. It may be doubted whether the present Laureate of England consumed more oxidable material in the shape of nourishment for every page of "Maud" or of "In Memoriam" than his predecessor Nahum Tate, whose masterpiece gets no better eulogy than that it is "the least miserable of his productions," in eliminating an equal amount of verse.[33]

As mental labor, in distinction from the passive flow of thought, implies an exercise of will, and as mental labor is shown to be attended by an increased waste, the presumption is that this waste is in some degree referable to the material requirements of the act of volition. We see why the latter should be attended by a sense of effort, and followed by a feeling of fatigue.

A question is suggested by the definition of the physicists. What is that which changes the form of force? Electricity leaves what we call magnetism in iron, after passing through it: what name shall we give to that virtue in iron which causes the force we know as electricity thus to manifest itself by a precipitate, so to speak, of new properties? Why may we not speak of a *vis ferrea* as causing the change in consequence of which a bar through which an electrical current has flowed becomes capable of attracting iron and of magnetizing a million other bars? And so why may not a particular brain, through which certain nutritious currents have flowed, fix a force derived from these currents in virtue of a *vis Platonica* or a *vis Baconica,* and thus become a magnet

---

[33] "Sur un même papier, avec la même plume et la même encre, en remuant tant soit peu le bout de la plume en certaine façon, vous tracez des lettres qui font imaginer des combats, des tempêtes, ou des furies à ceux qui les lisent, et qui les rendent indignés ou tristes; au lieu que si vous remuez la plume d'une autre façon presque semblable, la seule différence qui sera en ce peu de mouvement leur peut donner des pensées toutes contraires, comme de paix, de repos, de douceur, et exciter en eux des passions d'amour et de joie."—Descartes, *Principes de Philosophie,* 4ème Partie, § 197.

in the universe of thought, exercising and imparting an influence which is not expended, in addition to that accounted for by the series of molecular changes in the thinking organ?

We must not forget that force-equivalent is one thing, and quality of force-product is quite a different thing. The same outlay of muscular exertion turns the winch of a coffee-mill and of a hand-organ. It has been said that thought cannot be a physical force, because it cannot be measured. An attempt has been made to measure thought as we measure force. I have two tables, one from the "Annales Encyclopédiques," and another, earlier and less minute, by the poet Akenside, in which the poets are classified according to their distinctive qualities; each quality and the total average being marked on a scale of twenty as a maximum. I am not sure that mental qualities are not as susceptible of measurement as the aurora borealis or the changes of the weather. But even measurable *quality* has no more to do with the correlation of forces than the color of a horse with his power of draught; and it is with quality we more especially deal in intellect and morals.

I have spoken of the material or physiological coefficient of thought as being indispensable for its exercise during the only condition of existence of which, apart from any alleged spiritualistic experience, we have any personal knowledge. We know our dependence too well from seeing so many gallant and well-freighted minds towed in helpless after a certain time of service,—razees at sixty, dismantled at seventy, going to pieces and sinking at fourscore. We recognize in ourselves the loss of mental power, slight or serious, from grave or trifling causes. "Good God," said Swift, "what a genius I had when I wrote that book!" And I remember that an ingenious tailor of the neighboring city, on seeing a customer leave his shop without purchasing, exclaimed, smiting his forehead, "If it had not been for this—emphatically characterized—headache, I'd have had a coat on that man before he'd got out over my doorstep." Such is the delicate adjustment of the intellectual apparatus by the aid of which we clothe our neighbor, whether he will or no, with our thoughts if we are writers of books, with our garments if we are artificers of habiliments.

The problem of memory is closely connected with the question of the mechanical relation between thought and structure. How intimate is the alliance of memory with the material condition of the brain, is shown by the effect of age, of disease, of a blow, of intoxication. I have known an aged person repeat the same question five, six, or seven times during the same brief visit. Everybody knows the archbishop's flavor of apoplexy in the memory as in the other mental powers. I was once asked to see to a woman who had just been injured in the street. On coming to herself, "Where am I? what has happened?" she asked. "Knocked down by a horse, ma'am; stunned a little: that is all." A pause, "while one with moderate haste might count a hundred;" and then again, "Where am I? what has happened?"—"Knocked down by a horse, ma'am; stunned a little: that is all." Another pause, and the same question again; and so on during the whole time I was by her. The same tendency to repeat a question indefinitely has been observed in returning members of those worshipping assemblies whose favorite hymn is, "We won't go home till morning."

Is memory, then, a material record? Is the brain, like the rocks of the Sinaitic Valley, written all over with inscriptions left by the long caravans of thought, as they have passed year after year through its mysterious recesses?

When we see a distant railway-train sliding by us in the same line, day after day, we infer the existence of a track which guides it. So, when some dear old friend begins that story we remember so well; switching off at the accustomed point of digression; coming to a dead stop at the puzzling question of chronology; off the track on the matter of its being of first or second cousin of somebody's aunt; set on it again by the patient, listening wife, who knows it all as she knows her well-worn wedding-ring,—how can we doubt that there is a track laid down for the story in some permanent disposition of the thinking-marrow?

I need not say that no microscope can find the tablet inscribed with the names of early loves, the stains left by tears of sorrow or contrition, the rent where the thunderbolt of passion has fallen, or any legible token that such experiences have formed a part of the life of the mortal, the vacant temple of whose thought it is exploring. It is only an inference, aided by an illustration which I will presently offer, that I suggest the possible existence, in the very substance of the brain-tissue, of those inscriptions which Shakespeare must have thought of when he wrote,—

"Pluck from the memory a rooted sorrow;
Raze out the written troubles of the brain."

The objection to the existence of such a material record—that we renew our bodies many scores of times, and yet retain our earliest recollections—is entirely met by the fact, that a scar of any kind holds its own pretty nearly through life in spite of all these same changes, as we have not far to look to find instances.

It must be remembered that a billion of the starry brain-cells could be packed in a cubic inch, and that the convolutions contain one hundred and thirty-four cubic inches, according to the estimate already given. My illustration is derived from microscopic photography. I have a glass slide on which is a minute photographic picture, which is exactly covered when the head of a small pin is laid upon it. In that little speck are clearly to be seen, by a proper magnifying power, the following objects: the Declaration of Independence, with easily-recognized fac-simile autographs of all the signers; the arms of all the original thirteen States; the Capitol at Washington; and very good portraits of all the Presidents of the United States from Washington to Polk. These objects are all distinguishable as a group with a power of fifty diameters: with a power of three hundred, any one of them becomes a sizable picture. You may see, if you will, the majesty of Washington on his noble features, or the will of Jackson in those hard lines of the long face, crowned with that bristling head of hair in a perpetual state of electrical divergence and centrifugal self-assertion. Remember that each of these faces is the record of a life.

Now recollect that there was an interval between the exposure of the negative in the camera and its development by pouring a wash over it, when all these pictured objects existed potentially, but absolutely invisible, and incapable of recognition, in a speck of collodion-film, which a pin's head would cover, and then think what Alexandrian libraries, what Congressional document-loads of positively intelligible characters, —such as one look of the recording angel would bring out; many of which we can ourselves develop at will, or which come before our eyes unbidden, like "Mene, Mene, Tekel, Upharsin,"—might be held in those convolutions of the brain which wrap the talent intrusted to us, too often as the folded napkin of the slothful servant hid the treasure his master had lent him! [34]

Three facts, so familiar that I need only allude to them, show much more is recorded in the memory than we may ever take cognizance of. The first is the conviction of having been in the same precise circumstances once or many times before. Dr. Wigan says, never but once; but such is not my experience. The second is the panorama of their past lives, said, by people rescued from drowning, to have flashed before them.[35] I had it once myself, accompanied by an ignoble ducking and scrambling self-rescue. The third is the revival of apparently obsolete impressions, of which many strange cases are related in nervous young women and in dying persons, and which the story of the dog Argus in the "Odyssey," and of the parrot so charmingly told by Campbell, would lead us to suppose not of rare occurrence in animals.[36] It is pos-

---

[34] "Eas mutationes in sensorio conservatas, *ideas* multi, nos vestigia rerum vocabimus, quæ non in mente sed in ipso corpore, et in medulla quidem cerebri ineffabili modo incredibiliter *minutis notis* et copia infinita inscriptæ sunt."—Haller, quoted by Dr. Laycock, *Brit. and For. Med. Rev.* XIX. 310.

"Different matters are arranged in my head," said Napoleon, "as in drawers. I open one drawer, and close another, as I wish. I have never been kept awake by an involuntary preoccupation of the mind. If I desire repose, I shut up all the drawers, and sleep. I have always slept when I wanted rest, and almost at will."—*Table-Talk and Opinions of Napoleon Buonaparte*, London, 1869, p. 10.

[35] The following story is related as fact. I condense it from the newspaper account. "A. held a bond against B. for several hundred dollars. When it came due, he searched for it, but could not find it. He told the facts to B., who denied having given the bond, and intimated a fraudulent design on the part of A., who was compelled to submit to his loss and the charge against him. Years afterwards, A. was bathing in Charles River, when he was seized with cramp, and nearly drowned. On coming to his senses he went to his bookcase, took out a book, and from between its leaves took the missing bond. In the sudden picture of his entire life, which flashed before him as he was sinking, the act of putting the bond in the book, and the book in the bookcase, had represented itself."

The reader who likes to hear the whole of a story may be pleased to learn that the debt was paid *with interest*.

[36] "A troop of cavalry which had served on the Continent was disbanded in York. Sir Robert Clayton turned out the old horses in Knavesmire to have their run for life. One day, while grazing promiscuously and apart from each other, a storm gathered; and, when the thunder pealed and the lightning flashed, they were seen to get together, and form in line, in almost as perfect order as if they had had their old masters on their backs."—Laycock, *Brit. and For. Med. Rev.* Vol. XIX. 309.

"After the slaughter at Vionville, on the 18th of August (last), a strange and

sible, therefore, and I have tried to show that it is not improbable, that memory is a material record; that the brain is scarred and seamed with infinitesimal hieroglyphics, as the features are engraved with the traces of thought and passion. And, if this is so, must not the record, we ask, perish with the organ? Alas! how often do we see it perish *before* the organ!—the mighty satirist tamed into oblivious imbecility; the great scholar wandering without sense of time or place among his alcoves, taking his books one by one from the shelves, and fondly patting them; a child once more among his toys, but a child whose to-morrows come hungry, and not full-handed,—come as birds of prey in the place of the sweet singers of morning. We must all become as little children if we live long enough; but how blank an existence the wrinkled infant must carry into the kingdom of heaven, if the Power that gave him memory does not repeat the miracle by restoring it!

The connection between thought and the structure and condition of the brain is evidently so close that all we have to do is to study it. It is not in this direction that materialism is to be feared: we do not find Hamlet and Faust, right and wrong, the valor of men and the purity of women, by testing for albumen, or examining fibres in microscopes.

It is in the moral world that materialism has worked the strangest confusion. In various forms, under imposing names and aspects, it has thrust itself into the moral relations, until one hardly knows where to look for any first principles without upsetting everything in searching for them.

The moral universe includes nothing but the exercise of choice: all else is machinery. What we can help and what we cannot help are on two sides of a line which separates the sphere of human responsibility from that of the Being who has arranged and controls the order of things.

The question of the freedom of the will has been an open one, from the days of Milton's demons in conclave to the recent most note-

---

touching spectacle was presented. On the evening-call being sounded by the first regiment of Dragoons of the Guard, six hundred and two riderless horses answered to the summons,—jaded, and in many cases maimed. The noble animals still retained their disciplined habits."—*German Post*, quoted by the *Spectator*.

worthy essay of Mr. Hazard, our Rhode Island neighbor.[37] It still hangs suspended between the seemingly exhaustive strongest motive argument and certain residual convictions. The sense that we are, to a limited extent, self-determining; the sense of effort in willing; the sense of responsibility in view of the future, and the verdict of conscience in review of the past,—all of these are open to the accusation of fallacy; but they all leave a certain undischarged balance in most minds.[38] We can invoke the strong arm of the *Deus ex machina*, as Mr. Hazard, and Kant and others, before him, have done. Our will may be a primary initiating cause or force, as unexplainable, as unreducible, as indecomposable, as impossible if you choose, but as real to our belief, as the *æternitas a parte ante*. The divine foreknowledge is no more in the way of delegated choice than the divine omnipotence is in the way of delegated power. The Infinite can surely slip the cable of the finite if it choose so to do.

It is one thing to prove a proposition like the doctrine of necessity in terms, and another thing to accept it as an article of faith. There are cases in which I would oppose to the *credo quia impossibile est* a paradox as bold and as serviceable,—*nego quia probatum est*. Even Mr. Huxley, who throws quite as much responsibility on protoplasm as it will bear, allows that "our volition counts for something as a condition of the course of events."

I reject, therefore, the mechanical doctrine which makes me the slave of outside influences, whether it work with the logic of Edwards, or the averages of Buckle; whether it come in the shape of the Greek's destiny, or the Mahometan's fatalism; or in that other aspect, dear to the band of believers, whom Beesly of Everton, speaking in the character of John Wesley, characterized as

[37] "Witness on him that any parfit clerk is,
That in scole is gret altercation
In this matere, and gret disputison,
And hath ben, of an hundred thousand men;
But I ne cannot boult it to the bren."
Chaucer, *The Nonne's Preeste's Tale*.

[38] "But, sir, as the doctrine of necessity, no man believes it. If a man should give me arguments that I do not see, though I could not answer them, should I believe that I do not see?"—Boswell's *Life of Johnson*, Vol. VIII. p. 331. London, 1848.

"What have you to do with liberty and necessity? or what more than to hold your tongue about it?"—Johnson to Boswell. *Ibid.* letter 396.

"The crocodile crew that believe in election." [39]

But I claim the right to eliminate all mechanical ideas which have crowded into the sphere of intelligent choice between right and wrong. The pound of flesh I will grant to Nemesis; but, in the name of human nature, not one drop of blood,—not one drop.

Moral chaos began with the idea of transmissible responsibility.[40] It seems the stalest of truisms to say that every moral act, depending as it does on choice, is in its nature exclusively personal; that its penalty, if it have any, is payable, not to bearer, not to order, but only to the creditor himself. To treat a mal-volition, which is inseparably involved with an internal condition, as capable of external transfer from one person to another, is simply to materialize it. When we can take the dimensions of virtue by triangulation; when we can literally weigh Justice in her own scales; when we can speak of the specific gravity of truth, or the square root of honesty; when we can send a statesman his integrity in a package to Washington, if he happen to have left it behind,—then we may begin to speak of the moral character of inherited tendencies, which belong to the machinery for which the

[39] Southey's *Life of Wesley*, Vol. II. note 28.

[40] "Il est sans doute qu'il n'y a rien qui choque plus notre raison que de dir eque le péché du premier homme ait rendu coupables ceux qui, étant si éloignés de cette source, semblent incapables d'y participer. Cet écoulement ne nous parait pas seulement impossible, il nous semble même très injuste; car qu'y-a-t-il de plus contraire au règles de notre misérable justice que de damner éternellement un enfant incapable de volonté, pour un péché où il paraît avoir si peu de part qu'il est commis six mille ans avant qu'il fût en être?"—Pascal, *Pensées*, c. x. § 1.

"Justice" and "mercy" often have a technical meaning when applied to the Supreme Being. Mr. J. S. Mill has expressed himself very freely as to the juggling with words. —*Examination of Sir. W. Hamilton's Philosophy*, I. 131.

The Romanists fear for the future welfare of babes that perish unborn; and the extraordinary means which are taken to avert their impending "punishment" are well known.

Thomas Shepard, our famous Cambridge minister, seems to have shared these apprehensions. See his Letter in *Young's Chronicles of the Pilgrims of Massachusetts*, p. 538. Boston, 1846.

The author of "The Day of Doom" is forced by his logic to hand the infants over to the official tormentor, only assigning them the least uncomfortable of the torture-chambers.

However these doctrines may be softened in the belief of many, the primary barbarism on which they rest—that is, the transfer of mechanical ideas into the world of morals, with which they are in no sense homologous—is almost universally prevalent, and like to be at present.

Sovereign Power alone is responsible. The misfortune of perverse instincts, which adhere to us as congenital inheritances, should go to our side of the account, if the books of heaven are kept, as the great Church of Christendom maintains they are, by double entry. But the absurdity which has been held up to ridicule in the nursery has been enforced as the highest reason upon older children. Did our forefathers tolerate Æsop among them? "I cannot trouble the water where you are," says the lamb to the wolf: "don't you see that I am farther down the stream?" —"But a year ago you called me ill names."—"Oh sir! a year ago I was not born."—"Sirrah," replies the wolf, "if it was not you, it was your father, and that is all one;" and finishes with the usual practical application.

If a created being has no rights which his Creator is bound to respect, there is an end to all moral relations between them. Good Father Abraham thought he had, and did not hesitate to give his opinion. "Far be it from Thee," he says, to do so and so. And Pascal, whose reverence amounted to theophobia,[41] could treat of the duties of the Supreme to the dependent being.[42] If we suffer for anything except our own wrongdoing, to call it punishment is like speaking of a yard of veracity or a square inch of magnanimity.

So to rate the gravity of a mal-volition by its consequences is the merest sensational materialism. A little child takes a prohibited friction-match: it kindles a conflagration with it, which burns down the house, and perishes itself in the flames. Mechanically, this child was an incendiary and a suicide; morally, neither. Shall we hesitate to speak as charitably of multitudes of weak and ignorant grown-up children, moving about on a planet whose air is a deadly poison, which kills all that breathe it four or five scores of years?

Closely allied to this is the pretence that the liabilities incurred by any act of mal-volition are to be measured on the scale of the Infinite, and not on that of the total moral capacity of the finite agent,—a

---

[41] I use this term to designate a state of mind thus described by Jeremy Taylor: "There are some persons so miserable and scrupulous, such perpetual tormenters of themselves with unnecessary fears, that their meat and drink is a snare to their consciences.

"These persons do not believe noble things of God."

[42] "Il y a un devoir réciproque entre Dieu et les hommes. . . . *Quid debui?* 'accusez moi,' dit Dieu dans Isaïe. Dieu doit accomplir ses promesses," etc.—*Pensées,* xxiii. 3.

mechanical application of the Oriental way of dealing with offences. The sheik or sultan chops a man's head off for a look he does not like: it is not the amount of wrong, but the importance of the personage who has been outraged. We have none of those moral relations with power, as such, which the habitual Eastern modes of speech seem to imply.

The next movement in moral materialism is to establish a kind of scale of equivalents between perverse moral choice and physical suffering. Pain often cures *ignorance*, as we know,—as when a child learns not to handle fire by burning its fingers,—but it does not change the moral nature.[43] Children may be whipped into obedience, but not into virtue; and it is not pretended that the penal colony of heaven has sent back a single reformed criminal. We hang men for our convenience or safety; sometimes shoot them for revenge. Thus we come to associate the infliction of injury with offences as their satisfactory settlement,— a kind of neutralization of them, as of an acid with an alkali: so that we feel as if a jarring moral universe would be all right if only suffering enough were added to it. This scheme of chemical equivalents seems to me, I confess, a worse materialism than making protoplasm master of arts and doctor of divinity.

Another mechanical notion is that which treats moral evil as bodily disease has so long been treated,—as being a distinct entity, a demon to be expelled, a load to be got rid of, instead of a condition, or the result of a condition.[44] But what is most singular in the case of moral disease is, that it has been forgotten that it is a living creature in which it occurs, and that all living creatures are the subjects of natural and spontaneous healing processes. A broken vase cannot mend itself; but a broken bone can. Nature, that is, the Divinity, in his every-day working methods, will soon make it as strong as ever.

Suppose the beneficent self-healing process to have repaired the wound in the moral nature: is it never to become an honest scar, but always liable to be reopened? Is there no outlawry of an obsolete

[43] "No troubles will, of themselves, work a change in a wicked heart."—Matthew Henry, *Com. on Luke*, xxiii. 29.

[44] "The strength of modern therapeutics lies in the clearer perception, than formerly, of the great truth, that diseases are but perverted life-processes, and have for their natural history, not only a beginning, but equally a period of culmination and decline."—*Medicine in Modern Times. Dr. Gull's Address*, p. 187.

self-determination? If the President of the Society for the Prevention of Cruelty to Animals impaled a fly on a pin when he was ten years old, is it to stand against him, crying for a stake through his body, *in sæcula sæculorum?* [45] The most popular hymn of Protestantism, and the "Dies Iræ" of Romanism, are based on this assumption: *Nil inultum remanebit.* So it is that a condition of conscious being has been materialized into a purely inorganic brute fact,—not merely dehumanized, but deanimalized and devitalized.

Here it was that Swedenborg, whose whole secret I will not pretend to have fully opened, though I have tried with the key of a thinker whom I love and honor,—that Swedenborg, I say, seems to have come in, if not with a new revelation, at least infusing new life into the earlier ones. *What we are* will determine the company we are to keep, and not the avoirdupois weight of our moral exuviæ, strapped on our shoulders like a porter's burden.

Having once materialized the whole province of self-determination and its consequences, the next thing is, of course, to materialize the methods of avoiding these consequences. We are all, more or less, idolaters, and believers in quackery. We love specifics better than regimen, and observances better than self-government. The moment our belief divorces itself from character, the mechanical element begins to gain upon it, and tends to its logical conclusion in the Japanese prayer-mill.[46]

Brothers of the Phi Beta Kappa Society, my slight task is finished. I

---

[45] There is no more significant evidence of natural moral evolution than the way in which children outgrow the cruelty which is so common in what we call their *tender* years.

> "As ruthless as a baby with a worm;
> As cruel as a schoolboy ere he grows
> To pity,—more from ignorance than will."
> Tennyson, *Walking to the Mail.*

[46] One can easily conceive the confusion which might be wrought in young minds by such teaching as this of our excellent Thomas Shepard:—

"The Paths to Hell be but two: the first is the Path of Sin, which is a dirty Way; Secondly, the Path of Duties, which (rested in) is but a cleaner Way."—Quoted by Israel Loring, Pastor of the West Church in Sudbury, in *A Practical Discourse*, etc. Boston: Kneeland & Green, 1749.

However sound the doctrine, it is sure to lead to the substitution of some easy mechanical contrivance,—some rite, penance, or formula,—for perpetual and ever-renewed acts of moral self-determination.

have always regarded these occasions as giving an opportunity of furnishing hints for future study, rather than of exhibiting the detailed results of thought. I cannot but hope that I have thrown some ray of suggestion, or brought out some clink of questionable soundness, which will justify me for appearing with the lantern and the hammer.

The hardest and most painful task of the student of to-day is to occidentalize and modernize the Asiatic modes of thought which have come down to us closely wedded to mediæval interpretations. We are called upon to assert the rights and dignity of our humanity, if it were only that our worship might be worthy the acceptance of a wise and magnanimous Sovereign. Self-abasement is the proper sign of homage to superiors with the Oriental. The Occidental demands self-respect in his inferiors as a condition of accepting their tribute to him as of any value. The *kotou* in all its forms, the pitiful acts of *creeping, crawling, fawning, like a dog at his master's feet* (which acts are signified by the word we translate *worship*, according to the learned editor of "The Comprehensive Commentary"),[47] are offensive, not gratifying to him. Does not the man of science who accepts with true manly reverence the facts of Nature, in the face of all his venerated traditions, offer a more acceptable service than he who repeats the formulæ, and copies the gestures, derived from the language and customs of despots and their subjects? The attitude of modern Science is erect, her aspect serene, her determination inexorable, her onward movement unflinching; because she believes herself, in the order of Providence, the true successor of the men of old who brought down the light of heaven to men. She has reclaimed astronomy and cosmogony, and is already laying a firm hand on anthropology, over which another battle must be fought, with the usual result, to come sooner or later. Humility may be taken for granted as existing in every sane human being; but it may be that it most truly manifests itself to-day in the readiness with which we bow to new truths as they come from the scholars, the teachers, to whom the inspiration of the Almighty giveth understanding. If a man should try to show it in the way good men did of old,—by covering himself with tow-cloth, sitting on an ash-heap, and disfiguring his person,—we should send him straightway to

[47] See note on Matthew xi. 11.

Worcester or Somerville; and if he began to "rend his garments" it would suggest the need of a strait-jacket.

Our rocky New England and old rocky Judæa always seem to have a kind of yearning for each other: Jerusalem governs Massachusetts, and Massachusetts would like to colonize Jerusalem.

> "The pine-tree dreameth of the palm,
> The palm-tree of the pine."

But political freedom inevitably generates a new type of religious character, as the conclave that contemplates endowing a dotard with infallibility has found out, we trust, before this time.[48] The American of to-day may challenge for himself the noble frankness in his highest relations which did honor to the courage of the Father of the Faithful.

And he may well ask, in view of the slavish beliefs which have governed so large a part of Christendom, whether it was an ascent or a descent from the Roman's

> *Si fractus illabatur orbis*
> *Impavidum ferient ruinæ*

to the monk's

> *Quid sum miser tunc facturus,*
> *Quem patronum rogaturus?*

Who can help asking such questions as he sits in the light of those blazing windows of the ritual *renaissance*, burning with hectic colors like the leaves of the decaying forest before the wind has swept it bare, and listens to the delicious strains of the quartet as it carols forth its smiling devotions?

Our dwellings are built on the shell-heaps, the kitchen-middens of the age of stone. Inherited beliefs, as obscure in their origin as the parentage of the cave-dwellers, are stronger with many minds than the evidence of the senses and the simplest deductions of the intelligence. Persons outside of Bedlam can talk of the "dreadful depravity of lunatics,"—the sufferers whom we have learned to treat with the tenderest care, as the most to be pitied of all God's children.[49] Mr. Gosse can believe that a fossil skeleton, with the remains of food in its

[48] We have since discovered that the dogma was a foregone conclusion.
[49] *Brit. and Foreign Med. Review* for July, 1841; Wigan, *op. cit.*

interior, was never part of a living creature, but was made just as we find it,[50]—a kind of stage-property, a clever cheat, got up by the great Manager of the original Globe Theatre. All we can say of such persons is, that their "illative sense," to use Dr. Newman's phrase, seems to most of us abnormal and unhealthy. We cannot help looking at them as affected with a kind of mental Daltonism.

"Believing ignorance," said an old Scotch divine, "is much better than rash and presumptuous knowledge." [51] But which is most likely to be presumptuous, ignorance, or knowledge? True faith and true philosophy ought to be one; and those disputes,—*à double vérité*,—those statements, "true according to philosophy, and false according to faith," condemned by the last Council of Lateran,[52] ought not to find a place in the records of an age like our own. Yet so enlightened a philosopher as Faraday could say in a letter to one of his correspondents, "I claim an absolute distinction between a religious and an ordinary belief. If I am reproached for weakness in refusing to apply those mental operations, which I think good in high things, to the very highest, I am content to bear the reproach."

We must bestir ourselves; for the new generation is upon us,—the marrow-bone-splitting descendants of the old cannibal troglodytes. Civilized as well as savage races live upon their parents and grandparents. Each generation strangles and devours its predecessor. The young Feejeean carries a cord in his girdle for his father's neck; the young American, a string of propositions or syllogisms in his brain to finish the same relative. The old man says, "Son, I have swallowed and digested the wisdom of the past." The young man says, "Sire, I proceed to swallow and digest thee with all thou knowest." There never was a sandglass, nor a clepsydra, nor a horologe, that counted the hours and days and years with such terrible significance as this academic chronograph which has just completed a revolution. The prologue of life is finished here at twenty: then come five acts of a decade each, and the play is over, with now and then a pleasant or a tedious afterpiece, when half the lights are put out, and half the orchestra is gone. . . .

---

[50] Owen, in *Encyc. Brit.* 8th edition, art. "Paleontology," p. 124, note.
[51] Buckle, *Hist. of Civilization*, II. 327, note.
[52] Leibnitz, *Consid. sur la Doctrine d'un Esprit Universel.*

16

NOAH PORTER

1811, born December 14, Farmington, Conn.
1831, was graduated from Yale
1831–33, rector of Hopkins Grammar School, New Haven
1833–35, tutor at Yale; student in Yale Divinity School
1836–43, pastor of church in New Milford, Conn.
1843–46, pastor of church in Springfield, Mass.
1846–71, Clark professor of moral philosophy and metaphysics at Yale
1853–54, travel abroad; study at University of Berlin
1868, *The Human Intellect*
1870, *The American Colleges and the American Public*
1871–86, president of Yale
1871, *The Sciences of Nature vs. the Science of Man*
1879–80, conflict with William Graham Sumner over use of Spencer's *Sociology*
    as a text
1880, *The Christian College, an Address*
1882, *Science and Sentiment*, collected papers
1885, *The Elements of Moral Science*
1886, *Kant's Ethics, a Critical Study*
1886, received degree of D.D. (honorary), Edinburgh
1892, died March 4

THE very next year after Oliver Wendell Holmes, Sr., had made his plea for a more mechanistic approach to the study of thought as a function of the brain, Noah Porter faced the Phi Beta Kappa Society of Harvard University with the assertion that the physical sciences could establish conclusions only on the basis of a more careful study of the nature of man, and especially of his knowing process. While Porter incidentally attacked the physiological psychologists, this was not the main point of his speech. To understand what was, it is necessary to learn a little bit about his life.

When he made this address, he was facing his sixtieth birthday and was about to enter on a fifteen-year tenure of the presidency of Yale. While he was a student at the Yale Divinity School, more than thirty-five years earlier, he became an adherent of the modified Calvinistic system of Nathaniel W. Taylor; Porter accepted this system throughout the rest of his life. Taylor's view, which was generally known as orthodox, presented a pattern of minimum essentials of belief for a Presbyterian.

After some years as a Congregational minister and as Clark professor of moral philosophy and metaphysics at Yale, Porter spent two years abroad, chiefly in the study of philosophy at the University of Berlin, where he came under the influence of Adolf Trendelenburg. This German influence was reinforced by his earlier close study of the works of Samuel Taylor Coleridge. Porter thus emerged from his long training as an orthodox Calvinist, whose fundamental background in Scottish thought was overlaid by an extensive familiarity with German transcendentalism.

From his German studies, too, Porter developed a conviction of the value of the historical study of philosophy, an approach which had not been prominent in the American colleges prior to his time. This is revealed in his address of 1871, but it is even more evident in *The Human Intellect,* which he published in 1868 and is one of the more important American texts. After an introductory essay on "Psychology and the Soul," designed to prove that a science of the human "soul" is possible, Porter enters on an elaborate historical, critical, and expository presentation of the faculty · psychology, of sensation, representation, thought, intuition, and ends in a partially knowable Absolute, which is a thinking agent and must be assumed to explain thought and science. "We are compelled to conclude our analysis of the human intellect with the assertion, that its various powers and processes suppose and assume that there is an uncreated thinker, whose thoughts can be interpreted by the human intellect which is made in His image."

Out of this background of study and of writing Porter spoke on "The Sciences of Nature *versus* the Science of Man" and made a plea for a developed science of man. Despite his title, he did not consider natural science and the science of man as opposed. His title was meant to be descriptive of the type of positivistic thinking represented by Comte and Mill, by physiological psychologists such as Bain, and by the evolutionary eclecticism of Herbert Spencer. All these philosophers and many scientists elaborated supposedly nonmetaphysical systems of knowledge, and all alike, in Porter's account, failed to realize that man is the knowing agent and thereby failed to ground their sciences of nature in the science of man. It must be remembered that "*nature* furnishes the materials, and *man* arranges them; more exactly, the observing man *collects* facts, and the reflecting man *explains* facts. . . . If we are sufficiently curious to ask what science is, every answer which we give must carry us back to man as an agent who thinks natural facts into scientific theories, who explains phenomena by laws, and founds systems on principles."

Science maintains broadly that it is inductive; that is to say, the facts of observation are connected by relations under more and more general laws. "But facts or phenomena do not connect themselves." An agent, "the inter-

preting mind," is required. The relationships "are at once the conditions of
thought to man, because they are the conditions of being in nature and God
as the wit of common sense and the research of the profoundest philosophy
declare." Other possible interpretations are eliminated by criticism. The
interpreter makes chaos into cosmos by utilizing his "underlying faiths" about
nature and God. An inductive science can only claim support from men by
justifying its method by appeal to these underlying faiths. In Porter's briefest
statement, "an inductive science of nature presupposes a science of induction,
and a science of induction presupposes a science of man."

This science of man cannot be unscientific. The student "will exact from
others, and impose upon himself, severe requirements in respect of clear
definition, rigorous logic, well-grounded analogies, and coherent arrangement." He will apply the methods of physics to the study of man and thus
prevent "the recurrence of that metaphysical romancing," which has dishonored the science of man. This science is not to be limited to psychology,
but is to include the study of the humanities. With this we come to Porter,
the college president, who, in 1870, had written a book called *The American
Colleges and the American Public*. This book opposed almost all the trends
which were then modern; the drift towards the teaching of science and
away from the "arts," elective courses, and the secular conception of college
education. In this light his Phi Beta Kappa address is seen as a piece of special
pleading for the stand-pat college course, by a speaker shrewd enough to
use a weakness in the case for science as a crevice into which to drive his
wedge—the science of man as a precondition of the sciences of nature at
the narrow end, the humanities in the middle, and at the conclusion of the
address the broad end of the wedge, the study of divinity.

THE SCIENCES OF NATURE VERSUS
THE SCIENCE OF MAN

A PLEA FOR THE SCIENCE OF MAN

"I walked on, musing with myself
. . . whether, after all,
A larger metaphysics might not help
Our physics."

MRS. E. B. BROWNING.

NOT many days ago, as I strayed into the study of an eminent
physicist, I observed hanging against the wall, framed like a
choice engraving, several dingy, ribbon-like strips of I knew not what,
arranged in parallel rows. My curiosity was at once aroused. What

were they? and why were they so carefully protected and so greatly honored by my realistic friend? They might be shreds of mummy-wraps, or bits of friable bark-cloth from the Pacific, and therefore needing to be guarded under glass; or perhaps, indeed, they were remnants from a grandmother's wedding-dress; or shoe-ties, out of which all color had faded, leaving a faint shimmer of satin finish on the water-stained surface. They were none of these; to have suggested any of which might have been resented by the grave philosopher, who solidly explained that they were carefully prepared photographs of portions of the solar spectrum.

I stood and mused, absorbed in the varying yet significant intensities of light and shade, bordered by mystic letters and symbolic numbers. As I mused, the pale legend began to glow with life. Every line became luminous with meaning. Every shadow was suffused with light shining from behind, suggesting some mighty achievement of knowledge,— of knowledge growing more daring in proportion to the remoteness of the object known,—of knowledge becoming more positive in its answers as the questions which were asked seemed unanswerable. No Runic legend, no Babylonish arrow-head, no Egyptian hieroglyph, no Moabite stone, could present a history like this, could suggest thoughts of such weighty import, or so stimulate and exalt the imagination.

Over against these symbolic bands—records of light by means of the light, and glowing with light to the soul—hung the portrait of Newton, with its wondrous forehead and eagle glance. I turned from the spectrum to the portrait, and from the portrait to the spectrum, still musing as I turned. Newton's daring suggestion,[1] that the force familiarly recognized on the earth might prevail as far as the moon, and possibly extend to the sun,—coming like inspiration, but held in abeyance for years, till careful and long-delayed measurements made it spring into an acknowledged fact,—this came to mind as it had never done before; with it the successive experiments of Newton upon the

---

[1] "As he sat alone in a garden [1666] he fell into a speculation on the power of gravity; that as this power is not found sensibly diminished at the remotest distance from the centre of the earth to which we can rise, neither at the tops of the loftiest buildings, nor even on the summits of the highest mountains, it appeared to him reasonable to conclude that this power must extend much farther than was usually thought. Why not as high as the moon? said he to himself; and, if so, her motion must be influenced by it: perhaps she is retained in her orbit thereby."—WHEWELL: *History of the Inductive Sciences*, Vol. I, bk. vii. chap. ii. § 3.

light,—his expansion of the colorless beam into the gay and many-colored spectrum, suggesting theories of rays and undulations and mystic powers in the several colors. There followed the thought of Wollaston and Young and of Fraunhofer, and his discovery of the lines that were afterwards to be interpreted as a mystic language from the far-off worlds. But, first, chemistry must come into being, to evolve the gases, and decompose the solids, that it might use the refracted light to determine the elements of whatever is consumed in the light-giving flame. Each one of these steps of progress involved bold invention and exact observation. But each was necessary to this latest, proudest achievement of our times, by which the scientist has connected the sun and the earth by the closest affinities, and learned not only to interpret the structure of the orb which for centuries had smitten with blindness the eye that had ventured to gaze familiarly upon its face, but even to resolve the nebulæ themselves into luminous gases.

I exclaimed in thought, "Would that Newton were now living, and could look with our open vision upon the blinding sun, the glowing stars, and the burning nebulæ!—those objects which Science first made so remote, and now brings so near, between which and the eye she first interposed such abysms of distance as appall the imagination, and at last made them so familiar and so near, that we now inspect the sodium or the hydrogen that burns in the lamp upon our table, with the same look with which we watch the sodium and the hydrogen that have been consuming for ages in the sun or the stars. Of all the kings and prophets of science, surely Newton would most have desired to see the things which we see, and to hear the things which we hear. Would, indeed, that he could live again, and witness the completion of the work which he so nobly began!"

I awake from my musing; and, abjuring any scepticism which I may have cherished, I confess my faith in modern science. Though hard-hearted as any metaphysician ought to be, I prostrate myself before her shrine; nay, so ardent is my neophytic zeal, that I am tempted to glorify the photographic spectrum into a fetich. Indeed, had I nothing else to reverence, I could easily worship this.

I return to my studies a wiser, perhaps a sadder, man. To refresh and assure my bewildered spirit, I think of Socrates. Turning to the "Memorabilia" of Xenophon, I find I was not mistaken in my memory;

for it is there set down to the credit of the philosopher, that "he never discoursed concerning the nature of all things,—how that which the sophists call the universe, ὁ κοσμός, is constituted, under what laws the heavenly bodies exist, etc., but invariably represented those who concerned themselves with inquiries of this sort as playing the fool. First of all, he inquired whether such persons thought they had so far mastered the facts which relate to man, as to be justified in proceeding to such investigations, or whether they considered it in order to leave human inquiries for physical researches." [2] Thus records Xenophon concerning Socrates. Poor deluded son of Sophroniscus! For such sentiments, the present times would be more against thee than were thine own, hard as they were. Even the defence of atheism would not have saved thee against so enormous a heresy respecting the sciences of nature. Had a society of modern scientists sat in judgment upon thee, they for once would have been unanimous, and voted thee worthy of death. Certainly thou wouldst have found a smaller minority than thou hadst in ancient Athens, in any modern scientific association, whether it were a society for mutual admiration or for reciprocal altercation. For is it not now an exploded idea that man, or what concerns him, is better worth regarding than what was called nature by the sophists in the time of Socrates? Is not man himself now in danger of being eliminated out of the Kosmos? And as to holding that man has any great significance in the universe, has not the doctrine become fixed, that Science has to do only with phenomena, i.e., with material phenomena and their relations? Has not man been satisfactorily resolved into nerve-substance and vibrating force, and thus brought under the laws of mechanism? And has it not come to unconscious speech, without even the suggestion of unconscious irony, that this is the only way in which man can be scientifically studied, even though by this process he is scientifically and summarily disposed of? Is it not now near being demonstrated that man, as body and spirit, as conscience and speech, has been evolved from lower forms of being, with all his furnishings of aspirations, categories, and principles? and is it not also a matter of grave question, whether he can long remain in his present transition state,—whether, having been evolved from some very indeterminate germ, he may not be sublimated into something

[2] Xenophon, *Memorabilia*, lib. I. cap. i. 11–16.

altogether attenuated and impalpable? In short, is not man ranked very low in the present estimates of comparative science, and is he not in danger of being very soon left out of them altogether?

Somewhat after this fashion ran our meditations respecting nature and man, according to which the two are brought into sharp antagonism as objects of certain and trustworthy knowledge, and as claiming attention from the modern philosopher and educator. Already, in the departments of study and of education, an active controversy has sprung up which threatens to bring on a sharp litigation, in which the parties are to be the Sciences of Nature and the Science of Man. At present, the odds are largely against man, and we fear that soon it may be claimed that man has no rights which the student of nature is bound to respect; in short, that, if Science requires it, man must go to the wall. There is no telling how soon he may be summoned to allow himself quietly to be shoved out of being under the operation of natural selection, or to be sublimated into some sort of impalpable incense upon the altar of scientific progress.

Under these unequal odds I bring to this ancient and honorable philosophical society—a society which originated when philosophy had another meaning than is claimed for it at present—a plea for the science of man; not as against the sciences of nature, to whose claims I have already confessed my allegiance, but as essential to these sciences, and as, therefore, incapable of being ever superseded, or set aside, or left behind, in their most splendid achievements. I would even be so audacious as to seek to show, that, in all these, man must be a constant quantity, and that the elements which he furnishes can never be dispensed with; that, as the sciences of nature make progress, these elements will come more and more distinctly into recognition; that, as nature is more profoundly studied, the results of this study will bring man's capacities and endowments more distinctly into view. I would demonstrate that man must be thoroughly understood and nobly confided in, if nature is to be interpreted in its widest relations, and our confidence in the principles and laws which are essential to the science of nature is to be surely established. I offer this plea, not in the interests of strife, but in the interests of peace; not to gain a one-sided victory, but to show that no action can hold between the two parties, because the sciences of nature and of man can never be at variance. I would also show, that as there can be no science of nature which does not recognize the science of man, and as the study of nature cannot be prosecuted to the neglect of man, so the study of man will be always furthered by a generous study of nature; that as, on the broader field of investigation and culture, so on the narrower field of education and discipline, the scientific study of nature and the scientific study of man are mutually dependent and mutually helpful.

We enforce our argument, first of all, by an *analysis of the conception of science*. What science is, is not so easily stated as would seem likely from the freedom with which the term is used, or the readiness, not to say the flippancy, with which its authority is enforced. The most cautious scientist would doubtless concede that *nature* furnishes the materials, and *man* arranges them; more exactly, the observing man *collects* facts, and the reflecting man *explains* facts. We speak freely of the careless glance of the one and the sagacious insight of the other. We talk of the *secrets* which Nature has been carefully hiding for generations, and has been reluctantly forced to yield at the bidding of one who had overheard the charmed words at which the doors of her treasure-house must fly open. If we are sufficiently curious to ask what science is, every answer which we give must carry us back to man as an agent who thinks natural facts into scientific theories, who explains phenomena by laws, and founds systems on principles. This question, it is true, may be curious rather than useful. It were too much to expect that Newton should pause in the tremulous suggestion that first connected the detention of the revolving moon with the force that brings down the falling stone, in order to ask whence the suggestion was inspired, and how it could be justified; or that the ardent Davy should have held back from the brave experiment that literally unearthed the bounding potassium, in order to perfect a metaphysical analysis of the processes which discovered, or the reasons which foretold it; [3] or that Kirchhoff should have been diverted from the daring

---

[3] For the details of this discovery and experiment, see *Life of Sir Humphry Davy*, chap. III. We quote the following: "I have been told by Mr. Edmund Davy, his relative and then assistant . . . that when he [Sir Humphry] saw the minute globules of potassium burst through the crust of potash, and take fire as they entered the atmosphere, he could not contain his joy, he actually bounded about the room in ecstatic delight; and that some little time was required for him to compose himself sufficiently to continue the experiments."

gaze by which he would read the secret of the sun, in order to interpret the thoughts which emboldened him to the effort. But how is it after a discovery has been made, or a great secret of nature has been mastered? Then not only curiosity turns from the result to the process by which it has been achieved, but the anxiety to make sure that the jewel wrested from nature has been lawfully obtained, and may be safely held, impels to the earnest inquiry whether the charm by which we won it was whispered us in our ear by the honest spirit of nature, or by some mischief-loving imp of the mocking fantasy. So it happens long after Newton's discovery has become a commonplace to the schoolboy, and Davy's experiment is repeated every day by the shop-lad, and the revelations of the spectrum analysis have enabled the novice glibly to discourse of the secrets of the sun, that the true and earnest philosopher is impelled carefully to retrace the path which has conducted Science to the dizzy heights on which she stands, and tremblingly inquires, How came I hither? Is the standing-ground firm? Are the objects which I seem to see the firm and solid land, or only a delusive mirage?

Now, if we ask these questions, we must answer them; and if we answer them, so far as we can see, we must study the nature of man. We cannot justify the processes by which we interpret nature, unless we scrutinize the processes of the human spirit which performs them, and search after the principles and faiths which these processes assume and rest upon. We cannot discover and vindicate the grounds on which our inquiries rest, without finding them embedded in man's being as axioms and principles, which, as the result of further scrutiny, we find that he can neither question nor set aside. In other words, the foundations of the science of nature in the last analysis are discovered in the ineradicable beliefs and convictions of the human spirit; and it is only by the earnest and careful study of this spirit that we can find them, and, having found them, can recognize them as the principles by which we interpret both nature and man.

Were we to proceed farther in the analysis of science, we should add, that science objectively viewed is universally conceived as *related knowledge*. Those who limit it most narrowly, assert that it gives us phenomena connected by relations. But facts or phenomena do not connect themselves. To conceive that they do or can, were to fall into the worst and emptiest trick of personifying an abstraction, against which this class of philosophers are, as they should be, the most earnest in their cautions. They require an agent to do this work, and to do it, not after the caprices of an infant's or an idiot's handling, but by wise and intelligent combinations. Whence do these relations, these mystic bonds of science, proceed? The interpreting mind does, in some sense, find them already in its hands. Whether they are evolved from its own experience, as the progressive acquisitions of association which cannot be broken, or perhaps hardened in the brain under physiological laws, as Mill, Bain, and Spencer would teach us; whether, like a mystic veil, they are thrown over the otherwise chaotic phenomena of both matter and spirit by the formative energy of man, as Kant confidently suggests; or whether they are at once the conditions of thought to man, because they are the conditions of being in nature and God, as the wit of common sense and the research of the profoundest philosophy declare,—these relations must, in the study of nature, be confidingly applied by man as fast and as far as the chaos which bewilders the infant, and overawes the savage, is thought into a kosmos by man's interpreting reason. If the inductive sciences claim allegiance from the common sense of mankind, the inductive method must be justified to its critical, and even to its sceptical analysis. But the inductive method can in no way be thus justified, except as the intellect falls back upon its own underlying faiths concerning God and nature. Briefly, *an inductive science of nature presupposes a science of induction, and a science of induction presupposes a science of man.*

We urge, still further, that the *history of the sciences of nature* illustrates their near relation to the science of man. Before Socrates, the physics were as crude as the metaphysics. Both alike were raw guesswork, founded on hasty resemblances more rudely interpreted and generalized. From such speculations about matter and spirit Socrates wisely withdrew his thoughts, that he might first understand himself as nearer and more intelligible to himself than nature. But, in learning how to study himself, he also learned the secret of knowing other things. If we may trust the brief expositions of Xenophon and the embellished dialogues of Plato, he learned the rules of cautious observation, wise definition, and comprehensive comparison, and rigidly enforced them as the conditions of all trustworthy knowledge. The

Socratic method was first applied by him to man and what concerns man. But the disciples of Socrates, having learned the secret of wise observation, could not but forthwith apply it to nature; and out of this Socratic school came the ambitious cosmogony of Plato, the perfected logic, and the sober, and, in many respects, solid physics of Aristotle, with the beginnings of that geometry which soon was so nearly perfected as not to be disdained by Newton and Laplace,—the geometry which the modern schools that are most jealous of the study of man, rightly and earnestly insist on as the only condition of science, writing over their portals, as Plato did, "*Let no one enter here who cannot geometrize.*"

As we trace the beginnings of modern physics, we find that the true method of interpreting nature was sought for by Bacon and Descartes in the nature of man, by the first impliedly and yet abundantly, by the second confessedly and formally. The present century, so distinguished for the achievements of physics, numbers not a few among the most successful students of nature whose attention has been given to the scrutiny of the methods of Science itself. We name Davy, Herschel, Whewell, Agassiz, Faraday, and Tyndall—all of whom have judged the science of induction to be the most fundamental, the most wide-reaching and fascinating, of sciences. Not a few, like Davy, have combined poetic and metaphysical tastes with a genius for physics. We may say almost universally, that men great in discovery, and profound in philosophic research, have always been forward to recognize that man must furnish the key to the mysteries of nature; he himself being the greatest mystery of all. There have been many so-called physicists who were content to find or take their formulæ and principles at second-hand, and work them out in problems and experiments,—many who have hastily borrowed or stolen them from some crude and effete metaphysics; but never was there a philosopher of nature who looked for a theory of his science, who did not believe in a science of man.

Our position is still further confirmed by the defects, in this regard, of some of *the recent philosophies* which are now attracting general attention. These philosophies have these features, in common: they all claim to be constructed in the spirit of the inductive method, and after the analogies of modern physics, and to be justified by actual experiment. But they all can be shown to be seriously defective, for the reason that their science of man is too narrow or erroneous to furnish a solid basis for any science of nature whatever.

We begin with the philosophy which is now in the mouth of every man, the so-called *Positive Philosophy;* and, to be both discriminating and just, we will first notice it in that form in which it was taught by its original expounder. The fundamental doctrines of Comte, and the characteristics of the positive philosophy, are thus summed up by Mill: "We have no knowledge of any thing but phenomena (and our knowledge of phenomena is relative, not absolute). We know not the essence nor the real mode of production of any fact, but only its relations to other facts in the way of succession or of similitude. These relations are constant, that is, always the same in the same circumstances. The constant resemblances which link phenomena together, and the constant sequences which unite them as antecedent and consequent, are termed their laws. The laws of phenomena are all we know respecting them. Their essential nature and their ultimate causes, either efficient or final, are unknown and inscrutable to us." [4] Of this positive philosophy, as thus expounded, we observe that it is properly, if not emphatically, metaphysical. Against this charge, Comte would earnestly protest in the words, "Have I not demonstrated, by a broad and decisive induction, that the human mind must have passed through the stages of theology and ·metaphysics before it could reach the apotheosis of positivism? If this induction is good, I cannot be remanded to the condition which I have already outgrown." We do not care to question whether this historic induction of Comte is correct, concerning which his own adherents hold diverse opinions; nor do we urge that he has no right, according to his fundamental principles, to make any *historic* induction at all: we simply assert the fact that the positive philosophy is a metaphysical phenomenon. To urge that it cannot be, because it does not occur in the right order of time, is to urge that a patient cannot have scarlet-fever or the measles, because the same patient, according to the theory of these diseases, can have neither a second time. It is, to apply the *à priori* method, to set aside a *positive* phenomenon or fact.

[4] J. S. Mill, *The Positive Philosophy of Comte*, pp. 7 and 8. Am. ed.

That the positive philosophy is metaphysical, in the proper sense of the term, is too obvious to admit of question. Its *problem* is metaphysical. It proposes not only to discover the criteria of the processes which are common to all the special sciences, but it sets these forth as the criteria of every true science. Its *method* is metaphysical in so far as it passes each of these sciences in review, and re-applies these principles to each for its subsequent reconstruction and correction. Like every other metaphysical system, it concerns itself with *relations*. But constant relations are what, in all systems, exalt observed phenomena to the dignity of science. Other systems recognize more relations,—those of causation or force, mayhap those of design. Comte's metaphysics hold to fewer,—those of sequence and similitude. To use a figure of clothing, while other systems honor, by recognition and use, the habiliments which obvious necessity and universal usage have sanctioned, this sect appear among the *sans culottes* of philosophers, on the principle, that, the fewer clothes we have, the nearer we come to naked truth, and the less occasion we have to look after our clothes, or the less we are tempted to think more of the clothes than of the man.

Mill, indeed, while he concedes (p. 8) that Comte, without knowing it, accepted and sought to solve the problem of metaphysics, contends that he rightly defined and avoided metaphysics in the technical sense of the habit of "conceiving of mental abstractions as real entities, which could exert power, and produce phenomena," etc. That this tendency to hypostasize abstractions into real agencies has prevailed in all ages, we admit; that Comte and Comte's disciples have not escaped its influence, it would be easy to show. No class of reasoners seem to exemplify it more eminently. Every question which you ask them, beyond the charmed circle of the formulæ which the master magician has drawn around them with wand and charm, is answered by the stereotype phrases of sequence and similitude, till it would seem as though these relations had become personified into those living forces on which the universe depends for its existence and ordering.

But all this is by the way: the only charge which we care at present to urge against Comte is, that he does not recognize the presence and the agency of man; that he attempts to furnish a philosophy of science which leaves entirely out of view the prime element in science,—the nature of knowledge as explained by the nature of men as qualified to know. Man is not recognized by Comte [5] as such a being at all, but only as a mass of nervous substance, incased in a material shell, the functions of which, so far as they are deemed worthy of notice, are simply physiological, with the added capacity to expand or modify the incasing skull. Even the poor compliment is not formally paid to this nervous substance of being able to respond to the relations of sequence and similitude in material phenomena. Much less is it honestly conceded, as Comte's own system would require, that this mass has the additional power to observe the relations of constant sequence and similitude between its own material condition and any one of these acts of response or observation. All this is overlooked, and superficially huddled away into the general statement, that what are called psychological processes are properly included under biological phenomena; and this by the man who claims for the functions of his own brain the magic power to discover the follies of all the preceding philosophies, and to prevent all error in succeeding ages! Man, as treated by Comte, is not even cavalierly bowed out from the ivory gate of this palace of magnificent pretensions, but the door is contemptuously and violently thrust in his face; and then, inasmuch as there can be no science and no philosophy of science in which the presence of man must not somehow be implied, he is smuggled in by the meanest of the servants through the narrowest postern that could easily be devised.

Much may be truly said in praise of Comte and the positive philosophy. The daring of his problem, his exact and manifold knowledge of the special sciences, the breadth of his generalizations (especially in mathematics and physics), the cool severity of his stony-eyed criticism,—all these deserve the highest commendation. But the *naïve* and narrow simplicity, which, in a philosophy of knowledge, leaves out of sight man, or the knowing agent, and the unconscious innocence of his metaphysical abnegation of metaphysics, should claim no man's admiration. The student of nature or of history who is content with a formula to work by, may be satisfied with the positive philosophy; but any one who looks for a well-rounded theory of all human knowledge, and a comprehensive statement of the axioms and the principles which

[5] *The Positive Philosophy of Auguste Comte*, translated by Harriet Martineau, Bk. V. chap. VII.

it involves, cannot but be disappointed with Comte's teachings, and reject him as a trustworthy expounder of philosophy.

John Stuart Mill, the follower, yet critic, of Comte, has distinctly recognized some of his defects, and has attempted to supply them. But he has failed in *four* essential particulars. He has neither given a satisfactory theory of the mind nor of matter, nor of the process, nor of the axioms, of induction itself. Though he contends most stoutly for the legitimacy of psychological observation, and the necessity of a correct theory of the soul as fundamental to induction, he provides no such theory: as how could he, if he limits this science, after the dictum of his master, to phenomena and the relations of sequence and similitude? The knowing agent that must not only build up science, but provide its foundation principles, Mill resolves into successive states of consciousness: he even calls these feelings, which are wrought by we know not what. He defines the agent that believes in the spectroscope, and is not dazed by the sun, "as a series of feelings with a background of possibilities of feeling." [6] We do not stay to inquire what the word "background" can mean, unless it be the knowing *ego* familiar to common sense, and not unnecessary to philosophy, which is smuggled in through the *back-door* of a vaguely metaphorical term; not whether "possibilities" does not involve, while it seems to hide, the relation of causation or force, against which Mill protests. We only observe, that it is more creditable to the candor of Mill than to his acuteness, that, on second-thought, he completes this definition of the soul by calling it also "a series of feelings which is aware of itself as past and future." [7] Here, again, we have another example of this subreption by a postern, of the notions of the soul itself, and its relations to time, both of which had formally been discharged by the front passage as superfluous. More amazing still is it, that, after making this correction, he recovers his sense of consistency, or rather, demonstrates his own insensibility to the absurdity of his position, by confessing that "we are reduced to the alternative of believing that the mind, or *ego,* is something different from any series of feelings, or possibilities of them, or of accepting the paradox, that something which, *ex hypothesi,* is but a series of feel-

[6] *Examination of Sir William Hamilton's Philosophy,* chap. XII.
[7] *Ibidem.*

ings, can be aware of itself as a series." [8] Which of these alternatives does he embrace? Does he adhere to the one construction which his formal definitions, as well as the whole drift of his philosophy, require him to support? or does he frankly concede that he believes in the mind as an agent,—an existing being which is something more than a series of feelings? He does neither, but proceeds to affirm, "The truth is, that we are here face to face with that final inexplicability at which we inevitably arrive when we reach ultimate facts." [9] But why not accept the facts, and shape one's definitions accordingly, instead of constructing a definition of the soul, and building a theory of induction upon it, which the facts can never sustain. He prefers to concede his failure in the extorted acknowledgment: "I do not profess to account for the belief in mind." [10] We had not expected such a confession without repentance, and, what is worse, without a sense of the need of repentance, from the modern lawgiver of scientific method; from the new Bacon, who has codified the rules for the inductive study of nature; from the plausible and pertinacious antagonist or what he calls *à priori* metaphysics!

Not only has Mill entirely failed, and by his own confession, to provide a mind which can interpret matter, but he has failed as signally to provide for our belief in matter, or the universe of nature, which man must interpret. Though he claims, by eminence, to be the philosopher of things; [11] though he denounces with a slight disdain those who prefer thoughts to things,—he makes no provision for our knowledge of things, or our belief in the material world. His formal definition of matter (while it is vastly more vague and unsatisfactory) is as purely idealistic as that of Berkeley or Collier. Matter he defines as "a permanent possibility of sensations." [12] He concedes that this definition would satisfy Berkeley, and that, in any other sense than this, he does not believe in matter. He did not seem at first to be aware, that, through the word "permanent," time has stealthily crept into his definition, and that "possibility" is not too narrow to let in causation,—that dreaded metaphysical entity. He makes a fearful nod, when he says squarely, "The possibilities are conceived as standing to the actual sensations in

---

[8] *Ibid.*   [9] *Examination of Sir William Hamilton's Philosophy*, chap. XII.
[10] *Ibid.* 3d Lond. edition. P. S.   [11] *Logic*, Bk. I. chap. II.
[12] *Exam.*, etc., chap. xi.

the relation of a cause to its effect." [13] His assurance culminates when he refers our faith in the permanence of these possibilities to the assumption that sensations similar to our own are experienced from material objects by other beings. "The world of possible sensations succeeding one another, according to laws, is as much in other beings as it is in me: it has, *therefore*, an existence outside of me, it is an external world." [14] As if the existence of other beings, with the relations of *outside* and *inside*, were not the things to be accounted for; and as if, through the door opened to admit this item of proof, space and its relations, including matter, had not marched boldly in, after both had been formally excluded, till they could be formally introduced by a philosophical ticket of leave!

But, allowing Mr. Mill to believe in man and nature as much or as little as he will, we inquire, with greater earnestness, what is his theory of induction, i. e., how does he explain the process? and on what foundations does he rest the resulting product? These questions are somewhat important when the scientist requires me to believe in the spectroscope. Especially are they important in the view of the neophyte, whose faith in science is weak, and who considers all at once the number of assumptions which enter into the result,—the truth of gravitation, the theory of light, the chemical analysis by light of burning bodies and gases, and, above all, when he takes into account the enormous distances, and the subtle indications. It is not wonderful that he asks, "How and why is it that I am justified in accepting this wonderful story, as enchanting, if it be not as fabulous, as the story of the 'Lamp of Aladdin'?" Pray, Mr. Mill, who knowest every word and syllable of the magic spell, repeat it to me letter by letter, and word by word, confirm the steps of my tottering faith, trace out for me the subtle and narrow path along which the philosopher has reached the stars, and even leaped into the abyss beyond.

How does Mr. Mill answer these entreaties? "Induction, my son, in philosophical language, is the result of repeated experiences of sensations so closely combined as to have become practically inseparable. We learn in this way to make the familiar and the near to represent the unfrequent and remote, according to certain axioms and principles concerning the uniformities and laws of nature and the relations of

[13] *Exam.*, chap. XI.   [14] *Ibid.*

time and space, which give mathematical truths and relations."—"But whence are these ultimate beliefs derived?" To this Mr. Mill has no other reply: "All these are derived from induction. Even the very principles that are used in induction, and the very beliefs that are most sacred concerning the sequences and similitudes of phenomena—these all are the products of induction, even though they are the conditions of induction and all come from inseparable associations."—"Is this all that can be said of them? How, then, can I trust them, supposing I have not yet learned to associate these things together; or what if they should be differently connected in other minds?" To this he would reply, "The last is supposable; and the consequence would be, that those minds would have different beliefs concerning the laws of nature, and even concerning the fixedness of any laws of nature, or the relations of number and magnitude. It is supposable, that, to the inhabitants of another planet, their inseparable associations should be so strangely mixed and re-adjusted, that they should multiply *three* and *four* into *eleven,* and should conceive that to issue ten per cent dividends signifies to steal the capital ten times over. Or the inhabitants of another might be trained to believe that two straight lines might so enclose a space, that a railway charter from New York to Erie might be mathematically demonstrated to cover all the adjacent territory indefinitely in every direction. But to correct all such abuses, he would add, "You can use experiments, and they will verify all correctly joined associations, and expose those which are false."—"But," urges the novice, "I can make but few experiments, and concerning objects of limited reach; and what I am required to believe is a long way off. I cannot test the assertion that sodium is actually burning in the sun, the indications are so very remote, though very plausible. I can burn the sodium in my lamp, and, as I watch the spectrum, I can refract another spectrum from the sun; but how shall I pass from what is united in the one to what is unknown in the other? Nay, how do I know that what you sometimes call causation, and at other times call sequence, prevails in the sun at all?" This question is so important, and the answer so fundamental to the neophyte's faith, that Mr. Mill would probably refer him to chapter and verse in his "System of Logic," which reads as follows: "In distant parts of the stellar regions, where the phenomena may be entirely unlike those with which we are acquainted, it would be folly to affirm confidently that this general law of causation prevails any more than those special ones which we have found to hold universally on our own planet. The uniformity in the succession of events, otherwise called 'the law of causation,' must not be received as a law of the universe, but of that portion of it only which is within the range of our means of sure observation, with a reasonable degree of extension to adjacent cases. To extend it farther is to make a supposition without evidence," etc.[15] "But, if all this is so, I may as well give up my faith in the solar spectrum. Sodium burns in the lamp, and its flame can be defined; but to conclude that sodium burns in the sun, because the sun emits a similar light, does not seem reasonable. The cases are far enough from being adjacent, and the circumstances are, in manifold particulars, very unlike. Mill's very slender basis for inductive reasoning would seem to be as suitable to confirm the doubter concerning some new discovery in physics as the writings of Colenso to strengthen faith in the Pentateuch, or of Strauss and Baur to lead to confidence in the gospel history. But the defects in Mill's philosophy of induction are necessary consequences of his defective and uncertain science of man's power to know. The signal failure of one of the most elaborate attempts that has ever been made to furnish a scientific foundation for the science of nature is explained by its defective and uncertain science of man.

The defects of Mill's philosophical writings are the more conspicuous, the more sharply they are contrasted with their manifold excellences. His rules for the practice of induction are comprehensive and sagacious, and they are amply illustrated and applied. His observations upon classification and language are rich contributions to philosophical literature. His acuteness in criticising, and his skill in exposing, the vulnerable points of antagonistic philosophies, as also his admirable candor in confessing the difficulties of his own, with his something more than admirable unconsciousness that his confessions amount to a complete surrender of every thing for which he would contend, force his reader at times to exclaim, *"Miranda simplicitas si non sancta!"* Like Comte, he protests that he does not expound metaphysics, but only logic, striving to set up a distinction between the reasons of the logical rules which he professes to expound, and the underlying philosophical axioms, which he styles "transcendental metaphysics." And yet these

[15] *System of Logic*, Bk. III. chap. XXI. sect. 5.

he is constantly obtruding, and endeavoring to account for; contending that our ideas of time and space, the conceptions and axioms of mathematics, the belief in causation, in induction, and in the uniformity of the laws of nature, are all derived from experience; while experience, with its authority for the distant and the future, is the product of associations that have become so inseparably blended that they cannot be got rid of.

From Mill, we proceed to the *Cerebralists*, to *Alexander Bain* and his school, who limit the science of man to the analysis of the brain and its functions, and claim that the so-called physiological psychology is the only basis for a solid science of the soul. This point we shall not contest: we urge only, that, if the basis is broad enough for a science of man, it is neither broad nor deep enough to support a science of nature. Let it be granted that brain convolutions, and nerve vibrations or nerve growths, may account for the differences and developments of the human soul; that vision is simply a nervous response to the undulating light, and touch is an adjustment of particles in the innerved cuticle in accordance with the molecular agitations in the solids with which it comes in contact. Let it be granted that memory, imagination, classification, and reasoning, are but material forces newly correlated in the forms of nervous movements, and that what is called self-consciousness is one set of brain fibres dancing a mazy antistrophe to similar fibres in a corresponding brain lobe. Granting that all of man which we call thought, emotion, and aspiration, is reducible to the workings of mechanical statics and dynamics, we fail altogether to explain how man so constituted and so acting can form a science of nature; how Newton came to connect the falling stone with the moon steadily detained and impetuously struggling in its path, and ventured to write down the law of each in a brief algebraic formula; nor how Kirchhoff happened to imagine, and was inspired to believe, that he could see the burning sodium in the molten furnace of the sun, and could follow the hydrogen that flashes in jets along its surface. Let cerebral physiology do what it will in its movements against a better theory of man; let it call in to its aid the portentous battalions of the correlated forces; let unconscious cerebration dart in and out of the conflict with its wily and quick-moving cavalry—one and all fail utterly to demolish the solid squares of convictions on which the intellectual soul must plant itself when it makes good a grand discovery, like those of Newton, or Davy, or Faraday, or Kirchhoff. The eloquent John Tyndall has truly said, more boldly perhaps than he was aware, and forgetful of consistency with many of his teachings, "It is by a kind of inspiration that we rise from the wise and sedulous contemplation of facts to the principles on which they depend." "This passage from facts to principles is called induction, which, in its highest form, is inspiration." [16] Whatever else may be true of the brain philosophy, it can never explain and validate induction, with the mystery of its insight into nature's secrets and the mastery of its power over nature's forces.

From Comte and Mill, and the cerebralists, we proceed to *Herbert Spencer*, who claims to be more profound and comprehensive than them all; for whom his adherents claim, that, like Kant, he is the *zermalmende Philosoph*,—the all-crushing of these times; of whom it is asserted, that he takes into his system all that is true in the old metaphysical and the new positive and brain philosophies, and causes every thing to re-appear with a profounder meaning and a more catholic application. We cannot charge against Spencer that he neglects or dishonors the science of man. He stands foremost among modern writers in recognizing psychology as fundamental to all philosophy, whether of matter or spirit. He may be said to accept spiritual phenomena as having existence in their own right, and as claiming authority over other facts, so far as they furnish the principles for every department of philosophy. He recognizes fully the necessity that certain principles should be necessary and axiomatic. So far all is hopeful, and seemingly all that a sound philosophy could desire. But we soon discover that these fair promises are sacrificed to the merciless requirements of a metaphysical hypothesis which is as remorseless in its exactions as it is usurping in its authority. The *law of evolution*, acting as a movement of differentiation and integration, is ushered upon the scene, destined, like Saturn, to devour its own children as fast as they are produced. It is itself not proved. It does not claim to be self-evident, but simply, that, like Mill's induction, it is capable of being verified in every individual instance in which it can be applied. Its terms, also, are so broad as to be capable of a great variety of significations. "Evolu-

[16] John Tyndall, *Fragments of Science*, p. 60.

tion," "differentiation," and "integration," are words of many-sided import, as Spencer's use of them satisfactorily illustrates. Evolution is now treated as though it were a living force, endowed with the energy, and invested with the wisdom, of a personal creator; and again it sinks to an innocent symbolic formula. Differentiation and integration now rise to the dignity and mystery of organizing forces, and anon they sink into the meaningless platitudes of insignificant logical generalizations. It is not surprising, that with phrases so vague in their import, and so plastic in their application, the mysteries of the universe are often explained by Spencer in the manner of a dexterous juggler,—as plausibly to the eye, and as unsatisfactorily to the mind.

But one thing, at least, Mr. Spencer has not explained, nor does he in any wise provide for; and that is the possibility of a science of nature, and simply because by his theory the principles on which such a science rests are themselves but transient waves thrown up for the moment by an ever-heaving and new-evolving sea. According to Spencer, man as a differentiated and integrated type of being is physiologically evolved from a less complex type of being. Intelligence is a more complex evolution of life, and life is the joint product of interior and exterior relations. Even the axioms of intelligence which Spencer had recognized as the necessary and ultimate laws of thinking—these obey the same law. At first they are sprouting tendencies towards scientific axioms, which are gradually fixed and hardened in the brain, so as to strengthen with the growth, and be transmitted with the progress, of successive generations. The conceptions of time and space, with the relations they involve, follow this rule, being perfected and adjusted by a long course of physiological evolutions. This is man according to Spencer. Is he competent to attain to a science of nature? Behold him, on some bright morning of the evolving æons, just ushered into being, "like the herald Mercury, new-lighted on some heaven-kissing hill," which he spurns with his impatient foot, as just about to leave the earth for some higher sphere. He looks out upon nature, that he may interpret its laws; he geometrizes among the stars like a god; he weighs the mountains in balances; he takes up the isles as a very little thing; he reads the history of the earth, turning back its rocky laminæ one by one, and interpreting the characters that speak from each. He catches the light, and unfolds it into spectra of beauty, finding in each one of its glowing bars some secret of nature's hidden magic. He studies the composition of matter, its crystalline orderings of method and symmetry, and its chemical affinities and transmutations. He attempts the more difficult problem of life: he pauses in astonishment before the profounder mystery of the soul. Next he essays to account for the origin of these varied forms of being; and, by one daring sweep of generalization, he thinks to comprehend and explain the universe. By the magic of a formula as vague as it is broad, he thinks he discovers that matter and spirit, that thoughts and things, are evolved by a self-moving tendency, after which life is lifted out from death, and intelligence springs forth from life. He is confident that the science of the universe is unravelled by a newly corrected science of man, adjusted to his metaphysical theory. But is it so? Has Spencer succeeded? Let it be granted that so long as man endures as a persistent type of knowing force, with his interior relations,—i. e., his powers, his categories, his time and space,—that so long the science of the universe, which is built up by the application of them all, may stand, and be trusted as true. But what is to happen at the next evolution of this ascending spiral, when another form of knowing energy is evolved, with its new and more complex furnishings? May not some new interior relations emerge, some powers and modes of thinking, some principles of science itself, which shall reverse the science of to-day, and cause the Principia of Newton, the Logic of Mill, and the First Principles of Spencer himself, to be but an empty babble, because they are all outgrown; the intellect newly evolved finding in them no import, and acknowledging in them no authority?

To this it will be replied, that Mr. Spencer assumes that there can be no new evolution of the power to know, which does not correspond to some new objective relation in that which is known; that, while it is true that the beliefs in time and space are themselves developed, he assumes that there correspond to them certain exterior relations; that, in fact, he even goes farther, and surrounds this finite universe with the incomprehensible somewhat, in whom he allows us to believe, provided we will concede that what we believe does not correspond to the truth, and summons us to worship, provided we will confess that we worship we know not what. He does, indeed, assume all this. But by what authority does he enforce these dogmas, except by the impressions of a being who is himself evolved, and whose power to believe that there are realities which answer to his own interior relations is itself a transient interior relation which has been evolved from the agencies which have chanced to produce it, and whose methods of knowing are themselves the products of an evolving and changing physiological growth? If the man of the present æon, as the philosophy of Spencer explains, is warranted in trusting the axioms of evolution and the persistence of force, then these axioms are something higher and more authoritative than physiological products, evolved by the coincidence of exterior and interior relations. If Mr. Spencer's "First Principles," or the first principles of any other philosopher, are to be received as the foundations of science, they are good for all time, for all the past and all the future. They have a higher and more permanent authority than his special theory can vouch for. The sciences of nature and spirit which he expounds cannot stand upon any foundations which he provides for their support in his science of man. Every such science is weak just in proportion to the sweep of its pretensions and the accumulation of its facts. It is like an imposing engine which is reared upon a pedestal that is massive to the eye, but which crushes its foundations into sand by the first movements of its ponderous and complicated structure.

The position which Spencer holds among the philosophers of our time is so unique as to justify, if not to require, special attention. Many-sided in his culture, especially on the side of physics, mathematics, and natural history, and apparently familiar with the history of human culture and human progress, he seems to command an inexhaustible fund of pertinent and attractive illustrations. If he is not always clear in announcing his principles, if his arguments do not always convince us of the truth of what we do understand, the wealth and variety of his facts never fail to delight and astonish the confiding reader, who cannot find it in his heart to distrust so well-furnished a writer. The apparent breadth and daring of his generalizations surprise the student who does not consider that philosophical genius is as strikingly displayed in the acute detection of subtle differences as in the vague suggestion of broad and meaningless similarities. The catholic spirit with which he seems to desire to do justice to every system of philosophy and religion prepares for an easy credence in the universal solvent which promises to decompose them all. The positiveness of his manner and the dogmatism of his assertions, which increase with the paradoxical character of his opinions, are elements of power with readers whose credulity rises with the daring of their admired and trusted leader. It would not be fair to say, that, so far as matter is concerned, Spencer writes like a sophist or a charlatan, for the reason that he instructs us in too many single and important truths. But it is not unjust to assert, that, in method and manner, he is master of the art of imposing exposition. The reader who has had some experience in the necessary art of searching for a meaning and method in writers in which neither is obvious, will often lay down Spencer in despair, if not with disgust, for his stealthy subreptions, his cool word-plays, his confounding of inductions with axioms, and his sacrifice of common sense to the requirements of an unproved theory. The clearness of his diction is no compensation for the lack of that earnestness and *verve* which are the never-failing indications of the highest qualities of genius. The coolness of his manner rather betrays than hides the consciousness of paradox. His attempt to reconcile philosophy with religion proves his conceptions of both to be superficial. No well-read student of philosophy can hesitate to believe, that, notwithstanding the zeal of his admirers, he will ere long cease to be the wonder of the hour; that, so soon as the secret of his plausibility is exposed, he will suffer a more complete neglect than he will fairly deserve.[17]

[17] The author takes the liberty to call the attention of his reader to the fact, that this is a metaphysical essay or meditation, the argument of which is directed to a single conclusion, and is in no sense a comprehensive treatise or criticism of any system of philosophy. While he claims no exemption from the obligation to interpret Spencer's doctrines correctly, and to state them honestly, he does not consider himself required to expound his system at length, or to show, that in many of the positions to which he attaches very great importance, and urges with the greatest persistence, he is flagrantly inconsistent with himself; that he not only goes beyond the range of knowledge and belief to which he had limited himself by his theory of evolution, but introduces assumptions for which his system makes no provision. With the most earnest desire to understand Spencer, and some effort to reconcile his doctrines with one another in logical and philosophical coherence, we can find no place in his theory for what he calls *Ultimate Religious Ideas*, for the reality of which he contends so earnestly, as against Hamilton and Mansel, with *naïve* unconsciousness of any inconsistency with his own theory of knowledge,—on which theory, however, he does not hesitate to fall back at once as soon as he seeks to demonstrate their perpetual *unknowableness* by man. Nor is it any easier to see how this theory allows him to distinguish between a *formulated and an unformulated consciousness*, after having shut himself up to that consciousness which is formulated; nor how his explanation of *the genesis* of the ideas

These arguments and criticisms must suffice. We do not urge that a profound study of man, or a formal recognition of the principles which underlie the study of nature, are essential to eminent attainments in special sciences, or to enlarged and liberal views of scientific research. The working formulæ of a single science, and, indeed, of many, may be mastered by an adept, and skilfully applied to brilliant achievements, almost without the suspicion that they can be justified by a philosophic method. The principles and methods of induction are practically taught by nature and common sense to every one who is willing to use them. But should any one be questioned or denied, either in obedience to the private maxims of a special philosophy, or the spirit of a narrow and special study of a part of nature called physics, it must be recognized and defended; and, in order that it may be defended and recognized, it must be carefully studied by a thorough examination of man.

For this study, the devotee of any special science may be the more disqualified in proportion to his zeal and success in his own department; but, for this very reason, the greater may be his confidence in pronouncing upon questions of this sort, and with a positiveness which is proportioned to his incompetence. Nothing is more arrogant, and nothing ought to be more offensive, than that the powers and principles on which all science and induction depend should be resolved by or after analogies derived from the mechanics of matter and the dynamics of life. To narrowness of this sort the sciences of nature offer special temptations. The objects are so real, the processes are so definite, the experiments are so satisfying, the enthusiasm is so contagious, that the devotee is tempted occasionally to forget that he is a man as well as a scientist, and to adjust his estimates of human science and culture, and even of man's power to know, by a standard taken from a single and a

---

of *space and time* by evolution can provide at all for his belief of the necessity or universality of these ideas, or of the realities which correspond to them; nor how the philosopher who has limited the researches of science to the relations of co-existence and sequence, and has thereby formally excluded the relation of causation, should abruptly introduce us to something which he denominates *force*, which he oracularly informs us is inscrutable, and concludes therefrom that matter and spirit may therefore be mutually convertible and interchangeable. The reader who chooses to make the experiment for himself, of explaining and reconciling these incoherences of Spencer, is referred to his *First Principles*, part I. chaps. ii. iii. and iv., part II. chap. v., and *The Principles of Psychology*, part IV. chap. vii. § 208.

narrow sphere. He that would converse with Nature with effect, in these times, must retire apart into a separate cave, that is lonely and far withdrawn. Within its recesses alone does Nature whisper her choicest secrets, and after a long and painful initiation of the devotee. To his uplifted torch alone does she reveal the starry roof and the brilliant vision. No wonder, that, when he emerges into the light of common day, he is as one dazed and bewildered, and talks of common things with strange and perverted speech. A one-sided cultivation, with its positiveness, and not ill-grounded conceit, is not barbarism indeed; but it is not culture in the large and generous sense of the term. A system of education which is bent upon training specialists in any department may be defective in proportion to the completeness with which it absorbs and limits the energies of its devotees. That the study of man is fitted to correct these exclusive tendencies has been demonstrated by the many eminent examples which modern physics has furnished of philosophers distinguished alike for imaginative genius, careful observation, and speculative interest concerning the nature of man and the methods of science. That these tendencies need to be corrected, is as strikingly proved by the number of scientists of another sort, who are not content with a well-earned reputation within their own departments, but set themselves to reform psychology and metaphysics after the law of the dissecting-room, and to correct theology in very extemporized "Lay Sermons." [18]

We do not overlook the truth, that the student of man is exposed to a narrowness and dogmatism of his own, and can learn much, if he will, from the sciences of nature. All these sciences are but the products of the varied applications of his spiritual power to the investigation of that truth which must be tested by experiment, and enforced as fact. A mistake in the investigation of nature is not only certain to issue in

[18] The writer has no desire to say hard things of Mr. Huxley, because he has chosen to adopt the title of Lay Sermons for certain of his discourses; but he cannot avoid the impression that he would have done much more wisely, had he pursued a course with respect to metaphysics and theology similar to that which he does not hesitate to recommend to clergymen and metaphysicians with respect to science,—i. e., had he let them alone. The confident utterances in respect to the fundamental problem of philosophy, and the truths and duties of religion, which are freely expressed in many of these discourses, appear to the greatest disadvantage when contrasted with the purely scientific expositions into which they are interwoven. They seem to have many of the worst characteristics of the most offensive descriptions of sensational preaching.

failure in discovery; but it at once attracts attention to the error of method in the experiment, or of principle in the theory. Nature is fearfully and sternly realistic. She abhors the brilliant vagaries, the imaginative rhapsodies, the cloudy phraseology and dreaming idealism, in which the one-sided student of man and of metaphysics is tempted to indulge. While she suggests an elevating and spiritual philosophy of her own, and hides a magnificent history in her past, as well as veils a more splendid romance in the future, she deals very summarily with the metaphysical cosmologies, the idealistic physics, and realistic logics, which imaginative students have put off as *à priori* philosophies of nature. The student of the mind and of man, who has been schooled by a close and stern wrestling with the forces and laws of matter, cannot but carry the lessons which he has learned into his study of the soul and of the methods of science. He will exact from others, and impose on himself, severe requirements in respect of clear definition, rigorous logic, well-grounded analogies, and coherent arrangement. The best security against the recurrence of that metaphysical romancing by which the science of man and the logic of science have been dishonored in the past is to be found in the methods to which physics are so vigorously held. Under the pressure of these lessons, the metaphysics of the future are likely to prove sober and discreet. If they should need any additional warning from this quarter, they can find them in the examples of extravagant metaphysics which are furnished by the physicists and physiologists who would develop man, and the inductive philosophy itself, from the crucible, a beanstalk, or the gorilla; or by the metaphysicians who solve all the problems of the universe by a formula of sequences and similitudes, and a law of evolution,— forever attempting, and forever failing, to discover and reveal the mystery that lies hidden in *the unknowable and the unknown*.

The study of man is not necessarily the study of psychology or speculative philosophy. Man is made manifest in history, philology, literature, art, politics, ethics, and theology. The thoughts of man have recognized and accepted those principles and institutions, those manners and laws, that civilization and culture, which give security and grace to the present life, while they awaken the anticipations, and confirm the faiths, which reach into another. The study of all these is a study of *the humanities*. It enables us to understand man, and to benefit man, not only as he interprets and controls what we call nature, but as he interprets and controls that which is highest in nature; i. e., man himself.

This suggests the thought, that the sciences of nature are not only related to the science of man because man interprets nature, but because man is a part of nature; and nature cannot be truly and liberally interpreted, unless man, in his higher capacities, is embraced within her plan, and made the end of her agencies. That is a very narrow view of nature which only finds in nature physical agencies, and limits her resources to mechanics and chemistry, but discovers no place in her broad expanses or her generous provinces for spirit or intelligence, accepting no man, but protoplasm. That is also a narrow view which recognizes man's higher endowments and destiny, but allows them a scanty place and meaning in the scientific interpretation of the physical arrangements of the universe. The science of man, and of man's higher nature in its highest developments, is essential to a science of nature, because nature itself cannot be interpreted, except as designed for the uses and culture and development of man as a spiritual being. Thus to interpret nature does indeed require that we assume design in nature. But all philosophy must assume this, so far as it interprets the past or forecasts the future. The positive philosophy does this, when it assumes that "the relations of sequence and similitude" are constant; that is, are always the same in the same circumstances. Darwin and Spencer both assume that there is a plan of successive development or evolution provided for in the infinite capacities of the undeveloped germs (if such began at all), or in their still more enlarged capabilities of successive evolution and disintegration, if the march of evolution is in cycles returning upon one another. It would seem that the wise intelligence assumed for this law of evolution would draw so heavily upon the faith of its defenders, as to leave them little courage to sneer at any theory of creation as "the carpenter theory." But, upon questions of consistency or taste, we have no room to enlarge. We contend, at present, only for the position that we cannot have a science of nature which does not regard the spirit of man as a part of nature.

But is this all? Do man and nature exhaust the possibilities of being? We cannot answer this question here. But we find suggestions from the spectrum and the spectroscope which may be worth our heeding. The materials with which we have to do in these most brilliant scientific

theories seem at first to overwhelm us with their vastness and complexity. The bulks are so enormous, the forces are so mighty, the laws
are so wide-sweeping and at times so pitiless, the distances are so overmastering, even the uses and beauties are so bewildering, that we bow
in mute and almost abject subjection to the incomprehensible All, of
which we hesitate to affirm aught, except what has been manifest to our
observant senses, and connected by our inseparable associations. We
forget what our overmastering thought has done in subjecting this
universe to its interpretations. Its vast distances have been annihilated;
for we have connected the distant with the near by the one pervading
force which Newton divined. We have analyzed the flame that burns
in our lamp and the flame that burns in the sun, and done this by the
same instrument, connecting by a common affinity, at the same instant
and under the same eye, two agents the farthest removed in place, and
the most subtle in essence. As we have overcome distances, so we have
conquered time, reading the story of antecedent cycles with a confidence
equal to that with which we forecast the future ages. The philosopher
who penetrates the distant portions of the universe by the *omnipresence* of his scientific generalizations, who reads the secret of the sun by
the glance of his penetrating eye, has little occasion to deny that
all its forces may be mastered by a single all-knowing and *omnipresent*
Spirit, and that its secrets can be read by one all-seeing Eye. The scientist who evolves the past in his confident thought, under a few grand
titles of generalized forces and relations, and who develops, and almost gives law to, the future, by his faith in the persistence of force,
has little reason to question the existence of an intellect capable of
deeper insight and larger foresight than his own, which can grasp
all the past and the future by an all-comprehending intelligence, and
can control all events by a personal energy, which may, perhaps, be
softened to personal tenderness and love.

We blame not the scientific discoverer, when, fresh from some triumphant experiment, he rejoices in the consciousness of power. We
wonder not that he rises from his feat of discovery with a sense of
mastery and dominion. Man by thought *is* THE KING of the universe,
so far as by thought he masters its secrets, and lays his hand upon its
forces. Let him be crowned as king by Science, and let no one dispute
his right to rule. But let him never forget that it is only by the right

which spirit asserts over matter, which thought assumes over things, that he has gained this dominion, and that he can extend it only as he learns more wisely how to know and use his own sagacious, self-relying mind.

But has nature no other king? To answer this question here lies not within our scope. The suggestions which we have made would, however, seem to justify the conclusion that the sciences of nature, when viewed in their fundamental philosophy, do not necessarily lead to atheism. The history of these sciences of nature, moreover, testifies, that while the dexterous workers in experiments may successfully apply the formulæ which the thinkers have furnished, and be content to look no farther, the architects and philosophers of nature have uniformly and necessarily recognized the only possible foundations of a philosophy of nature in the spirit of man, as capable of thinking the thoughts of God. The nature of science as justified to the mind of man, also reveals the truth that its methods and assumptions are but varied acknowledgments of an originating Intelligence whose thoughts and purposes we interpret just so far as we discover the forces, determine the laws, or explain the history, of the universe. So far as man as a thinking being thinks the facts of nature into science, so far does he complete the cycle by recognizing the discoveries which he makes and verifies as the living thoughts of the living God.

17

JAMES WOODROW

1828, born May 30, at Carlisle, England
1837, moved to Chillicothe, Ohio
1849, graduated from Jefferson College, Canonsburg, Pa.
1849–53, taught in secondary school
1853–61, professor of natural science, Oglethorpe University
1853–54, studied under Agassiz at Harvard
1854–56, studied at University of Heidelberg
1856, received the degree of Ph.D., Heidelberg
1860, ordained to Presbyterian ministry
1861–86, professor of natural science in connexion with revelation, Presbyterian Seminary, Columbia, S.C.
1861–65, chief of Confederate Chemical Laboratories, Columbia, S.C.
1861–72, treasurer for missions of the Southern General Assembly
1861–85, editor of *Southern Presbyterian Review*
1865–93, publisher of the *Southern Presbyterian*, a weekly
1869–91, professor of science, University of South Carolina
1884, *Evolution*
1891–97, president of University of South Carolina
1901, moderator of Presbyterian Synod of South Carolina
1907, died January 17, at Columbia, S.C.

CHARLES DARWIN's *Origin of Species* was published in 1859. For a decade after its publication it appeared to raise a purely technical issue in biological science. A few reviews were published; a few men of science approved or opposed the theory of evolution set forth in Darwin's work. From 1870 to 1890 and beyond, however, after the publication of *The Descent of Man*, the development hypothesis became the storm center of American intellectual life. As late as 1925 the state of Tennessee forbade by law the teaching of evolution in her schools, and the Scopes trial for violation of this law again brought the matter into prominence. The intervening half century had made this difference: in 1870 few, even among the scientists, positively espoused the Darwinian theory; in 1925 the only opponents of the evolutionary hypothesis were to be found among the ignorant, the fanatical, and the bigoted. Dayton, Tennessee, was the last stand of the fundamentalists on this issue.

The many personal adjustments of scientists, theologians, and philosophers to the coming of Darwinism have recently been made the subjects of a number of tentative studies which have succeeded in grouping the adjustments into several major varieties. Here we are concerned with the terms in which dogmatic theologians were able to make some kind of peace with evolutionary theory. The basis of this peace was the assertion that religion and science have different subject matters. Therefore the dogmatic theologians were able to accept any scientific discoveries without admitting any possibility of their affecting religious faith. Science was religiously neutral, and religion scientifically neutral. Religious belief remained the same and remained true whether Ptolemaic or Copernican astronomy was accepted as scientific truth; the nebular hypothesis had no effect on religious belief; the evolutionary hypothesis could be believed or not on scientific evidence with no change whatever in the dogmas of religion. Religion had for its sphere declaring the truth about God, the soul, and the relations between God and the soul. This area science could invade only at its own peril; for the rest, natural science might have its way without opposition. This solution, comparable to political spheres of influence, seems comparatively easy, except that it limits severely the scope of both scientist and theologian.

James Woodrow, uncle of Woodrow Wilson, and Perkins professor of natural science in connexion with revelation in the Presbyterian Seminary at Columbia, South Carolina, found to his sorrow that the acceptance of the irenic, dogmatic solution was not always acceptable. The Board of Directors had apparently heard that he was not unreceptive to evolution and had therefore requested him to make a full statement of his views. An invitation to address the Alumni Association having come to him at the same time, he combined the invitation and the request by presenting his views on evolution to the Alumni. As a result of the views he expressed, he was dismissed from his position.

Before entering on his immediate topic, Woodrow made an excellent statement of the general position of the dogmatic theologian. He objected to the constant attempt to harmonize the teachings of science and the Scriptures. One does not harmonize two sciences or attempt to reconcile their contradictions. "We would confine ourselves to the task of removing the contradiction by seeking the error which caused it, and which it proved to exist; for we know that, as truth is one, two contradictories cannot both be true." The reason for making no attempt at harmony is that the subject matter of each science is different from that of the others. The application of this analogy of the different sciences indicates "the probable relations between the Bible and science." Their contents are entirely different. The

Bible does not teach science; science does not teach religion. All that we may expect is that the Bible and science should not contradict each other. "Believers in the Bible as such are indifferent to what form of astronomy may prevail. Calvin's belief in the geocentric system no more interfered with his confidence in the Bible than does our belief in the heliocentric system interfere with our confidence in the same sure word."

The Bible describes "phenomenal truth" in expressions which indicate with varying degrees of clarity exactly what is being described. Science has its concern in the explanation of the relations between phenomena. Again it is evident that the Bible and the scientist are talking of two distinct matters. There may be parts of the Bible which, because of the antiquity of the language in which they were written, cannot be understood; there is nothing in the Bible "which contradicts other known truth." Again, it is important to note that where there are "supposed to be inconsistencies," it is in matters which "cannot possibly directly affect any moral or religious truth."

After this statement of his general approach to science and religion, Woodrow presented his belief in evolution as "mediate creation," insisting that the hypothesis has reference only to the mode of origination of organic beings, not to the power which produces the origination. Creation and evolution are not mutually exclusive; evolution is a mode of the creative power of the Divinity. Thus, belief in evolution is not atheism; it is not contradictory to what is to be found in the Scriptures; it is supported by the scientific evidence. All in all, Woodrow found it hard "to see how any one could hesitate to prefer the hypothesis of mediate creation to the hypothesis of immediate creation." Finally, although the hypothesis itself is religiously neutral, "is not and cannot be either Christian or anti-Christian, religious or irreligious, theistic or atheistic," yet to view the universe through the glass of evolutionary theory is to become convinced that evolution is "God's plan of creation."

EVOLUTION

AT the same time that you honored me with an invitation to deliver an address before you on this occasion, the Board of Directors at the Theological Seminary, in view of the fact that "Scepticism in the world is using alleged discoveries in science to impugn the word of God," requested me "to give fully my views, as taught in this institution, upon Evolution, as it respects the world, the lower animals and man." Inasmuch as several members of the Board are also members of this Association, and both Board and Association feel the same interest in the Seminary, I have supposed that I could not select a subject more likely to meet with your approval than the one suggested to me by the Directors.

I am all the more inclined to make this choice, as it will afford me the opportunity of showing you that additional study has, in some respects, to a certain extent modified my views since I expressed them to many of you in the class-room.

As is intimated in the Board's request, I may assume that your chief interest in the topic is not in its scientific aspects, but in relations it may bear to the word of God; and therefore I will speak mainly of these relations. Not that I regard you as indifferent to science; from my past acquaintance with you, I have too high an appreciation of your intelligence to regard that as possible; for no intelligent person can be indifferent to knowledge, and especially can no intelligent child of God be indifferent to a knowledge of his Father's handiwork, or of the methods by which he controls the course of his universe. Still, on the present occasion it is doubtless the relations between science, or that which claims to be science, and the Bible, and not science itself, that should receive our attention.

Before entering on the discussion of the specific subject of Evolution in itself and in its relations to the Sacred Scriptures, it may be well to consider the relations subsisting between the teachings of the Scriptures and the teachings of natural science generally. We hear much of the harmony of science and Scripture, of their reconciliation, and the like. Now, is it antecedently probable that there is room for either agreement or disagreement? We do not speak of the harmony of mathematics and chemistry, or of zoology and astronomy, or the reconciliation of physics and metaphysics. Why? Because the subject-matter of each of these branches of knowledge is so different from the rest. It is true we may say that some assertion made by astronomy cannot be correct, because it contradicts some known truth of mathematics or of physics. But yet, in such a case, we would not proceed to look for harmony or reconciliation; we would confine ourselves to the task of removing the contradiction by seeking the error which caused it, and which it proved to exist; for we know that, as truth is one, two contradictories cannot both be true.

May it not be that we have here a representation of the probable relations between the Bible and science—that their contents are so entirely different that it is vain and misleading to be searching for harmonies; and that we should confine our efforts to the examination of real or seeming contradictions which may emerge, and rest satisfied, without attempting to go farther, when we have discovered that there is no contradiction, if it was only seeming, or have pointed out the error that caused it, if real?

Let us test this point by examining special cases which have arisen, and with regard to which conclusions satisfactory to all believers in the Bible have now been reached.

In Genesis i. 16, the Bible speaks of the two great lights, the sun and the moon, and of the stars as if these were of comparatively insignificant size and importance. It says further, Joshua x. 13, that "the sun stood still, and the moon stayed"; "the sun stood still in the midst of the heaven, and hasted not to go down about a whole day." In these and other passages the Bible has been thought to teach that the sun and the moon are larger than any of the stars, and that sun, moon, and stars, having been created for the benefit of man, revolve around the earth as a centre. On the scientific side, two forms of astronomy have been presented: the Ptolemaic, teaching that the earth is the centre of the universe; the Copernican, teaching that the sun is the centre of our planetary system. Those who asked for harmony between science and the Bible found wonderful confirmation of the Bible in the Ptolemaic astronomy, and of the Ptolemaic astronomy in the Bible. But gradually it came to be seen and admitted that, whatever might be its teachings on other subjects, the Bible was at least not intended to teach astronomy; and for centuries general assent has been given to the words of Calvin: "Moses does not speak with philosophical acuteness on occult mysteries, but relates those things which are everywhere observed, even by the uncultivated." . . . "He who would learn astronomy, and other recondite arts, let him go elsewhere." Thus it has come to be believed that all are entitled to ask, as regards the relations between astronomy and the Bible, is that they shall not contradict each other; not that they shall agree with each other. Believers in the Bible as such are indifferent as to what form of astronomy may prevail. Calvin's belief in the geocentric system no more interfered with his confidence in the Bible than does our belief in the heliocentric system interfere with our confidence in the same sure word.

Geography furnishes another illustration of this same kind of harmony between the Bible and science, which is not less instructive. For centuries geographers taught as science that which was claimed to be in perfect accord with the Bible in such passages as these: "They shall gather together his elect from the four winds, from one end of heaven to the other"; "I saw four angels standing on the four corners of the earth, holding the four winds of the earth"; "And shall go out to deceive the nations of the four quarters of the earth." So the Bible and science were thus found further to confirm each other. But, again, in process of time it came to be seen that neither the words of the Bible nor the phenomena of the earth taught what had been supposed; that the Bible taught nothing about the shape or other characteristics of the earth in these or other passages; and that the phenomena of the earth, rightly understood, did not teach that it is a four-cornered immovable plain. Here, again, it is seen that all we should ask for is not harmony, but absence of contradiction. The examination of other cases would lead to the same conclusion.

The Bible does not teach science; and to take its language in a scientific sense is grossly to pervert its meaning.

Yet it is not correct in any of these cases to say that the language of the Bible does not express the exact truth; that it is accommodated to the weakness of the popular mind, to the ignorance of the unlearned. We are often told by some defenders of the Bible that it speaks inaccurately when it says that the sun rises and sets, or that it stood still upon Gibeon. But what is accurate speech? It is speech which conveys exactly the thought intended. Now, if to say that the sun rises conveys exactly the thought intended, wherein can this expression be called inaccurate? There is no intention to explain the cause of the fact of rising. This fact exists equally, whether produced by the sun's absolute motion in space or by the rotation of the earth on its axis. The meaning is, that the relative position of our horizon and the sun has changed in a certain way; and in stating that the change has taken place, there is not the remotest reference to the cause. In passing from Europe to the United States, we say that we go westward. But we are met by the assertion, uttered in a patronising tone of superior wisdom: "Oh no;

you speak erroneously; you show that you are not acquainted with the real state of the facts; or if you are, you are speaking inaccurately for the sake of accommodating yourself to your ignorant hearers; you make a false statement because your hearers could not otherwise gain any idea from you on the subject. The truth is, that when you thought you were going westward, you were going eastward at a rapid rate; what you call your going westward was merely stopping a small part of the eastward motion you had in common with the surface of the earth." Now it would probably be hard to discuss this sage utterance in a perfectly respectful manner. But wherein does it differ from the tone of those who apologise for the "gross form" in which the Scriptures convey instruction, for their not speaking with "greater exactness," and the like? A phenomenal truth is as much a truth as is the so-called scientific explanation of it; and words which accurately convey a knowledge of the phenomenon are as exactly true as those which accurately convey a knowledge of the explanation. Science has to do almost exclusively with the explanation; it is interested in phenomenal truths only on account of their relations to each other; while the Bible speaks solely of the phenomenal truths involved in natural science for their own sake, and never for the sake of the explanation of them or their scientific relations to each other.

Admitting these principles, which are so readily admitted in their application to the cases already considered, many difficulties usually regarded as of the gravest character at once disappear. For example, in Leviticus xi. and Deut. xiv. the divinely inspired lawgiver classes the coney and the hare as animals that chew the cud; he places the bat amongst the birds; he speaks of the locust, the beetle, and the grasshopper as flying creeping things that go upon all four. Now if these representations are to be taken as scientific statements, we must without hesitation say there is here a sad batch of blunders: for the coney and the hare do not chew the cud; the bat is not a bird; the locust, the beetle, the grasshopper, and other flying creeping things, do not go upon four, but upon six. But now suppose that the words used conveyed exactly the knowledge that was intended, are they not correctly used? *We* understand by "chewing the cud" bringing back into the mouth, for the purpose of being chewed, food which had been previously swallowed; but if those to whom the words in question were addressed understood by them that motion of the mouth which accompanies chewing, then they would recognise by this motion the hare and the coney as rightly characterised. So with the bat—in a scientific sense it is not a bird; it is a mammal; hence, if we are teaching natural history, we would grievously err in making such a classification. But in describing flying things which do not creep, the bat was rightly placed where it is. Two years ago the Legislature of South Carolina enacted that "it shall not be lawful for any person . . . to destroy any bird whose principal food is insects, . . . comprising all the varieties of birds represented by the several families of *bats,* whip-poor-wills, . . . humming birds, blue birds," etc. Does this law prove that the Legislature did not know that the bat in a natural history sense is not a bird? They were not undertaking to teach zoology: they wished to point out the flying animals whose principal food is insects, and with all propriety and accuracy they did it. So "going on all four," when used in reference to the motion of animals, may fairly be taken as applying to the prone position of the animal which is common to the quadruped and the insect, and not at all to the number of feet. In this sense the phrase with perfect accuracy applies to the horizontal position of the locust and other insects; while the important natural history fact, that the insect has six feet, and not four, is perfectly immaterial.

In all these instances I think it has been made to appear that there is no contradiction; but he would be bold indeed who would claim that there is here harmony between science and the Bible. On the contrary, is it not most pointedly suggested that any exposition of Scripture which seems to show that natural science is taught, is thereby proved to be incorrect? For this reason, I may say in passing, I am strongly inclined to disbelieve the popular interpretations of the first chapter of Genesis, which find there a compendium of the science of geology.

As in the example above given, so in all other cases of supposed contradiction of the Bible by science, I have found that the fair honest application of such principles has caused the contradiction to disappear. I have found nothing in my study of the Holy Bible and of natural science that shakes my firm belief in the divine inspiration of every word of that Bible, and in the consequent absolute truth, the absolute inerrancy, of every expression which it contains, from beginning to end. While there are not a few things which I confess myself wholly unable to understand, yet I have found nothing which contradicts other known truth. It ought to be observed that this is a very different thing from saying that I have found everything in the Sacred Scriptures to be in harmony with natural science. To reach this result it would be necessary to know the exact meaning of every part of the Scriptures, and the exact amount of truth in each scientific proposition. But to show that in any case there is no contradiction, all that is needed is to show that a reasonable supposition of what the passage in question may mean does not contradict the proved truth in science. We do not need to show that our interpretation *must* be correct, but only that it *may* be correct—that it is not reached by distortion or perversion, but by an honest application of admitted principles of exegesis.

It should be noted that the matters respecting which there are supposed to be inconsistencies between the teachings of science and the Bible are such as cannot possibly directly affect any moral or religious truth; but that they derive their importance to the Christian believer solely from the bearing they may have on the truthfulness of the Scriptures. In the name of Christianity, belief in the existence of people living on the other side of the earth has been denounced as absurd and heretical; but how is any moral duty or any doctrine of religion affected by this belief? unless, indeed, it may be from doubt it may cast upon the truthfulness of the Bible. And with this exception, what difference can it make with regard to any relation between ourselves and our fellow-men, or between ourselves and God and the Lord Jesus Christ, whether the earth came into existence six thousand years or six thousand million years ago; whether the earth is flat or round; whether it is the centre of the universe or on its edge; whether there has been one creation or many; whether the Noachian deluge covered a million or two hundred million square miles; and last of all, I may add, whether the species of organic beings now on the earth were created mediately or immediately?

After these preliminary observations, I proceed to discuss the main subject of this address.

Before answering the question, What do you think of Evolution? I must ask, What do you mean by Evolution?

When thinking of the origin of anything, we may inquire, Did it come into existence just as it is? or did it pass through a series of changes from a previous state in order to reach its present condition? For example, if we think of a tree, we can conceive of it as having come immediately into existence just as we see it; or, we may conceive of it as having begun its existence as a. minute cell in connexion with a similar tree, and as having reached its present condition by passing through a series of changes, continually approaching and at length reaching the form before us. Or thinking of the earth, we can conceive of it as having come into existence with its present complex character; or we may conceive of it as having begun to exist in the simplest possible state, and as having reached its present condition by passing through a long series of stages, each derived from its predecessor. To the second of these modes, we apply the term "Evolution." It is evidently equivalent to "derivation"; or, in the case of organic beings, to "descent."

This definition or description of Evolution does not include any reference to the power by which the origination is effected; it refers to the mode, and to the mode alone. So far as the definition is concerned, the immediate existence might be attributed to God or to chance; the derived existence to inherent uncreated law, or to an almighty personal Creator, acting according to laws of his own framing. It is important to consider this distinction carefully, for it is wholly inconsistent with much that is said and believed by both advocates and opponents of Evolution. It is not unusual to represent Creation and Evolution as mutually exclusive, as contradictory: Creation meaning the immediate calling out of non-existence by divine power; Evolution, derivation from previous forms or states by inherent, self-originated or eternal laws, independent of all connexion with divine personal power. Hence, if this is correct, those who believe in Creation are theists; those who believe in Evolution are atheists. But there is no propriety in thus mingling in the definition two things which are so completely different as the power that produces an effect, and the mode in which the effect is produced.

The definition now given, which seems to me the only one which can be given within the limits of natural science, necessarily excludes the possibility of the questions whether the doctrine is theistic or atheistic, whether it is religious or irreligious, moral or immoral. It would be as plainly absurd to ask these questions as to inquire whether the doctrine is white or black, square or round, light or heavy. In this respect it is like every other hypothesis or theory in science. These are qualities which do not belong to such subjects. The only question that can rationally be put is, Is the doctrine true or false? If this statement is correct,—and it is almost if not quite self-evident—it should at once end all disputes not only between Evolution and religion, but between natural science and religion universally. To prove that the universe, the earth, and the organic beings upon the earth, had once been in a different condition from the present, and had gradually reached the state which we now see, could not disprove or tend to disprove the existence of God or the possession by him of a single attribute ever thought to belong to him. How can our belief in this doctrine tend to weaken or destroy our belief that he is infinite, that he is eternal, that he is unchangeable, in his being, or his wisdom, or his power, or his holiness, or his justice, or his goodness, or his truth? Or how can our rejection of the doctrine either strengthen or weaken our belief in him? Or how can either our acceptance or rejection of Evolution affect our love to God, or our recognition of our obligation to obey and serve him—carefully to keep all his commandments and ordinances?

True, when we go outside the sphere of natural science, and inquire whence this universe, questions involving theism forthwith arise. Whether it came into existence immediately or mediately is not material; but what or who brought it into existence? Did it spring from the fortuitous concurrence of eternally-existing atoms? Are the matter and the forces which act upon it in certain definite ways eternal; and is the universe, as we behold it, the result of their blind unconscious operation? Or, on the other hand, was the universe in all its orderly complexity brought into existence by the will of an eternal personal spiritual God, one who is omniscient, omnipresent, omnipotent? These questions of course involve the very foundations of religion and morality; but they lie wholly outside of natural science; and are, I repeat, not in the least affected by the decision of that other question, Did the universe come into its present condition immediately or mediately; instantly, in a moment, or gradually, through a long series of intermediate stages? They are not affected by, nor do they affect, the truth or falsehood of Evolution.

But, admitting that the truth of Theism is not involved in the question before us, it may fairly be asked, Does not the doctrine of Evolution contradict the teachings of the Bible? This renders it necessary to inquire whether the Bible teaches anything whatever as to the mode in which the world and its inhabitants were brought into their present state; and if so, what that teaching is.

It does not seem to be antecedently probable that there would be any specific teaching there on the subject. We have learned that "the Scriptures principally teach what man is to believe concerning God, and what duty God requires of man"; and that "the whole counsel of God, concerning all things necessary for his own glory, man's salvation, faith, and life, is either expressly set down in Scripture, or by good and necessary consequence may be deducted from Scripture." But this does not include the principles of natural science in any of its branches. We have already seen that it certainly does not include the teaching of astronomy or of geography; it does not include anatomy or physiology, zoology or botany—a scientific statement of the structure, growth, and classification of animals and plants. Is it any more likely that it includes an account of the limits of the variation which the kinds of plants and animals may undergo, or the circumstances and conditions by which such variation may be affected? We would indeed expect to find God's relation to the world and all its inhabitants set forth; but he is equally the Creator and Preserver, however it may have pleased him, through his creating and preserving power, to have brought the universe into its present state. He is as really and truly your Creator, though you are the descendant of hundreds of ancestors, as he was of the first particle of matter which he called into being, or the first plant or animal, or the first angel in heaven.

So much at least seems clear—that whatever the Bible may say touching the mode of creation, is merely incidental to its main design, and must be interpreted accordingly. Well may we repeat with Calvin, "He who would learn astronomy and other recondite arts, let him go elsewhere."

It is further to be observed, that whatever may be taught is contained in the first part of the oldest book in the world, in a dead language, with a very limited literature; that the record is extremely brief, compressing an account of the most stupendous events into the smallest compass. Now the more remote from the present is any event recorded in human language, the more completely any language deserves to be called dead, the more limited its contemporaneous literature, the briefer the record itself, the more obscure must that record be—the more difficult it must be to ascertain its exact meaning, and especially that part of its meaning which is merely incidental to its main design. As to the portions which bear on that design, the obscurity will be illuminated by the light cast backwards from the later and fuller and clearer parts of the Bible. But on that with which we are now specially concerned no such light is likely to fall.

To illustrate this point, I may refer to other parts of this early record. In the account of the temptation of Eve, we have a circumstantial and apparently very plain description of the being that tempted her. It was a serpent; and we read that "the serpent was more subtil than any beast of the field." Further, it was a beast which was to go upon its belly, and whose head could be bruised. Surely, it might be said, it is perfectly plain that the record should cause us to believe that it was a mere beast of the field, a mere serpent, that tempted Eve. But to narrate the fall of man is not simply incidental to the design of the Bible; on the contrary, its chief design may be said to be to record that fall and to show how man may recover from it. Hence, from the later parts of the Bible we learn that the tempter was no beast of the field, as seems to be so clearly stated; but it was "the dragon, the old serpent, which is the devil, even Satan," whatever may have been the guise in which he appeared to our first mother.

Then from the sentence pronounced upon the serpent, "I will put enmity between thee and the woman, and between thy seed and her seed; it shall bruise thy head, and thou shalt bruise his heel,"—from this it would seem to be clear that what we are here taught, and all that we are here taught, is that the woman's son was to crush the head of the beast, whilst his own heel would be bruised; whereas we learn from books which come after that this sentence really contains the germ of the entire plan of salvation; and that the woman's son who was to bruise the serpent's head at such cost to himself is Jesus the Saviour, who on Calvary through his death destroyed "him that had the power of death, that is, the devil." Now, since in these cases, where the meaning seems to be so unmistakeably clear, and where the subject matter belongs to the main design of the book, and yet where the real meaning is so entirely different, as we learn from the later Scriptures, how cautious we should be not to feel too confident that we have certainly reached the true meaning in cases where the subject-matter is merely incidental, and where no light falls back from the later Scriptures to guide us aright!

The actual examination of the sacred record seems to me to show that the obscurity exists which might have been reasonably anticipated. It is clear that God is there represented as doing whatever is done. But whether in this record the limitless universe to the remotest star or nebula is spoken of, or only some portion of it, and if the latter, what portion, I cannot tell. And if there is an account of the methods according to which God proceeded in his creative work, I cannot perceive it. It is said *that* God created; but, so far as I can see, it is not said *how* he created. We are told nothing that contradicts the supposition, for example, that, in creating our earth and the solar system of which it forms a part, he brought the whole into existence very much in the condition in which we now see the several parts; or, on the other hand, that he proceeded by the steps indicated in what is called the nebular hypothesis. Just as the contrary beliefs of Calvin and ourselves touching the centre of the solar system fail to contradict a single word in the Bible, so the contrary beliefs of those who accept and those who reject the nebular hypothesis fail to contradict a single word of the Bible.

I regard the same statements as true when made respecting the origin of the almost numberless species of organic beings which now exist and which have existed in the past. In the Bible I find nothing that contradicts the belief that God immediately brought into existence each form independently; or that contradicts the contrary belief that, having originated one or a few forms, he caused all the others to spring from these in accordance with laws which he ordained and makes operative.

If that which is perhaps the most commonly received interpretation of the biblical record of creation is correct, then it is certain that the Bible, implicitly yet distinctly, teaches the doctrine of Evolution. According to this interpretation, the record contains an account of the first and only origination of plants and animals, and all that exist now or that have existed from the beginning are their descendants. If, then, we have the means of ascertaining the characteristics of these ancestors of existing kinds, we can learn whether they were identical with their descendants or not. If the early forms were the same as the present, then the hypothesis of Evolution or descent with modification is not true; but if they were different, then it is true. Now, not indeed the very earliest, but great numbers of the earlier forms of animals and plants have been preserved to the present day, buried in the earth, so that we can see for ourselves what they were. An examination of these remains makes it absolutely certain that none of the species now existing are the same as the earlier, but that these were wholly unlike those now living; and that there have been constant changes in progress from the remote ages of the past, the effect of which has been by degrees to bring the unlike forms of a distant antiquity into likeness with those which are now on the earth. Hence all who believe that the creation described in the Bible was the origination of the ancestors of the organic forms that have since existed, cannot help believing in the hypothesis of Evolution. This is so obvious that it is surprising that it has been so generally overlooked.

There seems to be no way of avoiding this conclusion, except by assuming that the so-called remains of animals and plants buried in the earth are not really remains of beings that were once alive, but that God created them just as we find them. But this assumption must be rejected, because it is inconsistent with a belief in God as a God of truth. It is impossible to believe that a God of truth would create corpses or skeletons or drift-wood or stumps.

If the interpretation which I have spoken of as perhaps most commonly received is rejected, then it may be thought that the Bible speaks only of the first origination of organic beings millions of years ago, but says nothing of the origin of the ancestors of those now on the earth; but that it may be supposed that when one creation became extinct, there were other successive immediate independent creations down to the beginning of the present era. There may be nothing in the Bible contradicting this supposition; but certainly there is nothing there favoring it. And if it is rejected in favor of Evolution, it is not an interpretation of Scripture that is rejected, but something that confessedly lies outside of it.

Or, in the next place, the interpretation may be adopted that the narrative in the Bible relates exclusively to the origination of existing forms, and that it is wholly silent respecting those of which we find the buried remains. It need hardly be said that, on this interpretation, as in the last case, there is nothing in the silence of the Scriptures that either suggests or forbids belief in Evolution as regards all the creations preceding the last. For anything that appears to the contrary, the multitudes of successively different forms belonging to series unmentioned in Scripture may have sprung from a common source in accordance with the doctrine of descent with modification.

When we reach the account of the origin of man, we find it more detailed. In the first narrative there is nothing that suggests the mode of creating any more than in the case of the earth, or the plants and animals. But in the second, we are told that "the Lord God formed man of the dust of the ground, and breathed into his nostrils the breath of life; and man became a living soul." Here seems to be a definite statement utterly inconsistent with the belief that man, either in body or soul, is the descendant of other organised beings. At first sight the statemen, that "man was formed of the dust of the ground," seems to point out with unmistakeable clearness the exact nature of the material of which man's body was made. But further examination does not strengthen this view. For remembering the principles and facts already stated, and seeking to ascertain the meaning of "dust of the ground" by examining how the same words are employed elsewhere in the narrative, the sharp definiteness which seemed at first to be so plainly visible somewhat disappears. For example, we are told in one place that the waters were commanded to bring forth the moving creature that hath life, and fowl that may fly above the earth; and the command was obeyed. And yet, in another place we are told that out of the ground the Lord God formed every beast of the field, and every fowl of the air. Now as both these statements are true, it is evident that there can be no intention to describe the material employed. There was some sort of connexion with the water, and some with the ground; but beyond this nothing is clear. Then further, in the sentence which God pronounced upon Adam, he says: "Out of the ground wast thou taken; for dust thou art, and unto dust shalt thou return." And in the curse uttered against the serpent, it was said: "Dust shalt thou eat all the days of thy life." Now Adam, to whom God was speaking, was flesh and blood and bone; and the food of serpents then as now consisted of the same substances, flesh and blood. The only proper conclusion in view of these facts seems to be that the narrative does not intend to distinguish in accordance with chemical notions different kinds of matter, specifying here inorganic in different states, and there organic, but merely to refer in a general incidental way to previously existing matter, without intending or attempting to describe its exact nature. For such reasons it does not seem to me certain that we have a definite statement which necessarily conveys the first meaning mentioned touching the material used in the formation of man's body. If this point is doubtful, there would seem to be no ground for attributing a different origin to man's body from that which should be attributed to animals: if the existing animal species were immediately created, so was man; if they were derived from ancestors unlike themselves, so may man have been. Just so far as doubt rests on the meaning of the narrative, just so far are we forbidden to say that either mode of creation contradicts the narrative. And as the interpretation suggested may be true, we are not at liberty to say that the Scriptures are contradicted by Evolution.

As regards the soul of man, which bears God's image, and which differs so entirely not merely in degree but in kind from anything in the animals, I believe that it was immediately created, that we are here so taught; and I have not found in science any reason to believe otherwise. Just as there is no scientific basis for the belief that the doctrine of derivation or descent can bridge over the chasms which separate the non-existent from the existent, and the inorganic from the organic, so there is no such basis for the belief that this doctrine can bridge over the chasm which separates the mere animal from the exalted being which is made after the image of God. The mineral differs from the animal in kind, not merely in degree; so the animal differs from man in kind; and while science has traced numberless transitions from degree to degree, it has utterly failed to find any indications of transition from kind to kind in this sense. So in the circumstantial account of the creation of the first woman, there are what seem to me insurmountable obstacles in the way of fully applying the doctrine of descent.

But it is not surprising that, even if Evolution is generally true, it should not be true of man in his whole being. Man, as the image of God, is infinitely above the animals; and in man's entire history God has continually been setting aside the ordinary operation of the laws by which he controls his creation. For man's sake, the course of the sun in the heavens was stayed; the walls of Jericho fell down at the sound of the trumpets; manna ordinarily decayed in one day, but resisted decay for two days when one of these was the day of man's sacred rest; for man's sake the waters of the Red Sea and of the River Jordan stood upright as an heap; iron was made to swim; women received their dead raised to life again; the mouths of lions were stopped; the violence of fire was quenched; water was turned into wine; without medicine the blind saw, the lame walked, the lepers were cleansed, the dead were raised; more than all, and above all, for man's sake God himself took on him our nature as the second Adam by being born of a woman, underwent the miseries of this life, the cursed death of the cross; was buried; he rose again on the third day, ascended into heaven; whence, as both God and man, he shall come to judge the world at the last day. Surely then, I repeat, it is not surprising that, though man in his body so closely resembles the animals, yet as a whole his origin as well as his history should be so different from theirs.

Having now pointed out the probable absence of contradiction between the Scripture account of creation and the doctrine of Evolution, except in the case of man so far as regards his soul, but without having at all considered the probable truth or falsehood of Evolution, I proceed next, as briefly as possible, to state a few of the facts which seem to be sufficient at least to keep us from summarily rejecting the doctrine as certainly false.

First, as to the earth, in connexion with the other members of our solar system.

Some inquirers into the past history of this system have been led to suppose that at one time the whole of the matter now composing the various separate bodies may have existed in a nebulous state, forming a vast sphere with a diameter far exceeding that of the orbit of Neptune, the outermost planet; that this sphere rotated about its axis, and that it was undergoing gradual contraction. If there ever was such a sphere, it is claimed by some of those who have most carefully studied these subjects, that, in accordance with the laws by which God is now governing his material works, just such a solar system as ours would necessarily have resulted. As the sphere contracted, the nebulous matter would

become more dense, and the rate of rotation would increase and would
thereby increase the centrifugal force so that at length a belt or ring
would be thrown off from the equatorial region of the sphere; which
belt might continue to rotate as an unbroken mass, or, if broken, would
be collected by the laws of attraction into a spheroidal body, which
would rotate upon its own axis and would also continue to revolve in a
path around the axis of the whole mass—both these revolutions being
in the same direction, the axis of the new spheroid being not far from
parallel with the general axis, and the orbit of revolution being not far
from parallel with the plane of the general equator. This process would
be repeated from time to time, new belts or spheroids with the same
characteristics being successively formed. So from each of these spheroids, as it continued to contract, similar secondary spheroids might be
successively formed, each assuming a shape determined by the rate of
rotation. At a certain stage in the cooling, the nebulous matter would
become a liquid molten mass, ultimately solid. As the solid spheroid
cooled still more, it would still continue to contract, but unequally in
the interior and on the exterior, and thus the surface would be covered
with successively formed wrinkles or ridges.

Now, in every particular, with very slight exception, the constitution of our solar system and our earth is exactly such as has just been
described. It consists of a number of spheroids, each rotating on its own
axis, and revolving around a central mass; and around the several
primary spheroids are others which rotate on their axes, and revolve
around their primaries as these do around the sun—all having a form
determined by the rate of rotation; the primaries or planets all rotate
on axes nearly parallel with the axis of the sun; the planes of their
orbits of revolution nearly coincide with the equatorial plane of the
sun; these revolutions and rotations are all in the same direction; in
the case of Saturn, in addition to revolving satellites are revolving belts
or rings. Coming to our earth, it exhibits the plainest marks of having
once been in a molten state; the great mountain chains, which certainly
have been formed during successive periods, are just such as would be
formed by the wrinkling of the earth's crust caused by unequal contraction. Hence it would seem not unreasonable to conclude that, if
the nebular hypothesis has not been proved to be certainly true, it
has at least been shown to be probable. The number and variety of

coincidences between the facts which we see and the necessary results of the supposition on which the nebular hypothesis is founded, are so very great that it must go far to produce the conviction that that supposition can hardly be wrong. As before intimated, the correspondence is not perfect; but the exceptions are not such as to disprove the hypothesis—they are merely the residual phenomena, which in the case of even the most firmly established principles await a full explanation.

If it should be objected that, as this scheme rests on a mere supposition, no part of the superstructure can be stronger than the foundation, and that therefore it must be supposition and nothing more throughout, I would say that this objection rests on a misapprehension of the nature of reasoning on such subjects. Let us examine, by way of illustration, the method by which the truth of the doctrine of gravitation was established. At first it was the gravitation hypothesis merely. Newton formed the supposition that the heavenly bodies are drawn towards each other by the same force which draws bodies towards each other on the earth. He calculated what the motions of the moon and the planets should be if this supposition is correct. After many efforts, he found that many of these motions were nearly what his supposition would require. Even the first observed coincidence was a step towards proving the truth of his hypothesis; and as these coincidences multiplied, his conviction of its truth was increased; until at length he and all who took the trouble to become acquainted with the facts of the case believed with the utmost confidence that it was absolutely true. But even when this conviction was reached, there were still many phenomena which Newton could not explain on his hypothesis; but these residual phenomena, formidable as they were, did not shake his confidence, and should not have done so. Now, if Newton's gravitation hypothesis was entitled to his confidence on account of the number and variety of coincidences, notwithstanding the apparently inconsistent facts, ought not the nebular hypothesis to be entitled to similar confidence, provided there should be similar coincidences in number and variety, even though there remain some apparently inconsistent facts? And as the gravitation hypothesis rests upon a mere supposition in the same sense with the nebular hypothesis, ought the superstructure for that reason to be rejected in the one case any more than in the other?

It deserves to be remarked here that, after Newton had framed his hypothesis, he was led for years to abandon it, inasmuch as with the measurements of the earth on the basis of which he made his first calculations the motions of the heavenly bodies were utterly inconsistent with it.

To conclude, then, as regards the earth, I would say in the terms of one definition of Evolution—terms which have furnished to witlings so much amusement, but yet which so accurately and appropriately express the idea intended—that I think it very probable that our earth and solar system constitute one case in which the homogeneous has been transformed by successive differentiations into the heterogeneous.

In the next place, respecting the origin of the various kinds of animals and organised forms generally, it has been supposed by some naturalists that existing forms, instead of having been independently created, have all been derived by descent, with modification, from a few forms or a single one. It is known that the offspring of a single pair differ slightly from each other and from their parents; it is further known that such differences or variations may be transmitted to subsequent generations; and it is self-evident that under changing conditions the varieties best fitted to the new conditions would be most likely to survive. Now, under the operation of these principles, it is held that all the immense variety of existing forms of plants and animals may have sprung from one or a few initial simple types.

In accordance with this supposition, the earliest inhabitants of the world would be very simple forms. Among the varieties produced in successive generations some would be more complex in their organisation than their parents; such complexity being transmitted would form kinds somewhat higher in rank; these in turn would give rise to others still more complex and higher; until at length at the present day the most complex and highest would exist. All would not undergo such modifications as to produce the higher forms; hence there would be at all times, along with the highest, every intermediate stage—though the existing low forms would differ in many particulars from their ancestors, unless, indeed, the conditions under which they lived remained unchanged.

Now, in the statement just made we have an outline of the facts made known to us by an examination of the animals and plants which are buried in the earth. The sediment in the waters all over the world sooner or later sinks to the bottom in the form of layers; this sediment contains remains of plants and animals carried down with it, and in various ways permanently preserves them. Of course only a very small part of the plants and animals could be thus preserved; still a few would be. If we could gain access to these layers and examine their contents, we would obtain a knowledge of the successive generations of the past—the lowest layer being the oldest. It happens that a vast number of such layers have been hardened into rock, and have been raised from the waters where they were formed, and so broken and tilted that we have ready access to them. Not less than nine-tenths of the dry land, so far as examined, is composed of sedimentary rocks; and of these a large part contain the remains of plants and animals which were living at the time the rocks were formed. Of course it is not to be supposed that a complete series is known of all that ever were formed; still enough are brought to view to lead to the belief that from an examination of their contents we may obtain a fair knowledge of the history of the succession of animals and plants from an early period down to the present. We cannot go back to the beginning, but we can go a long way. The outline thus obtained shows us that all the earlier organic beings in existence, through an immense period, as proved by an immense thickness of layers resting on each other, were of lower forms, with not one as high or of as complex an organisation as the fish. Then the fish appeared, and remained for a long time the highest being on the earth. Then followed at long intervals the amphibian, or frog-like animal, the reptile, the lowest mammalian, then gradually the higher and higher, until at length appeared man, the head and crown of creation. The plants present a similar history—the first known being simple forms, like the seaweed, followed as we pass upwards through the later layers, by forms of higher and higher type, until we reach the diversity and complexity of existing vegetation. It is seen, too, that when a new type is first found, it does not present the full typical characters afterwards observed, but along with some of these also some of the characters belonging to other types. The earliest reptiles, for example, present many of the characters of the fish, the earliest birds and mammals many of the characters of the reptile; and so throughout the series. It is true there are many gaps, but not more than might be expected from the fact that the series of layers contain-

ing the remains is incomplete. When the layers show that the circumstances existing during the period while they were forming remained
unchanged, then the kinds of animals underwent little or no change;
but if the layers show rapid changes in climate, depth of water, etc.,
then the species of animals changed rapidly and frequently.

It would further follow, from the supposition under consideration,
that, all animals being related to each other by descent, they must resemble each other. In the organic world every one knows that likeness
suggests relationship, and that relationship usually accompanies likeness—the nearer the relationship, the closer generally is the likeness.
Now, careful observation makes known to us that the various animals
are surprisingly like each other. In the highest class of vertebrate animals, and also in man, for example, the skeleton, the nervous system,
the digestive system, the circulatory system, are all constructed on
exactly the same plan. If the skull of a man is compared with the skull
of a dog, or a horse, each will be seen to be composed of the same bones
similarly situated. Where the number differs, the difference will be
seen to result from the growing together of several bones in one case
which were separate in the others. So the human arm, the leg of the
quadruped, the wing of the bird, the paddle of the whale, will be
found to be formed on exactly the same plan. When the form of the
animal is such as to render unnecessary any part belonging to the
general plan, it is not omitted at once, but is reduced in size and so
placed as not to be in the way, and then in other similar animals by
degrees passes beyond recognition. And so it is with every part. There
are also the same kinds of resemblance between the lowest animals;
and, further, between any section of the lower animals and those which
are just above or just below them in rank. Thus we may arrange all
the forms in the entire animal kingdom, from highest to lowest, according to their resemblances; and while the highest is indeed very
unlike the lowest—a man very unlike a simple cell—yet at every step
as we pass through the entire series we find the resemblances vastly
greater than the differences.

We thus have another set of facts which plainly would follow from
descent with modification.

The existence of rudimentary organs is still another fact which would
follow very naturally from this mode of creation, but which seems not

very likely to have occurred if each species was independently created. For example, though a cow has no upper front teeth, a calf has such teeth some time before it is born. The adult whalebone whale has no teeth at all, but the young before birth is well supplied with them. In the blind worm, a snake-like animal, there are rudimentary legs which never appear externally. In the leg of a bird, the bone below the thigh-bone, instead of being double as in the general plan, has the shin-bone, and a rudimentary bone welded into it representing the small outer bone, but not fulfilling any of its uses. The blind fish of the Mammoth Cave have optic nerves and rudimentary eyes. So in the leg of the horse, of the ox, and indeed in many parts of the body of every kind of animal, will be found rudimentary organs, apparently not of the least use to the animal itself, but of great use to those animals which they closely resemble. All these facts are just such as the doctrine of descent with modification would lead us to expect, but which seem hard to understand on the supposition that each species was independently and immediately created.

Again, the changes through which an animal passes in its embryonic state are just such as the doctrine of descent requires. All animals begin life in the lowest form, and all in substantially the same form. Each at first is a simple cell. Beginning with this cell in the case of the higher animals, we find that, in the course of embryonic development, at successive stages the general forms are presented which characterise the several groups in which animals are placed when classified according to their resemblance to each other, ascending from the lowest to the highest. While it cannot be said that the human embryo is at one period an invertebrate, then a fish, afterwards a reptile, a mammalian quad-ruped, and at last a human being, yet it is true that it has at one period the invertebrate structure, then successively, in a greater or less number of particulars, the structure of the fish, the reptile, and the mammalian quadruped. And in many of these particulars the likeness is strikingly close.

The last correspondence which I shall point out between the results of the doctrine of descent and actual facts is that which is presented by the geographical distribution of animals. In this wide field I must confine myself to a few points.

By examining the depths of the channels which separate islands from each other or from neighboring continents, the relative length of time during which they must have been without land communication between them may be approximately ascertained. Where the channel is shallow, they may have formed parts of a single body of land recently; but where it is deep, they must ordinarily have been separate for a long time. For example, Great Britain is separated from the continent of Europe by a very shallow channel; Madagascar is cut off from Africa by one that is very deep. In the East Indies, Borneo is separated from Java by a sea not three hundred feet deep; it is separated from Celebes, which is much nearer than Java, by a channel more than five thousand feet deep. Now, if the theory of descent with modification is true, it should be expected that in the regions recently separated, the animals would differ but slightly; in regions separated long ago, the animals would differ more widely; and that, just in proportion to the length of separation. This is exactly what we find in the regions mentioned. The animals of Great Britain differ little from those on the adjacent continent; while the animals of Madagascar differ greatly from those of the neighboring coast of Africa. There are few kinds found in Java which are not also found in Borneo; while on the other hand very few kinds are found in Celebes which exist in Borneo. So it is the world over.

And this is not all. When we examine the kinds of animals which have recently become extinct in each country, we find that they correspond exactly with those which now inhabit that country; they are exactly such as should have preceded the present according to the doctrine of descent. For example, lions, tigers, and other flesh-eating animals of the highest rank, are found scattered over the great Eastern continent. In Australia the kangaroo and other pouched animals like the opossum abound, but none of any higher rank. In South America are found the sloth, the armadillo, and other forms which we meet with no where else on the earth. Now, in the Eastern continent we find buried in caves and the upper layers of the earth extinct kinds of lions, bears, hyenas, and the like, which differ from existing kinds, but yet closely resemble them. But we find nothing like the kangaroo or other pouched animals, or like the sloth or armadillo. Whereas if we examine the extinct buried animals in Australia, we find they are all pouched, with not a single example of anything of as high rank as the lion or the bear; and if we do the same in South America, we see extinct kinds of armadillos and sloths, but nothing at all like the animals of Asia or Australia. It is equally true that wherever regions of the world are separated by barriers which prevent the passage of animals—whether these barriers are seas, or mountain ranges, or climatic zones—the groups of animals inhabiting the separated regions differ more or less widely from each other just in proportion to the length of time during which the barriers have existed. If the barrier is such that it prevents the passage of one kind of animal and not another, then the groups will resemble each other in the animals whose passage is not prevented, and will differ in the rest. All this is independent of climate, and other conditions of life: two regions may have the same climate, may be equally favorable to the existence of a certain group of animals; but if these regions are separated by impassable barriers, the groups differ just as previously stated.

In view of all the facts now presented—the way in which animals have succeeded each other, beginning as far back as we can go, and coming down to the present; the series of resemblances which connect them from the lowest to the highest, exhibiting such remarkable unity of plan; the existence of rudimentary organs; the geographical distribution of animals, and the close connexion of that distribution now and in the past;—in view of all these facts the doctrine of descent with modifications, which so perfectly accords with them all, cannot be lightly and contemptuously dismissed. In the enumeration made, I have been careful to state none but well-ascertained facts, which any one who wishes to take the time can easily verify. Are not the coincidences such as must almost compel belief of the doctrine, unless it can be proved to be contradictory of other known truth? For my part I cannot but so regard them; and the more fully I become acquainted with the facts of which I have given a faint outline, the more I am inclined to believe that it pleased God, the Almighty Creator, to create present and intermediate past organic forms not immediately but mediately, in accordance with the general plan involved in the hypothesis I have been illustrating.

Believing, as I do, that the Scriptures are almost certainly silent on the subject, I find it hard to see how any one could hesitate to prefer the hypothesis of mediate creation to the hypothesis of immediate creation. The latter has nothing to offer in its favor; we have seen a little of what the former may claim.

I cannot take time to discuss at length objections which have been urged against this hypothesis, but may say that they do not seem to me of great weight. It is sometimes said that, if applied to man, it degrades him to regard him as in any respect the descendant of the beast. We have not been consulted on the subject, and possibly our desire for noble origin may not be able to control the matter; but, however that may be, it is hard to see how dirt is nobler than the highest organisation which God had up to that time created on the earth. And further, however it may have been with Adam, we are perfectly certain that each one of us has passed through a state lower than that of the fish, then successively through states not unlike those of the tadpole, the reptile, and the quadruped. Hence, whatever nobility may have been conferred on Adam by being made of dust has been lost to us by our passing through these low animal stages.

It has been objected that it removes God to such a distance from us that it tends to atheism. But the doctrine of descent certainly applies to the succession of men from Adam up to the present. Are we any farther from God than were the earlier generations of the antediluvians? Have we fewer proofs of his existence and power than they had? It must be plain that, if mankind shall continue to exist on the earth so long, millions of years hence the proofs of God's almighty creative power will be as clear as they are to-day.

It has been also objected that this doctrine excludes the idea of design in nature. But if the development of an oak from an acorn in accordance with laws which God has ordained and executes, does not exclude the idea of design, I utterly fail to see how the development of our complex world, teeming with co-adaptations of the most striking character, can possibly exclude that idea.

I have now presented briefly, but as fully as possible in an address of this kind, my views as to the method which should be adopted in considering the relations between the Scriptures and natural science, showing that all that should be expected is that it shall be made to appear by interpretations which may be true that they do not contradict each other; that the contents and aims of the Scriptures and of natural science are so different that it is unreasonable to look for agreement or harmony; that terms are not and ought not to be used in the Bible in a scientific sense, and that they are used perfectly truthfully when they convey the sense intended; that on these principles all alleged contradictions of natural science by the Bible disappear; that a proper definition of Evolution excludes all reference to the origin of the forces and laws by which it works, and therefore that it does not and cannot affect belief in God or in religion; that, according to not unreasonable interpretations of the Bible, it does not contradict anything there taught so far as regards the earth, the lower animals, and probably man as to his body; that there are many good grounds for believing that Evolution is true in these respects; and lastly, that the reasons urged against it are of little or no weight.

I would say in conclusion, that while the doctrine of Evolution in itself, as before stated, is not and cannot be either Christian or anti-Christian, religious or irreligious, theistic or atheistic, yet viewing the history of our earth and its inhabitants, and of the whole universe, as it is unfolded by its help, and then going outside of it and recognising that it is God's PLAN OF CREATION, instead of being tempted to put away thoughts of him, as I contemplate this wondrous series of events, caused and controlled by the power and wisdom of the Lord God Almighty, I am led with profounder reverence and admiration to give glory and honor to him that sits on the throne, who liveth for ever and ever; and with fuller heart and a truer appreciation of what it is to create, to join in saying, Thou art worthy, O Lord, to receive glory and honor and power; for thou hast created all things, and for thy pleasure they are and were created.

— III —

PHILOSOPHY OF RELIGION

18

JONATHAN EDWARDS

1703, born October 5, East Windsor, Conn.

1720, was graduated from Yale

1720–22, studied theology in New Haven

1722–23, minister of a Presbyterian church in New York City

1724–26, tutor at Yale

1726–50, pastor of Congregational Church, Northampton, Mass.

1731, *God Glorified in Man's Dependence*

1734, *A Divine and Supernatural Light*

1737, *A Faithful Narrative of the Surprising Work of God in the Conversion of Many Hundred Souls in Northampton, and the Neighboring Towns and Villages*

1738, *Discourses on Various Important Subjects*

1741, *The Distinguishing Marks of a Work of the Spirit of God*

1741, *Sinners in the Hands of an Angry God*

1742, *Some Thoughts concerning the Present Revivals of Religion in New England*

1746, *A Treatise concerning Religious Affections*

1749, *An Account of the Life of the late Reverend Mr. David Brainerd*

1750, *Farewell Sermon* at Northampton Church

1751–57, pastor of church in Stockbridge, Mass., and missionary to the Indians

1754, *A Careful and Strict Enquiry into the Modern Prevailing Notions of That Freedom of Will Which Is Supposed to Be Essential to Moral Agency, Vertue and Vice, Reward and Punishment, Praise and Blame*

1758, became president of the College of New Jersey

1758, *The Great Christian Doctrine of Original Sin Defended*

1758, died March 22, at Princeton, N.J.

1765, posthumous, *Two Dissertations on the Nature of True Virtue and the End for Which God Created the World*

THE conditions of New England at the time of its settlement, the hardships and difficulties which the settlers had to overcome, were such as made their belief in man's total dependence upon God a source of comfort and inspiration. After a while, however, their developing prosperity, the general amelioration of their situation, the increase of social security and moral institutions, led to a degree of falling away from the literal acceptance of total dependence. True, the theological formulation in the doctrine of man's salvation by the free and arbitrary grace of God was retained and given at least lip service. A growing number of the descendants of the first settlers, however, even those in high places, developed a kind of smugness towards this doctrine in particular.

The Reverend Samuel Willard was vice-president of Harvard College; in the Old South Church, in Boston, his congregation composed of the cream of Boston, the dignified and prosperous "elect," he preached a series of two hundred and fifty *Expository Lectures on the Assembly's Shorter Catechism*. Willard expounded the first question of the catechism, "What is the chief end of man?" to the favored few who made up his audience.

Answer: Man's chief end is to glorify God, and enjoy Him forever. . . . If we could speak exactly there is but One of these, viz. to glorify God, which is man's chief end; the other is immediately subordinated. . . . It is man's duty to seek his own best good, which consists in enjoying of God; but he is to do it in and for the Glory of God. . . .

The object of man's happiness is out of himself. Man cannot be his own felicity. He is a dependent creature; his being and his blessedness are two things. He cannot dwell at home. He doth not enjoy in himself a self-sufficiency. . . . Neither can the body or soul be at rest, till they meet with and fall upon an object that may give them satisfaction. This is it that hath made the whole world a company of seekers asking for Good. . . .

The whole creation affords no such object, the fruition whereof can make a man happy. . . . There are three defects in the creature, rendering it insufficient for our perfect well-being. (1) Its unsuitableness. If there were enough of it, yet it is not accommodated to all a man's wants; nay, those which are his greatest wants and make him truly miserable. . . . (2) Its scantiness. Were it never so suitable, yet there is not enough of it. The reaches of a man's soul are so vast, that they can grasp in the whole creation and scarce feel it. The desire of man, that horseleeches daughter, is still crying Give, Give. The bed is too narrow, and the covering too short. The world looks bulky but it is empty, void and waste. Many have had too much, but never yet any had enough. . . . (3) Its short continuance and uncertainty. Man is a creature made for perpetuity, and if his object be not stable, and durable, it will sooner or later leave him under horrible disappointment, and so will these things. They are broken cisterns. They are certain in nothing but uncertainty. . . . How then can they make a man happy?

God and He only is such an object, in the enjoyment of whom, there is perfect satisfaction and blessedness. . . . Every action in man's life that doth not serve to this great end is a vain action. . . . There are but a few that know what they were made for. . . . The greatest number of the children of men live in vain.[1]

---

[1] *A Compleat Body of Divinity in 250 Expository Lectures*, Boston, 1726, pp. 1, 4, 8; quoted in H. W. Schneider, *The Puritan Mind*, New York, 1930, pp. 99–100.

The "boundless imagination and occasional eloquence" of the preacher touched all but the exceptionally irresponsive among his hearers. He made them see the world as empty, void, and waste, full of horrible disappointments and broken cisterns. For their own best good and enjoyment they turned to the glory of God, and in him they were at home. Then church was over, and they were plunged into the heart of Boston, the metropolis of New England, growing, enterprising, exciting, absorbing. It was not empty, void, or waste. God himself must find his own best good and enjoyment in dwelling at home in Boston. The theory of the utter dependence of man on his sovereign God ceased to have any relevance to the facts of Puritan experience.

In his *Essays to Do Good* Cotton Mather stalwartly insists that he is not shifting from a doctrine of salvation by grace to one of salvation by works. His emphasis, however, had shifted in practice from the grace to the works. He maintained that doing good was evidence of election, not the occasion for election, but he stressed the benevolence rather than the salvation. Similarly, in his *Christian Philosopher* he weakened the element of arbitrariness in the Puritan account of grace by arguing the benevolence of the divine intentions towards men; God designs the happiness of mankind rather than being interested in his own glory. Mather's views move in the direction of the secular morality of the Enlightenment.

The Great Awakening was in large measure a protest against this conceit. It returned from an anthropocentric to a theocentric universe. Jonathan Edwards, in whose congregation at Northampton one of the early revivals began, had preached in Boston a year or two earlier on the text "that no flesh should glory in his presence" (I Corinthians i: 29). This sermon was published at the request of his hearers and is reprinted here under the title *God Glorified in Man's Dependence*. Here Edwards insists that God's aim in redemption is that man shall glorify Him and that this aim is attained "by that absolute and immediate dependence which men have upon God in that work, for all their good." Not only is God the first cause of redemption, "but he is the only proper cause."

Edwards insists that "the redeemed have all from the grace of God," which is free because God was "under no obligation to bestow" it. "Those that are called and sanctified are to attribute it alone to the good pleasure of God's goodness by which they are distinguished." It is arbitrarily bestowed; "He is sovereign, and hath mercy on whom he will have mercy." When man in the primal state was created holy, he was indebted to the goodness of God. In man's fallen state, when he is restored to holiness, "it is from mere and arbitrary grace."

This universal dependence of man upon God in the work of redemption redounds to the glory of God, "The greater the creature's dependence is on God's perfections, and the greater concern he has with them, so much the greater occasion he has to take notice of them." Man's total dependence upon God keeps the glory of God constantly in man's view. God has man's undivided respect; God is the center about whom all man's attentions move and in whom all unite.

Any doctrines which fall short in any respect of "such an absolute and universal dependence on God, derogate from his glory, and thwart the design of our redemption." This includes any doctrine which, by its emphasis on man's good works, tend to "put the creature in God's stead," to lead men to glory in themselves rather than in God. It can readily be seen that in this sermon Edwards is reviving the doctrine of total dependence, not so much in intellectual terms as in terms of a philosophical justification of the sense of dependence, and thus defending to the "sober minds" of Boston the "raised affections" of the frontier.

Edwards's sermon created a sensation among its auditors; the young preacher attracted great attention. In the "Advertisement to the Reader," prefaced to the published sermon, the ministers who caused its printing are quoted as rejoicing "that our churches (notwithstanding all their degeneracies) have still a high value for such principles, and for those who publicly own and teach them." Yet, though Edwards had the words of the traditional and by that time old-fashioned doctrines, he set them to a new tune. His words, produced out of his inner struggles, had an emotional appeal; this new intimacy of soul talking to soul was popularized by the Great Awakening. Its fruit was a religious individualism which in the long run helped to sap the foundations of the congregational system and thus to weaken the theory of the church covenant. Edwards himself and his followers, the "New Lights," played increasingly into the hands of the Presbyterians, who were both less democratic and less philosophical than the New England Puritans.

Edwards tried to turn back the clock towards dependence in a society which was becoming increasingly self-reliant. After the Great Awakening and the Presbyterian invasion, the New England conscience became more clearly bivalent, cultivating the doctrinal orthodoxy of dependence side by side with the common-sense practicality, self-reliance, and independence of the Yankee.

GOD GLORIFIED IN MAN'S DEPENDENCE

1 Cor. i. 29–31

That no flesh should glory in his presence. But of him are ye in Christ Jesus, who of God is made unto us wisdom and righteousness, and sanctification, and redemption. That according as it is written, He that glorieth, let him glory in the Lord.

THOSE Christians to whom the apostle directed this epistle, dwelt in a part of the world where human wisdom was in great repute; as the apostle observes in the 22d verse of this chapter, "The Greeks seek after wisdom." Corinth was not far from Athens, that had been for many ages the most famous seat of philosophy and learning in the world. The apostle therefore observes to them how God by the gospel destroyed, and brought to nought, their wisdom. The learned Grecians and their great philosophers, by all their wisdom did not know God, they were not able to find out the truth in divine things. But, after they had done their utmost to no effect, it pleased God at length to reveal himself by the gospel, which they accounted foolishness. He "chose the foolish things of the world to confound the wise, and the weak things of the world to confound the things which are mighty, and the base things of the world, and things that are despised, yea, and things which are not, to bring to nought the things that are." And the apostle informs them in the text why he thus did, *That no flesh should glory in his presence,* &c. In which words may be observed,

1. What God aims at in the disposition of things in the affair of redemption, *viz.* that man should not glory in himself, but alone in God; *That no flesh should glory in his presence,—that according as it is written, He that glorieth, let him glory in the Lord.*

2. How this end is attained in the work of redemption, *viz.* by that absolute and immediate dependence which men have upon God in that work, for all their good. Inasmuch as,

First, All the good that they have is in and through Christ: He *is made unto us wisdom, righteousness, sanctification, and redemption.* All the good of the fallen and redeemed creature is concerned in these four things, and cannot be better distributed than into them; but

Christ is each of them to us, and we have none of them any otherwise than in him. *He is made of God unto us wisdom:* In him are all the proper good and true excellency of the understanding. Wisdom was a thing that the Greeks admired; but Christ is the true light of the world; it is through him alone that true wisdom is imparted to the mind. It is in and by Christ that we have *righteousness:* It is by being in him that we are justified, have our sins pardoned, and are received as righteous into God's favour. It is by Christ that we have *sanctification:* We have in him true excellency of heart, as well as of understanding; and he is made unto us inherent as well as imputed righteousness. It is by Christ that we have *redemption,* or the actual deliverance from all misery, and the bestowment of all happiness and glory. Thus we have all our good by Christ, who is God.

Secondly, Another instance wherein our dependence on God for all our good appears, is this, That it is God that has given us Christ, that we might have these benefits through him: he *of God is made unto us wisdom, righteousness,* &c.

Thirdly, It is of him that we are in Christ Jesus, and come to have an interest in him, and so do receive those blessings which he is made unto us. It is God that gives us faith whereby we close with Christ.

So that in this verse is shown our dependence on each person in the Trinity for all our good. We are dependent on Christ the Son of God, as he is our wisdom, righteousness, sanctification, and redemption. We are dependent on the Father, who has given us Christ, and made him to be these things to us. We are dependent on the Holy Ghost, for it is *of him that we are in Christ Jesus;* it is the Spirit of God that gives faith in him, whereby we receive him, and close with him.

DOCTRINE

"God is glorified in the work of redemption in this, that there appears in it so absolute and universal a dependence of the redeemed on him." —Here I propose to show, 1st, That there is an absolute and universal dependence of the redeemed on God for all their good. And 2dly, That God hereby is exalted and glorified in the work of redemption.

I. There is an absolute and universal dependence of the redeemed on God. The nature and contrivance of our redemption is such, that the redeemed are in every thing directly, immediately, and entirely dependent on God: They are dependent on him for all, and are dependent on him every way.

The several ways wherein the dependence of one being may be upon another for its good, and wherein the redeemed of Jesus Christ depend on God for all their good, are these, *viz.* That they have all their good of him, and that they have all through him, and that they have all in him: That he is the *cause* and original whence all their good comes, therein it is *of* him; and that he is the *medium* by which it is obtained and conveyed, therein they have it *through* him; and that he is the *good itself* given and conveyed, therein it is *in* him. Now those that are redeemed by Jesus Christ do, in all these respects, very directly and entirely depend on God for their all.

First, The redeemed have all their good *of* God. God is the great *author* of it. He is the *first* cause of it; and not only so, but he is the *only* proper cause. It is of God that we have our Redeemer. It is God that has provided a Saviour for us. Jesus Christ is not only of God in his person, as he is the only begotten Son of God, but he is from God, as we are concerned in him, and in his office of Mediator. He is the gift of God to us: God chose and anointed him, appointed him his work, and sent him into the world. And as it is God that *gives,* so it is God that *accepts* the Saviour. He gives the purchaser, and he affords the thing purchased.

It is of God that Christ becomes ours, that we are brought to him and are united to him. It is of God that we receive faith to close with him, that we may have an interest in him. Eph. ii. 8. "For by grace ye are saved, through faith; and that not of yourselves, it is the gift of God." It is of God that we actually receive all the benefits that Christ has purchased. It is God that pardons and justifies, and delivers from going down to hell; and into his favour the redeemed are received, when they are justified. So it is God that delivers from the dominion of sin, cleanses us from our filthiness, and changes us from our deformity. It is of God that the redeemed receive all their true excellency, wisdom, and holiness: and that two ways, *viz.* as the Holy Ghost by whom these things are immediately wrought is from God, proceeds from him, and is sent by him; and also as the Holy Ghost himself is God, by whose operation and indwelling the knowledge of God and divine things, a holy disposition and all grace, are conferred and upheld. And though means are made use of in conferring grace on men's souls, yet it is of God that we have these means of grace, and it is he that makes them effectual. It is of God that we have the holy scriptures: they are his word. It is of God that we have ordinances, and their efficacy depends on the immediate influence of his Spirit. The ministers of the gospel are sent of God, and all their sufficiency is of him.—2 Cor. iv. 7. "We have this treasure in earthen vessels, that the excellency of the power may be of God, and not of us." Their success depends entirely and absolutely on the immediate blessing and influence of God.

1. The redeemed have all from the *grace* of God. It was of mere grace that God gave us his only begotten Son. The grace is great in proportion to the excellency of what is given. The gift was infinitely precious, because it was of a person infinitely worthy, a person of infinite glory; and also because it was of a person infinitely near and dear to God. The grace is great in proportion to the benefit we have given us in him. The benefit is doubly infinite, in that in him we have deliverance from an infinite, because an eternal misery, and do also receive eternal joy and glory. The grace in bestowing this gift is great in proportion to our unworthiness to whom it is given; instead of deserving such a gift, we merited infinitely ill of God's hands. The grace is great according to the manner of giving, or in proportion to the humiliation and expense of the method and means by which a way is made for our having the gift. He gave him to dwell amongst us; he gave him to us incarnate, or in our nature; and in the like though sinless infirmities. He gave him to us in a low and afflicted state; and not only so, but as slain, that he might be a feast for our souls.

The grace of God in bestowing this gift is most free. It was what God was under no obligation to bestow. He might have rejected fallen man, as he did the fallen angels. It was what we never did any thing to merit; it was given while we were yet enemies, and before we had so much as repented. It was from the love of God who saw no excellency in us to attract it; and it was without expectation of ever being requited for it.—And it is from mere grace that the benefits of Christ are applied to such and such particular persons. Those that are called and sanctified are to attribute it alone to the good pleasure of God's goodness by which they are distinguished. He is sovereign, and hath mercy on whom he will have mercy.

Man hath now a greater dependence on the grace of God than he had before the fall. He depends on free goodness of God for much more than he did then. Then he depended on God's goodness for conferring the reward of perfect obedience; for God was not obliged to promise and bestow that reward. But now we are dependent on the grace of God for much more; we stand in need of grace, not only to bestow glory upon us, but to deliver us from hell and eternal wrath. Under the first covenant we depended on God's goodness to give us the reward of righteousness; and so we do now: But we stand in need of God's free and sovereign grace to give us that righteousness; to pardon our sin, and release us from the guilt and infinite demerit of it.

And as we are dependent on the goodness of God for more now than under the first covenant, so we are dependent on a much greater, more free and wonderful goodness. We are now more dependent on God's arbitrary and sovereign good pleasure. We were in our first estate dependent on God for holiness. We had our original righteousness from him; but then holiness was not bestowed in such a way of sovereign good pleasure as it is now. Man was created holy, for it became God to create holy all his reasonable creatures. It would have been a disparagement to the holiness of God's nature, if he had made an intelligent creature unholy. But now when fallen man is made holy, it is from mere and arbitrary grace; God may for ever deny holiness to the fallen creature if he pleases, without any disparagement to any of his perfections.

And we are not only indeed more dependent on the grace of God, but our dependence is much more conspicuous, because our own insufficiency and helplessness in ourselves is much more apparent in our fallen and undone state, than it was before we were either sinful or miserable. We are more apparently dependent on God for holiness, because we are first sinful, and utterly polluted, and afterward holy. So the production of the effect is sensible, and its derivation from God more obvious. If man was ever holy and always was so, it would not be so apparent, that he had not holiness necessarily, as an inseparable qualification of human nature. So we are more apparently dependent on free grace for the favour of God, for we are first justly the objects of his displeasure, and afterward are received into favour. We are more apparently dependent on God for happiness, being first miserable, and afterward happy. It is more apparently free and without merit in us, because we are actually without any kind of excellency to merit, if there could be any such thing as merit in creature-excellency. And we are not only without any true excellency, but are full of, and wholly defiled with, that which is infinitely odious. All our good is more apparently from God, because we are first naked and wholly without any good, and afterward enriched with all good.

2. We receive all from the *power* of God. Man's redemption is often spoken of as a work of wonderful power as well as grace. The great power of God appears in bringing a sinner from his low state from the depths of sin and misery, to such an exalted state of holiness and happiness. Eph. i. 19. "And what is the exceeding greatness of his power to us-ward who believe, according to the working of his mighty power."—

We are dependent on God's power through every step of our redemption. We are dependent on the power of God to convert us, and give faith in Jesus Christ, and the new nature. It is a work of creation: "If any man be in Christ, he is a new creature," 2 Cor. v. 17. "We are created in Christ Jesus," Eph. ii. 10. The fallen creature cannot attain to true holiness, but by being created again, Eph. iv. 24. "And that ye put on the new man, which after God is created in righteousness and true holiness." It is a raising from the dead, Colos. ii. 12, 13. "Wherein also ye are risen with him through the faith of the operation of God, who hath raised him from the dead." Yea, it is a more glorious work of power than mere creation, or raising a dead body to life, in that the effect attained is greater and more excellent. That holy and happy being, and spiritual life which is produced in the work of conversion, is a far greater and more glorious effect, than mere being and life. And the state from whence the change is made—a death in sin, a total corruption of nature, and depth of misery—is far more remote from the state attained, than mere death or non-entity.

It is by God's power also that we are preserved in a state of grace. 1 Pet. i. 5. "Who are kept by the power of God through faith unto salvation." As grace is at first from God, so it is continually from him, and is maintained by him, as much as light in the atmosphere is all day long from the sun, as well as at first dawning, or at sun-rising.—Men are dependent on the power of God for every exercise of grace, and for carrying on that work in the heart, for subduing sin and corruption, increasing holy principles, and enabling to bring forth fruit in good works. Man is dependent on divine power in bringing grace to its perfection, in making the soul completely amiable in Christ's glorious likeness, and filling of it with a satisfying joy and blessedness; and for the raising of the body to life, and to such a perfect state, that it shall be suitable for a habitation and organ for a soul so perfected and blessed. These are the most glorious effects of the power of God, that are seen in the series of God's acts with respect to the creatures.

Man was dependent on the power of God in his first estate, but he is more dependent on his power now; he needs God's power to do more things for him, and depends on a more wonderful exercise of his power. It was an effect of the power of God to make man holy at the first; but more remarkably so now, because there is a great deal of opposition and difficulty in the way. It is a more glorious effect of power to make that holy that was so depraved, and under the dominion of sin, than to confer holiness on that which before had nothing of the contrary. It is a more glorious work of power to rescue a soul out of the hands of the devil, and from the powers of darkness, and to bring it into a state of salvation, than to confer holiness where there was no pre-possession or opposition. Luke xi. 21, 22. "When a strong man armed keepeth his palace, his goods are in peace; but when a stronger than he shall come upon him, and overcome him, he taketh from him all his armour wherein he trusted, and divideth his spoils." So it is a more glorious work of power to uphold a soul in a state of grace and holiness, and to carry it on till it is brought to glory, when there is so much sin remaining in the heart resisting, and Satan with all his might opposing, than it would have been to have kept man from falling at first, when Satan had nothing in man.—Thus we have shown how the redeemed are dependent on God for all their good, as they have all of him.

Secondly, They are also dependent on God for all, as they have all *through* him. God is the medium of it, as well as the author and fountain of it. All we have, wisdom, the pardon of sin, deliverance from hell, acceptance into God's favour, grace and holiness, true comfort and happiness, eternal life and glory, is from God by a Mediator; and this Mediator is God; which Mediator we have an absolute dependence upon, as he through whom we receive all. So that here is another way wherein we have our dependence on God for all good. God not only gives us the Mediator, and accepts his mediation, and of his power and grace bestows the things purchased by the Mediator; but he the Mediator is God.

Our blessings are what we have by purchase; and the purchase is made of God, the blessings are purchased of him, and God gives the purchaser; and not only so, but God is the purchaser. Yea, God is both the purchaser and the price; for Christ who is God, purchased these blessings for us, by offering up himself as the price of our salvation. He purchased eternal life by the sacrifice of himself. Heb. vii. 27. "He offered up himself." And chap. ix. 26. "He hath appeared to take away sin by the sacrifice of himself." Indeed it was the human nature that was offered; but it was the same person with the divine, and therefore was an infinite price.

As we thus have our good through God, we have a dependence on him in a respect that man in his first estate had not. Man was to have eternal life then through his own righteousness; so that he had partly a dependence upon what was in himself; for we have a dependence upon that through which we have our good, as well as that from which we have it: and though man's righteousness that he then depended on was indeed from God, yet it was his own, it was inherent in himself; so that his dependence was not so *immediately* on God. But now the righteousness that we are dependent on is not in ourselves, but in God. We are saved through the righteousness of Christ: he *is made unto us righteousness;* and therefore is prophesied of, Jer. xxiii. 6, under that name, "the Lord our righteousness." In that the righteousness we are justified by is the righteousness of Christ, it is the righteousness of God. 2 Cor. v. 21. "That we might be made the righteousness of God in him."—Thus in redemption we have not only all things of God, but by and through him, 1 Cor. viii. 6. "But to us there is but one God, the Father, of whom are all things, and we in him; and one Lord Jesus Christ, by whom are all things, and we by him."

Thirdly, The redeemed have all their good *in God.* We not only have it of him, and through him, but it consists in him; he is all our good.—The good of the redeemed is either objective or inherent. By their objective good, I mean that extrinsic object, in the possession and enjoyment of which they are happy. Their inherent good is that excellency or pleasure which is in the soul itself. With respect to both of which the redeemed have all their good in God, or, which is the same thing, God himself is all their good.

1. The redeemed have all their *objective* good in God. God himself is the great good which they are brought to the possession and enjoyment of by redemption. He is the highest good, and the sum of all that good which Christ purchased. God is the inheritance of the saints; he is the portion of their souls. God is their wealth and treasure, their food, their life, their dwelling-place, their ornament and diadem, and their everlasting honour and glory. They have none in heaven but God; he is the great good which the redeemed are received to at death, and which they are to rise to at the end of the world. The Lord God is the light of the heavenly Jerusalem; and is the "river of the water of life" that runs, and "the tree of life that grows, in the midst of the paradise of God." The glorious excellencies and beauty of God will be what will for ever entertain the minds of the saints, and the love of God will be their everlasting feast. The redeemed will indeed enjoy other things; they will enjoy the angels, and will enjoy one another: but that which they shall enjoy in the angels, or each other, or in any thing else whatsoever, that will yield them delight and happiness, will be what shall be seen of God in them.

2. The redeemed have all their *inherent* good in God. Inherent good is two-fold; it is either excellency or pleasure. These the redeemed not only derive from God, as caused by him, but have them in him. They have spiritual excellency and joy by a kind of participation of God. They are made excellent by a communication of God's excellency. God puts his own beauty, *i. e.* his beautiful likeness, upon their souls. They are made partakers of the divine nature, or moral image of God. 2 Pet. i. 4. They are holy by being made partakers of God's holiness, Heb. xii. 10. The saints are beautiful and blessed by a communication of God's holiness and joy, as the moon and planets are bright by the sun's light. The saint hath spiritual joy and pleasure by a kind of effusion of God on the soul. In these things the redeemed have communion with God; that is, they partake with him and of him.

The saints have both their spiritual excellency and blessedness by the gift of the Holy Ghost, and his dwelling in them. They are not only caused by the Holy Ghost, but are in him as their principle. The Holy Spirit becoming an inhabitant, is a vital principle in the soul. He, acting in, upon, and with the soul, becomes a fountain of true holiness and joy, as a spring is of water, by the exertion and diffusion of itself. John iv. 14. "But whosoever drinketh of the water that I shall give him, shall never thirst; but the water that I shall give him, shall be in him a well of water springing up into everlasting life." Compared with chap. vii. 38, 39. "He that believeth on me, as the scripture hath said, out of his belly shall flow rivers of living water; but this spake he of the Spirit, which they that believe on him should receive." The sum of what Christ has purchased for us, is that spring of water spoken of in the former of those places, and those rivers of living water spoken of in the latter. And the sum of the blessings, which the redeemed shall receive in heaven, is that river of water of life that proceeds from the throne of God and the Lamb, Rev. xxii. 1. which doubtless signifies the same with those rivers of living water, explained John vii. 38, 39. which is elsewhere called the "river of God's pleasures." Herein consists the fulness of good, which the saints receive of Christ. It is by partaking of the Holy Spirit, that they have communion with Christ in his fulness. God hath given the Spirit, not by measure unto him; and they do receive of his fulness, and grace for grace. This is the sum of the saints' inheritance; and therefore that little of the Holy Ghost which believers have in this world, is said to be the earnest of their inheritance, 2 Cor. i. 22. "Who hath also sealed us, and given us the Spirit in our hearts." And chap. v. 5. "Now he that hath wrought us for the self same thing, is God, who also hath given unto us the earnest of the Spirit." And Eph. i. 13, 14. "Ye were sealed with that Holy Spirit of promise, which is the earnest of our inheritance, until the redemption of the purchased possession."

The Holy Spirit and good things are spoken of in scripture as the same; as if the Spirit of God communicated to the soul, comprised all good things. Matt. vii. 11. "How much more shall your heavenly Father give good things to them that ask him?" In Luke it is, chap. xi. 13. "How much more shall your heavenly Father give the Holy Spirit to them that ask him?" This is the sum of the blessings that Christ died to procure, and the subject of gospel-promises. Gal. iii. 13, 14. "He was made a curse for us, that we might receive the promise of the Spirit through faith." The Spirit of God is the great promise of the Father. Luke xxiv. 49. "Behold, I send the promise of my Father upon you." The Spirit of God therefore is called "the Spirit of promise;" Eph. i. 33. This promised thing Christ received, and had given into his hand, as soon as he had finished the work of our redemption, to bestow on all that he had redeemed; Acts ii. 13. "Therefore being by the right hand of God exalted, and having received of the Father the promise of the Holy Ghost, he hath shed forth this, which ye both see and hear." So that all the holiness and happiness of the redeemed is in God. It is in the communications, indwelling, and acting of the Spirit of God. Holiness and happiness are in the fruit, here and hereafter, because God dwells in them, and they in God.

Thus God has given us the Redeemer, and it is by him that our good is purchased. So God is the Redeemer and the price; and he also is the good purchased. So that all that we have is of God, and through him, and in him. Rom. xi. 36. "For of him, and through him, and to him, (or in him,) are all things." The same in the Greek that is here rendered *to him*, is rendered *in him*, 1 Cor. viii. 6.

II. God is glorified in the work of redemption by this means, *viz.* By there being so great and universal a dependence of the redeemed on him.

1. Man hath so much the greater occasion and obligation to notice and acknowledge God's perfections and all-sufficiency. The greater the creature's dependence is on God's perfections, and the greater concern he has with them, so much the greater occasion he has to take notice of them. So much the greater concern any one has with and dependence upon the power and grace of God, so much the greater occasion has he to take notice of that power and grace. So much the greater and more immediate dependence there is on the divine holiness, so much the greater occasion to take notice of and acknowledge that. So much the greater and more absolute dependence we have on the divine perfections, as belonging to the several persons of the Trinity, so much the greater occasion have we to observe and own the divine glory of each of them. That which we are most concerned with, is surely most

in the way of our observation and notice; and this kind of concern with any thing, *viz.* dependence, does especially tend to command and oblige the attention and observation. Those things that we are not much dependent upon, it is easy to neglect; but we can scarce do any other than mind that which we have a great dependence on. By reason of our so great dependence on God, and his perfections and in so many respects, he and his glory are the more directly set in our view, which way soever we turn our eyes.

We have the greater occasion to take notice of God's all-sufficiency, when all our sufficiency is thus every way of him. We have the more occasion to contemplate him as an infinite good, and as the fountain of all good. Such a dependence on God demonstrates his all-sufficiency. So much as the dependence of the creature is on God, so much the greater does the creature's emptiness in himself appear; and so much the greater the creature's emptiness, so much the greater must the fulness of the being be who supplies him. Our having all *of* God, shows the fulness of his power and grace; our having all through him, shows the fulness of his merit and worthiness; and our having all in him, demonstrates his fulness of beauty, love, and happiness. And the redeemed, by reason of the greatness of their dependence on God, have not only so much the greater occasion, but obligation to contemplate and acknowledge the glory and fulness of God. How unreasonable and ungrateful should we be, if we did not acknowledge that sufficiency and glory which we absolutely, immediately, and universally depend upon!

2. Hereby is demonstrated how great God's glory is considered comparatively, or as compared with the creature's.—By the creature being thus wholly and universally dependent on God, it appears that the creature is nothing, and that God is all. Hereby it appears that God is infinitely above us; that God's strength, and wisdom, and holiness, are infinitely greater than ours. However great and glorious the creature apprehends God to be, yet if he be not sensible of the difference between God and him, so as to see that God's glory is great, compared with his own, he will not be disposed to give God the glory due to his name. If the creature in any respects sets himself upon a level with God, or exalts himself to any competition with him, however he may apprehend that great honour and profound respect may belong to God

from those that are at a greater distance, he will not be so sensible of its being due from him. So much the more men exalt themselves, so much the less will they surely be disposed to exalt God. It is certainly what God aims at in the disposition of things in redemption, (if we allow the scriptures to be a revelation of God's mind,) that God should appear full, and man in himself empty, that God should appear all, and man nothing. It is God's declared design that others should not "glory in his presence;" which implies that it is his design to advance his own comparative glory. So much the more man "glories in God's presence," so much the less glory is ascribed to God.

3. By its being thus ordered, that the creature should have so absolute and universal a dependence on God, provision is made that God should have our whole souls, and should be the object of our undivided respect. If we had our dependence partly on God, and partly on something else, man's respect would be divided to those different things on which he had dependence. Thus it would be if we depended on God only for a part of our good, and on ourselves, or some other being, for another part: Or, if we had our good only from God, and through another that was not God, and in something else distinct from both, our hearts would be divided between the good itself and him from whom, and him through whom we received it. But now there is no occasion for this, God being not only he from or of whom we have all good, but also through whom, and is that good itself, that we have from him and through him. So that whatsoever there is to attract our respect, the tendency is still directly towards God, all unites in him as the centre.

USE

1. We may here observe the marvellous wisdom of God, in the work of redemption. God hath made man's emptiness and misery, his low, lost and ruined state, into which he sunk by the fall, an occasion of the greater advancement of his own glory, as in other ways, so particularly in this, that there is now much more universal and apparent dependence of man on God. Though God be pleased to lift man out of that dismal abyss of sin and wo into which he has fallen, and exceedingly to exalt him in excellency and honour, and to a high pitch of

glory and blessedness, yet the creature hath nothing in any respect to glory of; all the glory evidently belongs to God, all is in a mere, and most absolute, and divine dependence on the Father, Son, and Holy Ghost. And each person of the Trinity is equally glorified in this work: There is an absolute dependence of the creature on every one for all: All is of the Father, all through the Son, and all in the Holy Ghost. Thus God appears in the work of redemption as all in all. It is fit that he who is, and there is none else, should be the Alpha and Omega, the first and the last, the all and the only, in this work.

2. Hence those doctrines and schemes of divinity that are in any respect opposite to such an absolute and universal dependence on God, derogate from his glory, and thwart the design of our redemption. And such are those schemes that put the creature in God's stead, in any of the mentioned respects, that exalt man into the place of either Father, Son, or Holy Ghost, in any thing pertaining to our redemption. However they may allow of a dependence of the redeemed on God, yet they deny a dependence that is so *absolute* and universal. They own an entire dependence on God for *some* things, but not for others; they own that we depend on God for the gift and acceptance of a Redeemer, but deny so absolute a dependence on him for the obtaining of an *interest* in the Redeemer. They own an absolute dependence on the Father for giving his Son, and on the Son for working out redemption, but not so entire a dependence on the Holy Ghost for *conversion*, and a being in Christ, and so coming to a title to his benefits. They own a dependence on God for *means* of grace, but not absolutely for the benefit and success of those means; a partial dependence on the power of God, for obtaining and exercising holiness, but not a mere dependence on the arbitrary and sovereign grace of God. They own a dependence on the free grace of God for a reception into his favour, so far that it is without any proper merit, but not as it is without being attracted, or moved with any excellency. They own a partial dependence on Christ, as he through whom we have life, as having purchased new terms of life, but still hold that the righteousness through which we have life is inherent in ourselves, as it was under the first covenant. Now whatever scheme is inconsistent with our *entire* dependence on God for all, and of having all of him, through him, and in him, it is repugnant to the design and tenor of the gospel, and robs it of that which God accounts its lustre and glory.

3. Hence we may learn a reason why faith is that by which we come to have an interest in this redemption; for there is included in the nature of faith, a sensible acknowledgment of *absolute dependence* on God in this affair. It is very fit that it should be required of all, in order to their having the benefit of this redemption, that they should be sensible of, and acknowledge their dependence on God for it. It is by this means that God hath contrived to glorify himself in redemption; and it is fit that he should at least have this glory of those that are the subjects of this redemption, and have the benefit of it.—Faith is a sensibleness of what is real in the work of redemption; and the soul that believes doth entirely depend on God for all salvation, in its own sense and act. Faith abases men, and exalts God; it gives all the glory of redemption to him alone. It is necessary in order to saving faith, that man should be emptied of himself, be sensible that he is "wretched, and miserable, and poor, and blind, and naked." Humility is a great ingredient of true faith: He that truly receives redemption, receives it as a little child, Mark x. 15. "Whosoever shall not receive the kingdom of heaven as a little child, he shall not enter therein." It is the delight of a believing soul to abase itself and exalt God alone: that is the language of it, Psalm cxv. 1. "Not unto us, O Lord, not unto us, but to thy name give glory."

4. Let us be exhorted to exalt God alone, and ascribe to him all the glory of redemption. Let us endeavour to obtain, and increase in, a sensibleness of our great dependence on God, to have our eye on him alone, to mortify a self-dependent, and self-righteous disposition. Man is naturally exceeding prone to exalt himself, and depend on his own power or goodness; as though from himself he must expect happiness. He is prone to have respect to enjoyments alien from God and his Spirit, as those in which happiness is to be found.—But this doctrine should teach us to exalt God *alone;* as by trust and reliance, so by praise. *Let him that glorieth, glory in the Lord.* Hath any man hope that he is converted, and sanctified, and that his mind is endowed with true excellency and spiritual beauty? that his sins are forgiven, and he received into God's favour, and exalted to the honour and blessedness of being his child, and an heir of eternal life? let him give God all the glory; who alone makes him to differ from the worst of men in this world, or the most miserable of the damned in hell. Hath any man much comfort and strong hope of eternal life? let not his hope lift

him up, but dispose him the more to abase himself, to reflect on his own exceeding unworthiness of such a favour, and to exalt God alone. Is any man eminent in holiness, and abundant in good works? let him take nothing of the glory of it to himself, but ascribe it to him whose "workmanship we are, created in Christ Jesus unto good works."

19

WILLIAM BENTLEY

1759, born June 22, at Boston
1777, graduated from Harvard
1777–80, taught in lower schools
1780–83, tutor of Latin and Greek at Harvard
1783–1819, pastor of East Church, Salem, Mass.
1784–1819, *Diary* (published 1905–14, in four volumes)
1790, *Sermon in Stone Chapel*
1791, *Sermon Occasioned by the Death of Jonathon Gardner, Esq.*
1793, *Oration, in Commemoration of the Birthday of Washington*
1796, *A Sermon Preached before the Ancient and Honourable Artillery Company, in Boston, June 6, 1796*
1819, died December 29, at Salem

AMONG the fruits of the Enlightenment was the widespread belief in natural religion. This belief was held in common by Deists, liberal Christians, and some orthodox Christians. It was natural religion as distinguished from revealed religion: those universal religious ideas which man holds independently of Scriptural authority. It was natural religion as distinguished from artificial religion: those universal religious ideas which man holds by virtue of his nature independently of the institutional sanctions given to human invention by churches. The lower limit, the least common denominator of religious ideas, seemed to the eighteenth century to be three: the idea of a creative first cause; the idea of a future life; and the idea of a universal moral order. Deists, in general, thought that it was necessary to break down the Christian churches in order to restore natural religion. Orthodox Christians tended to the belief that natural religion and revelation could not contradict each other or come into conflict. Liberal Christians saw the primitive religion of Jesus as the ideal expression of natural religion, and sought by purification of the church to return to that ideal. "Is it not time," said Bentley, "to recur to the instructions of this wise friend of mankind, and to accept them uncorrupted by traditions, creeds or councils?"

In this instance, at least, liberality and tolerance went hand in hand. The Deists were intolerantly anticlerical and antiecclesiastical; orthodox Christians were intolerantly anti-Deistic. Liberal Christians could and did tolerate every shade of opinion. William Bentley, the Salem liberal, for example, regarded Paine's *Age of Reason* as a "contemptible publication," but was able to make a sane and just comment on Paine himself. He loaned copies of Deistic books to members of his congregation and bore with equanimity the attacks made on him for infidelity. Fortunately for his peace of mind, Bentley's Salem was a town of cosmopolites, whose acquaintance for purposes of trading with the inhabitants of far corners of the earth had broadened their outlook and made them receptive to the latitudinarianism of their minister.

Bentley's eulogy of one of his parishioners might well have been an account of his own tolerance. "He never thought men who differed from him, were fools or knaves. He had a persuasion that religious opinions depend not on names, but upon sincere inquiry, for their best influence, and that an honest mind might be so circumstanced, as to admit the most absurd doctrines, and be uncharitable in the defence of them, while there might be great benevolence in the native purposes of the heart. . . . He loved men, rather than opinions, . . . and he desired to know more of their actions, than of their professions." [1]

Bentley was a Unitarian; he believed that Jesus had lived an ideal which others might benefit by following, but he did not accept Jesus as a divine savior. He substituted Priestley's catechism for the Westminster catechism in his congregation. He accepted the Unitarian hypothesis after careful study and became an open proponent of the belief that Jesus is not God. He believed that God intended the good of his creatures, and he therefore leaned towards Universalism; not that he believed that all men would be saved, but that he was convinced that "all men are, and always have been, capable of salvation." "Heaven and happiness were not designed by God as the exclusive rights of learned priests, or ingenious doctors; they are the end which God has proposed for all mankind, and are therefore, by the same means, attainable by all men."

If salvation is attainable by all, it cannot be based on such a particularist doctrine as the Puritan doctrine of election, nor can it be the reward of riches, honors, learning, birth, or breeding, not all of which are the possession of all men. "Virtue alone is the moral happiness of the world, and personal virtue alone secures heaven"; and virtue is within the powers of all men, for "the different capacities of men may admit degrees of virtue, but all are consistent with religious integrity."

[1] *A Funeral Discourse . . . on . . . Major General John Fiske*, Salem, 1797, pp. 16, 24.

When religion is thus judged, not by professions of faith, by external advantages, or by learning, but by its fruits in right actions or obedience to the will of God, "we are able to see how all men are accountable for their respective advantages; and hereby we leave not God as a respecter of persons." When we define religion by "sober action," "how much more acceptable is the honest devotion of an heathen, than the hypocrisy of a Christian! How much more pure the charity of a savage, than the pulpit-anathemas of a priest against churches which differ from his own." "All the exercises of instrumental religion are not worth one good deed, and a dishonest act is more than a balance for them all."

If the goodness of men's lives is the basis on which they are to be happy here and saved hereafter, if the ceremonies and dogmas of religions are incidental to salvation, "we may . . . infer the original dignity of natural religion" which "is still the most excellent religion," and which "consists in doing the will of God, as our inquiries may make it known to us, and our knowledge of its agreement with our nature confirms us in our affection for it." The original law is the law of nature as established by nature's God, and "neither this law, nor its authority is weakened by Christianity . . . Natural law is always right. Christianity will always assist men to go right." Christianity supplements, not supplants, natural religion.

As for revelation, we are faced with a dilemma. If revelation supersedes the original law, it must do so because of some defect in the original law, which is to argue a defect in God, which is impossible, or, if it does not supersede the original law, it must be a temporary adjunct to the original law, subservient to it, until such time as its aid is no longer necessary. Christianity, founded on revelation, is thus merely "an help to recover the full force of natural law," and therefore only temporary. In this way Bentley weakened Christianity as an institutional religion at the same time as he emphasized the accord between the moral principles of the natural law and Christian morality.

Finally, it should be noted that in common with the enlightened thought of his age, Bentley placed a high value on human life and human concerns. The noble end proposed by religion is "to perfect the constitutions which God has given us." God was "pleased to constitute us for happy, natural action in the present being, and yet render us capable of future life." Whatever the degree to which men may place importance on status, all men are "sufficient for wise action." Thus, he was predisposed to Jeffersonianism in politics and did, in fact, incur the enmity of conservatives for his unfailing support of republican ideas.

A SERMON PREACHED AT THE STONE CHAPEL
IN BOSTON, SEPTEMBER 12, 1790

Not every one that saith unto me, Lord, Lord, shall enter into the Kingdom of
Heaven; but he that doth the will of my father, who is in Heaven.

THE ingenuous simplicity, which recommends the doctrines and
precepts of Jesus Christ, forms a very pleasing evidence of his
design to reform the world. Should an impartial stranger consider the
history of his religion at its most favorable periods, he could hardly
imagine that it had so pure an origin; that the language of condescen-
sion, and the simple precepts of life, inspired by an hope of immortality, could produce various and contending sects, who had lost all affection for each other, had neglected the best virtues of life, and had
built their hopes of glory on zeal and contention. Still the melancholy
proofs of such conduct have not prevented the belief, that nothing
could be more benevolent than the character of Jesus Christ. Every
thing kind flowed from his lips. He was born in humble life, and never
rose in his distinctions beyond what humble life could suggest and
comprehend. Affection was recommended in every discourse; points
never debated with passion; the history of his religion, so offensive to
his countrymen, intimated in parables; and every idea of limited design excluded from his heart. Is it not time to recur to the instruction
of this wise friend of mankind, and to accept them uncorrupted by
traditions, creeds or councils? Should a preacher appear in this assembly, of venerable piety, or simple manners, and with all the marks
of humble birth, and declare, as the introduction to his religious service,
a zeal for the most important moral truths, and declare that by their
fruits men should be known; and to our text should he subjoin, Many
will say to me, Lord, Lord, have we not prophesied in thy name, and
in thy name done many wonderful works, and then I will profess to
them, I never knew you; and should he close with the memorable
words which represented only those who obeyed his precepts as founded
on a rock; could you suppose his design mysterious, or his doctrine
partial, or illiberal? Judge ye then of yourselves, what is right.

Let us then, in the consideration of the text, endeavour to obtain
the most obvious sense of the several expressions, that we may be sure
of the general sentiment they contain.

What could he have intended, in saying, that many would say, Lord, Lord? The words subjoined, very fully explain the intention. He that doth the will of my Father, shall be preferred. And the pretensions of such persons are cited in the next verse, in which the exercise of even supernatural powers is considered as in itself unavailing. We have corresponding expressions in Paul, who considered distinctly, all the evident endowments, of which the mind is capable, both miraculous and natural, and declared them insufficient without charity, which he defined to be practical godliness, to deserve the Christian character. They then, who cry, Lord, Lord, are they who do not obey the gospel, how far so ever they may go in pretensions of affection for it. Though they hold the first ranks, and the first gifts in the church; if they have the most commanding eloquence in delivering truth to others, or the most availing external sanctity, to gain them respect and confidence: Yea, if God should even supernaturally endue them for the most noble ends of his providence; yet, if they have not a right, moral temper, the whole shall not avail to place them among the meanest of those who have been obedient. What a check this is to the presumptuous, to the uncharitable, to the hypocritical, and to the unfaithful! Heaven and happiness were not designed by God as the exclusive rights of learned priests, or ingenious doctors; they are the end which God has proposed for all mankind, and are therefore, by the same means, attainable by all men. Riches and honors cannot ensure the purchase; neither can learning, pompous titles, respect nor dignity. Virtue alone is the moral happiness of the world, and personal virtue alone secures heaven. Let then priests declaim, this is sure, that the increase of virtue is the increase of happiness; and whatever sound may be made in this world, virtue alone will distinguish us in the next.

Having seen how our religious advantages may render us happy, by rendering us virtuous, let us, in the next place, inquire, what Jesus intended by doing the will of his Father. And he has so connected his discourse, that whatever sense may be applied to his words, in themselves considered, they here admit only one explanation. When he announced his last blessing, it is upon those who keep these sayings and do them; and these sayings or precepts are the will of God. As no new ritual is proposed, or doctrine which does not require action, something to be done, we may safely infer, that when he propounded his salvation to his countrymen, proposed his own rewards, upon doing the will of God, he intended his commandments. What the nature and extent of these commands were, he has determined by the preceding parts of his discourse; so that his rewards are offered to all who conformed to their conceptions of their moral obligations, and the foundation of his religion is placed in this disposition. For whatever consisted in belief, public profession, and zeal, they were supposed to perform, while the most important end of religion was neglected.

Such as were obedient, were of the kingdom of heaven. This expression very frequently occurs, and never when it may not in some sense apply to the history of Christianity. By some it has been thought to denote the commencement of a future state, but never is so necessarily limited to this sense, as to prevent its general design to represent the progress of Christian truth in the world. When they, who do the will of God, are pronounced to be of the kingdom of heaven, it intends, that as to them, religion has its true and most acceptable effect: That the proper way to secure divine blessing, was to obey, to act most agreeably to our obligations, and from the best motives reason or revelation could furnish. This obedience depends on our habitual inclination, connected with reasonable pursuits after knowledge. The different capacities of men may admit degrees of virtue, but all are consistent with religious integrity.

From the sentiments of the text, it is then inferred, that all men are, and always have been, capable of salvation. For if no external advantages, or personal knowledge of a revelation, can avail, without an habitual disposition to obedience, and this obedience is to be judged by its fruits, then this disposition is preferred to all those advantages, in themselves considered. And as the will of God implies the obligations of his creatures to all moral duties; so far as they are sensible of them, and conform, they do, in their measure, which is all that can be required, perform his will, the end proposed in the kingdom of God by Jesus Christ. This is an obvious doctrine of Jesus; and perhaps the reason why any have been taught to overlook it, has been, that it favors not those comparative, if not exclusive advantages to which some pretend, as it certainly does not their hopes, who cry, Lord, Lord, with affected devotion, and for their accomplishments, real or pretended, would be thought better than others, without any just claims. When men can inform us of a more noble end in revelation, than to perfect the constitutions which God has given us, we may suspect our argument; but when all the various opinions may accord with this end, in the judgments of their several advocates, we cannot be blamed for accepting the conclusion as free from their intricacies, or absurdities, as is possible. For while objects and powers are so admirably connected in the whole system, to make an abstruse religion, in order to introduce a distinction, which is internal; since the exclusive help attributed to the Christian religion makes no outward distinction in the moral world, and the effects of the different motives may account for all we see, is to affront the simplicity of the Christian faith. But by placing religion in sober action, we are able to see how all men are accountable for their respective advantages; and hereby we leave not God as a respecter of persons, and prevent not the equitable distribution of his favors. God, we all know, has variously bestowed his gifts upon the human race; in equal variety he may have bestowed his moral as his other benefits; but as neither are in their relations unequal, and both, may have a worthy end, there is no injustice with him. Without such sentiments, our most evident conceptions of justice may be violated.

What evidence should we consider as sufficient to prove this to be a doctrine of the Christian religion? At the critical moment when this truth was to be declared, should an heathen, possessed of devout respect to heaven, and exemplary in his life, be declared acceptable to God, and revelation assist this true light with miraculous testimony, would it be conclusive? Can any evidence be better adapted? This we can produce, without any forced or critical construction, in positive terms. Peter was taught to call nothing unclean, because the Jews thought other nations without the favor of God. Cornelius, a Roman officer in the province, was, for his devotion and alms, accepted of God. He was not proselyted to the Jewish religion, because Peter says, it was unlawful to keep company with him. Yet upon this evidence Peter exclaims, Of a truth I perceive that God is no respecter of persons, for in every nation, he that feareth him, and worketh righteousness, is accepted of him. Nor was this truth questioned in the disputes respecting the use of the Hebrew ritual. If evidence, in such circumstances, produces not conviction, arguments may be applied in vain. And what a generous idea does this truth give us of God! He was the friend of

Israel; that in the end he might advance a universal religion; but for a distant good, he never disregarded a present benefit. He knew the capacity he had given, and the several means by which it might be improved. He knew the distance of our most pure conceptions from truth, in all its relations, and could easily pardon the little varieties in those opinions, which were, at best, imperfect. If he took care for ravens, how much more would he take care of mankind! How much more acceptable is the honest devotion of an heathen, than the hypocrisy of a Christian! How much more pure the charity of a savage, than the pulpit-anathemas of a priest against churches which differ from his own. Blush, O Christian, that thy illiberal heart can call thy God to justify thy insolent attacks on other men, and fear lest thy fate, more miserable than their own, teach thee, with sorrow, to renounce the execrable idea.

And what may we infer more readily from this truth, than that the natural advantages of men constitute their only probation? Their gratitude is to arise from blessings they do really receive, their only devotion from the glory they behold, and their only obedience from the obligations they perceive. And do not our minds revolt, at the first reflection, on any other constitution? Let misery, in any degree, be increased by the guilt of men, that they should not rise beyond the strength of their powers in such state, is curse enough. But to superadd a gift which man has no natural power or inclination to accept, even when connected with his highest happiness, is a policy unworthy the bounty of heaven. As revelation shews us the motives adapted to strengthen and improve our virtue, will not God direct the natural powers to the best advantage, if he intends a bounty? Our most familiar ideas of goodness, especially such as the gospel recommends, assure us of it, and we dishonor God by any other supposition. We are all his offspring.

We may also infer the original dignity of natural religion. For what good ends Christians have shaken the foundations of their own religion, by depreciating natural religion, may not be easy to determine; but if the text is rightly explained, natural religion is still the most excellent religion. This consists in doing the will of God, as our inquiries may make it known to us, and our knowledge of its agreement with our nature confirms us in our affection for it. Neither this law, nor its authority, is weakened by Christianity; for as Christianity has the same object, it can, at best, but claim to assist us in the knowledge, and confirm us in the practice of it. For to suppose an original law so defective in itself as not to be sufficient to direct us, is to admit, at once, a defect in our constitution, which is as dishonorable to God, as to charge him with changes in the constitution of any other part of nature, because his original laws were not sufficient. Revelation cannot then be admitted but as a part of the original plan, or rather as such a spring as may act in subserviency to the original law, till a variety of causes, wisely fitted to act, may render this assistance unnecessary. Christianity is an help to recover the full force of natural law. The Son himself shall then be put under, and God, by perfecting human nature, be all in all.

If this be true, there is not an absolute, but only a relative difference in the condition of men. Natural law is always right. Christianity will assist men to go right. There is nothing beyond our conceptions in this view of Christianity. If God was pleased to constitute us for happy, natural action in the present being, and yet render us capable of future life, but not place the evidence of this future life so certainly in our natural condition as not to admit other evidence, we may not doubt of the benefit, and that he is able to make the evidence appear wise and fit. And when it concurs with natural religion, by our present good, to promote our final good, it may assist some, while it offers no injury to others; and as all things may be in a progressive state, it may, at some future time, be as universal as natural religion itself. But whatever our opinions of such things may be, we should be careful not so to frame them as to exclude natural law, and injure one of our first and most noble ideas of perfection, an impartial regard to the capacities of creatures which God has created for happiness. However we may magnify our relative advantages, let us leave all men sufficient for wise action; and if our just and exalted ideas of our own privileges do produce as just and exalted improvements, we are more sure not to be found among those boasting professors, who have said much and done little, and may have our reward in ample glory for doing the will of God.

The practical use of our text should be, to teach us to place religion in those things in which it really consists. However numerous our doctrines, whether simple or mysterious; whether we receive all the dogmas of the Church or not, let us consider that we should produce good fruits. To have accurate and well defined sentiments, is not unworthy of our most serious attention. To be distinguished, may be most laudable ambition. But let us not mistake either of them for religion, without regard to our actions. All the orthodoxy in the world will not vindicate a dishonest man. If we believe in supernatural gifts, and that we possess them, let us doubt our religion, if we allow ourselves to violate justice, defame or injure other men. However God may produce his desired regeneration in the mind, let it not have a visionary, but an active operation, that we may shew, out of a good understanding, the works of meekness and love. But all the exercise of instrumental religion are not worth one good deed, and a dishonest act is more than a balance for them all. We cannot be too careful to assist our virtue by the simple institutions of religion; these ought to have been done, and not the other left undone; but we are guilty of heinous iniquity, if we make them a cloke to our vices. Let us then reflect on the various duties of external religion, which we have attended with such deception. How many solemn sounds without sober thought! how many gracious words and ill actions! how many attempts to deceive by assumed gravity! how many tears in vain! and let us learn to despise such hypocrisy. Let the language of our countenances express the cheerful devotion of our hearts. Let our gravity arise from a just sense of religious truth, and all our actions have an undisputed testimony to our sincerity. The cries, and groans, and complaints of dangerous errors, disturb the weak, the credulous and superstitious. But the single act of injustice speaks louder to a discerning man than all this cant and hypocrisy. When a man is found, who does not profess much, nor despise all, who is pure from guile, peaceable in his life, gentle in his manners, easily dissuaded from revenge, with an heart to pity and relieve the miserable, impartial in his judgement, and without dissimulation, this is the man of religion. This is an apostolic description of a good man; and whatever opinions he may have, he ought to have some, and he has a right to chuse for himself; this man is after God's own heart.

The candid sentiment of the text demands also a practical effect. The opinions of men belong to God, and the consciences of men are subject to no human tribunal. But wherever they have a virtuous effect, we ought in charity to suppose the favor of God. When the Mahomedan journies to Mecca, as his acts of self-denial spring from his serious belief, we have no authority to determine in God's stead. But when we see his devotion, his zeal, and the acts of his unfeigned obedience, our affection should teach us with what tenderness the Universal Parent views his creatures innocently erring before him. And we should dismiss all the partialities, which arise from our own particular connections. We should be particularly kind to virtue, wherever we may behold it; and prefer, in this regard, the distant stranger, who practises it, to the child of our bosom, who neglects it. By considering religion in this amiable view, we may increase our love for it, and be induced to consider ourselves, not of small societies only, under the formal obligations of social contracts, but as belonging to the household of the faithful, who dwell in every nation, and in every clime, with one God and Father, who hateth nothing that he has made, but loveth and cherisheth it.

While we consider religion in connection with the unnumbered ceremonies of superstition, spread in strange confusion over the earth, we may be inclined to forget the reverence we owe to it, and despise the true excellence and glory of our nature. When we observe how often the various incidents of life tear asunder the mask, and expose the dreadful features concealed under it, we may be induced to curse the religion which assisted the disguise. But when we familiarise the reflection, that true religion is true virtue, and that it is only superstition which lends the false appearance, we shall detest the imposition, not more as an insult to man, than to religion itself. And how happy should we be, if we could attain that Christian perfection, when we may love to appear what we are, and yet deserve the character of true Christians. We cannot be too cautious. A form of prayer will easily pass upon us as devotion. We may easily mistake our gifts for divine fervor, and pass on with our neighbours, and be as zealous as they, without the least virtue. Our caution should increase with our danger, and we should remember, that our great obligation is to keep the heart with all diligence, since from that alone are the issues of life.

20

EZRA STILES ELY

1786, born June 13, Lebanon, Conn.

1803, was graduated from Yale College

1803–6, studied theology with his father, Zebulon Ely

1806, ordained pastor of Presbyterian Church in Colchester, Conn.

c. 1810, served as chaplain of New York City Hospital

1811, *The Contrast between Calvinism and Hopkinsianism*

c. 1815, awarded degree of D.D. by Washington College, Tenn.

1819, *Conversations on the Science of the Human Mind*

c. 1825, pastor of Third Presbyterian Church, Philadelphia, Pa.

1825–36, edited the weekly publication *The Philadelphian*

1834, failed in an attempt to establish a college and theological seminary in Missouri

1835, *Endless Punishment*

1835–44, pastor of Pine St. Church, Philadelphia, Pa.

1844–51, pastor of Northern Liberties Church, Philadelphia, Pa.

1861, died

THE fiftieth anniversary of the Declaration of Independence found America superficially a united nation. She had weathered the post-Revolutionary disorders and developed an effective, flexible government under the Constitution. She had lived through the stresses and strains of the French Revolution. She had prosecuted a second and for much of the country an unwanted war against Great Britain, and had survived it. She was in the full flush of early expansion into the West. Under the surface, however, there was trouble brewing.

One reason was that the national leaders of both parties were men who made little display of concern for the fate of organized religion. There were many, especially in post-Puritan New England, who resented this and looked back longingly, as did David Daggett, to a time when "the minister with two or three principal characters were supreme in each town." Others, many of them, argued that Christianity and democracy needed each other; that "there never was a republic worthy of the name, unless among a people who were in a considerable degree under the influence of Christianity." Still others took a more active course and formed national denominational organizations or interdenominational groups such as the American Board of Foreign Missions, the American Bible Society, and the American Sunday School Union. Such activities, they thought, would halt the trend toward Deism, Unitarianism, and Universalism. There was a strong movement for rigid Sunday observance, which was marked by the extreme demand put before Congress that the government should forbid by law the transportation of the mails on Sunday; this demand was twice rejected, each time with an excellent majority report written by Colonel Richard M. Johnson, congressman from Kentucky. The movement was not halted; the demand became more and more vociferous that the United States avow itself legally what it was actually, a Christian nation.

At the height of this agitation Ezra Stiles Ely, a learned and pious Presbyterian minister, took the opportunity presented by the Fourth of July celebration in 1827 to suggest a political device by means of which orthodox Calvinist religious groups might gain control of American life without technical violation of the constitutional provisions against state interference in religious life. The key to his idea is given in the title of his speech; it is "The Duty of Christian Freemen to Elect Christian Rulers." More directly stated, the primary criterion of a candidate's qualification for office should be his Christianity, not his ability. Ely proposed an informal union of the major orthodox trinitarian denominations, to which he gave the name of "a Christian party in politics," to assure the election of candidates who met his qualification. It is noteworthy that Ely defended his plan by referring to the rights and liberties of Christians as Christians, rather than to those of men. He also attacked by parody the ideal of toleration in civil matters which Jefferson had stated in the *Notes on Virginia*.

Ely was a leader of Presbyterian thought. His fundamental beliefs involved the necessary interrelation of civil and religious life. From this he consistently argued that as the infidel had the political liberty to be an infidel, so the Christian had the political liberty to be a Christian. He went farther, however, and argued that the Christian had the obligation to be "as conscientiously religious at the polls as in the pulpit or house of worship." This made of his proposal an abuse of freedom of religion, because in it he advocated political action to gain religious ends. He may or may not have desired the ultimate union of church and state. He obviously did not desire an immediate establishment. He was concerned, as is clear from the appendix to the speech here reprinted, with the development of a militant group of voters who would prevent the election of liberal religionists, generally Deists, Unitarians, or Universalists, to public office.

The narrowness of Ely's definition of a Christian weakened his argument. He met opposition not only from such "free thinkers" as Robert Dale Owen and Frances Wright but also from leaders of the liberal Christian denominations. The Universalists were the most outspoken of the excluded groups. In Providence, Rhode Island, in 1828, David Pickering attacked Ely's plan as an "unhallowed attempt to effect a coalition of Church and State." He warned that unless an organized resistance were to be opposed to "the disciplined forces of the enemy," "the unprecedented efforts which are now employed, will ultimately succeed in the utter subversion of all the principles of civil and religious liberty." Again, in 1829, William Morse, pastor of the First Universalist Church in Nantucket, declared that Ely's efforts were an attempt "to rivet upon his fellow-man the chains of mental slavery." It is clear that Morse was concerned with the position of his own denomination, for he asked "What would liberty be, or the right of suffrage, but a name to such as belonged not to the union, if five of the most popular religious sects in this country should unite, and succeed in getting the reins of government into their own hands?"

The best of the Universalist attacks on Ely was that delivered by Zelotes Fuller in a Washington's Birthday address entitled "The Tree of Liberty," delivered in Philadelphia in 1830. The theme of this address was set in the brief preface, where the author wrote:

> If there ever was a time, when our civil and religious liberties were in danger —if there ever was a time, when the political sons of the illustrious Washington, should be inspired with fresh zeal, in behalf of the cause of freedom—if ever a time, when the united exertions of the friends of equal rights were called for, to suppress clerical intolerance, and to defeat priestly finesse, that time is the present.
>
> The only apology we have to make to a certain "Christian party in politics," is, that we mean just what we say.

Fuller's speech began with a defense of the natural rights doctrine; among the natural rights he included freedom of conscience. His discussion of Ely's plan centered in its attack on this natural right. He pointed out that a distinction must be made between the ostensible and the actual motives of Ely's supporters. Ostensibly, they designed merely to halt the transportation of the mail on Sunday or some other specific object. Actually, they intended to bring about a union of church and state and "to infuse the spirit of religious intolerance and persecution into the political institutions of our country and in the end completely to annihilate the political and religious liberty of the people." He continued with a challenge to the American people to defend their liberties against such encroachments, basing his challenge upon the thought that since sovereignty resides in the people, the people can remain free if they will to remain free.

Notable Unitarian opposition to Ely was an address by the constitutional authority Joseph Story, commemorating the first settlement of Salem. The theme of Story's attack is that "there is not a truth to be gathered from history more certain, or more momentous, than this, that civil liberty cannot long be separated from religious liberty without danger, and ultimately without destruction to both." The Puritan doctrine that a union of church and state was necessary Story called "the fundamental error of our ancestors." Those who tried to justify exclusion from political rights on religious grounds, "whatever badge they may wear . . . are enemies to us and our institutions."

Because of opposition such as this, Ely's "Christian Party in Politics" seems never to have materialized; his speech is worthy of reprinting here as an indication that the political theory of the Enlightment was on its way out. In the interest of the slaveholders Calhoun was already attacking the belief in equality; Everett denied the validity of the social contract theory; Ely attempted to whittle down the doctrine of natural rights; soon Thomas Dew and others were to try to recast the belief in liberty in order to justify slavery. The political philosophy of the Declaration of Independence, the Constitution, and the *Federalist* papers, was increasingly to be called into question, and Ely, whatever his practical success, was one of the questioners.

THE DUTY OF CHRISTIAN FREEMEN TO ELECT CHRISTIAN RULERS

THE FOLLOWING PAGES
ARE RESPECTFULLY INSCRIBED TO THOSE MEMBERS OF THE
SENATE OF THE STATE OF PENNSYLVANIA, WHO,
IN FEBRUARY, 1828,

SIGNALIZED THEMSELVES,
BY REFUSING TO GRANT AN ACT OF INCORPORATION TO
"THE AMERICAN SUNDAY SCHOOL UNION."

Extracts from the Sermon having been submitted to your Honourable Branch of the Legislature, your attention is solicited to the Discourse itself,

BY THE AUTHOR.

PSALM II. 10–12

"Be wise now therefore, O ye kings: be instructed, ye judges of the earth. Serve the Lord with fear, and rejoice with trembling. Kiss the Son, lest he be angry, and ye perish from the way; when his wrath is kindled but a little. Blessed are all they that put their trust in him."

THIS Psalm represents the Lord Jesus Christ as the rightful sovereign of all lands. The nations may rage, and the people imagine vain things; the kings and other rulers of the earth may take counsel and perseveringly oppose the Lord and his anointed, saying, "Let us break their bands asunder, and cast away their cords from us," for we neither feel, nor will regard, the obligations imposed by christianity; but it is all fruitless rebellion, for "He that sitteth in the heavens shall laugh: the Lord shall have them in derision." He will exercise his government over them, with, or without their consent; and if they are refractory, "then shall he speak unto them in his wrath, and vex them in his sore displeasure. Yet have I set my King upon my holy hill of Zion. I will declare the decree: the Lord hath said unto me, Thou art my son; this day have I begotten thee. Ask of me, and I shall give the heathen," i. e., *all the* nations, "for thine inheritance, and the uttermost parts of the earth for a possession. Thou shalt break them with a rod of iron; thou shalt dash them in pieces, like a potter's vessel."

On this exhibition of Messiah's reign over all the inhabitants of the earth, whether Jews or Gentiles, the exhortation and benediction of our text are founded. Let all princes, kings, judges, and rulers of every description, says the Psalmist, be exhorted to be wise for themselves and their people; let them learn true wisdom; and act in conformity with their duty and privilege in serving the Lord with filial fear and reverential joy. Let them render to the Son of God, in their private character and public stations, that submission of the heart, and homage of their lives, which he claims, "lest he be angry and they perish from the way, when his wrath is kindled but a little." The benediction follows: "Blessed are all they," whether nations or individuals; whether public rulers or private citizens, "that put their trust in him;" who is the Saviour of sinners and Governor among the nations.

Yes, "happy is that people that is in such a case: yea, happy is that people whose God is the Lord."

We have assembled, fellow citizens, on the anniversary of our Nation's birth day, in a rational and religious manner, to celebrate our independence of all foreign domination, and the goodness of God in making us a free and happy people. On what subject can I, on the present occasion, insist with more propriety, than on the duty of all the

rulers and citizens of these United States in the exercise and enjoyment of all their political rights, to honour the Lord Jesus Christ.

Let it then be distinctly stated and fearlessly maintained IN THE FIRST
PLACE, that every member of this Christian nation, from the highest to
the lowest, ought to serve the Lord with fear, and yield his sincere
homage to the Son of God. Every ruler *should be* an avowed and a
sincere friend of Christianity. He should know and believe the doctrines of our holy religion, and act in conformity with its precepts.
This *he ought* to do; because as a man he is required to serve the Lord;
and as a public ruler he is called upon by divine authority to "kiss the
Son." The commandment contained in Proverbs iii. 6. *"in all thy ways
acknowledge him,"* includes public as well as private ways, and political
no less than domestic ways. It is addressed equally to the man who
rules, and to the person who is subject to authority. If we may not disown our God and Saviour in *any* situation, it will follow that we are to
own him in *every* situation. Infinite wisdom has taught us, that *he who
ruleth over men must be just, ruling in the fear of God.* No *Christian*
can gainsay this decision. Let all then admit, that our civil rulers ought
to act a religious part in all the relations which they sustain. Indeed,
they ought pre-eminently to commit their way unto the Lord that he
may direct their steps; delight themselves in him, and wait patiently
for him; because by their example, if good, they can do more good than
private, less known citizens; and if evil, more harm. Their official
station is a talent entrusted to them for usefulness, for which they
must give account to their Maker. They are like a city set on a hill,
which cannot be hid; and it is a fact indisputable, that wickedness in
high places does more harm than in obscurity.

I would guard, however, against misunderstanding and misrepre-
sentation, when I state, that all our rulers ought in their official stations to serve the Lord Jesus Christ. I do not wish any religious test
to be prescribed by constitution, and proposed to a man on his acceptance
of any public trust. Neither can any intelligent friend of his country
and of true religion desire the establishment of any one religious sect
by civil law. Let the religion of the Bible rest on that everlasting rock,
and on those spiritual laws, on which Jehovah has founded his kingdom: let Christianity by the spirit of Christ in her members support
herself: let Church and State be for ever distinct: but, still, let the

doctrines and precepts of Christ govern all men, in all their relations and employments. If a ruler is not a Christian he ought to be one, in this land of evangelical light, without delay; and he ought, being a follower of Jesus, to honour him even as he honours the FATHER. In this land of religious freedom, what should hinder a civil magistrate from believing the gospel, and professing faith in Christ, any more than any other man? If the Chief Magistrate of a nation may be an irreligious man, with impunity, who may not? It seems to be generally granted, that our political leaders in the national and state governments ought not to be notoriously profane, drunken, abandoned men in their moral conduct; but if they may not be injurious to themselves and their fellow men, who shall give them permission to contemn God? If they ought to be just towards men, ought they not also to abstain from robbing God, and to render unto him that honour which is HIS due?

Our rulers, like any other members of the community, who are under law to God as rational beings, and under law to Christ, since they have the light of divine revelation, ought to search the scriptures, assent to the truth, profess faith in Christ, keep the Sabbath holy to God, pray in private and in the domestic circle, attend on the public ministry of the word, be baptized, and celebrate the Lord's supper. None of our rulers have the consent of their Maker, that they should be Pagans, Socinians, Mussulmen, Deists, the opponents of Christianity; and a religious people should never think of giving them permission, as public officers, to be and do, what they might not lawfully be and do, as private individuals. If a man may not be a gambler and drink to intoxication in the western wilds, he may not at the seat of government; if he may not with the approbation of his fellow citizens, in a little village of the north, deny "the true God and eternal life," he may not countenance, abet, and support those who deny the Deity of our Lord Jesus Christ at Washington. In other words, our Presidents, Secretaries of the Government, Senators and other Representatives in Congress, Governors of States, Judges, State Legislators, Justices of the Peace, and City Magistrates, are just as much bound as any other persons in the United States, to be orthodox in their faith, and virtuous and religious in their whole deportment. They may no more lawfully be bad husbands, wicked parents, men of heretical opinions, or men of dissolute lives, than the obscure individual who would be sent to Bridewell for his blasphemy or debauchery.

God, my hearers, requires a Christian faith, a Christian profession, and a Christian practice of all our public men; and we as Christian citizens ought, by the publication of our opinions, to require the same.

SECONDLY, Since it is the duty of all our rulers to serve the Lord and kiss the Son of God, it must be most manifestly the duty of all our Christian fellow-citizens to honour the Lord Jesus Christ and promote Christianity by electing and supporting as public officers the friends of our blessed Saviour. Let it only be granted, that Christians have the same rights and privileges in exercising the elective franchise, which are here accorded to Jews and Infidels, and we ask no other evidence to show, that those who prefer a Christian ruler, may unite in supporting him, in preference to any one of a different character. It shall cheerfully be granted, that every citizen is eligible to every office, whatever may be his religious opinions and moral character; and that every one may constitutionally support any person whom he may *choose;* but it will not hence follow, that he is without accountability to his Divine Master for his choice; or that he may lay aside all his Christian principles and feelings when he selects his ticket and presents it at the polls. "*In all* thy ways acknowledge him," is a maxim which should dwell in a Christian's mind on the day of a public election as much as on the Sabbath; and which should govern him when conspiring with others to honour Christ, either at the Lord's table, or in the election of a Chief Magistrate. In elucidating the duty of private Christians in relation to the choice of their civil rulers, it seems to me necessary to remark,

1. That every Christian who has the right and the opportunity of exercising the elective franchise ought to do it. Many pious people feel so much disgusted at the manner in which elections are conducted, from the first nomination to the closing of the polls, that they relinquish their right of voting for years together. But if all *pious* people were to conduct thus, then our rulers would be wholly elected by the *impious*. If all *good men* are to absent themselves from elections, then the *bad* will have the entire transaction of our public business.

If the wise, the prudent, the temperate, the friends of God and of their country do not endeavour to control our elections, they will be controlled by others: and if *one* good man may, without any reasonable excuse, absent himself, then *all* may. Fellow Christians, the love of Christ and of our fellow-men should forbid us to yield the choice of our civil rulers into the hands of selfish office hunters, and the miserable tools of their party politics. If all the truly religious men of our nation would be punctual and persevering in their endeavours to have good men chosen to fill all our national and state offices of honour, power and trust, THEIR WEIGHT would soon be felt by politicians; and those who care little for the religion of the Bible, would, for their own interest, consult the reasonable wishes of the great mass of Christians throughout our land. If any good men in the community ought to abstain from the exercise of their rights in relation to the choice of civil rulers, they are those clergymen whose hearers are unhappily divided by the bitterness of party spirit. If it would prevent their usefulness as ministers of the gospel to show that they have any judgment and choice about public concerns, *they may,* doubtless, from expediency, refrain from voting for any one—but none have a right to disfranchise them, (as the state of New York has done,) for fearing God and working righteousness.

It is a pleasure to be able to say, however, that the people of my pastoral care never interfered with my personal rights as a citizen and a Christian; and in most instances I am persuaded, that even a divided congregation will be perfectly willing that their pastor shall *vote* as he thinks best, if he will do it without becoming a preacher of party politics.

Some connect the idea of giving a vote, with the electioneering tricks which are too commonly the disgrace of a free people, but there is no necessary connection between voting and the suborning of votes. Let all the good set a worthy example in this matter, and discountenance those who would purchase to themselves places, by promises, lies, strong drink, and noisy declamation at taverns, grog-shops and the polls, and these abominations, which have become too common in our land, will in a great measure cease. I could wish to see every professing Christian in attendance on elections; but rather let him never give a vote, than receive *a treat* for his suffrage.

I propose, fellow-citizens, a new sort of union, or, if you please, *a Christian party in politics,* which I am exceedingly desirous all good men in our country should join: not by *subscribing a constitution* and the formation of a new society, to be added to the scores which now exist; but by adopting, avowing, and determining to act upon, truly religious principles in all civil matters. I am aware that the true Christians of our country are divided into many different denominations; who have, alas! too many points of jealousy and collision; still, a union to a very great extent, and for the most valuable purposes is not impracticable. For,

2. All Christians, of all denominations, may, and ought to, agree in determining, that they will never wittingly support for any public office, any person whom they know or believe to sustain, at the time of his proposed election, a bad moral character. In this, thousands of moralists, who profess no experimental acquaintance with Christianity, might unite and co-operate with *our Christian party*. And surely, it is not impossible, nor unreasonable for all classes of Christians to say within themselves, no man that we have reason to think is a liar, thief, gambler, murderer, debauchee, spendthrift, or openly immoral person in any way, shall have our support at any election. REFORMATION should not only be allowed, but encouraged; for it would be requiring too much to insist upon it, that a candidate for office *shall always have sustained an unblemished moral character,* and it would be unchristian not to forgive and support one who has proved his repentance by recantation and a considerable course of new obedience.

Some of the best of men were once vile; but they have been washed from their sins. Present good moral character should be considered as essential to every candidate for the post of honour. In this affair I know we are very much dependent on testimony, and that we may be deceived; especially in those controverted elections in which all manner of falsehoods are invented and vended, wholesale and retail, against some of the most distinguished men of our country: but after all, we must exercise our candour and best discretion, as we do in other matters of belief. We must weigh evidence, and depend most on those who appear the most competent and credible witnesses. It will be natural for us to believe a man's neighbours and acquaintances in preference to strangers. When we have employed the lights afforded us for the illumination of our minds, we shall feel peace of conscience, if we withhold our vote from every one whom we believe to be an immoral man.

Come then, fellow Christians, and friends of good morals in society, let us determine thus far to unite; for thus far we may, and ought to, and shall unite, if we duly weigh the importance of a good moral character in a ruler. Let no love of *the integrity of a party* prevent you from striking out the name of every dishonest and base man from your ticket. You have a right to choose, and you glory in your freedom: make then your own election: and when all good men act on this principle it will not be a vain thing. Candidates then, must be moral men, or seem to be, or they will not secure an election.

Moral character has now *some* influence in our elections, but not that place which it deserves. The law of public opinion excludes confirmed sots, and persons judicially convicted of high crimes and misdemeanors against the State; but it ought to render the election of all profane swearers, notorious Sabbath breakers, seducers, slanderers, prodigals and riotous persons, as well as *the advocates of duelling*, impracticable. I humbly entreat, that all who reverence the Lord's day, will abstain from supporting by their suffrages the open violators of the fourth commandment; that no sober man would vote for a tippler; that no lover of domestic purity would vote for one whom he knows to be lewd; and that no lover of order would support the profligate. Is this asking too much from the friends of good morals? Are the openly wicked fit to rule a moral and religious people? Cannot drunkenness, gambling, debauchery, and habitual contempt for the Sabbath, be banished, by the suffrages of a moral people, from our halls of legislation and benches of justice? "When the righteous are in authority, the people rejoice; but when the wicked beareth rule, the people mourn." "If a ruler hearken to lies, all his servants are wicked."

3. All who profess to be Christians of any denomination ought to agree that they will support no man as a candidate for any office, who is not professedly friendly to Christianity, and a believer in divine Revelation. We do not say that true or even pretended Christianity shall be made a constitutional test of admission to office; but we do affirm that Christians may in their elections lawfully prefer the avowed friends of the Christian religion to Turks, Jews, and Infidels. Turks, indeed, might naturally prefer Turks, if they could elect them; and Infidels might prefer Infidels; and I should not wonder if a conscientious Jew should prefer a ruler of his own religious faith; but it would

be passing strange if a Christian should not desire the election of one friendly to his own system of religion. While every religious system is tolerated in our country, and no one is established by law, it is still possible for me to think, that the friend of Christianity will make a much better governor of this commonwealth or President of the United States, than the advocate of Theism or Polytheism. We will not pretend to search the heart; but surely all sects of Christians may agree in opinion, that it is more desirable to have a Christian than a Jew, Mohammedan, or Pagan, in any civil office; and they may accordingly settle it in their minds, that they will never vote for any one to fill any office in the nation or state, who does not profess to receive the Bible as the rule of his faith. If three or four of the most numerous denominations of Christians in the United States, the Presbyterians, the Baptists, the Methodists and Congregationalists for instance, should act upon this principle, our country would never be dishonoured with an *avowed infidel* in her national cabinet or capitol. The Presbyterians alone could bring *half a million of electors* into the field, in opposition to any known advocate of Deism, Socinianism, or any species of avowed hostility to the truth of Christianity. If to the denominations above named we add the members of the Protestant Episcopal church in our country, the electors of these five classes of true Christians, united in the sole requisition of apparent friendship to Christianity in every candidate for office whom they will support, could govern every public election in our country, without infringing in the least upon the charter of our civil liberties. To these might be added, in this State and in Ohio, the numerous German Christians, and in New York and New Jersey the members of the Reformed Dutch Church, who are all zealous of the fundamental truths of Christianity. What should prevent us from co-operating in such a union as this? Let a man be of good moral character, and let him profess to believe in and advocate the Christian religion, and we can all support him. At one time he will be a Baptist, at another an Episcopalian, at another a Methodist, at another a Presbyterian of the American, Scotch, Irish, Dutch, or German stamp, and always a friend to our common Christianity. Why then should we ever suffer an enemy, an open and known enemy of the true religion of Christ, to enact our laws or fill the executive chair? Our Christian rulers will not oppress Jews or Infidels; they will *kiss the Son and serve the Lord;* while we have the best security for their fidelity to our republican, and I may say scriptural forms of government.

It deprives no man of his right for me to prefer a Christian to an Infidel. If Infidels were the most numerous electors, they would doubtless elect men of their own sentiments; and unhappily such men not unfrequently get into power in this country, in which ninety-nine hundredths of the people are believers in the divine origin and authority of the Christian religion. If hundreds of thousands of our fellow citizens should agree with us in an effort to elect men to public office who read the Bible, profess to believe it, reverence the Sabbath, attend public worship, and sustain a good moral character, who could complain? Have we not as much liberty to be the supporters of the Christian cause by our votes, as others have to support anti-christian men and measures?

Let us awake, then, fellow Christians, to our sacred duty to our Divine Master; and let us have no rulers, with our consent and co-operation, who are not known to be avowedly Christians.

It will here be objected, that frequently we must choose between two or more candidates who are in nomination, or must lose our votes; and that no one of the candidates may be of the right religious and moral character.

I must answer, that every freeman is bound to give his voice in such a manner as he judges will best conduce to the public good; and that it is not usually beneficial to give the suffrage for one whose election is wholly out of the question. If no good man is in nomination he must choose the least of two natural evils, and support the better man to exclude the worse. But I pray you, who make, or should make, our nominations? Are they not the people who select their own candidates? And are not the majority of the people in profession Christians? The influence of the friends of Christ ought to be exerted, known, and felt *in every stage* of our popular elections. If we intend to have our civil and religious liberty continued to us, and to transmit our institutions unimpaired to posterity, we must not suffer immoral, unprincipled, and irreligious men to nominate themselves to office, and then tell us, that we must elect them or have no rulers.

We have good men in abundance to fill all civil offices, from the highest to the lowest; and it is the fault of all the numerous Christians of our country if such are not elected.

It will be objected that my plan of a truly Christian party in politics will make hypocrites. We are not answerable for their hypocrisy if it does. There is no natural tendency in the scheme to make men deceivers; and if real enemies of the Christian religion conceal their enmity, that concealment is for the public good. We wish all iniquity, if not exterminated, may, as if ashamed, hide its head. It will be well for our country when all men who expect office are under the necessity of appearing honest, sober, pure, benevolent, and religious. It will be well for us when men cannot expect to retain, if they for a time occupy high places, by bribery, deception, coalition, and hypocrisy. It is most of all desirable that public officers SHOULD BE good men, friends of God, followers of Jesus Christ, and lovers of their country; but it is a matter of thankfulness if they are constrained TO SEEM such persons; for in this way vice, and the propagation of vice by evil example, is prevented. It will be objected, moreover, that my scheme of voting on political elections according to certain fixed religious principles, will create jealousies among the different denominations of Christians. But why should it? Our rulers which we have elected are of some, or of no religious sect. If they are of no religious denomination, they belong to the party of infidels. If they are of any one of the denominations of true Christians, it is better, in the judgment of all true Christians, that they should be of that one company than in the fellowship of infidels. Let a civil ruler, then, be a Christian of *some sort*, we will all say, rather than not a Christian of any denomination. If we fix this as a principle of our political morality, we shall all be gratified in turn, and in part, by having Christian rulers of our own description.

I am free to avow, that other things being equal, I would prefer for my chief magistrate, and judge, and ruler, a sound Presbyterian; and every candid religionist will make the same declaration concerning his own persuasion; but I would prefer a religious and moral man, of any one of the truly Christian sects, to any man destitute of religious principle and morality.

Suffer, my Christian fellow-citizens, a word of exhortation. Let us all be Christian politicians; and govern ourselves by supreme love to our blessed Master, whether we unite in prayers or in the election of our civil rulers. Let us be as conscientiously religious at the polls as in the pulpit, or house of worship. This course of conduct will promote good government and true religion in our country at the same time. Our public rulers then will prove a terror to them who do evil, and a praise to them who do well. Let us choose men who dare to be honest in their own religious creed, while they are too much of Christians and of republicans, to attempt to lord it over the faith of others. Let us never support by our votes any immoral man, or any known contemner of any of the fundamental doctrines of Christ, for any office: and least of all for the Presidency of the United States; for "blessed are they who put their trust in Christ." The people who with their rulers *kiss the Son,* shall experience special divine protection, and be a praise in the whole earth. Let us elect men who dare to acknowledge the Lord Jesus Christ for their Lord in their public documents. Which of our Presidents has ever done this? It would pick no infidel's pocket, and break no Jew's neck, if our President should be so singular as to let it be known, that he is a *Christian* by his Messages, and an advocate for the Deity of Christ by his personal preference of a Christian temple to a Socinian conventicle. It would be no violation of our national constitution, if our members of Congress should quit reading of newspapers and writing letters on the Lord's day, at least during public worship in the Hall of Representatives.

If all our great men should set a holy example of reverence for the Sabbath and the worship of Almighty God, it would not convert them into tyrants; it would not make our national government a religious aristocracy; it would not violate our federal constitution.

We are a Christian nation: we have a right to demand that all our rulers in their conduct shall conform to Christian morality; and if they do not, it is the duty and privilege of Christian freemen to make a new and a better election.

May the Lord Jesus Christ for ever reign in and over these United States, and call them peculiarly his own. *Amen.*

21

WILLIAM ELLERY CHANNING

1780, born April 7, at Newport, R.I.
1798, was graduated from Harvard College
1798–1800, tutor in Randolph family, Richmond, Virginia
1800–1802, studied theology
1802–1803, regent of Harvard College
1803–42, pastor of Federal Street Church, Boston
1819, *Unitarian Christianity*
1820, received the degree of D.D., Harvard
1820, organized Berry Street Conference of Liberal Ministers
1821, *Lecture on the Evidences of Christianity*
1822–23, traveled in Europe
1825, one of organizers of the American Unitarian Association
1828, *Remarks on the Life and Character of Napoleon Bonaparte*
1828, *Likeness to God*
1830, *Remarks on National Literature*
1835, *Slavery*
1836, *The Abolitionists*
1837, *An Open Letter to Henry Clay*
1842, *The Duty of the Free States*
1842, died October 2, at Boston

THE defense of Puritan ideas by the post-Edwardean theologians was persistent and ultimately became petty. Pushed by their critics, "new light" theologians, such as Joseph Bellamy, Samuel Hopkins, Nathaniel Emmons, Jonathan Edwards, Jr., and their Presbyterian abettors, such as Timothy Dwight, were forced to restate the doctrine of man's total depravity in such strong terms that it became inconsistent to the point of absurdity with the strongly moral secular attitude of adherents of natural religion. It became incredible that men of professed morality, making every attempt to live up to their professions and considering moral actions as the center of their religious lives, should regard themselves as by nature utterly depraved.

Edwards himself, in his *Great Christian Doctrine of Original Sin Defended*, had pointed out that the various acts of an individual are not to be considered in isolation from each other, but together constitute the outward expression of an inner and fundamental character. This is true not of individuals only but also of the nature of mankind in general. All men sin in Adam, their "federal head" or representative, not by the imputation of Adam's sin to them, but by sharing as fallible human beings in Adam's fall. This is a fine distinction, but it is one based on the facts of human nature as men come into contact with them in daily life. It was a strong defense of the doctrine.

After Edwards, however, the defenses became more and more apologetic, less and less philosophical, less and less the expression of genuine faith. "Edwards believed what he said; Hopkins said what he thought ought to be believed." [1] When Samuel Webster, in his *Winter Evening's Conversation upon the Doctrine of Original Sin* (New Haven, 1757), concentrated his emotional attack on infant damnation, the defenders were cornered by the sentimental problem he raised. Peter Clark, for example, in the *Summer Morning's Conversation* (Boston, 1758), yielded the point, and asserted that most men believe that God deals differently with the natural sinfulness of the young and the conscious depravity of the old. This led Charles Chauncy, for the liberals, to point out that any theory of eternal punishment for young or old, was inconsistent with God's infinite goodness. Now the Edwardeans had to justify their theory of punishment; Hopkins and Bellamy led the attempts; Jonathan Edwards, Jr., and Timothy Dwight followed after. In the end Dwight was forced to the statement that sinners go on sinning endlessly in hell and that their punishment must therefore continue without end. The controversy with this had descended to petty arguments about the torture of damned infants and the cruelty of eternal punishment. The defense of the moral order had become a matter of mere logical wrangling, which seemed to have lost all sense of human values.

The time was ripe for a theology of "respect for the human soul." Essays in that direction were made by liberals such as Bentley, Universalists like Chauncy, but it was in the work of William Ellery Channing that this theology reached mature statement. He did not abandon the Puritan doctrine of the glory of God; he subordinated it to a new gospel of self reliance. In other ways, too, he tried to keep the faith, but he fell into a number of contradictions: "God's sovereignty is limitless; still man has rights. God's power is irresistible; still man is free. On God we entirely depend; yet we can and do act from ourselves, and determine our own character." [2] There was no contradiction, however, when he came to talk about those who would contribute their mite to the glory of God by derogating from man.

[1] H. W. Schneider, *The Puritan Mind.* New York, 1930, p. 223.
[2] William E. Channing, *Works,* 8th ed., Boston, 1848, "Introductory Remarks," p. ix.

From the direction which theology has taken, it has been thought that to ascribe anything to man was to detract so much from God. The disposition has been to establish striking contrasts between man and God, and not to see and rejoice in the likeness between them. It has been thought that to darken the creation was the way to bring out more clearly the splendor of the Creator.[3]

This was not Channing's way. He carried his emphasis on "Likeness to God" to the verge of mysticism. He affirmed that the chief end of true religion was to develop in men "a growing likeness to the Supreme Being," a likeness "which has its foundation in the original and essential capacities of the mind." Only by virtue of this likeness can God or God's world be known and enjoyed. Even heathen philosophers realized that "to understand a great and good being, we must have the seeds of the same excellence."

"God unfolds himself in his works to a kindred mind." This is the central insight of transcendentalism; it is the heart of Emerson's *Nature,* and of all absolute idealism. Religion for Channing, as for the later transcendentalists, is full of "perpetual testimonies to the divinity of human nature," and the creation is a "birth and shining forth of the Divine Mind." Therefore is man able to enjoy and to understand the universe.

Channing uses the transcendental, rather than the mystical, method to prove that man has a natural kinship with God from the consideration that our ideas of God are derived from our own souls, "first developed in ourselves and thence transferred to our Creator." Even the awful and sublime idea of God himself is an extension of our spiritual nature. "In ourselves are the elements of the Divinity." The divine intelligence and the divine goodness are comprehended by us only through our own minds; our own moral natures. We do not derive our idea of God from his works, but through our thoughts. "We see God around us because he dwells within us."

This is a far cry from Dwight, Hopkins, and Bellamy, but it is also far from the natural religion and Unitarianism of Joseph Priestley. As such it has been used by the New England Unitarians to show that, in New England, Unitarianism has always been an idealistic, almost a Platonic faith, in no way akin to materialism and rationalism. In fact, this sermon, which was preached in 1828, may be regarded as a reassertion of New England idealism in the face of a growing Unitarian rationalism. For after Channing's crucial sermon on *Unitarian Christianity,* delivered at the Baltimore convention in 1819, had precipitated the breach within Congregationalism, Channing was increasingly concerned to defend the "catholic" humanitarianism of New England against the purely theological polemics of Unitarian sectarianism.

[3] William E. Channing, *Works,* 8th. ed., Boston, 1848, "Introductory Remarks," p. vii.

LIKENESS TO GOD

Ephesians v. 1: "Be ye therefore followers of God, as dear children."

TO PROMOTE true religion is the purpose of the Christian ministry. For this it was ordained. On the present occasion, therefore, when a new teacher is to be given to the church, a discourse on the character of true religion will not be inappropriate. I do not mean, that I shall attempt, in the limits to which I am now confined, to set before you all its properties, signs, and operations; for in so doing I should burden your memories with divisions and vague generalities, as uninteresting as they would be unprofitable. My purpose is, to select one view of the subject, which seems to me of primary dignity and importance; and I select this, because it is greatly neglected, and because I attribute to this neglect much of the inefficacy, and many of the corruptions, of religion.

The text calls us to follow or imitate God, to seek accordance with or likeness to him; and to do this, not fearfully and faintly, but with the spirit and hope of beloved children. The doctrines which I propose to illustrate, is derived immediately from these words, and is incorporated with the whole New Testament. I affirm, and would maintain, that true religion consists in proposing, as our great end, a growing likeness to the Supreme Being. Its noblest influence consists in making us more and more partakers of the Divinity. For this it is to be preached. Religious instruction should aim chiefly to turn men's aspirations and efforts to that perfection of the soul, which constitutes it a bright image of God. Such is the topic now to be discussed; and I implore Him, whose glory I seek, to aid me in unfolding and enforcing it with simplicity and clearness, with a calm and pure zeal, and with unfeigned charity.

I begin with observing, what all indeed will understand, that the likeness to God, of which I propose to speak, belongs to man's higher or spiritual nature. It has its foundation in the original and essential capacities of the mind. In proportion as these are unfolded by right and vigorous exertion, it is extended and brightened. In proportion as these lie dormant, it is obscured. In proportion as they are perverted and overpowered by the appetites and passions, it is blotted out. In truth, moral evil, if unresisted and habitual, may so blight and lay waste these capacities, that the image of God in man may seem to be wholly destroyed.

The importance of this assimilation to our Creator, is a topic which needs no labored discussion. All men, of whatever name, or sect, or opinion, will meet me on this ground. All, I presume, will allow, that no good in the compass of the universe, or within the gift of omnipotence, can be compared to a resemblance of God, or to a participation of his attributes. I fear no contradiction here. Likeness to God is the supreme gift. He can communicate nothing so precious, glorious, blessed, as himself. To hold intellectual and moral affinity with the Supreme Being, to partake his spirit, to be his children by derivations of kindred excellence, to bear a growing conformity to the perfection which we adore, this is a felicity which obscures and annihilates all other good.

It is only in proportion to this likeness, that we can enjoy either God or the universe. That God can be known and enjoyed only through sympathy or kindred attributes, is a doctrine which even Gentile philosophy discerned. That the pure in heart can alone see and commune with the pure Divinity, was the sublime instruction of ancient sages as well as of inspired prophets. It is indeed the lesson of daily experience. To understand a great and good being, we must have the seeds of the same excellence. How quickly, by what an instinct, do accordant minds recognise one another! No attraction is so powerful as that which subsists between the truly wise and good; whilst the brightest excellence is lost on those who have nothing congenial in their own breasts. God becomes a real being to us, in proportion as his own nature is unfolded within us. To a man who is growing in the likeness of God, faith begins even here to change into vision. He carries within himself a proof of a Deity, which can only be understood by experience. He more than believes, he feels the Divine presence; and gradually rises to an intercourse with his Maker, to which it is not irreverent to apply the name of friendship and intimacy. The Apostle John intended to express this truth, when he tells us, that he, in whom a principle of divine charity or benevolence has become a habit and life, "dwells in God and God in him."

It is plain, too, that likeness to God is the true and only preparation for the enjoyment of the universe. In proportion as we approach and resemble the mind of God, we are brought into harmony with the creation; for, in that proportion, we possess the principles from which the universe sprung; we carry within ourselves the perfections, of which its beauty, magnificence, order, benevolent adaptations, and boundless purposes, are the results and manifestations. God unfolds himself in his works to a kindred mind. It is possible, that the brevity of these hints may expose to the charge of mysticism, what seems to me the calmest and clearest truth. I think, however, that every reflecting man will feel, that likeness to God must be a principle of sympathy or accordance with his creation; for the creation is a birth and shining forth of the Divine Mind, a work through which his spirit breathes. In proportion as we receive this spirit, we possess within ourselves the explanation of what we see. We discern more and more of God in every thing, from the frail flower to the everlasting stars. Even in evil, that dark cloud which hangs over the creation, we discern rays of light and hope, and gradually come to see, in suffering and temptation, proofs and instruments of the sublimest purposes of Wisdom and Love.

I have offered these very imperfect views, that I may show the great importance of the doctrine which I am solicitous to enforce. I would teach, that likeness to God is a good so unutterably surpassing all other good, that whoever admits it as attainable, must acknowledge it to be the chief aim of life. I would show, that the highest and happiest office of religion is, to bring the mind into growing accordance with God; and that by the tendency of religious systems to this end, their truth and worth are to be chiefly tried.

I am aware that it may be said, that the Scriptures, in speaking of man as made in the image of God, and in calling us to imitate him, use bold and figurative language. It may be said, that there is danger from too literal an interpretation; that God is an unapproachable being; that I am not warranted in ascribing to man a like nature to the Divine; that we and all things illustrate the Creator by contrast, not by resemblance; that religion manifests itself chiefly in convictions and acknowledgments of utter worthlessness; and that to talk of the greatness and divinity of the human soul, is to inflate that pride through which Satan fell, and through which man involves himself in that fallen spirit's ruin.

I answer, that, to me, Scripture and reason hold a different language. In Christianity particularly, I meet perpetual testimonies to the divinity of human nature. This whole religion expresses an infinite concern of God for the human soul, and teaches that he deems no methods too expensive for its recovery and exaltation. Christianity, with one voice, calls me to turn my regards and care to the spirit within me, as of more worth than the whole outward world. It calls us to "be perfect as our Father in heaven is perfect;" and everywhere, in the sublimity of its precepts, it implies and recognises the sublime capacities of the being to whom they are addressed. It assures us that human virtue is "in the sight of God of great price," and speaks of the return of a human being to virtue as an event which increases the joy of heaven. In the New Testament, Jesus Christ, the Son of God, the brightness of his glory, the express and unsullied image of the Divinity, is seen mingling with men as a friend and brother, offering himself as their example, and promising to his true followers a share in all his splendors and joys. In the New Testament, God is said to communicate his own spirit, and all his fulness to the human soul. In the New Testament man is exhorted to aspire after "honor, glory, and immortality"; and Heaven, a word expressing the nearest approach to God, and a divine happiness, is everywhere proposed as the end of his being. In truth, the very essence of Christian faith is, that we trust in God's mercy, as revealed in Jesus Christ, for a state of celestial purity, in which we shall grow for ever in the likeness, and knowledge, and enjoyment of the Infinite Father. Lofty views of the nature of man are bound up and interwoven with the whole Christian system. Say not, that these are at war with humility; for who was ever humbler than Jesus, and yet who ever possessed such a consciousness of greatness and divinity? Say not that man's business is to think of his sin, and not of his dignity; for great sin implies a great capacity; it is the abuse of a noble nature; and no man can be deeply and rationally contrite, but he who feels, that in wrong-doing he has resisted a divine voice, and warred against a divine principle, in his own soul.—I need not, I trust, pursue the argument from revelation. There is an argument from nature and reason, which seems to me so convincing, and is at the same time so fitted to explain what I mean by man's possession of a like nature to God, that I shall pass at once to its exposition.

That man has a kindred nature with God, and may bear most important and ennobling relations to him, seems to me to be established by a striking proof. This proof you will understand, by considering, for a moment, how we obtain our ideas of God. Whence come the conceptions which we include under that august name? Whence do we derive our knowledge of the attributes and perfections which constitute the Supreme Being? I answer, we derive them from our own souls. The divine attributes are first developed in ourselves, and thence transferred to our Creator. The idea of God, sublime and awful as it is, is the idea of our own spiritual nature, purified and enlarged to infinity. In ourselves are the elements of the Divinity. God, then, does not sustain a a figurative resemblance to man. It is the resemblance of a parent to a child, the likeness of a kindred nature.

We call God a Mind. He has revealed himself as a Spirit. But what do we know of mind, but through the unfolding of this principle in our own breasts? That unbounded spiritual energy which we call God, is conceived by us only through consciousness, through the knowledge of ourselves.—We ascribe thought or intelligence to the Deity, as one of his most glorious attributes. And what means this language? These terms we have framed to express operations or faculties of our own souls. The Infinite Light would be for ever hidden from us, did not kindred rays dawn and brighten within us. God is another name for human intelligence raised above all error and imperfection, and extended to all possible truth.

The same is true of God's goodness. How do we understand this, but by the principle of love implanted in the human breast? Whence is it, that this divine attribute is so faintly comprehended, but from the feeble development of it in the multitude of men? Who can understand the strength, purity, fulness, and extent of divine philanthropy, but he in whom selfishness has been swallowed up in love?

The same is true of all the moral perfections of the Deity. These are comprehended by us, only through our own moral nature. It is conscience within us, which, by its approving and condemning voice, interprets to us God's love of virtue and hatred of sin; and without conscience, these glorious conceptions would never have opened on the mind. It is the lawgiver in our own breasts, which gives us the idea of divine authority, and binds us to obey it. The soul, by its sense of right, or its perception of moral distinctions, is clothed with sovereignty over itself, and through this alone, it understands and recognises the Sovereign of the Universe. Men, as by a natural inspiration, have agreed to speak of conscience as the voice of God, as the Divinity within us. This principle, reverently obeyed, makes us more and more partakers of the moral perfection of the Supreme Being, of that very excellence, which constitutes the rightfulness of his sceptre, and enthrones him over the universe. Without this inward law, we should be as incapable of receiving a law from Heaven, as the brute. Without this, the thunders of Sinai might startle the outward ear, but would have no meaning, no authority to the mind. I have expressed here a great truth. Nothing teaches so encouragingly our relation and resemblance to God; for the glory of the Supreme Being is eminently moral. We blind ourselves to his chief splendor, if we think only or mainly of his power, and overlook those attributes of rectitude and goodness, to which he subjects his omnipotence, and which are the foundations and very substance of his universal and immutable Law. And are these attributes revealed to us through the principles and convictions of our own souls? Do we understand through sympathy God's perception of the right, the good, the holy, the just? Then with what propriety is it said, that in his own image he made man!

I am aware, that it may be objected to these views, that we receive our idea of God from the universe, from his works, and not so exclusively from our own souls. The universe, I know, is full of God. The heavens and earth declare his glory. In other words, the effects and signs of power, wisdom, and goodness, are apparent through the whole creation. But apparent to what? Not to the outward eye; not to the acutest organs of sense; but to a kindred mind, which interprets the universe by itself. It is only through that energy of thought, by which we adapt various and complicated means to distant ends, and give harmony and a common bearing to multiplied exertions, that we understand the creative intelligence which has established the order, dependencies, and harmony of nature. We see God around us, because he dwells within us. It is by a kindred wisdom, that we discern his wisdom in his works. The brute, with an eye as piercing as ours, looks on the universe; and the page, which to us is radiant with characters of greatness and goodness, is to him a blank. In truth, the beauty and glory of God's works, are revealed to the mind by a light beaming from itself. We discern the impress of God's attributes in the universe, by accordance of nature, and enjoy them through sympathy.—I hardly need observe, that these remarks in relation to the universe apply with equal, if not greater force, to revelation.

I shall now be met by another objection, which to many may seem strong. It will be said, that these various attributes of which I have spoken, exist in God in Infinite Perfection, and that this destroys all affinity between the human and the Divine mind. To this I have two replies. In the first place, an attribute, by becoming perfect, does not part with its essence. Love, wisdom, power, and purity do not change their nature by enlargement. If they did, we should lose the Supreme Being through his very infinity. Our ideas of him would fade away into mere sounds. For example, if wisdom in God, because unbounded, have no affinity with that attribute in man, why apply to him that term? It must signify nothing. Let me ask what we mean, when we say that we discern the marks of intelligence in the universe? We mean, that we meet there the proofs of a mind like our own. We certainly discern proofs of no other; so that to deny this doctrine would be to deny the evidences of a God, and utterly to subvert the foundations of religious belief. What man can examine the structure of a plant or an animal, and see the adaptation of its parts to each other and to common ends, and not feel, that it is the work of an intelligence akin to his own, and that he traces these marks of design by the same spiritual energy in which they had their origin?

But I would offer another answer to this objection, that God's infinity places him beyond the resemblance and approach of man. I affirm, and trust that I do not speak too strongly, that there are traces of infinity in the human mind; and that, in this very respect, it bears a likeness to God. The very conception of infinity, is the mark of a nature to which no limit can be prescribed. This thought, indeed, comes to us, not so much from abroad, as from our own souls. We ascribe this attribute to God, because we possess capacities and wants, which only an unbounded being can fill, and because we are conscious of a tendency in spiritual faculties to unlimited expansion. We believe in the Divine infinity, through something congenial with it in our own breasts. I hope I speak clearly, and if not, I would ask those to whom I am obscure, to pause before they condemn. To me it seems, that the soul, in all its higher actions, in original thought, in the creations of genius, in the soarings of imagination, in its love of beauty and grandeur, in its aspirations after a pure and unknown joy, and especially in disinterestedness, in the spirit of self-sacrifice, and in enlightened devotion, has a character of infinity. There is often a depth in human love, which may be strictly called unfathomable. There is sometimes a lofty strength in moral principle, which all the power of the outward universe cannot overcome. There seems a might within, which can more than balance all might without. There is, too, a piety, which swells into a transport too vast for utterance, and into an immeasurable joy. I am speaking, indeed, of what is uncommon, but still of realities. We see, however, the tendency of the soul to the infinite, in more familiar and ordinary forms. Take, for example, the delight which we find in the vast scenes of nature, in prospects which spread around us without limits, in the immensity of the heavens and the ocean, and especially in the rush and roar of mighty winds, waves, and torrents, when, amidst our deep awe, a power within seems to respond to the omnipotence around us. The same principle is seen in the delight ministered to us by works of fiction or of imaginative art, in which our own nature is set before us in more than human beauty and power. In truth, the soul is always bursting its limits. It thirsts continually for wider knowledge. It rushes forward to untried happiness. It has deep wants, which nothing limited can appease. Its true element and end is an unbounded good. Thus, God's infinity has its image in the soul; and through the soul, much more than through the universe, we arrive at this conception of the Deity.

In these remarks I have spoken strongly. But I have no fear of expressing too strongly the connexion between the Divine and the human mind. My only fear is, that I shall dishonor the great subject. The danger to which we are most exposed, is that of severing the Creator from his creatures. The propensity of human sovereigns to cut off communication between themselves and their subjects, and to disclaim a common nature with their inferiors, has led the multitude of men, who think of God chiefly under the character of a king, to conceive of him as a being who places his glory in multiplying distinctions between himself and all other beings. The truth is, that the union between the Creator and the creature surpasses all other bonds in strength and intimacy. He penetrates all things, and delights to irradiate all with his glory. Nature, in all its lowest and inanimate forms, is pervaded by his power; and, when quickened by the mysterious property of life, how wonderfully does it show forth the perfections of its Author! How much of God may be seen in the structure of a single leaf, which, though so frail as to tremble in every wind, yet holds connexions and living communications with the earth, the air, the clouds, and the distant sun, and, through these sympathies with the universe, is itself a revelation of an omnipotent mind! God delights to diffuse himself everywhere. Through his energy, unconscious matter clothes itself with proportions, powers, and beauties, which reflect his wisdom and love. How much more must he delight to frame conscious and happy recipients of his perfections, in whom his wisdom and love may substantially dwell, with whom he may form spiritual ties, and to whom he may be an everlasting spring of moral energy and happiness! How far the Supreme Being may communicate his attributes to his intelligent offspring, I stop not to inquire. But that his almighty goodness will impart to them powers and glories, of which the material universe is but a faint emblem, I cannot doubt. That the soul, if true to itself and its Maker, will be filled with God, and will manifest him, more than the sun, I cannot doubt. Who can doubt it, that believes and understands the doctrine of human immortality?

The views which I have given in this discourse, respecting man's participation of the Divine nature, seem to me to receive strong confirmation, from the title or relation most frequently applied to God in the New Testament; and I have reserved this as the last corroboration of this doctrine, because, to my own mind, it is singularly affecting. In the New Testament God is made known to us as a Father; and a brighter feature of that book cannot be named. Our worship is to be directed to him as our Father. Our whole religion is to take its character from this view of the Divinity. In this he is to rise always to our minds. And what is it to be a Father? It is to communicate one's own nature, to give life to kindred beings; and the highest function of a Father is to educate the mind of the child, and to impart to it what is noblest and happiest in his own mind. God is our Father, not merely because he created us, or because he gives us enjoyment; for he created the flower and the insect, yet we call him not their Father. This bond is a spiritual one. This name belongs to God, because he frames spirits like himself, and delights to give them what is most glorious and blessed in his own nature. Accordingly, Christianity is said, with special propriety, to reveal God as the Father, because it reveals him as sending his Son to cleanse the mind from every stain, and to replenish it for ever with the spirit and moral attributes of its Author. Separate from God this idea of his creating and training up beings after his own likeness, and you rob him of the paternal character. This relation vanishes, and with it vanishes the glory of the Gospel, and the dearest hopes of the human soul.

The greatest use which I would make of the principles laid down in this discourse, is to derive from them just and clear views of the nature of religion. What, then, is religion? I answer; it is not the adoration of a God with whom we have no common properties; of a distinct, foreign, separate being; but of an all-communicating Parent. It recognises and adores God, as a being whom we know through our own souls, who has made man in his own image, who is the perfection of our own spiritual nature, who has sympathies with us as kindred beings, who is near us, not in place only like this all-surrounding atmosphere, but by spiritual influence and love, who looks on us with parental interest, and whose great design it is to communicate to us for ever, and in freer and fuller streams, his own power, goodness, and joy. The conviction of this near and ennobling relation of God to the soul, and of his great purposes towards it, belongs to the very essence of true religion; and true religion manifests itself chiefly and most conspicuously in desires, hopes, and efforts corresponding to this truth. It desires and seeks supremely the assimilation of the mind to God, or the perpetual unfolding and enlargement of those powers and virtues by which it is constituted his glorious image. The mind, in proportion as it is enlightened and penetrated by true religion, thirsts and labors for a god-like elevation. What else, indeed, can it seek, if this good be placed within its reach? If I am capable of receiving and reflecting the intellectual and moral glory of my Creator, what else in comparison shall I desire? Shall I deem a property in the outward universe as the highest good, when I may become partaker of the very mind from which it springs, of the prompting love, the disposing wisdom, the quickening power, through which its order, beauty, and beneficent influences subsist? True religion is known by these high aspirations, hopes, and efforts. And this is the religion which most truly honors God. To honor him, is not to tremble before him as an unapproachable sovereign, not to utter barren praise which leaves us as it found us. It is to become what we praise. It is to approach God as an inexhaustible Fountain of light, power, and purity. It is to feel the quickening and transforming energy of his perfections. It is to thirst for the growth and invigoration of the divine principle within us. It is to seek the very spirit of God. It is to trust in, to bless, to thank him for that rich grace, mercy, love, which was revealed and proffered by Jesus Christ, and which proposes as its great end the perfection of the human soul.

I regard this view of religion as infinitely important. It does more than all things to make our connexion with our Creator ennobling and happy; and, in proportion as we want it, there is danger that the thought of God may itself become the instrument of our degradation. That religion has been so dispensed as to depress the human mind, I need not tell you; and it is a truth which ought to be known, that the greatness of the Deity, when separated in our thoughts from its parental character, especially tends to crush human energy and hope. To a frail, dependent creature, an omnipotent Creator easily becomes a terror, and his worship easily degenerates into servility, flattery, self-contempt, and selfish calculation. Religion only ennobles us, in as far as it reveals to us the tender and intimate connexion of God with his creatures, and teaches us to see in the very greatness which might give alarm, the source of great and glorious communications to the human soul. You cannot, my hearers, think too highly of the majesty of God. But let not this majesty sever him from you. Remember, that his greatness is the infinity of attributes which yourselves possess. Adore his infinite wisdom; but remember that this wisdom rejoices to diffuse itself, and let an exhilarating hope spring up, at the thought of the immeasurable intelligence which such a Father must communicate to his children. In like manner adore his power. Let the boundless creation fill you with awe and admiration of the energy which sustains it. But remember that

God has a nobler work than the outward creation, even the spirit within yourselves; and that it is his purpose to replenish this with his own energy, and to crown it with growing power and triumphs over the material universe. Above all, adore his unutterable goodness. But remember, that this attribute is particularly proposed to you as your model; that God calls you, both by nature and revelation, to a fellowship in his philanthropy; that he has placed you in social relations, for the very end of rendering you ministers and representatives of his benevolence; that he even summons you to espouse and to advance the sublimest purpose of his goodness, the redemption of the human race, by extending the knowledge and power of Christian truth. It is through such views, that religion raises up the soul, and binds man by ennobling bonds to his Maker.

To complete my views of this topic, I beg to add an important caution. I have said that the great work of religion is, to conform ourselves to God, or to unfold the divine likeness within us. Let none infer from this language, that I place religion in unnatural effort, in straining after excitements which do not belong to the present state, or in any thing separate from the clear and simple duties of life. I exhort you to no extravagance. I reverence human nature too much to do it violence. I see too much divinity in its ordinary operations, to urge on it a forced and vehement virtue. To grow in the likeness of God, we need not cease to be men. This likeness does not consist in extraordinary or miraculous gifts, in supernatural additions to the soul, or in any thing foreign to our original constitution; but in our essential faculties, unfolded by vigorous and conscientious exertion in the ordinary circumstances assigned by God. To resemble our Creator, we need not fly from society, and entrance ourselves in lonely contemplation and prayer. Such processes might give a feverish strength to one class of emotions, but would result in disproportion, distortion, and sickliness of mind. Our proper work is to approach God by the free and natural unfolding of our highest powers, of understanding, conscience, love, and the moral will.

Shall I be told that, by such language, I ascribe to nature the effects which can only be wrought in the soul by the Holy Spirit? I anticipate this objection, and wish to meet it by a simple exposition of my views. I would on no account disparage the gracious aids and influences which

God imparts to the human soul. The promise of the Holy Spirit is among the most precious in the Sacred Volume. Worlds could not tempt me to part with the doctrine of God's intimate connexion with the mind, and of his free and full communications to it. But these views are in no respect at variance with what I have taught, of the method by which we are to grow in the likeness of God. Scripture and experience concur in teaching, that, by the Holy Spirit, we are to understand a divine assistance adapted to our moral freedom, and accordant with the fundamental truth, that virtue is the mind's own work. By the Holy Spirit, I understand an aid, which must be gained and made effectual by our own activity; an aid, which no more interferes with our faculties, than the assistance which we receive from our fellow-beings; an aid, which silently mingles and conspires with all other helps and means of goodness; an aid, by which we unfold our natural powers in a natural order, and by which we are strengthened to understand and apply the resources derived from our munificent Creator. This aid we cannot prize too much, or pray for too earnestly. But wherein, let me ask, does it war with the doctrine, that God is to be approached by the exercise and unfolding of our highest powers and affections, in the ordinary circumstances of human life?

I repeat it, to resemble our Maker we need not quarrel with our nature or our lot. Our present state, made up, as it is, of aids and trials, is worthy of God, and may be used throughout to assimilate us to him. For example, our domestic ties, the relations of neighbourhood and country, the daily interchanges of thoughts and feelings, the daily occasions of kindness, the daily claims of want and suffering, these and the other circumstances of our social state, form the best sphere and school for that benevolence, which is God's brightest attribute; and we should make a sad exchange, by substituting for these natural aids, any self-invented artificial means of sanctity. Christianity, our great guide to God, never leads us away from the path of nature, and never wars with the unsophisticated dictates of conscience. We approach our Creator by every right exertion of the powers he gives us. Whenever we invigorate the understanding by honestly and resolutely seeking truth, and by withstanding whatever might warp the judgment; whenever we invigorate the conscience by following it in opposition to the passions; whenever we receive a blessing gratefully, bear a trial patiently, or encounter peril or scorn with moral courage; whenever we perform a disinterested deed; whenever we lift up the heart in true adoration to God; whenever we war against a habit or desire which is strengthening itself against our higher principles; whenever we think, speak, or act, with moral energy, and resolute devotion to duty, be the occasion ever so humble, obscure, familiar; then the divinity is growing within us, and we are ascending towards our Author. True religion thus blends itself with common life. We are thus to draw nigh to God, without forsaking men. We are thus, without parting with our human nature, to clothe ourselves with the divine.

My views on the great subject of this discourse have now been given. I shall close with a brief consideration of a few objections, in the course of which I shall offer some views of the Christian ministry, which this occasion and the state of the world, seem to me to demand.— I anticipate from some an objection to this discourse, drawn as they will say from experience. I may be told, that, I have talked of the godlike capacities of human nature, and have spoken of man as a divinity; and where, it will be asked, are the warrants of this high estimate of our race? I may be told that I dream, and that I have peopled the world with the creatures of my lonely imagination. What! Is it only in dreams, that beauty and loveliness have beamed on me from the human countenance, that I have heard tones of kindness, which have thrilled through my heart, that I have found sympathy in suffering, and a sacred joy in friendship? Are all the great and good men of past ages only dreams? Are such names as Moses, Socrates, Paul, Alfred, Milton, only the fictions of my disturbed slumbers? Are the great deeds of history, the discoveries of philosophy, the creations of genius, only visions? O! no. I do not dream when I speak of the divine capacities of human nature. It is a real page in which I read of patriots and martyrs, of Fenelon and Howard, of Hampden and Washington. And tell me not that these were prodigies, miracles, immeasurably separated from their race; for the very reverence, which has treasured up and hallowed their memories, the very sentiments of admiration and love with which their names are now heard, show that the principles of their greatness are diffused through all your breasts. The germs of sublime virtue are scattered liberally on our earth. How often have I seen in the obscurity of domestic life, a strength of love, of endurance, of pious trust, of virtuous resolution, which in a public sphere would have attracted public homage. I cannot but pity the man, who recognises nothing godlike in his own nature. I see the marks of God in the heavens and the earth, but how much more in a liberal intellect, in magnanimity, in unconquerable rectitude, in a philanthropy which forgives every wrong, and which never despairs of the cause of Christ and human virtue. I do and I must reverence human nature. Neither the sneers of a worldly skepticism, nor the groans of a gloomy theology, disturb my faith in its godlike powers and tendencies. I know how it is despised, how it has been oppressed, how civil and religious establishments have for ages conspired to crush it. I know its history. I shut my eyes on none of its weaknesses and crimes. I understand the proofs, by which despotism demonstrates, that man is a wild beast, in want of a master, and only safe in chains. But, injured, trampled on, and scorned as our nature is, I still turn to it with intense sympathy and strong hope. The signatures of its origin and its end are impressed too deeply to be ever wholly effaced. I bless it for its kind affections, for its strong and tender love. I honor it for its struggles against oppression, for its growth and progress under the weight of so many chains and prejudices, for its achievements in science and art, and still more for its examples of heroic and saintly virtue. These are marks of a divine origin and the pledges of a celestial inheritance; and I thank God that my own lot is bound up with that of the human race.

But another objection starts up. It may be said, "Allow these views to be true; are they fitted for the pulpit? fitted to act on common minds? They may be prized by men of cultivated intellect and taste; but can the multitude understand them? Will the multitude feel them? On whom has a minister to act? On men immersed in business, and buried in the flesh; on men, whose whole power of thought has been spent on pleasure or gain; on men chained by habit and wedded to sin. Sooner may adamant be riven by a child's touch, than the human heart be pierced by refined and elevated sentiment. Gross instruments will alone act on gross minds. Men sleep, and nothing but thunder, nothing but flashes from the everlasting fire of hell, will thoroughly wake them."

I have all along felt that such objections would be made to the views

I have urged. But they do not move me. I answer, that I think these views singularly adapted to the pulpit, and I think them full of power. The objection is that they are refined. But I see God accomplishing his noblest purposes by what may be called refined means. All the great agents of nature, attraction, heat, and the principle of life, are refined, spiritual, invisible, acting gently, silently, imperceptibly; and yet brute matter feels their power, and is transformed by them into surpassing beauty. The electric fluid, unseen, unfelt, and everywhere diffused, is infinitely more efficient, and ministers to infinitely nobler productions, than when it breaks forth in thunder. Much less can I believe, that in the moral world, noise, menace, and violent appeals to gross passions, to fear and selfishness, are God's chosen means of calling forth spiritual life, beauty, and greatness. It is seldom that human nature throws off all susceptibility of grateful and generous impressions, all sympathy with superior virtue; and here are springs and principles to which a generous teaching, if simple, sincere, and fresh from the soul, may confidently appeal.

It is said, men cannot understand the views which seem to me so precious. This objection I am anxious to repel, for the common intellect has been grievously kept down and wronged through the belief of its incapacity. The pulpit would do more good, were not the mass of men looked upon and treated as children. Happily for the race, the time is passing away, in which intellect was thought the monopoly of a few, and the majority were given over to hopeless ignorance. Science is leaving her solitudes to enlighten the multitude. How much more may religious teachers take courage to speak to men on subjects, which are nearer to them than the properties and laws of matter, I mean their own souls. The multitude, you say, want capacity to receive great truths relating to their spiritual nature. But what, let me ask you, is the Christian religion? A spiritual system, intended to turn men's minds upon themselves, to frame them to watchfulness over thought, imagination, and passion, to establish them in an intimacy with their own souls. What are all the Christian virtues, which men are exhorted to love and seek? I answer, pure and high motions or determinations of the mind. That refinement of thought, which, I am told, transcends the common intellect, belongs to the very essence of Christianity. In confirmation of these views, the human mind seems to me to be turning itself more and more inward, and to be growing more alive to its own worth, and its capacities of progress. The spirit of education shows this, and so does the spirit of freedom. There is a spreading conviction that man was made for a higher purpose than to be a beast of burden, or a creature of sense. The divinity is stirring within the human breast, and demanding a culture and a liberty worthy of the child of God. Let religious teaching correspond to this advancement of the mind. Let it rise above the technical, obscure, and frigid theology which has come down to us from times of ignorance, superstition, and slavery. Let it penetrate the human soul, and reveal it to itself. No preaching, I believe, is so intelligible, as that which is true to human nature, and helps men to read their own spirits.

But the objection which I have stated not only represents men as incapable of understanding, but still more of being moved, quickened, sanctified, and saved, by such views as I have given. If by this objection nothing more is meant, than that these views are not alone or of themselves sufficient, I shall not dispute it; for true and glorious as they are, they do not constitute the whole truth, and I do not expect great moral effects from narrow and partial views of our nature. I have spoken of the godlike capacities of the soul. But other and very different elements enter into the human being. Man has animal propensities as well as intellectual and moral powers. He has a body as well as mind. He has passions to war with reason, and self-love with conscience. He is a free being, and a tempted being, and thus constituted he may and does sin, and often sins grievously. To such a being, religion, or virtue, is a conflict, requiring great spiritual effort, put forth in habitual watchfulness and prayer; and all the motives are needed, by which force and constancy may be communicated to the will. I exhort not the preacher, to talk perpetually of man as "made but a little lower than the angels." I would not narrow him to any class of topics. Let him adapt himself to our whole and various nature. Let him summon to his aid all the powers of this world, and the world to come. Let him bring to bear on the conscience and the heart, God's milder and more awful attributes, the promises and threatenings of the divine word, the lessons of history, the warnings of experience. Let the wages of sin here and hereafter be taught clearly and earnestly. But amidst the various motives to spiritual effort, which belong to the minister, none are more quickening than those drawn from the soul itself, and from God's desire and purpose to exalt it, by every aid consistent with its freedom. These views I conceive are to mix with all others, and without them all others fail to promote a generous virtue. Is it said, that the minister's proper work is, to preach Christ, and not the dignity of human nature? I answer, that Christ's greatness is manifested in the greatness of the nature which he was sent to redeem; and that his chief glory consists in this, that he came to restore God's image where it was obscured or effaced, and to give an everlasting impulse and life to what is divine within us. Is it said, that the malignity of sin is to be the minister's great theme? I answer, that this malignity can only be understood and felt, when sin is viewed as the ruin of God's noblest work, as darkening a light brighter than the sun, as carrying discord, bondage, disease, and death into a mind framed for perpetual progress towards its Author. Is it said, that terror is the chief instrument of saving the soul? I answer, that if by terror, be meant a rational and moral fear, a conviction and dread of the unutterable evil incurred by a mind which wrongs, betrays, and destroys itself, then I am the last to deny its importance. But a fear like this, which regards the debasement of the soul as the greatest of evils, is plainly founded upon and proportioned to our conceptions of the greatness of our nature. The more common terror, excited by vivid images of torture and bodily pain, is a very questionable means of virtue. When strongly awakened, it generally injures the character, breaks men into cowards and slaves, brings the intellect to cringe before human authority, makes man abject before his Maker, and, by a natural reaction of the mind, often terminates in a presumptuous confidence, altogether distinct from virtuous self-respect, and singularly hostile to the unassuming, charitable spirit of Christianity. The preacher should rather strive to fortify the soul against physical pains, than to bow it to their mastery, teaching it to dread nothing in comparison with sin, and to dread sin as the ruin of a noble nature.

Men, I repeat it, are to be quickened and raised by appeals to their highest principles. Even the convicts of a prison may be touched by kindness, generosity, and especially by a tone, look, and address, expressing hope and respect for their nature. I know, that the doctrine of ages has been, that terror, restraint, and bondage are the chief safeguards of human virtue and peace. But we have begun to learn, that affection, confidence, respect, and freedom are mightier as well as nobler agents. Men can be wrought upon by generous influences. I would that this truth were better understood by religious teachers. From the pulpit, generous influences too seldom proceed. In the church, men too seldom hear a voice to quicken and exalt them. Religion, speaking through her public organs, seems often to forget her natural tone of elevation. The character of God, the principles of his government, his relations to the human family, the purposes for which he brought us into being, the nature which he has given us, and the condition in which he has placed us, these and the like topics, though the sublimest which can enter the mind, are not unfrequently so set forth as to narrow and degrade the hearers, disheartening and oppressing with gloom the timid and sensitive, and infecting coarser minds with the unhallowed spirit of intolerance, presumption, and exclusive pretension to the favor of God. I know, and rejoice to know, that preaching in its worst forms does good; for so bright and piercing is the light of Christianity, that it penetrates in a measure the thickest clouds in which men contrive to involve it. But that evil mixes with the good, I also know; and I should be unfaithful to my deep convictions, did I not say, that human nature requires for its elevation, more generous treatment from the teachers of religion.

I conclude with saying, let the minister cherish a reverence for his own nature. Let him never despise it even in its most forbidding forms. Let him delight in its beautiful and lofty manifestations. Let him hold fast as one of the great qualifications for his office, a faith in the greatness of the human soul, that faith, which looks beneath the perishing body, beneath the sweat of the laborer, beneath the rags and ignorance of the poor, beneath the vices of the sensual and selfish, and discerns in the depths of the soul a divine principle, a ray of the Infinite Light, which may yet break forth and "shine as the sun" in the kingdom of God. Let him strive to awaken in men a consciousness of the heavenly treasure within them, a consciousness of possessing what is of more worth than the outward universe. Let hope give life to all his labors. Let him speak to men, as to beings liberally gifted, and made for God. Let him always look round on a congregation with the encouraging trust, that he has hearers prepared to respond to the simple, unaffected utterance of great truths, and to the noblest workings of his own mind. Let him feel deeply for those, in whom the divine nature is overwhelmed by the passions. Let him sympathize tenderly with those, in whom it begins to struggle, to mourn for sin, to thirst for a new life. Let him guide and animate to higher and diviner virtue, those in whom it has gained strength. Let him strive to infuse courage, enterprise, devout trust, and an inflexible will, into men's labors for their own perfection. In one word, let him cherish an unfaltering and growing faith in God as the Father and quickener of the human mind, and in Christ as its triumphant and immortal friend. That by such preaching he is to work miracles, I do not say. That he will rival in sudden and outward effects what is wrought by the preachers of a low and terrifying theology, I do not expect or desire. That all will be made better, I am far from believing. His office is, to act on free beings, who, after all, must determine themselves; who have power to withstand all foreign agency; who are to be saved, not by mere preaching, but by their own prayers and toil. Still I believe that such a minister will be a benefactor beyond all praise to the human soul. I believe, and know, that, on those who will admit his influence, he will work deeply, powerfully, gloriously. His function is the sublimest under heaven; and his reward will be, a growing power of spreading truth, virtue, moral strength, love, and happiness, without limit and without end.

22

RALPH WALDO EMERSON

1803, born May 25, in Boston
1821, was graduated from Harvard College
1821–28, Harvard Divinity School
1829, became pastor of Second Church of Boston
1832, resigned pastorate
1833–35, in Europe; met Carlyle
1835, settled in Concord
1836, *Nature*
1837, *The American Scholar*
1838, *The Divinity School Address*
1841, *Essays, First Series*
1842–44, editor of the *Dial*
1844, *Essays, Second Series*
1847, *Poems*
1849, *Nature, Addresses and Lectures*
1850, *Representative Men*
1856, *English Traits*
1860, *Conduct of Life*
1867, *May Day* (poems)
1870, *Society and Solitude*
1875, *Letters and Social Aims*
1882, died April 27, in Concord

ON July 15, 1838, Ralph Waldo Emerson addressed the graduating class of the Harvard Divinity School. He took advantage of the occasion to apply to religion the method and the point of view which he had set forth in *Nature* (1836) and *The American Scholar* (1837). Novel as was his approach, it had caused no great controversy in the two earlier works, for it trod on few toes; when applied to religion, however, its radicalism became apparent. Tongues and pens rushed to oppose Emerson, and Harvard University banned him from its halls for about thirty years and did not readmit him until the glow of radicalism had become a feeble flicker in his mind, until he himself had become an institution.

What was so dangerous about the doctrine taught by Emerson in his Divinity School Address? What frightened liberal Unitarians and their liberal University? Simply this: that Emerson envisioned and presented here the minister as "Man preaching." He sought to stimulate his auditors, each of whom was now technically prepared to go forth and preach, to preach each one out of his own heart, his own life, his own experience. The "respectable deism" of the early Unitarians, despite the passion of Channing, had degenerated into a moribund, dogmatic orthodoxy. Emerson, who had left his own Unitarian pulpit in 1832 because he was cramped by the doctrinal rigidity and religious frigidity of formalized Unitarianism, was trying to prevent these young ministers from parroting a crystallized gospel.

Like the earlier adherents of a religion of nature, Emerson found the heart of religion in the moral law. Unlike them, however, he did not find the moral law in external nature any more than he found it in revelation. The moral law he found in the inner nature of man; his was a religion of human nature. In the "Divinity School Address" he said, "The intuition of the moral sentiment is an insight of the perfection of the laws of the soul. These laws execute themselves. They are out of time, out of space, and not subject to circumstance." A half century later, in an address entitled "Natural Religion," he again pointed to the superiority of soul-religion over traditional faith: "You can never come to any peace or part till you put your whole reliance in the moral constitution of man, and not at all in the historical doctrine." [1] The theme was constant in his thought.

Attacking traditionalism, historicism, a completed revelation, Emerson sought and found God, not in churches, institutions, or gospels, but in his own soul. God is the indwelling moral principle in man; "If a man is at heart just, then insofar is he God; the safety of God, the immortality of God, the majesty of God, do enter into that man with justice." This supreme and primary faith must be intuited anew by every soul. "It cannot be received at second hand. Truly speaking, it is not instruction but provocation that I can receive from another soul. What he announces, I must find true in me, or reject." This faith rejected, the divine-human nature forgotten, "a sickness infects and dwarfs the constitution. . . . Miracles, prophecy, poetry, the ideal life, the holy life, exist as ancient history merely. . . . Man becomes near-sighted and can only attend to what addresses the senses." When men hold to the faith in "the indwelling Supreme Spirit," each preacher will be "a newborn bard of the Holy Ghost," casting conformity to the winds in order to "acquaint man at first hand with the Deity." Here, then, in terms of "Man preaching," is Emerson's doctrine of self-reliance.

Was Emerson conscious of his radicalism, even as he talked? Indeed he

[1] Ralph Waldo Emerson, *Uncollected Lectures*, ed. by Clarence Gohdes, New York, 1932, p. 57.

was, and he gloried in it. "Wherever a man comes, there comes revolution. The old is for slaves. When a man comes, all books are legible, all things transparent, all religions are forms." He felt it his prophetic mission to restore religion to man, God to the soul. He knew that "it is the office of a true teacher to show us that God is, not was, that He speaketh, not spake." Later, indeed, the sense of a mission became less acute; an old man, he could temporize.

The leaders of society don't wear their hearts on their sleeves—a shrewdness natural and pardonable. They don't talk infidelity. . . . It were unwise, perhaps mischievous, to shake the settled faith of another until a new shall appear to take the place of the old. . . . It is not well to utter any deep conviction of the soul in any company when it will be contested. A truth polemically said loses half its effect.[2]

In youth he had no such hesitations about speaking his thoughts in any company. Only by speaking one's full thought is it possible to live up to the highest conception of preaching, "the speech of man to men," and to dare to love the God who speaks through man's soul "without mediator or veil."

The little men, like Andrews Norton and Henry Ware, were horrified. Ware asked Emerson for his arguments; Emerson, to whom reasons seemed irrelevant, replied that he hadn't any, that he didn't know "what arguments mean in reference to any expression of a thought." Andrews Norton, a year later, occupied the same platform to reply to Emerson in a defense of the historic faith. Some there were, however, who vibrated to the string that Emerson had plucked and carried on the work of revitalizing the Christian faith, using the remedy Emerson had suggested—"first, soul, and second, soul, and evermore, soul." Of these, Theodore Parker was the chief, calling men to "manly religion," to knowledge of the God within them.

DIVINITY SCHOOL ADDRESS

IN this refulgent summer, it has been a luxury to draw the breath of life. The grass grows, the buds burst, the meadow is spotted with fire and gold in the tint of flowers. The air is full of birds, and sweet with the breath of pine, the balm-of-Gilead, and the new hay. Night brings no gloom to the heart with its welcome shade. Through the transparent darkness the stars pour their almost spiritual rays. Man under them seems a young child and his huge globe, a toy. The cool

[2] *Ibid.*, pp. 55–56.

night bathes the world as with a river and prepares his eyes again for the crimson dawn. The mystery of nature was never displayed more happily. The corn and the wine have been freely dealt to all creatures, and the never-broken silence with which the old bounty goes forward has not yielded yet one word of explanation. One is constrained to respect the perfection of this world in which our senses converse. How wide; how rich; what invitation from every property it gives to every faculty of man! In its fruitful soils; in its navigable sea; in its mountains of metal and stone; in its forests of all woods; in its animals; in its chemical ingredients; in the powers and path of light, heat, attraction and life, it is well worth the pith and heart of great men to subdue and enjoy it. The planters, the mechanics, the inventors, the astronomers, the builders of cities, and the captains, history delights to honor.

But when the mind opens and reveals the laws which traverse the universe and make things what they are, then shrinks the great world at once into a mere illustration and fable of this mind. What am I? and What is? asks the human spirit with a curiosity new-kindled, but never to be quenched. Behold these outrunning laws, which our imperfect apprehension can see tend this way and that, but not come full circle. Behold these infinite relations, so like, so unlike; many, yet one. I would study, I would know, I would admire forever. These works of thought have been the entertainments of the human spirit in all ages.

A more secret, sweet, and overpowering beauty appears to man when his heart and mind open to the sentiment of virtue. Then he is instructed in what is above him. He learns that his being is without bound; that to the good, to the perfect, he is born, low as he now lies in evil and weakness. That which he venerates is still his own, though he has not realized it yet. *He ought.* He knows the sense of that grand word, though his analysis fails to render account of it. When in innocency or when by intellectual perception he attains to say, "I love the Right; Truth is beautiful within and without forevermore. Virtue, I am thine; save me; use me; thee will I serve, day and night, in great, in small, that I may be not virtuous but virtue"; then is the end of the creation answered, and God is well pleased.

The sentiment of virtue is a reverence and delight in the presence of certain divine laws. It perceives that this homely game of life we play, covers, under what seem foolish details, principles that astonish. The child amidst his baubles is learning the action of light, motion, gravity, muscular force; and in the game of human life, love, fear, justice, appetite, man, and God, interact. These laws refuse to be adequately stated. They will not be written out on paper, or spoken by the tongue. They elude our persevering thought; yet we read them hourly in each other's faces, in each other's actions, in our own remorse. The moral traits which are all globed into every virtuous act and thought, in speech we must sever, and describe or suggest by painful enumeration of many particulars. Yet, as this sentiment is the essence of all religion, let me guide your eye to the precise objects of the sentiment, by an enumeration of some of those classes of facts in which this element is conspicuous.

The intuition of the moral sentiment is an insight of the perfection of the laws of the soul. These laws execute themselves. They are out of time, out of space, and not subject to circumstance. Thus in the soul of man there is a justice whose retributions are instant and entire. He who does a good deed is instantly ennobled. He who does a mean deed is by the action itself contracted. He who puts off impurity thereby puts on purity. If a man is at heart just, then in so far is he God; the safety of God, the immortality of God, the majesty of God, do enter into that man with justice. If a man dissemble, deceive, he deceives himself and goes out of acquaintance with his own being. A man in the view of absolute goodness adores with total humility. Every step so downward is a step upward. The man who renounces himself comes to himself.

See how this rapid intrinsic energy worketh everywhere, righting wrongs, correcting appearances, and bringing up facts to a harmony with thoughts. Its operation in life, though slow to the senses, is at last as sure as in the soul. By it a man is made the Providence to himself, dispensing good to his goodness and evil to his sin. Character is always known. Thefts never enrich; alms never impoverish; murder will speak out of stone walls. The least admixture of a lie—for example, the taint of vanity, any attempt to make a good impression, a favorable appearance—will instantly vitiate the effect. But speak the truth, and all nature and all spirits help you with unexpected furtherance. Speak the truth, and all things alive or brute are vouchers, and the very roots of the grass underground there do seem to stir and move to bear you witness. See again the perfection of the Law as it applies itself to the affections and becomes the law of society. As we are, so we associate. The good, by affinity, seek the good; the vile, by affinity, the vile. Thus of their own volition, souls proceed into heaven, into hell.

These facts have always suggested to man the sublime creed that the world is not the product of manifold power but of one will, of one mind; and that one mind is everywhere active, in each ray of the star, in each wavelet of the pool; and whatever opposes that will is everywhere balked and baffled, because things are made so and not otherwise. Good is positive. Evil is merely privative, not absolute: it is like cold, which is the privation of heat. All evil is so much death or nonentity. Benevolence is absolute and real. So much benevolence as a man hath, so much life hath he. For all things proceed out of this same spirit, which is differently named love, justice, temperance, in its different applications, just as the ocean receives different names on the several shores which it washes. All things proceed out of the same spirit, and all things conspire with it. Whilst a man seeks good ends, he is strong by the whole strength of nature. In so far as he roves from these ends, he bereaves himself of power, or auxiliaries; his being shrinks out of all remote channels, he becomes less and less, a mote, a point, until absolute badness is absolute death.

The perception of this law of laws awakens in the mind a sentiment which we call the religious sentiment and which makes our highest happiness. Wonderful is its power to charm and to command. It is a mountain air. It is the embalmer of the world. It is myrrh and storax, and chlorine and rosemary. It makes the sky and the hills sublime, and the silent song of the stars is it. By it is the universe made safe and habitable, not by science or power. Thought may work cold and intransitive in things and find no end or unity; but the dawn of the sentiment of virtue on the heart gives, and is, the assurance that Law is sovereign over all natures; and the worlds, time, space, eternity, do seem to break out into joy.

This sentiment is divine and deifying. It is the beatitude of man. It makes him illimitable. Through it, the soul first knows itself. It corrects the capital mistake of the infant man, who seeks to be great by following the great and hopes to derive advantages *from another*—by showing the fountain of all good to be in himself, and that he, equally with every man, is an inlet into the deeps of Reason. When he says, "I ought"; when love warms him; when he chooses, warned from on high, the good and great deed; then deep melodies wander through his soul from Supreme Wisdom. Then he can worship and be enlarged by his worship; for he can never go behind this sentiment. In the sublimest flights of the soul, rectitude is never surmounted, love is never outgrown.

This sentiment lies at the foundation of society and successively creates all forms of worship. The principle of veneration never dies out. Man fallen into superstition, into sensuality, is never quite without the visions of the moral sentiment. In like manner, all the expressions of this sentiment are sacred and permanent in proportion to their purity. The expressions of this sentiment affect us more than all other compositions. The sentences of the oldest time, which ejaculate this piety, are still fresh and fragrant. This thought dwelled always deepest in the minds of men in the devout and contemplative East; not alone in Palestine, where it reached its purest expression, but in Egypt, in Persia, in India, in China. Europe has always owed to oriental genius its divine impulses. What these holy bards said, all sane men found agreeable and true. And the unique impression of Jesus upon mankind, whose name is not so much written as ploughed into the history of this world, is proof of the subtle virtue of this infusion.

Meantime, whilst the doors of the temple stand open, night and day, before every man, and the oracles of this truth cease never, it is guarded by one stern condition; this, namely: it is an intuition. It cannot be received at second hand. Truly speaking, it is not instruction but provocation that I can receive from another soul. What he announces, I must find true in me, or reject; and on his word or as his second, be he who he may, I can accept nothing. On the contrary, the absence of this primary faith is the presence of degradation. As is the flood, so is the ebb. Let this faith depart, and the very words it spake and the things it made become false and hurtful. Then falls the church, the state, art, letters, life. The doctrine of the divine nature being forgotten, a sickness infects and dwarfs the constitution. Once man was all; now he is an appendage, a nuisance. And because the indwelling

Supreme Spirit cannot wholly be got rid of, the doctrine of it suffers this perversion, that the divine nature is attributed to one or two persons and denied to all the rest, and denied with fury. The doctrine of inspiration is lost; the base doctrine of the majority of voices usurps the place of the doctrine of the soul. Miracles, prophecy, poetry, the ideal life, the holy life, exist as ancient history merely; they are not in the belief, nor in the aspiration of society; but, when suggested, seem ridiculous. Life is comic or pitiful as soon as the high ends of being fade out of sight, and man becomes near-sighted and can only attend to what addresses the senses.

These general views, which, whilst they are general, none will contest, find abundant illustration in the history of religion, and especially in the history of the Christian church. In that, all of us have had our birth and nurture. The truth contained in that, you, my young friends, are now setting forth to teach. As the Cultus, or established worship of the civilized world, it has great historical interest for us. Of its blessed words, which have been the consolation of humanity, you need not that I should speak. I shall endeavor to discharge my duty to you on this occasion by pointing out two errors in its administration which daily appear more gross from the point of view we have just now taken.

Jesus Christ belonged to the true race of prophets. He saw with open eye the mystery of the soul. Drawn by its severe harmony, ravished with its beauty, he lived in it and had his being there. Alone in all history he estimated the greatness of man. One man was true to what is in you and me. He saw that God incarnates Himself in man and evermore goes forth anew to take possession of His World. He said, in this jubilee of sublime emotion, 'I am divine. Through me, God acts; through me, speaks. Would you see God, see me; or see thee, when thou also thinkest as I now think.' But what a distortion did his doctrine and memory suffer in the same, in the next, and the following ages! There is no doctrine of the Reason which will bear to be taught by the Understanding. The understanding caught this high chant from the poet's lips and said, in the next age, 'This was Jehovah come down out of heaven. I will kill you, if you say he was a man.' The idioms of his language and the figures of his rhetoric have usurped the place of his truth; and churches are not built on his principles, but on his tropes.

Christianity became a Mythus, as the poetic teaching of Greece and of Egypt, before. He spoke of miracles; for he felt that man's life was a miracle, and all that man doth, and he knew that this daily miracle shines as the character ascends. But the word Miracle, as pronounced by Christian churches, gives a false impression; it is Monster. It is not one with the blowing clover and the falling rain.

He felt respect for Moses and the prophets, but no unfit tenderness at postponing their initial revelations to the hour and the man that now is; to the eternal revelation in the heart. Thus was he a true man. Having seen that the law in us is commanding, he would not suffer it to be commanded. Boldly, with hand, and heart, and life, he declared it was God. Thus is he, as I think, the only soul in history who has appreciated the worth of man.

1. In this point of view we become sensible of the first defect of historical Christianity. Historical Christianity has fallen into the error that corrupts all attempts to communicate religion. As it appears to us, and as it has appeared for ages, it is not the doctrine of the soul, but an exaggeration of the personal, the positive, the ritual. It has dwelt, it dwells, with noxious exaggeration about the *person* of Jesus. The soul knows no persons. It invites every man to expand to the full circle of the universe, and will have no preferences but those of spontaneous love. But by this eastern monarchy of a Christianity which indolence and fear have built, the friend of man is made the injurer of man. The manner in which his name is surrounded with expressions which were once sallies of admiration and love, but are now petrified into official titles, kills all generous sympathy and liking. All who hear me feel that the language that describes Christ to Europe and America is not the style of friendship and enthusiasm to a good and noble heart but is appropriated and formal—paints a demigod, as the Orientals or the Greeks would describe Osiris or Apollo. Accept the injurious impositions of our early catechetical instruction, and even honesty and self-denial were but splendid sins, if they did not wear the Christian name. One would rather be "A pagan, suckled in a creed outworn" than to be defrauded of his manly right in coming into nature and finding not names and places, not land and professions, but even virtue and truth foreclosed and monopolized. You shall not be a man even. You

shall not own the world; you shall not dare and live after the infinite Law that is in you, and in company with the infinite Beauty which heaven and earth reflect to you in all lovely forms; but you must subordinate your nature to Christ's nature; you must accept our interpretations and take his portrait as the vulgar draw it.

That is always best which gives me to myself. The sublime is excited in me by the great stoical doctrine, Obey thyself. That which shows God in me fortifies me. That which shows God out of me makes me a wart and a wen. There is no longer a necessary reason for my being. Already the long shadows of untimely oblivion creep over me, and I shall decease forever.

The divine bards are the friends of my virtue, of my intellect, of my strength. They admonish me that the gleams which flash across my mind are not mine, but God's; that they had the like and were not disobedient to the heavenly vision. So I love them. Noble provocations go out from them, inviting me to resist evil; to subdue the world; and to Be. And thus, by his holy thoughts, Jesus serves us, and thus only. To aim to convert a man by miracles is a profanation of the soul. A true conversion, a true Christ, is now, as always, to be made by the reception of beautiful sentiments. It is true that a great and rich soul, like his, falling among the simple, does so preponderate that, as his did, it names the world. The world seems to them to exist for him, and they have not yet drunk so deeply of his sense as to see that only by coming again to themselves, or to God in themselves, can they grow forevermore. It is a low benefit to give me something; it is a high benefit to enable me to do somewhat of myself. The time is coming when all men will see that the gift of God to the soul is not a vaunting, overpowering, excluding sanctity but a sweet, natural goodness, a goodness like thine and mine, and that so invites thine and mine to be and to grow.

The injustice of the vulgar tone of preaching is not less flagrant to Jesus than to the souls which it profanes. The preachers do not see that they make his gospel not glad and shear him of the locks of beauty and the attributes of heaven. When I see a majestic Epaminondas, or Washington; when I see among my contemporaries a true orator, an upright judge, a dear friend; when I vibrate to the melody and fancy of a poem; I see beauty that is to be desired. And so lovely, and with yet more entire consent of my human being, sounds in my ear the severe music of the bards that have sung of the true God in all ages. Now do not degrade the life and dialogues of Christ out of the circle of this charm, by insulation and peculiarity. Let them lie as they befell, alive and warm, part of human life and of the landscape and of the cheerful day.

2. The second defect of the traditionary and limited way of using the mind of Christ is a consequence of the first; this, namely: that the Moral Nature, that Law of laws whose revelations introduce greatness —yea, God himself—into the open soul, is not explored as the fountain of the established teaching in society. Men have come to speak of the revelation as somewhat long ago given and done, as if God were dead. The injury to faith throttles the preacher; and the goodliest of institutions becomes an uncertain and inarticulate voice.

It is very certain that it is the effect of conversation with the beauty of the soul to beget a desire and need to impart to others the same knowledge and love. If utterance is denied, the thought lies like a burden on the man. Always the seer is a sayer. Somehow his dream is told; somehow he publishes it with solemn joy; sometimes with pencil on canvas, sometimes with chisel on stone, sometimes in towers and aisles of granite, his soul's worship is builded; sometimes in anthems of indefinite music; but clearest and most permanent, in words.

The man enamored of this excellency becomes its priest or poet. The office is coeval with the world. But observe the condition, the spiritual limitation of the office. The spirit only can teach. Not any profane man, not any sensual, not any liar, not any slave can teach, but only he can give who has; he only can create who is. The man on whom the soul descends, through whom the soul speaks, alone can teach. Courage, piety, love, wisdom, can teach; and every man can open his door to these angels, and they shall bring him the gift of tongues. But the man who aims to speak as books enable, as synods use, as the fashion guides, and as interest commands, babbles. Let him hush.

To this holy office you propose to devote yourselves. I wish you may feel your call in throbs of desire and hope. The office is the first in the world. It is of that reality that it cannot suffer the deduction of any falsehood. And it is my duty to say to you that the need was never greater of new revelation than now. From the views I have already expressed you will infer the sad conviction, which I share, I believe, with numbers, of the universal decay and now almost death of faith in society. The soul is not preached. The Church seems to totter to its fall, almost all life extinct. On this occasion, any complaisance would be criminal which told you, whose hope and commission it is to preach the faith of Christ, that the faith of Christ is preached.

It is time that this ill-suppressed murmur of all thoughtful men against the famine of our churches—this moaning of the heart because it is bereaved of the consolation, the hope, the grandeur that come alone out of the culture of the moral nature—should be heard through the sleep of indolence and over the din of routine. This great and perpetual office of the preacher is not discharged. Preaching is the expression of the moral sentiment in application to the duties of life. In how many churches, by how many prophets, tell me, is man made sensible that he is an infinite Soul; that the earth and heavens are passing into his mind; that he is drinking forever the soul of God? Where now sounds the persuasion that by its very melody imparadises my heart, and so affirms its own origin in heaven? Where shall I hear words such as in elder ages drew men to leave all and follow—father and mother, house and land, wife and child? Where shall I hear these august laws of moral being so pronounced as to fill my ear, and I feel ennobled by the offer of my uttermost action and passion? The test of the true faith, certainly, should be its power to charm and command the soul, as the laws of nature control the activity of the hands—so commanding that we find pleasure and honor in obeying. The faith should blend with the light of rising and of setting suns, with the flying cloud, the singing bird, and the breath of flowers. But now the priest's Sabbath has lost the splendor of nature; it is unlovely; we are glad when it is done; we can make, we do make, even sitting in our pews, a far better, holier, sweeter, for ourselves.

Whenever the pulpit is usurped by a formalist, then is the worshiper defrauded and disconsolate. We shrink as soon as the prayers begin which do not uplift, but smite and offend us. We are fain to wrap our cloaks about us and secure, as best we can, a solitude that hears not. I once heard a preacher who sorely tempted me to say I would go to church no more. Men go, thought I, where they are wont to go, else had no soul entered the temple in the afternoon. A snowstorm was falling around us. The snowstorm was real, the preacher merely spectral, and the eye felt the sad contrast in looking at him, and then out of the window behind him into the beautiful meteor of the snow. He had lived in vain. He had no one word intimating that he had laughed or wept, was married or in love, had been commended, or cheated, or chagrined. If he had ever lived and acted, we were none the wiser for it. The capital secret of his profession, namely, to convert life into truth, he had not learned. Not one fact in all his experience had he yet imported into his doctrine. This man had ploughed and planted and talked and bought and sold; he had read books; he had eaten and drunken; his head aches, his heart throbs; he smiles and suffers; yet was there not a surmise, a hint, in all the discourse that he had ever lived at all. Not a line did he draw out of real history. The true preacher can be known by this, that he deals out to the people his life—life passed through the fire of thought. But of the bad preacher, it could not be told from his sermon what age of the world he fell in; whether he had a father or a child; whether he was a freeholder or a pauper; whether he was a citizen or a countryman; or any other fact of his biography. It seemed strange that the people should come to church. It seemed as if their houses were very unentertaining, that they should prefer this thoughtless clamor. It shows that there is a commanding attraction in the moral sentiment that can lend a faint tint of light to dullness and ignorance coming in its name and place. The good hearer is sure he has been touched sometimes; is sure there is somewhat to be reached, and some word that can reach it. When he listens to these vain words, he comforts himself by their relation to his remembrance of better hours, and so they clatter and echo unchallenged.

I am not ignorant that when we preach unworthily it is not always quite in vain. There is a good ear, in some men, that draws supplies to virtue out of very indifferent nutriment. There is poetic truth concealed in all the commonplaces of prayer and of sermons, and though foolishly spoken, they may be wisely heard; for each is some select expression that broke out in a moment of piety from some stricken or jubilant soul, and its excellency made it remembered. The prayers and even the dogmas of our church are like the zodiac of Denderah and the astronomical monuments of the Hindoos, wholly insulated from anything now extant in the life and business of the people. They mark the height to which the waters once rose. But this docility is a check upon the mischief from the good and devout. In a large portion of the community, the religious service gives rise to quite other thoughts and emotions. We need not chide the negligent servant. We are struck with pity, rather, at the swift retribution of his sloth. Alas for the unhappy man that is called to stand in the pulpit and *not* give bread of life. Everything that befalls accuses him. Would he ask contributions for the missions, foreign or domestic? Instantly his face is suffused with shame, to propose to his parish that they should send money a hundred or a thousand miles, to furnish such poor fare as they have at home and would do well to go the hundred or the thousand miles to escape. Would he urge people to a godly way of living; and can he ask a fellow-creature to come to Sabbath meetings, when he and they all know what is the poor uttermost they can hope for therein? Will he invite them privately to the Lord's Supper? He dares not. If no heart warm this rite, the hollow, dry, creaking formality is too plain than that he can face a man of wit and energy and put the invitation without terror. In the street, what has he to say to the bold village blasphemer? The village blasphemer sees fear in the face, form, and gait of the minister.

Let me not taint the sincerity of this plea by any oversight of the claims of good men. I know and honor the purity and strict conscience of numbers of the clergy. What life the public worship retains, it owes to the scattered company of pious men, who minister here and there in the churches and who, sometimes accepting with too great tenderness the tenet of the elders, have not accepted from others but from their own heart the genuine impulses of virtue, and so still command our love and awe, to the sanctity of character. Moreover, the exceptions are not so much to be found in a few eminent preachers as in the better hours, the truer inspirations of all—nay, in the sincere moments of every man. But, with whatever exception, it is still true that tradition characterizes the preaching of this country; that it comes out of the memory and not out of the soul; that it aims at what is usual and not at what is necessary and eternal; that thus historical Christianity destroys the power of preaching, by withdrawing it from the exploration of the moral nature of man, where the sublime is, where are the resources of astonishment and power. What a cruel injustice it is to that Law, the joy of the whole earth, which alone can make thought dear and rich—that Law whose fatal sureness the astronomical orbits poorly emulate—that it is travestied and depreciated, that it is behooted and behowled, and not a trait, not a word of it articulated. The pulpit, in losing sight of this Law, loses its reason and gropes after it knows not what. And for want of this culture the soul of the community is sick and faithless. It wants nothing so much as a stern, high, stoical, Christian discipline to make it know itself and the divinity that speaks through it. Now man is ashamed of himself; he skulks and sneaks through the world, to be tolerated, to be pitied, and scarcely in a thousand years does any man dare to be wise and good, and so draw after him the tears and blessings of his kind.

Certainly there have been periods when, from the inactivity of the intellect on certain truths, a greater faith was possible in names and persons. The Puritans in England and America found in the Christ of the Catholic Church and in the dogmas inherited from Rome scope for their austere piety and their longings for civil freedom. But their creed is passing away, and none arises in its room. I think no man can go with his thoughts about him into one of our churches without feeling that what hold the public worship had on men is gone or going. It has lost its grasp on the affection of the good and the fear of the bad. In the country, neighborhoods, half parishes are *signing off*, to use the local term. It is already beginning to indicate character and religion to withdraw from the religious meetings. I have heard a devout person, who prized the Sabbath, say in bitterness of heart, "On Sundays it seems wicked to go to church." And the motive that holds the best there is now only a hope and a waiting. What was once a mere circumstance, that the best and the worst men in the parish, the poor and the rich, the learned and the ignorant, the young and old, should meet one day as fellows in one house, in sign of an equal right in the soul, has come to be a paramount motive for going thither.

My friends, in these two errors, I think, I find the causes of a decaying church and a wasting unbelief. And what greater calamity can fall upon a nation than the loss of worship? Then all things go to decay. Genius leaves the temple to haunt the senate or the market. Literature becomes frivolous. Science is cold. The eye of youth is not lighted by the hope of other worlds, and age is without honor. Society lives to trifles, and when men die we do not mention them.

And now, my brothers, you will ask, What in these desponding days can be done by us? The remedy is already declared in the ground of our complaint of the Church. We have contrasted the Church with the Soul. In the soul then let the redemption be sought. Wherever a man comes, there comes revolution. The old is for slaves. When a man comes, all books are legible, all things transparent, all religions are forms. He is religious. Man is the wonderworker. He is seen amid miracles. All men bless and curse. He saith yea and nay only. The stationariness of religion; the assumption that the age of inspiration is past, that the Bible is closed; the fear of degrading the character of Jesus by representing him as a man—indicate with sufficient clearness the falsehood of our theology. It is the office of a true teacher to show us that God is, not was; that He speaketh, not spake. The true Christianity—a faith like Christ's in the infinitude of man—is lost. None believeth in the soul of man but only in some man or person old and departed. Ah me! no man goeth alone. All men go in flocks to this saint or that poet, avoiding the God who seeth in secret. They cannot see in secret; they love to be blind in public. They think society wiser than their soul and know not that one soul, and their soul, is wiser than the whole world. See how nations and races flit by on the sea of time and leave no ripple to tell where they floated or sunk, and one good soul shall make the name of Moses, or of Zeno, or of Zoroaster, reverend forever. None assayeth the stern ambition to be the Self of the nation and of nature, but each would be an easy secondary to some Christian scheme, or sectarian connection, or some eminent man. Once leave your own knowledge of God, your own sentiment, and take secondary knowledge, as St. Paul's, or George Fox's, or Swedenborg's, and you get wide from God with every year this secondary form lasts, and if, as now, for centuries, the chasm yawns to that breadth that men can scarcely be convinced there is in them anything divine.

Let me admonish you, first of all, to go alone; to refuse the good models, even those which are sacred in the imagination of men, and dare to love God without mediator or veil. Friends enough you shall find who will hold up to your emulation Wesleys and Oberlins, Saints and Prophets. Thank God for these good men, but say, 'I also am a man.' Imitation cannot go above its model. The imitator dooms himself to hopeless mediocrity. The inventor did it because it was natural to him, and so in him it has a charm. In the imitator something else is natural, and he bereaves himself of his own beauty, to come short of another man's.

Yourself a newborn bard of the Holy Ghost, cast behind you all conformity and acquaint men at first hand with Deity. Look to it first and only, that fashion, custom, authority, pleasure, and money, are nothing to you—are not bandages over your eyes, that you cannot see —but live with the privilege of the immeasurable mind. Not too anxious to visit periodically all families and each family in your parish connection, when you meet one of these men or women, be to them a divine man; be to them thought and virtue; let their timid aspirations find in you a friend; let their trampled instincts be genially tempted out in your atmosphere; let their doubts know that you have doubted and their wonder feel that you have wondered. By trusting your own heart, you shall gain more confidence in other men. For all our penny-wisdom, for all our soul-destroying slavery to habit, it is not to be doubted that all men have sublime thoughts; that all men value the few real hours of life; they love to be heard; they love to be caught up into the vision of principles. We mark with light in the memory the few interviews we have had, in the dreary years of routine and of sin, with souls that made our souls wiser; that spoke what we thought; that told us what we knew; that gave us leave to be what we inly were. Discharge to men the priestly office, and, present or absent, you shall be followed with their love as by an angel.

And, to this end, let us not aim at common degrees of merit. Can we not leave, to such as love it, the virtue that glitters for the commendation of society, and ourselves pierce the deep solitudes of absolute ability and worth? We easily come up to the standard of goodness in society. Society's praise can be cheaply secured, and almost all men are content with those easy merits; but the instant effect of conversing with God will be to put them away. There are persons who are not actors, not speakers, but influences; persons too great for fame, for display; who disdain eloquence; to whom all we call art and artist seems too nearly allied to show and by-ends, to the exaggeration of the finite and selfish and loss of the universal. The orators, the poets, the commanders encroach on us only as fair women do, by our allowance and homage. Slight them by preoccupation of mind, slight them, as you can well afford to do, by high and universal aims, and they instantly feel that you have right and that it is in lower places that they must shine. They also feel your right; for they with you are open to the influx of the all-knowing Spirit, which annihilates before its broad noon the little shades and gradations of intelligence in the compositions we call wiser and wisest.

In such high communion let us study the grand strokes of rectitude: a bold benevolence, and independence of friends, so that not the unjust wishes of those who love us shall impair our freedom, but we shall resist for truth's sake the freest flow of kindness and appeal to sympathies far in advance; and—what is the highest form in which we know this beautiful element—a certain solidity of merit that has nothing to do with opinion, and which is so essentially and manifestly virtue that it is taken for granted that the right, the brave, the generous step will be taken by it, and nobody thinks of commending it. You would compliment a coxcomb doing a good act, but you would not praise an angel. The silence that accepts merit as the most natural thing in the world is the highest applause. Such souls, when they appear, are the Imperial Guard of Virtue, the perpetual reserve, the dictators of fortune. One needs not praise their courage—they are the heart and soul of nature. O my friends, there are resources in us on which we have not drawn. There are men who rise refreshed on hearing a threat; men to whom a crisis which intimidates and paralyzes the majority—demanding not the faculties of prudence and thrift, but comprehension, immovableness, the readiness of sacrifice—comes graceful and beloved as a bride. Napoleon said of Massena that he was not himself until the battle began to go against him; then, when the dead began to fall in ranks around him, awoke his powers of combination, and he put on terror and victory as a robe. So it is in rugged crises, in unweariable endurance, and in aims which put sympathy out of question, that the angel is shown. But these are heights that we can scarce remember and look up to without contrition and shame. Let us thank God that such things exist.

And now let us do what we can to rekindle the smoldering, nigh-quenched fire on the altar. The evils of the church that now is are manifest. The question returns, What shall we do? I confess, all attempts to project and establish a Cultus with new rites and forms seem to me vain. Faith makes us, and not we it, and faith makes its own forms. All attempts to contrive a system are as cold as the new worship introduced by the French to the goddess of Reason—today pasteboard and fili-gree, and ending tomorrow in madness and murder. Rather let the breath of new life be breathed by you through the forms already existing. For if once you are alive, you shall find they shall become plastic and new. The remedy to their deformity is first, soul, and second, soul, and evermore, soul. A whole popedom of forms one pulsation of virtue can uplift and vivify. Two inestimable advantages Christianity has given us; first the Sabbath, the jubilee of the whole world, whose light dawns welcome alike into the closet of the philosopher, into the garret of toil, and into prison-cells and everywhere suggests, even to the vile, the dignity of spiritual being. Let it stand forevermore, a temple which new love, new faith, new sight shall restore to more than its first splendor to mankind. And secondly, the institution of preach-ing—the speech of man to men—essentially the most flexible of all organs, of all forms. What hinders that now, everywhere, in pulpits, in lecture rooms, in houses, in fields, wherever the invitation of men or your own occasions lead you, you speak the very truth, as your life and conscience teach it, and cheer the waiting, fainting hearts of men with new hope and new revelation?

I look for the hour when that supreme Beauty which ravished the souls of those Eastern men, and chiefly of those Hebrews, and through their lips spoke oracles to all time shall speak in the West also. The Hebrew and Greek Scriptures contain immortal sentences that have been bread of life to millions. But they have no epical integrity; are fragmentary; are not shown in their order to the intellect. I look for the new Teacher that shall follow so far those shining laws that he shall see them come full circle; shall see their rounding complete grace; shall see the world to be the mirror of the soul; shall see the identity of the law of gravitation with purity of heart; and shall show that the Ought, that Duty, is one thing with Science, with Beauty, and with Joy.

23

HORACE BUSHNELL

1802, born April 14, at Bantam, Conn.
1827, was graduated from Yale
1827–28, on the editorial staff of New York *Journal of Commerce*
1829–31, tutor and law student at Yale
1831–33, student at Yale Divinity School
1833, ordained as pastor of North Church, Hartford, Conn.
1837, *The True Wealth and Weal of Nations*
1845–46, travel in Europe
1847, *Christian Nurture*
1847, *Barbarism the First Danger*
1849, *God in Christ*
1851, *Christ in Theology*
1851, *The Age of Homespun*
1853, *Common Schools*
1858, *Sermons for the New Life*
1858, *Nature and the Supernatural as together Constituting One System of God*
1861, resigned pastorate
1864, *Popular Government by Divine Right*
1864, *Work and Play*
1864, *Christ and His Salvation*
1866, *The Vicarious Sacrifice*
1868, *Moral Uses of Dark Things*
1869, *Women's Suffrage; the Reform against Nature*
1872, *Sermons on Living Subjects*
1874, *Forgiveness and Law*
1876, died February 17
1881, posthumous, *Building Eras in Religion*
1903, posthumous, *The Spirit in Man*

THERE is one important respect in which Horace Bushnell, the founder in America of the so-called "new theology," of which Ritschl in Germany and Erskine, Campbell, McLeod, and Maurice in the British Isles were outstanding representatives, approached the position taken by Emerson. He agreed with Emerson that instruction cannot be derived from communication. Bushnell and Emerson both believed that *all* thinking had to be *original* thinking. Bushnell's statement of this point is given in his discussion of the Trinity in *God in Christ*. He said:

Words are the *signs* of thought to be expressed. They do not literally convey or pass over a thought out of one mind into another, as we commonly speak of doing. They are only hints or images held up before the mind of another, to put *him* on generating or reproducing the same thought; which he can only do as he has the same personal contents, or the generative power out of which to bring the thought required.[1]

Both Emerson and Bushnell, then, were opponents of received dogmas and of transmitted dogmatisms. Both devoted themselves to rethinking old problems and reaching new solutions.

Another parallel between these two nineteenth-century American thinkers is that neither was known as a student of the ideas of others; neither was a great reader. Emerson, of course, read far more than he liked to say, but he read for "hints or images," for suggestions which stimulated his own thought. Of Bushnell, the complaint was made by his disciple and biographer, Theodore T. Munger, that "he not only wrote, but published first, and read later." Perhaps the best explanation is that neither Emerson nor Bushnell was an academic lecturer; Emerson was the dean of the lyceum, and Bushnell was an active minister. Neither lost connection with the vitality of men.

Bushnell's thinking on religious matters came at a time when the New England theology of the followers of Jonathan Edwards had largely outlived its relevance in American life. Its original ethical basis had been distorted, for the average person, at least, beyond recognition by the refinements of the later Hopkinsians and Old Calvinists at both Andover and Yale. In fact, in Nathaniel Emmons, grace became not merely supernatural but also invisible; there was no way in which "internal grace" could be externally evidenced. Thus, the whole empirical basis of Edwards's doctrine was lost, and the doctrine of election was reduced to a theological subtlety. The doctrine of election had been paralleled by a theory of revivalism. The religious enterprise had two facets: first, and often neglected, was the proclamation to men of their sinful nature; second, the proclamation of the terms of redemption, and the preparation in whatever ways were possible for the divine work of regeneration of the human heart. According to the doctrine, redemption was entirely a supernatural affair; in practice, however, revivalistic techniques were thought of great value in preparing for the accession of divine grace. Ebenezer Porter, of Andover, wrote for the

[1] Horace Bushnell, *God in Christ*, Hartford, 1852, p. 46.

Andover Revival Association in 1832 a series of *Letters on the Religious Revivals Which Prevailed about the Beginning of the Present Century* (published, Boston, 1858), which analyzed systematically the techniques and results of earlier revivals as a guide for future work along these lines. Emphasis was placed upon the conversion experience; the center of religious activity came in early adult life; much care had to be given to assuring the permanence and stability of catastrophic conversion.

To this distortion Bushnell opposed his conception of Christian nurture. He wished to reinstate religious emphasis on the moral nature of man, and to abate the abuse of revivalism. He did not abandon the doctrine of innate sinfulness. "The natural pravity of man is plainly asserted in the Scriptures, and, if it were not, the familiar laws of physiology would require us to believe, what amounts to the same thing." He emphasized, however, the possibility that innate sinfulness might be mitigated even before the infant was able to speak, if a Christian atmosphere pervaded its environment. Christian nurture by example and later by precept might so far modify the original tendency to sin that, on reaching years of discretion the child would find himself a Christian without struggle. "Assuming the corruption of human nature, when should we think it wisest to undertake or expect a remedy? When evil is young and pliant to good, or when it is confirmed by years of sinful habit?"

This belief in the power of Christian nurture to make Christians involves the wish and desire to improve Christian education, much of which "only serves to make the subject of religion odious, and that, as nearly as we can discover, in exact proportion to the amount of religious teaching received." This criticism was directed not only at "ostrich nurture," Bushnell's vivid term for improper religious instruction in the home, but also, and more specifically at improper religious instruction in Bible schools. This "miseducation, called Christian" discourages piety by "making enmity itself a necessary ingredient in the struggle of conversion, conversion no reality without a struggle." The religious education of children should not consist of warmed-over revival sermons, but of a practical infusion of Christ into the infant mind, "the house, having a domestic Spirit of grace dwelling in it, should become the church of childhood. . . . Something is wanted that is better than teaching, something that transcends mere effort and will-work —the loveliness of a good life, the repose of faith, the confidence of righteous expectation, the sacred and cheerful liberty of the Spirit—all glowing about the young soul, as a warm and genial nurture, and forming in it, by methods that are silent and imperceptible, a spirit of duty and religious obedience to God."

Approaching Bushnell's thought from a different point of view, one sees that he believes that parents and children were spiritually as well as physically in organic unity. The development of the child's individuality takes place gradually within the family organism. "We seem to fancy that there is some definite moment when a child becomes a moral agent, passing out of a condition where he is a moral nullity, and where no moral agency touches his being. Whereas he is rather to be regarded, at the first, as lying within the moral agency of the parent, and passing out, by degrees, through a course of mixed agency, to a proper independency and self-possession." Because of this organic connection, it is possible "that the Christian life and spirit of the parents shall flow into the mind of the child." There is interconnectedness even beyond the family, which influences the child in like ways. "All society is organic—the church, the state, the school, the family." The child differs from the adult in being more within the power of organic laws. By taking church, state, school, and family as parts of an organic society, Bushnell opened a path for later thinkers who saw in secular institutions the proper field for spiritual activity.

Thus, Bushnell turned his attention to the development of piety and morality in the young, and away from the tactics of revivalism. His work was sharply criticized, although it contained no departure from "sound evangelical theology." Despite the criticism, it marked a turning point in the Congregational religious enterprise, which had become distorted in its concern for conscious conversion; Bushnell and those who followed his steps restored it to wholesome balance.

CHRISTIAN NURTURE, I

"Bring them up in the nurture and admonition of the Lord."

Ephesians vi. 4.

THERE is then some kind of nurture which is of the Lord, deriving a quality and a power from Him, and communicating the same. Being instituted by Him, it will of necessity have a method and a character peculiar to itself, or rather to Him. It will be the Lord's way of education, having aims appropriate to Him, and, if realized in its full intent, terminating in results impossible to be reached by any merely human method.

What then is the true idea of Christian or divine nurture, as distinguished from that which is not Christian? What is its aim? What its method of working? What its powers and instruments? What its contemplated results? Few questions have greater moment; and it is one of the pleasant signs of the times, that the subject involved is beginning to attract new interest, and excite a spirit of inquiry which heretofore has not prevailed in our churches.

In ordinary cases, the better and more instructive way of handling this subject, would be to go directly into the practical methods of parental discipline, and show by what modes of government and instruction we may hope to realize the best results. But unhappily the public mind is pre-occupied extensively by a view of the whole subject, which I must regard as a theoretical mistake, and one which must involve, as long as it continues, practical results systematically injurious. This mistaken view it is necessary, if possible, to remove. And accordingly what I have to say will take the form of an argument on the question thus put in issue; though I design to gather round the subject, as I proceed, as much of practical instruction as the mode of the argument will suffer. Assuming then the question above stated, What is the true idea of Christian education?—I answer in the following proposition, which it will be the aim of my argument to establish, viz:

THAT THE CHILD IS TO GROW UP A CHRISTIAN. In other words, the aim, effort, and expectation should be, not, as is commonly assumed, that the child is to grow up in sin, to be converted after he comes to a mature age; but that he is to open on the world as one that is spiritually renewed, not remembering the time when he went through a technical experience, but seeming rather to have loved what is good from his earliest years. I do not affirm that every child may, in fact and without exception, be so trained that he certainly will grow up a Christian. The qualifications it may be necessary to add will be given in another place, where they can be stated more intelligibly.

This doctrine is not a novelty, now rashly and for the first time propounded, as some of you may be tempted to suppose. I shall show you, before I have done with the argument, that it is as old as the Christian church, and prevails extensively at the present day in other parts of the world. Neither let your own experience raise a prejudice against it. If you have endeavored to realize the very truth I here affirm, but find that your children do not exhibit the character you have looked for;

if they seem to be intractable to religious influences, and sometimes to display an apparent aversion to the very subject of religion itself, you are not of course to conclude that the doctrine I here maintain is untrue or impracticable. You may be unreasonable in your expectations of your children.

Possibly, there may be seeds of holy principle in them, which you do not discover. A child acts out his present feelings, the feelings of the moment, without qualification or disguise. And how, many times, would all you appear, if you were to do the same? Will you expect of them to be better, and more constant and consistent, than yourselves; or will you rather expect them to be children, human children still, living a mixed life, trying out the good and evil of the world, and preparing, as older Christians do, when they have taken a lesson of sorrow and emptiness, to turn again to the true good?

Perhaps they will go through a rough mental struggle, at some future day, and seem, to others and to themselves, there to have entered on a Christian life. And yet it may be true that there was still some root of right principle established in their childhood, which is here only quickened and developed, as when Christians of a mature age are revived in their piety, after a period of spiritual lethargy; for it is conceivable that regenerate character may exist, long before it is fully and formally developed.

But suppose there is really no trace or seed of holy principle in your children, has there been no fault of piety and constancy in your church? no want of Christian sensibility and love to God? no carnal spirit visible to them and to all, and imparting its noxious and poisonous quality to the Christian atmosphere in which they have had their nurture? For it is not for you alone to realize all that is included in the idea of Christian education. It belongs to the church of God, according to the degree of its social power over you and in you and around your children, to bear a part of the responsibility with you.

Then, again, have you nothing to blame in yourselves? no lack of faithfulness? no indiscretion of manner or of temper? no mistake of duty, which, with a better and more cultivated piety, you would have been able to avoid? Have you been so nearly even with your privilege and duty, that you can find no relief but to lay some charge upon God, or comfort yourselves in the conviction that he has appointed the failure you deplore? When God marks out a plan of education, or sets up an aim to direct its efforts, you will see, at once, that he could not base it on a want of piety in you, or on any imperfections that flow from a want of piety. It must be a plan measured by Himself and the fullness of his own gracious intentions.

Besides, you must not assume that we, in this age, are the best Christians that have ever lived, or most likely to produce all the fruits of piety. An assumption so pleasing to our vanity is more easily made than verified, but vanity is the weakest as it is the cheapest of all arguments. We have some good points, in which we compare favorably with other Christians, and Christians of other times, but our style of piety is sadly deficient, in many respects, and that to such a degree that we have little cause for self-congratulation. With all our activity and boldness of movement, there is a certain hardness and rudeness, a want of sensibility to things that do not lie in action, which cannot be too much deplored, or too soon rectified. We hold a piety of conquest rather than of love. A kind of public piety, that is strenuous and fiery on great occasions, but wants the beauty of holiness, wants constancy, singleness of aim, loveliness, purity, richness, blamelessness, and—if I may add another term not so immediately religious, but one that carries, by association, a thousand religious qualities—wants domesticity of character; wants them, I mean, not as compared with the perfect standard of Christ, but as compared with other examples of piety that have been given in former times, and others that are given now.

For some reason, we do not make a Christian atmosphere about us— do not produce the conviction that we are living unto God. There is a marvelous want of savor in our piety. It is a flower of autumn, colored as highly as it need be to the eye, but destitute of fragrance. It is too much to hope that, with such an instrument, we can fulfill the true idea of Christian education. Any such hope were even presumptuous. At the same time, there is no so ready way of removing the deficiencies just described, as to recall our churches to their duties in domestic life; those humble, daily, hourly duties, where the spirit we breathe shall be a perpetual element of power and love, bathing the life of childhood.

Thus much it was necessary to say, for the removal of prejudices, that are likely to rise up in your minds, and make you inaccessible to the arguments I may offer. Let all such prejudices be removed, or, if this be too much, let them, at least, be suspended till you have heard what I have to advance; for it cannot be desired of you to believe any thing more than what is shown you by adequate proofs. Which also it is right to ask, that you will hear, if offered, in a spirit of mind, such as becomes our wretched and low attainments, and with a willingness to let God be exalted, though at the expense of some abasement in ourselves. In pursuing the argument, I shall—

I. Collect some considerations which occur to us, viewing the subject on the human side, and then—

II. Show how far and by what methods God has justified, on his part, the doctrine we maintain.

There is then, as the subject appears to us—

1. No absurdity in supposing that children are to grow up in Christ. On the other hand, if there is no absurdity, there is a very clear moral incongruity in setting up a contrary supposition, to be the aim of a system of Christian education. There could not be a worse or more baleful implication given to a child, than that he is to reject God and all holy principle, till he has come to a mature age. What authority have you from the Scriptures to tell your child, or, by any sign, to show him that you do not expect him truly to love and obey God, till after he has spent whole years in hatred and wrong? What authority to make him feel that he is the most unprivileged of all human beings, capable of sin, but incapable of repentance; old enough to resist all good, but too young to receive any good whatever? It is reasonable to suppose that you have some express authority for a lesson so manifestly cruel and hurtful, else you would shudder to give it. I ask you for the chapter and verse, out of which it is derived. Meantime, wherein would it be less incongruous for you to teach your child that he is to lie and steal, and go the whole round of the vices, and then, after he comes to mature age, reform his conduct by the rules of virtue? Perhaps you do not give your child to expect that he is to grow up in sin; you only expect that he will yourself. That is scarcely better: for that which is your expectation, will assuredly be his; and what is more, any attempt to maintain a discipline at war with your own secret expectations, will only make a hollow and worthless figment of that which should be an open, earnest reality. You will never practically aim at

what you practically despair of, and if you do not practically aim to unite your child to God, you will aim at something less, that is, something unchristian, wrong, sinful.

But my child is a sinner, you will say; and how can I expect him to begin a right life, until God gives him a new heart? This is the common way of speaking, and I state the objection in its own phraseology, that it may recognize itself. Who then has told you that a child cannot have the new heart of which you speak? Whence do you learn that if you live the life of Christ, before him and with him, the law of the Spirit of Life may not be such as to include and quicken him also? And why should it be thought incredible that there should be some really good principle awakened in the mind of a child? For this is all that is implied in a Christian state. The Christian is one who has simply *begun* to love what is good for its own sake, and why should it be thought impossible for a child to have this love begotten in him? Take any scheme of depravity you please, there is yet nothing in it to forbid the possibility that a child should be led, in his first moral act, to cleave unto what is good and right, any more than in the first of his twentieth year. He is, in that case, only a child converted to good, leading a mixed life as all Christians do. The good in him goes into combat with the evil, and holds a qualified sovereignty. And why may not this internal conflict of goodness cover the whole life from its dawn, as well as any part of it? And what more appropriate to the doctrine of spiritual influence itself, than to believe that as the Spirit of Jehovah fills all the worlds of matter, and holds a presence of power and government in all objects, so all human souls, the infantile as well as the adult, have a nurture of the Spirit appropriate to their age and their wants? What opinion is more essentially monstrous, in fact, than that which regards the Holy Spirit as having no agency in the immature souls of children, who are growing up, helpless and unconscious, into the perils of time?

2. It is to be expected that Christian education will radically differ from that which is not Christian. Now, it is the very character and mark of all unchristian education, that it brings up the child for future conversion. No effort is made, save to form a habit of outward virtue, and, if God please to convert the family to something higher and better, after they come to the age of maturity, it is well. Is then Chris-

tian education, or the nurture of the Lord, no way different from this? Or is it rather to be supposed that it will have a higher aim and a more sacred character?

And, since it is the distinction of Christian parents, that they are themselves in the nurture of the Lord, since Christ and the Divine Love, communicated through him, are become the food of their life, what will they so naturally seek as to have their children partakers with them, heirs together with them in the grace of life? I am well aware of the common impression that Christian education is sufficiently distinguished by the endeavor of Christian parents to teach their children the lessons of Scripture history, and the doctrines or dogmas of Scripture theology. But if they are given to understand, at the same time, that these lessons can be expected to produce no fruit till they are come to a mature age—that they are to grow up still in the same character as other children do, who have no such instruction—what is this but to enforce the practical rejection of all the lessons taught them? And which, in truth, is better for them, to grow up in sin under Scripture light, with a heart hardened by so many religious lessons; or to grow up in sin, unvexed and unannoyed by the wearisome drill of lectures that only discourage all practical benefit? Which is better, to be piously brought up to sin, or to be allowed quietly to vegetate in it?

These are questions that I know not how to decide; but the doubt in which they leave us will at least suffice to show that Christian education has, in this view, no such eminent advantages over that which is unchristian, as to raise any broad and dignified distinction between them. We certainly know that much of what is called Christian nurture, only serves to make the subject of religion odious, and that, as nearly as we can discover, in exact proportion to the amount of religious teaching received. And no small share of the difficulty to be overcome afterwards, in the struggle of conversion, is created in just this way.

On the other hand, you will hear, for example, of cases like the following: A young man, correctly but not religiously brought up, light and gay in his manners, and thoughtless hitherto in regard to any thing of a serious nature, happens accidentally one Sunday, while his friends are gone to ride, to take down a book on the evidences of Christianity. His eye, floating over one of the pages, becomes fixed, and he is surprised to find his feelings flowing out strangely into its holy truths. He is conscious of no struggle of hostility, but a new joy dawns in his being. Henceforth, to the end of a long and useful life, he is a Christian man. The love into which he was surprised continues to flow, and he is remarkable, in the churches, all his life long, as one of the most beautiful, healthful, and dignified examples of Christian piety. Now, a very little mis-education, called Christian, discouraging the piety it teaches, and making enmity itself a necessary ingredient in the struggle of conversion, conversion no reality without a struggle, might have sufficed to close the mind of this man against every thought of religion to the end of life.

Such facts (for the case above given is a fact and not a fancy) compel us to suspect the value of much that is called Christian education. They suggest the possibility also that Christian piety should begin in other and milder forms of exercise, than those which commonly distinguish the conversion of adults; that Christ himself, by that renewing Spirit who can sanctify from the womb, should be practically infused into the childish mind; in other words, that the house, having a domestic Spirit of grace dwelling in it, should become the church of childhood, the table and hearth a holy rite, and life an element of saving power. Something is wanted that is better than teaching, something that transcends mere effort and will-work—the loveliness of a good life, the repose of faith, the confidence of righteous expectation, the sacred and cheerful liberty of the Spirit—all glowing about the young soul, as a warm and genial nurture, and forming in it, by methods that are silent and imperceptible, a spirit of duty and religious obedience to God. This only is Christian nurture, the nurture of the Lord.

3. It is a fact that all Christian parents would like to see their children grow up in piety; and the better Christians they are, the more earnestly they desire it; and, the more lovely and constant the Christian spirit they manifest, the more likely it is, in general, that their children will early display the Christian character. This is current opinion. But why should a Christian parent, the deeper his piety and the more closely he is drawn to God, be led to desire, the more earnestly, what, in God's view, is even absurd or impossible. And, if it be generally seen that the children of such are more likely to become Christians early, what forbids the hope that, if they were better Christians still, living a more single and Christ-like life, and more cultivated in their views

of family nurture, they might not see their children grow up in piety towards God? Or, if they may not always see it as clearly as they desire, might they not still be able to implant some holy principle, which shall be the seed of a Christian character in their children, though not developed fully and visibly till a later period in life?

4. Assuming the corruption of human nature, when should we think it wisest to undertake or expect a remedy? When evil is young and pliant to good, or when it is confirmed by years of sinful habit? And when, in fact, is the human heart found to be so ductile to the motives of religion, as in the simple, ingenuous age of childhood? How easy is it then, as compared with the stubbornness of adult years, to make all wrong seem odious, all good lovely and desirable. If not discouraged by some ill-temper, which bruises all the gentle sensibilities, or repelled by some technical view of religious character, which puts it beyond his age, how ready is the child to be taken by good, as it were, beforehand, and yield his ductile nature to the truth and Spirit of God, and to a fixed prejudice against all that God forbids.

He cannot understand, of course, in the earliest stage of childhood, the philosophy of religion as a renovated experience, and that is not the form of the first lessons he is to receive. He is not to be told that he must have a new heart and exercise faith in Christ's atonement. We are to understand, that a right spirit may be virtually exercised in children, when, as yet, it is not intellectually received, or as a form of doctrine. Thus, if they are put upon an effort to be good, connecting the fact that God desires it and will help them in the endeavor, that is all which, in a very early age, they can receive, and that includes every thing—repentance, love, duty, dependence, faith. Nay, the operative truth necessary to a new life, may possibly be communicated through and from the parent, being revealed in his looks, manners, and ways of life, before they are of an age to understand the teaching of words; for the Christian scheme, the gospel, is really wrapped up in the life of every Christian parent, and beams out from him as a living epistle, before it escapes from the lips, or is taught in words. And the Spirit of truth may as well make this living truth effectual, as the preaching of the gospel itself.

Never is it too early for good to be communicated. Infancy and childhood are the ages most pliant to good. And who can think it necessary that the plastic nature of childhood must first be hardened into stone, and stiffened into enmity towards God and all duty, before it can become a candidate for Christian character! There could not be a more unnecessary mistake, and it is as unnatural and pernicious, I fear, as it is unnecessary.

There are many who assume the radical goodness of human nature, and the work of Christian education is, in their view, only to educate, or educe the good that is in us. Let no one be disturbed by the suspicion of a coincidence between what I have here said and such a theory. The natural pravity of man is plainly asserted in the Scriptures, and, if it were not, the familiar laws of physiology would require us to believe, what amounts to the same thing. And if neither Scripture nor physiology taught us the doctrine, if the child was born as clear of natural prejudice or damage, as Adam before his sin, spiritual education, or, what is the same, probation, that which trains a being for a stable, intelligent virtue hereafter, would still involve an experiment of evil, therefore a fall and a bondage under the laws of evil; so that, view the matter as we will, there is no so unreasonable assumption, none so wide of all just philosophy, as that which proposes to form a child to virtue, by simply educing or drawing out what is in him.

The growth of Christian virtue is no vegetable process, no mere onward development. It involves a struggle with evil, a fall and a rescue. The soul becomes established in holy virtue, as a free exercise, only as it is passed round the corner of fall and redemption, ascending thus unto God through a double experience, in which it learns the bitterness of evil and the worth of good, fighting its way out of one, and achieving the other as a victory. The child, therefore, may as well begin life under a law of hereditary damage, as to plunge himself into evil by his own experiment, which he will as naturally do from the simple impulse of curiosity, or the instinct of knowledge, as from any noxious quality in his mold derived by descent. For it is not sin which he derives from his parents; at least, not sin in any sense which imports blame, but only some prejudice to the perfect harmony of his mold, some kind of pravity or obliquity which inclines him to evil. These suggestions are offered, not as necessary to be received in every particular, but simply to show that the scheme of education proposed, is not to be identified with another, which assumes the radical goodness of human nature, and according to which, if it be true, Christian education is insignificant.

5. It is implied in all our religious philosophy, that if a child ever does any thing in a right spirit, ever loves any thing because it is good and right, it involves the dawn of a new life. This we cannot deny or doubt, without bringing in question our whole scheme of doctrine. Is it then incredible that some really good feeling should be called into exercise in a child? In all the discipline of the house, quickened as it should be by the Spirit of God, is it true that he can never once be brought to submit to parental authority lovingly and becaue it is right? Must we even hold the absurdity of the scripture counsel—"Children, obey your parents in the Lord, for this is right"? When we speak thus of a love to what is right and good, we must of course discriminate between the mere excitement of a natural sensibility to pleasure in the contemplation of what is good, (of which the worst minds are more or less capable,) and a practical subordination of the soul to its power, a practical embrace of its law. The child must not only be touched with some gentle emotions towards what is right, but he must love it with a fixed love, love it for the sake of its principle, receive it as a vital and formative power.

Nor is there any age, which offers itself to God's truth and love, and to that Quickening Spirit whence all good proceeds, with so much of ductile feeling and susceptibilities so tender. The child is under parental authority too for the very purpose, it would seem, of having the otherwise abstract principle of all duty impersonated in his parents, and thus brought home to his practical embrace; so that, learning to obey his parents in the Lord, because it is right, he may thus receive, before he can receive it intellectually, the principle of all piety and holy obedience. And when he is brought to exercise a spirit of true and loving submission to the good law of his parents, what will you see, many times, but a look of childish joy, and a happy sweetness or manner, and a ready delight in authority, as like to all the demonstrations of Christian experience, as any thing childish can be to what is mature?

6. Children have been so trained as never to remember the time when they began to be religious. Baxter was, at one time, greatly troubled concerning himself, because he could recollect no time when there was a gracious change in his character. But he discovered, at

length, that "education is as properly a means of grace as preaching," and thus found the sweeter comfort in his love to God, that he learned to love him so early. The European churches, generally, regard Christian piety more as a habit of life, formed under the training of childhood, and less as a marked spiritual change in experience. In Germany, for example, the church includes all the people, and it is remarkable that, under a scheme so loose, and with so much of pernicious error taught in the pulpit, there is yet so much of deep religious feeling, so much of lovely and simple character, and a savor of Christian piety so generally prevalent in the community. So true is this, that the German people are every day spoken of as a people religious by nature; no other way being observed of accounting for the strong religious bent they manifest. Whereas it is due, beyond any reasonable question, to the fact that children are placed under a form of treatment which expects them to be religious, and are not discouraged by the demand of an experience above their years.

Again, the Moravian Brethren, it is agreed by all, give as ripe and graceful an exhibition of piety, as any body of Christians living on the earth, and it is the radical distinction of their system that it rests its power on Christian education. They make their churches schools of holy nurture to childhood, and expect their children to grow up there, as plants in the house of the Lord. Accordingly it is affirmed that not one in ten of the members of that church, recollects any time when he began to be religious. Is it then incredible that what has been can be? Would it not be wiser and more modest, when facts are against us, to admit that there is certainly some bad error, either in our life, or in our doctrine, or in both, which it becomes us to amend?

Once more, if we narrowly examine the relation of parent and child, we shall not fail to discover something like a law of organic connection, as regards character, subsisting between them. Such a connection as makes it easy to believe, and natural to expect that the faith of the one will be propagated in the other. Perhaps I should rather say, such a connection as induces the conviction that the character of one is actually included in that of the other, as a seed is formed in the capsule; and being there matured, by a nutriment derived from the stem, is gradually separated from it. It is a singular fact, that many believe substantially the same thing, in regard to evil character, but have no thought of any such possibility in regard to good. There has been much speculation, of late, as to whether a child is born in depravity, or whether the depraved character is superinduced afterwards. But, like many other great questions, it determines much less than is commonly supposed; for, according to the most proper view of the subject, a child is really not born till he emerges from the infantile state, and never before that time can he be said to receive a separate and properly individual nature.

The declaration of Scripture, and the laws of physiology, I have already intimated, compel the belief that a child's nature is somehow depravated by descent from parents, who are under the corrupting effects of sin. But this, taken as a question relating to the mere *punctum temporis,* or precise point of birth, is not a question of any so grave import as is generally supposed; for the child, after birth, is still within the matrix of the parental life, and will be, more or less, for many years. And the parental life will be flowing into him all that time, just as naturally, and by a law as truly organic, as when the sap of the trunk flows into a limb. We must not govern our thoughts, in such a matter, by our eyes; and because the physical separation has taken place, conclude that no organic relation remains. Even the physical being of the child is dependent still for nutrition on organic processes not in itself. Meantime, the mental being and character have scarcely begun to have a proper individual life. Will, in connection with conscience, is the basis of personality, or individuality, and these exist as yet only in their rudimental type, as when the form of a seed is beginning to be unfolded at the root of a flower.

At first, the child is held as a mere passive lump in the arms, and he opens into conscious life under the soul of the parent, streaming into his eyes and ears, through the manners and tones of the nursery. The kind and degree of passivity are gradually changed as life advances. A little farther on it is observed that a smile wakens a smile: any kind of sentiment or passion, playing in the face of the parent, wakens a responsive sentiment or passion. Irritation irritates, a frown withers, love expands a look congenial to itself, and why not holy love? Next the ear is opened to the understanding of words, but what words the child shall hear, he cannot choose, and has as little capacity to select the sentiments that are poured into his soul. Farther on, the parents begin to govern him by appeals to will, expressed in commands, and whatever their requirement may be, he can as little withstand it, as the violet can cool the scorching sun, or the tattered leaf can tame the hurricane. Next they appoint his school, choose his books, regulate his company, decide what form of religion, and what religious opinions he shall be taught, by taking him to a church of their own selection. In all this, they infringe upon no right of the child, they only fulfill an office which belongs to them. Their will and character are designed to be the matrix of the child's will and character. Meantime, he approaches more and more closely, and by a gradual process, to the proper rank and responsibility of an individual creature, during all which process of separation, he is having their exercises and ways translated into him. Then, at last, he comes forth to act his part in such color of evil, and why not of good, as he has derived from them.

The tendency of all our modern speculations is to an extreme individualism, and we carry our doctrines of free will so far as to make little or nothing of organic laws; not observing that character may be, to a great extent, only the free development of exercises previously wrought in us, or extended to us, when other wills had us within their sphere. All the Baptist theories of religion are based in this error. They assume, as a first truth, that no such thing is possible as an organic connection of character, an assumption which is plainly refuted by what we see with our eyes, and, as I shall by and by show, by the declarations of Scripture. We have much to say also, in common with the Baptists, about the beginning of moral agency, and we seem to fancy that there is some definite moment when a child becomes a moral agent, passing out of a condition where he is a moral nullity, and where no moral agency touches his being. Whereas he is rather to be regarded, at the first, as lying within the moral agency of the parent, and passing out, by degrees, through a course of mixed agency, to a proper independency and self-possession. The supposition that he becomes, at some certain moment, a complete moral agent, which a moment before he was not, is clumsy, and has no agreement with observation. The separation is gradual. He is never, at any moment after birth, to be regarded as perfectly beyond the sphere of good and bad exercises; for the parent exercises himself in the child, playing his emotions and sentiments, and working a character in him, by virtue of an organic power.

And this is the very idea of Christian education, that it begins with nurture or cultivation. And the intention is that the Christian life and spirit of the parents shall flow into the mind of the child, to blend with his incipient and half-formed exercises; that they shall thus beget their own good within him—their thoughts, opinions, faith, and love, which are to become a little more, and yet a little more, his own separate exercise, but still the same in character. The contrary assumption, that virtue must be the product of separate and absolutely independent choice, is pure assumption. As regards the measure of personal merit and demerit, it is doubtless true that every subject of God is to be responsible only for what is his own. But virtue still is rather a *state* of being than an act or series of acts; and, if we look at the causes which induce or prepare such a state, the will of the person himself, may have a part among these causes more or less important, and it works no absurdity to suppose that one may be even prepared to such a state, by causes prior to his own will; so that, when he sets off to act for himself, his struggle and duty may be rather to sustain and perfect the state begun, than to produce a new one. Certain it is that we are never, at any age, so independent as to be wholly out of the reach of organic laws which affect our character.

All society is organic—the church, the state, the school, the family; and there is a spirit in each of these organisms, peculiar to itself, and more or less hostile, more or less favorable to religious character, and to some extent, at least, sovereign over the individual man. A very great share of the power in what is called a revival of religion, is organic power; nor is it any the less divine on that account. The child is only more within the power of organic laws than we all are. We possess only a mixed individuality all our life long. A pure, separate, individual man, living *wholly* within, and from himself, is a mere fiction. No such person ever existed, or ever can. I need not say that this view of an organic connection of character subsisting between parent and child, lays a basis for notions of Christian education, far different from those which now prevail, under the cover of a merely fictitious and mischievous individualism.

Perhaps it may be necessary to add, that, in the strong language I have used concerning the organic connection of character between the parent and the child, it is not designed to assert a power in the parent to renew the child, or that the child can be renewed by any agency of the Spirit less immediate, than that which renews the parent himself. When a germ is formed on the stem of any plant, the formative instinct of the plant may be said in one view to produce it; but the same solar heat which quickens the plant, must quicken also the germ, and sustain the internal action of growth, by a common presence in both. So, if there be an organic power of character in the parent, such as that of which I have spoken, it is not a complete power in itself, but only such a power as demands the realizing presence of the Spirit of God, both in the parent and the child, to give it effect. As Paul said, "I have begotten you through the gospel," so may we say of the parent, who, having a living gospel enveloped in his life, brings it into organic connection with the soul of childhood. But the declaration excludes the necessity of a divine influence, not more in one case than in the other.

Such are some of the considerations that offer themselves, viewing our subject on the human side, or as it appears in the light of human evidence—all concurring to produce the conviction, that it is the only true idea of Christian education, that the child is to grow up in the life of the parent, and be a Christian, in principle, from his earliest years.

24

EDWARDS AMASA PARK

1808, born December 29, at Providence, R.I.

1826, was graduated from Brown University

1826–28, elementary teaching

1828–31, student at Andover Theological Seminary

1831–35, pastor of Congregational Church, Braintree, Mass.

1835–36, professor of mental and moral philosophy and instructor of Hebrew at Amherst College

1836–47, Bartlett professor of sacred rhetoric at Andover

1839, edited and translated, with B. B. Edwards, *Selections from German Literature*

1844, received the degree of D.D., Harvard

1844–52, co-editor, with B. B. Edwards, of *Bibliotheca Sacra*

1846, received the degree of LL.D., Brown

1847–81, Abbot professor of Christian theology at Andover

1850, *The Theology of the Intellect and That of the Feelings*

1851, *The Indebtedness of the State to the Clergy;* an election sermon

1852–84, editor of *Bibliotheca Sacra*

1858, co-editor of *The Sabbath Hymn Book*

1859, editor of *The Atonement: Discourses and Treatises by Edwards, Smalley, Maxcy, Emmons, Griffin, Burge, and Week*

1881–1900, professor emeritus, Andover

1884–1900, associate editor of *Bibliotheca Sacra*

1885, *Discourses on Some Theological Doctrines*

1900, died June 4, at Andover

1902, *Memorial Collection of Sermons*

NEW ENGLAND Congregationalism in the first half of the nineteenth century was torn between piety and theology. Driven by the Unitarian and Universalist controversies and other liberalizing Arminian tendencies within its own ranks and by the split between the "Hopkinsians" and the "Old Calvinists," the theologians sharpened their dialectical weapons and produced distinction after distinction to build the system of the New England theology. This was a tightly reasoned, deductive system even in such a late exponent, "the last outstanding exponent and champion of the New England Theology," as Edwards Amasa Park, of Andover, who never published his theology, but whose pathetic attempt to derive it inductively has been carefully and faithfully described by Frank Hugh Foster, his pupil.

At the same time, emphasis on conscious conversion and the revivalism which was considered a necessary part of the preparation of men for receiving the influx of divine grace had produced a demand for an emotional expression which had the power to stimulate men's souls, rather than to appeal to their minds. Even at the beginning of the development the divergent needs of the theological mind and the pious soul were realized by Jonathan Edwards, whose treatise on the will had purely intellectual reference and whose sermon "Sinners in the Hands of an Angry God" was intended purely as an appeal to the emotions. Indeed, it was not at all rare to find theologian and revivalist in the same person, as in Edwards. Park himself had been a revival preacher during his pastorate at Braintree, Massachusetts, and frequently illustrated his theological discussions with examples drawn from his pastoral experiences. He once called the New England theology a system "fit to be preached." [1]

Ultimately, then, it became necessary for such a consistent thinker to justify himself to himself. In doing so, he escaped the dialectical difficulties which had haunted the Andover school by reconciling the Calvinist theology of regeneration with the evangelical theology of conversion. God, he said, is the "sole author" of regeneration; man is the sole author of conversion. This permitted him to remain a determinist with respect to the entire process of regeneration, while retaining freedom for the human will. One of the stumbling blocks of the New England theology was that if the will is divinely determined in the act of conversion, God, being responsible for this one act of the will, is responsible for all acts of the will and therefore for sin. Park's distinction left open to the pastor the duties of removing obstacles from the path of the sinner, stimulating him to repentance and, in short, forwarding the act of conversion in every possible way.

Another, and more radical, self-justification was Park's celebrated sermon, "The Theology of the Intellect and That of the Feelings," preached in Boston before the convention of Congregational ministers in 1850. It was partly an attempt to effect a reconciliation of the different groups represented in his mixed audience, an attempt to mediate between Harvard and Unitarian intellectualism and popular revivalism; the sermon is, however, as much a reconciliation of the two aspects of intellectualism and pietism in his own make-up. It was intended as a broad defense of the older theologies of Congregationalism. Park's emphasis on the emotional and moral side of religious life makes the sermon stand out as one of the precursors of such a "new" theology as did in fact develop out of the thought of his contemporary

[1] Daniel D. Williams, *The Andover Liberals*, New York, 1941, p. 19.

Horace Bushnell. Indeed, Williams points out that two years earlier Bushnell had talked at Andover on "Dogma and Spirit," and had made a distinction which closely parallels that made by Park; Bushnell had spoken of opinion, which is of the head, and knowledge of Christian truth, which is of the heart.

By the theology of the intellect Park meant a theology which is rational, exact, accurate, based on evidence, and scientific, preferring the general to the specific statement. The theology of the feelings, on the other hand, is emotional, suggestive, approximate, sensitive, and poetic, preferring the specific to the general statement. The theology of the intellect insists upon clear and complete expression; the theology of the feelings accentuates and exaggerates now one aspect, now another, according to the emotional needs of the moment. Each partial expression "is embraced as involving the substance of truth, although, when literally interpreted it may or may not be false." Much of the Bible, said Park, is an expression of the theology of the feelings. The confusion of the two types of theology spoils both, especially in the pulpit.

It is this crossing of one kind of theology into the province of another kind . . . which mars either the eloquence or else the doctrine of the pulpit. The massive speculations of the metaphysician sink down into his expressions of feeling and make him appear cold-hearted, while the enthusiasm of the impulsive divine ascends and effervesces into his reasonings and causes him both the *appear*, and to *be* . . . hot-headed.

Park's particular application of the distinction between the two types of theological expression was to attack the literal interpretation of some of the traditional doctrines, especially those of total depravity, and of the imputation of Adam's sin, on the ground that the moral sense of humanity was against them. Out of a heart repentant and overflowing with a sense of sin may come the words "Behold! I was shapen in iniquity, and in sin did my mother conceive me."

But when a theorist seizes at such living words as these, and puts them into his vice, and straightens or crooks them into the dogma that man is blamable before he chooses to do wrong . . . really sinful before he actually sins, then the language of motion, forced from its right place and treated as if it were a part of a nicely measured syllogism, hampers and confuses his reasoning.

In short, then, Park modified the traditional Calvinism of the New England theology with the softer, more humane elements suited to his time, making the moral sentiment of "choice men and women" the standard by which all theology must be judged.

THE THEOLOGY OF THE INTELLECT
AND THAT OF THE FEELINGS

The strength of Israel will not lie nor repent: for he is not a man that he should repent.—1 Sam. 15:29.

And it repented the Lord that he had made man on the earth, and it grieved him at his heart.—Gen. 6:6.

I HAVE heard of a father who endeavored to teach his children a system of astronomy in precise philosophical language, and although he uttered nothing but the truth, they learned from him nothing but falsehood. I have also heard of a mother who, with a woman's tact, so exhibited the general features of astronomical science that although her statements were technically erroneous, they still made upon her children a better impression, and one more nearly right than would have been made by a more accurate style. For the same reason many a punctilious divine, preaching the exact truth in its scientific method, has actually imparted to the understanding of his hearers either no idea at all or a wrong one; while many a pulpit orator, using words which tire the patience of a scholastic theologian, and which in their literal import are false, has yet lodged in the hearts of his people the main substance of truth. John Foster says, that whenever a man prays aright he forgets the philosophy of prayer; and in more guarded phrase we may say, that when men are deeply affected by any theme, they are apt to disturb some of its logical proportions, and when preachers aim to rouse the sympathies of a populace, they often give a brighter coloring or a bolder prominence to some lineaments of a doctrine than can be given to them in a well compacted science.

There are two forms of theology, of which the two passages in my text are selected as individual specimens, the one declaring that God never repents, the other that he does repent. For want of a better name these two forms may be termed, the theology of the intellect, and the theology of feeling. Sometimes, indeed, both the mind and the heart are suited by the same modes of thought, but often they require dissimilar methods, and the object of the present discourse is, to state some of the differences between the theology of the intellect and that of feeling, and also some of the influences which they exert upon each other.

What, then, are some of the differences between these two kinds of representation?

The theology of the intellect conforms to the laws, subserves the wants and secures the approval of our intuitive and deductive powers. It includes the decisions of the judgment, of the perceptive part of conscience and taste, indeed of all the faculties which are essential to the reasoning process. It is the theology of speculation, and therefore comprehends the truth just as it is, unmodified by excitements of feeling. It is received as accurate not in its spirit only, but in its letter also. Of course it demands evidence, either internal or extraneous, for all its propositions. These propositions, whether or not they be inferences from antecedent, are well fitted to be premises for subsequent trains of proof. This intellectual theology, therefore, prefers general to individual statements, the abstract to the concrete, the literal to the figurative. In the creed of a Trinitarian it affirms, that he who united in his person a human body, a human soul and a divine spirit, expired on the cross, but it does not originate the phrase that his soul expired, nor that "God the mighty Maker died." As it is a science, strict and severe, it aims not to be fascinating or impressive, but plain, instructive, defensible. Hence it insists on the nice proportions of doctrine, and on preciseness both of thought and style. Its words are so exactly defined, its adjustments are so accurate, that no caviller can detect an ambiguous, mystical or incoherent sentence. It is, therefore, in entire harmony with itself, abhorring a contradiction as nature abhors a vacuum. Left to its own guidance, for example, it would never suggest the unqualified remark that Christ has fully paid the debt of sinners, for it declares that this debt may justly be claimed from them; nor that he has suffered the whole punishment which they deserve, for it teaches that this punishment may still be righteously inflicted on themselves; nor that he has entirely satisfied the law, for it insists that the demands of the law are yet in force. If it should allow those as logical premises, it would also allow the salvation of all men as a logical inference, but it rejects this inference and accordingly, being self-consistent, must reject those when viewed as literal premises. It is adapted to the soul in her inquisitive moods, but fails to satisfy her craving for excitement. In

order to express the definite idea that we are exposed to evil in consequence of Adam's sin, it does not employ the passionate phrase, "we
are guilty of his sin." It searches for the proprieties of representation,
for seemliness and decorum. It gives origin to no statements which require apology or essential modification; no metaphor, for example,
so bold and so liable to disfigure our idea of the divine equity, as that
Heaven imputes the crime of one man to millions of his descendants,
and then imputes their myriad sins to him who was harmless and undefiled. As it avoids the dashes of an imaginative style, as it qualifies
and subdues the remark which the passions would make still more
intense, it seems dry, tame to the mass of men. It awakens but little
interest in favor of its old arrangements; its new distinctions are easily
introduced, to be as speedily forgotten. As we might infer, it is suited
not for eloquent appeals, but for calm controversial treatises and bodies
of divinity; not so well for the hymn-book as for the catechism; not so
well for the liturgy as for the creed.

In some respects, but not in all, the theology of feeling differs from
that of intellect. It is the form of belief which is suggested by, and
adapted to the wants of the well-trained heart. It is embraced as involving the substance of truth, although, when literally interpreted,
it may or may not be false. It studies not the exact proportions of
doctrine, but gives especial prominence to those features of it which
are and ought to be most graceful to the sensibilities. It insists not on
dialectical argument, but receives whatever the healthy affections crave.
It chooses particular rather than general statements; teaching, for
example, the divine omnipotence by an individual instance of it; saying, not that God can do all things which are objects of power, but that
He spake and it was done. It sacrifices abstract remarks to visible and
tangible images; choosing the lovely phrase that 'the children of men
put their trust under the shadow of Jehovah's wings,' rather than the
logical one that his providence comprehendeth all events. It is satisfied with vague, indefinite representations. It is too buoyant, too
earnest for a moral result, to compress itself into sharply-drawn angles.
It is often the more forceful because of the looseness of its style, herein
being the hiding of its power. It is sublime in its obscure picture of the
Sovereign who maketh darkness his pavilion, dark waters and thick
clouds of the sky. Instead of measuring the exact dimensions of a
spirit, it says, "I could not discern the form thereof: an image was be-

fore mine eyes; there was silence and I heard a voice;" and in the haziness of this vision lies its fitness to stir up the soul. Of course, the theology of feeling aims to be impressive, whether it be or not minutely accurate. Often it bursts away from dogmatic restraints, forces its passage through or over rules of logic, and presses forward to expend itself first and foremost in affecting the sensibilities. For this end, instead of being comprehensive, it is elastic; avoiding monotony it is ever pertinent to the occasion; it brings out into bold relief now one feature of a doctrine and then a different feature, and assumes as great a variety of shapes as the wants of the heart are various. In order to hold the Jews back from the foul, cruel vices of their neighbors, the Tyrian, Moabite, Ammonite, Egyptian, Philistine, Babylonian; in order to stop their indulgence in the degrading worship of Moloch, Dagon, Baal, Tammuz, they were plied with a stern theology, well fitted by its terrible denunciations to save them from the crime which was still more terrible. They were told of the jealousy and anger of the Lord, of his breastplate, helmet, bow, arrows, spear, sword, glittering sword, and raiment stained with blood. This fearful anthropomorphism enstamped a truth upon their hearts; but when they needed a soothing influence, they were assured that "the Lord shall feed his flock like a shepherd, he shall gather the lambs with his arm and carry them in his bosom, and shall gently lead those that are with young." Thus does the theology of feeling individualize the single parts of a doctrine; and, so it can make them intense and impressive, it cares not to make them harmonious with each other. When it has one end in view, it represents Christians as united with their Lord; now, they being branches and he the vine-stock; again, they being members and he the body; still again, they being the body and he the head; and once more, they being the spouse and he the bridegroom. But it does not mean to have these endearing words metamorphosed into an intellectual theory of our oneness or identification with Christ; for with another end in view it contradicts this theory, and teaches that he is distinct from us, even as separate as the sun or morning star from those who are gladdened by its beams; the door or way from those who pass through or over it, the captain from his soldiers, the forerunner from the follower, the judge from those arraigned before him, the king from those who bow the knee to him. In order to make us feel the strength of

God's aversion to sin, it declares that he has repented of having made our race, has been grieved at his heart for transgressors, weary of them, vexed with them. But it does not mean that these expressions which, as inflected by times and circumstances, impress a truth upon the soul, be stereotyped into the principle that Jehovah has ever parted with his infinite blessedness; for in order to make us confide in his stability, it denies that he ever repents, and declares that he is without even the shadow of turning. It assumes these discordant forms, so as to meet the affections in their conflicting moods. Its aim is not to facilitate the inferences of logic, but to arrest attention, to grapple with the wayward desires, to satisfy the longings of the pious heart. And in order to reach all the hiding-places of emotion, it now and then strains a word to its utmost significancy, even into a variance with some other phrase and a disproportion with the remaining parts of the system. We often hear that every great divine, like Jonathan Edwards, will contradict himself. If this be so, it is because he is a reasoner and something more; because he is not a mere mathematician, but gives his feelings a full, an easy and a various play; because he does not exhibit his faith always in the same form, straight like a needle, sharp-pointed and one-eyed.

The free theology of the feelings is ill fitted for didactic or controversial treatises or doctrinal standards. Martin Luther, the church fathers, who used it so often, became thereby unsafe polemics. Anything, everything, can be proved from them; for they were ever inditing sentences congenial with an excited heart, but false as expressions of deliberate opinion. But this emotive theology *is* adapted to the persuasive sermon, to the pleadings of the liturgy, to the songs of Zion. It is eloquence, but not that alone. By no means can it be termed *mere* poetry, in the sense of a playful fiction. It is no play, but solemn earnestness. It is no mere fiction, but an outpouring of sentiments too deep, or too mellow, or too impetuous to be suited with the stiff language of the intellect. Neither can its words be called *merely* figurative, in the sense of arbitrary or unsubstantial. They are the earliest, and if one may use a comparison, the most natural utterances of a soul instinct with religious life. They are forms of language which circumscribe a substance of doctrine, a substance which, fashioned as it may be, the intellect grasps and holds fast; a substance which arrests the more attention and prolongs the deeper interest by the figures which bound it. This form of theology, then, is far from being fitly represented by the term imaginative, still further by the term fanciful, and further yet by the word capricious. It goes deeper; it is the theology both of and for our sensitive nature; of and for the normal emotion, affection, passion. Much of it, however, may be called poetry, if this word be used, as it should be, to include the impulsive developments of a heart moved aright and to its depths by the truth. And as it is animated with the true poetic life, so it avails itself of a poetic license, and indulges in a style of remark which for sober prose would be unbecoming, or even, when associated in certain ways, irreverent. All warm affection, be it love or hatred, overleaps at times the proprieties of a didactic style. Does not the Bible make this obvious? There are words in the Canticles and in the imprecatory Psalms, which are to be justified as the utterances of a feeling too pure, too unsuspicious, too earnest to guard itself against evil surmises. There are appearances of reasoning in the Bible, which the mere dialectician has denounced as puerile sophisms. But some of them may never have been intended for logical proof; they may have been designed for passionate appeals and figured into the shape of argument, not to convince the reason but to carry the heart by a strong assault, in a day when the kingdom of heaven suffered violence and the violent took it by force. In one of his lofty flights of inspiration, the Psalmist cries, "Awake! why sleepest thou, oh Lord?" and Martin Luther, roused more than man is wont to be by this example, prayed at the Diet of Worms, in language which we fear to repeat, "Hearest thou not, my God; art thou dead?" And a favorite English minstrel sings of the "dying God," of the "sharp distress," the "sore complaints," of God, his "last groans," his "dying blood;" of his throne, also, as once a "burning throne," a "seat of dreadful wrath;" but now "sprinkled over" by "the rich drops" of blood "that calmed his frowning face." It is the very nature of a theology framed for enkindling the imagination and thereby inflaming the heart, to pour itself out, when a striking emergency calls for them, in words that burn; words that excite no congenial glow in technical students, viewing all truth in its dry light, and disdaining all figures which would offend the decorum of a philosophical or didactic style, but words which wake the deepest sympathies of quick-moving, wide-hearted, many-sided men, who look through a superficial impropriety and discern under it a truth which the nice language of prose is too frail to convey into the heart, and breaks down in the attempt.

Hence it is another criterion of this emotive theology that when once received, it is not easily discarded. The essence of it remains the same, while its forms are changed; and these forms, although varied to meet the varying exigencies of feeling, are not abandoned so as never to be restored; for the same exigencies appear and reäppear from time to time, and therefore the same diversified representations are repeated again and again. Of the ancient philosophy the greater part is lost, the remnant is chiefly useful as an historical phenomenon. Not a single treatise, except the geometry of Euclid, continues to be used by the majority of students for its original purpose. But the poetry of those early days remains fresh as in the morning of its birth. It will always preserve its youthful glow, for it appeals not to any existing standard of mental acquisition, but to a broad and common nature which never becomes obsolete. So in the *theology* of reason the progress of science has antiquated some, and will continue to modify other refinements; theory has chased theory into the shades; but the theology of the heart, letting the minor accuracies go for the sake of holding strongly upon the substance of doctrine, need not always accommodate itself to scientific changes, but may often use its old statements, even if, when literally understood, they be incorrect, and it thus abides as permanent as are the main impressions of the truth. While the lines of speculation may be easily erased, those of emotion are furrowed into the soul, and can be smoothed away only by long-continued friction. What its abettors feel, they feel and cling to, and think they know, and even when vanquished they can argue still; or rather, as their sentiments do not come of reasoning, neither do they flee before it. Hence the permanent authority of certain tones of voice which express a certain class of feelings. Hence, too, the delicacy and the peril of any endeavor to improve the style of a hymn-book or liturgy, to amend one phrase in the common version of the Bible, or to rectify any theological terms, however inconvenient, which have once found their home in the affections of good men. The heart loves its old friends, and so much the more if they be lame and blind. Hence the fervid heat of a controversy when it is provoked by an assault upon the words, not the truths but the words, which have been embosomed in the love of the church. Hence the Pilgrim of Bunyan travels and sings from land to land, and will be, as he has been, welcome around the hearthstone of every devout household from age to age; while Edwards on the Will and Cudworth on Immutable Morality, knock at many a good man's door, only to be turned away shaking the dust from off their feet.

Having considered some of the differences between the intellectual and the emotive theology, let us now glance, as was proposed, at some of the influences which one exerts on the other.

And *first*, the theology of the intellect illustrates and vivifies itself by that of feeling. As man is compounded of soul and body, and his inward sensibilities are expressed by his outward features, so his faith combines ideas logically accurate with conceptions merely illustrative and impressive. Our tendency to unite corporeal forms with mental views, may be a premonition that we are destined to exist hereafter in a union of two natures, one of them being spirit, and the other so expressive of spirit as to be called a spiritual body. We lose the influence of literal truth upon the sensibilities, if we persevere in refusing it an appropriate image. We must add a body to the soul of a doctrine, whenever we would make it palpable and enlivening. It is brought, as it were, into our presence by its symbols, as a strong passion is exhibited to us by a gesture, as the idea of dignity is made almost visible in the Apollo Belvedere. A picture may, in itself, be superficial; but it expresses the substantial reality. What though some of the representations which feeling demands be a mere exponent of the exact truth; they are, *as it were*, that very truth. What though our conceptions be only the most expressive signs of the actual verity; they are *as if* the actual verity itself. They are substantially accurate when not literally so; moral truth, when not historical. The whole reality is at least *as* good, *as* solid as they represent it, and our most vivid idea of it is in their phases.

The whole doctrine, for example, of the spiritual world, is one that requires to be made tangible by an embodiment. We have an intellectual belief that a spirit has no shape, and occupies no space; that a human soul, so soon as it is dismissed from the earth, receives more decisive tokens than had been previously given it of its Maker's com-

placency or displeasure, has a clearer knowledge of him, a larger love
or a sterner hostility to him, a more delightful or a more painful experience of his control, and at a period yet to come will be conjoined
with a body unlike the earthly one, yet having a kind of identity with
it, and furnishing inlets for new and peculiar joys or woes. It is the
judgment of some that the popular tract and the sermons of such men
as Baxter and Whitefield ought to exhibit no other than this intellectual
view of our future state. But such an intellectual view is too general to
be embraced by the feelings. They are balked with the notion of a
spaceless, formless existence, continuing between death and the resurrection. They regard the soul as turned out of being when despoiled
of shape and extension. They represent the converted islander of the
Atlantic as rising, when he leaves the earth, to the place where God
sitteth upon his throne, and also the renewed islander of the Pacific as
ascending, at death, from the world to the same prescribed spot. When
pressed with the query, how two antipodes can both rise up, in opposite
directions, to one locality, they have nothing to reply. They are not
careful to answer any objection, but only speak right on. They crave a
reality for the soul, for its coming joys or woes, and will not be defrauded of this solid existence by any subtilized theory. So tame and
cold is the common idea of an intangible, inaudible, invisible world, that
few will aspire for the rewards, and many will imagine themselves
able to endure the punishments which are thus rarified into the
results of mere thought. Now a doctrine of the intellect need not, and
should not empty itself of its substance in the view of men because
it is too delicate for their gross apprehension. "God giveth" to this
doctrine "a body as it hath pleased him," and it should avail itself of
this corporeal manifestation for the sake of retaining its felt reality. If
it let this scriptural body go, all is gone in the popular consciousness.
It is not enough for the intellect to prove that at the resurrection a new
nature will be incorporated with the soul, and will open avenues to new
bliss or woe; it must vivify the conception of this mysterious nature
and its mysterious experiences by the picture of a palm-branch, a harp,
a robe, a crown, or of that visible enginery of death which, in the
common view, gives a substance to the penalties of the law. Our demon-
strable ideas of the judgment are so abstract, that they will seemingly
evaporate unless we illustrate them by one individual day of the grand

assize, by the particular questionings and answerings, the opened book, and other minute formalities of the court. The emotions of a delicate taste are, of course, not to be disregarded; but it is a canon of criticism—is it not?—that we should express all the truth which our hearers need, and express it in the words which they will most appropriately feel. The doctrine of the resurrection, also, seems often to vanish into thin air by an over-scrupulous refinement of philosophical terminology. The intellect allows the belief that our future bodies will be identical with our present, just as really as it allows a belief that our present bodies are the same with those of our childhood, or that our bodies ever feel pleasure or pain, or that the grass is green or the sky blue, the fire warm or the ice cold, or that the sun rises or sets. The philosopher may reply, The sun does not rise nor set, the grass is not green nor the sky blue, the fire is not warm nor the ice cold, and our physical nature in itself is not sensitive. The man responds, They are so for all that concerns me. The philosopher may affirm that our present bodies are not precisely identical with those of our childhood; the man answers, They are so to all intents and purposes; and when we practically abandon our belief in our physical sameness here, then we may modify our faith in our resumed physical identity at the resurrection. But while man remains *man* upon earth, he will not give up the forms of belief which he feels to be true. He must vivify his abstractions by images which quicken his faith; and even if these images should lose their historical life, they shall have a resurrection in spiritual realities. Through our eternal existence, the biblical exhibitions of our future state will be found to have a deeper and deeper significance. They will be found to be literal truth itself, or else the best possible symbols by which that truth can be shadowed forth to men incapable of reaching either its height or its depth. In the Bible is a profound philosophy which no man has fully searched out. As this volume explains the essence of virtue by the particular commands of the law, the sinfulness of our race by incidents in the biography of Adam, the character of Jehovah by the historical examples of his love, and especially by portraying God manifest in the flesh; so, with the intent of still further adapting truth to our dull apprehension, it condescends to step over and beyond the domain of literal history, and to use the imagination in exciting the soul to spiritual research; it enrobes itself in fabrics woven

from the material world, which seems as if it were formed for elucidating spiritual truth; it incarnates all doctrine, that the wayfaring
man, though a fool, need not err, and that all *flesh* may see the salvation of God.

But the sensitive part of our nature not only quickens the percipient,
by requiring and suggesting expressive illustrations, it also furnishes
principles from which the reasoning faculty deduces important inferences. I therefore remark in the *second* place,

The theology of the intellect enlarges and improves that of the feelings, and is also enlarged and improved by it. The more extensive and
accurate are our views of literal truth, so much the more numerous
and salutary are the forms which it may assume for enlisting the
affections. A system of doctrines logically drawn out, not only makes
its own appeal to the heart, but also provides materials for the
imagination so to clothe as to allure the otherwise dormant sensibility.
The perceptive power looks right forward to the truth, (for this end
was it made), from it turns to neither side for utilitarian purposes, but
presses straight onward to its object; yet every doctrine which it discovers is in reality practical, calling forth some emotion, and this emotion animating the sensitive nature which is not diseased, deepening its
love of knowledge, elevating and widening the religious system which
is to satisfy it. Every new article of the good man's belief elicits love or
hatred, and this love or hatred so modifies the train and phasis of his
meditations, as to augment and improve the volume of his heart's
theology.

It is a tendency of pietism to undervalue the human intellect for the
sake of exalting the affections; as if sin had less to do with the feelings
than with the intelligence; as if a deceived heart had never turned men
aside; as if the reason had fallen deeper than the will. Rather has the
will fallen *from* the intellectual powers, while they remain truer than
any other to their office. It cannot be a *pious* act to underrate these
powers, given as they were by him who made the soul in his image.
Our speculative tendencies are original, legitimate parts of the constitution which it is irreverent to censure. We *must* speculate. We must
define, distinguish, infer, arrange our inferences in a system. Our
spiritual oneness, completeness, progress, require it. We lose our
civilization, so far forth as we depreciate a philosophy truly so called.

Our faith becomes a wild or weak sentimentalism if we despise logic. God has written upon our minds the ineffaceable law that they search after the truth, whatever, wherever it be, however arduous the toil for it, whithersoever it may lead. Let it come. Even if it should promise nothing to the utilitarian, there are yet within us the *mirabiles amores* to find it out. A sound heart is alive with this curiosity, and will not retain its health while its aspirations are rebuffed. It gives no unbroken peace to the man who thwarts his reasoning instinct; for amid all its conflicting demands, it is at times importunate for a reasonable belief. When it is famished by an idle intellect, it loses its tone, becomes bigoted rather than inquisitive, and takes up with theological fancies which reduce it still lower. When it is fed by an inquiring mind it is enlivened, and reaches out for an expanded faith. If the intellect of the church be repressed, that of the world will not be, and the schools will urge forward an unsanctified philosophy which good men will be too feeble to resist, and under the influence of which the emotions will be suited with forms of belief more and more unworthy, narrow, debasing.

But the theology of reason not only amends and amplifies that of the affections, it is also improved and enlarged by it. One tendency of rationalism is, to undervalue the heart for the sake of putting the crown upon the head. This is a good tendency when applied to those feelings which are wayward and deceptive, but an *irrational* one when applied to those which are unavoidable and therefore innocent, still more to those which are holy and therefore entitled to our reverence. Whenever a feeling is constitutional and cannot be expelled, whenever it is pious and cannot but be approved, then such of its impulses as are uniform, self-consistent and persevering are data on which the intellect may safely reason, and by means of which it may add new materials to its dogmatic system. Our instinctive feelings in favor of the truth, that all men in the future life will be judged, rewarded or punished by an all-wise lawgiver, are logical premises from which this truth is an inference regular in mood and figure. Every man, atheist even, has certain constitutional impulses to call on the name of some divinity; and these impulses give evidence that he ought to pray, just as the convolutions of a vine's tendrils and their reaching out to grasp the trellis, signify that in order to attain its full growth the vine must cling to a support. The wing or the web-foot of an animal is no more conclusive proof of its having been made with the design that it should fly or swim, than the instinctive cravings of the soul for a positive, an historical, a miraculously attested religion, with its Sabbaths and its ministry, are arguments that the soul was intended for the enjoyment of such a religion. If the Bible could be proved to be a myth, it would still be a divine myth; for a narrative so wonderfully fitted for penetrating through all the different avenues to the different sensibilities of the soul, must have a moral if not a literal truth. And so it appears to me, that the doctrines which concentre in and around a vicarious atonement are so fitted to the appetences of a sanctified heart, as to gain the favor of a logician, precisely as the coincidence of some geological or astronomical theories with the phenomena of the earth or sky, is a part of the syllogism which has these theories for its conclusion. Has man been created with irresistible instincts which impel him to believe in a falsehood? Or has the Christian been inspired with holy emotions which allure him to an essentially erroneous faith? Is God the author of confusion;—in his word revealing one doctrine and by his Spirit persuading his saints to reject it? If it be a fact, that the faithful of past ages, after having longed and signed and wrestled and prayed for the truth as it is in Jesus, have at length found their aspirations rewarded by any one substance of belief, does not their unanimity indicate the correctness of their cherished faith, as the agreement of many witnesses presupposes the verity of the narration in which they coincide? In its minute philosophical forms, it may not be the truth for which they yearned, but in its central principles have they one and all been deceived? Then have they asked in tears for the food of the soul, and a prayer hearing Father has given them a stone for bread.

Decidedly as we resist the pretension that the church is infallible, there is one sense in which this pretension is well founded. Her metaphysicians as such are not free from error, nor her philologists, nor any of her scholars, nor her ministers, nor councils. She is not infallible in her bodies of divinity, nor her creeds, nor catechisms, nor any logical formulae; but underneath all her intellectual refinements lies a broad substance of doctrine, around which the feelings of all renewed men cling ever and everywhere, into which they penetrate and take root, and this substance must be right, for it is precisely adjusted to the soul, and the soul was made for it.

These universal feelings provide us with a test for our own faith. Whenever we find, my brethren, that the words which we proclaim do not strike a responsive chord in the hearts of the choice men and women who look up to us for consolation, when they do not stir the depths of our own souls, reach down to our hidden wants, and evoke sensibilities which otherwise had lain buried under the cares of time; or when they make an abiding impression that the divine government is harsh, pitiless, insincere, oppressive, devoid of sympathy with our most refined sentiments, reckless of even the most delicate emotion of the tenderest nature, then we may infer that we have left out of our theology some element which we should have inserted, or have brought into it some element which we should have discarded. *Somewhere it must be wrong.* If it leave the sensibilities torpid, it needs a larger infusion of those words which Christ defined by saying, they are spirit, they are life. If it merely charm the ear like a placid song, it is not the identical essence which is likened to the fire and the hammer. Our sensitive nature is sometimes a kind of instinct which anticipates many truths, incites the mind to search for them, intimates the process of the investigation, and remains unsatisfied, restive, so long as it is held back from the object toward which it gropes its way, even as a plant bends itself forward to the light and warmth of the sun.

But while the theology of reason derives aid from the impulses of emotion, it maintains its ascendancy over them. In all investigations for truth, the intellect must be the authoritative power, employing the sensibilities as indices of right doctrine, but surveying and superintending them from its commanding elevation. It may be roughly compared to the pilot of a ship, who intelligently directs and turns the rudder, although himself and the entire vessel are also turned by it. We are told that a wise man's eyes are in his head; now although they cannot say to the hand or the foot, we have no need of you, it is yet their prerogative to determine whither the hand or foot shall move. The intellectual theology will indeed reform itself by suggestions derived from the heart, for its law is to exclude every dogma which does not harmonize with the well-ordered sensibilities of the soul. It regards a a want of concinnity in a system, as a token of some false principle. And as it will modify itself in order to avoid the error involved in a contradiction, so and for the same reason it has authority in the last resort to rectify the statements which are often congenial with excited emotion. I therefore remark in the *third* place,

The theology of the intellect explains that of feeling into an essential agreement with all the constitutional demands of the soul. It does this by collating the discordant representations which the heart allows, and eliciting the one self-consistent principle which underlies them. It places side by side the contradictory statements which receive, at different times, the sympathies of a spirit as it is moved by different impulses. It exposes the impossibility of believing all these statements, without qualifying some of them so as to prevent their subverting each other. In order to qualify them in the right way, it details their origin, reveals their intent, unfolds their influence, and by such means eliminates the principle in which they all agree for substance of doctrine. When this principle has been once detected and disengaged from its conflicting representations, it reäcts upon them, explains, modifies, harmonizes their meaning. Thus are the mutually repellent forces set over against each other, so as to neutralize their opposition and to combine in producing one and the same movement.

Seizing strongly upon some elements of a comprehensive doctrine, the Bible paints the unrenewed heart as a stone needing to be exchanged for flesh; and again, not as a stone, but as flesh needing to be turned into spirit; and yet again, neither as a stone nor as flesh, but as a darkened spirit needing to be illumined with the light of knowledge. Taking a vigorous hold of yet other elements in the same doctrine, the Bible portrays this heart not as ignorant and needing to be enlightened, but as dead and needing to be made alive; and further, not as dead but as living and needing to die, to be crucified, and buried; and further still, not as in need of a resurrection or of a crucifixion, but of a new creation; and once more, as requiring neither to be slain, nor raised from death, nor created anew, but to be born again. For the sake of vividly describing other features of the same truth, the heart is exhibited as needing to be called or drawn to God, or to be enlarged or circumcised or purified, or inscribed with a new law, or endued with new graces. And for the purpose of awakening interest in a distinct phase of this truth, all the preceding forms are inverted and man is summoned to make himself a new heart, or to give up his old one, or to become a little child, or to cleanse himself, or to unstop his deaf ears and hear, or to open his blinded eyes and see, or to awake from sleep, or rise from death. Literally understood, these expressions are dissonant from each other. Their dissonance adds to their emphasis. Their emphasis fastens our attention upon the principle in which they all agree. This principle is too vast to be vividly uttered in a single formula, and therefore branches out into various parts, and the lively exhibition of one part contravenes an equally impressive statement of a different one. The intellect educes light from the collision of these repugnant phrases, and then modifies and reconciles them into the doctrine, that *the character of our race needs an essential transformation by an interposed influence from God.* But how soon would this doctrine lose its vivacity, if it were not revealed in these dissimilar forms, all jutting up like the hills of a landscape from a common substratum.

We may instance another set of the heart's phrases, which, instead of coalescing with each other in a dull sameness, engage our curiosity by their disagreement, and exercise the analytic power in unloosing and laying bare the one principle which forms their basis. Bowed down under the experience of his evil tendencies, which long years of painful resistance have not subdued, trembling before the ever recurring fascinations which have so often enticed him into crime, the man of God longs to abase himself, and exclaims without one modifying word: "I am too frail for my responsibilities, and have no power to do what is required of me." But in a brighter moment, admiring the exuberance of divine generosity, thankful for the large gifts which his munificent Father has lavished upon him, elevated with adoring views of the equitable One who never reaps where he has not sown, the same man of God offers his unqualified thanksgiving: "I know thee, that thou art *not* an hard master, exacting of me duties which I have no power to discharge, but thou attemperest thy law to my strength, and at no time imposest upon me a heavier burden than thou at that very time makest me able to bear." In a different mood, when this same man is thinking of the future, foreseeing his temptations to an easily besetting sin, shuddering at the danger of committing it, dreading the results of a proud reliance on his own virtue, he becomes importunate for aid from above, and pours out his entreaty, with not one abating clause: "I am nothing and less than nothing; I have no power to refrain from the sin which tempts me: help, Lord, help; for thou increasest strength to him who hath no might." But in still another mood, when the same man is thinking of the past, weeping over the fact that he has now indulged in the very crime which he feared, resisting every inducement to apologize for it, blaming himself, himself alone, himself deeply for so ungrateful, unreasonable, inexcusable an act, he makes the unmitigated confession; with his hand upon his heart, he dares not qualify his acknowledgment: "I could have avoided that sin which I preferred to commit; woe is me, for I have not done as well as I might have done; if I had been as holy as I had power to be, then had I been perfect; and if I say I have been perfect, that shall prove me perverse." Thus when looking backward, the sensitive Christian insists upon his competency to perform an act, and fears that a denial of it would banish his penitence for transgression; but when looking forward, he insists upon his incompetency to perform the same act, and fears that a denial of this would weaken his feeling of dependence on God. Without a syllable of abatement, he now makes a profession, and then recalls it as thus unqualified, afterward reiterates his once recalled avowal, and again retracts what he had once and again repeated. It is the oscillating language of the emotions which, like the strings of an Æolian harp, vibrate in unison with the varying winds. It is nature in her childlike simplicity, that prompts the soul when swayed in opposing directions by dissimilar thoughts, to vent itself in these antagonistic phrases awakening the intenser interest by their very antagonism. What if they do, when unmodified, contradict each other? An impassioned heart recoils from a contradiction, no more than the war-horse of Job starts back from the battle-field.

The reason, however, being that circumspect power which looks before and after and to either side, does not allow that of these conflicting statements, each can be true save in a qualified sense. It therefore seeks out some principle which will combine these two extremes, as a magnet its opposite poles; some principle which will rectify one of these discrepant expressions by explaining it into an essential agreement with the other. And the principle, I think, which restores this harmony, is the comprehensive one, that man with no extraordinary aid from Divine grace is obstinate, undeviating, unrelenting, persevering, dogged, *fully set* in those wayward preferences which are an abuse of his freedom. His unvaried wrong choices imply a full, unremitted, "natural power" of choosing right. The emotive theology therefore, when it affirms this power, is correct both in matter and style; but when it denies this power, it uses the language of emphasis, of impression, of intensity; it means the certainty of wrong preference by declaring the inability of right; and in its vivid use of *cannot* for *will not* is accurate in its substance though not in its form. Yet even here, it is no more at variance with the intellectual theology than with itself, and the discordance, being one of letter rather than of spirit, is removed by an explanation which makes the eloquent style of the feelings at one with the more definite style of the reason.

But I am asked, Do you not thus explain away the language of the emotions? No. The contradictoriness, the literal absurdity is explained out of it, but the language is not explained away; for even when dissonant with the precise truth, it has a significancy more profound than can be pressed home upon the heart by any exact definitions. Do you not make it a mere flourish of rhetoric? I am asked again. It is no flourish; it is the utterance that comes welling up from the depths of our moral nature, and is too earnest to wait for the niceties of logic. It is the breathing out of an emotion which will not stop for the accurate measurement of its words, but leaves them to be qualified by the good sense of men.

If, however, this language be not exactly true, I am further asked, how can it move the heart? We are so made as to be moved by it. It is an ultimate law of our being, that a vivid conception affects us by inspiring a momentary belief in the thing which is conceived. But, the objector continues, can the soul be favorably influenced by that which it regards as hyperbolical? Hyperbolical! What is hyperbolical? Who calls this language an exaggeration of the truth? If interpreted by the letter, it does indeed transcend the proper bounds; but if interpreted as it is meant, as it is felt, it falls far short of them. To the eye of a child the moon's image in the diorama may appear larger than the real moon in the heavens, but not to the mind of a philosopher. The literal doctrines of theology are too vast for complete expression by man, and our intensest words are but a distant approximation to that language, which forms the new song that the redeemed in heaven sing; language which is unutterable in this infantile state of our being, and in comparison with which our so-called extravagances are but feeble and tame diminutives.

Astronomers have recommended, that in order to feel the grandeur of the stellary system we mentally reduce the scale on which it is made; that we imagine our earth to be only a mile in diameter, and the other globes to be proportionally lessened in their size and in their distances from each other; for the real greatness of the heavens discourages our very attempt to impress our hearts by them, and we are the more affected by sometimes narrowing our conceptions of what we cannot at the best comprehend. On the same principle, Christian moralists have advised us not always to dilate our minds in reaching after the extreme boundaries of a doctrine, but often to draw in our contemplations, to lower the doctrine for a time, to bring our intellect down in order to discern the practical truth more clearly, to humble our views in order that they may be at last exalted, to stoop low in order to pick up the keys of knowledge;—and is this a way of exaggerating the truth? *We do err, not knowing the Scriptures nor the power of God,* if we imagine that when for example he says, the enemies that touch his saints "touch the apple of his eye," and "he will lift up an ensign to the nations from far and will hiss unto them from the ends of the earth," he uses a mere hyperbole. No. Such anthropopathical words are the most expressive which the debilitated heart of his oriental people would appreciate, but they fail of making a full disclosure, they are only the foreshadowings of the truths which lie behind them. These refined, spiritual truths, the intellect goes round about and surveys, but is too faint for graphically delineating, and it gives up the attempt to the imagination, and this many-sided faculty multiplies symbol after symbol, bringing one image for one feature, and another image for another feature, and hovers over the feeble emotions of the heart, and strives to win them out from their dull repose, even as 'the eagle stirreth up her nest, and fluttereth over her young, and spreadeth abroad her wings, and taketh up her little ones, and beareth them on her out-stretched pinions.' Into more susceptible natures than ours the literal verities of God will penetrate far deeper than, even when shaped in their most pungent forms, they will pierce into our obdurate hearts. So lethargic are we, that we often yield no answering sensibilities to intellectual statements of doctrine; so weak are we, that such passionate appeals as are best accommodated to our phlegmatic temper are after all no more than dilutions of the truth, as "seen of angels;" and still so fond are we of harmony with ourselves, that we must explain these diluted representations into unison with the intellectual statements which, however unimpressive, are yet the most authoritative.

We are now prepared for our *fourth* remark,—the theology of the intellect and that of feeling tend to keep each other within the sphere for which they were respectively designed, and in which they are fitted to improve the character. Both of them have precisely the same sphere with regard to many truths, but not with regard to all. When an intellectual statement is transferred to the province of emotion, it often appears chilling, lifeless; and when a passionate phrase is transferred to the dogmatic province, it often appears grotesque, unintelligible, absurd. Many expressions of sentiment are *what* they ought to be, if kept *where* they ought to be; but a narrow creed *displaces* and thus spoils them. It often becomes licentious or barbarous, by stiffening into prosaic statements the free descriptions which the Bible gives of the kindliness or the wrath of God. The very same words are allowed in one relation, but condemned in a different one, because in the former they do, but in the latter do not harmonize with the sensibilities which are at the time predominant. When we are enthusiastic in extolling the generosity of divine love, we feel no need of modifying our proclamation that God desires all men to be saved, and in these uninquisitive moods we have no patience with the query which occupies our more studious hours, "whether he desire this good all things, or only itself considered." Often, though not in every instance, the solid philosophy of doctrine, descending into an exhortation, makes it cumbrous and heavy; and as often the passionate forms of appeal, when they claim to be literal truth, embarrass the intellect until they are repelled by it into the circle distinctively allotted them.

At the time when the words were uttered, there could not be a more melting address than, "If I, your Lord and Master, have washed your feet, ye also ought to wash one another's feet;" but when this touching sentiment is interpreted as a legal exaction, an argument for a Moravian or Romish ceremony, its poetic elegance is petrified into a prosaic blunder. There are moments in the stillness of our communion service, when we feel that our Lord is with us, when the bread and the wine so enliven our conceptions of his body and blood as, according to the law of vivid conception, to bring them into our ideal presence, and to make us *demand* the saying, as more pertinent and fit than any other, 'This *is* my body, this *is* my blood.' But no sooner are these phrases transmuted from hearty utterances into intellectual judgments, than they merge their beautiful rhetoric into an absurd logic, and are at once repulsed by a sound mind into their pristine sphere. So there is a depth of significance which our superficial powers do not fathom, in the lamentation: "Behold! I was shapen in iniquity, and in sin did my mother conceive me." This will always remain the passage for the out-flow of *his* grief, whose fountains of penitence are broken up. The channel is worn too deep into the affections to be easily changed. Let the schools reason about it just as, and as long as they please. Let them condemn it as indecorous, or false, or absurd, and the man who utters it as unreasonable, fanatical, bigoted. Let them challenge him for his meaning, and insist with the rigidness of the judge of Shylock, that he weigh out the import of every word, every syllable, no more, no less:—they do not move him one hair's breadth. He stands where he stood before, and where he will stand until disenthralled from the body. "My meaning," he says, "is exact enough for me, too exact for my repose of conscience; and I care just now for no proof clearer than this: 'Behold! I *was* shapen in iniquity, and in sin *did* my mother conceive me.' Here, on my heart the burden lies, and I *feel* that I am vile, a man of unclean lips, and dwell amid a people of unclean lips, and I went astray as soon as I was born, and am of a perverse, rebellious race, and there is a tide swelling within me and around me, and moving me on to actual transgression, and it is stayed by none of my unaided efforts, and all its billows roll over me, and I am so troubled that I cannot speak; and I am not content with merely saying that I am a transgressor; I long to heap infinite upon infinite, and crowd together all forms of self-reproach, for I am clad in sin as with a garment, I devour it as a sweet morsel, I breathe it, I live it, I *am* sin; my hands are stained with it, my feet are swift in it, all my bones are out of joint with it, my whole body is of tainted origin, and of death in its influence and end; and here is my definition and here is my proof, and, definition or no definition, proof or no proof, here I plant myself, and here I stay, for this is my feeling, and it comes up from the depths of an overflowing heart: '*Behold! I was shapen in iniquity, and in sin did my mother conceive me.*' "—But when a theorist seizes at such living words as these, and puts them into his vice, and straightens or crooks them into the dogma that man is blamable before he chooses to do wrong; deserving of punishment for the involuntary nature which he has never consented to gratify; really sinful before he actually sins, then the language of emotion, forced from its right place and treated as if it were a part of a nicely measured syllogism, hampers and confuses his reasonings, until it is given back to the use for which it was first intended, and from which it never ought to have been diverted. When men thus lose their sensitiveness to the discriminations between the style of judgment and that of feeling, and when they force the latter into the province of the former, they become prone to undervalue the conscience, and to be afraid of philosophy, and to shudder at the axioms of common sense, and to divorce faith from reason, and to rely on *church government* rather than on fraternal discussion.

It is this crossing of one kind of theology into the province of another kind differing from the first mainly in fashion and *contour*, which mars either the eloquence or else the doctrine of the pulpit. The massive speculations of the metaphysician sink down into his expressions of feeling and make him appear cold-hearted, while the enthusiasm of the impulsive divine ascends and effervesces into his reasonings and causes him both to *appear*, and to *be*, what our Saxon idiom so reprovingly styles him, hot-headed. The preacher ought to lay a solid basis on which he may rear a bold superstructure. He ought to prove with a clear mind, what he is to enforce with a free love. There are intellectual critics ready to exclude from our psalms and hymns all such stanzas as are not accurate expressions of dogmatic truth. Forgetting that the effort at precision often mars the freeness of song, they would condemn the simple-hearted bard to joint his metaphors into a syllogism, and to sing as a logician tries to sing. In the same spirit, they would expurgate the Paradise Lost of all phrases which are not in keeping with our chemical or geological discoveries. But it is against the laws of our sensitive nature to square the effusions of poesy by the scales, compasses and plumb-lines of the intellect. The imagination is not to be used as a dray horse for carrying the lumber of the schools through the gardens of the Muses. There are also poetical critics who imagine that the childlike breathings of our psalmody are the exact measures, the literal exponents of truth, and that every doctrine is false which cannot be transported with its present bodily shape into a sacred lyric. But this is as shallow an idea of theology as it is a mechanical, spiritless, vapid conception of poetry. If this be true, then my real belief is, that 'God came from Teman and the Holy One from Mount Paran; that he did ride upon his horses and chariots of salvation; the mountains saw him and they trembled; the sun and the moon stood still; at the light of his arrows they went and the shining of his glittering spear; he did march through the land in indignation, he did thresh the heathen in anger.' And if this be the language of a creed, then not only is the suggestion of Dr. Arnold a right one, that 'in public worship a symbol of faith should be used as a triumphal hymn of thanksgiving, and be chanted rather than read,' but such is the original and proper use of such a symbol at all times. And if this be true, then I shall not demur at phrases in a Confession of Faith, over which, in my deliberate perusal, I stagger and am at my wit's end. Wrap me in mediaeval robes; place me under the wide-spreading arches of a cathedral; let the tide of melody from the organ float along the columns that branch out like the trees of the forest over my head; then bring to me a creed written in illuminated letters, its history redolent of venerable associations, its words fragrant with the devotion of my fathers, who lived and died familiar with them; its syllables all of solemn and goodly sound, and bid me cantilate its phrases to the inspired notes of minstrelsy, my eye in a fine phrenzy rolling,—and I ask no questions for conscience' sake. I am ready to believe what is placed before me. I look beyond the antique words, to the spirit of some great truth that lingers somewhere around them; and in this nebulous view, I believe the creed *with my heart*. I may be even so rapt in enthusiasm as to believe it because it asserts what is impossible. Ask me not to prove it,—I am in no mood for proof. Try not to reason me out of it,—reasoning does me no good. Call not for my precise meaning,—I have not viewed it in that light. I have not taken the creed so much as the creed has taken me, and carried me away in my feelings to mingle with the piety of by-gone generations.—But can it be that this is the only, or the primitive, or the right idea of a symbol of faith? For *this* have logicians exhausted their subtleties, and martyrs yielded up the ghost, disputing and dying for a song? No. A creed, if true to its original end, should be in sober prose, should be understood as it means, and should mean what it says, should be drawn out with a discriminating, balancing judgment, so as to need no allowance for its freedom, no abatement of its force, and should not be expressed in antiquated terms lest men regard its spirit as likewise obsolete. It belongs to the province of the analyzing, comparing, reasoning intellect; and if it leave this province for the sake of intermingling the phrases of an impassioned heart, it confuses the soul, it awakens the fancy and the feelings to disturb the judgment, it sets a believer at variance with himself by perplexing his reason with metaphors and his imagination with logic; it raises feuds in the church by crossing the temperaments of men, and taxing one party to demonstrate similes, another to feel inspired by abstractions. Hence the logomachy which has always characterized the defence of such creeds. The intellect, no less than the heart, being out of its element, wanders through dry places, seeking rest and finding none. Men are thus made uneasy with themselves and therefore acrimonious against each other; the imaginative zealot does not apprehend the philosophical explanation, and the philosopher does not sympathize with the imaginative style, of the symbol; and as they misunderstand each other, they feel their weakness, and "to be weak is miserable," and misery not only loves but also makes company, and thus they sink their controversy into a contention and their dispute into a quarrel; nor will they ever find peace until they confine their intellect to its rightful sphere and understand it according to what it says, and their feeling to *its* province and interpret its language according to what it means, rendering unto poetry the things that are designed for poetry, and unto prose what belongs to prose.

The last clause of our fourth proposition is, that the theology of intellect and that of feeling tend to keep each other within the sphere in which they are fitted to improve the character. So far as any statement is hurtful, it parts with one sign of its truth. In itself or in its relations it must be inaccurate, whenever it is not congenial with the feelings awakened by the Divine Spirit. The practical utility, then, of any theological representations is one criterion of their propriety. Judged by this test, many fashionable forms of statement will sooner or later be condemned. Half of the truth is often a falsehood as it is impressed on the feelings; not always, however, for sometimes it has the good, the right influence, and is craved by the sensibilities which can bear no more. The heart of man is contracted, therefore loves individual views, dreads the labor of that long-continued expansion which is needed for embracing the comprehensive system. Hence its individualizing processes must be superintended by the judgment and conscience, which forbid that the attention be absorbed by any one aspect of a doctrine at the time when another aspect would be more useful. If the wrong half of a truth be applied instead of the right, or if either be mistaken for the whole, the sensibilities are mal-treated, and they endure an evil of which the musician's rude and unskilful handling of his harp, gives but a faint echo. The soul may be compared to a complicated instrument which becomes vocal in praise of its Maker when it is plied with varying powers, now with a gradual and then with a sudden contact, here with a delicate stroke and there with a hard assault; but when the rough blow comes where should have been the gentle touch, the equipoise of its parts is destroyed, and the harp of thousand strings all meant for harmony, wounds the ear with a harsh and grating sound. The dissonance of pious feeling with the mere generalities of speculation or with any misapplied fragments of truth, tends to confine them within their appropriate, which is their useful sphere. In this light, we discern the necessity of right feeling as a guide to the right proportions of faith. Here we see our responsibility for our religious belief. Here we are impressed by the fact, that much of our probation relates to our mode of shaping and coloring the doctrines of theology. Here also we learn the value of the Bible in unfolding the suitable adaptations of truth, and in illustrating their utility, which is, on the whole, so decisive a touchstone of their correctness. When our earthly hopes are too buoyant we are reminded 'that one event happeneth to all,' and "that a man hath no preëminence above a beast;" but such a repressing part of a comprehensive fact is not suited to the sensual and sluggish man who needs rather, as he is directed, to see his 'life and immortality brought to light.' When we are elated with pride we are told that "man is a worm;" but this abasing part of a great doctrine should not engross the mind of him who despises his race, and who is therefore bidden to think of man as 'crowned with

glory and honor.' If tempted to make idols of our friends, we are
met by the requisition to 'hate a brother, sister, father and mother;'
but these are not the most fitting words for him who loves to persecute
his opposers, and who requires to be asked, "He that loveth not his
brother whom he hath seen, how can he love God whom he hath not
seen?" In one state of feeling we are stimulated to "work out our
salvation with fear and trembling," but in a different state we are encouraged to be neither anxious nor fearful, but to "rejoice in the Lord
always." I believe in the "final perseverance" of all who have been
once renewed, for not only does the generalizing intellect gather up
this doctrine from an induction of various inspired words, but the
heart also is comforted by it in the hour of dismal foreboding. Yet
when I wrest this truth from its designed adjustments, and misuse it
in quieting the fears of men who are instigated to 'count the blood
of the covenant wherewith they were sanctified an unholy thing,' I
am startled by the threat that 'if they shall fall away, it will be impossible to renew them *again* unto repentance.' This threat was not designed, like the promise of preserving grace, to console the disconsolate,
nor was that promise designed like this threat, to alarm the presumptuous. Let not the two appeals cross each other. My judgment, and,
in some lofty views in which I need to be held up by the Divine Spirit
lest I fall, my feelings also are unsatisfied without the biblical announcement that "the Lord hardened Pharaoh's heart;" but at my
incipient inclination to pervert these words into an excuse for sin, or a
denial of my entire freedom, or of my Maker's justice or tenderness, I
regard them as a "form of sound words" from which my depravity has
expelled their spirit, and I flee for safety to the other words, which are
a complement to the first, that "Pharaoh hardened his own heart."
When even a Puritan bishop is inflated with his vain conceits, it is
perilous for him to concentrate his feelings upon the keys with which
he is to open or shut the door of heaven. Such a man should oftener
tremble lest having been a servant of servants here, he be cast away
hereafter. But with a melancholic though faithful pastor this application of Scriptures may be reversed. We delight in the thought,
that he who hath made everything beautiful in its season, who sendeth
dew upon the earth when it has been heated by the sun,—and again,
when it has been parched by drought, sendeth rain; who draweth the

curtains of darkness around us when the eye is tired of the bright heavens, and irradiates the vision when the night has become wearisome; who intermingleth calm with tempest and parteth the clouds of an April day for the passage of the sun's rays,—hath also adopted a free, exuberant, refreshing method of imparting youth to the soul; giving us a series of revelations flexile and pliant, flitting across the mental vision with changeful hues, ever new, ever appropriate, not one of its words retaining its entire usefulness when removed from its fit junctions, not one of them being susceptible of a change for the better in the exigency when it was uttered, but each being "a word spoken in due season, how good is it."

There is a kind of conjectural doctrine, (which in the Swedenborgian and Millenarian fancies is carried to a ruinous excess, but) which within, not beyond the limit of its practical utility may be either justified or excused. Our feelings, for example, impel us to believe that we are compassed about with some kind of superior and ever wakeful intelligence. To meet this demand of the heart, Paganism has filled the air with divinities, but a wiser forecast has revealed to us the omnipresence of an all-comprehending mind. Still our restless desires would be sometimes gratified by a livelier representation of the spiritual existence around us, and accordingly in the more than paternal compassion of Jehovah, he maketh his angels ministering spirits, sent forth to attend upon the heirs of salvation, and to animate our spiritual atmosphere with a quick movement. But even yet, there are times when the heart of man would be glad of something more than even these cheering revelations. We are comforted with the thought that our deceased companions still mingle with us, and aid us in our struggles to gain their purity, and that, after we have left the world to which thus far we have been so unprofitable, we shall be qualified by our hard discipline here, for more effective ministries to those who will remain in this scene of toil. Such a belief however is not one which the reason, left to itself, would fortify by other than the slightest hints. It is a belief prompted by the affections, and the indulgence in it is allowed by the intellectual powers no further than it consoles and enlivens the spirit wearied with its earthly strifes. If we begin to think more of friends who visit us from heaven, than of Him who always abideth faithful around and over and within us, if we begin to search out witty inventions and to invoke the aid of patronizing saints, if we imagine that she who once kept all her child's sayings in her heart will now lay up in her motherly remembrance the *Ave Marias* of all who bless her image, then we push an innocent conjecture into the sphere of a harmful falsehood. The intellectual theology recognizes our felt need of a tenderness in the supervision which is exercised over us, but instead of meeting this necessity by picturing forth the love of one who after all may forget her very infant, it proves that we are ever enveloped in the sympathies of him who will not give away to his saints the glory of answering our feeble prayers. The intellectual theology does not indeed recognize our felt want of a Mediator, through whose friendly offices we may gain access to the pure, invisible, sovereign, strict lawgiver. But instead of an unearthly being canonized for his austere virtues, it gives us him who ate with sinners, who called around him fishermen rather than princes, and lodged with a tax-gather instead of the Roman governor, so as to remind us that he is not ashamed to call us brethren. Where men looked for a taper, it gives a light shining as the day, and hides the stars by the effulgence of the sun; where they looked for a friend it gives a Redeemer, where for a helper, a Saviour, where for hope, faith. It takes away in order to add more, thwarts a desire so as to give a fruition. It not so much unclothes as clothes upon, and swallows up our wish for patron saints in the brotherly sympathies of him who ever liveth to make intercession for us.

In conclusion allow me to observe, that in some aspects our theme suggests a melancholy, in others a cheering train of thought. It grieves us by disclosing the ease with which we may slide into grave errors. Such errors have arisen from so simple a cause as that of confounding poetry with prose. Men whose reasoning instinct has absorbed their delicacy of taste, have treated the language of a sensitive heart as if it were the guarded and wary style of the intellect. Intent on the sign more than on the thing signified, they have transubstantiated the living, spiritual truth into the very emblems which were designed to portray it. In the Bible there are pleasing hints of many things which were never designed to be doctrines, such as the literal and proper necessity of the will, passive and physical sin, baptismal regeneration, clerical absolution, the literal imputation of guilt to the innocent, transubstantiation, eternal generation and procession. In that graceful volume, these metaphors bloom as the flowers of the field; *there* they toil not neither do they spin. But the schoolman has transplanted them to the rude exposure of logic; here they are frozen up, their fragrance is gone, their juices evaporated, and their withered leaves are preserved as specimens of that which in its rightful place surpassed the glory of the wisest sage. Or, if I may change the illustration, I would say that these ideas, as presented in the Bible, are like oriental kings and nobles, moving about in their free, flowing robes; but in many a scholastic system they are like the embalmed bodies of those ancient lords, their spirits fled, their eyes, which once had speculation in them, now lack lustre; they are dry bones, exceeding dry. Not a few technical terms in theology are rhetorical beauties stiffened into logical perplexities; the exquisite growths of the imagination pressed and dried into the matter of a syllogism in Barbara. Many who discard their literal meaning retain the words out of reverence to antique fashions, out of an amiable fondness for keeping the nomenclature of science unbroken, just as the modern astronomer continues to classify the sweet stars of Heaven under the constellations of the Dragon and the Great Bear.

In this and in still other aspects our theme opens into more cheering views. It reveals the identity in the essence of many systems which are run in scientific or aesthetic moulds unlike each other. The full influence of it would do more than any World's Convention, in appeasing the jealousies of those good men who build their faith on Jesus Christ as the chief cornerstone, and yet are induced, by unequal measures of genius and culture, to give different shapes to structures of the same material. There are indeed kinds of theology which cannot be reconciled with each other. There is a life, a soul, a vitalizing spirit of truth, which must never be relinquished for the sake of peace even with an angel. There is (I know that you will allow me to express my opinion,) a line of separation which cannot be crossed between those systems which insert, and those which omit the doctrine of justification by faith in the sacrifice of Jesus. This is the doctrine which blends in itself the theology of intellect and that of feeling, and which can no more be struck out from the moral, than the sun from the planetary system. Here the mind and the heart, like justice and mercy, meet and embrace each other; and here is found the specific and ineffaceable difference between the Gospel and every other system. But among those who admit the atoning death of Christ as the organific principle of their faith, there are differences, some of them more important, but many far less important, than they seem to be. One man prefers a theology of the judgment; a second, that of the imagination; a third, that of the heart; one adjusts his faith to a lymphatic, another to a sanguine, and still another to a choleric temperament. Yet the subject matter of these heterogeneous configurations may often be one and the same, having for its nucleus the same cross, with the formative influence of which all is safe. Sometimes the intellectual divine has been denounced as unfeeling by the rude and coarse preacher, who in his turn has been condemned as vulgar or perhaps irreverent by the intellectual divine; while the one has meant to insinuate into the select few who listened to him, the very substance of the doctrine which the other has stoutly and almost literally *inculcated* into the multitudes by which he was thronged. The hard polemic has shown us only his visor and his coat of mail, while beneath his iron armor has been often cherished a theology of the gentle and humane affections. Dogmas of the most revolting shape have no sooner been cast into the alembic of a regenerated heart, than their more jagged angles have been melted away. We are cheered with a belief, that in the darkest ages hundreds and thousands of unlettered men felt an influence which they could not explain, the influence of love attracting to itself the particles of truth that lay scattered along the symbols and scholastic forms of the church. The great mass of believers have never embraced the metaphysical refinements of creeds, useful as these refinements are; but have singled out and fastened upon and held firm those cardinal truths, which the Bible has lifted up and turned over in so many different lights, as to make them the more conspicuous by their very alternations of figure and hue. The true history of doctrine is to be studied not in the technics, but in the spirit of the church. In unnumbered cases, the real faith of Christians has been purer than their written statements of it. Men, women, and children have often decided aright when doctors have disagreed, and doctors themselves have often felt aright when they have reasoned amiss. "In my heart," said a tearful German, "I am a Christian, while in my head I am a philosopher." Many who now dispute for an erroneous creed have, we trust, a richer belief imbedded in their inmost love. There are discrepant systems of philosophy pervading the sermons of different evangelical ministers, but often the rays of light which escape from these systems are so refracted, while passing through the atmosphere between the pulpit and the pews, as to end in producing about the same image upon the retina of every eye. Not seldom are the leaders of sects in a real variance when the people, who fill up the sects, know not why they are cut off from their brethren, and the people may strive in words while they agree in the thing, and their judgments may differ in the thing while their hearts are at one.

Thus divided against itself, thus introverting itself, thus multiform in its conceptions, so quick to seize at a truth as held up in one way, and spurn at it as held up in another, so marvellous in its tact for decomposing its honest belief, disowning with the intellect what it embraces with the affections, so much more versatile in regulating its merely inward processes than in directing the motions of an equilibrist, thus endued with an elastic energy more than Protean,—thus great is the soul, for the immense capabilities of which *Christ died*. Large-minded, then, and large-hearted must be the minister, having all the sensibility of a woman without becoming womanish, and all the perspicacity of a logician without being merely logical; having that philosophy which detects the substantial import of the heart's phrases, and having that emotion which invests philosophy with its proper life,—so wise and so good must the minister be, who applies to a soul of these variegated sensibilities the truth, which may wind itself into them all, as through a thousand pores; that truth, which God himself has matched to our nicest and most delicate springs of action, and which, so highly does he honor our nature, he has interposed by miracles for the sake of revealing in his written word; that word, which by its interchange of styles all unfolding the same idea, by its liberal construction of forms all enclosing the same spirit, prompts us to argue more for the broad central principles, and to wrangle less for the side, the party aspects of truth; that word, which ever pleases in order to instruct, and instructs in such divers ways in order to impress divers minds, and by all means to save some. Through the influence of such a Bible upon such a soul, and under the guidance of Him who gave the one and made the other, we do hope and believe, that the intellect will yet be enlarged so as to gather up all the discordant representations of the heart and employ them as the complements, or embellishments, or emphases of the whole truth; that the heart will be so expanded and refined as to sympathize with the most subtile abstractions of the intellect; that many various forms of faith will yet be blended into a consistent knowledge, like the colors in a single ray; and thus will be ushered in the reign of the Prince of peace, when the lion shall lie down with the lamb, when the body shall no more hang as a weight upon the soul, and the soul no longer wear upon its material framework, when the fancy shall wait upon rather than trifle with the judgment, and the judgment shall not be called as now to restrain the fancy, when the passions shall clarify rather than darken the reasoning powers, and the conscience shall not be summoned as now to curb the passions, when the intellect shall believe, not without the heart, nor against the heart, but *with the heart unto salvation;* and the soul, being one with itself, shall also be one with all the saints, in adoring one Lord, cherishing one faith, and being buried in one baptism; and when we who are united unto Christ on earth, he dwelling in us and we in him, shall, in answer to his last prayer for us, be made perfect with him in God.

25

THEODORE PARKER

1810, born August 24, at Lexington, Mass.
1827–30, taught in elementary schools
1831, taught in a Boston school
1832–34, established his own school in Watertown
1834–36, studied at Harvard Divinity School
1837–45, pastor at West Roxbury, Mass.
1840, M.A. (honorary), Harvard
1841, *The Transient and the Permanent in Christianity*
1842, *A Discourse of Matters Pertaining to Religion*
1843, *Translation of DeWette's Einleitung in das Alte Testament*
1843–44, traveled in Europe
1845–60, minister of the Twenty-Eighth Congregational Society in Boston
1848, *A Letter to the People of the United States Touching the Matter of Slavery*
1858, "The Philosophical Idea of God"; one of four sermons before the Society
of Progressive Friends
1860, died May 10, in Florence, Italy

RALPH WALDO EMERSON left the ministry when he found his beliefs at
odds with those of his Unitarian colleagues. Emerson's disciple, Theodore
Parker, not only refused to leave the ministry, he flatly refused to resign
from the Boston Association of Ministers and thus placed his colleagues in a
quandary. Four years after having been ordained, he preached, at an ordina-
tion in South Boston (May 19, 1841), his noted sermon on "The Transient
and the Permanent in Christianity," which marked his break with formal
Unitarianism and his full espousal of an Emersonian position. A year later
he published *A Discourse of Matters Pertaining to Religion,* where he used
his great knowledge to support the positions he had taken in the earlier
sermon. He presented Christianity, not as ultimate religion, but as the
furthest development to his time of the direct experience of divine reality by
the individual. He proclaimed the need for a new theology, superseding the
old, which should be a science of religion using the immanence of God in
nature and in man as its canon of interpretation. After these two complementary works, he was asked to resign from the Boston Association of
Ministers. When he refused, expulsion was suggested. Unitarians, however,
had long argued their liberalism and their disbelief in the "exclusive system,"

and could not permit themselves the luxury of expelling Parker. On the other hand, if they continued to associate with him, they furnished their orthodox opponents with evidence for the charge that infidelity was the logical consequence of Unitarianism. To escape this dilemma, some members of the Association actually suggested its dissolution. "Most of my clerical friends fell off; some would not speak to me in the street, and refused to take me by the hand; in their public meetings they left the sofas or benches when I sat down, and withdrew from me as Jews from contact with a leper. In a few months most of my former ministerial coadjutors forsook me." [1]

It is worth while to examine in some detail the views of one who could so upset the worthy Boston clergy. It is certainly refreshing to turn from the quibblings of the Congregationalists of Andover or New Haven, even when these were informed by an earnest moralism, to the honest radicalism of Parker. A mature expression of Parker's views was presented in a series of four sermons which he delivered on May 30 and 31, 1858, in the annual meeting of Progressive Friends, at Longwood, Pennsylvania. The atmosphere was suitable for the speaker; he was favorably regarded by the group he addressed, with whose antislavery views and absence of religious exclusiveness he was completely in agreement. When the call for the formation of this group was issued, in 1853, its purposes and spirit were thus stated:

The chief characteristic of the Progressive Friends . . . is seen in the fact that they prescribe no system of theological belief as a test of membership, but invite to equal co-operation all who regard mankind as one brotherhood, and who acknowledge the duty of showing their faith in God, not by assenting to the lifeless propositions of a man-made creed, but by lives of personal purity and a hearty devotion to the welfare of their fellowmen.

To such a group Parker found no difficulty in communicating his ideas. His reply to their invitation to the 1853 meeting expressed his immediate sympathy with their "movement for real religion. . . . There is only [he said] one religion in the world. . . . There are various helps to the acquisition of this one religion, and various hindrances with the name of helps. . . . I rejoice in your movement."

Of the four sermons, the first two are critical, the last two constructive. In introducing the series Parker alluded to the liberality of his audience and to the universality of God, and he announced his intention of speaking of men's various ideas of God and of the results of these ideas.

With the catholic spirit of Universal Religion one of your Clerks has just read from the Scriptures of the Chinese, the Hindoos, the Persians, the Mohammedans, the

<hr>

[1] *Works*, XIII, 324.

Hebrews, and the Christians. There is one Material Nature about us all, one Human Nature in us all, one Divine Nature, one Infinite God above us all, immanent in each, and equally near to the Buddhist and the Christians, equally loving to all. He is no respecter of sects more than of persons.

After this introduction Parker spoke of "The Progressive Development of the Conception of God in the Books of the Bible." Here he develops the concept of development, of progress, which is one of the constants in his thought.

In the human race nothing is ever still; the stream of humanity rolls continually forward, change following change; nation succeeds to nation, theology to theology, thought to thought. Taken as a whole, this change is a Progress, an ascent from the lower and ruder to the higher and more comprehensive. . . . The Progress of Mankind is continuous and onward, as much subject to a natural law of development as our growth from babyhood to adult life.

This law of development Parker illustrated by showing how even during the span of years of the composition of the Bible the idea of God had improved. Yet even the highest Biblical conception in the New Testament "is quite unsatisfactory to a thoughtful and deeply religious man today," because of the particularism still associated with the idea of God.

The Bible does not know that Infinite God, who is immanent in the World of matter and man . . . who works everywhere by law, a constant mode of operation of natural power in Matter and in Man.

For men of the nineteenth century to accept the Biblical idea would be impious.

It would be contrary to the spirit of Moses, and still more contrary to the spirit of Jesus, to attempt to arrest the theological and religious progress of mankind.

If men cannot accept the God of Genesis, can they accept the God of ecclesiastical tradition? This was the question posed in Parker's second sermon at Longwood, "The Ecclesiastical Conception of God, and Its Relation to the Scientific and Religious Wants of Man." Here Parker defines theology as the intellectual part of the religion of civilized man, as piety is the sentimental part and morality the practical part—a clear echo of the faculty psychology of intellect, sensibilities, and will. The theology accepted by any man will influence for good or ill both his piety and his morality. "There are two methods of creating a Theology . . . the Ecclesiastical and the Philosophical." All Christian sects pursue the ecclesiastical method, which is to take the Bible as "a miraculous and infallible revelation," as the final truth and ultimate authority on all matters, and thence to draw all the theological doctrines. The supernatural authority of the Bible exempts it from all standards; "the test of inspiration is not in man; it is not Truth for things reasonable, nor Justice for things moral, nor Love for things affectional." The ecclesiastical conception of God makes no account of the development of the God-idea through the books of the Bible. It is ethically unsatisfactory, because God "is immensely inferior to the average of men in justice and benevolence." It is scientifically unsatisfactory, because the ecclesiastical God operates spasmodically. "To explain the World of Matter, the naturalist wants a sufficient power which is always there, acting by a constant mode of operation; not irregular, vanishing, acting by fits and starts; but continuous, certain, reliable; an intelligent power which acts by law, not caprice and miracle." Finally the ecclesiastical conception of God is religiously unsatisfactory, because the religious consciousness demands a God on whom men can put absolute reliance, "who is always at hand, not merely separate and one side from the World of Matter or the World of man."

With this rejection of the Biblical and ecclesiastical ideas of God, Parker comes, in his third sermon, which is reprinted here, to "The Philosophical Idea of God and Its Relation to the Scientific and Religious Wants of Mankind Now." Beginning with the two assertions that the need of God is instinctive in men and that the idea of God is progressive, Parker states that "religious progress cannot be wholly prevented; it may be hindered and kept back for a time . . . Men form an ecclesiastical organization, and take such a conception of God as satisfies them at the time, stereotype it, and declare all men shall believe that forever." Over against this ecclesiastical conception of God, he sets the philosophic idea of God derived from the "Facts of instinctive and reflective Consciousness within him, and the Facts of Observation without." The philosophic theologian will build on the God-idea of the past, but will cast aside its errors, regardless of the presumed sanctity of their source. By this method he will arrive at the idea of the "God of Infinite Perfection . . . Perfect Cause and Perfect Providence, creating all things from a perfect motive, of a perfect material, for a perfect purpose, and as a perfect means, and to a perfect end. . . . There is no absolute Evil in the world, either for the whole as all, nor for any one as part." As Perfect Cause, this idea of God is adequate for science, as Perfect Providence, adequate for religion, theologically, morally, and pietistically. Such a God-idea will develop a form of worship suitable to it and in conformity with the nature of man, in whom there is a religious faculty of which God is the proper object, as light is of the faculty of vision, and sound of the faculty of hearing. This conception of God, suited to the times, will make religion the center of all life, not a concern apart from daily duties. It will not support tyranny and oppression and wrongdoing.

To close this brilliant series of sermons, summing up his mature ideas on the nature of God and of religion, Parker spoke "Of the Soul's Normal Delight in the Infinite God." Here he tells of the joy of religion to the heart of man and offers some autobiographical fragments which are interesting as showing that he went through no struggle to achieve faith. He generalized from his own experience to the belief that all men naturally love and feel a delight in God. Herein is a passage on the religious culture of the child the thought of which parallels Bushnell's *Christian Nurture.*

It has been said that Parker was "influenced" by Schleiermacher, Fries, De Wette, and others. He did read the works of these writers, and suggestions from them may have entered into his mind and been taken up into the fabric of his own thought. Let this not be considered a detraction from his originality. It must be admitted that he lived ahead of his time; reviled as an infidel by his fellow-Unitarians in 1843, less than a hundred years later he was being hailed by Francis A. Christie, in the *Journal* of the Meadville Theological School, as "a prophet of our modernism and . . . one of its best exponents," an anticipator of the "social gospel," "a great Humanist just as he was a great Theist." Some Unitarian theology has caught up with Theodore Parker.

THE PHILOSOPHICAL IDEA OF GOD AND ITS RELATION TO THE SCIENTIFIC AND RELIGIOUS WANTS OF MANKIND NOW

Perfect love casteth out fear.—1 John iv. 18.

THE religious element is so strong that it always will act both in its instinctive and its reflective form, for though here and there an eccentric man neglect or treat it with scorn, no race of men ever does so; nay, no nation, no little tribe, no considerable company of men. There are a thousand devotees who give up all to the religious faculty where there is not a single atheist who sacrifices that to something besides. Like the two other great Primal Instincts—the hunger for bread, which keeps the individual alive, and the hunger for posterity, which perpetuates mankind—this hunger for God is not to be put down. Here and there an individual man neglects the one or the other, the instinct of food, of kind, of religion; but the human race nor does, nor can. In Mankind instinctive nature is stronger than capricious will. Whimsy alters the cut of Ahab's beard, or the shape of Jezebel's ringlets; but the beard itself grows on Ahab's cheek and chin, will he or nill he, and Jezebel's head is herbaged all over with curls, growing while she sleeps.

Soon as Man outgrows the wild state of infancy, where he first appeared, in his primitive sense of dependence he has always felt his need of God, as in his instinctive perception he has always felt the Being of God reflected therein, and formed some Notion of God, better or worse. Go where you will, you find that men know God. The notions they form of him vary from land to land, from age to age. They are the test of the people's civilization; how rude with the savage! how comprehensive with the enlightened, thoughtful, religious man! But no nation is without them, or without a sense of obligation towards God or the practice of some form of service of him.

The notion men form of God, and the corresponding service they pay, are both proportionate to the people's civilization. The Indian Massasoit's conception of God, two hundred and fifty years ago, fitted him as well as ours fits us. Let us never forget this, nor think that we are proportionately more favored than our fathers were. Little baby Jimmy in Pennsylvania, some seventy years ago, was as much pleased with a penny trumpet, which worried his aunts and uncles, as President Buchanan now is with the Presidency of the United States and power to scare all Democrats into obedience. To us our fathers in 858 are barbarians, and we wonder how they stood it in the world, so poorly furnished and provisioned as they were. You will be barbarians to your sons and daughters in 2858, and they will wonder how you continued to live and have a good time of it. Yet you and I think life is decent and worth having. Milk and a cradle are as good for babies as meat and railroad engines for men. Small things suit little folks. So is it in religion as all else besides. I love to read the religious stories of rude nations—the Hebrews, the Philistines, the New England Indians. The Iroquois thought there were three Spirits, the Spirit of Beans, of Squashes, and of Indian Corn, and these made an Agricultural Trinity, three beneficent persons in one rude conception of a Mohawk God. Such a notion served their souls as well as the stone tomahawk and snowshoe their hands and feet. Let us never forget that each age is as sufficient to itself as any other age, the first as the last. The immense progress between the two is also the law of God, who has so furnished men that they shall find satisfaction for their wants, when they are babies of savage wildness and when they are grown men of civilization.

From the beginning of human history there has been a continual progress of man's conception of God. It did not begin with Jacob, Isaac and Abraham; it will not end with you and me. Yesterday I mentioned some of the facts of this progress in the Bible, and pointed out the Jehovah of the Pentateuch eating veal with Abraham and Sarah, wrestling with Jacob, trying to kill Moses and not bringing it to pass; I showed the odds between that conception of God and "Our Father who art in heaven," which filled up the consciousness of Jesus, and the God who is Perfect Love, which abode in the consciousness of another great man. This progress is observable in all other people, in the literature of every nation.

Religious progress cannot be wholly prevented; it may be hindered and kept back for a time. This is the mischief;—men form an ecclesiastical organization, and take such a conception of God as satisfies them at the time, stereotype it, and declare all men shall believe that forever. They say "This is a finality; there shall never be any other idea of God but this same, no progress hereafter." Then priests are made in the image of that Deity, and they misshape whole communities of men and women; and especially do they lay their plastic hand on the pliant matter of the child, and mismould him into deformed and unnatural shapes. What an absurdity! In 1780, in a little town of Connecticut, Blacksmith Beecher, grim all over with soot, leather-aproned, his sleeves rolled above his elbows, with great, bare, hairy arms, was forging axes "dull as a hoe," and hoes "blunt as a beetle," yet the best that men had in Connecticut in those days. What if the Connecticut lumberers and farmers had come together, and put it into their Saybrook Platform, that to the end of time all men should chop with Beecher's axes and dig with Beecher's hoes, and he who took an imperfection therefrom, his name should be taken from the Lamb's Book of Life, and he who should add an improvement thereto, the seven last plagues should be added unto him! We all see the absurdity of such a thing. In 1830, in Boston, Minister Beecher, grim with Calvinism, surpliced from his shoulders to his feet, Geneva-banded, white-choked, a stalwart and valiant-minded son of the old blacksmith, was making a theology—notions of Man, of God, and of the Relation between them. His theological forge was in full blast in Hanover Street, then in Bowdoin Street, and he wrought stoutly thereat, he striking while his parish blew. But his opinions were no more a finality than his father's axes and hoes. Let Blacksmith Beecher, grim with soot, and Minister Beecher, grim with theology, hammer out the best tools they can make, axes, hoes, doctrines, sermons, and thank God if their work be of any service at that time; but let neither the blacksmith over his forge, his triphammer going, nor the minister over his pulpit, his Bible getting quoted, ever say to mankind, "Stop, gentlemen! thus far and no farther! I am the end of human history, the last milestone on the Lord's highway of progress; stop here, use my weapon, and die with it in your hand, or your soul." Depend upon it, mankind will not heed such men; they will pass them by; whoso obstructs the path will be trodden down. Progress is the law of God.

At an early age the Christian Church accepted the Ecclesiastical Method of theology, namely—that every word between the lids of the Bible is given by God's miraculous and infallible inspiration, which contains the religious truth, the whole truth, and nothing but the truth, and to get doctrines, men must make a decoction of Bible, and only of Bible, for that is the unique herb out of which wholesome doctrines can be brewed. By that method it formed its conception of God. First, it fixed the Ethical Substance of God's character, the quality of God, with all the contradictions which you find in the Old Testament and the New. Next it fixed the Arithmetical Form of God's character, the quantitative distribution into three persons, Father, Son, and Holy Ghost, like in their Godhead, diverse in their function. Thus the capability to produce was in the Father; the capacity of being produced was in the Son; the capacity of being proceeded from was in the Father and the Son, and the capability of proceeding was in the Holy Ghost. These are the *differentia* of the total Godhead. All that was fixed well-nigh fifteen hundred years ago.

Since that time there have been three great movements within the Christian Church. First, an attempt to centralize ecclesiastical power in the Bishop of Rome; that was the Papal movement. Next was the attempt to explain the ecclesiastical doctrines by human reason, not to alter but expound and demonstrate by intellect what was accepted by faith; that was the Scholastic movement. Then came at last the attempt to decentralize ecclesiastical power, and bring back from the Roman Bishop to the common people what he had filched thence away; that was the Protestant movement. It split the Western world in twain, following the ethnological line of cleavage; and since that there is a Roman Church with a Pope, and a Teutonic Church with a People. But the Papists and their opponents the Laists, the Scholastics and their enemies the Dogmatists, the Protestants and Catholics, all accepted the Ecclesiastical Method of theology, and so the Ecclesiastical Notion of God. So within the borders of the Christian Church, from the Council at Nice in 325 to the Council at North Woburn in 1857, there has been no revision of the Conception of God, no improvement thereof. Protestant and Catholic, Scholastic and Dogmatists, Laist and Papist, agree in the ethical substances of God and in the arithmetical form. The Athanasian creed set forth both; in the fourth century it was appointed to be read in the churches. What is called the "Apostles' Creed" has little apostolic in it save its name; yet it has been held orthodox for sixteen hundred and fifty years. All this time there has been no progress in the ecclesiastical conception of God, as set forth in the great sects of the Christian Church; the same creed which answered for the third century suffices the Church today. So long as the Church holds to this ecclesiastical method of theology there can be no progress in the notion of God, for only Biblical plants may be put into the ecclesiastical caldron, and from them all only that conception can be distilled, though it may be flavored a little, diversely here and there, to suit the taste of special persons.

But shall Mankind stop? We cannot if we would. We can stereotype a creed and hire men to read it, or scare, or coax them; but a new Truth from God shines straight down through creed and congregation, as that sunlight through the sky. In the last four hundred years what a mighty development has there been of human knowledge! In three hundred and sixty years the geographic world has doubled; and what a development in astronomy, chemistry, botany, zoology; in mathematics, metaphysics, ethics, history! How comprehensive is science now! But there has been no development in the Church's conception of God. The ecclesiastical God knows nothing of modern science—chemistry, geology, astronomy; even the geographic extent of the earth is foreign thereto; neither Jehovah nor the ecclesiastical Trinity ever heard of Australia, of the Friendly Islands, nor even the Continent of America. The ecclesiastical conception of God was formed before the discovery of America, before modern science was possible. The two are not to be reconciled. Which shall yield, the Fact of Science, or the Fiction of Theology?

Outside of the orthodox Christian Church there has been a great development of the conception of God, a revision of it more or less complete, certainly a great improvement. Thus the Unitarians rejected the Trinitarian arithmetic, and said, "God is one nature in one person." The Universalists rejected the devilish element and said, "God is love all over, and is not hate anywhere." Once it seemed as if these two sects would make a revolution in the Church's notion of God: but alas! the Unitarians and Universalists both accept the ecclesiastical method of theology, and when they appeal to the miraculous and infallible Bible in support of their more reasonable and religious notion of God, they are always beaten in that court where Genesis is of as much value as the four Gospels, and murderous Joshua as great a theological authority as beneficent Jesus. So when they rely on the Bible, these sects are defeated, and draw back toward the old Church with its belief of a ferocious Deity; this explains the condition and character of these two valuable sects. Accordingly, little good has come from their movement, once so hopeful. They would change Measures and Doctrines, but they would not alter the Principle which controls the measure, nor the Method whereby the doctrines are made; and so these sects leaven only a little of the whole lump; they do not create that great fermentation which is necessary to make the whole Church take a new form. How much depends on the first Principle, and the right Method!

Now, by the Philosophic Method, a man takes the Facts of instinctive and reflective Consciousness within him, and the Facts of Observation without, and thence forms his Idea of God. He will be helped by the labors of such as have gone before him, and will refuse to be hindered by the errors of the greatest men. He will take the good things about God in this blessed Bible, because they are good, but not a single ill thing will he take because it is in the Bible. "God is love," says a writer in the New Testament, and our thoughtful man will accept that; but he will not feel obliged to accept that other statement, in the Old Testament, that "God is a consuming fire;" or yet a kindred one in the New Testament, "These shall go away into everlasting punishment," "prepared for the devil and his angels." He will understand and believe that "He that loveth is born of God, and knoweth God;" but he will not assent to this, which the Christian Church teaches, "He that believeth and is baptized shall be saved, but he that believeth not shall be damned." Because he accepts the good and true of the Bible, he will not fall down and accept the false and ill; for the ultimate standard of appeal will not be to a Book writ with pens, as a minister interprets it, but to the Facts of the Universe, as the human mind interprets them.

In philosophic men the reflective element prevails; but I do not think they often have much intuitive power to perceive religious truths directly, by the primal human instinct; nor do I think that they in the wisest way observe the innermost activities of the human soul. Poets like Shakespeare observe the play of human passion and ambition better than metaphysicians like Berkeley and Hume, better than moralists like Butler and Paley. Commonly, I think, men and women of simple religious feeling furnish the facts which men of great thoughtful genius work up into philosophic theology. It is but rarely that any man has a genius for instinctive intuition, and also for philosophic generalization therefrom. Such a man, when he comes, fills the whole sky, from the nadir of special primitive religious emotion up to the zenith of universal philosophic thought. You and I need not wait for such men, but thankfully take the Truth, part by part, here a little and there a little, and accept the service of whoso can help, but taking no man for master—neither Calvin, nor Luther, nor Paul, nor John, nor Moses, nor Jesus—open our soul to the Infinite God, who is sure to come in without bell, book, or candle.

When a man pursues this natural, philosophic method of theology, takes his facts from consciousness in his own world, and observation in the world of matter, then he arrives at the Philosophical Idea of the God of Infinite Perfection. That God has all the qualities of complete and perfect being; He has Infinite Power to do, Infinite Mind to know, Infinite Conscience to will the right, Infinite Affection to love, Infinite

Holiness to be faithful to his affections, conscience, mind, power. He has Being without limitation, Absolute Being; he is present in all space, at all times; everywhere always, as much as sometimes anywhere. He fills all spirit, not less than all matter, yet is not limited by either, transcending both, being alike the materiality of matter, and the spirituality of spirit—that is, the substantiality which is the ground of each, and which surpasses and comprehends all. He is Perfect Cause and Perfect Providence, creating all things from a perfect motive, of a perfect material, for a perfect purpose, and as a perfect means, and to a perfect end. So, of all conceivable worlds he makes the best possible, of all conceivable degrees of welfare he provides the best in kind and the greatest in bulk, not only for all as a whole, but for each as an individual, for Jesus of Nazareth who is faithful, for Judas Iscariot who turns traitor. There is no Absolute Evil in the world, either for the whole as all, nor for any one as part.

That is the Philosophic Idea of God and of his relation to the Universe. To-day I state it short, for I have dwelt on it often before, and perhaps at some other time I shall take up the idea part by part, and speak of God as Infinite Power, then as Infinite Wisdom, then as Infinite Justice, as Infinite Love, Infinite Integrity, and so on.

I think this Idea of God as Infinite Perfection, Perfect Power, Wisdom, Justice, Love, Holiness, is the grandest thought which has ever come into mortal mind. It is the highest result of human civilization. Let no man claim it as his original thought; it is the result of all mankind's religious experience. It lay latent in human nature once, a mere instinctive religious feeling. At length it becomes a bright particular thought in some great mind; and one day will be the universal thought in all minds, and will displace all other notions of God—Hindoo, Egyptian, Hebrew, Classic, Christian, Mohammedan, just as the true theory of astronomy, which actually explains the stars, displaced the Ptolemaic and all the other theories which were only approximate; just as the iron axe displaced the tomahawk of stone.

The Evidence of this God is in man's Consciousness and in the World of Matter likewise outside of him. When the idea is presented to a thoughtful man, he at once says, "Yes, God is Infinite Perfection, Power, Wisdom, Justice, Holiness, Love," for human nature is too strong for his theologic prejudice. To prove there is such a being as

Jehovah, who met Moses in a tavern between Midian and Egypt some thirty-three hundred years ago, and vainly tried to kill him, you must know Hebrew, and understand the antiquities of the Jews, know who wrote the Book of Exodus, where he got his facts, what he meant by his words, what authority he rested on; and when you have made that investigation, the story will turn out to be. wind, and none the better because Hebrew wind thirty-three hundred years old; and after all that, you do not come to a fact of the Universe, but only the fiction of a story-teller. But to prove the Infinite Perfection of God, you have the facts in your own nature; you are to sit down beside that primeval well and draw for yourself, and drinking thence, you shall thirst no longer for heathen Abana and Pharpar, the rivers of Gentile Damascus, nor for the Hebrew Jordan itself, for you shall find there is a well of living water within you, springing up to everlasting life; and as you drink, the scales of theologic leprosy fall off from your eyes, and you stand there a clean man, full of the primitive, aboriginal vigor of Humanity. As you look down into that depth of consciousness do you behold the eternal and immutable Idea of the Infinitely Perfect God forever mirrored there. This depends on no subjective peculiarities of the individual, but on the objective forces of the Universe. So, by its name to distinguish it from all other notions of God, I will call this the Philosophical or Natural Idea of God; it seems to me a fact given in Humanity itself, a self-evident truth of spiritual consciousness, something we discover in the Universe, not something we invent and project thereon. So, while I name the others Conceptions of God, I call this the Idea of God—the Philosophical Idea, because derived by that Method—the Natural, because it corresponds to Nature. To this men will also add conceptions of their own invention, which partake of the subjective peculiarity of John or Jane.

I. This Idea of God is adequate to the Purposes of Science. First of all things the philosopher wants an Adequate Cause for the Facts of the Universe, both the World of Matter out of him, and the World of Spirit in him. He is to explain facts by showing their mode of operation, and tracing them back to the cause—to the proximate cause first, to the ultimate cause at last. Now, as I showed before, the Ecclesiastical Conception of God furnishes no adequate cause for the Facts of the

Universe. To the theologian it is cause sufficient for Noah's flood, for the ark, for the downfall of Jericho when the rams'-horns blew, for the standing still of the sun and moon while a Hebrew army slew their victims;—it explains such things as are not authenticated facts of history, but only anonymous fictions of mythology. It is no adequate cause for the earth under our feet, for the heavens over our head, and, least of all, for this earth and heaven of human consciousness within us. The ecclesiastical God is sufficient cause for the Westminster Catechism, for baptism, by sprinkling or plunging, for belief in eternal damnation, for admission to Dr. Banbaby's Church—but it does not explain a mother's love for her wicked, profligate girl; nor David's wailing over his worthless, handsome boy: "O Absalom, my son! my son Absalom! would God that I had died for thee!"—there is no fact in the ecclesiastical God's consciousness which corresponds to that. It is not cause for such a man as Socrates, or Franklin, nor such women as Miss Dix and Miss Nightingale, and others not less noble, only less known. It explains Pharaoh's dream about fat and lean kine; the story of Elisha's cursing the children who cried after him, "Go up, thou bald head, go," and of the two she-bears out of the woods who tore two and forty of those children to atoms in Divine and bearish wrath—but it does not explain the life of such a man as Jesus of Nazareth, nor his lament, "O Jerusalem, Jerusalem!" It does not account for that grandest of human triumphs, "Father, forgive them, for they know not what they do." To explain such characters the ecclesiastical conception of God is no more adequate cause than the penny-trumpet in a little boy's mouth is sufficient to explain the world of music which Beethoven dreamed into thought and then poured forth, gladdening the earth with such sweet melody. Read the Book of Genesis, then read Newton's Principia, Humboldt's Kosmos, nay, any college manual of chemistry, and ask if the theologic God is cause adequate to the chemic composition of a single flower! Nay, read the stories in Genesis, or the sermons in Jonathan Edwards, and then in some starry night look up to the sky, and ask if that form of Deity could have conceived the heavens? You see at once how insufficient it is.

But the God of Infinite Perfection is Adequate Cause for all the facts in the Universe. In the world of matter you find Power resident on the spot; Mind resident on the spot, a Plan everywhere, things working together in order. The world of matter is a "team of little atomies," thing yoked to thing, and skilfully are they drove afield by that Almighty One whose thoughtful road is everywhere. All is orderly—never a break in the line of continuity. In the fossil animals which perished a million of years ago you find proximate formations which point to man; nay, yet further back in the structure of the earth, the fashion of the solar system itself, do we find finger-posts which indicate the road to humanity—distinctly pointing unto man. There is Law always, a constant mode of operation, never a miracle; no chemist, geologist, astronomer, can show proof of the "intervention of God," but the Power, Mind, Law, constant mode of operation, these show the presence of God always, everywhere, ordering all things "by number and measure and weight." The chemist analyzes matter into some sixty primitive substances, oxygen, hydrogen, nitrogen, carbon, and the rest; but of all that "team of atomies" not a single brute creature ever thinks a thought; it is in God that the Mind resides, in him is the Power and the Plan. Mr. Whewell, a theological man indeed, but yet also, I think, certainly one of the ablest and most dispassionate men of science in these days, writes a book against the Plurality of Worlds, and declares there is no conscious life analogous to man's in any planet, in sun, or moon, or star: it is a dead world up there; the sun is a dead sun, the moon is dead as brass, and there is no life in any star. Why so? It is not consistent with the Ecclesiastical Notion of God; the Book of Miraculous Revelation never gives us a hint of a living thing in sun or moon or star; the Plan of Atonement applies only to the earth, it cannot reach an inch beyond the atmosphere, which extends about fifty-two miles from the surface! Mr. Whewell is right—a plurality of worlds is wholly inconsistent with the ecclesiastical God; there is no record that such a thought ever crossed the mind of Moses, Jesus, Paul or John, that it ever occurred to Hebrew Jehovah or Christian Trinity. But it is not inconsistent with the Infinite God, and the philosopher who believes in him will not correct the facts of Nature by the fictions of Genesis. To him, how different the World of Matter appears, one grand act of creative power, which is everywhere active at all times.

Then when this Idea is accepted no philosopher will be bid to look for a miracle, and called an "infidel" because he finds only Law—law in the botanic growth of plants, law in the chemic composition of minerals, law in the mechanic structure of the earth, the sun, the solar system, the Universe itself. Then there will be no atheistic Lagranges and La Places to deny all God, because they do not find the phantom which theologians bid them seek, and because their telescope bores through the spot where the New Jerusalem was said to be, and finds but blank celestial space! From the scheme of matter and of mind no brilliant Schelling, no cautious, erudite Von Buch, no comprehensive, magnificent, generous, and thousand-minded Von Humboldt shall ever omit the Cause and Providence of matter and of mind!

Then, too, how different will the great complex world of Human History appear! Men will study it without hindrance, asking only for facts, for the law of the facts, and the human meaning of the law. They will find no miracle in man's religious history, but a continual development of a faculty common to all mankind, a gradual progress in religious feeling, religious thought, religious act; no savage nation without consciousness of God, a sense of dependence, obligation, gratitude— aye, and trust in him, and something of love for him "even in savage bosoms"—all this proportionate to the people's civilization. The philosopher will find God in all human history, in the gradual elevation of mankind from the low state of the wild man, to higher and higher types of excellence.

Jehovah is the God of Abraham, Isaac, and Jacob; he inspires only Jews, them not much. He hates Esau, and butchers the Canaanites. To the Gentiles he is not a loving God, but a hating Devil. The ecclesiastical God is a Redeemer only to the redeemed—a handful of men, rather mean men too, I fear, most of them. What is he to babies dying unbaptized? What to the wicked whom death cuts down in their unrepented naughtiness? He is not God, but a "consuming fire;" he is "the Devil and his angels" to such; not the God of love, but a "great and dreadful God," who laughs when their fear cometh, and crushes Sodom and Gomorrah under his fiery hail; and, all bloody with battle, tramples populous Idumea under foot, as a Bacchanalian treads the wine-press full of purple-blooded grapes!

With the philosophical Idea, there is a God for all nations, for all men, inspiring liberal Greece and prudent Rome not less than pious Judea—a God for babies sprinkled, and for babies all unsmooched by priestly hands; a God for Jacob and Esau, Jew and Gentile; a God to whom mankind is dear, Father and Mother to the human race! Then you can explain human history: the diverse talents of Egyptian, Hindoo, Persian, Hebrew, Greek, Teuton, Celt, American, these are various gifts, which imply no partial love on the part of him who makes yon oak a summer green, yon pine a winter green. You find the Infinite God in human history, as in the world of matter; for as the plan of material combination, mineral, vegetable, animal, did not reside in any one of the sixty primitive substances, nor in the world of minerals, plants, animals, but in God, who is the thoughtful substance to these unthinking forms—so the plan of human history is not in Abraham, Isaac, Jacob; it is not in the whole world of men, but in the Infinite God, who is the Providence that shapes our ends to some grand purpose which we know not of. Thus the true idea of God is adequate to the Purposes of Science both of matter and man.

II. This Idea of God is also adequate to the Purposes of Religion. For that I want not merely a cause sufficient to my intellect, but much more. I want a God I can trust and have absolute confidence in, so that I am sure of him. Now the savage may confide in a God of blood, a partial God, who loves Jacob and hates Esau; an inconstant and irregular God, who works by fits and starts, who is absent now for a long time, and then comes in with miraculous pomp, signs, and wonders. A malignant man may be content for a moment with his vengeful Deity, who hates the wicked and will torment them forever; but soon as a man is considerably enlightened in his mind, conscience, heart and soul, soon as he comprehends the Power that is everywhere always, active and acting for good, then that savage deity is not enough for him. He wants not only infinite Ability,—power of Force to do, power of Mind to plan, and Will to execute, but also power of Conscience to will right, and the Infinite power of Affection to love all men and all things, using this energy of will, mind, force, for the welfare of each man—nay, of every mote that peoples this little leaf. That quality is not in the ecclesiastical God; here it is in the true God of earth and heaven and human consciousness. He is perfect creating Cause, making all things of the best possible material, from the best possible motives, for the best possible purpose, and as the best possible means to achieve that purpose. He is perfect conserving Providence, who is as perfectly, completely and essentially present in this little rosebud which I hold in my hand, as he was when, as the Biblical poet has it, "the morning stars sang together, and all the sons of God shouted for joy," at the creation of the earth, just springing into new-born stellar life. He administers all things by the perfect method, with the best of means, and will secure the best of ends for you and me, for each man, saint and sinner, for the poor widow who supplicates and the unjust judge who fears not God, neither regards man.

By the ecclesiastical notion there is Absolute Evil in God, a dark deep background, out of which comes evil in the nature of things; and hence comes the total depravity of man, hence the wrath of God, enlivening forever the fire of hell, which no deluge of human tears and blood can ever quench. So the Evil in the world is eternal, not reconciled, not atoned for; it cannot be removed, neither in this life nor that to come, because it is an essential part of God. Nine hundred and ninety-nine men out of a thousand are sinners, and their sin is eternal, not to be removed; so their agony has no end. Trace it back logically to its ultimate cause, and it is all God's fault. So every sin not repented of that you and I commit, is not only perpetual wretchedness for us, but likewise an eternal blot on the character of the ecclesiastical God. Under the parlor windows of his little Heaven, where the elect loll on their couches and look out, indolently touching their harps of gold, there lies the immeasurable Sink of Hell, where the Devils, those unclean beasts of the infernal world, wallow continual, rending the souls of men, while the reek of their agony ascends up forever and ever!

But by the true and philosophic or natural Idea of God, all the Evil of the world is something incident to man's development, and no more permanent than the stumbling of a child who learns to walk, or his scrawling letters when he first essays to write. It will be outgrown, and not a particle of it or its consequences shall cleave permanent to mankind. This is true of the individual wrongs which you and I commit; and likewise of such vast wickedness as war, political oppression, and the hypocrisy of priesthoods. These are blots in mankind's writing-book, which we make in learning to copy out God's Eternal Rule of Right in fair round letters, so clear that he may read who runs. The very pain the error gives is remedial, not revengeful; it is medicine to cure and save and bless, not poison to kill and torture with eternal smart. Here then is a God you can trust—Power, Wisdom, Will, Justice also, and likewise Love. What quality is there a man can ask for that is not in the Infinite, Perfect God?

Then there will be a Form of Religion adapted to represent such an idea of God. It will conform to Man's Nature, his body and soul, doing justice to every part, for as God made man with such faculties as would best serve his own great end, so it is clear that it is man's duty to use these faculties in their natural way, for their normal purpose. God did not make man with something redundant to be cut off, or lacking something to be sought elsewhere and tied on; he gave us such faculties as are fit for our work.

1. See the effect this idea has on Piety. A natural religious instinct inclines us to love God. If we have an Idea of him which suits that faculty, then the soul loves God as the eye loves light, the ear sound, as the mind loves truth, use and beauty, the conscience justice, and the affections men and women. The hungry religious faculty seeks for itself bread, finds it, and is filled with strength and delight. If it find it not, then we are tortured by Fear, that ugly raven which preys on the dissatisfied heart of man. Now the Infinite God is the object of entire and complete satisfaction to the Soul. You want perfect power for your reverence, perfect wisdom for your intellect, perfect justice for your conscience, perfect love for your affections, perfect integrity for your soul: and here they all are in the infinitely perfect God. So piety will be complete in all its parts, and perfect too in each. I cannot love a wicked man as a good man, nor a foolish and unjust man as one wise and just; no more can I love a foolish God, nor an unjust God, nor a hating God. In proportion as I am wise, just, humane, shall I hate such a God, and repudiate the shameful thought. But the perfect God—I cannot help loving him just in proportion to my excellence. He made me so. I put it to the consciousness of every one of you, is it not so? When God is thus presented as infinitely perfect, can you refrain from loving him with your intellect, your conscience, heart and soul? No more than the healthy eye can fail to enjoy the light; no more than the hungry, healthy appetite can help rejoicing in its natural food, the maiden in her lover, or the bridegroom in his bride!

2. Not less does this Idea of God affect Morality, the other part of

religion. I find certain ideal rules of conduct writ on my body and in my spirit. By inward and outward experience gradually I learn these rules—the laws of God, enacted by him into my flesh and soul. I shall try to keep these laws; I know they are his commandment. I shall turn every faculty to its special work. My general piety, the love of God, shall come out in my normal daily work, in temperance and chastity, the piety of the body; in knowledge of the true, the useful, the beautiful, the piety of the intellect; in justice for all men, the piety of the conscience; in affection for all in their various relations to me, in love for my friend, kindred, wife and child, which is the piety of the heart; yes, it will appear in continual trust, in absolute reliance on the Infinite God, which is the great total generic piety of the soul.

Then Religion will not be away off, one side of my life, separate from my daily duty as brother, sister, son, father, mother; not apart from my work as blacksmith, governor, shoemaker, minister, nurse, seamstress, baby-tender, cook, editor, judge, or whatever I may be; but the soul of piety will make religion in all these things. It will not be an exception in my life, condensed into a single moment of morning or of evening prayer; it will be the instance of my life, spread as daylight over all my work.

One day this Idea of God will shine in human consciousness, and all the rude conceptions which now prevail will vanish as Moloch, Baal, Zeus, Jupiter, Odin, and Thor have faded out from the religion of all live mankind. To-day nobody prays to, nor swears by these names, whereunto millions of men once fell prostrate and poured out such sacrificial blood. One day the God of Infinite Perfection shall be felt and known by all mankind! Then no bigot, ignorant as a beast, shall essay to rebuke thoughtful men where he knows nothing and they know much. No longer shall priests—ill-born to little talent, ill-bred to superstition, ignorance and bad manners—thrust their anointed stupidity in between man and God; no longer shall fanaticism pinch the forehead of the people; no longer shall it mutilate the fair body of man, nor practise yet more odious emasculation on the soul. Religion shall not mildew and rot the fruit of manhood; nor blast the bloom of youth; nor nip the baby bud: but the strongest force in our nature shall warm and electrify the whole plant of humanity, helping the baby bud swell into youthful bloom, and ripen into manly fruit, golden and glorious amid the sheltering leaves of human life. To youth, religion shall give a rosier flush of healthy joy; to maid and man shall it bring strength, more stalwart and a lovelier beauty, cheering them through their single or their married toilsome life; and it shall set its kingliest diadem, a crown of heavenly stars, on the experienced brow of age.

To-day "all Christendom is Christian." Why? It has the ecclesiastical method, the ecclesiastical conception of God, a mode of salvation by another man's religion, not our own. Let me do no injustice. It has the best form of religion the world has devised yet on any large scale, which has done great service; but in all Christendom ecclesiastical Christianity hinders no war, it breaks no tyrant's rod, it never liberates a slave, emancipates no woman, shuts up no drunkery, removes no cause of ignorance, poverty, or crime, cherishes the gallows; it is no bar to the politician's ambition, all reckless of the natural rights of man; it never checks a pope or priest in his hypocrisy. Every monster is sure to have this ecclesiastical form of religion on his side, and when Napoleon or President Buchanan wishes to do a special wicked deed, he bends his public knees and supplicates his ecclesiastic God, the name in which all evil begins.

But the true Idea of God, the Religion which is to come of it, which is love of that God and keeping all his commandments, will work such a revolution in man's affairs as Luther, nor Moses, nor yet mightiest Jesus ever wrought. God everywhere, Infinite Wisdom, Justice, Love, and Integrity, Religion in all life, over the anvil, in the pulpit, beside the cradle, on the throne—what a new world shall that make, when the great river of God runs in the channel he made for it, singing melodies as it runs, and sending the spray up from its bosom to fertilize whole continents, which shall break out into flowers, that ripen into fruit, the very leaves for the healing of the nations!

26

FRANCIS ELLINGWOOD ABBOT

1836, born November 6, Boston, Mass.
1859, was graduated from Harvard College
1859, attended Harvard Divinity School
1860–63, attended Meadville Theological School
1864, Unitarian pastor, Dover, N.H.
1867, an organizer of the Free Religious Association
1868, resigned his pastorate
1869–73, leader of Independent Church, Toledo, Ohio
1869–80, editor of the *Index*
1874, *Religion and Science*
1876, organizer and first president of National Liberal League
1881, received the degree of Ph.D. from Harvard
1881–92, conducted a classical school at Cambridge
1885, *Scientific Theism*
1888, substituted for Josiah Royce at Harvard
1890, *The Way Out of Agnosticism; or, The Philosophy of Free Religion*
1903, died October 23
1906, posthumous, *The Syllogistic Philosophy*

THE protestant tradition in American Christianity, its radicalism, was the legitimate inheritance of the American people. Their English and European ancestors were Protestants; their immediate forebears were protestants within Protestantism. No sooner had any brand of religious radicalism gained position than there were found within its ranks those who felt that it was too conservative, that it did not go far enough. The history of American religion was on the side of Moses Stuart when he insisted to William Ellery Channing that the Unitarian movement would spawn infidelity. Once the appeal to authority was made impossible, the only appeal was to the religious sense and the religious experience of the individual. Where this might lead, no one could predict.

When Emerson dismissed the appeal to the Scriptures, infidelity was thought to have come out of Unitarianism. But Emerson remained at least nominally a Christian, and, towards the end of his life he even lost some of the extreme emphasis on self-reliance of his earlier days. When Parker went beyond Emerson in dismissing the traditional God-idea, everyone thought that now Unitarianism had emerged into infidelity. But Parker remained a Christian and led a Unitarian congregation to the end of his life. And yet Moses Stuart was right. Out of the transcendental Unitarianism of Emerson and Parker there developed a genuine and serious attempt to found a non-Christian religion in America, and, to a great extent, of America.

Among the men of various liberal denominations who met together in Boston in 1867 to form the Free Religious Association or joined the movement soon afterward, there were two who stand out both for their earnestness and for the direction which their constructive labors in religion took. One of these men was the young Felix Adler, whose contribution to free religion is the Society for Ethical Culture, still vigorous at three score and ten. Adler's ethical idealism was an original contribution to American thought; his ethical practicality led to many and various contributions to American social welfare. If the test of a religious movement is to be found in the inspiration it gives its adherents to live a better life in and for society, then the movement begun by Adler passes the test with flying colors. The second of these free religionists was the Unitarian minister Francis Ellingwood Abbot, who served the cause as lecturer and as editor of two of the movement's periodicals, the *Index* and the *Radical*. Abbot was expelled from his pulpit by an injunction issued against him by the Supreme Court of New Hampshire soon after his entry into the Free Religious Association.[1] His feeling that the association was not sufficiently militant in its program led him to organize the National Liberal League, later known as the American Secular Union. Abbot, like Adler, developed a philosophic rationale for free religion; in Abbot's work the emphasis was placed on the alteration in outlook involved in an acceptance of the results of science, particularly of evolution (*Religion and Science*, 1874; *Scientific Theism*, 1885; *The Way Out of Agnosticism; or, The Philosophy of Free Religion*, 1890).

Abbot's address "The Genius of Christianity and Free Religion," which is reprinted here, is an excellent statement of the left, or infidel, wing of the free religionists, those who believed it to be necessary to abandon Christianity completely in order to have free religion. Free religion, according to Abbot, meets, as the Church does not, the needs of those who show their spiritual health by a "hunger for truth and life." As age follows age, humanity progresses, and what provided suitable nourishment for this hunger in the past does not do so now. Each religious movement of the past had "its own special historic form, determined by the personality of its founder, by the spirit of the age in which it arose and by the character of the historic forces

[1] See Hale v. Everett, 53 New Hampshire Reports, p. 1.

by which it was developed." Yet each was at its core an expression of the "universal aspiration of humanity." Thus, in each religion there is an element of diversity, which is its own and an element of universality which is not its own, but belongs, rather, to human nature. Any particular religion must, therefore, be defined historically if its individuality is to be discovered.

Historically defined, "Christianity is religion as taught in the New Testament, developed in the history of the Christian Church, and based on faith in Jesus of Nazareth as the Christ of God." Radical religious thought sometimes abandons the historic ground by trying to develop a Christianity without a Christ; this, to Abbot, is to "identify Christianity with Religion, and annihilate the specific difference between Christianity and all other historical faiths," to reduce all to forms of Christianity and Christianity to natural religion. Now, what is specific to the Christian religion is the development of the Christ-idea out of Jewish Messianism and Greek speculation, and the institutional embodiment of the Christ-idea in the Roman Church. All the other elements of Christianity are universal; this alone is specific. This is "the great tap root of Christianity." "The Romish Church . . . is the ripened fruit of the Messianic germ, the supreme culmination of Christianity. . . . The Protestant Reformation was simply the first stage in the decay of Christianity." The reformers were, "although unwittingly, the first apostles of Free Religion." The strength of liberal Christianity indicates a "next step . . . outside of Christianity altogether." Christianity lies "at Death's door in the Unitarian Church," because its specific feature, homage to and worship of the Christ, is minimized.

Recognizing "the transcendent greatness of Jesus," whose spiritual insight was "so pure and piercing . . . that, once possessed with the Messianic idea, he entered into the best that was in it," Abbot still finds a problem impossible of solution in the need to reconcile the "supreme self-emphasis" of Jesus "with his supreme self-sacrifice," since, as a humanistic thinker, he cannot accept the orthodox solution, the doctrine of the divinity of Christ. As for liberal Christianity, it is a misnomer. "Christianity is based on forgetfulness of liberty," because the Lordship which Jesus claimed is "no Lordship at all, if it leaves the soul supreme Lord over itself." Voluntary servitude of the spirit is the cornerstone of Christianity; "the love of perfect freedom is not in it." The only justification for this slavery is the Messianic idea; "the Christian Confession remains the boundary line which no Christian can overstep." Christianity becomes something else when it abandons the Christ-idea.

It becomes, in Abbot's case, something he thinks superior to Christianity.

Free Religion, the higher faith I hold, has no history, save the history of the human spirit, striving to work out its destiny in freedom. . . . It is the soul's deep resolve to love the truth, to learn the truth, and to live the truth, uncoerced and free. It is Intellect daring to think. . . . It is Conscience daring to assert a higher law. . . . It is Will setting at naught the world's tyrannies. . . . It is Heart resting in the universal and changeless Law as eternal and transcendent Love.

The superiority of this doctrineless faith over Christian belief he establishes by a series of direct comparisons of Christianity and Free Religion.

The cornerstone of Christianity is the Christ, while that of free religion is the universal soul of man; the Christian fellowship includes all Christians, while that of free religion is "as wide as humanity itself"; the Christian social ideal is to "Christianize the world," that of free religion, to "humanize" it. The highest spiritual ideal of Christianity is Christ-likeness; that of free religion is self-development. "The spiritual idea of Free Religion is to develop the individuality of each soul in the highest, fullest, and most independent manner possible." Finally, the essential spirit of Christianity is that of self-abnegation; that of free religion is self-reliance; "God in Christ is God outside of self, and devotion to him must be self-suppression; but God in Humanity is God in every soul; and devotion to him becomes the putting forth of every energy to attain freely the individual ideal."

Thus, to Abbot, free religion was the religion of democracy. The faith of the evolutionist in progress led him to see its development as inevitable. Even the light yoke of Jesus seemed to him an unbearable slavery; he could not even wear the name of Christian, even though his best ideas were those of the best and rarest Christians.

THE GENIUS OF CHRISTIANITY
AND FREE RELIGION

TO say that the age we live in is preëminently an era of revolution, is to utter a stale and profitless truism. The fact mirrors itself on every open eye, and voices itself to every unstopped ear. Not merely in the forms of government, the adjustments of society, and other external matters, constant changes occur which are perceptible by all; but the more observing also detect indications of some profound and hidden movement in the depths of the human spirit. The world's heart is ill at ease. Miseries and oppressions and crimes are, it is true, like the poor, ever with us; but cancel these, and the world's unrest will still remain. Its secret inquietude betrays itself even in the tone of the popular poems and novels of the day; and although the Church, abundantly assiduous with prescriptions and pill, promises to cure the distemper, she encounters a most alarming symptom in the patient's distrust of the physician. In fact, the patient refuses to be a patient; and what the Church accounts disease turns out to be a new-born hunger for truth and life,—a most excellent sign of spiritual health. The world needs, not to be doctored, but to be fed; and whoso brings substantial food fairly cooked finds a hearty welcome.

The old faiths, like cotyledons well stored with starch, are perishing as the spring advances, yet only to yield their contents as nourishment for a better faith. Although there are no "new truths" except as the discovery, or riper development in human thought and life, of truths old as God, yet in this sense new truths are creating to-day a new faith in the world before which the elder faiths lose their power. The grounds of human hope, the motives of human action, the objects of human aspiration, are slowly changing; and because change in these respects involves corresponding change in all the relations of public and private life, the great visible movements of the age are but indices of the greater invisible movements in the spiritual consciousness of mankind. Because all questions of immediate interest in the amelioration of society depend ultimately on deeper questions in the soul, there can be no theme of profounder practical importance than that to which I now invite your attention,—the "Genius of Christianity and Free Religion." In the conflict between these two faiths, and in the law of spiritual development by which the one must increase and the other decrease, lies, as I believe, the secret of the religious restlessness of the times. With the seriousness befitting so great a subject, and yet with no shrinking from the plainness of speech which equally befits it, I wish to express convictions neither hastily formed nor weakly held, for which I ask from you only a calm and candid hearing. Whether right or wrong, they must affect profoundly the well-being of every one who makes them the basis of intelligent and fearless action. Let them, then, be intelligently and fearlessly judged.

A savage coming to the sea shore at several distant points might perhaps imagine that he had come to several disconnected seas, not knowing that the sea is one. So he who beholds without reflection the great religions of the world might conceive these to be separate and distinct, not knowing that religion is one. It must have been from some such conception, as this that men used to class Christianity by itself as wholly true, and all other religions in a group by themselves as wholly false. But this distinction cannot stand. The question of the truth or falsity of different religions is purely a question of degree. They are all expressions of the universal aspiration of humanity and are so far all based on eternal truth. But each of them has its own special historic form, determined by the personality of its founder, by the spirit of the age in which it arose, and by the character of the historic forces by which it was developed; and so far it must share the error which clings to all things human. The worst religion has its truth,—the best has its error. Thus all religions are *one*, in virtue of their common origin in the aspiring and worshiping spirit of man; while they are *many*, in virtue of the historic form peculiar to each. The universal element in each belongs, not to it, but to universal human nature; while its special element, its historic form, is its own.

Whoever, therefore, would find the oneness of all religions must seek it in the universal spiritual consciousness of the race; while he who would learn the characteristics of any particular religion must seek this in its history and origin. The object of the first seeker is generic unity, —the object of the second is specific difference. Their methods, consequently, must correspond with their objects, and be the converse of each other. The one must neglect peculiarities, and attend to resemblances; the other must neglect resemblances, and attend to peculiarities. To claim as peculiar to one religion what is common to all religions, a claim often made in behalf of Christianity,—is unreasonable; but it is equally unreasonable to ignore its actual peculiarities. No estimate of a great historical religion can be just, unless formed by the impartial, scientific application of the historical method.

In attempting, therefore, to determine what Christianity actually is, as a great fact in human history, I shall not endeavor to frame a transcendental or mystical formula, and thus, spider-like, evolve a definition of it out of my own consciousness. On the contrary, believing Christianity to be the loftiest of all historical religions, I believe that, like all other historical religions, it can only be understood by the study of its sacred books, its traditions, its institutions, its origin, its history. What were the ideas, purposes, and character of Jesus, and what was the nature of the faith which took its name from him and became Christianity as we see it in the world to-day, must be learned historically or not at all. Abstract speculation can throw no light on these questions of fact. History is the key to the problem of Christianity.

Viewed, then, as one of the world's great historical faiths, Christianity is religion as taught in the New Testament, developed in the history of the Christian Church, and based on faith in Jesus of Nazareth as the Christ of God.

If we attempt to make Christianity independent of its founder, and of the only records we possess of his life and teachings (an attempt sometimes made by modern radical thinkers), we simply abandon the historical ground altogether, identify Christianity with Religion, and annihilate the specific difference between Christianity and all other historical faiths. It thereby becomes impossible to distinguish it from them on the same level; we resolve it into "natural religion," and must treat all other religions as merely various modifications of it. I need not say how arbitrary and irrational this seems to me. If Christianity is itself "natural religion,"—only love to God and love to man, —how can we escape calling Brahmanism and Buddhism and Confucianism and the rest *different forms of Christianity?* Would there be nothing absurd in that? If, on the other hand, we say that religion is always natural, and that Christianity, Brahmanism, Buddhism, Confucianism, Zoroastrianism, Mahometanism, and so forth, are all diverse historical forms of this one natural religion, I think we take the only sensible ground. We then put all historical faiths on the same level, and can distinguish them one from another by their different historical characters. But to do this is at once to sweep away all the fine-spun metaphysical, transcendental, and purely ethical definitions of Christianity, in order to make room for its only historical definition, namely religion as taught in the New Testament, developed in the history of the Christian Church, and based on faith in Jesus of Nazareth as the Christ of God.

The ethical and spiritual teachings of the New Testament are not peculiar to it; as is well known, they can all be paralleled in other ancient writings. These, therefore, will not help us to comprehend that which is peculiar to Christianity and makes it a distinct historical religion; they belong to the universal religion of man, appear in the sacred books of all religions, and are the private property of none. In accordance with the true historical method, therefore, I shall pass by these universal truths, which find perhaps their best expression in the New Testament, in order to concentrate our attention on the fundamental characteristic of Christianity, namely, its faith in the Christ. It is this which separates it from all other religions, constitutes its prime peculiarity, and serves as foundation to the other leading doctrines of Christian theology. Purity, benevolence, mercy, forgiveness, humility, self sacrifice, love, and so forth, are nowhere more beautifully taught than in the discourses, conversations, and parables of Jesus; but these make the universal, not the special, element in the New Testament,—these make its religion, not its Christianity,—and it is now its Christianity that we seek to comprehend.

So far as our present object is concerned, we need not be embarrassed by the doubts resting over the authorship, the dates, and the historic credibility of the various books of the New Testament. No critical scholar of the present day regards the gospels as wholly mythical. Yet, unless they are wholly mythical, it is impossible to doubt that Jesus did actually claim to be the Christ or Messiah, that is, the founder and sovereign of the "kingdom of heaven." So all-pervading is this claim, that to eliminate it from the gospels is to reduce them at once to unadulterated myth. If misunderstood on this point, there is no reason to suppose that Jesus has been understood on any point; if his reported sayings on this subject are ungenuine, there is no reason to suppose any of his sayings to be genuine. In the words of James Martineau [*National Review*, April, 1863]: "Whoever can read the New Testament with a fresh eye must be struck with the prominence everywhere of the Messianic idea. It seems to be the ideal framework of the whole,— of history, parable, dialogue; of Pauline reasoning; of Apocalyptic visions. *'Art thou he that should come?'* This question gives the ideal standard by which on all hands,—on the part of disciples, relations, enemies, of Saul the persecutor and Paul the apostle,—the person and pretensions of Christ are tried. His birth, his acts, his sufferings, are so disposed as to 'fulfil what was spoken' by the prophets: so that the whole programme of his life would seem to have preëxisted in the national imagination."

That these words of Martineau are true, I am profoundly convinced. The Messianic faith is the soul of the entire New Testament, giving unity to the gospels, epistles, and apocalypse, and making Christianity a vital organism. In vain shall we seek to comprehend the spiritual power of Christianity, and determine its agency in the evolution of modern civilization, until we have first comprehended the Messianic idea, and discovered the sources, the channels, and the limitations of its power. In vain shall we seek to solve the mystery of that spiritual Nile which has fertilized the centuries; until we discover its Lake Nyanza in the Messianic hope of Judaism and its widening Delta in the advent of Free Religion. History, not theology, must reveal the true origin of Christianity; and when we are prepared to accept her calm instructions, we shall learn that the greatest of the world's historical religions is no bastard with the bar sinister of miracle athwart its scutcheon, but the lawful offspring of Jewish faith and Greek thought. In the New Testament, if we will but read aright, is ample proof of its pedigree. In the first three gospels we find the Jewish Messiahship assumed by Jesus; in the fourth gospel, we find it interpreted by the Logos doctrine, and thus rationalized by Greek philosophy; in the book of Acts and in the Epistles we find it stripped by Peter and Paul of its local and national limitations, and thus fitted to become the basis of a world-wide church. The organizing genius of Rome supplied the element necessary to convert the idea into an institution; and the triumph of Christianity was assured.

Here, then, in the New Testament itself, the Messianic idea appears as the great tap root of Christianity; and we see, already fulfilled, all the intrinsic spiritual conditions of its subsequent growth. Given the corresponding extrinsic historical conditions, what need of a miracle to account for its wonderful development? It would have been a miracle indeed, if, in the actual state of the Roman Empire at the time, Christianity had failed to become the State Religion. Into what a melancholy and senile decrepitude had fallen its pagan competitors! The decaying mythologies of Persia, Egypt, Greece, Rome, were the spiritual compost whence the vigorous young plant derived its sap. Universal putrefaction is a powerful fertilizer. To the spread of every religion, however rapid (and Christianity is in this respect no more remarkable than Buddhism or Mahometanism), the same explanation applies,—adaptation to the spirit and circumstances of the times. It is customary among Unitarians to extol the purity of "primitive Christianity," and to bewail what they call its theological and ecclesiastical "corruption" during the first three centuries. This is to praise the blossom at the expense of the fruit,—to indulge in that idealization of childhood which is practical depreciation of manhood. The triumph of Athanasius over Arius, and of Augustine over Pelagius, was not accidental. On the contrary, the gradual formation of the Athanasian and Augustinian theology was the strictly logical and natural development of the claim made by Jesus of being the Savior of the world; while the gradual erection of the Romish hierarchy was the equally logical and natural result of the attempt to found a universal church upon this claim. How could a *man* be the Savior of the world? Only by being also *God*. The Romish Church, with its theology of salvation through the God-Man, so far from being a "corruption of primitive Christianity," was its necessary historical evolution; the Messianic idea, freed from its merely Hebrew application, enfolded mediaeval Catholicism as the acorn enfolds the oak. As the Jewish theocracy was at last obliged to enthrone an earthly king as the representative of Jehovah, so the Christian Church was obliged at last to enthrone the Pope as the representative of the Christ. It betrays therefore, a lack of the philosophical, the scientific, the historical spirit, to call that a corruption which was in truth a development.

As the history of philosophical systems is the truest exponent of their logical tendencies, so the history of religions is the truest interpreter of their genius and innermost spirit. The Romish Church, whether in its hierarchy, its institutions, its architecture, its painting, its music, its literature, its theology, its spiritual power, its type of spiritual character, or its missionary zeal, is the ripened fruit of the Messianic germ, the supreme culmination of Christianity. Christian poetry and art, no less than Christian character and faith, have reached their zenith in the Catholic Church. The cathedrals, the Madonnas, the anthems, Dante's *Divine Comedy* (the great poem of Christianity, setting it to eternal music), were born in the souls of Catholics. The Protestant Reformation was simply the first stage in the decay of Christianity. In Wick-liffe and Huss, in Luther and Calvin and their compeers, the modern spirit came to self-consciousness. These men were, although unwittingly, the first apostles of Free Religion. Socinus, Priestley, Channing, Parker, and the other reformers of the Reformation, carried the work of disintegration still farther, and gave voice to the deepening demand of humanity for spiritual freedom. "Liberal Christianity," which means Christianity as liberal as it can be, has reduced the Messianic idea to its minimum dimensions and its minimum power; the next step is outside of Christianity altogether. Gradual in its growth and gradual in its decay,—coming to its prime in the Romish, and lying at Death's door in the Unitarian Church,—Christianity has realized the highest possibilities of the Messianic faith, has accomplished the utmost which that faith can accomplish for man, and is now destined to wane before a faith higher and purer still. Its history, from beginning to end, is the history of men's faith in the Christ; its first and last word is, by the law of its being,—"Come to Jesus." In proportion as the name of Jesus grows infrequent on its lips,—in proportion as his person fails to attract its supreme homage and worship,—in that proportion it ceases to be Christianity, and becomes merged in that universal religion whose only history is the history of the soul. Let me repeat, with emphasis, that, while Christianity is the perishing form, religion is the eternal substance,—that the universal truths, the inspiring hopes, the tender consolations, the quickening impulses, the divinely beautiful spirit, which have made and still make the name of Christianity so dear to the undistinguishing many, belong to the eternal substance and not to the perishing form. Religion must endure; but as Christianity came into history, so it must go out from history. Its inspiration and life have come in and through its faith in the Christ, the one Lord and Master and Savior of the world, and its church, or visible embodiment in a social and spiritual fellowship, has planted itself from the beginning on this faith as its own eternal rock and cornerstone.

There is no clearer recognition of the fundamental character of the Christian Confession than in the following words of Dr. Hedge, a Unitarian clergyman, who perceives how much is involved in the apparent truism that Christianity has a history:—

"I am far from maintaining that Christianity must stand or fall with the belief in miracles; but I do maintain that Christian churches, as organized bodies of believers, must stand or fall with the Christian Confession,—that is, the Confession of Christ as divinely human Master and Head . . . Things exist in this world by distinction one from another. Enlarge as you will the idea and scope of a church, there must be somewhere, whether stated or not in any formal symbol, a line which defines it, and separates those who are in it from those who are without. The scope of the Liberal Church is large; but everything and everybody cannot be embraced in it. The Christian Confession is its boundary line, within which alone it can do the work which Providence has given it to do . . . The distinction involved in the Christian Confession is organic and vital; its abolition would be the dissolution of the ecclesiastical world and the end of Christendom." [*Reason in Religion*, pp. 218, 219.]

This statement of Dr. Hedge is the verdict of history itself. On the Christian Confession, Jesus himself founded his church; on the Christian Confession, Peter, John, Paul, and the rest, built up its walls; on the Christian Confession, Augustine, Athanasius, and their fellow-workers, roofed and completed the great historic edifice. From the vast ecclesiastical hierarchy of Rome to the puny "National Conference of Unitarian and other Christian Churches," all the sects and sub-sects of Christendom, with one consenting voice, confess that Jesus is the Christ, the Savior of the world, the spiritual King of mankind by the grace of God. In all the endless controversies respecting doctrines, forms, or politics, all parties have accepted the Christian Confession as the universal creed of Christians. Whatever differences of opinion exist or have existed concerning the nature, the official function, or the spiritual mission of the Christ, the Christian Confession has remained the cornerstone of the Christian Church; and a Christian will no more challenge the Christian Confession that "Jesus is the Christ," than a Mahometan will challenge the Mahometan Confession that "there is but one God, and Mahomet is his prophet."

It is in the first gospel, not the fourth, that Jesus says to Peter, on his confessing him to be "the Christ, the Son of the living God,"— "Blessed art thou, Simon Bar-jona; for flesh and blood have not revealed it unto thee, but my Father who is in heaven. And I say also unto thee, That thou art Peter, and upon this rock [i. e., your faith in me as the Christ] I will build my church; and the gates of hell shall not prevail against it." It is in the first gospel, not the fourth, that Jesus replies to the high priest, adjuring him to declare whether he is the Christ,—"I am. Moreover I say to you, Henceforth ye will see the Son of Man sitting on the right hand of Power, and coming on the clouds of heaven" [Noyes's translation]. It is in the first gospel, not in the fourth, that Jesus explicitly makes the Christian Confession the necessary condition of salvation: "Whosoever, therefore, shall confess me before men him will I also confess before my Father who is in heaven; but whosoever shall deny me before men, him will I also deny before my Father who is in heaven." It would be easy to cite scores of passages to the same effect; but these are amply sufficient.

In the same spirit, Peter declares, in the book of Acts, that "there is no other name given under heaven whereby men can be saved." In the same spirit, Paul declares to the Galatians, "There be some that trouble you and would pervert the gospel of Christ. But though we, or an angel from heaven, preach any other gospel unto you than that which we have preached unto you, let him be accursed"; and to the Romans, "If thou shalt confess with the mouth that Jesus is Lord, and shalt believe in thy heart that God has raised him from the dead, thou shalt be saved; for with the heart man believeth so as to obtain righteousness, and with the mouth confesseth so as to obtain salvation." In the same spirit, John exclaims in his first epistle, "Who is a liar, but he that denieth that Jesus is the Christ? Whosoever denieth the Son, the same has not the Father." And so on. Sayings such as these meet the eye on almost every page of the New Testament; and so far from being accidental or non-essential, they utter the heart faith, the inmost spirit of Christianity, as a distinct religion.

The one grand aim of Jesus was to establish the "kingdom of heaven"; and this, however universalized and spiritualized, was in essence the ancient ideal theocracy, in which the Christ was to be the God-appointed king. From the day when, on the very eve of death, Jesus boldly affirmed before Pilate and the high priest his title to the Messianic throne, the highest and deepest prayer of his disciples has been that his throne may be established for ever in the hearts of all mankind. Was it an *accident* that the new faith took its name, not from the individual Jesus, but from his royal office? Christianity was the faith of the Christians, and the Christians were those who believed in the Christ. Hence the condition of Christian fellowship has always been fealty to Jesus as common Lord and Master; and in this, the organic bond of union in all branches of the Christian Church, the innermost life of Christianity has, by the very law of its being, only expressed itself outwardly in social form. In short, the history of Christianity is simply the history of the Messianic faith, deepened and widened, developed and spiritualized, in the highest possible degree—the history of the varying fortunes which have befallen the attempt of Jesus to found a universal spiritual empire in the hearts of men; and he will seek in vain to fathom the depths of Christianity who looks elsewhere than to this Messianic faith for the secret of its peculiar religious power.

Furthermore, unless liberal thinkers cease to philosophize loosely about Christianity and learn to do complete justice to its Messianic or special element, a problem of great importance will remain permanently insoluble. It is only by tracing the course of the Messianic idea back to its fountain-head in the living faith of Judaism, that it becomes possible to discover the *natural origin* of Christianity. If the sources of Christianity reach no further back than to the individual soul of Jesus; if so mighty a power in the world's history was born of one man's single life, and owed nothing to earlier ancestors; if no deep unity can be discovered between Jesus and the spirit of his age, in virtue of which he became the natural representative of humanity in his day and generation, and brought to a living focus the religious forces of his times,—then is Christianity indeed a miracle, and Jesus may well have been God. The naturalistic interpretation of Christianity fails utterly, unless it can reveal an adequate cause for its tremendous influence on the course of history. Once admit that a Jewish peasant lifted the whole world up to a higher spiritual level, not by embodying in himself the best religious life of his era, but by the sheer strength of his own individuality,—and I, for one, must perforce admit him to have been Omnipotence in disguise. The incarnation of God would be a less miracle than the upheaval of the planet by a human arm. But if Jesus was a man, and acted under natural human conditions, then his power must have been the power of humanity; behind him, beneath him, within him, must have been the spirit of his age, concentrating in his word the vitality of his race. Somewhere must he have found a foot-hold in the profoundest faith of his own nation, or he could not have moved the universal consciousness of man. The secret of success, with every great soul, lies in sympathy with his times, without which his most magnificent utterance perishes on the air. Given, therefore, the humanity of Jesus, it is imperatively necessary to discover the faith which he and his countrymen must have held in common. Where shall we search for this except in that Messianic idea which is the core and heart of his religion?

Here we find established a vital relation between Jesus and the Hebrew people. The moment we accept the clew here offered, the labyrinth ceases to bewilder,—our path is clear. It would be at the same time tedious and pedantic, were I to rehearse in detail the evidence which has convinced my own mind that *Christianity is only a developed Judaism.* From the time of the Babylonish Captivity, the narrow the-ocracy of earlier ages began to develop in Hebrew thought into the dazzling dream of a universal "kingdom of heaven," designed to suc-ceed the great empires of antiquity and to embrace in its dominions all the nations of the globe. The so-called Jewish Apocalyptic literature, which sprang up as a transformation of the primitive prophetism, and of which the most important writings are the book of Daniel, the Sibylline oracles, the book of Enoch, and the fourth book of Esdras, enables us to distinguish successive stages in the formation of the Mes-sianic faith. At first an aristocracy of the saints rather than the mon-archy of the Messiah, the conception of the "kingdom of heaven" in-corporated into itself more and more of the personal element, until this at last came to predominate. Long before the birth of Jesus, the chief features of the Messianic idea as contained in the New Testament were strongly marked, both with regard to the "end of the world" and the "coming of the Son of Man." The same place, Jerusalem; the same time, the immediate future; the same symptomatic signs, wars and rumors of wars, and the gathering of Gentile armies against Jerusalem; the same coming of the Messiah with his angels on the clouds of heaven; the same solemn Judgment, with the Son of man on the throne of his glory and all nations before his tribunal; the same sentences to the wicked and the righteous; the same resurrection of the dead from Hades; the same passing away of the old earth and appearance of the new,—all these, and more, were definite Messianic beliefs in the century before Jesus. Nor this alone. The "kingdom of heaven," as conceived in the later of these Apocalyptic writings, was highly spiritual in its character, bringing at once happiness and holiness to all mankind. The "kingdom of heaven" was to ultimate in a universal brotherhood of man, an era of universal peace and righteousness, introduced through universal submission to the Hebrew Messiah or Christ. Every generous aspiration for spiritual perfection and the welfare of humanity thus found its satisfaction in the vision of Messianic redemption to the chosen people of God.

Into this circle of ideas and national aspirations Jesus was born; and were they not also his own? They were the very atmosphere he breathed; they filled his soul from the earliest days of childhood. The gospels represent him as not wholly illiterate, being able at least to read. He undoubtedly was ignorant of Greek, which even at Jerusalem was but little known and regarded as dangerous in its tendencies; and there is no trace in the gospel narratives of the influence of the Hellenic culture upon his mind. The study of the Mosaic Law was alone considered reputable and safe by devout Jews. The Rabbi Hillel, however, who fifty years before Jesus anticipated his Golden Rule and others of his finest sayings, in all probability exerted a deep influence upon his development. It is evident from the evangelists that Jesus had earnestly pondered the Old Testament, especially Isaiah and the book of Daniel,—perhaps the book of Enoch also, and other Apocalyptic writings. "The advent of the Messiah," says Renan, "with his glories and his terrors, the nations dashing one against another, the cataclysm of heaven and earth, were the familiar food of his imagination; and as these revolutions were thought to be at hand, so that a multitude of people were seeking to compute their times, the supernatural order of things into which such visions transport us appeared to him from the first perfectly natural." The conception of universal and invariable laws of nature which had been developed to a considerable degree in the Greek mind by the philosophy of Epicurus, and which, nearly a century before the birth of Jesus, had been admirably stated by Lucretius in his great poem on "The Nature of Things," was utterly foreign to the thought of Jesus and his countrymen, who believed in the habitual agency of demons and evil spirits, and had unwavering faith in miracles. The great idea of Jesus, the immediate advent of the "kingdom of heaven," was also the dominant idea of his times; but, various attempts to realize it by political means having ended in utter failure, especially that of Judas the Gaulonite or Galilean, he early perceived the folly of military Messianism, and replied implicitly on the establishment of his Messianic throne by the miraculous display of the divine power. Thus was Jesus educated by his age.

Repelled though he was by the vulgar conception of the Christ as a mere warlike prince, the idea of spiritual supremacy through the religious reformation of his people struck a responsive chord in his soul. His deep nature was thrilled and kindled by his country's hope, and with intense earnestness must he have asked himself,—"Can I fulfil it? Am I the Called, the Anointed of God?" The consciousness of his wonderful religious genius, fertilized and developed by the spirit of his age, fanned the wish into a prayer, and the prayer into a conviction, and the conviction into an enthusiasm, and the enthusiasm into a calm and omnipotent faith, that he was indeed the Messiah,—singled out from all eternity by the will of God, foretold by prophets and kings, and awaited for weary centuries by humanity in tears. Impossible as it is for the cool intellect of the West to comprehend the mystic fervor, the religious intensity of the Semitic race, it is yet evident that Jesus acquired faith in his Messianic destiny by an inward experience analogous to that which convinced the prophets of their divine missions. Fathom it or analyze it we cannot; but we can yet perceive that the phenomenon of Hebrew prophetism, with its sublime identification of impassioned thought with the direct mandate of God, repeats itself in the history of the young Galilean carpenter. It is a fact to be studied,—not to be denied.

Let no one meet me here with the bigot's wornout dilemma, "If Jesus was not in reality the Messiah he claimed to be, he was either a madman or an impostor!" Was John Brown a madman or an impostor, when he aspired to be the redeemer of an enslaved race? The moral sublimity of such an aim is not to be measured by the six-inch rule of vulgar souls, but by the astronomic spaces of the heavens above. There is a madness that is more than sanity,—a veritable inspiration to dare the impossible, and by bloody failure to achieve a somewhat greater than "success." The hero is always a fool in the eyes of him who counts the cost. If it be madness to obey the enthusiasm of ideas without stopping to count the cost, God grant us all the wisdom to go mad! Such madness is the glory of humanity. The insane man is he whose thought fatally contradicts his surroundings; but he who comprehends the profoundest, though it may be the unconscious, movement of his age, and carries its underlying ideas into fuller and higher development,—this man, I say, is the sanest of the sane. To his contemporaries, the idealist is always crazy; to posterity, he appears as the only practical man of his times,—the guide of his generation in the pathway of progress. In the soul of Jesus, the great aspiration of the Hebrew race became purified from its alloys, and stamped forever with the impress of his superior spirit. But, being essentially Hebrew still, it is incapable of expansion into the aspiration of universal humanity; and Jesus, though endowed with that sanity of genius which is madness in the eyes of mediocrity, is no longer in the van.

To him, however, who in the face of sincerity like that of Jesus, ventures to whisper the word *imposture*, I will not do insult to my own reverence for human greatness by addressing any defence of Jesus from such a charge. It should blister the mouth that makes it. Enough for me that in the privacy of his own self-communings Jesus believed he heard the summons to a work of unparalleled sublimity,—that he valued not his blood in comparison with obedience,—that he claimed the Messianic diadem with death for its Koh-i-noor. Surely, the suspicion of duplicity as the root of such vast historic influence, betrays in the suspecter a disgraceful faith in the power of knavery.

The transcendent greatness of Jesus appeared in this, that the popular hope of a Priest-King ruling by the sword transformed itself in his musing soul into the sublime idea of a spiritual Christ ruling by love,— that he sought to establish the "kingdom of heaven," not over the bodies, but deep in the hearts, of men. So pure and piercing was his spiritual insight, that, once possessed with the Messianic idea, he entered into the best that was in it, and forgot the rest; seized on the elder and diviner meaning of the prophets, and cast away as rubbish the popular selfishness with which this was overlaid. Believing himself to be the Anointed of God, he aspired to become, not merely king of the Jewish theocracy after its miraculous restoration by God at the great "day of judgment," but also king of the very heart of regenerated humanity.

I would fain put upon this ambition the noblest possible construction; for, so far from wishing to make out a case against him, I am only anxious to do him exact justice, and penetrate the spirit of the faith which he bequeathed to mankind. To become the object of human imitation and the quickening ideal of human aspiration,—to be the One Way to purity and love and peace,—to reign in men's souls, as the sun reigns in the solar system, by developing the seeds of all goodness and beauty;—this, and no selfish empire, was the ambition of Jesus. He aimed to be Lord and King by drawing all men to God, and thus to make himself the great centre of the world's divinest life. To reconcile his supreme self-emphasis with his supreme self-sacrifice, is the great perplexing problem of the gospels. The doctrine of his Deity, which is the Orthodox solution, is not a possible one to humanitarian thinkers. Where shall we find another?

On the one hand, the claim of Jesus to the Messianic crown did not grow out of a vulgar lust of power, but out of a profound faith that it was God's will that he should wear it. Belief in the "divine right of kings" was universal in the Jewish world, and Jesus fully shared it. How it happened that he first became convinced of his own divine election to the throne of the "kingdom of heaven," will never, I think, be explained: that is a secret, buried with him. But that he did become convinced of it, and that this profound conviction, rather than any desire of personal aggrandizement, was the root of his Messianic claim, seems to me the simple verdict of justice. His self-emphasis, therefore, was the necessary product of his education, his spiritual experience, and his faith in God; and in the necessity of this connection between cause and effect, lies his defence against the charge of overweening and selfish egotism. But there was nothing original in this conviction of a special Divine mission; every founder of a religion shares it. The true originality of Jesus lies, I conceive, in the means he adopted to accomplish his end and realize his ambition. Here he stands alone. Strange as it may seem, he aimed to win absolute power by absolutely renouncing it. This is the identification of contradictories,—the very Hegelianism of conscience. With a new conception of what constitutes true royalty of soul, he sought to earn his kingship by the more than regal majesty of his service. The "great Masters" have been rare indeed; yet how much rarer have been the great Servants! It is the grandest and most original trait in Jesus' character, that he sought to realize his supreme Mastership through a supreme Servantship. Here lies the reconciliation of his self-emphasis and self-renunciation. Here, also, I find the secret of his wonderful success in subduing souls to his sway. He would govern, yet through love; he would secure absolute allegiance, yet bind men to it by the spontaneous outgush of their own gratitude; he would wear a crown, yet bow his head to receive it from the hands of subjects burning with eagerness to place it there. Thus, and thus alone, he aspired to reign, the welcome Sovereign of every human soul.

What astounding, yet sublime, audacity! How mean, compared with this, the ambitions of Alexanders and Caesars and Napoleons! How brutal is the ambition that relies on force, compared with the ambition that relies on love! Yet because it involved his own elevation to a throne, albeit a spiritual throne, his ambition was ambition still, the "last infirmity" of a most noble mind. It precluded the possibility of self-forgetfulness in service,—of that supreme modesty which teaches that the value of the grandest soul is not personal, but inheres in the universal humanity it contains, and the universal ideas it represents. There is but one ambition sublimer than to REIGN BY SERVING,—and that is, to SERVE WITHOUT REIGNING. I cannot shut my eyes to the nobler purpose; I cannot forget that Socrates both lived and died to make it real.

In vain is all the modern noise and bustle about a "Liberal" Christianity. Christianity is based on forgetfulness of liberty; the love of perfect freedom is not in it. Spiritual servitude is its cornerstone,—none the less hurtful, if voluntary. Many a slave has loved his chains. Interpret as loosely as you may the Lordship which Jesus claimed,—it is no Lordship at all, if it leaves the soul supreme Lord over itself. Run down the scale from slavish imitation to simple deference,—it avails nought; there is no spiritual freedom but in reverence for the still, small voice within the soul, as supreme above all other voices. This made the greatness of Jesus himself; would that he had fostered it in his disciples! Yet no! Even the mistakes of lofty spirits help on the great cause of human development; and, mistaken as was the Messianic ambition of Jesus, the world's debt is immense to this magnificent mistake. Mankind were not yet ripe for self-government in spiritual freedom,—are not wholly ripe for it to-day,—will not be wholly ripe for it this many a long year. The overpowering influence of a spiritual King whose law was love met the world's wants as the freedom of self government could not then have done; and thus the gospel of authority accomplished a work not yet possible to the modern gospel of spiritual liberty. The grave responsibilities of independence befit only the ripe maturity of the soul.

Whether we consider Christianity with regard to its essence, its origin, or its history, we are thus led to one and the same conclusion,— that its fundamental characteristic as a distinct religion is its faith in Jesus as the Christ. Faith in a Christ or Messiah as "the coming man" had become, long prior to the birth of Jesus, an integral part of Hebrew monotheism; and Christianity, historically considered, is only the complete development of Judaism into its highest possibilities. "In its earliest aspect," says Martineau, "Christianity was no new or universal religion; Judaism had found the person of its Messiah, but else remained the same." All of high truth and spiritual power that are compatible with the Messianic idea, Jesus, I believe, put into it, when he made it the cornerstone of his religion. The Christian Church has expressed outwardly the genuine character of Messianism, and realized, both in their best and in their worst directions, its necessary historical tendencies. Gradually developing until the Papacy reached the zenith of its prosperity, and gradually decaying from that day to this, Christianity becomes daily more and more discordant with modern civilization and modern religion; and those sects that dream of adapting it to modern life are unconsciously officiating at its funeral. Construe it as largely or as loosely as you please, Christianity, as a great historical and spiritual power, will nevertheless remain *religion within the limits of the Messianic idea*. Idealize or transcendentalize the Christ as highly as you may, his practical power is gone the moment you make him aught less than a person. It is the vitality of Jesus that has made, and still makes, the vitality of his religion. Pass beyond the circle of its supreme influence, and, whether you know it or not, you have passed outside of Christianity. Detach Christianity wholly from the person of Jesus, and you destroy all meaning in the Christian name by destroying the historic root from which it sprang. The Christian Confession remains the boundary line which no Christian can overstep.

However some may yearn, having lost all faith in the Messianic idea, to retain nevertheless the Christian name, whether from love for its venerable associations or from reluctance to bear the odium of its distinct rejection, I believe that the proprieties of language and increasing perception of what consistency requires will slowly wean them from this desire. The world at large can never be made to understand what is meant by a Christian who in no sense has faith in the Christ. If Jesus really claimed to be the Christ,—if he made this claim the basis of the Christian religion,—and if through this claim he still infuses into his Church all its Christian life,—then the world is right, and may well marvel at a Christianity that denies the Lord, yet wears his livery. For myself, I cannot evade the practical consequences of my thought. The central doctrine of Christianity is for me no longer the highest or the best; and with the reality, I resign the name. Far be it from me to do this in levity or mockery or defiance! Far be it from me to turn my back in scorn on my own most hallowed experiences in the past! Once I felt the full power of the Christian faith; now I cleave to a faith diviner still. If I am in fatal error, and rush madly into the woes denounced against the Anti-Christ, even so must it be; but come what may, let me never plunge into the deeper damnation of moral faithlessness, or make my heart the coffin of a murdered truth!

If, then, there is a higher faith than Christianity, he who shall cherish it is bound to make known what it is, and how it is higher than Christianity. Bear with me while I endeavor to discharge this duty. It is no easy thing to do. Free Religion, the higher faith I held, has no history, save the history of the human spirit, striving to work out its destiny in freedom. It is spiritual, not historical,—universal, not special,—inward, not outward. It has no list of doctrines to teach, no Church to extend, no rites to perform, no Bible to expound, no Christ to obey. With none of these things, it is the soul's deep resolve to love the truth, to learn the truth, and to live the truth, uncoerced and free. It is Intellect daring to think, unawed by public opinion. It is Conscience daring to assert a higher law, in face of a corrupted society and a conforming church. It is Will setting at naught the world's tyrannies, and putting into action the private whispers of the still, small voice. It is Heart resting in the universal and changeless Law as eternal and transcendent Love. It is the soul of man asserting its own superiority to all its own creations, burning with deep devotion to the true and just and pure, and identifying its every wish with the perfect order of the universe. It is neither affirmation nor negation of the established, but rather a deep consciousness that all the established is inferior to that which has established it. It is the spirit of self-conscious freedom, aiming evermore at the best, and trusting itself as the architect of character. In fine, it is that sense of spiritual unity with boundless Being which fills the soul with reverence for human nature, and disables it from worshiping aught but the formless, indwelling, and omnipresent One.

But the difference between Christianity and Free Religion will best be made evident by a direct comparison between the two, with respect to their leading characteristics. This will show that by the intrinsic truth or falsity of the Christian Confession, that "Jesus of Nazareth is the Christ of God," Christianity must stand or fall. Let the issue be met fairly and squarely. The heart of the great controversy which is now shaking the world to its profoundest depths can be found nowhere, in the last analysis, but in this question of the truth or falsity of the Christian Confession. Here lies the battle ground between freedom and authority, the vast Christian Church and the spirit of the nineteenth century, the great historical faith of the Old World and the genius of American liberty,—in one word, between Christianity and Free Religion. The time has come to see and to say that the Christian Confession is not a truth, *Jesus was not the "Christ of God."* The "Christ" prophesied and longed for has never come, and will never come. The office and function is a mythical, an impossible one. No individual man has ever stood, or can ever stand, in the relation of Lord, King, and Savior to the whole world. It would be an infinite usurpation for any man to occupy that office, either in a temporal or spiritual sense. A comparison between the Christian idea as it has always been and must ever remain, on the one hand, and the ideas which are now asserting eminent domain over the development of humanity on the other hand, will show that this issue between Christianity and Free Religion is an absolute and irreconcilable one, and that the former is doomed by the very nature of things to fade away and make room for the latter.

The cornerstone of Christianity is the Christ himself, believed to have actually come in the flesh as the Divinely appointed Savior of the world, the one "Life, Truth, and Way." His mission is unique, not to be accounted for by historical causes, but only by a special miraculous influx of Divine Power into the course of history. However this conception is refined and subtilized by the more thoughtful minds in the Christian Church, Jesus remains still, in the religion it teaches, the one Vine of which all his followers are merely branches.

But the cornerstone of Free Religion is the universal soul of man, the common nature of humanity, as the source and origin of the world's religious life. Out of this have sprung, in accordance with unchanging spiritual laws, all churches, faiths, and religions. Nothing less than the entire history of humanity can reveal all its possibilities; and through its own inherent possibilities alone can the world ever be "saved" from its own miseries and imperfections. The spontaneous energies of human nature, which is the great fountain-head of all history, all civilization, all religion, are the power of God gushing up and revealing in each soul afresh the Infinite Life that fills all space and time. It is faith in these human yet divine spontaneities, wherever and whenever and however manifested, that inspires the free soul to its highest life, and bids it realize its own inborn ideal as the consummation of its noblest possibilities. Faith in the individual Jesus; faith in universal human nature: these are the two cornerstones.

As is the basis of faith, so is the fellowship built upon it. The Christian fellowship is as wide as all Christians, but no wider. Those are Christian brethren who acknowledge the same common Lord, and thus drink at the same general fountain of Christian life. It was their love *for each other* that made the ancients marvel at the early Christians; and they who forget this limitation of their love fail to understand the spirit of the primitive Church as impressed on the New Testament. From that day to this, the same limitation of fellowship has existed; and so long as the Christian Church continues to survive, its organic bond of union must still be the original Christian Confession.

But the fellowship of Free Religion is as wide as humanity itself. All who are born of woman are brothers and peers in virtue of their common nature. There is no right of spiritual primogeniture, no monopoly of inspiration, no precedence of creed; all men are but seekers after truth, and despite all pretensions and delusions they reach it only by using the natural faculties of the mind. The impartial God sends his sunshine and his rain to all. There is no privileged or commissioned interpreter of Divine oracles.

> Now there bubbled beside them, where they stood,
> A fountain of waters sweet and good;
> The youth to the streamlet's brink drew near,
> Saying "Ambrose, thou maker of creeds, look here!"
> Six vases of crystal then he took,
> And set them along the edge of the brook.

> "As into these vases the water I pour,
> There shall one hold less, another more,
> And the water unchanged in every case
> Shall put on the figure of the vase:
> O thou who wouldst unity make through strife,
> Canst thou fit this sign to the Water of Life?"

These beautiful lines of our own American poet breathe the true spirit of Free Religion,—a deep humility in the presence of infinite truth which forbids any one to despise another's earnest faith. How all dogmatic arrogance fades away, when reverence for our own souls begets an equal reverence for the souls of others! It is out of this profound sentiment of human equality in respect to all spiritual privileges that a profound regard for all other human equalities is born, nor do I see how it can have any other origin. Yet in the conscious equality of all human rights, whether before God or man, must be found the seed of all universal brotherhood that deserves the name. These, then, are the two contrasted fellowships,—the brotherhood of the Christian Church limited by the Christian Confession, the great brotherhood of man without limit or bound.

A similar contrast meets us in the social ideals held up as the great end of collective human activity. The supreme object of the Christian Church is to *Christianize the world,* and thus secure the salvation of all in the world to come. That is, its efforts are all directed to the one aim of bringing all men within its fold, of making its brotherhood universal on the basis of the Christian Confession, of absorbing the world into itself, and thus including all men under the sceptre of its Lord. In the prime of its glory the mediaeval Papacy went far towards accomplishing this object; and, although now the Christian Church is shattered into fragments, each separate piece or "sect" endeavors to accomplish it anew. "Church extension" is the primary aim of all denominations as such, the evidence and measure of all denominational life. To evangelize or Christianize the world is the ideal end of all Christian activity of a social kind; and this means to make conterminous with the globe that "kingdom of heaven" in which the Christ is the Divinely appointed king.

But the supreme object of Free Religion is to *humanize the world*. That is, it aims to liberate, to educate, to spiritualize, in one word, to develop the race. To bring out of man the best that is in him,—the best in thought, in feeling and sentiment, in moral action, in social, political, and religious life,—this is the work it proposes. Whatever inward or outward conditions favor this symmetrical development of human nature, it strives unceasingly to secure; and thus all high philanthropies and all generous reforms and all noble endeavors to ameliorate society grow out of the essential purpose and dominant idea of Free Religion. Man does not need to be Christianized: he does need to be humanized. While thus the social ideal of the Christian Church is that of a "kingdom of heaven" on earth with the Christ for its king, the social ideal of Free Religion is that of a Commonwealth of Man, in which there is neither king nor lord, but all are free and equal citizens.

A profounder contrast still exists between the two spiritual ideals held up to the private soul. The highest possible exhortation of Christianity is—"Be like Christ"; its highest eulogy is to say—"He is Christlike." By rigid self-examination and laborious imitation to model the character after the pattern set by the "Great Exemplar," is the crowning achievement of the Christian saint. The little work of Thomas à Kempis, called the *Imitation of Christ*, which is said to have passed through more editions than any other book except the Bible alone, is chiefly a devoutly passionate outpouring of the Christian aspiration to attain the character of Jesus. Suppression of the stubborn individuality and complete reproduction of the Master's likeness is the spiritual ideal of the Christian mystic; and the heroes of Christian history are precisely those who, like Fénelon or St. Francis of Assisi, are supposed to have most successfully imitated it.

But the highest exhortation of Free Religion is —"Be thyself"; its highest praise—"He was true to himself, and therefore true to humanity and to God." It recognizes no absolute ideal in Jesus; it perceives that, even were it possible (which it is not), the successful imitation of Jesus by all mankind would extinguish individuality, make original and independent character impossible, and destroy the very roots of all civilization. It proclaims the servility, nay, the utter irreligion, of spiritual imitation. The character of Jesus exhibits but one out of an infinite number of spiritual types, and could be an ideal to no one but himself, even supposing that he had made his own ideal identical with his own real. The law of endless variety in natural temperaments and organizations, and in the relative strength of elementary faculties, involves another law of endless variety in individual ideals. A single absolute ideal for all mankind would be an appalling curse, if it were possible to hold all to it. Each soul must have its own ideal according to the balance of its natural capacities and powers, the nature of its surroundings and conditions in the world, and the quantity and quality of its being; and as the soul grows in attainment, so must its ideal evermore enlarge. It is supremely mischievous to be a copyist in character. Facsimiles of Jesus are impossible; good imitations of him are excessively rare; caricatures of him are plentiful. The ideal of another, like a die stolen from the mint, can at the best make me only a counterfeit. Hence the highest maxim in this matter is simply this: "Be true to yourself." Thus, while the spiritual ideal of Christianity is to sacrifice all individuality in the reproduction of the character of Jesus, the spiritual ideal of Free Religion is to develop the individuality of each soul in the highest, fullest, and most independent manner possible.

But the profoundest contrast of all lies in the fundamental unlikeness of spirit and tone. The spirit of Christianity, as manifested in the chief saints of Christian history, has always been on the one hand that of self-abnegation, self-distrust, self-contempt, and on the other hand that of utter spiritual prostration before Jesus, and utter submission to his authoritative will. To be absolutely obedient to the Christ, and to find this obedience made easy by a divine passion of love for his person and his character, has always been, and must always be, the governing secret aspiration of every Christian heart. Whether believed to be the Incarnate God, or simply the one Divinely ordained Way to God, the supreme motive to holy living has always been, in the deeply devout Christian, absorbing love for his Savior; and this love always tends to produce the suppression of the free self, the paralysis and humiliation of the individual will, in order that the will of the Master may be accomplished in heart and life. Meekness, patience, submission, resignation, passivity, absence of self-will, complete surrender of the whole soul to a will outside of itself,—these are the especial graces and virtues of the Christian character, and determine the types of the "Christian spirit."

But the spirit of free religion is fundamentally different. The same self-consecration to God, which in the Christian soul produces self-surrender and self-humiliation, produces in the free soul self-reliance and self-respect. God in Christ is God outside of self, and devotion to him must be self-suppression; but God in Humanity is God in every soul; and devotion to him becomes the putting forth of every energy to attain freely the individual ideal. The spirit of Free Religion, as the name imports, is the spirit of freedom, of manly and womanly self respect, of deep religious trust in human nature; and because its faith in self is, at bottom, faith in the divineness of universal nature, it is the perfect blending of sturdy self-reliance with noble humanity, and devout repose in God.

Thus, from a thoughtful and independent comparison of the great faith of the past, and the greater faith of the present, it becomes clear, I think, that there is a deep spiritual antagonism between them. The one must wane as the other waxes. The one must die that the other may live. *God in Christ* is the spiritual centre of Christianity; hence in Christ himself must Christianity ever have its basis and cornerstone,— in the Christian Confession it must ever have its bond and limit of fellowship,—in the universal extension of the Christian Church it must ever have its social ideal,—in the imitation of Jesus it must ever have its spiritual ideal,—in the suppression of self, and utter submission to the will of Jesus, it must ever manifest its essential spirit. But *God in Humanity* is the spiritual and central faith of free religion; which has thus its cornerstone in universal human nature, its fellowship in the great brotherhood of man, its social ideal in a free republican commonwealth, its spiritual ideal in the highest development of each individual soul, its essential spirit in a self-respect which is at once profound reverence for human nature, and profound repose in universal Nature.

Am I not right in calling this the higher and diviner faith,—the faith of manhood as contrasted with that of childhood? I recognize the great services rendered to man by the Christian Church; I appreciate the peculiar beauty of the Christian character; I know the mighty power of the Christian spirit. But I cannot conceal from myself that Christianity is not adapted to the present as it has been to the past, and that a deeper, broader, and higher faith is to-day silently entering the heart of humanity. If, out of all the sayings attributed to Jesus in the New Testament, I were asked to select that one which most profoundly utters the spirit of his religion, I should select these beautiful, gracious, and tender words:—

"Come unto me, all ye that labor and are heavy-laden, and I will give you rest. Take my yoke upon you, and learn of me; for I am meek and lowly of heart, and ye shall find rest unto your souls. For my yoke is easy, and my burden is light."

How many aching hearts and wounded spirits have taken upon them the easy yoke of Jesus, and found the promised rest! And how many more will find repose and peace in the same gentle bondage! If the free spirit could indeed wear a yoke,—if it could indeed purchase rest on such terms without abjuring that spiritual independence which is its very life and breath,—then might it wear the yoke of Jesus. Once I rejoiced to wear it; but I can wear it no longer. The rest I need comes no longer from spiritual servitude, but must be sought and found in the manly exercise of spiritual freedom. It is to those who feel this Anglo-Saxon instinct of liberty stirring in their hearts that my words are addressed,—not to those who feel no galling pressure from the easy yoke. My duty is discharged; my task is done; and, as I have freely spoken, so do you freely judge my words.

27

THEODORE T. MUNGER

1830, born March 5, at Bainbridge, N.Y.
1851, was graduated from Yale
1855, was graduated from Yale Divinity School
1855, spent one term at Andover Theological Seminary
1856–85, served as minister in various Congregational churches in New England and California
1883, *The Freedom of Faith*
1885–1900, minister of the United Church, New Haven
1887, *The Appeal to Life*
1897, *Character through Inspiration*
1899, *Horace Bushnell, Preacher and Theologian*
1904, *Essays for the Day*
1910, died January 11, at New Haven, Conn.

ABBOT made explicit in his thinking the tendencies of liberal Unitarian leaders like Frothingham, Bellows, and Parker. He gave their ideas systematic expression and translated their spiritual insights into a program for religious action. Among the Trinitarian Calvinists, too, there was a liberal movement, departing in several essential respects from the traditional theology of Andover and Yale, which awaited systematization. An early attempt at synthesis was made by Theodore T. Munger, disciple and biographer of Bushnell, who had, like Bushnell, both the advantages and the disadvantages of a pastoral rather than an academic position.

Like Abbot, Munger accepted two basic ideas which determined his religious theories: the evolutionary hypothesis and the historical approach. By accepting these ideas he was prepared to discuss religions as events in time, rather than eternal ordinations, and to bring revelation to the bar of criticism. In utilizing the evolutionary hypothesis as added proof of the glory of God and maintaining that evolution strengthens the design argument, Munger took the line that liberal Christianity has taken since Darwin; in readiness to accept an historical interpretation of the Scriptures, he stood in the main stream of modern religious development, but he was not interested in textual criticism. His method of dealing with the Scriptures explains them as "a continually unfolding revelation of God . . . . a book of eternal laws and facts that are evolving their truth and reality in the process of history"; [1] thus he accepted the text of the Bible as given, but allowed for changing interpretations of the revelation.

Munger's most systematic and careful statement of his position is incorporated in an essay titled "The New Theology," prefaced to his collection of sermons *The Freedom of Faith.* To attempt to convey a clear idea of the pattern of this statement, in Munger's own words, this series of extracts is given.

What is called New Theology . . . justifies itself by the belief that it can minister to faith, and by a conviction that the total thought of an age ought to have the greatest possible unity, or, in plainer phrase, that its creed ought not to antagonize its knowledge. . . . It does not propose to do without a theology. . . . It does not resolve belief into sentiment, nor etherealize it into mysticism, nor lower it into mere altruism; yet it does not deny an element of sentiment, it acknowledges an element of mysticism, and it insists on a firm basis in ethics. . . . While it believes in a harmony of doctrines, it regards with suspicion what have been known as systems of theology, on the ground that it rejects the methods by which they are constructed. . . . It regards theology as an induction from the revelations of God—in the Bible, in history, in the nation, in the family, in the material creation, and in the whole length and breadth of human life . . . The New Theology does not part with the historic faith of the church, but rather seeks to put itself in its line while recognizing a process of development. . . . It holds to progress by slow and cosmic growth rather than by cataclysmal leaps. . . . It does not reject the specific doctrines of the church of the past. It holds to the Trinity . . . to the divine sovereignty . . . to the Incarnation . . . to the Atonement . . . to the Resurrection . . . to Judgment . . . to Justification by faith . . . to Regeneration and Sanctification by the Spirit. . . . It is not iconoclastic in its temper. . . . Believing that revelation is not so much *from* God as *of* God, its logical attitude is that of seeing and interpreting. . . . It is not disposed to find a field and organization outside of existing churches. . . . It claims only that liberty whereunto all are called in the church of Christ. . . .

It claims for itself a somewhat larger and broader use of the reason that has been accorded to theology. . . . Especially it makes much of the intuitions—the universal and spontaneous verdicts of the soul; and in this it deems that it allies itself with the Mind through which the Christian revelation is made. . . . If Christianity has any human basis it is its entire reasonableness. It must not only sit easily on the mind, but it must ally itself with it in all its normal action. . . . In the last analysis, revelation—so far as its acceptance is concerned—rests on reason, and not reason on revelation. The logical order is, first reason, and then revelation— the eye before sight. . . . The New Theology seeks to interpret the Scriptures in what may be called a more natural way, and in opposition to a hard, formal, un-

[1] Theodore T. Munger, *The Freedom of Faith*, Boston, 1883, p. 19.

sympathetic, and unimaginative way. . . . The New Theology is not disposed to limit its interpretation of the Scriptures by the principle contained in the phrase "the plain meaning of the words." . . . This principle must be enlarged, until it becomes something quite different. There must be recognized the principle of moral evolution or development,—a principle that removes whatever difficulties some may feel as to Hebrew anthropomorphism. . . . The New Theology seeks to replace an excessive individuality by a truer view of the solidarity of the race. It does not deny a real individuality, it does not predicate an absolute solidarity, but simply removes the emphasis from one to the other. It holds that every man must live a life of his own, build himself up into a full personality, and give an account of himself to God: but it also recognizes the blurred truth that man's life lies in its relations; that it is a derived and shared life; that it is carried on and perfected under laws of heredity and of the family and the nation. . . . It does not submerge the individual in the common life, nor free him from personal ill desert, nor take from him the crown of personal achievement and victory. It simply strives to recognize the duality of truth, and hold it well poised. . . . Hence an apparently secular tone, which is, however, but a widening of the field of the divine and spiritual. This theology recognizes a new relation to natural science; but only in the respect that it ignores the long apparent antagonism between the kingdoms of faith and of natural law. . . . It accepts the theory of physical evolution as the probable method of physical creation, and as having an analogy in morals; but it accepts it under the fact of a personal God who is revealing himelf, and of human freedom. . . . The New Theology chooses for its field the actual life of men in the world in all their varying conditions, rather than as massed in a few ideal conditions. It finds its methods in the every-day processes of humanity, rather than in a formal logic. . . . This full and direct look at humanity induces what may be called the ethical habit of thought. The New Theology seeks to recover spiritual processes from a magical to a moral conception. . . . The word "eternal," it does not regard wholly as a time-word, but as a word of moral and spiritual significance. . . . There is no more and no other relation between time and eternity in the future world than there is in the present world. . . . The Faith is not a finite thing, but an infinite; its truths are not conditional but absolute; the play of its laws is not within time, but above time; its processes are not hedged about by temporal limits,—*in* time it may be, but not bounded by it. . . . Such are some of the features of this fresh movement in the realm of theology, for it can scarcely be called more than a movement, an advance to meet the unfolding revelation of God. . . . It makes no haste, it seeks no revolution, but simply holds itself open and receptive under the breathing of the Spirit that has come, and is ever coming, into the world; passive, yet quick to respond to the heavenly visions that do not cease to break upon the darkened eye of humanity.

Within this theological framework Munger composed his sermon, "Man the Final Form in Creation," which is reprinted here. Munger suggests here that with the development of species, evolution has run its course; as evolution is a process which begins in time, it may be expected to end in time. As a creative method, evolution has produced the perfect creature, man; its goal has been achieved; its purpose is complete. "The effort of nature seems to have been to produce a *person*, and, having done this, the work of evolving creation ceases and rests from its labors." Any further evolution will not be material, but spiritual, "but there is more reason for expecting growth than evolution, because man is already a perfect creature,—the image of God, as near and like to God as a created being can be." Though physical evolution ends with man, the methods of evolution may continue to affect him. "His history may go on under laws analogous to those of physical evolution, but he himself will be the theatre of them." That is to say, the methods of physical evolution will be adapted to moral evolution. Within the moral realm, however, man is a free agent. Although "the methods and features are evolutionary . . . he himself is the force presiding over them." This moral evolution has already been lived by Jesus, who "lived out the life of man in its highest degree and to its last form on the earth," and "upon the basis of it, and as it were out of its nature, predicated another life." The Resurrection and the Ascension are earnests to man that resurrection and ascension would "not only be a worthy end of the long blind upward struggle of creation, but an explanation of it."

MAN THE FINAL FORM IN CREATION

The earth beareth fruit of herself; first the blade, then the ear, then the full corn in the ear.—ST. MARK iv. 28.

OUR Lord nowhere defines the kingdom of Heaven, but many times over tells us what it is like. A great teacher does not indulge in definitions; for a definition by its nature implies logical processes and conclusions that shut one up within one's own mind, subject to its weaknesses and limitations. Christ put himself in contrast with the dogmatist who frames a definition that necessarily imprisons him, by opening a universe—undefinable, but clearly apprehended. Search it throughout, he says, and you will find that all things are in harmony, one truth in all truths. The dogmatist proves a point, Christ reveals the universe of truth; one drives us to some definite action, the other inspires us with a sense of duty; one binds us, the other leaves us in freedom. A great truth can be conveyed only by a great illustration; but Christ's method went farther and connected the truth with the process and fact he uses: the same force, the same order, the same movement, are in the illustration and in the truth illustrated; and one sets forth the other because they have such a relation. The kingdom of Heaven is like growing corn, not because the Oriental fancy discerns an external likeness, but because the same power lies behind the springing corn and the unfolding kingdom inducing their likeness; they correspond, because both are ordained by one mind and put into one order.

Christ likened the kingdom of Heaven to two fields of action,— growth in the organic world, and the spontaneous action of the human heart in the natural and every-day relations of life. It is like seed sown, like growing corn, like working leaven, like mustard-seed and a fig-tree, like wheat and tares, and fermenting wine. It is like the play of the mind when men lose sheep or money or sons, when they are intrusted with money, when they go to feasts and weddings, when they pray, when they catch fish, and barter, and mend garments, and build houses. The world of unfolding nature and the world of human life,— here are set down the laws, the methods, and the outcome of this great order named the Kingdom of Heaven. Understand one and you will know the other. The likeness is not rhetorical but essential; the revelation of one is through the other, and they match each other because both rest on one Will that works in harmony with itself.

It would be pressing language too far to seek in the phrase, "the earth beareth fruit of herself," a reference to any scientific theory; still there is a recognition of the fact that there is lodged in the world of nature a force that works, as it were, of itself, and so brings forth fruit. It does not assert, but it admits of, an evolutionary process in the organic world.

The theory of evolution in some form is now so widely accepted that it no longer stirs offense nor awakens suspicion to name it in connection with questions of theology. One may do so without thereby committing one's self to any special theory of evolution, or to any conclusion that may be drawn from it. It may be well, whether it is accepted or rejected, to lay it beside the problems of religion in a tentative way, in order to see if it will aid in solving them, or add to their force and clearness. A multitude of inquiring and not wholly believing minds are thinking upon the themes of evolution, who are eager to discover if they can retain both their faith and their science. The practical divorce between this popular theory and theology, that is often insisted on, reacts against faith, for we are so closely bound to this world that its apparent verdicts take precedence of those of the spiritual world. They may be specially blessed who believe without seeing, but others are not to be condemned who ask to lay their finger upon the proof that life is stronger than death. There is a great deal of incipient infidelity that might be cured if it were properly dealt with. The limitations that make theology an isolated science, and the common assertion that religion and science have nothing to do with each other, are the actual sources of this infidelity. We know ourselves too well to assent to the claim that we are compartment-beings, thought-tight, and can shut religion up in one part, and philosophy in another, and science in still another. When a truth enters into man it has the range of his whole nature, and makes its appeal to every faculty; if shut within the heart it will mount to the brain, or if held there it will steal down to the heart. Man is the completest unit in nature. The divisions set up between mind and will and sensibility are like the great circles which astronomy puts into the heavens,—imaginary, and for convenience only; if insisted on as real, they might check the planets in their orbits.

No harm, at least, can come from a hypothetical discussion of evolution in its relations to religion, and it is possible that much good will be gained. It is certainly well for all to have some general knowledge of it and to trace its varying stages in the world of thought, if for no other reason than to find out what is settled and what is still undetermined.

While evolution is now so generally accepted that no one thinks in any department of study except under the evolutionary idea, there is as yet no accurate definition and no special theory of it which is not open to criticism. It is immediately urged: How can there be a consensus of belief in evolution without some settled theory of it? What is the foundation of your belief? If it consists of facts, cannot these facts be formulated? These are forceful questions and can be strongly pressed, but may be met by an appeal to the actual attitude of the thinking world,—holding to evolution without a definite theory of it beyond its bare principle and general method. This is not without precedent. The Copernican system was believed by all the men of science contemporary with its framer long before he stated it; and the system waited for centuries, and waits still, for full statement. Gravitation was held under an imperfect formula before Newton discovered the correct one, and was held as local before it was known to be universal; nor do we yet know much about it. Nearly every great truth precedes its theory; it is believed before it is formulated. Christianity itself was a fact and a power in the world before it became a system; nor have we yet, nor shall we ever have, a definition of it. There is reason to think it will be the same with evolution. It is certainly true to-day that there is no closely defined theory of evolution that covers its facts. Universal laws are asserted, but they are found to be particular and limited in their field. Evolution and Darwinism have been used as interchangeable terms and are still popularly so used; but the men of science to-day regard Darwin as a great student of evolution who discovered the law of natural selection to which his followers gave a wider scope than was claimed for it by himself. Natural selection, though a law of wide reach, does not cover the facts of evolution.

Roughly defined, evolution is the theory that life in the organic world is developed or evolved from preceding life by descent and variation. So far, there is nearly universal agreement because the fact is so evident. But when we ask why, or by what law, offspring is like parents, we get various answers, and none are satisfactory; and when we ask why offspring varies from parents, we get still more divergent answers that are even less satisfactory. Some theories explain variation by natural selection; others by migration; others by an "internal tendency," which is quite probable, but it is a mere phrase and explains nothing; others still by "extraordinary births" which become the progenitors of new species,—true in part doubtless, but how far true is not known, and, whether partial or universal, it is no explanation of the fact. Another, and just now popular, theory of variation is that it is caused by the active efforts of animals in certain directions; but it is questioned if tendencies so caused are sufficiently persistent to form a permanent species.

These are examples of attempts to explain a fact upon which all are agreed, but are wide apart in their explanations. They touch each other at certain points and run into each other at other points, and all rest on certain well-attested phenomena; but no one covers, nor do all, taken in their points of agreement, cover the facts, nor do they get beyond a certain limit where observation ends,—reaching a dead-wall behind which their great fact lies in unattainable mystery. This condition of the subject is of great significance. It does not indicate an imperfect state of science. Lamarck was perhaps as near right as any man since; and science has chiefly provided old theories with a few more facts: the microscope has only added to the vision of the eye. It rather indicates two things: first, that life is a very complex thing, and is too wide to be brought under a theory,—that while innumerable things may be asserted of it, it cannot be put into a single category; second, that an explanation of life must be sought in a region that technical science does not recognize. A point of immense significance, I repeat, because the theories break down one after another at just those points where they must threaten morals and religion, leaving the great fact of evolution to be explained, if explained at all, by theories that admit of morals and religion. The men of science demur, and say, "Give us time and we will unravel the tangled thread of creation." We do not cast at science its disagreements, nor remind it that so far it has worked at cross purposes, for we well know that such confusion is no sign of error; science seldom starts on the right path, but it often reaches its end, or some better end than it aimed at. Instead, we assert that science will fail in its quest because it always brings up against ultimate facts in both the material and physical worlds. When it is found that some countless millions of vibrations of luminiferous ether upon the retina of the eye give the color red, we have reached an ultimate fact; go one step farther and you are in a world that physical science does not recognize; namely, the consciousness of vision. So when we say, I think, I will, I remember, we assert actual processes that physical science cannot measure; the effort to do so is an attempt to get outside of mind to find mind; it is going outside of the ship to discover where it is bearing you. These ultimate facts form barriers that physical science cannot pass. It may crowd them back and make ever-widening fields for itself, but they remain; they exist in every grain of sand, in every begotten and conceived thing, in every acting intelligence. There cannot therefore be any theory of creation that is scientific, in the ordinary sense of the word. Science covers only a section of creation. It begins with a homogeneous fluid disturbed by force, but what the force is, and why it begins to act, it does not undertake to determine; it simply strikes in at a given point upon an existing order. What is back of this, what may be over it and under it and in it, science does not recognize, but cannot deny. Now here are great realities, orders, forces already existing and at work when science begins its examination. They exist and act still, and are the materials with which science works; they are the ocean out of which science has filled the cup over which it is busy; but no measurement or analysis of the contents of the cup will explain the ocean. It is in this, so to speak, preëxisting world, this *supra et sub et intra* existing world, that theology and philosophy have their fields, which are not only outside of the physical world but inclusive of it. Physical science can no more settle a question of morals than it can settle the question of creation. It adduces many illuminating facts in respect to both, but it brings up against the same barriers in either case, giving us methods and processes but never causes and explanations. Hence it can determine no question in morals or religion or philosophy, simply because they reach beyond its domain while they have a considerable play within it.

But the theistic evolutionist refuses to think within this domain, and holds that it is unscientific and empirical to start in at a given point and then attempt an explanation of creation and morals. He boldly enters the wider domain of ultimate cause and original force, and there attempts to think. He can, at least, offer explanations that cannot be disproved, and more and more seems he to be marshaling the forces the way they are going. Postulate a creative Power, an eternal Will, a moral Being, and you can have a coherent system, which is certainly better than a scientific theory that cannot carry the facts.

The point at which I am aiming is this: as natural science starts in at a given point and abandons all that is before it to the theist, so a point will be reached where science fails and must leave the problems of existence to be solved by the theist. As science cannot determine origin, so it cannot determine destiny; as it presents a sectional view of creation, so it gives only a sectional view of everything in creation. It is not only a sectional view in time but in scope and reach. Everything rises out of its domain, and disappears from its view in that larger world which is about it; a crystal and a man are equally inexplicable within its necessarily limited vision.

Such reflections leave with us the clear conviction that physical science cannot settle the problems of religion, though it may furnish important factors in their solution. It can trace a few of the external features of their history for a limited time, the most important of which is that man is included in the evolutionary process so far as the limited vision of science can observe him. But as this covers his entire visible history, the question arises, What will be his future history? If he has been evolved in his physical nature from the lower orders, may he not develop into a higher order, and so become a simple factor of an ascending series—as much below what is to be as he is now above what has been? More briefly: granting evolution, may not man develop, by the law of descent and variation, into a superior species of being?

The question is worthy of discussion, because evolutionary conceptions prevail so generally that it is wise to discuss man under them, and a question so legitimate as this must be met; and also because it leads to a lofty conception of man, and throws possible light upon certain great Christian facts.

I shall attempt to suggest a few reasons tending to show that man has reached the end of his physical evolution, and will not develop into another and higher species.

Evolution does not imply that any given evolutionary process has no limits or end.

Evolution may be a general law or method, but it does not follow that each thing or species evolved will forever go on developing into higher forms. It is quite as probable that evolution is working towards a fixed end as towards a forever ascending end; it begins in time and space, and because it so begins it may so end. If we find a tendency to develop, we find also a tendency to cease developing. There is a strife and effort to produce a species, but, having produced it, there is a disposition to rest and go no farther, and it is only by great struggle that nature is crowded on to the production of another species out of existing ones. Hence the apparent permanence of species; there is undoubtedly a tendency to such permanence, and there is much reason to believe that it will be reached. Creation presents itself in that aspect—species produced and obstinately remaining such; and the only reason we believe that one species has been evolved from another is because the facts require such belief as we study the past. We do not now behold the evolutionary process going on except in embryology, where the whole story of creation is perpetually repeated; and in artificial experiments with certain animals, which are not wholly satisfactory, as they show a tendency to sterility and reversion. Evidently the end of a process has been reached, or nearly reached. The struggle for existence and natural selection go on, and environment changes, but plant and tree and animal remain the same, and wear an aspect of finality. Nature has done what she strove to do, namely, evolved species, and, having gained her end, ceases from effort in that direction. The oak and the maple intertwine their boughs for a thousand years, but do not modify each other. The rose and the poppy blossom in the same garden for countless generations, but the rose distills no sleep and the poppy does not rob the rose of its perfume.

We not only have the fact of permanence of species before us, but it is explicable if we can be content to regard evolution as a simple process, and decline to grant unlimited sweep to the laws of natural selection and variation. It is neither good logic nor good science to assert that the observed processes of evolution are equal to evolution. Logic and science indicate that evolution is the working out of a definite design with reference to a definite end; the laws themselves are the merest slaves of the design. This design and end is the production of species. When these are produced, the laws either cease to act, or show a tendency to cease,—if not wholly in the lower species, an ever-increasing tendency to do so in the higher,—thus indicating that an end of physical variation will be reached.

For the sake of entire clearness, let me say again that science itself does not require us to assign unlimited and endless sweep to the laws of struggle for existence, natural selection, and variation; they work towards definite ends, then stop and give way to other laws that may be analogous to them in some respects, but in others are the reversal of them. It is equally scientific, and it is far more reasonable because it takes in a larger group of facts, to assert that evolution, having produced man, has done what it was set to do and goes no farther.

The effort of nature seems to have been to produce a *person*, and, having done this, the work of evolving creation ceases and rests from its labors.

What is a person? A being having intellect, feeling, and will, and consciousness of itself as such. The brute world produces individuals but not persons. An individual is one of a class, distinct from it but not to the point of consciousness; a person is not only one of a class, but knows himself as one. An individual is not free because it is not wholly detached from its species, but a person is wholly detached, and therefore is wholly free; a person only can say *I* and *Thou*. The brutes certainly have mind and feeling and will, but only in a rudimentary and partial way. Suppose a brute of a higher order were capable of self-analysis, it would be obliged to say of itself: "I think, but I have not a full mind; I do nothing reflectively, but because I feel that I must; I love, but I see that I cease to love after a little, nor can I tell why I love; I have will up to a certain point,—I can defend myself and seek food, and I can learn to obey, but I feel myself driven by a power that I do not understand, nor can I resist doing what I am moved to do; I am a part of that which is around me, and I cannot detach myself from it." Man is not obliged to speak of himself in such terms. He can think perfectly, that is, reflectively and up to the verge of his knowledge; if he could see farther and know more facts, he is conscious that he could reflect upon them. He can love perfectly because he can choose to die for what he loves; that is, he can cast the whole of himself into the act of love. He can will perfectly; that is, when he makes a choice he knows that it is a real choice: he knows and weighs the motives on either side. He knows himself as distinct from creation,—drawn out from it and still bound to it by a thousand cords, but still so separate from it that he can say: "I am *I*, and am not *it*."

These full attributes and this full consciousness constitute personality. We need not hesitate to say that man, ideal man, is a perfect being. He may go on indefinitely towards an enlargement of his powers; he may think more widely, love more intensely, choose more wisely, and grow into an ever-deepening sense of selfhood; but there is no occasion for his changing into another kind of being. His limitations are not indications that he is not already a perfect being. A greater and more complex physical development would not necessarily yield a superior creature. Voltaire points one of his severest gibes at human nature in the fable in which he transfers an inhabitant of the earth to one of the larger planets, and sets him to talking with the people he finds there,—a very discontented lot, who grumble over their limitations: "We have only sixty senses, and cannot be expected to know much;" and so quite put to confusion the earthly visitor, who is forced to confess that he has only five. Voltaire was too eager in his sarcasm to see that knowledge does not depend upon the senses but upon mind. If mind is absolute, five senses may be as good as sixty. Indeed, it is probable that the physical universe is correlated to the five senses; that these inlets are sufficient to let in the whole material creation upon man, provided there is a true mind behind them. With five senses and mind we have already come to the verge of matter, and stand looking off into a world of spirit: what we now want is, not more senses,—more or better eyes and ears and hands,—but a better use of mind. Nay, it seems probable that what we now need for larger knowledge is to drop what senses we have, and go off into that world of the spirit to the borders of which we have come, and explore it simply as minds, or with spiritual bodies. There is not the slightest reason for believing that a superior physical being would gain a better knowledge of the world than man has or will have.

And so it would seem that nature, having produced a being who is capable of understanding it, who is separate from matter, and is allied to an order above it, will make no more efforts in a physical direction, but will move in the direction of this other order to which man belongs. If there is to be further evolution, it will not be material but spiritual; but there is more reason for expecting growth than evolution, because man is already a perfect creature,—the image of God, as near and like to God as a created being can be.

There is in man no premonition of a development into a higher physical life.

In every antecedent order, we may well suppose there is a sympathetic forecast of, and movement towards, that which is about to come. The embryonic bird must have some sense or limited consciousness of wings and flight. As one species or variety is about to pass into another, there is doubtless some prior hint or yearning or movement towards the functions awaiting development. Nature makes no sudden changes in its order, but always sends forward some announcing herald: the force sets towards its destiny. But in man this does not point in a physical direction. He does not dream of better hands and feet and eyes and ears. Instead, all the inward movements of his nature are mind-ward, and towards that world of thought in which he can secure all the results which a more highly organized body might possibly give. He does not yearn for swifter feet, but rather for such use of his mind that he can make engines which shall not only outrun all possible feet, but supersede them; nor for stronger hands, but for inventive power to create machines that shall do the work of many hands; nor for better eyes, but for skill to make telescopes and microscopes that shall outreach the power of all possible eyes. The set and bent of our nature is not towards more senses, but towards mental faculties that either supplement or supersede the senses. Indeed, more senses, that is, more avenues into the physical world, would imply that man was to turn his attention backward and downward towards matter, whereas the whole effort of nature has been to get him out of and away from it. His lessons do not now lie there, but in the moral and spiritual world to the borders of which he has come. Were man to develop physically into a superior animal, it might result in binding this finer creature faster in matter; for such a being would either be more perfectly correlated to the world, and so might come into a fatal satisfaction with a transient order; or it would be out of true correlation with the world, and so would despise it. Either result would be fatal: gross contentment with a world wholly mastered, or pessimistic contempt for a world too far removed or too alien to be of service. Man occupies just that relation to the physical world in which he can make the best use of it preparatory to leaving it behind him. One step short of man, the being cannot extricate itself from matter; one step beyond might throw the being back into matter, either as content with it or as hating it, in which case the world would no longer serve it.

The actual movement and effort of man is not in the direction of physical development, but is towards a moral and spiritual development. The effort of nature points away from the physical world and seems about to overleap it, and to lift its last creation into a world of thought and spirit.

Man will, indeed, perfect his body and make the most of it, but only as a basis for an intellectual and spiritual life. He has already done much in this way, but there is no hint of organic change. There is reason to believe that the modern eye has a better perception of the chromatic scale than the Greek eye. Homer is devoid of color, but a landscape, to the last touch, could be painted from the pages of George Eliot or Charles Craddock. So of music: the Greek ear knew little of it beyond rhythm. "Old Timotheus" might lead a military company, but he could not lift a modern "mortal to the skies." But these improvements of eye and ear are not organic changes, and only carry man over into a spiritual world. It is the thought and feeling in color and sound that we care for; they literally transport us into a world where eye and ear have no function. Hence we infer that the next step for man is not some superior physical form, but an elevation into a true spiritual world. Already he stands on its borders; he enters within it by thought and feeling; he cares for little else when thought and feeling have once been awakened; he yearns for it with real or unconscious desire. He knows that he issued from that world, that he is the creature of mind and not of matter, of spirit and not of force. Behind this long evolution of struggling nature lies this world of idea and thought and feeling and creating energy, a real world of which this physical world is only the show or semblance, as the statue is only the poor shadow of the sculptor's ideal which is the real thing. Having been brought through the long process of evolving creation, and made a partaker of every stage of it for some inscrutable reason, to the verge of another world, so that it can be said of him that he has a true mind and a true spirit, his next step will be into that world to which he is thus correlated. He already moves in it; he has its freedom; he knows its language; he can pronounce the ineffable Name, and can receive upon his face the rays of the divine glory. He can hear the eternal hymn of creation, and knows that it is keyed to joy and righteousness. He can feel in full measure the throb of that supreme, genetic impulse out of which creation sprang—love. If there is any significance or fitness in the order of things, the next step for man will be into this world of realities, and not into a physical order in which nothing more could be done than has been done for him.

In saying that physical or creative evolution probably ends with man, it is not meant that he is exempt from the methods of evolution. His history may go on under laws analogous to those of physical evolution, but he himself will be the theatre of them. The law of the struggle for existence and the survival of the fittest may continue, not as a physical process in relation to others, but as a moral process within the circle of his own powers. For man, being the end and head of creation, has in himself the whole history of creation; the entire past in all its forms lives and its processes work in him, but always within the fixed and stable limits of personality. The atoms still whirl in tissue and blood; the gases and fluids of primeval ages are a part of his composition; his bones are built out of the elemental solids; the habits and motives of the animal world linger within him, and show their lineaments in his own; the appetites and passions and tempers of beasts still assert themselves in him, even as we name them,—beastly. Being such, the whole process of evolving nature is repeated in him as a free moral being. He becomes, as it were, the whole creation, and its whole struggle is repeated in him and by him, but in conjunction with other factors and on another stage. Heredity conserves and strives to fix the past, but the moral within him, and the spiritual environment made for him, contend against heredity, and select and nourish that which is best. The animal is kept down and crowded out, giving place to intellectual and moral and spiritual habits and qualities. In this process man himself is a free actor, sinking backward into brute conditions, or rising into the divine life of which he has become conscious. The methods and features are evolutionary, but he himself is the force presiding over them—resisting or coöperating with him who is over and in all. Hence the process is moral, and embraces the whole circle of moral truths,—sin, repentance, conversion, regeneration, aspiration, and struggle after the highest; for all of these turn on, and have their meaning in, a yielding to the animal nature or a striving after the spiritual nature. Tennyson, whose poems are impregnated with the evolutionary idea,—an idea that corrects and redeems what otherwise would be a pessimistic muse,—puts the truth into the lines of *In Memoriam*, where he ascribes a high destiny to man:—

> "If so he type this work of time
> Within himself, from more to more."

Such thoughts do not invalidate any moral duty, or contradict any Christian doctrine. Instead they provide a rational philosophy for sin, conscience, regeneration, and life in the Spirit. They open a path from lower life to higher, and pave a way between this world and the next. They fortify Christian truths by universal truth, and put underneath their problems the base-line that runs through creation as a basis for expectations that converge in heaven. Man needs the whole world to stand on, and all truth to support him; for so only is he the head of creation, and so only can he find his way out of its lower forms into that higher order from which creation sprang.

Still, such considerations might be considered as mere speculations were it not for the fact that we have them in the form of a reality. Man's nature and destiny are not only matters of theory but of fact; his history and its stages have been gone through and ultimated in One who was Humanity itself. It is possibly more than a religious fact that Christ lived out the life of man in its highest degree and to its last form on the earth, and that he thus illustrated the movement and destiny of humanity. The presiding feature of that life was his consciousness of another world from which he came and into which he returned. If it was a dream, then all is a dream and all may go. But we have no right to pass by that life and consciousness without testing them to see if they will not fit into and explain this lofty hypothesis of man that we are considering.

The reality and fullness of Christ's human life, and the consciousness of another world, each interpenetrating and swelling the volume of the other, this is the fact that holds the eye of the world and challenges its thought. He lived a perfectly human life, and yet upon the basis of it, and as it were out of its nature, predicated another life. He does not bring immortality into the world as the far-off secret of highest heaven, but he instinctively predicated it because he was perfectly the Son of Man. It was no problem for discussion to him, but simply a natural assertion,—the outcome of his insight and outlook as he turned to the world and measured it, and then into heaven and saw what was there, and then upon himself, and found that he belonged both to this world and to heaven, Son of man and Son of God, each because he was perfectly the other. He saw all things; he pierced to the meaning of the world; he understood day and night; he comprehended the morning and the evening; he looked into the heart of the rose; he knew the secret of history; he entered into the depths of humanity, and knew life and man; he saw all things and himself in God, and God in all; and out of such vision sprang the spontaneous conviction of eternal life as the key to all and the end of all. Life in another world is what nature and man and God mean, and he was the illustration and realization of it. The destiny of man is thus outlined in the Christ. His resurrection was a real entrance into that world, and is the next stage in the development of humanity. His history between that event and his ascension cannot be understood and measured until it is connected with some theory of man and made a part of it. As mere attestation to previous works and words, it has no weight with thought, and no dignity in a large theology. The facts are too great for such an end; they must have in them the scope and swing of human destiny. What if the natural history of humanity on this world be finished not by evolution into some finer form of physical life, not by death, but by resurrection and ascension! Such would not only be a worthy end of the long, blind upward struggle of creation, but an explanation of it. Towards some high end creation has been pressing with age-long steps and yearning throes. Does the uniform process that has wrought to ever-finer issues till it has produced man, cease on the borders of the grave, when, if at all, it is taken up by forces of which we know nothing, and man is transported across the bottomless gulf of death by the sheer force of Omnipotence? or is it probable that this process—working ever to finer issues—completes the history of man, and lifts him by resurrection and ascension into his final state, returning him as a perfect creation to the world whence his life was drawn, and to the God in whom all along he has lived and moved and had his being?

Three objections may be suggested: First, that such a view identifies man with nature, and leaves him in its grasp. Whether this is an evil thing or not, depends upon the conception of nature. It is a fact that we are in nature, and there seems to be no way of getting out of it; but under a conception of it as rooted in God, and as mounting ever towards the spiritual, there is no need to be delivered from it; it might be separation from God himself. Nothing is gained for man by disdainful thought of nature; it is the mother of whom we were born, over whom the begetting spirit broods perpetually. Second, it is objected that it represents Christ as the product of nature, and the mere culmination of an evolutionary process. But what if this process be met by one in the heavens, so that the phrase, Son of Man and Son of God, becomes one that takes in perfect man and real God,—the revelation of the mystery of eternity? Give full and equal sweep and reverence to each, and no violence will be done to faith and revelation: rather are they thus fulfilled. Third, it is said that if such a destiny awaits humanity, no room is left for the full play of character, and for its final destiny as turning on morals. To this it may be said that, while the line of destiny for humanity runs in the direction named, it is complicated by the great fact of freedom which may modify its action in the case of individuals. The eternal march is in this direction: woe be to him who falls out of its line!

Theology must not disdainfully separate itself from science while it refuses to be measured by it. It must come into harmony with nature, if it would be true to itself. It is not apart from nature, nor is it parallel with it, nor is it superinduced upon it; it is rather the projection or extension of nature into the world of the spirit,—that left behind which cannot be carried forward, that added which could not earlier be included, but nature still in its essential meaning and purpose, and in that larger sense in which nature is the revelation of God in all his works.

There has been a fatal tendency in the past to make theology a thing by itself,—a play of divine forces in the air or above it, or a by-play to the drama of creation. It has already come somewhat nearer the world, but it must come nearer still, and cast itself into the stream of human life, where, if it is true to itself, it will not be submerged and lost, but instead will ride on the waves, point out the direction they are moving, and preside over the destiny of every child of humanity borne on the mysterious tide that sets towards eternity.

INDEX

INDEX